Also by Michael A. Bellesiles

*Revolutionary Outlaws: Ethan Allen and the
Struggle for Independence on the Early
American Frontier* (1993)

EDITOR

*Lethal Imagination: Violence and Brutality
in American History* (1999)

*Ethan Allen and His Kin: Correspondence,
1772–1819* (1998)

DEVELOPER

BiblioBase (1996)

Arming America

Arming

The Origins of a

America

National Gun Culture

Michael A. Bellesiles

Alfred A. Knopf

New York

2000

THIS IS A BORZOI BOOK
PUBLISHED BY ALFRED A. KNOPF

Copyright © 2000 by Michael A. Bellesiles

All rights reserved under International and Pan-American Copyright Conventions.
Published in the United States by Alfred A. Knopf, a division of Random House, Inc.,
New York, and simultaneously in Canada by Random House of Canada Limited,
Toronto. Distributed by Random House, Inc., New York.

www.aaknopf.com

Knopf, Borzoi Books, and the colophon are registered trademarks of Random House, Inc,

ISBN 0 375-40210-1
LC 00-106191

Manufactured in the United States of America
First Edition

For

Lilith Claire

with love.

Veritas vel silentio

consumpitur vel mendacio.

Contents

Arming America

Introduction

In Search of Guns

"I am only looking for one word," said Father Brown.
"A word that isn't there."

... "Right you are," said the big man called Flambeau
cheerfully. "Let us begin at the wrong end. Let's
begin with what everybody knows, which isn't true."

—G. K. Chesterton, "The Sign of the Broken Sword"

On April 6, 1998, the nation's two leading news magazines featured cover photographs of a young boy with a gun. The photograph on the cover of *Time* magazine was of a toddler named Andrew Golden, dressed in camouflage and clutching a high-powered rifle. *Newsweek* featured a slightly older Andrew Golden, still in camouflage, now clutching a pistol. The two magazines chronicled the brief lives of Golden and Mitchell Johnson, boys growing up in a culture in which parents thought it a good idea to pose their three-year-olds with deadly weapons and said, "Santa gave Drew Golden a shotgun when he was six." These two children were raised with guns, and with God. Mitchell Johnson had just "made a profession of faith and decided to accept Jesus Christ as his savior." He was active in his church and impressed the adults with his piety. But the temptation of a gun can trump a claim of faith in God and all dreams of childhood innocence.

On March 24, 1998, these two boys, aged eleven and thirteen, set off the fire alarm at their school in Jonesboro, Arkansas, and then shot at the other children as they filed out of the building. Between them the boys had three rifles and seven pistols. In less than four minutes, they fired twenty-two shots, killing eleven-year-old Brittheny Varner, twelve-year-olds Natalie Brooks, Stephanie Johnson, and Paige Ann Herring, and their young teacher Shannon Wright, who was shielding one of her students. Golden and Johnson wounded ten other people, mostly children.[1]

The questions asked repeatedly after the Jonesboro tragedy—as after the shootings at Columbine High School in Littleton, Colorado, on April 20, 1999, and after every similar mass shooting—seem depressingly familiar: How did we get here? How did the United States reach a point where children shoot and kill? How did we acquire a culture in which Santa Claus gives a six-year-old boy a shotgun for Christmas? For Christmas!

An astoundingly high level of personal violence separates the United States from every other industrial nation. To find comparable levels of interpersonal violence, one must examine nations in the midst of civil wars or social chaos. In the United States of America in the 1990s, two million violent crimes and twenty-four thousand murders occurred on average every year. The weapon of choice in 70 percent of these murders was a gun, and thousands more are killed by firearms every year in accidents and suicides. In a typical week, more Americans are killed with guns than in all of Western Europe in a year. Newspapers regularly carry stories of shootings with peculiar causes, like the case of the Michigan man who shot at a coworker who took a cracker from him at lunch without asking. In no other industrial nation do military surgeons train at an urban hospital to gain battlefield experience, as is the case at the Washington Hospital Center in the nation's capital. It is now thought normal and appropriate for urban elementary schools to install metal detectors to check for firearms. And when a Denver pawnshop advertised a sale of pistols as a "back-to-school" special, four hundred people showed up to buy guns.[2]

The manifestations of America's gun culture are well known: the sincere love and affection with which American society views its weapons are demonstrated daily on television and movie screens. Every form of the media reinforces the notion that the solution to your problems can be held in your hand and provides immediate gratification. Just as there are flight simulators that re-create the experience of flying a plane, so do video games make available to any child in America a killing simulator that will train him or her to shoot without a moment's hesitation. An entire generation, as Dave Grossman has astutely argued, is being conditioned to kill. And since the United States does not register guns, no one knows how many there are or who actually buys them. The FBI estimates that there are 250 million firearms in private hands, with five million new guns purchased every year. The National Sporting Goods Association estimates that men buy 92 percent of all rifles and 94 percent of the shotguns. Most of these men fall into the 25- to 34-year-old age group, earn between $35,000 and $50,000 annually, and do not need to kill animals for their survival.[3]

That efforts to solve violence are subject to volatile contention should not be surprising. Solutions require a knowledge of origins, and that search for historical understanding has politicized the past as well. Many if not most Americans seem resigned to, or find comfort in, the notion that this violence is immutable, the product of a deeply imbedded historical experience rooted in the frontier heritage. Frequent Indian wars and regular gun-battles in the streets of every Western town presumably inured Americans to the necessity of violence. That frontiers elsewhere did not replicate America's violent culture is thought irrelevant. In the imagined past, "the requirements for self-defense and food-gathering had put firearms in the hands of nearly everyone."[4] With guns in their hands and bullets on their belts, the frontiersmen conquered the wilderness with a deep inward faith that, as Richard Slotkin so eloquently put it, regeneration came through violence. In short, we have always been killers.[5] From this Hobbesian heritage of each against all emerged the modern American acceptance of widespread violence. Its fixed character has the political implication that little if anything can be done to alter America's gun culture.[6]

Such statements are often presented as logically obvious, sociological equivalents of Thomas Jefferson's self-evident truths. Yet an examination of the social practices and cultural customs prevalent in early America suggests that we have it all backward. This book argues that gun ownership was exceptional in the seventeenth, eighteenth, and early nineteenth centuries, even on the frontier, and that guns became a common commodity only with the industrialization of the mid nineteenth century, with ownership concentrated in urban areas. The gun culture grew with the gun industry. The firearms industry, like so many others, relied on the government not just for capital development but for the support and enhancement of its markets. From its inception, the U.S. government worked to arm its citizens; it scrambled to find sources of weapons to fulfill the mandate of the Second Amendment. From 1775 until the 1840s the government largely failed in this task, but the industrialization of the arms industry allowed the government to move toward its goal with ever-increasing speed, though in the face of residual public indifference and even resistance.

While this book is dedicated to examining the creation of America's gun culture, it is important to clarify that culture's current nature. Gun magazines offer the most immediate insight into contemporary attitudes toward firearms. These journals are hardly examples of disinterested journalism. Unlike car magazines, which often publish articles highly critical of the automotive industry or its latest models, the gun magazines never have an unkind word to say about American-made guns—all guns are thought to be above average. Special feature stories rave about the superiority of one gun manufacturer after another, allowing the corporate spokespeople to describe their companies' many virtues.[7]

These articles and advertisements open a window onto the values of America's most enthusiastic gunowners and gunmakers. The December 1998 issue of *Guns & Ammo* offered its recommendations for Christmas gifts with a large photo of Santa, in camouflage and with rifles sticking out of his bag, putting pistols and ammunition under the tree while a little girl smiles in surprise. Features explore the best means of carrying concealed guns, and promote the new smaller guns as "Fire-Spittin' Kittens." There are pistols that can fit in the palm of the hand, like the 3.25-inch Downsizer WSP that fires .357 Magnum bullets. There are even diminutive pistols made especially for ladies; "one of the virtues of these pistols" is that they "offer the power of" a larger gun "in a highly concealable package." Then there is Kel-Tec's "Mighty Mite," a semiautomatic weighing 4.6 pounds, praised by *Guns & Ammo* for being "good enough for a head shot at 100 yards" and "far easier to stow away or hide" than its larger cousins. Its only "flaw" is its ten-round magazine, and "Who wants a 10-round carbine?" But one can slap on a thirty-rounder.[8]

These smaller guns are very important in modern society, for "There are times when packing a sidearm on the hip is just plain inconvenient. This does not mean that one is forced to venture out naked upon the world." To insure against nakedness, there are a number of new accoutrements, such as the Gard-Her, a gun holster that doubles as a garter for stockings. As the ad for one leading manufacturer, Beretta, states: "Easy to Conceal. Easy to Fire. Easy to Acquire."[9]

And yet many gunowners in America feel that the easy availability of firearms is under sustained attack. Many citizens hold that the most essential American right of all, the unhindered ownership of firearms, is threatened by the federal government and liberal fanatics who want to disarm everyone, even the police. In 1998 Chuck Klein wrote, "The Second Amendment . . . means that anyone may literally own and carry any type of 'arms' anywhere, *sans* licenses, permits or special taxes." Klein admits that some people, "mental incompetents or children," should be excepted from this sweeping right, but "federal, state and local ordinances and judicial rulings arc *not* the legal and correct method of enacting exceptions." If we do not want "citizens to have .303 Vickers machine guns mounted on their SUVs, then changing the Constitution is the only way to incorporate the exceptions." Constitutional amendments would be required to place any limitations on gun ownership, including ownership by "mental incompetents or children," for Americans' unhindered access to any weapon desired "is set in stone." Five days before the shootings in Littleton, Colorado, Supreme Court Justice Antonin Scalia agreed with this view that citizens have a constitutionally protected right to own machine guns.[10]

Charlton Heston, president of the National Rifle Association (NRA), has fought to protect this understanding of the Second Amendment. Heston often warns that the United States must avoid "England's Orwellian nightmare" of gun control. As part of that continuing battle against the *1984* nightmare, Heston recently suggested that, when it comes to journalists, it is time to "re-think" the axiom that "you should never kill a messenger bearing bad news." "The national media," Heston wrote, "in their obsessive addiction to ever-more terror, brutality and gore . . . may be contributing to the violence that they broadcast and publish." The media, it seems, wants to "shift blame" for America's gun violence "from themselves onto gun owners." Heston does not actually call for the murder of journalists, but he does insist that "for gun owners who care about their rights . . . it's time to put blame where it's due"—on the media. It is difficult, and perhaps dangerous, to argue with such logic. [11]

Heston clearly expresses the hostility toward dissent evident within this single-minded ideology. As writer Warren Cassidy of the NRA told Osha Gray Davidson, "You would get a far better understanding if you approached us as if you were approaching one of the great religions of the world." *Guns & Ammo* recently tested the effectiveness of the "world's hottest pistol round" on a piece of ballistic gelatin wrapped in a police-issue Kevlar vest. These bullets, called "cop-killers" by some and "anti-terrorist" by *Guns & Ammo,* passed through the vest, producing an "impressive channel" in the gelatin. It would have been interesting to have heard the view of an urban chief of police on this test.[12]

By the end of the twentieth century, any American could acquire a private arsenal, consisting of an astonishing array of weapons. The .700

Nitro Express is so powerful that the "recoil from it will actually make your brain bounce off your skull." When fired, the Browning M2 .50 caliber rifle—a sniper's rifle known to kill at twenty-five hundred yards—can cause permanent hearing loss to unprotected ears. Navegar, Inc., describes its TEC-DC9, used to deadly effect at Columbine High School, as a "high spirited . . . fun gun." The Henry Company proclaims its .22 rifle "The *perfect* Christmas present." Also available is a wide range of accessories to embellish the gun culture, from lasergrips that place "a high-density red dot where the bullet will strike," to a replica of the Derringer that killed Abraham Lincoln, to a bulletproof leather jacket. Supposedly, none of these items conveys any lethal intent. As one advertisement boldly proclaims: "Just for fun. 10 shots in 2 seconds." What could be more fun than that? Obviously, sexy women with guns. The variety of calendars available is impressive, including "Guns 'n' Babes" and the "Hunting & Fishing Lingerie Calendar." As the advertisement for G. Gordon Liddy's "1999 Stacked and Packed Calendar" asks, "Where do you mix lingerie and guns?" The answer says it all, "Only in America!"[13]

America's fascination with guns involves more than a peripheral subculture. It is not just a small minority of individuals who idolize and even fetishize firearms. Guns are central to the identity of Americans, to their self-perception as a rugged and violent people, as well as to their perception of others. Most of the world associates the United States with firearms, if not as the world's leading maker of guns, then for such global cultural icons as the cowboy, the gangster, the street thug, and the heroic cop. At every level of American culture, through all the layers of culture from lowbrow to highbrow, firearms abound. From television to opera, trashy novels to elite literature, guns are employed to relate the essential American character: impatient, forthright, loud, independent, and subject to explosive brutality. The signs of this gun culture are everywhere, from movie posters to the daily newspaper, book jackets to CD covers, emergency rooms to police blotters. When the velvet-voiced D'Angelo sings, "I'll tell ya what's on my mind / I'm 'bout to go get my nine / And kill both ya'lls behind," his audience understands that he means his .9 mm semiautomatic pistol, and that using it is an understandable response to catching his best friend and wife together in bed. D'Angelo is only updating older cultural references such as the classic "Forty-four Blues," about a man walking the streets with his .44, looking for his woman and the friend who stole her away. "I walked all night long, with my .44 in my hand. / Looking for my woman, looking for her other man." The caliber may change, but the sentiment remains the same.[14]

Guns are absolutely fundamental to the way Americans understand themselves. In a society that regulates and registers almost every commodity, the gun leads a charmed life of perfect freedom. In the United States teddy bears are subject to four different types of safety standards, and the Toy Manufacturers Association established voluntary toy-safety standards in 1976. In contrast, there are no federal safety standards on American-made firearms, nor any voluntary safety standards. Several state legislatures have passed bills specifically prohibiting their own citizens from bringing suit against the gun industry; no other manufacturer receives such state protection of its interests. Legislatures have even encouraged gun use, as when Louisiana passed a law granting its citizens the right to shoot to kill anyone attempting to steal their car. In 1996 Congress cut $2.6 million from its appropriation for the Centers for Disease Control (CDC), the exact amount the CDC spent on firearm injury research. Congress also instructed that "none of the funds made available for injury prevention and control at the Centers for Disease Control and Prevention may be used to advocate or promote gun control." This legislation has been understood by those who work at the CDC as a gag order, and it has effectively terminated research on gun-related injuries. Likewise the Washington state legislature was so concerned over the statistical evidence that gun ownership increased the likelihood of being shot that it placed its police files off-limits to epidemiologists. The gun must be protected from research.[15]

The gun is so central to American identity that the nation's history has been meticulously reconstructed to promote the necessity of a heavily armed American public. In the classic telling, arms ownership has always been nearly universal, and American liberty was won and maintained by the actions of privately armed citizens. The gun culture has been read from the present into the past. Franklin Orth, executive vice president of the NRA, told a Senate subcommittee in 1968, "There is a very special relationship between a man and his gun—an atavistic relation with its deep roots in prehistory, when the primitive man's personal weapon, so often his only effective defense and food provider, was nearly as precious to him as his own limbs."[16] What, then, of the man who does not have such a special relationship with his gun? What kind of man is he? And even more frightening, what if we discover that early American men did not have that special bond with their guns?

Historians have joined actively in the mythmaking. Book after book proclaims that Americans all had guns because they had to have them. Frontier settlers especially would have been armed because of the need to hunt, and to defend themselves from one another and from skulking Indians. Yet nineteenth-century historians somehow missed this special relationship of Americans with their guns, and twentieth-century historians often question their own evidence when it contradicts what is assumed to have always existed. Thus, in a wonderful book, William C. Davis refutes the familiar vision of the frontier as the site of repeated Indian attacks and murderous conduct. But he then adds: "Of course, every cabin had at least one rifle, and perhaps an old pistol or two. . . . They put meat on the table, defended the home against intruders, and provided some entertainment to the men. . . . A man was not a man without knowledge of firearms and some skill in their use." The rifle was fundamental, as every frontier father "taught his sons to use it from the age of ten or earlier. . . . They went with him to hunt the deer and bear that filled their dinner plates, and in the worst extremities, when the Indians came prowling or on the warpath, the boys became men all too soon in defending their lives and property." As supportive evidence, Davis cites a receipt showing how expensive it was to buy lead.[17]

While many historians have accepted this formulation of America's past without too many doubts, a few have claimed originality in discovering the presence of guns. Wesley Frank Craven maintained "a point that too often has been overlooked, or simply taken for granted, and that is that every able free male inhabitant of an English settlement in North America was armed." Yet Craven fails to provide even one example of this widespread gun ownership.[18] For some reason these assertions seem beyond the usual need of historians for supportive evidence, even when the author notes the absence of such evidence. Harold L. Peterson, an outstanding scholar of the history of firearms, wrote, "At no time in American history have weapons been more important than they were from 1620 to 1690. They protected the early colonist from the attack of wild beast or savage, and were the means of providing him with food and clothing and with many of the commodities which he sent back to England." And then comes the odd twist: "Because of this importance of arms, the colonists were forced to purchase the most efficient arms that Europe produced." They produced none themselves, so they had to import them all, and as a consequence, "Americans soon outdistanced the Europeans in superiority of weapons and in skill in using them." This logic, while difficult to fol-

low, is supported in the next sentence with the observation that "the contemporary writers only occasionally refer specifically to the type of arms
used," leaving the historian with no choice but "indirect reference."[19]

It often seems that historians lack confidence in their research. Many
have noted that Americans did not have very many guns, only to fall back
on an insistence that most men must have owned guns. On the basis of
extensive research in the source materials, one scholar of gunsmithing,
James B. Whisker, observed that there was a "scarcity of firearms" in early
America, which became evident "in times of national emergency." After
providing ninety pages of evidence attesting to that scarcity, Whisker concluded, "It is probably [sic] that most urban and nearly every rural household in the United States had at least one gun. . . . With the exception of a
few religious pacifists, every american [sic] was tied to firearms in some
way: they hunted, they sought protection and they enjoyed sport, all with
guns."[20] Elsewhere, Whisker writes about Americans' unfamiliarity with
firearms, citing Jeffrey Amherst's shock when he discovered that most
Colonial militiamen had no idea how to use a gun, and remarking on "the
generally unarmed civilians" of Revolutionary America. Defying his own
research, Whisker then declared that "Americans, accustomed to firearms since birth, realized the importance of good guns." No one could
be familiar with a ten-pound, four-and-a-half-foot-long flintlock from
birth, though it is a favorite image within the myth of American gun
ownership.[21]

The power of image and myth repeatedly overwhelms reality in
discussions of early American firearms. Paul B. Jenkins, a prominent
gun expert in the first half of the twentieth century, wrote that the Sharps
rifle "accompanied every wagon train from the Mississippi to the Rio
Grande, . . . and taught alike Pawnee, Ute, . . . and Blackfoot that . . .
their Canutelike attempts to check the incoming tide of white men were
predestined to be a losing game." Harold F. Williamson similarly noted
that "the Sharps rifle was one of the most widely used guns in America"
during the antebellum period, even though he had previously stated that
Sharps invented his gun in 1848 and produced only a few hundred of
them prior to 1860.[22] A few scholars have observed that powder, ammunition, and guns were rare, and then suggest that these shortages meant
that Americans *had* to be good shots, because they could not waste lead
and powder by missing, or practicing. From that arises the notion that
Americans are born able to shoot, and also that they used their guns when
farming. "Most American citizens entered the nineteenth century with

firearms still at their sides. Men and boys carried arms into the farm fields to work." There is little evidence for this assertion, nor any indication of what good a gun might be when plowing except to hinder the work.[23]

One explanation for the perpetuation of this myth of a comprehensively armed America may be a tendency to confuse law with practice. Though John M. Dederer did a fine job demonstrating the many flaws with firearms and the inactivity of the American militia, and even noted "the dire shortage of arms suffered by the Americans throughout the Revolution," he nonetheless concluded that "by the eighteenth century, colonial Americans were the most heavily armed people in the world; not only did colonial law mandate owning and maintaining a firearm, but through the Revolution most colonials still shot for the table." Unfortunately, the evidence for this statement appears to be deductive logic, working backward from the fact that laws calling for settlers to arm themselves existed to an assumption that they had done so.[24]

The most likely explanation for a continuing faith in an unchanging American gun culture despite evidence to the contrary is the assumption that what *is* must *have been*. It is nearly impossible to believe that the current, advanced civilization of the United States could be so violent unless its more primitive predecessors had been even more enamored of guns. Or as John Milton more cleverly put it:

> We know no time when we were not as now;
> Know none before us, self-begot, self-rais'd
> By our own quick'ning power.[25]

How else could a civilized democratic society place guns at the center of its identity with such passionate devotion unless this is an essential quality of its culture? The source must be deep in history, too deep even for evidence to emerge. Early Americans did not talk about their guns because they all had guns. They did not know how to use those guns because, well, just because. And that is the rub: What to do with the evidence of ignorance? Jeff Cooper, the "gunner's guru," wrote in a 1999 *Guns & Ammo* column, "I discover to my surprise that personal firearms amongst the pioneers were not nearly as common as I had thought. For example, the majority of recruits volunteering for Stonewall Jackson's command in the Civil War showed up not only without shoes, but also without guns. . . . We think of the American pioneer as invariably in possession of his ax and his rifle. That was obviously the way it should have been, but sometimes was not." Cooper's comment, "That was obviously the way it should have been," is unusually honest.[26]

Military historians have certainly noticed the paucity of firearms and Americans' inexperience with guns. As John K. Mahon observed, "folklore has enshrined the sharpshooting frontiersman as the conqueror of North America." But the reality, as military scholars have long argued, was that English settlers of North America relied on British Regulars for protection, and after Independence, on the U.S. Army.[27] Though it may currently be difficult to imagine, that is the core contention of this book: that America has not always been subject to a gun culture. It has not always been this way.

The evidence for this contrary thesis began with the dog that did not bark. In Sir Arthur Conan Doyle's "Silver Blaze," the Scotland Yard inspector asked Sherlock Holmes, was there "any other point to which you would wish to draw my attention?" Holmes responded, "To the curious incident of the dog in the night-time." "The dog did nothing in the night-time," noted the inspector. "That," said Holmes, "was the curious incident."[28]

While studying county probate records (inventories of property after a death) for a project on the legal and economic evolution of the early American frontier, I was puzzled by the absence of something that I assumed would be found in every record: guns. Probate records list every piece of personal property, from acreage to broken cups. An examination of more than a thousand probate records from the frontiers of northern New England and western Pennsylvania for the years 1765 to 1790 revealed that only 14 percent of the inventories included firearms; over half (53 percent) of these guns were listed as broken or otherwise defective. A musket (there were only three rifles mentioned) in good condition often drew special notice in the probate inventories and earned a high evaluation. Obviously guns could have been passed on to heirs before the death of the original owner. Yet wills generally mention previous bequests, even of minor items, and only four mentioned firearms. That was the beginning of this project, a ten-year search for "a word that isn't there."

America's gun culture is an invented tradition.[29] It was not present at the nation's creation, whenever we fix that point. Rather, it developed in a single generation, among those who experienced the onset of the Civil War and that disaster itself. All cultural attributes have a starting point, and a path of development. America's gun culture is unusual only in that one can determine the precise period in which a specific artifact became central to a nation's identity and self-conception. Prior to the 1860s, guns were not perceived as a significant component of America's national identity, essential to its survival. The literature on early American culture repeatedly locates the core values of most Americans in either religious or liberal sensibilities, though this is obviously a sweeping generalization. The prosperity and survival of the United States depended on the grace of God, or civic virtue, or the individual's pursuit of self-interest. The notion that a well-armed public buttressed the American dream would have appeared harebrained to most Americans before the Civil War. But starting in the 1850s, cultural and social standards began a fairly rapid shift that soon placed guns in ever more American hands and at the core of essential cultural values. By the mid-1870s, males in the United States had a fixation with firearms that any modern enthusiast would recognize and salute. That is the story that this book attempts to tell, the path of North America from indifference to a widespread use and acceptance of firearms.

This book does *not* argue that guns did not exist in early America, nor that gun violence did not occur. Nor does this book seek to pull out a few quotations scattered through America's long historical record to strengthen a current political position. This book is concerned with the normative, with what most people did, owned, and thought in reference to guns, most of the time. The question is one of cultural primacy: What lies at the core of national identity? The modern United States, even after the various efforts to tighten restrictions on federal firearms licenses with the 1994 Crime Bill, has more than 140,000 authorized sellers of firearms. There are far fewer bookstores and schools than gunshops, a situation that would have shocked the toughest resident of the early American frontier. For the modern United States, guns are determinative; for early America, they served an often limited function. It is possible, of course, to extract a few ripe quotations here and there that argue otherwise, and reference will be made to several. But the perspective of this work is that the aggregate matters.[30]

This book seeks to examine the relationship of Americans and their guns from a number of different angles. Legal, probate, military, and business records, travel accounts, personal letters, fiction, hunting magazines, legislation, and the guns themselves are all examined. And it is the guns that often make the most compelling case. Most people have no idea how difficult it is to use and care for a black-powder muzzle loading musket, or how haphazard and dangerous these weapons can be when fired. One indication can be found in records of any of the many states that set aside a separate deer season for muzzle-loaders. During New York's 1994 season, for instance, only 3.5 percent of the licensed hunters using muzzle-loaders bagged their deer. Far more deer—19,430 to be exact—were killed by archers.[31] Likewise, no scholar has yet made an effort to count how many guns were actually produced or imported into North America prior to the Civil War, though a few scholars have drawn attention to the fact that almost no guns were made in America prior to the 1820s. The Civil War is the pivot of this cultural development; it was the moment when a large proportion of the country tried to replace elections with gunfire, and when millions of Americans first learned the art of war—and how to use a gun.

An exact historic coincidence of increased productivity of and demand for guns occurred during the Civil War. American armsmakers took advantage of the latest technological breakthroughs to mass-produce firearms, reaching levels of production that for the first time matched those in Europe. From that precise historical moment emerged a distinctive American gun culture, by which is meant not only a shared and widespread culture idolizing firearms, but also a fascination distinct from and unlike the popular attitude toward guns in all other cultures with which the United States shared basic values.

In many ways, then, this is the story of what was not. This work studies the absence of that which was thought to be eternally and universally present—an American gun culture—and its slow, and largely intended, emergence in the nineteenth century. By the end of this book, the gun will be seen as the axial symbol of American culture, absolutely integral to the nation's self-image and looming ever larger in plans for its future development. In a society justly proud of its contributions to human freedom, the gun became the icon of a savage civilization. But it was not always that way. That which was once thought exceptional is now routine. That which was once perceived as subject to communal regulation is now seen as an individual right. There exists a fear of confronting the specifics of these cultural origins, for what has been made can be unmade.

All historical investigation is tentative. Historians build upon one another's research and test sources against generalizations. This study is hardly unique in being, to borrow the wonderful words of R. G. Collingwood, an "interim report on the progress of our historical inquiries." History, Gordon Wood reminds us, is "an accumulative science, gradually gathering truth through the steady and plodding efforts of countless practitioners turning out countless monographs."[32] What an historian says has little impact on present conditions. As Hegel wrote, "Amid the pressure of world events, neither a general principle nor the remembrance of similar circumstances is of any help. . . . Something like pale recollection has no power against the vitality and freedom of the present."[33] And yet, at the very least, the study of the past may impart this one valuable lesson: that nothing in history is immutable.

Chapter One

The European
Gun Heritage

Those blessed ages were fortunate which wanted
the dreadful fury of the devilish and murdering
pieces of ordnance, to whose inventor I am verily
persuaded that they render in hell an eternal
guerdon [reward] for his diabolical invention, by
which he hath given power to an infamous, base,
vile, and dastardly arm to bereave the most
valorous knight.

—Miguel de Cervantes, *Don Quixote*

The Gun in
Early Modern Europe

Handheld firearms developed slowly
and in the face of great suspicion
and even hostility in Europe. Airguns—tubes that fired darts by the use of
compressed air—first appeared in India around the beginning of the
Christian era and were in use in thirteenth-century Persia, finding their
way to Europe by the late fifteenth century.[1] Of far greater long-term significance was the Byzantine development of copper tubes for launching
Greek fire in the ninth century.[2] The idea that gunpowder could be used
to propel a projectile of some kind "seems to have dawned almost simultaneously upon Europeans and Chinese artificers." The earliest drawings
of such weapons are from 1326 in Europe and 1332 in China; both show a
"vase-shaped vessel, armed with an oversized arrow that projects from its
mouth."[3]

Europeans certainly experimented far more with the technology of
firearms than did any other culture. But most of the truly remarkable

technological advancements were seen as little more than curiosities. The Italian Giovanni da Fontana experimented with rockets in the early fifteenth century, without notable impact. The rifle itself was first used in Germany at the very end of the fifteenth century, but its expense and difficulty of use kept it from general acceptance until the nineteenth century. Similarly, in 1650 Otto von Guericke's *Madeburger Windbusche,* an intriguing construction of vacuum chambers that could fire a shot with astounding speed, attracted great interest. But it was an inventive cul-de-sac that produced no further developments.[4]

Those concerned with military armaments had no idea that firearms represented the future. Technological innovations in weaponry followed a number of different trajectories, any one of which seemed to show promise at the time. After all, bladed weapons improved in quality markedly in the medieval period while the more traditional arrow weaponry demonstrated enormous potential; thirteenth-century Chinese crossbows were lethal up to four hundred yards and thus more dangerous than eighteenth-century muskets. Though less accurate than its Chinese counterpart, the European crossbow proved effective in warfare. In 1139 the second Lateran Council banned the crossbow as "a weapon hateful to God" and "too lethal for Christians to use against one another," yet it remained a mainstay of many European military forces.[5] Catapult technology also improved considerably during the medieval period and remained superior to cannon until the mid-fifteenth century.[6]

At the same time, many problems with firearms remained unsolved. For instance, if gunpowder was shaken during transit, the heavier saltpeter sank to the bottom while the carbon remained on top and the sulfur settled in the middle. If gunpowder became too compacted, the lack of air space between the particles limited its explosive power. So common were these problems that the practice of placing padding over the gunpowder in the barrel emerged. The padding contained the gas released by the burning powder, allowing the buildup of pressure. The German "corning" method—wetting the powder, baking it, and then sifting it into granules—allowed for a more even distribution of the three components, which lessened but did not eliminate the problems of transport. But corning, though developed in the fifteenth century, did not become common until 1700, and it remained a dangerous procedure.[7]

In fact many scholars have been struck by the peculiar fascination that drove many Europeans to persist in tinkering with a weapon that showed little real promise until the eighteenth century, and then mainly because of the advent of the bayonet.[8] William McNeill has even speculated that "sexual symbolism . . . goes far to explain the European artisans' and rulers' irrational investment in early firearms." An English scholar has stated that "it is difficult to understand the increasing popularity abroad of the miserably ineffective hand-gun," except as a part of a desperate search for "a rival to the English longbow." Less controversial is the notion that the militaristic habits of the urban Europeans who manufactured and purchased the new guns account for this obsession. It is worth noting that, from its earliest stage, the fascination with the gun has been an urban phenomenon.[9]

Nonetheless, not everyone welcomed the new technology with enthusiasm. In the 1570s, Michel de Montaigne noted the psychological value of firearms, but found little else to celebrate about that weapon. "As for the pistol," he wrote, "except for the shock to the ear, with which everyone has become familiar, I think it is a weapon of very little effect, and hope that some day we shall abandon the use of it." The horse seemed to Montaigne a far superior tool in warfare.[10] Writing in 1605, Miguel de Cervantes stated that firearms cheapened life and honor: "it grieves me to have ever undertaken this exercise of a knight-errant in this our detestable age; for although no danger can afright me, yct . . . I live in jealousy to think how powder and lead might deprive me of the power to make myself famous and renowned by the strength of my arm and the edge of my sword."[11] Many shared this view that the new firearms were just not fair, though more common was a skepticism of their efficacy. The French Marshal Blaise de Monluc complained that "poltroons that had not dared look those men in the face at hand, which at distance they had laid dead with their confounded bullets." Many engravers pictured the makers of firearms and gunpowder working with the devil lurking just behind their shoulder. Erasmus called guns "the engines of hell," and exclaimed, "Who can believe that guns were the invention of man?" Milton was less subtle in having Satan invent the gun in revenge for his fall. Others reacted more strenuously. The first use of handheld guns in battle came in 1439 when a party of Bolognese opened fire on their Venetian opponents, killing a few Venetians. However, the Venetians emerged victorious, and immediately massacred all those found with this "cruel and cowardly innovation" in their possession. Francesco Sforza did the same after the Battle of Lonigo a few years later.[12]

Among the landed gentry of Europe, the belief that firearms were not fit for a gentleman persisted into the seventeenth century. Many aristocrats and professional soldiers felt that guns undermined martial skill and manliness. Combat, this view held, should be a test of strength, courage, and ability. In contrast, they feared that anyone could be trained in the use of a gun, lending itself to dangerous leveling ideas, with the possibility that common people might someday level those weapons at their social betters.[13]

But there was another reason why professionals hated guns: they were deadly. Many battles in the late Middle Ages ended with few casualties, the game being won by one party outmaneuvering the other, ending in a surrender of one group of professionals to another. Machiavelli, citing a pair of early fifteenth-century battles that took three lives between them, observed that "the mercenaries devoted all their professional skill to eliminating hardship and anxiety for themselves and their own troops; they did not kill one another in battle, but rather took each other prisoner."[14] But firearms threw a strange randomness into the equation. As Don Quixote said, "without knowing how or from whence, . . . there arrives a wandering bullet (shot off, perhaps, by him that was afraid, and fled at the very blaze of powder, as he discharged the accursed engine), and cuts off and finisheth in a moment the thoughts of him who merited to enjoy it many ages." There was no telling who might be killed by a shot from these wild new weapons that could pierce armor at forty yards. Certainly the person aimed at was in no more danger than someone standing ten yards away, so inaccurate were these early guns.[15]

Firearms transformed warfare throughout the world, but not immediately.[16] Even in Europe, the center of firearms development and production, soldiers carried a wide variety of weapons through the end of the eighteenth century. European artisans and scientists continued to experiment, fine-tuning the nature of the first guns, but failing to make the dramatic technological leaps that would come only in the nineteenth century. Likewise, military leaders experimented with the use of firearms in warfare, discovering the advantages of massed musket fire in the seventeenth century. Where the English longbow had established distance combat and given military status to the common yeoman, the gun returned combat to relatively close quarters and placed a command of weaponry back in the hands of professionals. It turned out that the gun was not quite so simple to use, requiring much time, money, training, and care.[17]

Firearms also introduced a greater degree of uncertainty to the battlefield. Even veteran troops could panic before a massed volley of musketry, and both victories and defeats became far more conclusive than in the past. The more farsighted military thinkers saw that firearms raised the stakes of combat while placing a premium on training, planning, and leadership. Using guns necessitated more preparation and organization than had previously been the case, and common soldiers had to pay far more attention to their officers. The battlefield would no longer be a collection of single combats; firearms required far more coordination and granted a capable commander far more control than any feudal chieftain had ever exercised. Here was a challenge and opportunity for the more clever military leaders who worked to transform warfare into an "art." And yet most commanders remained suspicious of the reliability and usefulness of firearms, usually seeing them as a supplement to traditional methods of warfare.[18]

Governments, too, remained deeply suspicious of firearms. Above all they feared the use of this new technology by individuals. There was no doubt that a single company of regulars could overwhelm and defeat any band of discontented subjects armed with a few guns; but no monarch wanted to test the validity of this theory. Ruling elites saw no reason to accept any level of unnecessary social disorder because of the availability of this new weaponry. Every state in Europe therefore placed strict restrictions on the use and availability of firearms. In England this legislation started as early as the reign of Henry VII (1485–1509), who feared the wheelock—the first gun to ignite the powder by producing a spark, in this case by a wheel striking a piece of iron—as giving far too much equality to the poor. As a consequence, Henry VII and Henry VIII both outlawed wheelocks. Henry VIII attempted to limit the use of other firearms to the elite, chartering the Fraternity of St. George in London to develop the "Science and Feate of Shootynge" longbows, crossbows, and firearms. This fraternity, which became the Ancient and Honourable Artillery Company of London, was the first group to be granted royal permission to shoot firearms. In 1541, Parliament limited the ownership of handguns to nobility and freeholders who earned more than £100 a year from their property; a threshold fifty times higher than the forty-shilling freehold needed to vote in county elections. Henry VIII continued to rely on archers to defend his ships at sea, buying tens of thousands of yew bows for that purpose. The bows found on the fighting deck of the *Mary Rose,* the recently excavated flagship of Henry VIII's fleet, indicate "that archers were preparing to defend the ship when she sank."[19]

The one advantage that any state found in the new firearm technology was that it was so easy to regulate. The longbow was generally held to be the equal of a matchlock or snaphance (which used a spark rather than a match to ignite the powder), and could easily be cut, fitted, and equipped with a large supply of arrows in a single day almost anywhere in England. But guns required metal, furnaces, a wide assortment of tools, and specially trained craftsmen. Guns required powder and metal for shot and needed constant maintenance and regular repairs; to use them well required training and practice. In short, it was an expensive and time-consuming enterprise. And best of all, the shops producing all these items and responsible for repair were supervised by the government. Consequently, most European states, England included, found it an easy matter to keep firearms the private preserve of the military and the elite.[20]

And still England hesitated to adopt this new technology beyond the level of a novelty. A basic ambivalence underlay the attitudes of most European governments in the sixteenth and seventeenth centuries. Military leaders remained divided on the usefulness of firearms in warfare, many feeling that they posed as much danger to those holding them as to those at whom they were aimed, if only for the false confidence they imparted. Yet public officials remained certain that they were dangerous in the hands of commoners. Crowds armed with even a few guns might think themselves the equal to trained troops and risk battles that they would have avoided if both sides held only pikes and swords, because regulars were understood to be superior in the use of both. As a result, governments proceeded slowly in the integration of firearms into their military forces, and maintained a watchful eye on the distribution of guns to civilians—if they allowed it at all.[21]

The Great Debate

In the 1590s, on the eve of English settlement in North America, a vigorous pamphlet debate raged over whether longbows should be replaced with firearms. Sparked by the conviction that England was falling behind its continental competitors, this debate involved most of the nation's leading military figures and transformed the English army.[22]

Most scholars agree that the longbow was in fact far superior to the firearms of the sixteenth century, as well as those of the seventeenth and eighteenth centuries. As one expert of the Napoleonic Wars pointed out, longbows were superior even to the muskets of that era, with a far greater range and accuracy, and five times the rate of fire. One obvious reason why so many English officers preferred to keep the longbow was financial. Arrows were not only inexpensive, but they could be used repeatedly in practice, while the powder required for guns literally went up in smoke. The interest in firearms may appear at first glance more mysterious. As the prominent military historian Charles Oman wrote, "Indeed, it is not easy to make out the reasons why [the musket] superseded the bow in the end of the reign of Elizabeth." There is little agreement as to why less efficient firearms replaced longbows; perhaps the very attractiveness of a new technology was sufficient justification.[23]

The pamphlets themselves, which are full of misinformation about each form of weaponry, do not completely clarify the attraction of firearms. The two primary forms of firearms at the turn of the seventeenth century were the harquebus and the musket. The former was not very large, though bulky and remarkably inaccurate, but far less expensive than the musket. The musket, a matchlock at this time, was a big, clumsy weapon that required touching a smoldering string to a pan of gunpowder in order to fire it, thus giving away one's position at all times and making it largely useless in the rain. In addition, matchlocks needed to be fired at a tilt, with the lock on top, to facilitate the ignition of the powder. Aiming the matchlock was thus nearly impossible. In contrast, the longbow was not only a superb weapon for its age, but also part of a long, romantic tradition in England, dating back at least to the Battle of Crécy in 1326, when English archers had decimated the ranks of the slower-firing Genoese crossbowmen. Some proponents of bows looked back even further, to the Battle of Hastings. It was, after all, archery that had cut down Harold III's Anglo-Saxons and led to the Norman conquest of England. For its adherents, the bow and arrow had demonstrable mastery as a weapon of war over the five centuries since Hastings.[24]

This debate rehearsed the discussions about the perceived flaws of firearms that would be repeated over the next two centuries. Guns took far too long to load and fire. A bow could release twelve arrows in the time it took to reload a musket, and all at a much greater range than firearms. A musket could fire about ten to twenty rounds an hour without risk of overheating—taking the risk could, according to gun proponent Humfrey Barwick, double that performance. Officers at the Battle of Kissingen in 1636 and the Battle of Wittenmergen in 1638 reported that their musketeers averaged just seven shots total in the roughly eight hours of each of these battles. If the powder were improperly mixed or corned, or became damp and shaken, or was not packed down properly in the piece, a misfire would ensue. There was no such thing as a misfired arrow. Rain and wind could both prevent the use of muskets; it would take a hurricane to hinder the flight of an arrow. A neutral observer of this debate, Robert Barret, added to the list of firearm flaws in noting all the equipment required in using them, and the absence of any room for error: too little powder and the shot was too feeble to have an effect, too much and the musket could blow up. In contrast, the only thing that could go wrong with a longbow was "the breaking of the Bowe or bowstring." The "unreadines, imperfections and small effects of the weapons of fire" meant that they hit few targets for the number of shots fired. And on top of these and other flaws, guns were expensive and took a long time to make well. Even Barwick acknowledged that crafting a good musket required fifty-four days.[25]

The foremost opponent of firearms at this time was Sir John Smythe, who had personally trained those militia units preparing to meet the Spanish invasion by the Armada.[26] Smythe insisted that most experienced officers "scorned and laughed at" these new weapons and knew of battles in which muskets had been fired much of the day with few killed by their shots. The supporters of firearms, Smythe charged, knew little of real war, basing their estimations of a gun's usefulness on shootings undertaken in perfect conditions.[27] Smythe acknowledged that these "toyes" frightened "yonglings and novices of warre, with smoake and noyse," and had demonstrated some real usefulness as defensive weapons fired from behind strong emplacements that allowed the musketeers the opportunity to reload. They could also exert a powerful impact in prepared ambushes, where the first volley often proved decisive. But even in these circumstances, the utility of guns was strictly limited by the need for constant practice and by an effective range of only six to ten yards, a distance granted by supporters of the new firearms. Beyond that range, "their bullets doo worke as much effect against the Moone, as against the Enemie that they shoote at."[28]

Many other problems plagued the matchlock and its successor, the snaphance, which came out of the Netherlands in the late sixteenth century. These early muskets generally weighed around twenty pounds and required a "fourquette," a forked stick that held up the weapon so that it could be fired. The shooter had to juggle the weapon in such a way so as to keep the match and powder far apart while still being able to use both. Easily ignited, black powder was very dangerous to the musketeer. Since burning embers often remained in the barrel after a shot, most guides recommended waiting before reloading and insisted on angling the gun away from the body. Loading a gun safely facing away from the shooter was a difficult physical arrangement. Even with these precautions, delayed discharge was common with all black-powder weapons. The delayed discharge is a source of humor now, but was a cause of real terror on the battlefield. All manuals of arms, then and now, agree that this was a task that only a fully grown, sober, and alert man should perform. Further, each black-powder musket required a slightly different load; a shooter needed to become familiar with the exact amount appropriate for the gun. The ball had to be seated on top of the powder in such a way as to compress it a little, but not too much. If contact was not made, the explosion of the powder could damage the barrel without propelling the ball with much force; if too tight, the barrel could explode. Such limitations remained true of the flintlock into the nineteenth century.[29]

Not surprisingly, guns were not in large demand in seventeenth-century England. Not only was access to these weapons limited by the government, they were also expensive and difficult to use. Humfrey Barwick was certainly correct in noting that using a firearm required extensive training. Even the simplest firing instructions for a matchlock consisted of fourteen steps. The most exact military directions had fifty-seven separate points. One late seventeenth-century instruction manual listed twenty steps to loading a carbine on horseback before one could "Give fire." And even then, "the Carbine is to be fired at about a twelve foot distance, and to be levelled at the knees of your Enemies Horse, because that by the strength of the Powder and motion of the Horse your shot may be at Random." After firing, the twenty-first instruction was to "Drop (or let fall) your Carbine," whereupon the horseman should draw his sword for the real combat.[30]

But there was a "new discipline" on the continent that captured the attention of English military enthusiasts in the 1590s and launched a debate in England.[31] This modern approach to warfare saw the cavalry armed with lances working in combination with pike-bearing infantry and companies of well-trained troops carrying muskets and harquebuses. In contrast, the English army, with its bows and halberds, just seemed old-fashioned. Smythe dismissed handheld firearms as just another indi-

cation of the effete nature of French society. It would not be the last time
that otherwise intelligent people would fall for nonsense coming out of
France.[32]

There was more to the arguments of gun advocates than fashion. The
essence of the pro-gun position is to be found in that phrase "well
trained." By 1590 England had enjoyed a century of relative peace, its
battles fought at sea rather than on land. The navy had become the
nation's prime defense, backed by the "trained bands," volunteer militia
units headed by the country gentry. For many in the English elite there
were two large problems with the militia ideal: the need for everyone to
own a bow and the absence of training. Contrary to Smythe's accusations,
the experience of many English officers serving on the continent convinced them that if England went to war against France or Spain again, as
they surely would, they would need a well-trained standing army to
match those countries. But there was a further advantage to a standing
army: militia armed with longbows might revolt, while standing armies
trained in the use of guns, which could be strictly regulated by the government, could put down such rebellions. This vision required, of course,
that the common yeoman not have access to firearms. The English government certainly saw no reason to encourage the poor to continue practicing the use of longbows, and what had been routine vanished.[33]

Robert Dudley, Earl of Leicester, who had served with the Dutch in
their long war against the Spanish (1568–1648), was a leader in this movement to replace the bow with the gun, and the militia with a standing
army. He had seen English militia turn and flee in battle in the Netherlands, and worried that they might do the same in a situation of greater
danger to England. Dudley and other military leaders prevailed in this
debate, convincing the English army to make the transition to firearms
and pikes. In 1595 the Privy Council finally voted to end the use of archers
in English military forces.[34]

Class attitudes lurked at the edge of this debate. For Smythe the longbow equaled the militia. Those nations that lacked one lacked the other,
and also lacked, as a consequence, liberty. So of course such nations as
France and Spain turned to the newfangled firearms, which negated forever, in Smythe's view, the possibility of the citizen-soldier. Only professional soldiers could afford the years it took to become proficient in the
use of firearms.[35] Smythe condemned the whole new system as aimed at
degrading the English commoner, reducing the English soldier to cannon
fodder, better killed in battle than preserved for the nation's security and

prosperity. Smythe's anger spilled over as he charged that the "excuse used by some of our [new] men of war, for the casting away and losse of such great numbers, and many thousands of our gallant English people in those Lowe countrie warres . . . [is] that all those brave people that have been lost . . . were the very scomme, theeves, and roges of England, and therefore have been well lost; and that the Realme (being too full of people) is very well ridde of them, and that if they had not beene consumed in those warres, they would have died under a hedge." With such attitudes, Smythe maintained, most soldiers were killed not in battle, but by their own commanders, who provided too little food and care, so that their troops were claimed by disease and malnourishment. Smythe astutely noted that the new military system carried with it a new vision of the poor as "surplus population."[36]

Humfrey Barwick, like Smythe a professional soldier, accepted these class distinctions but focused instead on what he saw as the practical issue of the deadliness of "the fiery shot." Much of his book is devoted to listing officers killed by firearms in order to show the effectiveness of muskets. Barwick had a great deal of difficulty with consistency, and veracity—he claimed that it took longer to shoot an arrow than to fire a musket, a patently false assertion. Barwick also argued that the use of guns in battle led to fewer deaths, since one side usually turned and fled at the first volley. On the other hand, he claimed that the gun was superior to the longbow because lead shot could pierce armor, unlike rusty arrowheads launched into flight by bowmen who did not always pull their bows all the way back. In fact, metal-tipped European arrows could and did pierce armor.[37]

The most difficult issue for supporters of the gun was its limited range. All their descriptions of the gun's usefulness were based on a range of eight to ten yards. Beyond that, they acknowledged, firearms were largely useless. Bows could fire their shafts two to three hundred yards. Reconstructions of the longbows found on the Mary Rose had "penetrative power at up to 300 yards." Even more amazing is the durability of these weapons; after lying underwater for more than four centuries, the Mary Rose bows could still be strung and pulled to their full extent. Muskets, in contrast, required constant care. In the end, Barwick and the other supporters of guns held to the simple assertion—really an article of faith—that guns were better.[38]

But then Barwick, like other supporters of firearms at the end of the sixteenth century, never claimed that the gun was decisive in battle.

Identifying three causes of military success—loyalty, intelligence, and training—Barwick addressed the latter. A musket "in the handes of a skilfull souldier, well practised and trained with the use thereof, is a most terrible and deadly weapon." Repeatedly Barwick insisted that the musket must be judged only "in the handes of skilfull men"; in fact "without practice they are not commodious but hurtful" to the shooter. The point of using firearms rather than longbows was not that the one was superior to the other on the field of battle, but that the modern weapon required trained soldiers to use them. The yeomen should be present as pikers— half the total force—protecting the musketeers while they reloaded. There was, in the estimation of all supporters of firearms, no way that amateurs could employ such weapons in battle; theirs was an argument for a professional army in place of the romantic vision of Smythe and other supporters of the archaic militia. If England hoped to compete internationally in the seventeenth century, it had to deploy modern, highly trained armies organized according to the continental model. Barwick asserted that England really needed only a force of five thousand professional musketeers and "a carte lode of billes for the labourers." Smythe could not really respond to this essential argument, for his was a medieval vision of an insular England protecting its island domain. Barwick spoke for the expansionists, and the modern professional army with modern weapons was to be their tool of conquest.[39]

But the expansionists understood the limitations of firearms, and did not make the mistake of placing sole reliance on them. One problem they discovered immediately was the absence of trained smiths capable of repairing guns. Writing from Ireland in 1590, Sir George Carew complained that nearly all of his firearms were "unserviceable; only 600 worth the repairing." Carew reported that there was little he could do even to fix those six hundred muskets, as "I know not but two [workmen] in this realm that have knowledge of how to stock a piece." Barwick thought there should be thirty muskets per hundred soldiers, while the continental practice was twenty-five, a number Robert Barret supported. But in 1600 Sir John Dowdall ordered that there be no more than twelve muskets per hundred, as his soldiers "being weak and ill fed, will not be able to carry them in his long and continued marches"; so they took turns hefting these twenty-pound weapons around. Probably as a consequence of such ill treatment, they were not very good with their guns. When troops mutinied in Ostend in 1588, ten of their marksmen shot at the governor, Sir John Conway, from six yards. All missed.[40]

Modern scholars tend to agree that the supporters of longbows had the better argument. As Thomas Esper summarized the case, "the replacement of the longbow by firearms occurred at a time when the former was still a superior weapon." There were even repeated efforts to bring back the longbow, most notably that led by Gervase Markham in 1634 and the Earl of Craufurd in the 1700s. One thing that the two types of weapons did have in common was that proficiency in either required a great deal of training. The difference was that bows and arrows were so cheap, and the arrows largely reusable, that any village could regularly host archery meets. Guns and powder were not only more expensive, but closely regulated by the Crown, which did not want common people training in their use.[41]

In 1365 Edward III had ordered that able-bodied men practice archery on every church holiday and prohibited all other games so as to insure his subjects' attention to this sport. These policies bore fruit at Agincourt in 1415.[42] Bows made from yew trees acted as natural springs, sending arrows with forged metal tips flying at France's great aristocrats. Sheets of arrows at Agincourt were reported to have ascended at five-second intervals; the descending arrows could pierce an inch of oak, and French mailed armor.[43] Later monarchs, Henry VII and VIII and Elizabeth I, encouraged archery practice, but James I made no such effort. Rather, James I used the nation's new game laws to place many obstacles in the path of those interested in archery.[44] His attitude, and that of most gun enthusiasts of the sixteenth century, was well summarized in his response to the suggestion that more of England's subjects should enjoy the right to hunt and own firearms: "it is not fit that clowns should have these sports."[45]

As England's government came to encourage the use of firearms among its troops, it not only outlawed the use of guns by commoners, but also discouraged their use of bows and arrows. Those members of the militia "levied for service abroad" were to be trained in the use of firearms, but their use was to be discouraged and even forbidden in all other contexts. To emphasize that point, all guns used by the militia were stored in government magazines. From 1600 on, the trained bands trained almost exclusively with pikes, though the gentlemen could carry firearms supplied by the state. Such volunteer groups would continue to keep the poor in line until the late eighteenth century.[46] In all, it was a tremendously effective policy not so much for disarming the public, as for making them largely indifferent to the whole issue of arms. By 1600 the trained bands, except those in London, were dormant. And by the dawn of the seventeenth century, firearms ownership in England had been limited to the elite and the government.[47]

The Gun in Seventeenth-Century England

From the government's perspective, there was one rarely stated advantage to guns: they were far more expensive than bows and arrows. Those military leaders who wisely associated themselves from the start with gun manufacturers found benefit in this greater expense. Smythe even charged a conspiracy to undermine the use of the arrow as a way of enhancing firearms production. It is absolutely correct that the triumph of the pro-gun forces in the great debate of the 1590s and the adoption of firearms by the English military offered an enormous boost to a struggling new industry, even if initially limited to a few thousand purchases. By the middle of the seventeenth century, England's few gunmakers would organize a highly effective lobby, establishing a profitable monopoly.[48]

At the start of the seventeenth century, gunmaking was still a new profession in England. Those making firearms—and there were only five gunmakers in London in 1607—could be found in many different guilds: usually the blacksmiths, but also cutlers, armorers, founders, and clockmakers. On the continent, gunmakers were generally seen as artists, and their works were regarded as luxury items for the rich. For instance, Martin le Bourgeoys, the seventeenth-century gunmaker popular with the European elite, was also a painter, sculptor, and musical-instrument maker.[49]

Starting in 1599 and continuing for forty years, a battle raged between the blacksmiths and the armorers over the right to proof guns (a test to insure that a gun met government standards). Each guild claimed that it alone could best judge the quality of firearms, and each arrested and fined in guild courts anyone who dared to make a gun without its proof mark. The first effort to bring order to gun production and to establish standardization came from the Crown in 1630, when the Council of War issued "Orders for the generall uniformitie of all sortes of armes." The following year Charles I appointed commissioners to oversee the repair of all the armor and arms of the militia and to regulate the fees that gunsmiths could charge for those repairs. Complaining that they were few in number, mostly aged and poor, and subject to constant harassment and even arrest by the armorers and blacksmiths, London's gunsmiths joined together to form the Gunmakers' Company in 1637. The need for a gunmakers' guild seemed obvious not only to those promoting their own interest, but also to a government worried about the poor state of English firearms production. The Armourers' and Blacksmiths' Companies filed suit against this new guild, which led to a hearing before the attorney general in 1638. Not only did the Crown award the Gunmakers' Company their charter, but it also offered its support by purchasing nearly every gun they had made and would make.[50]

Despite their efforts at professionalization, most gunmakers did not find it profitable to specialize. Until the mid-eighteenth century gunsmiths continued to work as blacksmiths or cutlers as well, belonging to both guilds. English guns were usually of the poorest quality in Europe and often unreliable even by the low standards of the day. Even after the formation of the Gunmakers' Company, individual gunmakers in and out of the guild produced inferior firearms, often on purpose. For instance, in the 1650s a group of gunmakers associated with the prominent gunsmith Edward Burrows, who "cared not a fart" for the efforts of any guild to regulate his guns, produced the profitable "Barbary guns," shoddy firearms for sale in the Mediterranean. These Barbary guns so damaged the reputation of English gunmakers that the Gunmakers' Company stepped in with government approval in 1658 and passed the first set of regulations on firearms production in England. Less intentional was the embarrassment caused when it was discovered in 1648 that the guns of William Burton, the company's proofmaster, could not pass his own proof. Despite government patronage, regulatory powers, and the lack of any real competition from elsewhere in Britain, English gunmaking remained well behind the continent until the late part of the century.[51]

Much of the unreliability in firearms in the seventeenth century was not the product of inferior workmanship, but inherent to the firearms themselves. Keeping a wheelock primed and ready for too long would generally disable the weapon, as Edmund Ludlow discovered during the English Civil War when, as governor of Wardour Castle, he faced the besieging royalists: "My pistols being wheel locks and wound up all night, I could not get to fire, so that I was forced to trust to my sword for the keeping down of the enemy." Even flintlocks were known to get stuck in the half-cocked position if left unfired for too long. As a result most seventeenth- and eighteenth-century texts that addressed firearms advised that the gun should not be loaded until it was time for its use. And even then, most seventeenth-century guns required cleaning between uses. The simplification of the lock, from the wheelock's thirty-five parts to the flintlock's seventeen, did not eliminate the basic problem of mechanical error.[52]

From its beginning the Gunmakers' Company appealed directly to the government for aid, promising in return to overcome these technical problems. On January 9, 1640, they petitioned the Privy Council for its custom. "Carrabines and Pistolls have not been here many yeares in use, nor long beene made, And we doubt not but hereafter upon Encouragement we shalbe more ready in the making of them."[53] The government provided this support, yet English arms production remained insufficient to meet domestic demands, especially once the conflict between Parliament and the Crown turned violent in 1642.

The Civil War was good for the gun business. Although both sides turned to the Netherlands and France for the bulk of their firearms, the war did provide a major boost to English weaponsmakers as they worked feverishly to meet the demands of all participants and frightened neutrals. Much of their labor was devoted to cleaning and repairing old firearms that had not seen use in years, and converting the old-fashioned sear lock to trigger locks; they were also called upon often to maintain recently produced firearms. Gunmakers throughout England became desperate for apprentices, and the London gunmakers began relying on the putting-out system* to get provincial gunsmiths to help them fill their orders. Gunsmiths outside of London had previously not been allowed to make guns, only to repair them. But now the London gunmakers were themselves so desperate for help that they ignored the laws they had previously insisted on enforcing. For instance, in 1645 seven members of the Gunmakers' Company received an order for 347 carbines. Each of these gunmakers had two or three apprentices, which allowed at least twenty-eight pairs of hands to produce the carbines within three months. But many charges of breach of contract were brought in these years, as the gunsmiths failed to fulfill the large orders they were tempted to take. And many gunmakers showed a willingness to sacrifice integrity for profit, selling cleaned, old muskets as new, shortening barrel lengths, skimping on the quality of

*In which the component parts were supplied to an artisan who finished production in his home.

locks, and even bribing procurement officers in the ordnance offices of both sides. Oliver Cromwell proved particularly harsh in punishing these miscreants. Those who could avoid prosecution and find sufficient well-trained labor enjoyed enormous success during the 1640s. By 1647 the majority of arms for the parliamentary forces were being made in England, a landmark in English firearms production.[54]

No matter how hard some early gunsmiths struggled to attain uniformity in arms production, it remained beyond their grasp. One of the best gunsmiths of the seventeenth century was Robert Murden of London. There exist five of his pistols from the same consignment made to the same specifications in 1642. Experts consider them "remarkably uniform," as close to identical as it is possible for guns made prior to the nineteenth century to be. And yet no two are alike. They look alike and share similar embellishments, yet they have different lengths and calibers, and differ in weight by as much as a third. Each gun was the product of individual labor and attention, the gunsmith taking the time to ornament the locks and the butt plate—even the stock bears its flourishes.[55]

Added to this amazing diversity among similar firearms was the larger issue of completely different types of guns. The matchlock was a favorite of the English military through most of the seventeenth century. Yet soldiers still stood side by side holding matchlocks and flintlocks, snaphances and wheelocks and sear locks, carbines and pistols, harquebuses and blunderbusses. Most amazingly, the English army seemed uninterested in systematizing their armaments; in fact throughout the seventeenth century the ordnance department would routinely order every kind of firearm made, assuming, incorrectly, that they served different functions.[56]

It is difficult to determine how many muskets a qualified gunsmith could make in a month. In any shop much depended on what other sort of work was being undertaken, from blacksmithing to swordmaking to cleaning and repairing old firearms. The Gunmakers' Company produced 385 guns per month in the 1650s, which is two and a half guns per gunsmith. But as Walter Stern has written, "gunmakers contracted out much of their work; they bought and even 'borrowed' guns from each other," and even bought guns from the continent in order to fulfill contracts. The Restoration government kept very close track of gunmaking in the realm, wanting to know precisely who made how many guns and for whom. Their account on one leading London gunmaker, Ralph Venn, indicates that in a six-month period in 1660, he produced twenty-two

muskets, six of which he sold. Venn seems to have had only one apprentice at this time, though the records are vague in this regard. That would
indicate that a master and his apprentice made three to four muskets a
month during a slow period. In the same six-month period, Robert Murden made three matchlocks, fifteen carbines, and twenty-five pistols. In
1665 William Parsons and two apprentices made twenty-four snaphance
muskets in just two months, a rate of four per month per worker.[57]

Complete records remain for the Watson Brothers of London. They
indicate that almost all of their work from the opening of their shop in
London in 1625 until 1655 was for the government, with only the occasional private order. In fact, with the granting of the charter of the Gunmakers' Company, the English government proclaimed all guns in
gunshops in England state property, subject to regulation and seizure
at any time. Even without a contract, gunsmiths worked for the government, and it did not matter which government. In 1655 Cromwell
ordered that all firearms of every type in London were to be seized and
stored in the Tower. Cromwell discouraged selling firearms to private
persons; Charles II regulated it carefully.[58]

One of the largest orders placed by the Ordnance Department in the
seventeenth century was for five thousand muskets, two thousand snaphances, and fifteen hundred pistols in 1652. Fifty-eight gunmakers shared
this contract, each devoting his shop to finishing his share of the order
within a year. Many had to turn to other gunsmiths to fulfill their part
of the commission of approximately 120 guns each, or 10 a month.[59] But
this was the last major contract for England's gunmakers until the century's end; the war was over and the government sat on a surplus of arms
of all types, stockpiling muskets, swords, and pikes by the thousands.
England's gunmakers were dependent on the government, and when
those contracts dried up in 1653, many of them closed shop or shifted their
labor to new objects, typically falling back on their skills as blacksmiths
or cutlers.[60]

The Restoration brought a rush of orders for aristocratic families
who no longer had to fear the Lord Protector of the Commonwealth
or his agents. But Charles II made certain that he knew where every firearm went. In 1660 he ordered gunmakers to inform the government of
all guns sold, and to whom, plus any remaining in stock. Fortunately
for historians, the government's agents were very thorough in checking
these returns. Gun production fell from a seventeenth-century high of

1,512 in the single month of March 1661, to an average of 310 per month in 1662.[61]

Perhaps as a result of this government monitoring, sales to individuals other than members of the ruling class remained insignificant. English firearms retained their poor reputation, one not aided when it was discovered in 1661 that the Gunmaker to the King, Harman Barne, had been importing guns from Liege and selling them as his own make. Even those who supported the English gunsmiths, such as the Duke of Richmond, generally preferred continental firearms for personal use. With no large government contracts taking up the slack, gun sales again plummeted and gunmakers looked frantically for any relief. In 1671 they gained the sole right to proof all firearms made in the London area and all arms made for the government—a privilege they maintained until 1813—and had authority to prosecute those who violated this rule. Though their proof mark was not required on guns made in Scotland or Ireland, the Gunmakers' Company did succeed in reducing provincial gunmaking to insignificant levels. They also called for outlawing the importation of foreign firearms. It took thirteen years of expensive effort to bring the prohibition into law, but in 1685 the new king, James II, outlawed the importation of "all Arms and utensils of warr." By that date the Gunmakers' Company of London had a near monopoly on gunmaking in England. They also acted to prevent the introduction of new types of firearms, such as breechloaders, in the eighteenth century. But then production levels in general remained very low, which was fine with the government, as it found "the armament industry . . . not only essential, but also dangerous."[62]

Despite these limitations on both production and ownership, there are those who have suggested that most English owned and used guns. Joyce Lee Malcolm has written that "many, if not most, common people had arms." This assertion is based on deductive logic: people must have been afraid for their lives and property, therefore they must have had guns. The late seventeenth century was "an age when these weapons were needed" because of all the highwaymen and "wealthy travelers" who carried guns for protection. If the elite owned guns, then surely the average Englishman did as well. Yet historians from the leftist E. P. Thompson to the conservative member of Parliament Ian Gilmour have found that nearly all English citizens were unarmed; in fact there were laws to that effect. Gilmour's massive study of eighteenth-century mobs located only a single instance of an armed crowd firing on the authorities. If they had owned guns, one would expect common people to have used firearms rather than farm implements to defend themselves against armed troops.[63]

Nor is there much evidence that criminals used guns. There is a long tradition in England, as in America, of associating crime with poverty. In the classic formulation, "forest dwellers were generally believed to be addicted to crime and violence." Yet the evidence indicates that much of that crime was squatting on commons and wastelands. In 1658 Parliament even considered limiting the use of paths through wooded areas as a way of controlling these dangerous poor. The actual level of violent crime was not higher in the forests than in the towns, but the perception persisted.[64]

Most personal violence in early modern England occurred not on lonely highways but at public festivals, often between competing teams of Morris dancers and such other representatives of communal pride. "Violence of this sort, like football a ritualized expression of communal rivalry, often occurred at revels: ''tis no festival unless there be some fightings' ran the popular saying."[65] There were a few dramatic exceptions, such as in 1628 when a London mob set upon Dr. Lamb, Lord Buckingham's astrologer, and beat him to death, shouting that they would do the same to Buckingham. But generally, English crowds, whether rural or urban, behaved with a notable lack of violence. For the gentry, as E. P. Thompson noted, "the insubordination of the poor was an inconvenience; it was not a menace."[66]

Armed citizens generally denoted social order. Public processions in the sixteenth and seventeenth centuries usually featured public officials in full regalia parading with citizens armed with pikes as a show of force and stability.[67] Yet England had another tradition of those citizens using their arms to intimidate the authorities, almost always in defense of traditional rights, with an appeal to custom and ancient laws—real and imagined.[68] For instance, between 1626 and 1628 residents of Gillingham Forest demonstrated in opposition to enclosures. On the latter date they even appeared bearing every sort of weapon, from scythe to halberd, but no guns, and drove the sheriff of Dorset to flee. There were similar "public disorders," as the government saw them, in other parts of England over the next decade. But it should be noted that displays such as this were more acts of aggression—displays of threatened force—than of violence. No one was injured and the demonstrators usually succeeded only in slowing down the process of enclosure. Most actions labeled "riots" by the government were little more than ritualized demonstrations of dissatisfaction. Riot was the final step in a process aimed at attaining aid from the government. Violence—real violence against people rather than property—was almost inconceivable, and popularly perceived as counterproductive. Owning a gun in order to prevent government tyranny, as some writers have suggested was the norm in early modern England, not only remained illegal but also seemed not to have occurred to many people.[69]

It is notable that the state turned to the militia first to deal with these uprisings. As would later be the case in the American colonies, the militia was seen as the preserver of social order. Yet it proved largely ineffective in England and America alike. Often it was the case that the militia was the crowd. "Commands to mobilize the militia were generally ignored, and on the one occasion when the trained bands did turn out, their house-to-house search in a part of Dean Forest known to be swarming with rebels was a fiasco." And again, like the American militia, when they did turn out, they were either unarmed or bore pikes and clubs.[70]

The state needed to arm the militia, when they were not busy disarming them, seeing them as a threat. On the one hand the state relied on the militia to maintain order; on the other hand the government feared a militia force joining rioters. The first necessity required some form of arms; the second demanded that the militia remain unarmed. The government therefore tacked carefully between these positions. Authority to disarm the militia was left in the hands of any regular army officer of senior rank.[71] And even when given arms, the militia often failed to use them, or, most tellingly, threatened to "surrender their arms" if a political objective went unmet. In short, refusing to bear arms was a form of resistance to the state.[72]

The English army proved little more effective than the militia, refusing to fire on "the mob," and, in at least one instance, even mutinying and joining the crowd.[73] Only the aristocrats among private citizens owned the frightening new firearms, and occasionally they put a stop to these demonstrations by arming their servants. But such occurrences were rare, as was violence by the crowd against the aristocrats. Insults and threats might be traded in these confrontations, but so were drinks in the local pubs.[74]

Violence against property was another matter. By the seventeenth century, the English had a long tradition of trashing the property of prominent individuals who were menacing their customary rights. Rural crowds did not hesitate to tear down the fences and walls of aristocrats attempting to enclose common land or traditional tenancies; on a few occasions they even smashed the windows of the gentry. But violence against persons remained the preserve of the state, which as a last resort would send the army in to clear up any confusion as to who ruled England.[75]

When Lord George Goring's army marched through Dorset in 1645, some one thousand civilians rose up in arms to oppose them. With this rising representing all classes, the question to be asked is, What kind of arms did they bear? Observers reported that the opponents of the Royalist army were armed with everything from clubs to guns, according to class.[76] Such diversity of weaponry based on class was noted in other crowd gatherings before and during the Civil War.[77] Uprisings that did not include members of the local gentry were a different matter. In 1631 a crowd of country people in the Forest of Dean "in a most dareinge and presumptious manner presented themselves unto us [the sheriff and his posse] with warlike weapons (vizt.) pikes, forrest bills, pitchforkes, swordes and the like."[78] A rising of local farmers seeking to drive off Hertford's Cavaliers in 1642 carried "pitchforks, dungpicks, and suchlike weapons."[79] As a Royalist said contemptuously of his opponents under Sir Lewis Dyve in Blackmore Vale in 1644, they were armed only with "hedge-stakes, prongs, sheep-hooks, tar-boxes, and such like rural implements."[80] Guns were in sufficiently short supply for a bailiff in Dorset to write to London requesting a brace of pistols, as they were unobtainable in the west, and he feared for his life in the face of these hostile crowds. Another complained that a mob tearing down enclosure fences "enforced him to work with them by threats of striking him down with a club if he did not."[81]

In short, the English people demonstrated real courage in battling even regulars, but rarely were they able to bring guns to bear. But then the regulars themselves were not routinely armed with muskets until well into the eighteenth century. For instance, there was the remarkable resistance to the quartering of the Scots army in Yorkshire between 1645 and 1647. On one occasion, some of the gunless troops took refuge in a church from an angry crowd armed with clubs and tools. There were similar confrontations in these years between civilians and troops in Hampshire, Hereford, and Berkshire. In none of these instances did the troops have firearms.[82]

But English crowds also attacked fellow civilians, especially those identified as religious deviants. Here again, however, there was no evidence of firearms. In 1656, five Anglican ministers led a crowd against the Quaker meeting at Martock. The crowd was armed with farm implements and clubs and attacked the Quakers by hurling "cow-dung, sticks, and dabs of earth" at them—a typical English assault.[83]

Englishmen took pride in their strength, and identified themselves with their ability to wield a sword. As Sir Dudley Digges boasted in Parliament in 1628, "In Muscovy one English mariner with a sword will beat five Muscovites that are likely to eat him."[84] The very image of the Cavalier was "the swordsman," romantic or swaggering, depending on political point of view, but waving a sword about in either case. When the members of seven volunteer companies from London disbanded in 1593, they stole fifty-five firearms and 495 swords, which, in the words of one scholar, "suggests that the sword was the most useful weapon for civilian life."* In popular imagination the English hero or oppressor carried a sword, not a gun.[85]

Such imagery aside, England began the seventeenth century as one of the least militaristic of European powers. As John Brewer has pointed out, the two central features of the English state were "its early centralization" and "its decline as a European military force in the sixteenth and seventeenth centuries." In the years from the end of the Hundred Years War in 1453 until "the outbreak of hostilities with Louis XIV in 1689, England ceased to be a major military power in Europe." Throughout England castles became country manors, and weapons of war rusted in forgotten armories. Lawrence Stone estimated that while three-fourths of Henry VIII's peerage joined him in various continental wars, by the early seventeenth century 80 percent of England's aristocracy lacked military experience of any kind.[86]

Like all European nations, England had its forms and rituals of violence. But guns did not enter into the common understanding of violence. Few common people, except those serving in the military, ever had occasion to even hold a gun, let alone own one. The English system of violence made the journey to North America in the early seventeenth century. Guns, which in England remained the preserve of aristocrats and the state, also made the trip to the New World.

---

*Of course, it could also suggest that firearms were less common and harder to maintain than swords.

Chapter Two

The Role of Guns
in the Conquest
of North America

We Beate the Salvages outt of the Island burned
their howses Ransaked their Temple Tooke down
the Corpes of their deade kings from [out] of
their Toambes And caryed away their pearles. . . .
The Salvages still contineweinge their mallice
Ageinste us.

—George Percy, "A Trewe Relacyon" (1612)

Cultures of Violence

Samuel de Champlain hoped to build Quebec in peace. In 1608 Champlain led the second French effort to establish a colony on the St. Lawrence River. Europeans did not find settling in North America a healthy enterprise, and half of the French succumbed to disease that first year. Champlain realized that his settlement could survive only if the colonists remained friendly with the local Indians, the Huron, who could have wiped them out with a single sustained attack. However, friendship with one group of Indians often meant hostility with another.

The Huron accepted the French as provisional allies. Champlain perceived their skepticism and knew that he had to prove the value of a French alliance. In the summer of 1609 Champlain and two of his soldiers accompanied a Huron expedition against their traditional enemy, the Mohawk. The Frenchmen each carried a harquebus, the smallest of the muskets then existing, three and a half feet long and weighing about ten pounds, firing a charge of ten to fifteen one-ounce pellets.[1]

On July 30, 1609, there occurred one of the very few battles in seventeenth-century North America in which European firearms proved decisive. On the shores of the lake that would soon bear Champlain's name, the Huron and Mohawk confronted one another. The Indians performed their usual rituals of singing and hurling insults, then moved threateningly toward one another. As they drew close together, Champlain stepped from behind the Huron, leveled his harquebus at three Mohawk chiefs walking in the lead of their forces, and fired. Two of the chiefs fell dead; the third was seriously wounded. At the firing of just one more harquebus the Mohawk fled. The Huron took ten or so prisoners, one of whom they tortured in their postbattle celebrations. Champlain reported himself disturbed by this sight, and so shot the victim. It was a fitting conclusion to a strange encounter. Champlain philosophically "pointed out to them [the Huron] that we did not commit such cruelties, but that we killed people outright." Ian Steele may have overstated the case in writing that "the impact of firearms was never as dramatic again on that frontier." But it is true that it would be decades before a group of Europeans would be able to terrify Indians so thoroughly with their firearms.[2]

At the start of the European conquest of the Americas, it is widely stated, firearms imparted a technological advantage that the natives could never hope to overcome. Yet firearms were rare curiosities in the sixteenth century when Spain conquered Mexico and much of South America, and they still appeared in very small numbers among the English, Dutch, and French when these nations established their first bases along the eastern seaboard of North America in the seventeenth century. As numerous military historians have noted, firearms did not dominate Western warfare until the nineteenth century. It was organization that mattered most. In Max Weber's words, "It was discipline and not gunpowder which initiated the [military] transformation" of the seventeenth century.[3] Not that any single cause sufficiently explains European successes in their invasion of the Americas. The victories of the European nations can be explained in many terms: surprise, centralized political control, a willingness to slaughter innocents, superiority of transportation, disease, and, as a consequence of the latter, the press of numbers. Though a future archbishop of Canterbury called them one of the "miracles of Christendome," guns appear well down a list of advantages enjoyed by the Europeans.[4]

Firearms did impart an initial psychological edge to their possessor, but their disadvantages were numerous. The debate in England in the

1590s had exposed these flaws, and though the technology of firearms improved somewhat, the experience of using guns in the Americas further clarified these deficiencies. In the mid-seventeenth century the flintlock, a descendant of the snaphance, became the dominant ignition system and it remained so until the mid-nineteenth century.[5] Flintlocks were lighter, weighing an average of fifteen pounds and measuring four to four and a half feet in length. Though the weapons were still heavy and clumsy to use, supporting stakes were no longer required. These guns were also easier to load. A cartridge for a flintlock consisted of powder wrapped in paper with a lead ball. The shooter would rip open the paper and pour a little of the powder in the flashpan where the flint struck, the rest going down the muzzle followed by the ball. The shooter then pulled the flint back to its full-cock position. Pulling the trigger released the flint, which then struck the steel in the flashpan, creating a spark that set off the little bit of priming powder. Obviously too much priming powder could explode in the face of the shooter, making the whole exercise an anxious occasion for inexperienced shooters. The flash from the priming powder went through the barrel's touchhole, setting off the powder tamped down there, which created an explosion, the expanding gas sending the ball forward out of the muzzle, if all went well. This elaborate procedure remained the basic mode of firing a gun for the next two hundred years, right into the Civil War.[6]

While no longer dependent on a smoldering match and much lighter than previous muskets, flintlocks remained ineffective in the rain and inaccurate beyond ten yards, required constant maintenance, and retained all the problems associated with the use of black powder. A further problem with the flintlock was the amazing variability of locks. Most manuals emphasized the need to make careful adjustments to avoid too weak a spring, which would not create a consistent spark, or one too strong, which could break the flint. And because the barrel filled with black powder, it was a common practice to use a smaller-caliber ball so that it would fit, which reduced both accuracy and range. Modern tests on flintlocks reveal that even in dry weather, with flints replaced every fifteen shots, they misfire one-fourth of the time. But then the gun becomes dangerously hot after eight consecutive shots, making it wise to take one's time reloading.[7]

The major problem with the flintlock remained the need to keep it clean inside and out. Powder accumulated from each shot in the barrel, forming a sludge like Turkish coffee. Such muck is not only highly corrosive, but also slows down the flight of a bullet, and can lead to explosions. And if the sludge accumulated in the touchhole, the gun simply would not fire. Thus a musket should be cleaned after every four shots, a difficult task to perform in the heat of battle. This problem was more pronounced in the rifle, which required that a bullet essentially be screwed into the muzzle, making its loading a much slower process than a musket's. The famous Kentucky rifle took, on average, three minutes to load. If the bullet became stuck, it required a special tool, a "bullet screw," to extract it. A stuck bullet rendered a rifle useless; this uncertainty and the slow firing rate led most military leaders to prefer the less accurate but less dangerous musket. Except as a tool for marksmen, the rifle did not really become practical until the late eighteenth century.[8]

Nonetheless, flintlocks were an enormous improvement over the snaphances, and they did get a little better with time, especially in terms of their effective ranges. Whereas a snaphance had an effective range of only ten to twenty yards, flintlocks increased in quality by the American Revolution to the point where soldiers could be fairly confident that their unaimed volleys might hit an enemy at sixty yards. But most of those familiar with guns agreed that it was useless to aim at any target beyond twenty yards with any expectation of hitting it. The bullet traveled down the muzzle at a high speed, glancing off the side. Its final course was determined by its last bounce, as it emerged like a curveball that might break in any direction (thus few muskets even bothered with sights until the 1850s). And as anyone in the eighteenth century could report, the smoke blinded the shooter, so even the best shot had only one real opportunity to demonstrate his accuracy. It was for this reason that the military command was: "Ready; level; fire!"[9] The Indians figured out this aspect of gunfire early on, but it took some time for the lesson to sink in as well with the settlers. The most famous soldier of Metacom's Rebellion, or King Philip's War, Colonial Benjamin Church, reported that he learned a basic Indian defensive tactic from some Indian members of his patrol: marching "at a wide distance from one another" so that musket fire was less likely to hit anyone.[10]

Firearms were most effective as defensive weapons. They were best used from behind entrenched positions, which allowed the time and protection necessary for reloading, and did the most damage against massed troops, with their bullets likely to hit someone, if the musket was properly leveled.[11] Neither of these situations applied very often in North America. The European nations sought not only to conquer territory, but to hold it. They therefore built many forts and blockhouses, both strongholds that maximized the advantages of gunfire. Yet the Indians, and even other European powers, rarely attacked these fortified sites, preferring to engage their enemies in the forests, where the gun proved least serviceable, and they seldom moved forward in neat European ranks. However, when the Indians did oblige by assaulting a fort, firearms usually demonstrated their defensive advantages.

Far more significant than as a weapon of war was the role guns played as trade objects. Though it became apparent only in the eighteenth century, firearms served to tie certain Indian tribes irrevocably to their European sources, making those Indians dependent on the manufacturers of arms. Guns were not like other trade goods that Indians acquired from Europeans in that they required a constant supply of other goods in order to function—powder, shot, flints. But more important, guns differed in their need for regular maintenance and occasional repair. The gun was therefore not simply a weapon that the Indian acquired, but also represented a necessary series of relations with the Europeans.

Those Indians who entered into this relationship could gain enormous power over traditional enemies. For instance, René Laudonnière, a French Huguenot from the settlement of Fort Caroline on Florida's St. Johns River, described a sixteenth-century alliance with the Utinas. In 1564 the Utinas and a few French gunners attacked the Potano in their village. The French fired a round that killed one of the Potano. The rest fled in horror.[12]

Historians have long debated whether the advent of the European musket made Indian warfare deadlier.[13] Much of the power imparted by firearms was symbolic, as in the case of a single death terrifying the Potano. But there was little way around the fact that the musket was inefficient and inaccurate. Indian warfare certainly became deadlier with the advent of Europeans, but as a consequence of methods rather than materials.

Recently historians working out of the source documents have perceived the limited applicability of the gun in the European conquest of the Americas, emphasizing instead the centrality of disease in decimating the native populations.[14] Yet Europeans, too, died in great numbers from disease and starvation at the beginning of colonization. The English settlement of the Chesapeake Bay area was, as one historian called it, a "charnel house" where half the settlers died the first year of 1607, and 90 percent of those who had arrived in the first fifteen years of settlement were not alive by 1622. Likewise, half the settlers of Plymouth Colony died during their first winter in New England. But whereas the Indians replaced their population losses very slowly, if ever, Europeans kept pouring into the Americas. As European settlements expanded, the percentage dying from disease decreased while Indians experienced repeated epidemics.[15]

In their initial contacts, American Indians and Europeans were fairly evenly matched in one-on-one combat. But Europeans enjoyed a number of specific advantages. In the Southwest and Florida the horse gave the Spanish an enormous edge; in the East the superiority of English longboats imparted a mobility that played a vital role in their eventual victory over the Powhatan. In all theaters, various forms of guns allowed the Europeans to enjoy an initial success, which they generally exploited. Yet once Indians realized that firearms were not the voice of some deity but only a very loud weapon, they adjusted accordingly, putting up a stiff resistance to European conquest. Only when European settlers in North America learned to deploy their own Indian allies against their immediate target were they able, step by bloody step, to conquer ever more territory. In short, it was not guns that insured the European conquest of North America, but a host of factors that collectively gave them strategic advantage.[16]

At the time of first contact, most of the eastern woodlands Indians used an open-field battle formation of massed troops, placing a premium on display over carnage. The settlers of Jamestown, Virginia, described the elaborate preparation of the Powhatan for battle, taking the time to paint their faces and array their tokens from previous victories, selecting their battle site carefully. At the beginning of battle the warriors were "leaping and singing" as they arranged themselves in "a halfe moone" and advanced in orderly ranks. In contrast, Europeans including Champlain and John Smith learned the advantages of hiding behind trees and firing at the exposed Indians from ambush.[17] As the English knew from Agincourt, flights of massed arrows could be devastating in open-field battles. In America they discovered the stunning impact of firearms fired at close quarters from ambush. Each side learned from the other, and the more they learned, the greater the slaughter.

First Encounters

Guns were one of many advantages
Europeans enjoyed in their conquest
of the Americas, but they proved far from decisive. The brief narratives
of historians that simply state that a battle produced a certain number of
casualties give the impression that European firearms mowed down their
victims. But contemporary battle descriptions demonstrate that other
weapons inflicted the majority of casualties. Specifically, swords, axes, and
fire proved to be the most deadly weapons in Colonial warfare.

In the initial conflicts between Indians and Europeans in the sixteenth
and early seventeenth centuries, armor and swords made the greatest difference. But neither was sufficient by itself. Indians found ways of shooting around the armor, aiming for exposed flesh; once they started using
European forged metal on the tips of their arrows they could pierce the
lighter, mailed armor.[18] Nonetheless, armor and the high-quality bladed
weapons of the Europeans account for the disparity in casualty figures in
the battles between the Europeans and their various Indian opponents.
But new forms of warfare redressed the balance.

The first four Spanish efforts to invade Florida offer ample evidence
of the Indians' ability to resist European incursions armed only with
bows. Between 1513 and 1562, the Spanish sent four well-armed expeditions to Florida, each as large as the force that Cortés took against the
Aztecs, and each defeated by the local Indians in combat.

In 1513 Juan Ponce de León's Spanish troops were driven off three
times by the Timucuan and Calusa of Florida. Though they had never
seen or heard the likes of the Spanish muskets, the Indians of Florida,
armed with bows and lances, were not intimidated. Four years later the
Calusa again drove off the Spanish under Francisco Hernández de Córdoba. Córdoba reported that the Spanish swords, being of a far superior
quality, triumphed in hand-to-hand combat, but their muskets and crossbows were useless before the greater range of the Indians' bows. Ponce de
León returned to Florida in 1521, and his two hundred soldiers were
again sent fleeing to the safety of their ships by the Calusa. The technological superiority of the Europeans proved irrelevant in these first confrontations with the American Indians.[19]

Pánfilio de Narváez tried his luck next in 1527, bringing a larger force
with more of the modern weapons. Yet in his first encounter, the Florida
Indians bested his forces until he could bring his mounted lancers into

play. Narváez was shocked to discover that the Indians' arrows pierced the Spanish armor and that their archers easily surpassed the skill of his crossbowmen and musketeers. This expedition also ended in failure.[20]

In 1539 Hernando de Soto invaded Florida with more than three hundred infantry, armed with crossbows and harquebuses, and nearly as many cavalry, armed with lances and swords. De Soto hoped to triumph by fighting at close quarters with the Indians, but he discovered that his matchlocks consistently gave away the Spanish position and regularly misfired. De Soto's initial attack on Chief Tascaloosa's fortified village was a disaster. But when the Spanish retreated, the cavalry was able to wheel about and fall on the pursuing Indians. The Spanish then set fire to the village, the flames killing far more Indians than had died in battle. The real advantage for the Spanish came not from their guns, but from their horses and armor. De Soto himself was apparently hit by twenty arrows, but suffered only some minor wounds. Later the Chickasaw would ruin De Soto's expedition, just as the Apalachee, Choctow, Calusa, and Timucuan defeated other Spanish forces.[21]

These experiences persuaded the Spanish government that there was no hurry in transporting large numbers of firearms to the Americas. Most of the first large shipment of firearms to the New World, one hundred muskets bound for Mexico, was lost at sea in 1559.[22]

In 1565 the Spanish sent what they were certain would be the decisive force to conquer Florida under Pedro Menendez de Avilés. Before they were done, the Spanish would end up devoting a fifth of the kingdom's military budget to this enterprise. Within two years all of the Spanish posts had been defeated by Indians and abandoned. But the Spanish kept trying. In 1576 Moyano de Morales, attempting to establish an outpost in the Carolinas, allowed his twenty-one musketeers to let their matches go out. They were immediately attacked by the Indians, who killed all but one Spaniard.[23] The Spanish were slow learners, and the inferiority of matchlocks was still being demonstrated in 1668, when the pirate Robert Searles attacked San Agustin with a force armed with flintlocks. The matches gave away the Spanish positions, and Searles's pirates fired volleys at any light they saw. Though they did not suffer heavy casualties, the Spanish fled to the safety of the fort, leaving Searles to loot the town.[24]

Through defeat after defeat, the Spanish kept trying to establish a permanent presence in the southeast of North America, relying on their superior firearms to decide the conflict. In 1647, with the Timucuan now their allies, a company of Spanish musketeers fought a daylong battle with the Apalachee, who had recently destroyed seven Spanish missions. Even though the musketeers reported firing at least ninety shots each over eight hours, the Apalachee won the day. It took Christian Apalachee to defeat their more traditionalist comrades who adhered to the native religion. Technology again proved indecisive.[25]

Part of the problem, of course, was that very few European-style pitched battles occurred in North America. Both the Europeans and the Indians had a heritage of fighting in the open, with their forces moving into close range. It was precisely such battles that displayed the musket to maximum advantage, so long as the musketeers were protected by pikers during the reloading process. But Indian archers negated much of this method of warfare, and so Europeans learned early the advantages of surprise attacks. During the Taino's twenty-year resistance to Spanish conquest there was only a single "battle," at Vega Real on Hispaniola in 1495. There two hundred armored Spanish swordsmen swooped down on their sleeping opponents and hacked hundreds of Indians to death. Likewise, once the Indians figured out how firearms worked, they began avoiding open-field battles and followed the Europeans in favoring surprise attacks on small groups and burning crops and settlements.[26]

The Spanish had an easier time of it in the Southwest, where the local spears and arrows glanced off Spanish armor. Battle descriptions indicate that even the Spanish leather armor deflected these arrows.[27] As a consequence, very few Spanish soldiers were killed in their reconquest of New Mexico in 1692, though many were wounded. What is more surprising is how few Indians were killed. The Spanish battle tactic was simple and effective, taking advantage of the psychological impact of a few guns to fire a single volley and then pursue their fleeing enemies with swords and pikes. The Spanish appreciated the advantages of their metal weapons in trained hands. For instance, in 1694 a Spanish contingent in New Mexico was surprised by a large group of Ute, who attacked with arrows and clubs, quickly wounding six Spanish. But the Spanish fought the Ute off with their swords, killing eight Ute and driving the rest into full retreat. Spanish metal was the technological advantage; their poled weapons with metal tips and their sturdy swords overwhelmed the Indians in the sort of close battle in which firearms were useless.[28]

The Spanish were not the only European nation to fail in their sixteenth-century efforts to settle North America as a consequence of Indian resistance. In 1541 Jean-François de La Rocque attempted to establish a French colony on the north shore of the St. Lawrence River. Armored French troops carrying matchlocks were defeated by the Iroquois and the settlement was abandoned. The French returned in 1608, founding Quebec. After Champlain's violent encounter with the Mohawk in 1609, he discovered that Indian tribes were actually willing to fight in order to gain access to European metal goods. Thus the Mohawk did not end their war with the Huron after witnessing the loud power of the harquebus; rather they accelerated their conflict to win the right to trade for French knives and axes.[29]

Historians often convey the impression that European firearms decimated the Indians. For instance, descriptions of Champlain's second battle alongside his Huron allies in June 1610 tend to note that the French, armed with matchlocks, "encountered two hundred Iroquois at the mouth of the Richelieu River, destroying them all." The actual description of the battle supplied by Champlain offers a different portrait. The first thing he noticed was that the Indians had already lost their fear of firearms. Every time his troops fired, the Indians simply dropped to the ground, taking advantage of the delay between the match setting off the powder and the actual explosion of the shot from the gun's muzzle. Champlain, who had been struck in the ear and neck by an arrow, and perceiving that the battle was deadlocked and his ammunition running out, ordered his men to charge the Ottawa with their swords. He thus won the battle, and massacred more than one hundred Indians, on the basis of superior European blades.[30]

Five years later, in 1615, Champlain again experienced the limitations of firearms. Joining the Huron to attack an Iroquois settlement, Champlain found that the enemy simply withdrew behind their stockade walls to avoid the musket fire. After spending most of his ammunition in a futile attempt to drive the Iroquois from their walls so that his men could charge in with their swords, Champlain was again hit by an arrow, this time in the leg. The Huron, seeing Champlain and two of their own chiefs felled by arrows, decided to retreat, and Champlain was carried from the battlefield to the taunts of the Iroquois. Those taunts reverberated in Champlain's memory in 1629 when three English ships under Gervase Kirke appeared off Quebec. Champlain had nineteen muskets to resist Kirke's landing party but lacked gunpowder and even matches for his matchlocks. When none of his Indian allies would agree to assist him, Champlain saw no choice but to surrender Quebec to the English. The

English returned the settlement to France two years later in the peace treaty, but the French had learned well the dangers of an undue reliance on firearms.[31]

Initially the French followed the Spanish policy of not trading guns to the Indians. As Samuel de Champlain wrote, it is "a most pernicious and mischievous thing thus to arm these infidels, who might on occasion use these weapons against us."[32] But in 1640 the French made an exception for Christian Indians, giving the Huron access to firearms. In an interesting twist on the enticements of Christianity, that religion now became attractive for those hoping to acquire the new European weaponry, and many families and tribes became divided as younger warriors converted to Christianity to acquire guns. A Jesuit report from 1644 stated that "The use of arquebusses, refused to the Infidels . . . and granted to the Christian Neophytes, is a powerful attraction to win them: it seems that our Lord intends to use this means in order to render Christianity acceptable in these regions."[33]

At first those few muskets gave the Huron a notable advantage. In 1648 most of the Christian Huron were on their way to Montreal to trade with the French when they were surprised by a large group of Mohawk who were stunned to discover that Indians could also fire muskets. The Mohawk fled in disarray. The French government began an active policy of supplying firearms to their Indian allies as a buffer against both other Indians and their new competitor to the south, the English.[34]

The English Invade
North America

Europeans drew great confidence from their firearms. Prior to actual settlement, Thomas Harriot proclaimed that the Indians posed no threat to the English because of the latter's "advantages against them [in] so many maner of waies, as by our discipline, our strange weapons, and devises else, especially by ordinance great and small." Lacking "skill and judgement in the knowledge and use of our things," the Indians found that "running away was their best defense."[35] This estimation came before the settlement at Roanoke vanished mysteriously in 1590.

The Virginia Company shared this faith in technological superiority. In their 1606 instructions, the company directors informed the settlers that the Indians feared only cannon and muskets, meaning that the settlers had better take good care of those weapons.[36] John Smith drew upon this European hubris by telling his troops that "God will so assist us, that if you dare stand but to discharge your pieces, the very smoake will bee sufficient to affright them." Lacking respect for his Indian adversaries, Smith described them as a "naked and cowardly . . . people, who dare not stand the presenting of a staffe . . . or peece, nor an uncharged peece in the hands of a woman." The actual history of Colonial Virginia proved otherwise; Indians quickly learned to stand up to gunfire.[37]

The pattern set in the Chesapeake Bay area was fairly typical for European settlement in North America. The Europeans and local tribes, in this case the Powhatan, pretended good relations while actually exercising the most careful scrutiny and viewing one another with suspicion. But as the Europeans ignored food production in their search for rapid wealth, they began making ever more insistent demands on the Indians for food, yet most North American Indians did not enjoy a crop surplus. Matters quickly degenerated, as Europeans began seizing food, coming into conflict with Indians, and then lashing out at any Indian they could reach. Europeans demonstrated a startling consistency in their willingness to kill innocent Indians for the crime of another Indian, despite the fact that such action almost always proved counterproductive. Indians usually responded to European terrorism with surprise attacks on isolated English settlements and an end to food gifts. On Hispaniola in the early sixteenth century, the Taino even destroyed their own food supplies in order to keep them away from the Spanish. In the Chesapeake Bay area the Indians would come within a few days of victory in 1610. Only the process of constant European reinforcements and supplies kept colonies going through their first fifty years.[38]

On May 26, 1607, the Powhatan tested the defensive capacities of the new Jamestown settlement. More than two hundred Indians attacked the unfinished fort, killing two colonists before being driven off by the ships' cannon, one shot from which brought down a tree among the astonished Powhatan.[39]

The two sides learned a great deal almost immediately. The English were stunned by the fighting skill of the Indians, while the Indians got a sense of the awesome power of English ships and the terrifying impact of cannon and even inaccurate muskets.[40] Both Indians and English were used to open-field battles; yet the ferocity of the Indians and the impact of muskets at close range convinced each that such encounters had to be avoided. The Indians adapted quickly, determining the short range of the muskets and always staying beyond that distance, making especially effective use of the sudden massed volley of arrows from hiding places.[41] The English took a little longer to determine their most effective strategy: slaughter. But until then, for the first two years of settlement, the English mostly tried to keep within their secure areas while patient Powhatan waited to pick off stragglers in the fields.

As the English hid in their fort through the summer of 1607, the Indians did not dare a direct assault, especially so long as a ship with its cannon lay in the river. The Powhatan appreciated that they would need the metal weapons of the English in order to launch effective attacks on their forts. The Virginia Company ordered that Indians were never to be allowed to handle European firearms and that they should witness the firing of muskets by only the best shots, for if they see any English "miss what they aim at, they will think the weapon not so terrible, and thereby will be bould to assault you." The company advised that it was best to scare the Indians off with their guns, for otherwise "they will easily kill all with their arrows."[42]

But such preventive measures were wasted, as the Powhatan found access to European metal through trade, exchanging food with the starving English for weapons. The Indians did not understand this seemingly irrational preference of the Jamestown settlers to trade or even starve rather than tend the fields or fish or hunt. In Europe hunting was a sport confined by law to landed gentlemen. Those who hunted to survive were not just undignified, they were by definition criminals, poachers. In the European perspective, a gentleman hunted only when he was in a position to leave the game to rot on the forest floor. On one occasion in 1608, Captain Newport traded twenty swords for twenty turkeys, a rather foolish exchange. More tragic for the Jamestown settlers was their tendency to steal company weapons to trade with the Indians in "Night Marts." As a consequence the settlement found itself with a diminishing supply of arms of all kinds, while the Powhatan gained a trove of useful metal hatchets, swords, pikes, and even a few muskets. The Powhatan learned how to use these latter weapons from some settlers who had "gone native" and joined the Indians in order to avoid starvation.[43]

Yet, oddly, it was the English who launched the surprise attack in 1609 that began the next stage in their devastating war with the Powhatan. The settlers were emboldened by the latest shipment of arms and armor direct from the Tower of London, bringing their total stock up to three hundred pistols and muskets of various kinds, as well as armor and more pikes and swords than there were men to use them. In retaliation for what the Powhatan saw as an unprovoked assault and the cruel burning of their homes and desecration of their temples, they encircled the English outpost at Nansemonds, killing half the garrison. The relief company of "30 good shotte" sent out by Captain John Smith found English corpses with as many as a dozen arrows in them, and their mouths stuffed with cornbread. The English muskets had apparently proved useless against such a barrage of arrows.[44]

There ensued a series of cruel attacks, as each side learned the most harmful military tactics of the other, brutalizing their traditional systems of violence in a desperate effort to survive. As Smith told the Powhatan at one of their encounters just before this slaughter began, fighting wars were the "chiefest pleasure" of the English. Again and again Indians and English betrayed, tricked, and slaughtered one other; the English targeting nonhostile Indians as the easiest prey, the Indians falling upon isolated families whenever possible. Any negotiation was usually a pretense for the latest massacre, and neither side was to be trusted. In one memorable encounter, the Appomattox Indians lured fourteen English ashore with a bevy of naked women and killed thirteen of the men.[45]

The Powhatan almost succeeded in their aims during the winter of 1609–10. For six months they kept the English confined to their settlement, despite the latter's muskets. More than half of the settlers died from starvation and disease in this brief period, leaving just sixty of the original five hundred settlers alive by the spring. When Governor Sir Thomas Gates arrived in early June, he found the survivors preparing to abandon Jamestown. After inspecting the colony and learning its recent history, the governor announced to "general acclamation and shouts of joy" that they were giving up on Virginia and heading back to England. They buried their cannon and almost burned the town. On June 8, just as they were about to sail away, Lord De La Warr's relief fleet arrived.[46]

Lord De La Warr saved Virginia by militarizing it, imposing a harsh martial law that made everyone part of the general effort to defeat the Powhatan. Every weapon in whatever hands became part of the colony's arsenal, a policy that would effectively remain in place throughout the Colonial period. The government of Virginia would "distribute Armes to those [who] were found most fit to use them." In the summer of 1610 the English hit upon the tactical formula that preserved their position in North America. In a series of quick strikes, the English surprised and destroyed four Indian villages, not caring that three of them were not hostiles. The point was to exterminate all Indians in the immediate vicinity of their settlements. Their method of attack soon became standard tactics in North America: firing a volley with their muskets and then rushing in with swords and halberds to drive off the inhabitants. The Indians almost always fled before this charge, reorganizing themselves in the forest. But in the meantime the English put the village to the torch, harvested all the crops they could carry, and burned the rest. The demoralization and starvation that ensued not only weakened the resistance of the survivors, but also drove many to flee for protection to neighboring tribes.[47]

When the new deputy governor, Sir Thomas Dale, arrived in 1611 with three hundred professional soldiers fresh from the Dutch wars, he brought the technological secret that would defeat the Powhatan: armor. His armored troops, armed with muskets or halberds, stood up well to the barrage of arrows. Contemporary accounts indicate the centrality of armor in preserving the lives of the English soldiers.[48] Although there were still many deaths from arrows hitting in the gaps in the armor or in the face, Dale's troops shocked the Powhatan with their ability to keep advancing against flights of arrows. And that shock gave the English the time they needed to move close enough to charge with their swords. According to George Percy, the English preferred to run the Indians "throwghe the body wth [their] sworde." Guns were fine for making a loud noise and providing a smoke screen, but to do the job right required a fine European blade.[49]

Dale, who placed his reliance in the professional soldiers who accompanied him, was shocked by the lack of military skill evident in the settlers. He could not believe that they spent their time bowling rather than drilling. He immediately turned his ferocity upon both the Indians and his fellow English. Those who would not meet his expectations fed his sadism. Dale's maxim was simple: "terrour . . . made short warres."[50]

Dale helped to instill among the English a bloodlust such as they had previously demonstrated only against the Irish. They brutally murdered women and children, ambushed peaceful parties of Indians as they were gathering berries in a desperate search for food, killed prisoners of all ages and both sexes, and destroyed every vestige of the Indian presence. Few of these deaths came in the initial volley of musketry; far more were killed as the Indians fled their burning huts or after they had surrendered, the majority dying of the privation that followed.[51]

The Powhatan did their best to respond in kind. In one attack on a blockhouse in 1610, the Indians goaded the English into counterattacking. Some twenty soldiers bearing muskets charged forth, and were met by arrows from several hundred bows. Every one of the English died without firing a shot; the "Salvages lett flye their Arrowes as thicke As hayle . . . and Cutt them all [down] in A moment." So effective were Indian arrows when tipped with European forged metal that the Virginia Company banned both metal-tipped arrows and longbows from Virginia for fear that they would fall into Indian hands.[52] More significant was the arrival of Governor Gates, in August 1611, with another fleet and reinforcements, bringing the English force of professional soldiers to near six hundred, with sufficient armor and muskets for them all. The English now moved methodically, clearing the Indians away from their settlements and ending the war in 1614, though they paid a heavy price for this victory. By May 1615 there were only four hundred English in the Virginia Colony. It was indeed a charnel house.[53]

It is appropriate that the English referred to their conflict with the Indians as "feed fights," a murderous effort to capture or destroy the sustenance of the other side. The English tended to prevail in these contests, though not easily. The Indians of the eastern woodlands planted enough food for immediate use and rarely stored a surplus. For meat they relied on trapping and hunting. The English did not turn their attention to agriculture for the first two decades of settlement. But once they began planting crops and raising livestock, which they did in great abundance, they could outlast the Indians by destroying their fields. The Indians could never get enough food from hunting alone, and the malnutrition that plagued those who did not die of starvation lowered their resistance to Old World diseases. The English exploited this relative weakness ruthlessly though inconsistently. But in the long run, European agriculture and livestock outlasted Indian farming and hunting.[54]

In 1616 the English colonists made an odd exchange with the Powhatan. In return for allowing Christian missionaries to work among the Indians, the English agreed to teach the Powhatan how to use muskets. The Powhatan also promised to hunt game for the English. Thus Kissarourr became the first Indian to own a snaphance, the new musket that created a spark by striking flint on steel. Within three years the English discovered they had made a poor bargain. Among other problems, by exchanging their firearms with the Indians, the white settlers reduced their own limited supplies. By 1618 the hundred men at Smythe's Hundred, Virginia's second settlement, had only twenty muskets and forty swords and daggers for their defense. The new governor, George Yeardley, immediately criticized this policy of allowing Indians the use of firearms so that they could hunt for the settlers. "The Indians mixing among 'em [the settlers], got Experience daily in Fire-Arms, and some of 'em were instructed therein by the English themselves, and employ'd to hunt and kill wild Fowl for them."[55]

Yeardley attempted to counteract the emerging Indian mastery of firearms—even though the Powhatan still had only a handful of guns—through trickery. First he paid one of the "white Indians" to steal the flints from the snaphances. Then he offered to repair the mysteriously disabled muskets. The Powhatan brought in their muskets for repair and the governor ordered that they not be given back. The House of Burgesses, in one of its first acts, followed up by ordering the death penalty for anyone caught selling firearms to the Indians and compiled a list of all Indians with a knowledge of their use. Deputy Governor Samuel Argall issued a proclamation declaring the death penalty for anyone teaching an Indian how to use firearms. But they missed the real point, admitted by even John Smith, that the Indians practiced the use of their weapons regularly, while the English settlers did everything they could to avoid such practice, as they were busy trying to make money from tobacco.[56]

Though effectively deprived of firearms by the English, the Powhatan under Opechancanough twice came close to defeating the English, in 1622 and 1644. The first war, organized in just two weeks to avenge the murder of an Indian mystic, began with a brutally effective surprise attack on March 22, 1622. English guns, whether matchlocks or snaphances, had little value against such an assault, as it took too long to prepare these firearms for defense. A few settlers fought off their attackers with axes and swords, but some 350 of the 1,240 settlers were not so fortunate, as the Indians "beat out their braines scarce any escaping," as the Reverend Joseph Mead wrote at the time. In a single day the Powhatan killed 28 percent of the English colony, "most of them falling by their own Instruments, and Working-Tools," as Robert Beverley wrote. It was a horrendous defeat for the Europeans, and Opechancanough expected the interlopers to appreciate that they were beaten and leave immediately, as would any sensible Indian people.[57]

But the English did not leave. Instead they entrenched themselves in a series of forts. The English used their greater seaborne mobility to attack the Indian towns, killing mostly noncombatants and destroying crops. As one ballad of 1623 put it, the English "Set fire to a town of theires, and bravely came away."[58] It was far easier to kill friendly Indians, as the English did to thirty of their Patawomec allies in a swift surprise attack. Following this latter attack, in April 1623, Captain Henry Spelman led a force of twenty-two armored and heavily armed soldiers up the Potomac River in an effort to purchase food for the starving colony. They were wiped out by their former allies the Patawomec, and their muskets, swords, and armor fell into Indian hands. So emboldened were these Patawomec by their possession of European weapons that they actually rowed out to attack the pinnace *Tiger,* the first such attack on a European ship by the North American Indians. The crew of the *Tiger* beat them off easily enough by firing their cannon, but it was a frightening indication of what could happen if the Indians bore European arms, as well as an indicator of the way in which those arms seemed to impart heightened self-confidence.[59]

The Powhatan began their war with no muskets, but captured ever more of them as the war proceeded. The English deeply resented the Powhatan for actually using European weapons against them, charging them with cowardice for abandoning their traditional ways. Some of the Indians "shot with Arrows manfully, till bullets answered them,"[60] but others "now steale upon us and wee Cannot know them from English [because of the armor], till it is too late."[61] By 1623 the settlers were complaining that "now the Rogues growe verie bold, and can use peeces, some of them, as well or better than an Englishman."[62] James I responded by issuing his own proclamation outlawing the trading of any kind of "warlike weapons" to the North American Indians.[63]

But such prohibitions proved largely irrelevant, as the Powhatan acquired more than one hundred firearms from dead Englishmen. Desperate for weapons, the settlers appealed to both the government and the Virginia Company for more muskets and pikes. A large group of settlers complained that they had never known a sufficiency of arms and ammunition, and what they did have was "in qualitie almost altogether uselesse." It took some time, but the Virginia Company was able to borrow twenty barrels of powder from the Crown, a certain indication of the unavailability of gunpowder in England at this time, and to purchase one hundred guns and fifty pikes for colonial use. The Crown contributed another one thousand pikes.[64]

Unable to defeat the Indians in battle, the English turned to betrayal.

At peace talks with the Powhatan, the colonists served, but did not drink, poisoned wine, thus killing two hundred Indians. They then ambushed those Indians they had not poisoned, taking scalps as trophies of their heroism. Robert Beverley described these events as giving "the English a fair Pretence of endeavouring the total Extirpation of the Indians, but more especially of Oppechancanough, and his Nation." The following year, 1624, sixty armored soldiers, carrying the entire supply of snaphances in Virginia, fought their only real battle against Opechancanough's forces. For two days on the York River the English fired their muskets at the Powhatan without any noticeable impact. Running low of ammunition, the English set fire to the fields and proclaimed victory.[65]

This war with the Powhatan lasted ten years, from 1622 to 1632, and proved almost a complete disaster for the English. By 1625 only fifty-seven of the near five hundred matchlocks sent to Virginia remained in English hands, the rest having fallen to the Indians or been lost or destroyed. The colonists discovered a further limitation in the use of firearms in a sustained war: they kept running out of powder. Nearly every year the English found themselves with only a thin reserve of powder left, and relied on swords and axes in battle while waiting for the next shipment from England. As a consequence, they surely noticed the one great advantage of bows: there were more than enough trees to supply arrows. The Virginia council warned the Crown that if the Indians knew how little powder remained, "they might easily in one day destroy all our people." Shortly before they lost control of the colony in 1624, the Virginia Company requested "certain old cast Armes remayning in the Tower." The Privy Council granted their request, though they thought these guns "altogether unfitt, and of no use for moderne Service, [they] might nevertheles be serviceable against that naked people." But the colonists did not make much use of these guns, King James taking the colony under his royal protection and sending over regular soldiers. A truce with the Powhatan was finally negotiated in 1632.[66]

One impact of the second Powhatan war followed from the importation of a great number of muskets. Though most remained in the hands of the government and its soldiers, the colony in 1644 had one musket for every four men in the colony—the highest percentage Virginia would attain until the American Civil War. Colonial officials feared that these firearms would fall into the hands of the Indians in one way or another. Not only was the gun trade with Indians outlawed, but every English settler was granted the authority to confiscate any firearm found in the possession of an Indian—not that enforcement would be easy.[67]

Colonial officials not only appreciated the importance of keeping firearms out of the hands of Indians, but also understood that in case of war these same weapons did most good in the hands of professionals. The wisdom of these policies became evident on April 18, 1644, when the Powhatan launched a reprise of their surprise attack of 1622. This time the Indians killed five hundred of the fourteen thousand settlers, again revealing the danger of a reliance on too few and clumsy firearms. But this time Virginia's government turned to a force of "rangers," specialists paid to protect the colony by hunting down and killing the enemy. In 1646 such a force captured and killed Opechancanough. Shortly thereafter the Powhatan sued for peace, handing over all their firearms to the English. Virginia had finally attained internal security, at least for the next thirty years. Victory came not out of the muzzle of a gun but from barren fields and the smoldering ruins of Indian villages.[68]

Soldiers of God

Muskets proved no more decisive in New England. In 1620 Thomas Dermer landed on Martha's Vineyard in search of a suitable settlement site. The Wampanoag, angry over the murder of some of their number by English sailors, did not wait for explanations. They attacked Dermer's crew, killing most of the English, including Dermer. The survivors hurriedly sailed back to England.[69]

Later that year another ship, the *Mayflower,* set down a group of one hundred settlers on the mainland. These Pilgrims, as they styled themselves, had recruited an experienced soldier in Myles Standish. His was one of only four snaphances held by the settlers, though there were also some battered old matchlocks. But Standish hoped to avoid conflict, and otherwise relied on his sword and armor. Until a shipment of snaphances arrived in 1645, Plymouth's forces relied on a simple and by now familiar tactic in battle: fire a single volley of all their available muskets and then throw down their guns and charge with swords and axes before the smoke had cleared. It was a method that proved effective, especially because of the security offered by English armor—metal at first, and heavy leather in the 1630s.[70]

The first encounter with the local Nauset came in late November 1620. A company of sixteen armored Pilgrims had stolen corn from the Nauset, who attacked a few days later. Arrows flew and the Pilgrims fired their four snaphances while the rest of the force lit their matches with a brand from the fire. They then let off a volley from these muskets and the Indians fled. No one was hurt, though the Nauset learned that the Europeans could make very loud noises.[71]

Once it became obvious that European firearms could do much more damage than simply making frightening noises, the New England Indians hoped to discover the secret of these new weapons. These efforts struck some Europeans as unfair. Thus Plymouth's Governor William Bradford whined in 1628, "O, the horribleness of this villainy! How many both Dutch and English have been lately slain by those Indians thus furnished, . . . and the blood of their brethren sold for gain." Bradford even complained that the Indians were "ordinarily better fitted and furnished than the English themselves." But the worst of it was that once "the very sight of [a gun] (though out of kilter) was a terror unto them," but they had now lost that fear.[72]

That fear did give way, though at first to a certain mockery. In 1631 a group of Indians chased the traveler Sir Christopher Gardiner, ignoring the gun he leveled at them. Gardiner jumped into a canoe and aimed his snaphance at the shouting Indians, but the effort to hold the heavy gun tipped Gardiner out of the canoe into the river. He came up "with a little dagger," but the Indians, "getting long poles . . . soon beat his dagger out of his hand." The Indians, feeling sorry for Gardiner, "used him kindly," in the expression of the day, sending "him to a lodging where his arms were bathed and anointed." This frontier encounter ended comically, with Gardiner shouting at the Indians for hitting him and the Indians responding "that they did but a little whip him with sticks," and had chased him because Governor Bradford of Plymouth had asked them to find him. Not all such meetings between Europeans and Indians ended so peacefully, and not all firearms ended up resting quietly at the bottom of rivers.[73]

Massachusetts was the most militant and often militaristic of the British colonies. The General Court declared in the preamble to their 1643 militia law that "as piety cannot bee maintained without church ordinances and officers, nor justice without lawes & magistracy, no more can our safety & peace be preserved without military orders & officers." The founders of both Plymouth and Massachusetts Bay understood that most settlers lacked knowledge of the use of arms, and both made careful plans for the training of the new militia. While England was moving to keep firearms out of the hands of commoners, Edward Winslow called for the arming of Plymouth's settlers. "Bring every man a musket or fowling piece," he wrote. "Let your piece be long in the barrel; and fear not the weight of it, for most of our shooting is from stands" (which is to say, on rests). On the other hand, the leadership did not want these same settlers to be too conversant in the use of modern weaponry, for that could lead to rebellion. Thus Governor Winthrop rejected the application of a group of leading gentlemen who sought to organize themselves into an artillery company as a challenge to the state's military authority.[74]

Despite Winslow's plea that each man bring a musket, most did not, and New England quickly faced a shortage of weapons. In 1634 the Massachusetts Bay Company sent over a store of arms that were distributed among the towns for use as a town stock. That still was far from sufficient, and in 1653 the New England colonies sent commissioners to England to purchase more guns and ammunition, which were distributed among the four colonies.[75] The colonies had been relying on other weaponry for their defense, particularly axes and pikes. Massachusetts militia laws required that two-thirds of each trained band be musketeers and one-third pikemen. The pikemen proved easier to find. In 1643 the Massachusetts General Court repealed an order that every man should be supplied by the government with a musket and encouraged the use of pikes instead. And even these most militant of colonies confronted resistance to the regular meeting of militia units for exercises and drills. In 1631 the general court ordered the militia to meet every Saturday for training. Faced with mass refusal to meet weekly, the court reduced trainings to once a month, and finally to six days a year. It remained at six days from 1637 until 1678, when it was reduced again to four times a year.[76]

As the English settlements in New England expanded, conflicts with the Indians intensified. In April 1637, the Pequot War began with an attack on Wethersfield, Connecticut. The Pequot killed nine settlers and took two girls captive. The Pequot, who had two or three captured muskets at this time, assumed that all the English could make gunpowder and were disappointed when it became evident that these girls did not have a clue how to go about it. The girls did produce some gunpowder when the Pequot traded them to the Dutch for powder; but it was evident that European arms offered little to the Indians unless they could acquire the powder in greater quantities.[77]

The very next month the New England settlers hit on the strategy they would employ repeatedly with great success. Led by John Mason, a force of ninety New Englanders, each armed with a musket, and seventy allied Mohegan Indians moved against the Pequot. Instead of meeting the Pequot warriors in battle, Mason deliberately eluded them. As Plymouth's governor William Bradford described it, Mason's forces then moved "with great silence and surrounded [Mystic Village] both with English and Indians, that they might not break out; and so assaulted them with great courage, shooting amongst them, and entered the fort with all speed. And those that first entered found sharp resistance from the enemy who both shot at [with arrows] and grappled with them." Some of the English grabbed torches and set the houses on fire. The houses "standing close together, with the wind all was quickly on a flame, and thereby more were burnt to death than was otherwise slain." Some did escape the flames, but "were slain with the sword, some hewed to pieces, others run through with their rapiers, so as they were quickly dispatched and very few escaped." According to John Underhill the English killed some four hundred Pequot while their Indian allies cried, "Mach it, mach it; that is, It is naught, it is naught, because it is too furious, and slays too many men." Bradford concluded that "it was a fearful sight to see [the Pequot] thus frying in the fire and the streams of blood quenching the same, and horrible was the stink and scent thereof, but the victory seemed a sweet sacrifice, and they gave the praise thereof to God, who had wrought so wonderfully for them, thus to enclose their enemies in their hands and give them so speedy a victory over so proud and insulting an enemy." When the Pequot warriors were discovered to be rushing to the spot of this carnage, the English retreated to their boats.[78] Edward Johnson, who attributed this and all other Puritan victories to God's grace, mentioned how only Captain Richard Davenport stayed behind to rescue a man taken prisoner by two Indians. He pursued these Indians not with a musket, but with the "severe cutlace" that he carried with him at all times. The very sight of this lethal cutlass intimidated the Indians into abandoning their captive.[79]

Neither Europeans nor Indians had a tradition of the mass murder of women and children, though such atrocities had occurred on occasion.[80] After the assault on Mystic Village in May 1637, such slaughter became rather routine on both sides. As Ian Steele put it, "This outrage served initially as a warning, and eventually as an invitation to imitation."[81] The English used a surprise first volley of musket fire followed by a charge with sword and the burning of the village, preferably with the huts inhabited. It was a prescription for extermination. Of course such a policy was backed with a profound religious justification. As the residents of the town of Milford put it, "Voted, that the earth is the Lord's and the fulness thereof; voted, that the earth is given to the Saints; voted, that we are the Saints."[82]

But even the Saints needed gunpowder. Through most of the seventeenth century the New England settlers were desperate for firearms and powder. As in the Chesapeake Bay area, the exception was in the first wave of settlement, when so many settlers died that there were enough guns for use by the survivors. In 1630 the Massachusetts Bay Company reported in their possession: "80 bastard musketts, with snaphances, 4 Foote in the barrill without rests; 6 long Fowlinge peeces . . . 6 foote longe; 4 longe Fowlinge peeces . . . 5-½ foote longe; 10 Full musketts, 4 Foote barrill, with matchlocks and rests," one hundred swords, and "5 peeces of ordnance, long sence bowght and payd For." There were thus exactly one hundred firearms for use among seven towns with a population of about one thousand.[83]

This need for guns led the New England settlers to concentrate their arms for use by volunteer forces, rather than scattering them among the several militia companies. They also did their best to acquire more from Europe. The New England colonies had little luck purchasing European firearms until 1673. In that year, the Massachusetts General Court sent Hezekiah Usher to England to buy five hundred "new snaphances, or fire lock musketts." He was able to acquire only 292 muskets, but they arrived just in time to see use in King Philip's War.[84]

The Gun in the New World

All of the European powers scrambling for possessions in North America fought wasting wars with the Indians. All of them initially assumed that their God, their technology, and their very way of life gave them enormous advantages that would make conquest an easy matter. Yet each found that the struggle absorbed resources and manpower and lasted decades.

To offer one final example in this regard, the Dutch also enjoyed little initial luck in North America. In 1628 a group of seven Dutch, each armed with muskets but not armor, accompanied a party of Mahican

Indians up the Hudson River. They were attacked and defeated by a party of Mohawk armed with nothing but bows and arrows. Four of the Dutch were killed in the first "discharge of arrows"; the rest fled without firing a shot.[85] Perhaps because of this initial exchange, the Mohawk at first showed little interest in trading for muskets. As with most other Indians, it was other metal objects, especially axes and knives, that they wanted from the Dutch. With a European ax they could cut down a tree in less than an hour, whereas it had taken most of a day with their primitive tools.[86]

The government of the Dutch colony did its best to arm its own soldiers while keeping muskets out of Indian hands, under penalty of death, until William Kieft arrived in 1640.[87] Kieft was a notable member of that small army of self-righteous fools who marched across the stage of Colonial America. In his first five years as governor, Kieft sold the Mohawk three hundred muskets, assuming that he could draw upon these forces as allies.[88] Kieft employed the Mohawk as enforcers, calling, for instance, on them to attack a group of River Indians along the southern Hudson River who refused to pay tribute to the Dutch governor. The River Indians fled to the Dutch for protection, who slaughtered them by the score in a surprise night attack. The Dutch settlers threw babies into the river and slashed their wailing mothers to pieces. It is difficult to determine Kieft's reasons for these actions, but he seems to have thought it best to remove or exterminate all Indians in the area. Instead he started a devastating war.[89]

Not content with his own murderers, Kieft imported John Underhill, veteran of the Pequot War, to work his magic in the colony of New Netherland. Replicating the attack on Mystic Village, Underhill gathered together all the muskets and armor he could for his force. Surrounding the Indian village near Poundridge, his troops fired one deafening volley and then charged in, slashing and burning everything in sight. It was another massacre. The Indians attempted to respond in kind, attacking farms and stockades, in one instance slaughtering a group of eighteen settlers who "had only one gun among them."[90]

Kieft's War, as it is known, ended in 1645 in a peace enforced by the Mohawk. Up until this point the Mohawk had enjoyed a real military advantage by being the only Indians along the Hudson with a large number of firearms. Their three hundred guns made them the best-armed tribe in North America at that time. But over the next fifteen years the French and English gave an equal number of guns to other tribes in an effort to balance Mohawk power. This miniature arms race grew out of the Dutch willingness to take the risk of trading guns for furs, at the rate of twenty beaver pelts per gun. The French were more cautious, giving arms only to Christian Indians, while the English allowed the trading of guns only with "friendly" Indians. Either way, by 1660, parity had been reached along the Hudson, and between 1661 and 1663 the Mohawk and their allies were defeated by the Mahican, Ottawa, Abenaki, Susquehannock, and Delaware. And they found that their Dutch source for guns and even powder had largely evaporated, as the Dutch were themselves engaged in a long struggle against English encroachments for which they were inadequately armed.[91]

In 1664 New Netherland's militia refused to fight the English, and the colony surrendered. (Interestingly, nine years later the English colony of New York surrendered to a Dutch fleet without a fight.[92]) It is hardly surprising that English officials did not trust these settlers. In every one of the colonies, the government kept firearms under its own control, if only because even loyal subjects were not to be relied upon to keep them in working order. For example, Major Edmund Andros, the new governor of New York after it was reclaimed from the Dutch in 1674, gathered together the city's six hundred working muskets into Fort James, where one hundred English Regulars were stationed. He did not intend to give the town's twelve hundred Dutch residents—out of a population of fifteen hundred—the opportunity to betray their loyalty to the Crown. While keeping guns away from his subjects, Andros restored the Dutch policy of supplying firearms to the Mohawk, only now with the intention of their serving as a buffer against the French. Andros and his successors found this policy cost-effective, as the Indians maximized their use of a few hundred muskets, something the English settlers seemed incapable of accomplishing. It was just plain cheaper. Thus, even while the government was trading another hundred muskets to the Mohawk in 1687, the garrison at Albany, New York, had one hundred soldiers but only forty muskets.[93]

The American militia of the seventeenth century proved largely ineffective against the Indians in open battle without the aid of allied Indians. No militia would even consider doing battle against a force of professional soldiers, no matter how small. As a consequence, British governors in the late seventeenth century developed a defensive strategy that relied on Indian allies and the occasional collection of hired rangers to protect their borders. The militia remained as little more than a political gesture, intended to convince settlers that they still played a role in their own defense.

This strategy fit in well with a number of practical considerations involving munitions. First and foremost was the fact that every gun present in seventeenth-century North America came from Europe. The various governments of Europe could perceive no reason for helping to develop arms manufacturing in America, especially as most were still busily supporting the creation of domestic gunmakers.[94] Given the complete failure of settlers to care for those guns they did receive or to learn their proper use, as well as the evident insufficiencies of the militia, any European nation would need some compelling reason to spend the money required to ship arms to America. And those arms that were sent were best directed to the types of people who would take the time to use and maintain them properly: professional soldiers and allied Indians.[95]

An equally compelling reason limiting the flow of firearms to North America was the absence of strong evidence that guns made any decisive difference in warfare. Seventeenth-century firearms offered two advantages: psychological impact and wounding power. The presence of a gun affected both its possessor and its intended victim; the former gained confidence from its bulk and deadly aura, the latter felt terror at its noise and the uncertainty of the bullet's path. Though many Indians doubted the military efficacy of firearms, they certainly appreciated the totemic qualities of guns, often displaying their few firearms to their enemies in hopes of scaring them off. On one notable occasion two Iroquois even dressed in French clothes in an effort to convince the Erie Indians that they possessed the terrifying European weapons. And there was certainly reason to be frightened. The wounding power of the gun was well known, tearing larger holes, spilling more blood, and smashing bones in excess of any other weapon. When a musket ball hit flesh, it expanded, causing enormous wounds that could not be closed by surgery, as could arrow and blade wounds. As William Strachey noted in his 1612 account of Virginia, the Indians had an amazing ability to mend wounds made with arrows or blades, but "a compound wound . . . where . . . any rupture is, or bone broken, such as our smale shott make amongest them, they know not easely how to cure, and therefore languish in the misery of the payne thereof."[96]

The effectiveness of firearms at close quarters had assuredly been

demonstrated, as when Captain John Smith held a pistol to Opechancanough's head until his warriors handed over a supply of corn—though
a razor would have worked just as well.[97] But given the European
method of fighting the Indians, it seemed best to limit the number of guns
exported to the New World as well as to restrict distribution. In battle the
gun was fired once and thrown aside for the ensuing charge with bladed
weapons, a method that lasted into the nineteenth century.[98] It is not too
surprising, then, that North Americans often perceived the ax as the
equal of a gun. In 1778 Daniel Trabue wrote of a neighbor named Lucust
looking forward to battle with the Indians. "He wanted so bad to have the
chance of killing them. He said he knew he could kill 5 him self. He
Could shoot. He could Tomerhack and make use of his butcher knife and
slay them." Such boasts were common throughout the entire Colonial
period. Equally common was Lucust's actual performance once on the
march. Ordered to watch the horses, he left them to join his companions,
stating that "I was afraid to stay by my silf." He never got a chance to kill
anyone, though his company did "plunder" some Indian goods.[99]

In North America two systems of violence had come into conflict. The
Europeans perceived violence as the monopoly of the state, while the
Indians held violence to be an individual action. Each side adjusted at
some level to the other, though neither abandoned its core understanding
of the responsible party. Right through the nineteenth century, Indians
continued to see violence as largely an issue of individual honor, while the
European Americans persisted in seeing the use of violence as the prerogative of the state.[100]

Yet European states seem to have had little interest in events in America before the mid-eighteenth century. After all, the battles and skirmishes of North America were minor affairs compared to the set-piece
battles of Europe. The largest battles in America prior to the French and
Indian Wars involved a few hundred troops at most, and as Daniel K.
Richter has written, "only 153 French lost their lives in conflict with the
Five Nations between 1608 and 1666." Contemporary European battles
pitted armies of thousands against one another. The Thirty Years War of
the early seventeenth century saw a devastation of Germany to match that
of the Chesapeake in the 1610s and 1620s. But in Germany tens of thousands of Christians hacked away at one another, producing thousands of
casualties in a single encounter. In America, a few score at most died in
battle. In such a context, it was an easy matter for European governments

to minimize the military needs of their colonies and to let them battle it out in small, face-to-face confrontations, for which knives, swords, and axes were far better suited than muskets.

One lesson mastered by the Europeans very quickly was the concentration of forces. This was neither an obscure nor a mysterious aspect of military strategy. It quickly became obvious to European commanders that the only way to defeat an elusive foe like the Indians was to concentrate a superiority of forces. In this regard, the English command of the sea proved crucial. Not only could the English move large numbers of men and supplies across the Atlantic and along the North American coast, but their longboats were far superior to Indian canoes as military transports, allowing the English to move their forces quickly up the tangled river system of the Chesapeake. European ships were floating fortresses, largely unassailable by Indians, a base from which the Europeans could launch their attacks at will, and to which they could retreat. This command of transportation gave the Europeans the added advantage of being able to bring the war home to the Indians, something the Indians could never hope to attain. As one group of Indians chased off the Spanish on the lower Mississippi their leader shouted that "If we possessed such large canoes as yours . . . we would follow you to your land and conquer it." But that remained an empty threat.[101]

The European concentration of forces was aided by their method of settlement, organizing compact communities along the coast. The Powhatan of the Chesapeake Bay area were scattered over a wide area; any organized effort against the English required the calling together of warriors from a large region. In contrast the English lived on a small peninsula, so compact that they were able to build a defensive fence running from shore to shore.[102]

Indians adapted to European technology, collecting metal weapons and using them, often with greater skill than their European opponents. But then the European settlers rarely practiced and seldom shot at specific targets. The basic European military method was to fire volleys, with timing, not accuracy, at a premium. Technological improvements through the seventeenth and eighteenth centuries focused on questions of reliability (especially the reduction of misfires) rather than accuracy.[103]

What may seem surprising today is that from the 1650s on the Indians did not have to take their firearms by force from the Europeans. There was a European standard, based on the centuries-long conflict with Islam, not to trade arms with infidels. The Spanish were particularly keen on this value and rigorously enforced it in those parts of the Americas that came under their control. The English were a little unreliable in this regard, and the Dutch and French unconcerned. The French, much to the anger of the Spanish and English, made a point of supplying their Indian allies with firearms, most particularly in the years 1725 to 1760.[104] An unintended consequence, therefore, of the European competition for North America was the arming of the Indians.

As George Raudzens has written, from the Aztecs on there was "a pattern of weapons shock followed by adaptation."[105] At first, the Indians were stunned by firearms and the other technological wonders of the whites, but not for long. Soon they were doing their best to acquire and master these new weapons. Some of these adaptations mixed new knowledge with traditional approaches to problems, as when the Powhatan prayed for their god Okee to rain on the English matchlocks so that they could not be fired.[106] The Indians understood that gunpowder, whether used in cannon or muskets, offered some real military advantages, but they struggled to understand its workings. Opechancanough, the inveterate opponent of the English in the Chesapeake Bay area, poignantly expressed this mixing of ancient and modern when, in 1622, he scattered some captured gunpowder in his cornfields, hoping to grow a crop of this strange and powerful new grain.[107]

Chapter Three

Guns in the Daily Life
of Colonial America

Considering wether the right or left Shoulder
Was the most proper to Cary the Arms of a Souldier
And after an hour was Spent and near
To Learn right from Left and the front from the rear
And often Questioning how and which way
They were drawn up at last into battle array.

—Popular eighteenth-century ballad[1]

The Law and the Gun

In 1705, Robert Beverley published his *History and Present State of Virginia* in London. An astute observer of his native Virginia, Beverley has long provided historians with a wealth of material on the attitudes of Colonial Americans. Probably no passage is as often cited as Beverley's description of gun use among his fellow Virginians: "The People there are very Skilful in the use of Fire-Arms, being all their Lives accustom'd to shoot in the Woods. This, together with a little exercizeing would soon make the Militia little inferior to Regular Troops." That would seem to resolve the issue—the settlers of British North America owned firearms and used them in their daily activities. It is worth noting, however, that two pages later Beverley defends the institutions of slavery and indentured servitude in a passage that also used to be widely quoted by historians: "the work of both, is no other than what the Overseers, the Freemen, and the Planters themselves do."[2]

Both passages are but assertions without demonstration, yet both are used in their turn as evidence for describing the nature of Colonial society. Both fly in the face of reality, as historians have come to realize about Beverley's description of slavery. Beverley made each of these statements for a reason. He was writing for a London audience, seeking to defend his province from what he saw as aspersions upon its honor. Thus, in the midst of his defense of slavery he admits that, "Because I have heard how strangely cruel, and severe, the Service of this Country is represented in some parts of England; I can't forbear affirming, that the work of the Servants, and Slaves, is no other than what every common Freeman do's." Beverley sought to reassure the English that this strange new labor system could fit within the English system. Though historians no longer take such defenses of slavery at face value, they do not hesitate to take similar generalizations about gun use as fundamental truths.[3]

But Beverley also had his reasons for twisting the truth about gun use in Virginia. He hoped to convince his English audience of Virginia's stability so that there would be no need to send British Regulars to maintain order. Interestingly, Beverley contradicts his own statements on the usefulness of the militia even while praising them. He notes that the militia is largely ornamental, their weapons are "but to fire upon some Joyful Occasions." On paper Virginia should have had a militia of some eighteen thousand men, but only ninety-five hundred of those were enrolled for the annual muster. This lack of employment for their firearms is simply explained, as the Virginians "are happy in the enjoyment of an Everlasting Peace." The Indians have all been driven from their borders and no foreign enemy threatens them. Thus Virginia had no need for those regulars, thank you very much.[4]

Beverley knew the truth and hinted at it. He hoped to keep the British government at a distance while making Virginia attractive to prospective settlers. In England a gun was a sign of status, limited by legislation to the elite. Beverley implied that every settler in America could carry this status symbol, and historians have seized upon this notion to argue that they did. This observation is supported more by deductive logic than by evidence. The early Americans must have enjoyed universal gun ownership because they needed firearms to hunt and to defend themselves from Indians. We will return to hunting, but generally such approaches to Colonial American history reify the entire period and treat it as a single chronological unit experiencing conflict from end to end. Thus one regularly encounters such statements as "Of the 156 years between the founding of Jamestown and the Treaty of Paris, more than one-third were years of warfare somewhere in the colonies." And certainly a listing of these wars looks most formidable.[5] Yet in this vast expanse of time from 1607 to

1775, peace was the norm, and the perception of those on the ground differs sharply from the Hobbesian vision crafted by historians. Thus Beverley could write of Virginia enjoying "Everlasting Peace" in the midst of one of the listed wars. Beverley is again not entirely accurate, but it is true that entire generations passed without knowing war, and entire regions, such as Pennsylvania and Maryland, knew little conflict in their long Colonial histories. Pennsylvania, which made every effort to get along and deal honestly with the Indians, enjoyed decades of peaceful relations with local tribes and did not develop a militia system until 1756.[6]

But there was a secret that Beverley kept to himself. The American colonies, just like England, legislated who could and who could not own firearms. In fact, Beverley's own father, Major Robert Beverley, had made use of one of these laws in 1676 to disarm militia members who refused to serve.[7]

English common law formed the basis for American colonial legislation. As J. A. Sharpe has said of eighteenth-century England, "the law had replaced religion as the main ideological cement of society."[8] From the first codes of law passed in the Chesapeake and New England colonies, gun ownership was carefully circumscribed. Possession of firearms was not understood as either an individual or a collective right, but rather as a collective duty necessary to the defense of society, with that collectivity precisely defined in far from inclusive terms. Colonial legislatures repeatedly passed laws requiring white Protestant adult male property holders to own guns as a support for the local militia. Just so there would be no misunderstanding, such laws forbade other groups from owning firearms. Only Protestants could own guns, and not always all Protestants; for instance, in 1637 Massachusetts disarmed the Antinomians. Maryland first disarmed its Catholics in 1670, but inconsistently enforced this prohibition because of the large number of Catholics in the colony. But in 1756, with the start of the Seven Years' War, the Maryland assembly noted that anomaly and expropriated all the arms and ammunition of Catholics and mandated prison terms for any Catholic found concealing arms. Maryland's militia law did not allow Catholics, indentured servants, or slaves to bear arms. In contrast, any qualified individual who refused to serve in the militia forfeited any arms and ammunition he might own. The upshot, though, was that if one did not own a gun, one could avoid militia duty.[9]

The English government supplied the majority of firearms to the Americans, hoping that the settlers would defend themselves and not need the expensive aid of regular troops. But the Crown did not provide anywhere near sufficient numbers of guns, passing the burden on to the Colonial governments. These governments in turn hoped to limit their expenses by requiring all freemen to own a gun. In its earliest years, Virginia even required all freemen to bring guns to church; each freeman had to be ready to serve as a sentinel, with "both ends of his match being alight, and his piece charged, and primed, and bullets in his mouth." Few freemen welcomed this duty, and fewer still could afford firearms, so it became necessary for governments to supply them, with laws passed to effect that purpose. At the same time, legislators feared that gun-toting freemen might, under special circumstances, pose a threat to the very polity they were supposed to defend. Colonial legislatures therefore strictly regulated the storage of firearms, with weapons kept in some central place, to be produced only in emergencies or on muster day, or loaned to individuals living in outlying areas. They were to remain the property of the government. The Duke of York's first laws for New York required that each town have a storehouse for arms and ammunition. Such legislation was on the books of colonies from New Hampshire to South Carolina.[10]

A few contemporary observers described different cultural attitudes toward firearms from one region of colonial North America to another. In the eighteenth century, New Englanders, even the wealthy who enjoyed the time and resources to practice shooting, were generally described as terrible shots. On the other hand, the southern elite were closely associated with guns and their deadly use. William Blathwayt stated in 1691 "that there is no Custom more generally to be observed among the Young Virginians than that they all Learn to keep and use a gun with a Marvelous dexterity as soon as ever they have strength enough to lift it to their heads." Yet there is much evidence that these perceived distinctions emerged from stereotype rather than observation. Southerners, for instance, were held to be deadly shots in a duel, the preferred method of conflict resolution in the mid-eighteenth-century South. But recent research on dueling finds far more bloodshed in literature than on the field of honor. There were three duels in the 1760s, none of them fatal; before that time, "no member of the Virginia elite had ever accepted a challenge let alone fought in a duel . . . since the spring of 1624," when George Harrison and Richard Stephens had dueled without loss of life. When William Byrd and Robert Bolling attempted to fight a duel, they were turned in by the shopkeeper from whom Byrd attempted to purchase the pistols for the duel. Community disapproval also led Thomas Mason to turn in his cousin, James Mercer, when the latter attempted to borrow a pistol in order to fight a duel with Arthur Lee in 1767. It is worth noting that these wealthy gentlemen did not own pistols at the time they sought to duel.[11]

Probate records indicate that, generally, more propertied white males owned firearms in the Chesapeake Bay area than anywhere else in Colonial America or England, yet this number represented only a small proportion of the total population. And government records from 1634 through the onset of the Revolution reveal that there were never enough guns in the whole colony to arm those serving in the militia. If Blathwayt's description was accurate for 1691, Governor Robert Dinwiddie and Colonel George Washington could find no indication that skill with firearms had survived among Virginians into the 1750s.[12] Despite possible regional differences, the presence and administration of restrictions on gun ownership can be traced through the history of each English colony.

Local communities and Colonial assemblies passed regulatory legislation affecting the use as well as the distribution of firearms throughout the Colonial period. As in England, American governments sought to regulate the quality, sale, and storage of firearms and munitions; the maintenance of arms used for public purposes; as well as where, when, and by whom firearms could be carried and fired. For instance, colonies generally forbade the use of firearms in connection with "drinkinge or enterteynments," while in times of emergency, prohibitions against the frivolous shooting of a musket were backed by the death penalty. Massachusetts outlawed "unprofitable fowlers" who wasted powder and lead by missing birds; South Carolina forbade anyone taking a gun out of the province without license from the government.[13] Colonial governments took a dim view of the misuse of guns, even those personally owned. Thus on a single day in October 1675, the Connecticut council—and it is notable that the council itself rather than a local constable addressed these matters—fined Thomas Trill "for unseasonably shooteing of his gun, owned by him," as well as Bartholomew Barnardt for allowing his son to shoot a militia musket in his possession.[14]

Legislatures also granted officials the right to expropriate firearms during internal or external crises, as when the Virginia governor and council gave General Robert Smith power to seize all the arms and ammunition in private possession so as to distribute them better and to conduct gun censuses.[15] And, most important, legislatures followed the

English example in denying the right to own guns to potentially dangerous groups: slaves, free blacks, Indians, propertyless whites, non-Protestants, and heterodox Protestants. These laws worked because the political community supported their enforcement, fearing the consequences of unregulated access to firearms and munitions. But a basic tension remained throughout the Colonial period between the need to arm trustworthy subjects for defense and the fear of seeing weapons fall into the hands of those most feared by the government.[16]

Colonial governments encouraged merchants to bring firearms into the colonies for sale either to the government or appropriate civilians. But many of those merchants sold firearms and powder to the Indians as well, despite numerous laws explicitly outlawing this practice. The severe punishment for violating these laws ran from the automatic loss of all property and imprisonment for life to death. Colonial legislatures even prohibited loaning or sharing arms or ammunition with Indians and teaching Indians to shoot. But these efforts failed for two reasons: the Colonial governments supplied firearms to "friendly Indians" as gifts, and other Europeans persisted in trading firearms to the Indians. Governments endeavored to deal with each problem through regulation. For instance, several colonies attempted to terminate the common practice of employing Indians as hunters, granting any white the authority to seize the firearms and ammunition of any Indian, friendly or hostile, caught hunting on English-owned land. Connecticut ordered that an Indian who refused to deliver up all his firearms or attempted to flee was to be shot.[17]

As early as 1632 Virginia's governing body recognized that, in addition to the Indians, they faced an internal threat from indentured servants. These unfree white laborers often had reason to resist the authority of the English elite, being exploited often unto death and having very little to lose by insurrection. Again there was the inherent ambiguity of attempting to keep firearms out of the hands of servants, while arming them with unfamiliar weapons in an emergency. Throughout the Colonial period, indentured servants in most colonies were not allowed to serve in the militia, an effective way of keeping them unarmed while minimizing knowledge of the use of firearms. And all the Colonial governors had the power to declare "Martill Law against mutinous and seditious persons," as the Maryland charter put it, with the authority to seize all arms for public use.[18]

The Virginia elite first acknowledged in law the inherent danger slavery posed to social order in 1640. In the midst of an Indian war, the

Virginia House of Burgesses recommended that "all masters of families . . . use their best endeavours for the firnishing of themselves and all those . . . capable of arms (excepting negroes) with arms." Yet the law's attitude toward free blacks remained ambiguous: sometimes all blacks were denied access to firearms; on other occasions some exceptions were allowed. In 1675 a county court clarified that a free black head-of-household could own a gun. The next year Nathaniel Bacon supplied arms to blacks who joined his insurgent forces. The legislature learned a valuable lesson from Bacon's Rebellion, and in 1680 it prohibited "any negroe or other slave" from carrying guns or any other weapon, ordering the confiscation of the guns and the whipping of the slave—a wording that may have still allowed free blacks to possess firearms. Later the assembly granted exceptions for blacks living in frontier regions, but only after the free black or master obtained a license from a justice of the peace. In 1723 the Virginia legislature closed any loopholes in its laws in "An Act for the better government of Negroes, Mulattoes, and Indians," which declared that "no negro, mulatto, or Indian whatsoever . . . shall hereafter presume to keep, or carry any gun, powder, shot, or any club, or other weapon whatsoever, offensive or defensive." The 1738 militia act further clarified this prohibition and ruled that free blacks could serve only "as drummers or trumpeters."[19]

Eventually, every southern colony legislated a complete prohibition of gun ownership by blacks, to be strictly enforced. By the beginning of the eighteenth century, the various legislatures forbade the carrying of firearms by a slave except when under the direct command or supervision of his owner. From time to time these laws were laxly enforced, and favored slaves could be seen hunting with their masters. But legislatures tightened these laws immediately following a slave uprising, such as South Carolina's Stono Rebellion of 1740. These slave uprisings—whether real or imagined—persuaded Colonial legislatures that blacks as a group, slave or free, should not be allowed to own firearms.[20]

The obverse of this fear of slaves owning guns was an insistence on whites using them to preserve slavery. In 1729 Governor William Gooch of Virginia, concerned over the threat of slave rebellion, instructed his officers to see that their men learned the use of firearms. In 1736 he revised an old law requiring members of the militia to attend church with their arms, this time out of fear not of Indian attack, but of a slave uprising. In the face of a number of complaints, the legislature allowed each militia commander to determine whether his troops should carry their guns to church. By 1742 Gooch could report to the British Board of Trade that he was making good progress training the "ordinary people" in "the use and exercise of their Arms." In Virginia, at least, guns were held at the service of slave owners.[21]

Racially determined prohibitions on gun use were not limited to the southern colonies. In 1675, at the beginning of King Philip's War, Plymouth made it a capital crime "to sell, barter, or give, directly or indirectly, any gun or guns, or ammunition of any kind, to any Indian or Indians." In 1690 the Connecticut assembly spoke for the first time on the racial dimension of gun ownership, though it may have just been regularizing common practice. As subjects without civic rights, Negroes and Indians, even Christian Indians, were excluded from the militia laws, essentially cutting off both from a legal right to own firearms. The Assembly simplified this prohibition, at least for Indians, in 1708, by forbidding selling, lending, or giving "to any of our friend Indian or Indians, any gun, for any time." Guns in the hands of Indians were expropriated. The assembly denied Indians, hostile or friendly, access to firearms, as the entire race was not to be trusted with guns.[22]

Colonial legislatures occasionally encouraged the private ownership of firearms by white male property owners, while appreciating how improbable it was for them to fulfill that goal. At one time or another, most assemblies threatened militia members with heavy fines if they did not provide themselves with a firearm. But the difficulty of finding firearms to buy, even if one had the surplus capital—equal to two months' pay for a skilled artisan—left these laws entirely unenforced. For instance, Connecticut's first militia act, passed in 1637, expected all Protestant males above the age of sixteen to own a firearm, "except they doe tender a sufficient excuse." The same act made each town responsible for supplying firearms and munitions, from flints to powder to lead for balls.[23] Every few years the Connecticut General Court observed that the towns were negligent in this duty and passed some nominal fine to demonstrate its continued concern and control, always acknowledging the towns' failure to meet the desired end of a well-armed militia.[24]

Several colonies tried the expedient of paying the militia to buy arms, holding back the per diem each militia member received until it equaled the cost of a firearm, and then presenting him with that gun. But there were two problems with this approach. First, the colonies themselves had great difficulty finding firearms. Second, soldiers who drilled once a year rarely bothered to maintain their firearms in working condition. The response to the first difficulty was the steady appropriation of funds to buy guns and the sending of agents to Europe for that purpose. The legislative records note each of these purchases, often of just a single gun, occasionally of scores. The guns purchased in Europe were always military weapons, intended for defense of the colony, not for private use. Virginia became so desperate for guns that it actually exempted from militia duty anyone who would supply two or more "complete sets of arms" for use by the militia. Thus the well-armed subject could avoid service in the militia entirely.[25] All the English colonies came to rely on the Crown to supply firearms, though there were still never enough. In 1675 the Connecticut General Court reported that most militia members did not have access to guns and therefore ordered the creation of "foot companies" bearing pikes.[26]

The second problem was the seeming indifference of so many of the favored property-owning white Protestant males toward firearms. All the colonies discovered, sooner or later, the insufficiency of requiring freemen to own firearms, and even the limitations of attempting to provide those guns. Firearms made of iron rusted and decayed quickly if not carefully serviced. In 1656 Connecticut, like so many other colonies, granted the clerk of each militia company the authority "to examin & censure all defects of armes" and to require repairs. The colony found these directions frustrated, however, by the paucity of trained gunsmiths. In response, the government granted local officials the power to impress the labor of anyone capable of repairing firearms.[27]

The Connecticut assembly did not trust its citizens to take pride in their possession of firearms nor to demonstrate sufficient enthusiasm for the militia ideal by actually holding regular musters. In 1724 the legislature ordered that the annual general inspection of all arms, public and private, "be held on one and the same day, to prevent deceit" by people passing the same guns from one town to another. It further instructed, yet again, that the towns were to see that all defective weapons were repaired immediately. Such insistence on annual inspections and on the care of firearms persisted through the Colonial period, as did efforts by the Colonial governments to repair firearms. In 1756 the legislature noted that, though the law required every householder to keep arms and ammunition, "yet for want of a due obedience thereto the true intention" of the act "is greatly frustrated." The assembly therefore ordered a second inspection of arms and ammunition, with stiffer fines for noncompliance, while granting commanding colonels greater authority to insure the care of militia arms.[28]

This lax attitude toward the condition of firearms annoyed British officials. In accordance with their Bill of Rights, the English preferred to maintain tight control of guns; English and Irish Catholics were not allowed to own even a part of a gun, and civil authorities throughout the empire were empowered to search for weapons in the hands of those deemed "dangerous to the peace of the realm." Gunsmiths could not have Catholic apprentices, and Protestants working for Catholics were forbidden from owning weapons, while those with arms in their homes were required to report the particulars to the local constable. William Blackstone clearly stated the purpose of these laws as "the prevention of popular insurrections and resistance to government by disarming the bulk of the people." And yet here were the Americans losing track of hundreds of guns, apparently selling them to the Indian allies of the French, and slacking off in the enforcement of the gun laws intended to secure the peace and order of these colonies.[29]

The eventual solution to the lack of care devoted to firearms was to make all guns into the property of the state, subject to storage in central storehouses where they could be cleaned and repaired by paid government gunsmiths. Thus the Connecticut assembly, annoyed that "complaints are still made of intolerable [guns] or insufficiencies and gross defects in arms and ammunition . . . notwithstanding all former lawes and orders," mandated the appointment of muster-masters in each county to inspect all arms and powder and to prescribe the necessary repairs. These muster-masters not only could compel the labor of anyone discovered to have a knowledge of firearms, but they also had the authority to seize property to pay for repairs or to impress any firearms needed for the community's defense and to command towns to purchase more firearms.[30]

Though the colonies supported and subsidized the private ownership of firearms, the government reserved to itself the right to impress arms on any occasion, either as a defensive measure against possible insurrection or for use by the state. No gun ever belonged unqualifiedly to an individual. It could not be seized in a debt case, could not be sold if that sale left a militia member without a firearm, had to be listed in every probate inventory and returned to the state if state-owned, and could be seized whenever needed by the state for alternative purposes. Guns might be privately owned, but they were state-controlled.[31]

In the seventeenth century, the Colonial militia's main duty was to protect the new settlements from the external danger of Indian attack. But at least in the southern colonies, that concern was consistently matched against an equivalent fear of internal subversion, particularly from indentured servants and slaves as a class. In the eighteenth century the main duty of southern militias was not public defense but internal security. The state drew its slave patrols, charged with keeping the slaves under strict control, from the militia, an arrangement institutionalized in Virginia with the 1726 militia act and maintained under the strictest state regulation with government-supplied arms until 1865. Until at least that latter date, guns were held in trust for the state, subject to the demands of fears generated by racism.[32]

Colonial America's culture did an excellent job directing its violence both outward, against perceived enemies, and inward, against those seen as a threat to social order. Lacking anything like a regular police force, Colonial society remained remarkably free of personal violence. Court records bear testament to this relative quiescence. Deep class divisions in Colonial society necessitated further laws prohibiting the ownership and use of firearms by the subservient classes. Compared to contemporary Europe, these efforts proved remarkably effective. But then guns were more readily available in Europe, where they were made.[33]

Dissent, Disruption, and Disorder

There is a popular perception that Americans have always resolved their conflicts with guns. This form of conflict resolution has been a favored American technique on both the personal and social level, from the first arrival of the Europeans in North America, or so we are assured. As one historian began her study of popular uprisings in early America, "Since the first adventurers waded ashore at Jamestown, Americans of all persuasions let their guns be heard when their voices in protest were ignored."[34]

And yet, with very few exceptions, colonists did not actually fire on one another in an effort to effect political or personal change. The reality was that firearm usage was strictly limited for most of the Colonial period. The ownership and use of firearms were constrained not merely by the law but also as a consequence of minimal availability and cultural attitudes. There were no gun manufactories in North America in the Colonial period—none. All American firearms—with a very few exceptions—came from Europe. France, and England, and the Netherlands led the world in gun production, with the lion's share of that production going to their armies. But in England, at least, that production was far from sufficient even for military purposes. The disappointment of Charles I with the unarmed state of his volunteers during the English Civil War is palpable. It is no wonder that Queen Henrietta rushed off to the Netherlands to trade her jewels for arms of all kinds.[35]

Those firearms made for private use tended to be works of great beauty, the product of skilled European craftsmen creating luxury goods for the rich. Few of these guns found their way to North America in the seventeenth century. The vast majority of firearms crossing the Atlantic were sent by the government for military use. It was not until the end of the Colonial period that any sort of market existed to justify the regular importation of firearms by merchants, or their production by the few gunsmiths scattered through North America. It is not surprising, then, that guns rarely saw use outside of warfare.[36]

This is not to say that Colonial America was a nonviolent society. It is to say that the vast majority of violence was state-sanctioned, as demanded by contemporary political and cultural attitudes, and that individuals rarely used guns in their personal quarrels. Just as a close examination of seventeenth-century battles undermines the notion that guns were the decisive weapon, so court records and contemporary accounts of crowd actions are notable for the absence of firearms. It is important here to distinguish between violence and aggression. The first is a commission of physical harm upon another person, while aggression is a posturing intended to frighten or intimidate without actual physical conflict.[37] Crowds in America were like those in Europe, relying primarily on intimidation to effect their ends, on the aggressive display of social power rather than on destructive injury. When they employed weapons, American crowds, like their European counterparts, wielded stones, clubs, and farm implements—not guns.

Whites rarely assaulted other whites in the colonies and almost never killed one another. This attitude toward violence was no different from England, except in that urban hothouse of London. Crime rates in

England remained very low through the eighteenth century, and it was not until 1829 that the English created their first police force.[38] Colonial court records offer very few cases of violence. There were 559 criminal actions in North Carolina between 1663 and 1740, 43 of which (7.7 percent) were murders, an average of one homicide every two years. A study of eighteen years of Virginia's seventeenth-century court records discovered twenty-three murder trials resulting in eleven homicide and four manslaughter convictions, or less than one murder a year. In the four years of 1736 to 1739, there were ten murders in Virginia, a notable increase to two and a half murders per year. Only one murder is mentioned in the records of New Haven Colony, while in forty-six years Plymouth Colony's courts heard five cases of assault, and not a single homicide. More common was Edward Jenkins's charge that Morris Truant threatened to "break his scythe." William Byrd exaggerated, but not much, when he wrote in 1726 that "We have neither publick Robbers nor private, which Your Ldsp will think very strange, when we have often needy Governors and pilfering Convicts sent among us."[39]

Until the 1760s, expressions of popular resistance to government authority remained localized, collapsing almost immediately and without violence in the face of a concerted display of force. Such a pattern was set early on. In the 1620s, the notorious "Lord of Misrule," Thomas Morton, made himself obnoxious to the leaders of Plymouth Plantation by enjoying himself with drunken parties and trading guns and powder to the local Indians in violation of James I's Proclamation of 1622 (which was reissued in 1630 at the request of the government of Massachusetts). Morton, who mocked the religiosity of the Pilgrims, refused to limit his trade or his festivals in any way. With evident reluctance, Plymouth sent a force of militia under Myles Standish to arrest Morton at his trading post of Merrymount. Morton and his followers vowed to defend their right to bear and trade arms, warning Standish that their muskets were loaded. According to William Bradford, it was fortunate that most of the muskets were not in fact properly loaded, for the people of Merrymount "were so steeled with drink as their pieces were too heavy for them." No one was hurt, "save that one was so drunk that he ran his own nose upon the point of a sword . . . but he lost but a little of his hot blood." And thus ended the story of free trade in firearms in Colonial America. From that date forth, the gun trade would be regulated by the Colonial legislatures and by the Crown.[40]

Probably the first Colonial civic uprising of any kind came in Virginia in 1635. Dr. John Pott, the man who had poisoned the Powhatan in 1623, led a number of the local elite in opposing the governor, Sir John Harvey. When Harvey charged most of his council with treason, Pott called in a band of forty armed men led by Captain William Pierce. No one was injured, or even threatened, and the assembly approved these actions by Pott and Pierce. Harvey agreed to resign and returned to England, where he acknowledged to the Commissioners for Foreign Plantations that Virginia's government lacked the force to maintain its authority, "nor had I the means or power to raise any force to suppress this meeting." He returned to Virginia in January 1637, with his powers clearly spelled out in his royal orders, and arrested and dispossessed the leaders of the uprising without resistance. In this, as in every succeeding conflict other than Bacon's Rebellion in which the province acted, the government's success was total and courts of law settled the issue.[41]

When Leonard Calvert, governor of Maryland, purchased land from the Yaocomicoe Indians, he found that they were far more interested in such metal goods as axes, hatchets, and rakes than in firearms. Calvert appreciated the advantages of the state's maintaining a monopoly on firearms, and not merely in the event of a possible Indian threat. In December 1636 he moved against the upstart William Claiborne on Kent's Island with a group of musketeers, kicking Claiborne out of the colony. Claiborne remained a thorn in the side of the Calvert family for two decades, but whenever the state moved against him and his supporters with force, Claiborne gave way without violence.[42]

In times of unrest in North America, competing sides jostled for control of public arms to supplement the few in private hands. During the English Civil War of the 1640s, for instance, Colonial adherents and opponents of King Charles never actually did battle, but they certainly maneuvered a great deal. While the English were busily hacking away at each other, most Americans waited and hoped for the best. But just in case, a few activists tried to prepare for the future by hoarding firearms. In Maryland in 1643 the acting governor, Giles Brent, seized a cargo of arms from the ship *Reformation,* captained by Richard Ingle, a known supporter of Parliament. Ingle managed to get his ship back and returned two years later to seize control of the colony from the Catholic Calvert family. A year later, Leonard Calvert gained the help of Virginia's Governor William Berkeley and had no trouble reclaiming control of the government. These actions occurred without loss of life. But in 1651 Parliament decided that Governors Berkeley and Calvert remained emotionally attached to monarchy and sent four commissioners and five hundred soldiers to the Chesapeake Bay area to reorganize government. The Virginia burgesses agreed with the governor that they should resist this force, especially in the face of the new Navigation Act, which eliminated all foreign trade with the North American colonies. Despite this incentive and the legislature's pledge, the entire colony, which boasted a militia of nearly seven thousand troops, collapsed before a small military force. Again, the government met no resistance, armed or otherwise.[43]

Maryland proved even easier to subdue, abandoning all resistance when faced with a force of two commissioners. The proprietor, Lord Baltimore, was charged with selling arms to the Indians and confiscating the arms of Protestants, and Governor William Stone was cast out of office. Oddly, in January 1655 Oliver Cromwell declared that the commissioners had gone too far in upsetting Baltimore's government. There followed a "petty civil war," as Stone seized the public arms in the name of Lord Baltimore and moved against the "Puritans" led by Captain William Fuller. On March 25, the two forces met at the Battle of the Severn. Stone was able to arm his roughly two hundred followers with the supplies he had seized from the provincial armory, but that did not make them effective soldiers. When confronted by a force of 120 well-trained troops from a Commonwealth ship, Stone's forces opened fire, killing the standard-bearer with their volley. Fuller's troops fired a single volley and then charged, most of the Royalists throwing down their guns and fleeing or begging for quarter. Forty men were killed, only a few by gunshot, and several executed on Fuller's orders after the battle. The supporters of the Commonwealth controlled the colony for the next five years, and then this government also collapsed without a fight at the restoration of Charles II.[44]

The pattern was little different in Dutch New Netherland. There, in 1653, John Underhill tried to rouse the English settlers on Long Island, New York, into rebellion. But there were few guns and no violence, and a Dutch official ordered Underhill to leave Long Island, which he did. This was one of three such rebellions on Long Island between 1653 and 1657, none of which exhibited any violence. In 1663 John Scott of Connecticut tried to seize the island for his province. He arrived with two hundred followers who waved their swords around a great deal and looted freely. As was almost always the case, the locals did not rise in self-defense. Their militia units did not rush onto the field to protect family and home. Instead, negotiations terminated this effort, with Governor John Winthrop Jr. of Connecticut arresting Scott and seizing the island with a body of troops. The whole farce came to an end in 1664 when Colonel Richard Nicholls arrived at Manhattan with four hundred regulars. Peter Stuyvesant surrendered when his militia refused to fight, and Dutch rule ended. The English confiscated what arms there were and looted the city.[45]

In 1669 the Dutch in New York attempted to reverse their fate with a rebellion, but the insurrection was quelled simply by arresting the leaders.[46] All these uprisings—except the one in Maryland—were thus short-lived, and in each the near uselessness of the militia comes across clearly. The militia's performance was equally unimpressive whether the enemy was internal or external. When the Dutch attacked the coast of Virginia in 1667 and seized several ships of the valuable tobacco fleet, they met no resistance from the militia, though Governor Berkeley did raise a force that then waited for the Dutch to come to them. Seven years later the Dutch returned and again raided the coast unhindered by local forces; only "the timely appearance of the royal navy saved the day."[47]

At the time of this latter crisis, in 1673, the governor ordered all arms and ammunition in the colony seized for use by the militia. But there was just not enough to go around; a "diligent search and inquiry" discovered that few Virginians owned serviceable arms. In desperation, the government offered to pay for the repair of all "unserviceable armes," and, for the first time since the 1630s, spent public funds to purchase weapons. But it was a slow process. Two years later they discovered that four companies of one regiment needed two hundred muskets and swords for their 280 men. Several other companies reported similar shortages, with three-quarters of their men owning no firearms. The guns purchased in England were stored in a communal center, generally the home of one of the local "great men." While these weapons arrived too late to do much good against the Dutch, they did serve to arm most of the followers of Nathaniel Bacon.[48]

Virginia enjoyed a long peace with the Indians from the end of the final Powhatan War until 1675. As the Royal Commissioners reported in 1677, "Few or none had bin the Damages sustained by the English from the Indians, other than occasionally had happen'd sometimes upon private quarells and provocations, untill in July, 1675, certain Doegs and Susquahanok Indians on Maryland side, stealing some Hoggs," from a settler named Matthews who had cheated them, "were pursued by the English . . . beaten or kill'd and the hoggs retaken."[49] In retaliation, some Doeg Indians killed two of Matthews's servants and his son. The Virginians responded by attacking an Indian village. The whites surprised the peaceful village with a volley and then moved in to slice and hack at the Indians with their axes and swords. Only later did they discover that this was not a Doeg but a Susquehannock village. Maryland's government was furious and Virginia's prepared for the expansion of the war, offering a coat to every Indian who brought in a scalp from a hostile Indian and calling on the king for help, appealing for arms and ammunition based on "their inability to furnish the same themselves." These actions by the settlers were an astounding case of projection. As Robert Beverley wrote, the Indians, "observing an unusual Uneasiness in the English, and being terrified of their rough Usage, immediately suspected some wicked Design against their Lives, and so fled to their remoter Habitations. This confirm'd the English in the Belief, that they had been the Murderers, till at last they provoked them to be so in Earnest."[50]

It was to combat these enemies they had just created that so many Virginians turned to the leadership of "that Imposture," Nathaniel Bacon. Bacon organized his followers around a demand for more guns and a more belligerent Indian policy, insisting that the government had failed to adequately arm its subjects—and he never suggested that they should arm themselves. Governor Berkeley should have arrested Bacon immediately, but he liked the young man, had appointed him to the council, and hated to admit such a lapse in judgment. Berkeley also hoped that Bacon might prove useful in channeling the passions of the lower orders, especially those on the frontier who were begging for arms. As Beverley wrote a few years later, the settlers, their "Minds already full of Discontent" because of the collapse of tobacco prices, were "ready to vent all their resentment against the poor Indians." Bacon led a large force against the Susquehannock, but the vast majority of his troops had little interest in any military activity beyond the alcohol that accompanied their musters. So Bacon hired the Occaneechee to attack the Susquehannock, who fled before this onslaught. Bacon and his followers then attacked the Occaneechee, probably to avoid paying them. The whites set fire to the Indian village and cut down everyone who fled the burning huts.[51]

Flushed with victory, Bacon marched on Williamsburg, Virginia, with six hundred followers to intimidate the burgesses. Fearful of "having their throats cut by Bacon," as Thomas Ludwell put it, the legislature and then Governor Berkeley submitted. Bacon followed this success with a looting expedition, his troops seizing all the guns they could find. Berkeley responded by secretly taking the arms and ammunition out of Tindall Fort on the York River, leaving it defenseless. But Berkeley did not move yet, nor did he intervene when Bacon sent a force into Dragon Swamp in pursuit of hostile Indians—and thanks to Bacon and his followers, there were only hostiles. Bacon's followers succeeded in hacking some women and children to death. A frustrated Bacon turned his attention on the peaceful Pamunkey, until recently allies of Virginia who, as the Royal Commissioners wrote, "had [never] at any time betray'd or injuryed the English." Even though they met no resistance, their queen having ordered "that they should neither fire a gun nor draw an arrow," the whites attacked viciously, killing or taking prisoner the entire tribe.[52]

Berkeley finally confronted Bacon at Jamestown with a force of unenthusiastic militiamen. Each side sat behind their defenses until the governor launched the only battle of the rebellion. The militia attacked "like scholers goeing to schoole . . . with hevie harts, but returnd hom with light heeles." Bacon's forces fired a single volley and Berkeley's men threw down their guns and ran, suffering about a dozen casualties. Bacon then set the capital on fire and fled as well. He died of disease shortly thereafter, his rebellion collapsing within days. Berkeley moved with alacrity to punish the Baconites, charging Sarah Grendon with high treason as the chief "encourager" of the rebellion for having supplied the rebels with gunpowder.[53]

In February 1677 twelve hundred British Regulars under the command of Colonel Herbert Jeffreys arrived to clean up the mess left by the rebellion. Jeffreys brought with him the largest arsenal the British had yet carried into North America: one thousand muskets, seven hundred carbines, one hundred barrels of gunpowder, and even a crate of hand grenades. England was taking this uprising very seriously—not that it mattered much. Governor Berkeley was now creating the most problems, denying Jeffreys's authority, seeking to punish all those who had supported Bacon, and refusing to return home as ordered by the king. But a quick show of force by Jeffreys settled the matter. Berkeley left for England and Jeffreys became acting governor.[54]

There was an unusual last act to Bacon's Rebellion. The uprising had begun in a debate over the lack of arms for colonial defense. In 1678 Jeffreys reduced the pay of his forces since the rebellion had been crushed and they were no longer on active duty. The troops began to mutter ominously. To forestall a mutiny, Jeffreys sent most of his forces home, leaving only a few hundred in Virginia until 1682. But he sent his troops home without their guns, distributing most of the seventeen hundred firearms he had brought with his force to the militia of Virginia. This act doubled the number of guns in the hands of the Virginians, who built two new armories for their storage.[55]

The militia almost had an opportunity to use these guns the same year they became available. In 1682 a number of planters threatened to revive the memory of Bacon by calling for a moratorium on the tobacco harvest as a way of raising its price. Those who did not go along with the "plant-cutters' rebellion" found their fields attacked by angry neighbors. Acting governor Sir Henry Chicheley responded to this "strange Insurrection" by calling on the militia rather than the regulars still in Virginia, but only "soe many of them as may, in this juncture, bee admitted to arms." The plant-cutters dispersed whenever the militia appeared but took to destroying crops at night. Despite the presence of the militia, two hundred plantations lost their tobacco crop in Gloucester County, and then the movement spread to Middlesex, York, and New Kent Counties. The movement just faded out after that with no violence, much like any of the contemporary fence-destroying movements in England.[56]

Though it came closer than any colony to civil war in the first 160 years of English settlement, Virginia itself suffered little from Bacon's Rebellion. With the exception of the one encounter at Jamestown, whites did not kill whites. They threatened and terrorized one another, but they reserved their murderous rage for the Indians. And the rebellion ended even before the arrival of British Regulars. In the 1630s the English had learned the danger of allowing firearms to fall into the hands of Indians; in 1676 they discovered that it was equally dangerous to let poor whites have access to guns. Yet battling the one seemed to necessitate the arming of the other. Unable to resolve this paradox, Colonial governments began every new crisis by begging the Crown for guns and troops, and ended it by frantically trying to recover those guns and get rid of the troops. The result, according to a careful student of the Colonial Virginia militia, was that the militia never recovered from Bacon's Rebellion but instead sank into insignificance.[57]

Roughly the same pattern was evident in the response of the New England colonies to the reign of James II (1685–88). James effectively overturned the entire system of government and social relations in New England by his creation of the Dominion of New England, and further alterations were promised. His officials were harsh and arrogant, their lack of respect for the Puritan way of life callous and offensive. The people of New England received every provocation, and yet they were unwilling to break out of the traditional modes of complaint via petition and noncompliance until they received word that William had invaded England in the name of Protestantism. It was in his name that many New Englanders finally acted, and then only to arrest James II's officials and appeal to William of Orange for the restoration of their charter. There is little evidence here of a tradition of an armed people defending their rights. Their resistance was expressed with words, not guns, and no shots were fired.[58]

The people of New York also put up with what was widely seen as arbitrary government until after William's invasion of England. In fact it was not until May 1689 that the public responded in any way to the perceived tyranny. Lieutenant Governor Francis Nicholson shocked the city by pulling a pistol on a militia lieutenant with whom he was arguing. Such an action alone was without precedent, but Nicholson compounded public anger by threatening to burn the city to the ground. A militia captain named Jacob Leisler led four hundred militiamen in a peaceful invasion of Fort James, a disappointing exercise. They had hoped for a stockpile of English guns, but found instead, as Leisler reported, only fifteen usable cannon and one barrel of powder "fit to sling a bullet halfway [to] the river."[59]

Leisler's forces then took over the city. They disarmed the Catholics, finding only four guns, and seized the arms of political opponents as well as gunpowder in private hands. One of his enemies wrote that "Capt. Leysler with a party of Men in Arms, and Drink, fell upon [the new customs officers] at the Custom-House, and with Naked Swords beat them thence, endeavouring to Massacree some of them, which was Rescued by Providence." These "arms" were swords and clubs, and no one was actually hurt, despite the effort "to Massacree some of them."[60]

When Albany refused to go along with the New York junto's claims to authority, Leisler sent some militia under the command of his son-in-law Jacob Milbourne. Milbourne spent a great deal of time talking with the leaders of Albany but was finally persuaded to return to New York by the presence of a group of Mohawk who promised to intervene on behalf of the people of Albany, with whom "they were in a firm Covenant chain." There were no casualties.[61]

The "rebellion" began to take on comic form. Desiring an end to the whole charade, a group of thirty-six prominent New Yorkers appealed to William and Mary to terminate this rule "by the sword." A group of thirty men confronted Leisler and some companions. Leisler was almost felled by a blow from a cooper's adz, but ducked just in time. Waving his sword before him, Leisler made good his escape—again no one was seriously hurt. It is surprising that none of these men, all of whom supposedly owned guns, thought to bring one with them.[62]

The only confrontation between these competing forces occurred in late 1690. Major Thomas Willett, a veteran of the assault with the adz, organized a march by 150 Long Island militia on New York. They were confronted by three hundred militia under Jacob Milbourne's command. The two sides began shoving one another, Milbourne using his musket as a club to knock down a militia captain. Suddenly, Milbourne's troops fired, an unheard-of action. Firing at point-blank range, roughly one hundred militiamen succeeded in killing one of their opponents. The rest ran before Milbourne's troops could reload.[63]

This violent encounter was the last straw. Unwilling to fight Leisler themselves, his opponents called in British Regulars. On January 31, 1691, two companies of English soldiers under the command of Major Richard Ingoldesby arrived at New York. Leisler called out the militia to defend the government in the name of William and Mary. For six weeks there was no confrontation between the militia and the regulars, but they did exchange proclamations. The soldiers were quartered in city hall, three hundred militia in Fort James. On March 16, for no apparent reason, Leisler's militia began firing their cannon at the city. A few civilians were killed, nine British Regulars wounded, and several of Leisler's followers killed when one of their misloaded cannon exploded. On March 19 the new governor, Sir Henry Sloughter, arrived. He immediately threatened to attack Fort James if the militia did not surrender. When Leisler hesitated, his forces threw down their guns and surrendered. And so Leisler's Rebellion came to an end, not with a battle, but a pathetic whimper as bystanders spat on Leisler as he was marched off to jail.[64]

Bacon's and Leisler's Rebellions were the only Colonial uprisings in which whites fired on whites. More typical were the brief little insurrections like those in Maryland in the last quarter of the seventeenth century. In June 1676 a group of sixty men in the Patuxent River region took advantage of the recent departure of Governor Charles Calvert to London to petition against taxes. When the governor's council rejected their petition, the group marched on St. Mary's, threatening to battle any militia called out. But no militia was called out. The council declared the group in rebellion but offered a pardon to those who went home. They all went home, except the two leaders, who were hanged.[65]

In 1681 former governor Josias Fendall of Maryland attempted to follow Nathaniel Bacon's example, using fear of Indian attacks and the failure of the proprietary government to supply arms to the settlers as a route to power. His effort never came anywhere near success. Fendall joined with the eternal gadfly John Coode, a landowner and merchant who opposed every Maryland government for thirty years, to attack the proprietor as an arbitrary governor who imposed excessive taxes and had failed to build the local arsenals required by law. Fendall and Coode apparently organized a large following along both banks of the Potomac, recruiting, as Calvert wrote, "most of the rascals" in the region. But the insurrection evaporated with the arrest of the two leaders.[66]

When news of William's invasion of England reached the Chesapeake Bay area in early 1689, the Maryland government ordered the recall of all arms that had been distributed to the militia. The council announced that the guns were just being brought in for routine maintenance and would be returned, but they intended to hold on to the firearms until they discerned which way the political winds were blowing. Maryland had still not built the county arsenals ordered by the legislature more than a decade earlier, so these recalled guns were brought to the central armory in St. Mary's, under the watchful eyes of the council.[67]

In July, John Coode, whom the government kept unwisely freeing, organized a protest demanding the return of the "public arms" to the militia. In the name of the new monarchs, William and Mary, he marched on St. Mary's with several hundred men armed with clubs, axes, hoes, and such. In response, the council called out the St. Mary's militia, arming them with the recalled guns, and declared the insurgents in rebellion. On July 27 the four hundred militiamen occupying Fort St. Mary announced that they would not fire upon their fellow citizens and turned the fort over to Coode's followers.[68]

With the fort, and the state's guns, now in Coode's hands, the council immediately reached a deal. All Catholics left office, and Coode took effective control of the new papist-free government. He immediately ordered the confiscation of all guns in Catholic hands. In July 1691 Maryland became a royal colony. The first royal governor arrived the following year and expelled Coode from power. Coode continued to complain for another fifteen years, but no force rose in opposition to this heavy-handed exercise of arbitrary authority.[69]

With the exception of Bacon's Rebellion, most encounters between dissidents and governors in that Colonial period were nonevents. In the 1660s a group of sword-waving opponents threatened but did not attack Governor Samuel Stephens of North Carolina. The only political uprising in the colony's first hundred years came in 1677, when the customs collector seized the ship *Carolina* for nonpayment of plantation duties. Aboard the ship was a small consignment of swords, guns, and ammunition intended for the colony. The sailors of the *Carolina* seized the collector and distributed the arms to the public.[70] The new governor died of a fever within days of his arrival, and the next governor was, amazingly, captured by Algerian pirates while on his way to America. The colonial proprietors chose to ignore the whole affair, afraid that if word got out that they had lost control of North Carolina, the king would take the colony for himself. No one was hurt, and not a single shot was fired in what historians call Culpeper's Rebellion. For two years the assembly ran the colony until a temporary governor arrived. It was as though the uprising had never occurred.[71]

What one mostly sees in Colonial America is calm and peace punctuated by some rather nasty Indian wars. Most settlers were too focused on the prosperity of their families and the health of their souls to bother about political and social issues. In January 1683 New Hampshire's Governor Edward Cranfield arbitrarily prorogued the assembly, a unique act in New England. One member of the assembly, Edward Gove, tried to start an uprising with the cry of "liberty and reformation." Traveling from town to town, Gove raised a force of sixteen men, half of whom ran away at the first sign of trouble. The governor arrested the remainder and charged them with treason. Thus ended that rebellion.[72]

Another insurrection started the following year, as Governor Cranfield ignored the tradition of assemblies voting taxes and ordered a series of new "fees," hoping the name change would baffle the public. There were a few sporadic attacks around the colony, and a great deal of noncompliance. In December 1684 a club-wielding crowd in Exeter chased off the sheriff attempting to collect the fees. In Hampton another crowd actually beat a sheriff. The militia was called out in Hampton, but no one showed up since the militia was the crowd. The deputy governor lost a tooth in a fight with an assemblyman, the chancellor of the colony was pushed into a fireplace, and a sheriff who entered a religious meeting in Dover to collect a fee was knocked flat by a woman wielding her Bible. There were no further casualties, and no guns in evidence during any of these battles. The governor resigned his position, and another rebellion reached a peaceful conclusion.[73]

These Colonial insurrections were conservative in nature. The sovereignty of Great Britain was never questioned, the goal of uprisings generally a return to some real or imagined traditional relation, or, more often, a dispute among factions over who would enjoy the perquisites of power, each side claiming to act in the interests of the monarch. As long as white Americans had difficulty acquiring firearms and ammunition, there would be little chance of a real threat to England's Colonial rule. As Gary Nash has written, the American lower class was "far more moderate in their proposals and far less violent" than the contemporary London crowd.[74]

And yet one historian of Colonial uprisings concluded that "The heavily armed adults of the provinces were far different from the domesticated residents of England. In Britain, guns and shot were reserved only for gentlemen, but in the colonies arms were the everyday tools of all citizens. Provincial men and women were well versed in fighting techniques and not to be trifled with."[75] But where were the guns? Where is the evidence that they were used in any circumstances other than war? At some level the image of the armed settler appears a grand mythology intended to formulate a portrait of Americans as many would like to see them: people not to be trifled with, not willing to put up with ill treatment, and very violent.[76] The history of the first 150 years of settlement in America is of a people fairly hesitant to act, and then usually in a nonviolent manner, except, tragically, when race was involved.

The Colonial Militia
and Its Guns

One searches in vain through the Colonial period for evidence of Americans armed with guns rising in great numbers to defend their liberties, whether in organized militia units or unorganized crowds. There were some insurrections, the first act of which was generally an effort to lay hands on English muskets. But these uprisings peaked in the period from Bacon's Rebellion through the Glorious Revolution, and there would not be another major domestic upheaval until the Stamp Act crisis in 1765.

White Americans would, however, rise up to defend slavery. Colonial governments were willing to distribute, use, and even give away their valuable firearms in support of slavery. Virginia was typical in its offer of a gun and two blankets to any Indian who returned a runaway slave to bondage; South Carolina offered two guns or four blankets.[77] Faced with the slightest threat to their system of slavery, white Americans did not hesitate to battle and kill black Americans. But then suppressing slave rebellions was the primary function of the militia in several colonies.[78]

In New York in 1712, a group of slaves spent weeks stockpiling weapons for an uprising against tyranny. But ironically, it was the very fact that the blacks had guns that doomed the effort. Their strategy was to set a fire and then kill whites rushing to put out the blaze, a tactic that initially worked, as the slaves killed or wounded with knives and axes the first fourteen whites who rushed to the scene. But they had a gun, and a fatal shot fired by that weapon gave away the ambush. Governor Robert Hunter acted very quickly in calling out the militia and crushing the rebellion. Tellingly, when faced with a slave uprising, militia units from other communities rushed to the scene to help the New Yorkers, an unusual event.[79]

The Stono Rebellion of 1739 tested the militia's ability to respond to domestic insurrection. The rebels began with a successful attack on a militia arsenal, and then, well armed with guns and ammunition, the slaves set off for Florida and freedom. But the blacks were completely unfamiliar with firearms, and their defense crumbled before Lieutenant Governor William Bull's first charge. A dozen insurgents were quickly killed and most of the rest taken prisoner. The colony spared no expense in pouring the militia onto the roads and into the swamps of South Carolina in search of escaped rebels, and even hired local Indians to help put down the uprising. Such sustained efforts contrast dramatically with the earlier feeble responses to local white insurrections. Slavery touched the way most whites lived in a manner that politics never could.[80]

In 1740 a second slave uprising was discovered. Rather than fleeing south to Florida, these insurgents, numbering between one hundred and two hundred, planned to seize the Charleston arsenal and then take over the government of the colony. An informant gave away the plan and the government hanged fifty rebels.[81]

That same year a similar conspiracy was broken up in Prince George

County, Maryland. Here again the initial target was the arsenal, this one at Annapolis. Whites understood that firearms had their uses, but could also pose a major threat if not carefully controlled and protected, leading southern colonies to keep regular guards on their armories.[82]

Jumping ahead a bit, a final indication of the basic racism inherent in the use of violence by Colonial whites can be found in the career of the notorious Paxton Boys. In 1763 this group of frontier thugs did not hesitate to kill dozens of friendly Christian Indians, for they were easier to get at than the hostiles who would put up a fight. The Paxton Boys mostly beat their victims to death, though they did not scruple at using axes. Yet when they marched on Philadelphia to press their claims for more funding and arms for a war against the Indians, they were met by an armed militia, and their forces melted away. Only some 250 Paxton Boys remained, and they were intellectually outnumbered by Benjamin Franklin, who offered these "white savages" a face-saving out. The western insurgents presented a promurder petition to the legislature, an amazing exercise in projection that argued that Indians should be killed because they were prone to massacre innocents. The point is, again, that these white rebels contented themselves with a petition and then went home. The legislature ignored their drivel.[83] In brief, then, personal violence in Colonial America appears to have been reserved for despised races.

And yet, it would appear that a great number of these settlers took seriously the injunctions of Christianity against killing, for they showed little interest in owning, maintaining, or even holding firearms.[84] One consequence was a long crisis in the maintenance of the militia system, which entered a period of decrepitude in the 1690s from which it would not emerge until the onset of the Seven Years' War in 1756.

Efforts by Colonial governments to correct the problems in the militia by arming and training them met one frustration after another. On the one hand was a seemingly widespread public indifference, as when the New Hampshire assembly flatly refused to vote funds to arm the militia. On the other hand, the insufficiency of supply played a role as well. Part of the latter concern may have been the product of corruption. A prime complaint of Bacon and his followers was that the government of Virginia was not spending the money allotted to buy arms for the militia but was instead diverting funds to individual use. Even the established garrisons along the coast had insufficient arms. But of far greater importance was the unavailability of guns in the colonies. In the 1670s the Virginia legislature appropriated funds for the purchase of firearms but had little success in acquiring them in England, while it was nearly impossible to purchase more than one or two guns at a time in North America.[85]

Virginia was the richest colony. Poorer colonies, such as North Carolina, had few militia and fewer firearms. The settlers complained often that the proprietors had not supplied them with arms and ammunition for self-defense—or offense—against the Indians, leaving them to rely on blades and axes. In 1672 the council sent Governor Peter Carteret to England to request arms, but he was rebuffed by the Privy Council. Fortunately for these settlers, the Indians seemed uninterested in waging war.[86]

Opponents of Sir Edmund Andros, governor of the Dominion of New England, accused him of deliberately supplying the New England troops marching against Indians in Maine with bullets so malformed that they could not be used. It emerged, however, that the inconsistency of shape in these bullets was fairly standard, just as the powder available in America tended to be weak or damaged. Andros had himself observed the shocking inferiority of Massachusetts's few usable guns and had written directly to the Crown begging for new muskets and ammunition. The Lords of Trade ignored his request.[87]

Andros detected what most contemporaries note but historians have missed: the shortage of firearms in the possession of the American militia. Unless these men were hiding their guns, it would seem that at no point in the Colonial period after the 1630s, when the population began its steady rise, did the American militia units own sufficient firearms. This paucity should not be too surprising, for nearly every single gun had to cross the Atlantic from Europe. Through the entire seventeenth century and the first half of the eighteenth, the English government reserved the majority of firearms production for its own army. As noted earlier, the American colonies tended to receive small shipments of the older, usually damaged military firearms, except in times of crisis, when the Crown would send over a few hundred usable muskets for the militia. These guns—numbering, according to government figures, some eleven thousand firearms in the seventeenth century—formed the bulk of guns available in the American colonies in 1700. Yet more than that many men were eligible to serve in the Virginia militia alone. Any additional arms were independently purchased directly from Europe by the richer planters and merchants.[88]

The reason for this misunderstanding on the part of historians seems to arise from a too casual reading of the word "arms." Thus an historian can read of people rushing to battle with their "arms" or "rising up in arms" in England as evidence that most people had guns in the mid-seventeenth century. But "arms" and "guns" are not exact synonyms. Thus slaves were often reported as "rising up in arms" despite the fact that they did not have a single gun.[89] Arms could be pikes, swords, hoes, and clubs, as well as firearms; thus the need for scholars to look very closely at the source documents for the militia. Those who have done so with care, the military historians, have long reported that it was well-known in the Colonial period that few firearms were available and militia units generally practiced with pikes, as they were required to do in England.[90]

All military service was ordained by the state, not by individuals. It was illegal in the British empire for groups of men to form themselves into military units without state sanction. Such an effort would be officially proclaimed a riot. As the first militia law in Plymouth stated, every adult male settler was "subject to such military order for trayning and exercise of armes as shall be thought meet, agreed on, and prescribed by the Governor and Assistants."[91] The government determined whether the colony had a militia or not, where it would meet, how often, who should belong, and what they should do. In practice, Colonial militias tended to meet in peacetime once a year for a parade, a counting and inspection of arms, and to drink.

Maryland was not unusual in starting with high ambitions for its militia, aspirations quickly abandoned. The proprietors ordered the first governor to organize the militia with musters weekly or monthly. In 1639 the legislature considered and rejected a militia bill following this standard, instead delegating authority for provincial defense to local captains. The next act in 1654 compounded this loose organization with an equally obscure charge that all eligible men would be provided with arms, but with no reference as to where those arms should come from. The first detailed militia act did not pass until 1661, yet even after that event, the governor called for volunteers when they were needed, with the towns to provide arms to each of these rangers. From that point on, Maryland kept a provincial armory with commissioners appointed to impress arms and men from the counties as needed, the government drafting mostly indentured servants, with their masters responsible for supplying arms. In 1675

Maryland abandoned the pretense of a militia and shifted to reliance on paid rangers, though they rarely called upon them. From time to time the legislature would request the proprietor or the Crown to supply arms for the militia, but the militia itself remained a spectral presence, not even existing on paper. Maryland tried to preserve its militia's arms by employing an armorer, Isaac Miller, who also served as an arms dealer purchasing guns in England for several colonies. In 1690 Lord Baltimore "thought fitt to call in all arms held by the Publick to fixe and make them fitt for Service & upon Occasion to Distribute the same until such Hands as shall faithfully serve the King." Yet when the legislature ordered a census of arms at the end of the seventeenth century, they found twenty muskets, thirty-eight carbines, sixteen bayonets, sixteen swords, fifty-six fusees, sixteen horse pistols, and seventy-eight barrels of powder accumulated over the previous twenty-five years but never used—not a formidable array of weapons.[92]

When a Colonial government made the militia a high priority, improvement was noticeable. Thus in 1632 Governor John Winthrop issued an alarm to test the readiness of the Massachusetts militia. He reported that this practice revealed "the weakness of our people, who, like men amazed, knew not how to behave themselves, so as the officers could not draw them into any order." Over the next decade the government exerted every effort to arm and train these men, so that by 1641 Winthrop could report with some pride that "about 1,200 men were exercised in most sorts of land service; yet it was observed that there was no man drunk, though there was plenty of wine and strong beer in the town, not an oath sworn, no quarrel, nor any hurt done."[93]

Massachusetts enjoyed a qualified success with its militia by expending money and energy on the effort. Other Colonial governments demonstrated less interest and produced lesser results. Francis Howard, Baron of Effingham and governor of Virginia in the 1680s, came up with an obvious solution to the problem of the militia. In 1672, according to muster reports, only one-tenth of those eligible for militia service owned guns. By 1680 the colony had purchased or been given by the Crown enough guns for one-half of the eighty-five hundred men in the Virginia militia. Effingham, observing that most Virginians "cannot afford to equip themselves," reversed the logic; rather than trying to arm the entire militia, he limited the militia to those who bore arms, either their own or the province's. In 1689 the militia consisted of forty-three hundred men, all of whom held guns. Thus, out of a population of fifty thousand, 8.6

percent possessed guns, or 28.7 percent of the adult white males who should have been serving in the militia; this number was reached only because England had just given more than one thousand muskets to Virginia. As William Shea has written, this "exclusionary trend" in the Virginia militia produced "an English-style 'bourgeois militia.' "[94] In 1688 William Fitzhugh observed that such a completely armed force "with a Soldier like appearance, is far more suitable & commendable, than a far greater number presenting themselves in the field with Clubs & staves, rather like a Rabble Rout than a well disciplin'd Militia." It is ironic that Fitzhugh did not include himself in that number. Though he owned thousands of acres, fifty-one slaves, and two stores, and was a colonel of the militia, Fitzhugh's role was entirely administrative. He did not own a gun himself.[95]

And yet, when Sir Francis Nicholson arrived as Effingham's successor in 1689, he was appalled at the condition of the militia, even in its supposedly more efficient form. With King William's War now in progress, Effingham called on the Crown to send over thousands of arms for the use even of the "poore and Indigent" who should also serve in the militia but could not afford to buy a gun even if the law did require such. The local elite, and the Crown, thought this idea bordered on insanity, and proposed instead the creation of a specialized force of rangers who would hunt down their enemies, without the need to arm the potentially dangerous poor. Nicholson found these efforts inadequate and worried that only a major infusion of arms from England could possibly save the militia, the vast majority of whom remained unfamiliar with the use of firearms. He was ignored, and the "militia naturally began to atrophy." By 1702 Robert Quary could report that the militia was "so undisciplined and unskillful and in such great Want of arms and ammunition proper and fit for action, that not one fourth of the militia is fit to oppose an Enemy." And this in the midst of Queen Anne's War. The Crown was so concerned over the lack of military readiness in Virginia that it sent a gift of fourteen hundred swords, one thousand muskets, and four hundred pistols in 1702 for use by the militia. The government attempted to sell the arms and ammunition to the militia members, but found few takers. Somehow this new weaponry failed to excite the Virginians with a proper willingness to fight and die for queen and empire.[96]

The 1710 panic in Virginia over the approach of a French fleet, as reported in William Byrd's diary, indicates the failure of previous efforts to reform the province's militia. On August 15 Governor Alexander

Spotswood ordered Byrd, commander of the militia in two counties, to call out his troops. Byrd sent directions to his captains and then went about his business for the next week, largely ignoring two further expresses from the governor about the crisis. Byrd talked with some of his captains but, by his own account, did nothing else until August 23, when the governor warned him that the French fleet was present on the James River. The next day Byrd "sent for my guns and ammunition from Appomattox," where the militia's arms were stored. Two days later he received a request from the settlement on the Potomac known as the Falls for powder, as the settlers feared an Indian attack. Byrd sent off a pound of powder, but saw no cause for concern. Twelve days after the alarm was sounded, Byrd finally met with all his officers, having received orders from Spotswood to march to Williamsburg. Unable to delay the matter further, Byrd called out the militia. The next day Byrd learned that the ships were English. "This was just as I suspected," he wrote, and ordered the militia not to bother to appear. Thus ended the crisis.[97]

In the aftermath of this nonevent, the governor ordered more inspections, and Byrd dutifully went around to the militia companies under his command and reviewed them. The first of these musters, Byrd reported, went very well. The officers were all "drunk and fighting all the evening, but without much mischief." Byrd found another company "in as good condition as might be expected," while at a third he "found several without arms." More dramatic was a review postponed because of poor attendance, leading Byrd and Captain Thomas Jefferson to spend a great deal of time drinking together. Finally, Byrd noted, "I caused the troops to be exercised by each captain and they performed but indifferently for which I reproved them." Shockingly, one of the soldiers "was drunk and rude to his captain, for which I broke his head in two places." At several musters the troops held contests, running and wrestling but not shooting. After one such muster, many of the whites watched some Indians shoot for prizes, but did not do the same themselves.[98]

In the last half of the seventeenth century all the European powers figured out that the settlers themselves were hardly capable of holding on to their colonies. Contingents of regulars that would have been considered insignificant by European standards, but which appeared as overwhelming demonstrations of power, arrived in North America. In 1665 the French sent twelve hundred veterans under General Alexandre de Prouville, all armed with the new flintlocks, to Quebec, immediately making it the largest and best-armed military force in North America.[99] England had no desire to follow suit, preferring to keep its expenses down by sending troops over only as a last resort. Unfortunately for the budget, that last resort arrived on many occasions.

The biggest problem with the militia was that they tended not to want to fight. In the winter of 1666 a starving French company stumbled into Schenectady, New York, and ransacked some houses. Thirty Mohawk attacked the French and drove them into retreat. At this point, in the classic formulation, the militia should have rushed to battle; instead, the mayor told the French commander that his town was undefended and offered to surrender. The French officer gratefully declined this offer, as he did not realize that the colony was now English, bought some provisions, and left. Neither side knew that England and France had been at war for a month. But with or without a declaration of war, Schenectady's militia had shown itself completely unwilling to defend the town against hostile forces.[100]

England's second problem was that when the militia showed a willingness to fight, they did not always have guns. Since only a limited number of any given militia company ever went on a military campaign, the governments generally requesting one or two soldiers from each company, this gun shortage was not too significant, as a gun could simply be loaned to the draftee. Thus when a member of the militia company in Salisbury, Massachusetts, was pressed into service for a winter campaign to Canada in 1706, Captain Henry True saw that the man "was fitted out by myself with a gunn flints bullits and a paire of good Snow shoose which he ingaged to returne to me againe and or to pay for them." But in a general crisis, as in New England in 1746, it would turn out that the majority of volunteers did not possess arms, and almost none of those conscripted had a gun. There was no consistent pattern in this regard, though Providence and Hartford had the highest percentage of ownership. Individual volunteer companies in these towns reported those entirely unarmed numbering between 16 percent and 54 percent. And again, the majority of those men with arms carried government guns. The New England colonies therefore had to spend hundreds of pounds to purchase arms for the unarmed militiamen.[101]

Even when armed, the militia showed an unfamiliarity with guns. At their greatest victory, the 1745 capture of Louisbourg, Nova Scotia, the New England troops, all paid volunteers, earned the contempt of their commander, William Pepperrell, who complained that his troops were entirely unfamiliar with any aspect of warfare and that "the unaccountable irregular behaviour of these fellows . . . is the greatest fatigue I meet with." When the New Hampshire troops arrived, Pepperrell found it necessary that they all be "Taught How to Use the firelock." At that first training, one of them fired his musket by accident, "the Bullet went thro a mans Cap on his head." In fact half of the casualties came from accidents with guns and artillery, and the New Englanders initially refused to attack Louisbourg. The victory itself was aided by the capture of the French munitions bound for the fortress, with which Pepperrell was able to arm his forces.[102]

Clearly some companies were better supplied than others, even within the same colony. It was the captain's responsibility to find weapons for those who lacked them. For many, that meant passing out pikes, which were in great supply. Other captains simply took note of the unarmed. At one muster in 1689 the clerk reported that he "did Acordingly go through the company and found the souldiers most of them furnished acording to Law with arms and amunition and thos that were not so furnished I gave acount of in writeing to the Leftenant." Another officer inspecting a Massachusetts company in 1744 reported that most of the soldiers had "arms yet I find several of them was borrowed." Both officers reported that nearly all of these guns were government-issued military muskets.[103]

Drill occurred at these musters, but the real importance of the militia lay in maintaining social connections: "The Foot-Companies, after having perform'd their Exercise, were discharged by their several Captains, but the Gentlemen Troopers with their officers return'd to the Bowling Green, where they and the Officers of the Foot Companies were regaled with a handsome dinner." Most musters demonstrated a predilection toward merriment. As the South Carolina *Gazette* reported in 1735, "four Companies mustered on Tuesday last, heads of Companies read their Commissions, and Concluded the Day in regaling and Merriment." One observer concluded that the militia drill was a "burlesque of everything military."[104]

By the start of the eighteenth century, the militia was the subject of some popular contempt. The author of a captivity narrative of 1748 changed the words of Dryden's popular "Cymon and Iphigenia" from "And raw in Fields the rude Militia swarms," to "And raw in Arms, the rude Melitia Swarms." At this time it became far more common for great numbers of men to attempt to avoid militia duty, often bargaining their way out. Thus Samuel Carter convinced the Salisbury, Massachusetts, militia company to "free him from paying any fins for Neglecting to trayn provided he give them a barrell of Sider yerely and to bring it" to where they were training so that "they may Conveniently drinke it." Even those who stayed in the militia came to treat it with a certain lack of respect. In July 1668 Governor Nicholls was so upset with the performance of the Flushing, New York, militia that he ordered it disarmed on the spot. Or as Samuel Sewall wrote in his diary, "Exercise Regimentally in the Afternoon; when concluded, Mr. Mather prayd." Sewall's next entry records his resignation as captain.[105]

Hunters and Gunsmiths

The records of the Colonial militia, and the story of their generally abysmal showing in early American wars, may seem counterintuitive. Surely there must have been more guns hiding someplace? After all, one of the most popular and persistent visions of the American past is that every settler owned a gun in order to hunt—"to put meat on the table," in the oft-repeated phrase. This is a very strange perception. Hunting is and always has been a time-consuming and inefficient way of putting food on the table. People settling a new territory have little time for leisure activities, and hunting was broadly understood in the European context to be an upper-class leisure activity. One of the most significant advantages that European settlers enjoyed over their Indian competitors for the land of North America was their mastery of domesticated animals.[106] If a settler wanted meat, he did not pull his trusty and rusty musket, inaccurate beyond twenty yards, off the hook above the door and spend the day cleaning and preparing it. Nor did he then hike miles to the nearest trading post to trade farm produce for powder and shot. To head off into the woods for two days in order to drag the carcass of a deer back to his family—assuming that he was lucky enough to find one, not to mention kill it—would have struck any American of the Colonial period as supreme lunacy. Far easier to sharpen the ax and chop off the head of a chicken or, as they all did in regular communal get-togethers, slaughter one of their enormous hogs, salting down enough meat to last months. Colonial Americans were famously well fed, based on their farming, not their hunting.[107]

There were restrictions on who could and could not hunt in America,

just as in England. But in America the privileged group was much larger
and there were few restrictions on when and where one could hunt. For
instance, most colonies banned hunting at night because it led to the death
of too many cows and horses. In England only the wealthy were allowed
to trap game. In the American colonies nearly everyone could trap, and
most free white landowners could hunt with firearms. Nonetheless, not
that many people did so. When John Lawson came to the Carolinas in
1701 to explore and hunt, one of his first observations was that "the meanest Planter" in America could enjoy hunting. Even "A poor Labourer,
that is Master of his Gun" might hunt under the law. Yet Lawson also
noticed that these settlers all worked hard on their land and devoted little
or no time to hunting, leaving that pleasure to the Indians. When Lawson
went exploring with two settlers, he discovered that his was the only gun:
"We had but one Gun amongst us [with] one Load of Ammunition."
"Relying wholly on Providence," the three men, like so many others in
early America, traveled among and with many different Indians for the
next few weeks without mishap.[108] Lawson concluded that journey by
noting that the local Indians were mostly friendly and "hunt and fowl for
us at seasonable rates." He thought no place "so free from Blood-shed, as
Carolina," though he warned his readers that they would have to bring
their own arms and ammunition with them to America.[109]

Account books, which offer very complete portraits of local econ-
omies, demonstrate that throughout the American colonies most merchants carried little gunpowder and shot—and almost never had a gun
for sale—and few of their customers purchased either in times of peace.
Outside of the few Colonial cities, merchants faced the danger of seeing
their gunpowder rot, as it had a short shelf life, especially in moist or
humid climates. But a very few people appear in these account books as
regular purchasers of gunpowder, buying an ounce or two every six
months. With the vast majority of people never bothering to buy powder,
it seems safe to say that they may have trapped animals, but they rarely
hunted them.[110]

Hunters were specialists. Individuals like Ethan Allen made their living by learning the routines of the forest, the best places to lay their traps,
following the old Indian trails, and often, as in Allen's case, getting to
know the local Indians and learning from them. Professional hunters
relied on their traps, not their guns. Traps were reliable and required little
time; one set them up and then checked them from time to time. Hunters
like Allen were not out to put meat on their table, though they might do

that as well. It was hides they were after. Every account of hunters prior to the nineteenth century speaks of their heading off on long journeys, generally of several weeks, checking their traps, trading with the Indians for furs and hides, seeking new areas that had not yet been developed, carrying their musket or rifle, but almost never using it. Again, it was not the most efficient way to kill an animal, and these were very practical people.[111]

But white hunters were the exceptions. Given the abundance of animals along the East Coast in the early eighteenth century, John Phillip Reid has pointed out, "it might be thought that the British settlers could have hunted them on their own." Yet the Indians did almost all the hunting, not only because they alone had the numbers and time to do so, but also because they were better at it and, as Reid says, only they "were willing to work for beads, guns, . . . blankets, and rum" (which is to say, for peanuts). In 1707 the Cherokee traded at the rate of thirty-five deerskins for a gun, thirty for a coat.[112] Given the wide availability of land and the demand for labor in the towns and cities, few free men could afford hunting as a livelihood, and those few generally did not succeed. Ethan Allen, for instance, gave up hunting in his early thirties and settled down to farming.

And that, after all, is what most European Americans did: they farmed. Historians have found that nearly 95 percent of the non-Indian population of Colonial America farmed, either by choice or through coercion as indentured servants and slaves. These farmers often had to deal with varmints, and laid traps, then as now, as the most efficient way of addressing that problem. Occasionally a pest eluded their traps, or they had a particularly bad bird problem. On those occasions they would certainly use a gun, if they had one. If not, they would borrow a musket or a fowling piece from a neighbor, often entering the exchange in their account books, noting that they owed that neighbor a return of some sort. But they certainly did not keep a gun to put meat on their tables. They kept knives and axes for that purpose.[113] And the other 5 percent of the population? They were mostly urban artisans. To put meat on their tables they behaved like their European contemporaries—they went to the market to purchase food.[114]

It was not easy to acquire a firearm, should an individual want one for some reason. The simplest route was to become an active member of the militia, and be supplied with one by the government from its stores, or the next time the Crown sent over a shipment. But these guns were supposed to be used only at musters and during emergencies. To purchase a gun was a more difficult and expensive matter. In an age when £3 a month was considered a very good income for any trade, skilled artisan or prosperous farmer, and the average wage for a worker was £18 a year, a flintlock cost £4 to £5. In addition, the American colonies were cash poor, and most merchants insisted on payment in cash for firearms, which were among the most expensive items they could carry. For the average free American in the Colonial period, who devoted half of his income to diet alone, a gun represented the equivalent of two months' wages and could easily claim all his currency.[115]

Adding to the difficulty of purchasing a firearm was the fact that almost every single one had to cross the Atlantic from Europe. There were only a handful of gunsmiths in America in its first century and a half of settlement. Most of their labor was devoted to making and repairing other forms of metalwork. These men were more smiths than gunsmiths, and in fact most labeled themselves blacksmiths.[116] Those few guns that were made in the British colonies were largely assembled from parts purchased in Europe. But then it was extremely rare to find a gunmaker who made an entire gun himself—it generally took three or four working together. Most European shops had one gunsmith specializing in locks, another in the stock, and a third in the barrel, while a fourth generally assembled and finished the gun.[117] No one in America could make the key part of the gun, its lock, until the Revolutionary era, and even tools had to be imported.[118] A very few gunsmiths did craft their own barrels, most notably for the famous Pennsylvania rifles, but their most common repair was stocking, putting new wood stocks on old firearms.[119] Simply finding someone to repair a gun required a major effort, as every Colonial government discovered at the beginning of every war.

For instance, there was only a single gunsmith in South Carolina's first quarter-century of European settlement. Thomas Archcraft understood his value to the colony as the only one capable of repairing its weapons, and he extorted preferential treatment from the government. Archcraft soon discovered that the real profit was not in weapons repair but in the manufacture of Indian hatchets, and the state council received many complaints that he was not repairing guns that had been "lying along time in [his] hands," but instead devoted his time to making axes. The council ordered Archcraft to stop making Indian hatchets until the necessary gun repairs were completed and then tried to set repair rates—another edict ignored by Archcraft. When the threat of imprisonment evoked no response, the council ordered Archcraft into custody, to finish his repairs in jail. But Archcraft went on strike, refusing to repair any firearms, so the council ordered his release and tried other forms of persuasion, none of which worked. They finally took away his tools. The amazing aspect of this story is that the government found Archcraft to be a terrible gunsmith. The council reported that he either "altogether neglects the mending of [guns], or else returnes them as ill, sometimes worse than when he received them." But they had no choice, as there was no one else in South Carolina with training as a gunsmith.[120]

Study after study reveals a surprisingly low number of gunsmiths in early America. There were a few German gunsmiths who emigrated to Pennsylvania and continued in the trade over many decades, the Henry family becoming something of a dynasty in this regard. But Lancaster County, Pennsylvania, was the great exception. No other area in North America could boast even half as many gunsmiths.[121] Harold B. Gill's exhaustive search of Virginia's records found three, possibly four, gunsmiths in the years from 1607 to 1676, with two additional artisans who performed the task of gunsmiths. In the following six decades, 1677 through 1739, there were seven gunsmiths and seven—possibly eight—more artisans working on guns. And it was one of these men, Charles Parkes, who is the first known to have made a gun in Virginia, though he probably stocked only parts made in England. The thirty years from 1740 through 1770 witnessed a jump to seven gunsmiths and seventeen artisans in a colony with a population of 447,000 in 1770 (259,000 white), including the Geddy brothers, the first Virginians able to rifle gun barrels. In other words, no more than eighteen gunsmiths served Virginia in its first 150 years. Gill's study further revealed that the major task of these gunsmiths was cleaning guns, which was seen by the government as a task requiring the services of a professional.[122]

Likewise, studies in other colonies reveal a rather muted—at best—enthusiasm for guns. In the fifty years from 1726 to 1776, only two gunsmiths advertised their services in New York City's fifteen newspapers. Guns were occasionally offered for sale in shops dealing in other goods, though never in a large number. The jeweler John Richardson advertised that he had some guns and a brace of pistols for sale. Similarly, repairs were undertaken by people in a variety of other trades. Thus James Yeomen and John Collins, watchmakers, advertised their ability to repair guns for "Gentlemen." All the advertisements targeted gentlemen and promised guns "as neat as in England."[123] This desire to link their goods to English quality appears in the advertisement of one of the two gun-smiths in the city, Edward Annely. He did not have a shop, but operated at the "fly market," selling guns and pistols, "all Tower proof" (meeting the standards of the Tower of London), and "Cheap." He also "makes Guns and Pistols as any Gentleman shall like, and does all Things belonging to the Gun-Smith's Trade; and engraves Coats of Arms on Plate."[124] A similar examination of three Boston newspapers from 1704 to 1775 reveals just four gunsmiths, two of whom advertised as importers of guns, and a third who did not have a shop.[125] And, most amazingly, Alfred C. Prime's examination of twenty-two Philadelphia newspapers during the Colonial period produced not a single gunsmith or ad for gun repairs.[126]

Unlike in Europe, there was no guild system in America to impose quality control over gun production. In England, each journeyman was rigorously examined, as was each gun, which required a government proof mark before it could be sold. In America anyone could claim to be a gunsmith, and any gun that could find a customer could be sold. Every American gun was thus not only different, but often very different, with bullet molds made to suit the individual gun and each repair specific to that gun—there was no standardization of any kind. It was little wonder that Americans often complained, as of Thomas Archcraft, that the gun-smith's work worsened the problem. Becoming a good gunsmith required years of study with a master of the craft, and there were few to study with in the colonies. It could also be a dangerous task, as the Virginia gunsmith John Brush made evident in 1723 when he petitioned the government for support after "his misfortune in being blown up and hurt in firing the Guns on his Majtys Birthday."[127]

But then not many Americans demonstrated much interest in becoming gunsmiths. In fact the opposite, keeping the few gunsmiths at their work, troubled the Colonial legislatures. Most gunsmiths who came to America found it more profitable to enter other lines of work. In 1633 the Virginia Assembly ordered that gunsmiths and other artisans "be compelled to worke at theire trades and [are] not suffered to plant tobacco or corne or doe any other worke in the ground." In 1662 the assembly tried incentives instead, exempting smiths from paying taxes if they followed their trade. But such extraordinary legislation did not prove sufficient, and in 1672 the legislature fined any smith who failed to "lay aside all other worke" and devote himself to the repair of firearms. Twenty years later the legislature had to repeat this expropriation of labor in ordering that every smith in Virginia "fix all Armes . . . brought them by any of the

Souldiers of this Countrey." In 1705 the Assembly granted all militia officers the authority to "impress any smith . . . or other artificer, whatsoever,
which shall be thought useful for the fixing of arms."[128]

One revealing aspect of this legislation is the way in which the Assembly lumped all smiths together as competent and needed to handle gun
repair. Repeatedly through the Colonial period governments turned to
artisans in other trades for assistance with their firearms.[129] These artisans cleaned and repaired guns; they did not make them. In 1692 the Virginia council reported that no guns were "to be had but from England,"
and they worried that this supply was erratic. In 1699 the council reported
that they had only three "good muskets" in the Jamestown armory and
begged for more guns. The Crown indicated little sympathy for Virginia's plight.[130]

Gunsmiths sought income elsewhere, it appears, because there was
just not a sufficient market for their services in Colonial North America.[131] As the probate records of the period evidence, gun ownership was
far less widespread than is generally assumed. It is vital to emphasize that
these probate inventories scrupulously recorded every item in an estate,
from broken glasses to speculative land titles to which the deceased
claimed title, including those that had already been passed on as bequests
before death.[132] It is a bit difficult to discover complete runs of these
inventories and wills (which would record any items given up until that
time) for the period prior to the 1760s. But gun ownership in those complete probate inventories that do exist run the range from 7 percent in
Maryland to, curiously, 48 percent in Providence, Rhode Island. Apparently gun ownership was linked to prosperity, not the frontier.

The Providence records serve well to indicate the nature of gun ownership in Colonial America. These 186 probate inventories from 1680 to
1730 are all for property-owning adult males, or the top quarter of Providence society. Ninety of them mention some form of gun, from pistols to
"a peice of a Gun Barrill." More than half of these guns are evaluated as
old and of poor quality. Two-thirds of those inventories containing guns
fall into the last twenty years of this fifty-year period, after the distribution of firearms by the British government to the New England militia in
Queen Anne's War. A great many inventories explicitly list "one of ye
Queens armes," which officially still belonged to the government. The
inventories also note when a gun was on loan, such as "A Gun at Henry
Mores." Fifty-one of these ninety men owned one gun of some kind,
twenty-five owned two, nine held three, three owned four guns, and two

owned five guns. Four of the five men holding four or five guns were militia officers. If one could imagine these 186 men as a militia company, half would be unarmed and a third armed with guns that were broken or too old for service. And yet they would have been one of the best-armed forces of their time.[133]

There is a traditional belief that gun owners were emotionally attached to their favorite weapon, passing them on to their eldest sons in moving ceremonies of manhood. There is no contemporary evidence for such rites of passage in the Colonial period. It is hard to imagine that Epenetus Olney felt a strong attachment to his only gun, "an old short Gunn without a lock," or John Whipple to his only weapon, a "pistol without a lock." Nor could William Ashley give his "Queenes Arm" to his son, since it officially remained government property. Just two of the 186 wills accompanying these probate files specifically mention a gun: Captain Joseph Jenckes left his only gun to his son; and William Vincent, who owned two guns, left "my shortest Gunn" to William Jr. The other wills are all silent on the distribution of guns.

It is difficult, therefore, to credit the unsupported statements of historians that "the callused hand of the pioneering settler cradled a musket as easily as a pitchfork, and military training of a sort was nearly as much a part of his diet as salt pork."[134] Contrary to the popular perception that imagines all settlers as hunters as well as farmers, the vast majority of those living in the British North American colonies had no use for firearms, which were costly, difficult to locate and maintain, and expensive to use.

For some wealthy individuals in America, a well-made gun was as much a status symbol as it was in England, with French guns particularly prized and carrying the highest evaluations in probate records. For others such a gun was a specialized tool, one of several used in hunting. For most of those who owned guns—and the evidence from the militia records is very compelling on this point—a gun was an object that sat rusting. Frantic repairs were made in the case of a war scare, but otherwise the weapons appeared in just one-fifth of the probate records as "gun, old, rusted," or "gun, broken." But for one group of people in the early eighteenth century, the gun became the center of their very way of life, a perceived necessity, a fulcrum of identity, and the image of their culture.

Chapter Four

Creation of the First American Gun Culture: Indians and Firearms

The rangers, "discerning Indians in the Edg of the Swamp, fired immediately upon them, who answering our Men in the same Language, retired presently into the Swamp."

—William Hubbard[1]

Hunters and Hunted

In 1681 Benjamin Henden, traveling through the woods near Providence, Rhode Island, saw an Indian carrying a gun. Connecticut and Massachusetts had laws on the books prohibiting Indians from possessing guns. Henden, unaware that Rhode Island had no such law, demanded the Indian's gun. The Indian ignored him, which so infuriated Henden that he fired his own gun "with an Intent to have killed him [the Indian]." But he missed. With an empty gun, Henden should have been an easy prey for the "savage" enemy he had just attempted to kill. But the Indian simply shook his head at the crazy white man, gave him "some words by way of Reproof; . . . blaming [Henden] for . . . his Violence and Cruelty, and wondering that English men should offer soe to shoot him and such as he was without cause." Then the Indian "went peacefully away." Henden was stunned to find himself charged by the province of Rhode Island with "rash turbulent and violent behavior." To make certain that no other travelers behaved in such an atrocious manner, the assembly passed an act "to prevent outrages against the Indians," ordering that whites must "behave themselves peaceably towards the Indians, in like manner as before [King Philip's] warr."[2]

Before leaping to any conclusions that the violence of Colonial America is entirely exaggerated, it is important to recall an incident that occurred just a few years earlier. In July 1677, following some violent exchanges between whites and Indians along the Maine coast, fishermen from Marblehead, Massachusetts, captured two hostile Indians who had tried to seize their boat. When they landed in Marblehead, a crowd gathered around the Indians and "demanded to know," one of the fishermen related, "why we kept them alive and why we had not killed them." Soon "the whole town flocked about [the Indians], beginning first to insult them, and soone after, the women surrounded them and drove us by force from them.... Then with stones, billets of wood, and what else they might, they made an end of these Indians. ... [W]e found them with their heads off and gone, and their flesh in a manner pulled from their bones." The women would not allow any man "to come near them, until they had finished their bloody purpose."[3]

One aspect of such stories is clear: the presence or absence of guns is irrelevant to the violence committed. Most English settlers feared and hated their Indian neighbors and hoped to cleanse their new homes of this "alien" race.[4] They did so, however, inconsistently and without coherent plan. When settlers did act violently, they used every weapon imaginable; the women at Marblehead used rocks, pieces of wood, and their bare hands. In 1676, women at Huntington, Massachusetts, used a cannon to fire on a group of Indians.[5] Neither act was usual and defied gender norms, yet both were applauded by many contemporaries. These women acted, in their eyes, to preserve their homes, which was of course exactly the same justification that drove many Indians to violence.

The long conflict between whites and Indians is one of the defining aspects of Colonial North America. Despite their firearms, the survival of the English colonies often appears highly improbable. Long after the initial disasters of Jamestown, it seemed that several colonies were intent on self-extermination. Their efforts at preservation led the settlers not only to launch wars against the Indians, but also to arm their enemies with theoretically advanced European weaponry.

In South Carolina in 1715 there were fifty-five hundred English barely controlling more than eighty-five hundred slaves and facing at least five thousand Indians. The governor reported that the militia could draw upon just 950 men "able to bear arms." And what arms they had came entirely from the proprietors, who sought to economize by sending over the cheapest matchlocks. As early as 1673, the state council had given up trying to get members of the militia to supply their own arms and ammunition, resolving that such supplies would in the future be supplied by the government, hopefully by way of the proprietors.[6] The proprietors sent over two hundred French matchlocks, thirteen fowling pieces, two hundred pikes, twelve suits of armor, one thousand flints, thirty barrels of powder, and ten pounds of musket shot—more than sufficient, the proprietors thought, for the four hundred free men in the colony in 1670. This was the largest shipment ever sent by the proprietors, and it had to last the colony for the rest of the century. Preserving these guns required a gunsmith, and in 1682 Robert Ferguson reported that none was to be found in the whole colony. In 1687, a desperate council passed the Powder Act, requiring ships entering a South Carolina port to pay a duty of a half pound of gunpowder for every ton of cargo. The law was renewed several times over the next eighty years as the colony tried to maintain a stock of gunpowder.[7]

In 1687 Governor Blake reported to the assembly that all his militia commanders complained of dangerously high absentee rates, as most freemen lacked both firearms and any interest in the militia. The assembly raised a tax on real and personal estates to purchase arms and ammunition for the colony and created a special paid force of thirty men who would always have arms and ammunition for pursuit of runaway slaves or Indians. The legislature tried several times to force its citizens to buy arms, requiring in 1696, for instance, those who could not supply their own arms to work as servants for six months for any person who would furnish a firearm. The state was thus not only telling the poor how to spend their money but also alienating the largest number of free whites. In 1702 the assembly's militia committee again recommended that the government supply those willing to serve with arms; it also proposed, noting the lack of arms in private hands, that all stores of arms and ammunition should be delivered to the militia captains "to be ready upon all occations of an Allaram." The full assembly evidently felt that it mattered little that some of the militia lacked firearms, and defeated the bill. As in most colonies, the militia of South Carolina was dormant by 1700, though special provision was made to arm the slave patrols "at ye Charge of the publick."[8]

South Carolina's militia served to maintain white dominance, functioning as the slave patrol that kept the black majority at work. Yet 200 of

their 350 serving members lacked arms in 1702, leading the government
to purchase arms in England to be held by the patrols' captains. But
within five years the colony had lost track of these guns and ordered the
captain to "Make Search . . . for ye Arms belonging to ye Publick Lost" in
the previous few years. Members of the militia had often demonstrated
not only their unwillingness to fight but also their incompetence at anything other than beating slaves.[9]

One would expect a people in so defenseless a situation to be particularly careful to avoid confrontation with possible enemies. Instead South
Carolina had a habit of inciting wars with the Indians. The colony came
close to total disaster in 1715 with the Yamasee War. The government of
South Carolina emulated its northern neighbors and hired a force of
rangers, who fled before a Yamasee ambush. Realizing that the only thing
standing between the Yamasee and the total destruction of South Carolina was the militia, the government frantically hired a private army. This
force of twelve hundred men included, ironically, five hundred black soldiers and one hundred Indians. But this army, too, lacked sufficient arms,
and South Carolina had no reserves. Virginia sent some militia to help,
earning this praise from a member of the assembly: "the most ignorant
creeping naked people that ever was seen for such a number together and
I verily believe that many of them did not know how to load a gun."[10]

When the government's plea to Virginia for more arms met with a
firm negative, South Carolina had no choice but to turn to diplomacy and
trickery.[11] They convinced the Catawba and Creek Indians to remain
neutral and the Cherokee to switch to their side. Despite their supposed
technological superiority and the famous universally armed militia, South
Carolina could not arm a force of twelve hundred or persuade the militia
to defend their own homes. White settlers fled instead to the safety of the
coastal towns. Even with a hired army, South Carolina could not beat the
Yamasee without Cherokee help, and the war dragged on for thirteen
years. This reliance on Indian allies and volunteer rangers saved money,
and English lives. But the Cherokee demanded guns in return.[12]

As the assembly concluded in 1720, when it asked the board of trade to
make South Carolina a royal province, the proprietors were unable "to
protect the Inhabitants . . . so that his Majesties Subjects are neither safe in
their lives, libertys or estates." They called on the Crown to provide the
necessary protection. The South Carolina elite wanted the British army,
not the militia, to protect them. The Crown finally took over the colony
and sent over one thousand muskets and three hundred pistols. With the

arrival of just a token force for permanent stationing in South Carolina in 1721, the assembly stopped worrying about arming their citizens, and with the exception of the immediate aftermath of the Stono Rebellion in 1740, spent little time debating militia affairs for the next fifty years.[13]

By the early eighteenth century all the colonies had adopted the practice of hiring soldiers to wage quasiwars against the Indians. These rangers were offered bounties of as much as £100 per Indian scalp. Rather than militia companies operating under the authority of the state, private companies of bounty hunters patrolled the frontier in hopes of scalping Indians, who could easily be claimed as hostiles since it was impossible to tell the attitude toward the English from a scalp. In August 1724 a group of these rangers descended on the Abenaki village of Norridgewock, Maine, taking thirty scalps, including that of the Catholic missionary Father Rale. The use of rangers made sense, given that the traditional settler method of attack now required forces able to travel greater distances in order to strike at Indian homes. But provincial governments had also altered the expectations of the common soldier. They now definitely expected pay, and good pay at that. When Virginia tried to organize a company of rangers in 1712, "nobody would accept of that place because the pay was too little," while the militia would not even muster, preferring to stay at home and tend to their crops. As Governor Alexander Spotswood told the board of trade, "The Militia of this Colony is perfectly useless without Arms or ammunition, and by an unaccountable infatuation, no arguments I have used can prevail upon these people to make their Militia more Serviceable," and the legislature would make "no provision for arming their Militia." Spotswood reminded the people of the danger from "Insurrections [by] our own Negroes, or the Invasions of the Indians," yet they remained "stupidly averse" to being well armed.[14]

The actual training in the use of firearms was a complicated and tedious task, especially as most recruits were unfamiliar with the use of guns. American militia adhered to European standards throughout the Colonial period, only the rangers striking out into new tactical fields.[15] Despite living "in a wilderness radically different from their homeland," as military historian Harold Selesky has written, "the colonists clung to the military training which reminded them they were Englishmen." Thus they tended to practice formal field movements and the "pushing of pikes," when they practiced at all. For "militiamen were inept," prone to hurt one another in their practices and not cultivating "the marksmanship and woodcraft which would have made them a match" for their

Indian opponents.[16] The failure of Indians to meet these European standards remained a prime reproach of their methods of war. As the Massachusetts minister Urian Oakes wrote after King Philip's War, they had just defeated "a despised & despicable Enemy, that is not acquainted with books of military Discipline, that observe no regular Order, that understand not the Souldier's Postures, and Motions, and Firings, and Forms of Battel, that fight in a base, cowardly, contemptible way." It was an oft repeated criticism.[17]

Again and again the Colonial militia proved totally unsuited for warfare. Legislatures would supply the necessary firearms, only to see them lost in battle or flight to the enemy. In 1656 an Indian tribe known as the Richahecrian appeared on the borders of the English settlements. The assembly sent one hundred militia with another hundred Indian allies to warn these strangers off. When five Richahecrian chiefs came to negotiate, the commander of the Virginia militia had them murdered. The Richahecrian responded by attacking. The militia fled without firing their government-supplied muskets, while their Indian allies stood their ground and were slaughtered. The legislature discovered that it was not sufficient to supply firearms; they needed to train their troops in both how to use them and how to fight.[18]

In 1675 a contingent of 750 Virginia and Maryland militia under the command of John Washington attacked, with no known cause, a settlement of one hundred Susquehannock warriors and their families, who took refuge in the abandoned Fort Piscataway. The militia again murdered five Indians who came out to negotiate. Rather than using their superior numbers and munitions to assault the fort, the militia determined to starve the Indians. Over the next seven weeks the besieged Indians killed fifty of the militia in daring nighttime raids, and then all fled one night, killing another ten militia on the way out. The whites then burned down the fort and declared victory. It was, in fact, a humiliating defeat that did honor to the Susquehannock.[19]

But the ultimate test of the American militia must certainly be that most violent and brutal of Colonial conflicts, King Philip's War. In March 1671 Metacom, called "Philip" by the whites,[20] demonstrated the power of his people by marching his warriors through Swansea. Plymouth officials were shocked to discover that some of his troops carried muskets. They demanded that Metacom turn over all the muskets owned by his people. He delivered seventy guns, most of those owned by his tribe, but did not let the lack of muskets deter him.[21] In June 1675 he struck first at

Swansea and then at frontier towns throughout New England with deadly efficiency. The government of Massachusetts negotiated the neutrality of the Narragansett and Nipmuck and sent arms and ammunition to Plymouth, which lacked, as always, sufficient firearms for its defense. With this aid, and as a consequence of the Indians capturing many of these muskets from the bodies of dead white soldiers, King Philip's War was the first fought in Colonial America with a large number of firearms on each side.[22]

It was in King Philip's War that the musket became the weapon of choice for American militia. Up until that time, the sword, ax, and pike were favored. The first two remained in active use through the Civil War, and even the pike would make occasional appearances, though lancers on horseback would be more common. Pikemen were present at nearly every encounter in King Philip's War, as there simply were not enough guns to go around. Nonetheless, in October 1675, the Massachusetts General Court ordered that, "Whereas it is found by experience that troopers & pikemen are of little use in the present warr with the Indians . . . It is ordered by the court . . . that all pikemen are hereby required . . . to furnish themselves with fire armes." But they could not locate sufficient guns, leading one Massachusetts soldier to recall in 1681, "I thought a pike was best for a young soldier, and so I carried a pike, and . . . knew not how to shoot off a musket." First, of course, the Massachusetts government had to find more firearms, and for that the colonies turned, as always, to the Crown, which supplied several hundred muskets.[23]

Despite their increased use of flintlocks in the late eighteenth century, militia companies throughout New England demonstrated little skill in battle against Indian warriors, finding themselves best able to defeat women and children, and far too willing to throw aside their muskets for a quicker retreat.[24] In one notorious attack on Metacom, the combined militia of Massachusetts and Plymouth became lost in the Pocasset swamp, suffered many casualties, and finally extricated themselves from the bogs seemingly without inflicting any damage on the enemy. Unable to locate Metacom, the colonies united their military efforts against the neutral Narragansett. The first English attack was defeated after suffering heavy casualties, but the second assault drove the Indians from their fort. The New Englanders then slaughtered all their captives, including women and children. The surviving Narragansett joined Metacom. This Battle of the Great Swamp of December 19, 1675, was the militia's only major battlefield victory.[25]

The Narragansett sought retribution by attacking Lancaster, Massachusetts, in February 1676. As onetime allies of the New Englanders, the Narragansett had a number of muskets and used them in their attack on Lancaster. But as Mary Rowlandson's famous account makes clear, setting the houses on fire proved the most effective weapon. As the New Englanders fled the flames they were cut down by Indian hatchets and arrows, both of which were more accurate than guns. Oddly, Rowlandson saw no settlers returning fire; apparently the surprise and panic were simply too extreme.[26]

Town after town suffered a similar fate; only Northampton succeeded in driving off the attackers. Repeatedly New Englanders lacking firearms confronted Indians in brutal encounters. Two white men traveling to Sudbury were attacked by a group of Indian women. They battled with sticks, until finally the men were overcome and beaten to death by the women. On March 26, 1676, a column of sixty-five Plymouth militia and twenty Christian Indians was cut to shreds by the Narragansett; only a few of the New Englanders fired before fleeing in terror. Just one of the militiamen and eight of their Indian allies survived. Clergyman Increase Mather stated that "as to Victoryes obtained, we have no cause to glory in any thing that we have done, but rather to be ashamed and confounded for our own wayes."[27]

On another occasion Colonel Benjamin Church, Plymouth's great war hero, led twenty militia in pursuit of some one hundred Indians. "But," Church reported, "before they saw any body they were saluted with a volley of fifty or sixty guns." Church was stunned by the number of firearms in the Indians' possession, especially as "Some bullets came very surprisingly near." Church turned, "expecting to have seen half of them [his men] dead; but seeing them all upon their legs, and briskly firing at the smokes of the enemies' guns; (for that was all that was then to be seen.)" The two sides fired at each other until the English ran out of gunpowder. Church's men "began to cry out, for God's sake to take them off, for their ammunition was spent!" Church used his last powder to fire one last shot "to bid them farewell," but the powder was not strong enough "to carry the bullet half way to them." Church was concerned that the Indians had more guns and powder than his force, but he also noted that none of his twenty men was wounded or killed, and he was sure that the Indians also escaped injury.[28]

It is impossible to know how many muskets Metacom's forces held during the war. He had some four thousand warriors fighting with him at one time or another, yet in few battles did guns play a significant role for the Indians. Benjamin Trumbull found three encounters at which the settlers were bested by Indians armed with guns: outside Springfield, Massachusetts, in January 1675; Church's shoot-out with the Indians in 1675; and the relief party to Lancaster in July 1676. Every other battle description from the war indicates that the Indians had few firearms. In 1676, one prisoner reported that Metacom's force of one thousand had "near one hundred" firearms. On another occasion, Captain William Brattle reported that a force of eighty Indians he attacked were armed solely with hatchets. At another battle the Indians "were in possession of but few firearms," yet "checked the progress of the cavalry with long spears." At least the Indians had a choice; they could use bows. The English were pretty much stuck with the musket.[29]

The settlers' superiority in firearms did not translate into automatic victory. In one of the first actions of the war, a group of Indians "discharged a shower of arrows" at Church's force, and then "rushed furiously upon them with knives and tomahawks." Being in the midst of a forest, Church's troops could not "use their fire-arms with any effect," and had to defend themselves with their own swords and axes. "Of sixty-four who entered the swamp, only seventeen escaped." It was at this time that Church came to appreciate a basic method of Indian warfare. He learned to order his forces "not to discharge all their guns at once, lest the enemy should take the advantage of such an opportunity to run upon them with their hatchets." Some commanders used their guns in a creative fashion, as when Major Simon Willard's forces "in a very heroic manner rushed upon the savages with clubbed muskets" and drove the Indians off after beating several to death. The "clubbed musket" turned out to be a rather effective weapon, being responsible for the death of the Wampanoag Sachem (chief) Pompham.[30]

The New Englanders also found it effective to surprise previously neutral tribes, such as the Abenaki. In May the commander of the garrison at Hatfield, William Turner, learned that there were only a few warriors in the Abenaki village of Peskeompscut, twenty miles north up the Connecticut River. Reassured by the absence of Indian warriors, 150 men joined Turner in a morning attack on the Indians. Sneaking among their sleeping prey, the New Englanders killed at least one hundred and perhaps as many as three hundred people, most in the traditionally noncombatant category of women and children. The New Englanders were stunned to discover that the Abenaki had built a pair of working forges for repairing muskets—perhaps the first among the Indians. Turner and his men quickly retreated from the burning village but were attacked by a group of returning Abenaki warriors, many of whom carried muskets. The New Englanders lost some forty men, including their commander, before making good their escape.[31]

With such miserable battlefield performances, it is amazing that the New Englanders won King Philip's War. Three major factors brought them victory. First, the Indians ran out of gunpowder. Though they were not yet entirely dependent on firearms in warfare, they had made good use of them in battle, but they had no source of new supplies. In contrast, the New England governments confiscated all guns and powder for public use and sent off to England for more of each. Second, the New Englanders somehow managed to find Indian allies, most particularly the Mohegan. As William Harris wrote, had "the Indeans not bin devided, they might have forced us to Som Islands." And third, the New England strategy of killing noncombatants demoralized and devastated the Indians. Most of Metacom's followers just gave up and drifted away. The rest were discovered by the Mohegan and slaughtered. Indians who surrendered were killed on the spot or sold into slavery. It seems appropriate somehow that a Christian Indian named Alderman shot and killed Metacom with an English musket on August 12, 1676.[32]

In battle the Colonial militia pursued the strategies developed at Jamestown, destroying the crops of the Indians and starving them into submission. Certainly that was the course of events in King Philip's War, with the New England forces burning the towns and fields of the Indians. And, as in most Colonial wars, the greatest number of Indian deaths came from disease and starvation rather than battle.[33] But a new dimension of American warfare appeared in King Philip's War: the avoidance of service by a great number of eligible young men. The practice of avoiding militia duty by constant moving became so extensive that the Massachusetts legislature had to prohibit men from moving from one town to another without a certificate of registration in a militia company. Other members of the militia showed their disapproval of the war by abandoning their posts. New England ministers found it necessary to deliver services reminding their congregations that military training was "a commendable practice, yea [a] Duty of Great Consequence." Many of the congregants did not share that view.[34]

King Philip's War demonstrated that the Indians had learned to use English military technology against the settlers. But that mastery was not so much firearms as fire. John Mason had proved the effectiveness of fire in warfare at Mystic Village in 1637; Metacom drove the point home. In the year from the summer of 1675 through 1676, Metacom's followers attacked and burned twenty-five English towns, shattered the economy of New England, and killed hundreds of people. The whites also burned every Indian community they could and wiped out Metacom's Wampanoag. The English settlers won the war, but it took them decades to rebuild.[35]

The French also imitated the English pattern of warfare. In February 1690, a force of two hundred French and Indians descended on Schenectady, setting fire to the houses, killing sixty people, and capturing twenty-seven, making it one of the bloodiest Indian raids of the entire Colonial period. Most of those killed were hacked to death with swords and tomahawks or burned to death in the ensuing fires. If those attacked owned guns, they made no move to use them; in fact the only French casualty was inflicted with a spear. In the coming year, the French and their Indian allies made brutal use of surprise attacks, finding that the vaunted English militia was useless against them. Fifty French and Indians burned Salmon Falls, New Hampshire, taking more than fifty captives and killing thirty-four people. Other relatively small parties of French and Indians burned Fort Casco and Fort Loyal in Maine, at the latter killing twenty-six of the thirty-man garrison in hand-to-hand fighting.[36]

Theoretically the English colonies should have been able to overwhelm the Canadians with superior military forces. New York alone had three thousand men eligible for militia duty, Connecticut and Massachusetts about seven thousand between them. But when an inter-Colonial force was organized to respond to these outrages, it consisted of 150 New Yorkers, 135 New Englanders, and 120 Indians. It was a rather pathetic army, though still larger than any of the forces that had attacked from Canada. But the Colonial commanders forgot to arrange for boats to take their forces down Lake Champlain, and so they turned back after burning La Prairie. Meanwhile a force of two thousand New England militia under Sir William Phips sailed up the St. Lawrence, took one look at Quebec's defenses, and sailed back to Boston. This grand enterprise collapsed without the militia firing a shot.[37]

The next year, 1691, another force of four hundred New Yorkers and Indians fought a long battle with "sword, knife, tomahawk, and clubbed musket" through the Canadian forests before retreating back to Albany. In the latter confrontation the English made almost no use of their muskets as anything other than clubs, fleeing on three separate occasions before a single volley from the French Regulars. It was their Indian allies who understood the advantage of rushing in after this volley and engaging the regulars in hand-to-hand combat before they could reload.[38]

The nature of warfare in these years is well revealed in the captivity narrative of settler Hannah Duston. In March 1697 her village of Haverhill, Massachusetts, was attacked by a small group of Abenaki. The Abenaki burned the houses and killed nearly thirty people as they fled the flames. One of a dozen captives from the village, Duston witnessed the barbaric murder of her five-day-old baby by the Abenaki. Duston marched 150 miles through the forest, where she and her friend Mary Neff were given to an Abenaki family that had already adopted an English boy, Samuel Lennardson. Six weeks later, Hannah, Neff, and Lennardson took axes and attacked the sleeping Abenaki, killing two men, two women, and six children. Duston took their scalps and returned to Massachusetts, where she was received and celebrated as a heroic role model. Guns appear nowhere in this story; it is entirely a tale of people brutally hacking one another to death. That was the nature of frontier warfare.[39]

Duston's exploits stand out as a rare victory for the English settlers in King William's War. They had proved completely incapable of defending themselves against French and Indian forces, which never exceeded two hundred. As the Lords of Trade and Plantations complained in 1696, "that little province [of New York], besides the losses sustained at sea, . . . [has] been at over £30,000 charge in securing its frontier against the French and Indians." They could not understand why the local militia forces could not do better; even—or especially—in time of war it proved difficult to find officers to lead these units in defense of their homes. "The King has subjects enough in those parts not only to defend themselves from any attack of French and Indians, but they are so crumbled into little governments and so disunited in their interests that they have hitherto afforded but little assistance to each other. . . . It is almost incredible that the Governor of New York, in the middle of above 40,000 English . . . should say, as he does, that he has only the companies in the King's pay that he can rely on for the defence of the frontier." And throughout the war, all the governors of the northern colonies had pleaded not only for English regulars, but also for firearms for their underarmed militia.[40]

This pattern of turning to the government for military aid would be repeated in all the Colonial wars. In 1704, during Queen Anne's War, the town of Deerfield, Massachusetts, knew an attack was coming and attempted to prepare for it. A poor town, most of its nearly three hundred inhabitants could not hope to afford arms and ammunition, so they appealed to the government for support. After two unarmed men guarding the town's animals were captured by some Indians who fired at them but missed, Massachusetts sent twenty-two soldiers with a supply of ammunition to Deerfield. On the morning of February 29, some 250 French Regulars and Indians approached the town. There was no watch. The Indians attacked "with axes and hatchets," setting fire to the houses. The Reverend John Williams had loaded his pistol before he went to bed and "put it to the breast of the first Indian that came up; but my pistol missing fire, I was seized by three Indians who disarmed me." Such misfires were extremely common with guns that had sat loaded for more than an hour. Only one house, made of brick and a storehouse for ammunition, resisted. For nearly three hours the seven men exchanged fire at near point-blank range with the French attempting to fire their house. "Some shot 40 tymes," for a rate of nearly one shot every five minutes. By their report, they hit five or six of the enemy, suffering three casualties themselves, and ran out of ammunition just as a relief column arrived from nearby towns. Forty-four of the town's inhabitants, 25 of them children, were killed, in addition to 12 soldiers, and another 109 people were taken captive. It was a mortifying defeat for the local militia.[41]

The militia neither prevented nor responded adequately to these small-scale attacks on isolated towns. When a conflict started, the first thing the militia did was appeal for arms and ammunition. When the Connecticut assembly ordered out select members of the militia to protect the state in 1703, they received the response that the militia knew not "the woods nor the manner of that work." The assembly received a similar refusal in 1709, necessitating an offer of serious inducements, including a new musket, to get their recruits. Two years later the assembly found it necessary to institute a draft in order to obtain sufficient militia for the colony's defense. About the best that one could say for this "disordered" Colonial militia, one scholar has pointed out, is that they "responded vigorously but ineffectively."[42]

Many historians have nonetheless concluded that the Colonial militia worked well. One reported it as a "fact that of the hundreds and thousands of Englishmen who began migrating to the new colonies, a large percentage had received some basic training in the militia or at least knew how to handle a gun." Yet this fact, like most such assertions on this subject, is not supported with a single piece of evidence. It is difficult to understand the origin of these statements that America's early settlers came with a familiarity with firearms when the militia system in England had been largely terminated by the end of the sixteenth century and in the face of the many English laws that effectively kept firearms out of the hands of nearly all civilians and required that pikes be used at militia musters. Those who came to North America knowing how to use firearms were primarily soldiers and former soldiers.[43]

Certainly no Colonial governor can be found who would have supported the myth of the mighty militia. Every experience they had with the militia demonstrated its relative uselessness for any purposes other than slave patrol. When Georgia was founded in the 1730s it institutionalized this nonreliance on the militia by sending over a regiment of seven hundred Highlanders to defend the colony. When the Spanish attacked Georgia in 1742, those Highlanders and the Creek ambushed the Spanish force and saved the colony. There was no militia. However, in addition to trained troops, James Oglethorpe also brought six hundred guns "For Presents to the Indians to purchase lands."[44] Supplying firearms to Indians with the best of intentions had a number of unintended long-term consequences.

The American Indians
Discover the Gun

Guns supposedly granted European settlers the technological edge in their conquest of North America. Yet in reality it was disease and the devastation wreaked by the continual flow of European immigrants that guaranteed their victory. Guns played a lesser, though interesting, role, especially as a trade object that tied many Indians to the Europeans. Paradoxically, the Europeans transformed those they most feared, the American Indians, into the world's first true gun culture.

That Indians developed a gun culture at all is a testament to the lack of resolve on the part of the Colonial governments. Colonial legislatures sought to limit Indian access to firearms and on some occasions passed universal bans on Indians purchasing or carrying firearms. In 1619 the Virginia House of Burgesses passed an act that "no man do sell or give any Indians any piece of shott, or pouder, or any other armes offensive or defensive, upon paine of being held a traitor to the colony & of being hanged." This law was revised in 1653. But the French from the north and the Spanish in Florida, and even some English merchants, consistently undermined these efforts to keep Indians unarmed. The reliance by the English on Indian allies in their wars against hostile Indians and competing European powers further complicated matters. As long as Colonial governments acknowledged that there were "good Indians" deserving guns, they jeopardized their own efforts to keep guns away from "hostile Indians" as well.[45]

Nevertheless, Colonial governments did try to maintain a distinction, time and again attempting to specify the fine line between friendly and hostile Indians in terms of the gun trade. Trade with the former was encouraged, with the latter forbidden. Maryland passed a law authorizing any English settler to "shoote or kill any Indian" found within the settled areas on the same day in 1643 that it legislatively attempted to protect friendly Indians from unjustified attacks by whites.[46] The one check the governments maintained on Indian gun ownership was regulation of gun repair, an act easier to enforce than that on the sale of guns. Thus the government of South Carolina kept a close account of Cherokee firearms by requiring that they all be repaired in Charleston, a process that inevitably took several months. Since few people could repair firearms, especially the easily damaged gun locks, a broken musket was good for little more than a club.

The Westo of South Carolina discovered the danger of an excessive dependence on firearms. Initially the Westo had found an efficient way around the prohibition on selling guns to Indians. Starting in 1674, they traded Indian slaves to the white settlers for guns. By 1680 the government of South Carolina feared that it had created a threat to their own security, and joined with Virginia in cutting off the Westo's supply of powder and access to repairs.[47] The government of South Carolina also armed the Savannah Indians, encouraging them to take Westo captives and sell them as slaves, leading to the eventual destruction of the Westo.[48] The South Carolina government learned from this experience that controlling access to firearms led to dominance of the frontier at a minimal cost. If "the nation we shall have set should misbehave, we shall be able to ruin them by cutting off the supply of ammunition and setting their neighbors at them." The Savannah Indians would therefore "be furnished with arms and ammunition" in order to "deter the Northern and Spanish Indians from daring to infest" the colony.[49] Like most Colonial governments, South Carolina's thought that arming some Indians "tyed them to soe strict a dependance upon us," that they would be reliable allies. Such an approach might have made sense if South Carolina were itself packed with guns. But at the same time that it was making these gifts, the government was lamenting the shortage of firearms.[50]

The late seventeenth century marked the transition among the Eastern Indians to a dependence on firearms. Until that time, as T. M. Hamilton has written, not enough "firearms were traded or given to the Indians in sufficient numbers to have served other than ceremonial or prestige purposes." It was only with the introduction of the flintlock "Indian trade gun" and the acceleration of the competition between England and France for domination of North America that the Eastern Indians were able to acquire a large number of guns, though they contin- ued to be of inferior quality through the nineteenth century and in need of regular repair.[51] As one Huron complained to a French traveler in 1685, "The French give us fusees that burst and lame us."[52]

This transition from bows and arrows to guns as the weapon of choice began around 1700 (though axes remained popular), but there were ear- lier signs of a change. In 1643, the New Englanders found no evidence that any of the Narragansett, numbering some one thousand warriors, carried a firearm.[53] Thirty years later Metacom shattered the white forces with bows and a small stock of guns, many of his followers having learned well the use of firearms. But when his forces ran out of ammunition, there was no way to replenish their supplies, and they had to fall back.[54] In the end it was the shortage of food that defeated them, but the New England Indians essentially gave up the fight because they no longer felt they had the means to carry on the struggle.[55]

In the years after King Philip's War, the eastern Indians not only acquired more guns, but also learned how to care for those weapons. Most European observers felt that the Indians were better shots than the Amer- icans, but that was not surprising, since they had more practice than the whites.[56] So common had guns become among the Indians in the Caroli- nas by the early eighteenth century that John Lawson found it notable that the Wateree were "very poor in English Effects," having few guns and still relying mostly on bows. Lawson thought an Indian who used a gun regularly could not miss more than one shot in twenty. Yet on one hunting trip Lawson and his Indian companions sighted "plenty of turkies, but perch'd upon such lofty Oaks, that our Guns would not kill them, tho' we shot very often, and our Guns were very good." A few days later a wolf came right into their camp. "One of our Company fir'd a Gun at the Beast; but, I believe, there was a Mistake in the loading of it, for it did him no Harm. The Wolf stay'd till he had almost loaded again," when Lawson's spaniel chased the animal off. Their reputation aside, little evidence exists to substantiate the claim that Indians, who had enormous difficulty acquiring a regular supply of powder and shot, were in fact more accurate with firearms.[57]

It is vital to stress that at no point did the musket become the sole Indian weapon. They continued to mix their weapons as available and appropriate to use. Whereas their common battle tactic at the time of King Philip's War had been to fire a volley of arrows and then rush in with tomahawks, by the beginning of the eighteenth century those who had muskets fired a volley, accompanied by arrows, and then all rushed in as before. After the Battle of Kingsbridge in 1778, Captain Johann Ewald walked among the corpses of the Stockbridge Indians who had fought on the side of the Revolutionaries. The most European of Indians, the Christian Stockbridge tribe, carried more than guns. "Their weapons," Von Ewald wrote, "were a rifle or musket, a quiver with some twenty arrows, and a short battle-axe which they know how to throw skillfully."[58] Though they continued to use traditional weapons, and appreciated that different weapons had distinctive uses, Indians placed a far higher value on the new firearms, centering much of their economic culture on guns in a way European settlers never did. Doing so meant that, though they were not exactly dependent on the whites, theirs was no longer an independent culture. Indians had to associate with the whites to maintain their adherence to firearms technology.[59]

For instance, the Cherokee first acquired guns around 1700. Once they started using them, the Cherokee traded hundreds of deerskins to acquire more. By 1715, the government of South Carolina believed that there were one thousand guns among the Cherokee, more than their own militia could get their hands on.[60] Of course these were mostly the inferior Indian trade guns known as "North West Guns," weapons generally around three feet long with a large bore that delivered a less powerful charge than the standard European musket. These guns broke and exploded easily. One would assume a great deal of intelligence on the part of the English government in trading such less-effective weapons to the Indians, but in fact it was simply a case that the gunmakers of England found that they could sell these far-cheaper guns in America for the same amount as a well made one, thus hiking their profits considerably. The Indians in turn actually preferred these muskets because they were far lighter. This coincidence of interests would have great long-term consequences for America.[61]

While it is odd that the European nations moved comparatively quickly to replace the longbow with the musket, there is little mystery in the case of the Eastern Woodland Indians, whose bows lacked the power of the longbow. It seems likely that many Indians turned to the gun for the same reason as did some Europeans: the prestige attached to them. Indians, like many members of the European elite, owned guns not simply because they served a function but as a symbol of power and wealth.[62] But, to quote Reid again, "A Cherokee man's most prized possession, the gun[,] was also his most disastrous acquisition, marking the beginning of Cherokee dependence." Reid summarizes the disadvantages succinctly: "No Cherokee could make a gun, keep it in repair, or manufacture powder." It was a bargain that handed all power to the whites.[63] When George Chicken visited the Cherokee in 1725, he heard Long Warrior warn that, having lost the old ways, the Cherokee "must Consider that they could not live without the English," for "they have all their goods of the English and Arms to Defend themselves (without wch) they could not go to Warr and that they'll always be ruled by them."[64] At roughly the same time Captain Tobias Fitch was telling the Creek much the same thing: "I must tell your Young Men that if it had not Been for us, you would not have known how to Warr Nor yet Have anything to Warr with. . . . You had no hoes or Axes [except] What you made of Stone. . . . But now you have Learn'd the use of Firearms As well to Kill Dear and other Provissions as to War agst your Enemies."[65]

Very early on, Indian tribes entered into treaties with the Europeans for gun repairs. These were basically service agreements, by which the Europeans agreed to fix any malfunctioning guns in return for the Indians' using these same guns on the behalf of the Europeans. The Onondaga agreed to such a treaty with the French as early as 1653. This agreement so frightened the Mohawk that they signed a similar treaty with the French.[66]

Some Indians grew skillful at makeshift repairs, particularly anything involving woodwork. They were also fairly successful making their own gunflints, matching the European average of twenty to thirty shots per flint. They had much less luck with metalwork, lacking the tools and the experience, while manufacturing gunpowder was completely beyond them. A common effort at repair that rarely worked was straightening a bent barrel by placing it in the crook of a tree and bending. Indians learned quickly that even the slightest bend in a barrel sent the shot on an even more erratic path. Indians could salvage guns, but not make them. Fitting parts from separate guns was no mean task, but it still marked a net loss in firearms.[67]

The development of the Indian gun culture was far from consistent, largely because European policies changed so often. Out West, Spanish armor served as a formidable advantage in battle, as long as the Indians were not armed with guns. It is hardly surprising that the Spanish carefully maintained their monopoly on firearms (a relatively easy task given the complexity of their manufacture), the expertise required in their use, and the absolute reliance of firearms on a steady supply of ammunition. Controlling the trade in gunpowder proved easier in the more centralized Spanish state, meaning that even Indians who had guns found it very difficult to acquire ammunition. The Spanish also took the added precaution of limiting the number of firearms employed by their own troops, ordering the greatest degree of security in their deployment so that they would not fall into Indian hands. These efforts worked. Western Indians adopted European horses and then leather armor, and the prized object of their trading efforts was European metal and metal goods, especially the metal-tipped weapons that gave any Indians who possessed them an enormous advantage over other tribes. But they only turned to firearms late in the eighteenth century, when European technology made guns practical for use from horseback. Doing so made the western Indians dependent on Europeans for the supply of guns and ammunition.[68]

Until 1779 the Spanish steadfastly and effectively enforced their laws against selling firearms to the Indians, unless they were enemies of the English. The result of this prohibition was that the Indians of the old Southwest did not acquire guns in any quantity until the mid-eighteenth century, while those in the far West had to wait for the nineteenth century. That policy matched the Spanish goal of integrating conquered peoples into their expanding empire, exercising political control while insisting that Indians adopt Spanish religious and social values. Such aims necessitated the Spanish government's maintaining as absolute a monopoly on firearms as possible so as to prevent rebellion.[69]

Because of the strict Spanish prohibition on the gun trade, the use of firearms among the Indians moved westward across the region that is now the Canadian border with the United States, and did not make its way into the southwest corner of the country until the nineteenth century. A British trader traveling among the western Cree and Blackfoot in 1773 did not see any guns among these people.[70]

One of the very first uses of firearms by Plains Indians came in a battle between the Snake and Blackfoot around 1740. According to the Blackfoot Saukamappee, "between us . . . we had ten guns and each of us about thirty balls, and powder for the war. . . . When we came to meet each other, as usual, each displayed their numbers, weapons and shields, in all of which [the Snake] were superior to us, except our guns which were not shown." After a great deal of posturing, the two sides closed. Those ten Blackfoot with guns "stood in the front line, and each of us [had] two balls in his mouth, and a load of powder in his left hand to reload. We noticed they had a great many stone clubs for close combat, which is a dangerous weapon, and had they made a bold attack on us, we must have been defeated as they were more numerous and better armed than we were, for we could have fired our guns no more than twice." Instead of attacking, though, the Snake set themselves to receive an attack, giving the Blackfoot a chance to move close before opening fire with their ten guns. The Snake were so surprised by the noise and the sight of a few of their number falling wounded, that they cowered behind their shields, giving the ten Blackfoot a chance to reload and fire again. Noticing that some of the Snake were starting to sneak away, the Blackfoot all "rushed on their line, and in an instant . . . the greater part of the enemy took to flight, but some fought bravely and we lost more than ten killed and many wounded." Thus even a few guns with only a little ammunition could quickly win a battle against superior numbers, so long as the opponent had no experience battling against firearms.[71]

But as Indians became familiar with guns and adjusted accordingly, that advantage vanished. Tribes without guns avoided pitched battles and conducted what amounted to guerrilla warfare against tribes armed with guns. After the Blackfoot had stunned their Snake enemies with a handful of guns, the latter learned to avoid battles "and our wars have since been carried by ambuscade and surprize, of small camps." Suakamappee noted that it was not only the guns that gave them military superiority, but also the metal axes, knives, and arrowheads, which they had obtained in trade with the French and English. Interestingly, the Snake came to understand guns well enough that they destroyed any they seized from the Blackfoot, realizing that they were useless without regular access to gunpowder. In contrast, the Blackfoot had to keep their forces concentrated to avoid ambush. The Blackfoot also preferred to fight their battles on foot, so as to make best use of their few guns.[72]

Later, as the fur trade died out, Indians learned to husband their firearms resources, using bows and arrows for hunting buffalo and saving their guns for warfare. Most Plains Indians continued to use the bow for hunting into the 1840s, and many questioned the value of guns even in warfare.[73] One observer reported in the winter of 1809 that the Plains Cree "take to the bow and arrows; firearms are scarce among them, and they use but little ammunition." Loading a musket was so cumbersome and time-consuming that the Assiniboin prohibited its use in hunting. Walter P. Webb noted that an "Indian could . . . ride three hundred yards and discharge twenty arrows" in the time it took to reload a musket.[74] And then there was the problem of ammunition. In 1829 Chief Tachee advised his group of Cherokee, newly arrived in Texas from the East, not to attack the Waco Indians who had just stolen their entire herd of horses. Though the Cherokee had brought many guns with them, "we have no ammunition so our guns are only clubs." In contrast the Waco "have bows and arrows and lances," making them formidable in battle.[75] As a consequence of such limitations, Joseph Jablow has written, "the gun never attained such imperative importance in subsistence activity" on the Great Plains as it did among eastern Indians.[76]

Horses were in far greater demand at this time, and Alexander Henry reported that "if they [Indians] procure a gun, it is instantly exchanged . . . for a horse." Frank Secoy noted that "the infrequency with which any guns at all were available prevented these weapons modifying the military technique pattern." In fact "after the full development of mounted war, these same few guns exercised a much less potent effect, since their accuracy was much diminished by the rapid mobility of the target, particularly when they were fired from horseback rather than from afoot." As a final limitation on the impact of firearms on the military methods of most Indian peoples, "the slowness of reloading, in conjunction with the extremely small number of guns" meant that the western Indians were never able to master the volley technique of the Europeans, making "the fire extremely discontinuous, with long vacant intervals during which the mobility and rapid fire of the mounted archer could have effect."[77] It was not until the third decade of the nineteenth century that the increase in the number of guns in the hands of western Indians allowed for a rotation of fire, giving those who fired first the chance to reload. Until that time, the horse, leather armor, and the metal-tipped lance had far greater impact on the military techniques of the western Indians. In the last two decades of the eighteenth century, a few western tribes—the Blackfoot, Atsina, Plains Cree, and Sarsi—expanded their territories with the aid of only a few guns. In one encounter between some Piegan and Kalispell, just two guns exerted a huge psychological impact, the Kalispell fleeing in the face of these "bad spirits."[78]

Events in the East differed as a consequence of the wars between the European powers, with each nation making a concerted effort to arm its Indian allies. During such wars, Indians could, for a brief time, direct concentrated fire on an enemy. But as soon as peace returned, the source of ammunition and repairs evaporated, and the Indians often found themselves trading unusable or broken guns for more useful metal weapons. The English and Dutch were far less consistent than the Spanish, and remarkably ineffective in their efforts to limit and control the Indian gun trade,[79] while the French gave the northern Indians guns as gifts in order to win them over.[80] The English and Dutch wanted to form alliances with those Indians they were not exterminating but desired to keep even "friendly" Indians at a distance from their settlements. In contrast, the French never had the numbers or system to conquer the Indians, and sought instead to work with them to maintain sovereignty over large areas of North America that had meaning only on the maps back in Europe. Most of the time it seemed that the real point of French Indian policy was to slow down English expansion. On the other hand, the French could not really afford to give away too many guns, which created a constant tension between them and their Indian allies.[81]

French guns were found even in Texas, where the Pawnee received their first guns in 1706. In 1720 the Pawnee surprised and defeated an Apache and Spanish force on the Platte River by dismounting and protecting the small number of the force carrying guns while they fired a volley and then reloaded. In effect the Pawnee had turned European methods upon the Spanish to prevent them from rallying their forces. The Apache also tried to turn the tables by sneaking into the Pawnee camp and stealing some of their guns. But they did not steal any ammunition and lacked access to it as well, since the Spanish would not sell any, even after they took the Apache under their protection. The Apache therefore found themselves with some rather extravagant clubs.[82] Like most southwestern Indians, the Apache did not acquire firearms in any numbers until the Mexican Republic was established in 1821, that government proving willing to trade guns with the Indians. But even into the 1840s, observers described the Apache relying on lances and bows, and wearing leather armor and carrying shields to deflect arrows.[83]

In 1779 Spain temporarily ended its policy of keeping firearms out of the hands of Indians. In 1786 the Indian gun trade was made a permanent part of official Spanish policy, part of Bernardo de Gálvez's "peace by deceit." "The vanquishment of the heathen" in the northern parts of the Spanish empire, Gálvez wrote, "consists in obliging them to destroy one another." Toward this end, he not only supported introducing Indians unfamiliar with alcohol to that dangerous product but also commanded that the Indians be given poorly made firearms that would be difficult to handle and likely to break often. Galvez ordered that the Indians be given lots of powder and shot, for then they would come to rely on the musket and "lose their skill in handling the bow." As David J. Weber has written, "Gálvez correctly believed" that the bow "was a more effective weapon than the firearm." The only hindrance to the full implementation of this policy was that Spain never had enough guns and ammunition for its own army in the Americas. But even in partial execution, Gálvez's plan helped push the Indians of the modern Southwest into a debilitating dependence on European arms.[84]

European powers had good reason for this seemingly counterproductive policy of supplying Indians with firearms. British officials discovered early on the uselessness of Colonial militia and relied primarily on Indian allies to fight their wars for them. The Indians in turn had every reason to prolong the wars between the European powers and to see that neither side enjoyed a decisive victory. So long as England was at war with France, both sides provided arms, supplies, and gifts to their various Indian allies.

Indians were warriors, while the English settlers, after the first few years, were almost entirely farmers. As the military historian Harold Selesky wrote, the settlers "had neither the training nor the skill to meet the Indians as military equals." And yet, somehow, many historians maintain that the colonists were the equal of the Indians based on the training they received at their annual muster.[85]

It is true that the early colonists gained a false confidence based on their first victories over the Indians, victories facilitated by widespread disease, starvation, and demoralization among the Indians, and the latter's shock over the brutality of the whites. The result, as a number of

military scholars have pointed out, was the failure of the settlers to prepare for the next war. Thus the Pequot War, won by Mason's ruthless
destruction of Mystic Village and aided by Indian allies who guided him
through Pequot territory, lulled the New Englanders into thinking that
they could easily meet any future Indian threat. While the whites slept,
the Indians "mated firearms with their superior knowledge of the land to
create a new style of hit-and-run fighting that emphasized speed, stealth,
and surprise."[86]

Still, the Europeans never supplied that many guns to the Indians. A
merchant was fortunate to acquire a complete crate of Indian trade guns,
which held thirty of the smaller flintlocks. The French rarely presented
more than twenty muskets at a time to a tribe. Richard White found the
French sending an average of 680 to 800 guns per year to the Indians in
the last twenty years of the seventeenth century, hardly enough to arm
any of the tribes adequately. In 1643 Sebastian Cramoisy reported that the
Iroquois had a total of thirty-six muskets, "the remainder are very well
armed in Savage fashion," and wanted an additional thirty guns; the government hesitated to supply that many more firearms to one tribe. In 1679
the French met a party of 120 Fox Indians who had eight muskets, while
the Illinois had "virtually no guns." In 1706 the Peoria attacked a French
party with arrows tipped with flint, an indication that they had not yet
gained access to European metals. The Hudson's Bay Company, the main
supplier of guns to the northern Indians, purchased an average of 480
muskets per year between 1675 and 1775. In 1694 the British government
delivered a total of fifty trade guns as gifts to four different Iroquois tribes
in an effort to win them as allies. Such small numbers often proved sufficient in diplomacy.[87]

Nonetheless, by the mid-seventeenth century several eastern Indian
tribes had learned that even a few guns gave them an enormous psychological advantage over those foes who had none. In fact, many
seventeenth-century Indians used guns only against opponents who did
not have guns, where the psychological impact would be greatest. Father
Claude Allois reported in 1677 that the Illinois "do not use guns, finding
them too cumbersome and slow. They carry them, nevertheless, when
they march against nations who do not understand the use of them, to
frighten them by the noise and put them to rout." The point was not to
kill their opponents, but to make them flee. When tribes with guns faced
one another, they often employed bows as the more reliable weapon. As
Father Allois noted, the Indians rely on "arrows, which they shoot with

such skill and rapidity as scarcely to give time to those who have guns to take Aim."[88]

The Iroquois especially discovered the secrets of European warfare: to stun the enemy with the first volley of firepower and then scatter them from the field with a massed charge. They also learned the reverse: to allow the enemy to fire the first volley and then charge them while they were reloading. However, the Iroquois, like many other tribes, seem to have paid a price for this knowledge in losing the ability to fight with clubs. On several occasions they were beaten in battle by Indians using weapons more primitive than the Iroquois' firearms. They became so dependent on European firearms that their prime complaint against the English in the early eighteenth century was the latter's inability to sell them even more guns and powder.[89]

The Iroquois were not alone in taking advantage of the gun's limitations in battle. As one observer of an early eighteenth-century battle between the Apache and Spanish described the encounter, the Apache "waited until the soldiers had discharged their guns, and then closed in with them in a hand-to-hand struggle." This technique of luring the Europeans into firing a volley and then attacking was copied by Indians throughout North America, and would continue to be described into the mid-nineteenth century. But this technique required the Indians to close with the armed European enemy and drive them off before they had a chance to reload.[90]

The only other way to deal with the presence of European firearms was the source of much calumny from European sources: the surprise attack. Indians found it to their advantage to attack white troops even before the latter had a chance to retrieve or load their firearms. (It was almost impossible to keep a gun permanently loaded prior to the development of the bullet.) But for almost the entire Colonial period, surprise attacks by Indians could hope to attain only a rough parity with the Europeans, who continued to battle with superior bladed weapons.[91]

Those Indians who lacked guns justly feared these weapons that "could launch a missile so fast that it could not be seen in flight and so powerful that it could penetrate a hide shield and kill its holder." Many Indians came to invest supernatural powers in firearms, joining the Lakota in labeling them "sacred irons."[92] And those Indians who had guns came, like their European counterparts, to feel great self-confidence from holding such a powerful weapon. Indians with guns seemed more willing to fight than those who possessed only bows and tomahawks. As

Frank R. Secoy discovered in his groundbreaking study, the spread of firearms among the Indians increased the number and violence of inter-tribal battles.[93]

By the mid-eighteenth century, the gun played a far larger role in Indian than in white culture. Guns were central to Indian relations with the whites. Lewis and Clark discovered some western Indians who spoke a few words of English, including "musket." One of the signs "that the Quera, or good Spirit, has been very kind to the English men," some Indians told John Lawson, is that Quera taught "them to make Guns, and Ammunition, besides a great many other Necessaries, that are helpful to man. All which, they say, will be deliver'd to them, when that good Spirit sees fit." The Good Spirit seems to have delivered, though the evidence for gun ownership among the Indians is far too scattered and inadequate for any certainty. However, it is possible that by the 1740s there were more guns per capita among the Indians than among the whites. Of primary importance to the Indian economy, the gun formed a fundamental part of Indian cultural relations.[94]

The majority of eastern tribes maintained a few guns in peacetime during the eighteenth century, exhausting the fur supply in an effort to acquire ammunition and pay for necessary repairs. All that changed in the mid-1770s, when the English made a greater effort to offer Indians a steady supply of ammunition, first to combat the revolting Americans, and then, after the victory of the United States, to compete with American merchants.

As many Indian peoples discovered, firearms could transform a balance of power in a very brief period. In 1684 the Scots of Stuart's Town on Point Royal Sound provided the Muskogean under Altamaha with twenty-three muskets and ammunition. Altamaha's force quickly became the most formidable Indian group in the area, destroying the mission of Santa Catalina de Afuyca, killing eighteen Timucuan in the process—a fatality rate that stunned neighboring Indian tribes.[95] But generally the Indians used only a few guns, since firearms appeared to be primarily a defensive weapon, and offensive actions earned far more honor. As John Heckewelder observed, "all the weapons which the Indians make use of in war are intended for *offence,* they have no breast-plates, helmets, nor any arms or accoutrements of the defensive kind."[96]

Though less honored, the defensive advantages of guns were too great to ignore for long. In 1797 the Mandan halted the Sioux advance by building strong barricades from which they could fire at the attacking forces. What is intriguing is that the Mandan did so with very few guns, while the Sioux probably had more firearms than any of the western tribes. (But then Sioux success was based more on the smallpox epidemics that devastated their opponents in the late 1770s than on their use of firearms.) As one Mandan told the English trader David Thompson, "[our] enemies have never been able to hurt us when we are in our Villages; and it is only when we are absent on large hunting parties that we have suffered; and which we shall not do again."[97] The Sioux, in turn, developed a shortbow and lance to use when they did not have guns or access to ammunition, limitations that increased the further west they went.[98]

In 1810 David Thompson, who had been providing the Blackfoot with guns, decided to trade with the Flathead as well. In exchange for furs, Thompson gave the Flathead "twenty guns . . . with several hundreds of iron arrow heads, with which they thought themselves a fair match for" the Piegan, one of the Blackfoot tribes. This stalemate ended with about a dozen killed. Thompson noted that the Indians tended to use bows and arrows, clubs, and lances when on the defensive, saving their guns for offensive purposes alone. He also was impressed by the ability of both groups of Indians to avoid gunfire simply by jumping around quickly. Four years later the two groups again joined battle, and again the two sides spent the whole day maneuvering, each trying to bring their guns to bear offensively with no clear result. The significant point is that the Flathead were able to stop the Blackfoot advance, which had been sweeping everything in its path, with just twenty guns and a pile of iron arrowheads.[99]

In the early nineteenth century the European fur market had been glutted, and the source of arms and ammunition evaporated. Some tribes had become so dependent on guns that they thought of attacking trading posts to seize the firearms there. When the Atsina heard, incorrectly, that the unarmed Crow were about to begin trading for guns with the Americans, they planned to launch a preemptive strike against the British Fort Augustus, killing the whites and taking their guns in order to defend themselves from the Crow. Other tribes had the idea of kidnapping whites and trading them for guns.[100] But then Indians realized the value of all forms of European metal in creating better weapons of war, and often stole what they could not buy, even the locks that Europeans used to prevent such thefts.[101]

The unevenness of the spread of the Indian gun culture became a particular problem for those tribes that had not yet obtained access to firearms, as they suddenly found themselves the target of the expansionist tendencies of those groups with guns. As with the eastern tribes a century earlier, the integration of firearms into the culture of the Plains Indians was inconsistent. The Cheyenne of the Dakotas first traded for guns with a Canadian merchant in 1804. As late as 1834 George Catlin and T. B. Wheelock were struck with how few guns they saw among the Kiowa and Comanche. The Comanche were essentially unarmed until frontiersman Jesse Chisholm sold them seventy-five rifles in 1856. Yet in 1840 a visitor could report that the Cheyenne had acquired enough guns in the previous few years that they exchanged them as gifts.[102]

There were a few Indian groups, such as the western Assiniboin, that tapped into the demand for pemmican to trade for a large number of guns (enough by 1810 to supply half of their two thousand warriors). Ammunition, however, remained a problem, and much of the energy of the Assiniboin was devoted to acquiring powder and shot. And tribes that operated as middlemen between Europeans and other Indians almost never allowed guns and ammunition to pass in trade.[103] There was even some contempt among Indians for those who did use firearms. As one Cree said of a battle between his people and the Sioux in the 1730s, "the Cree [fight] in the open like brave men, the Sioux hiding behind trees." Eventually, however, all the Indian tribes came around to the use and glorification of guns.[104]

As guns became more common among western Indians in the 1820s, armor was abandoned in favor of the shield, which was lighter and still useful against arrows and blows from clubs.[105] The gun changed Indian warfare—in the early eighteenth century in the East, and the early nineteenth century in the West—accentuating the warrior's individualism in battle. Guns led to smaller Indian formations and the diminution of cooperation among groups of Indians. The fatal impact of massed gunfire on concentrated troops convinced Indians to move in smaller numbers stretched over larger areas. The "shock weapons," the club and lance, had inspired the close support of massed formations, while defense against the gun necessitated a dive for cover. Indians held that even the offensive use of firearms, which for Europeans consisted of massed troops, worked best from behind some form of cover. The exception was in the massed cavalry battles of the plains. But there the rapid movement of the warriors combined with their slow-loading and inaccurate guns, as well as the difficulty in acquiring fresh supplies of powder and shot, kept fatalities low.[106] And even then, the basic Indian strategy remained surprise. Any form of resistance generally led to the offensive party retreating, often in panic. In the 1880s, a Blackfoot described a battle in which a joint Crow–Gros Ventre surprise attack was discovered by their Piegan prey. "When the attacking party came tearing over the little rise of ground just east of the camp they were met by such an overwhelming force of determined and well-mounted men that they turned and fled, firing but few shots. They were utterly panic stricken; their only thought was to escape." Those Gros Ventre who were caught fleeing in panic "were brained with war clubs."[107]

In 1755, South Carolina's governor James Glen insensitively reminded the Cherokee of their dependence. In his "Advise to such of your Warriors as are too young to remember when you first had a Trade with the English," Glen recommended, "Let them consult your old Men what was the Condition of your Country at that Time and compare it with your Circumstances now. Instead of the admirable Fire Arms that you are now plentifully supplied with, your best Arms was bad Bows and wretched Arrows headed with Bills of Birds and Bones of Fishes or at best with sharp Stones." As if that were not bad enough, Glen pressed on: "Your knives were split Canes and your Hatchets of Stone, so that you spent more Days in felling a Tree than you now do Minutes." His audience was less than appreciative, yet there is no record of anyone disputing his word.[108]

Four years later Governor William Lyttelton of South Carolina again demonstrated this dependence of many Indians on European firearms and metals by forbidding the trading of guns and powder to the Cherokee. When many Cherokee called for war against South Carolina over this prohibition, one chief asked if they had "found a mountain of powder? Had their women learned to make clothes and their men to make knives?" It was a pointed question. With the English blockade keeping gunpowder from the French, Indians hostile to the English, or being made so, had no alternative source of metal weapons or gunpowder.[109] Repeatedly, Indians throughout North America discovered that the gun was a very effective offensive weapon but a constant drain on a tribe's resources.[110] As John P. Reid summarized the case, "South Carolina could survive without Cherokee deerskins; the Cherokees could not survive without Carolina-supplied ammunition." Any threat to that supply brought the Cherokee into line with white policy.[111]

By the mid-eighteenth century the Eastern Woodlands Indians possessed more firearms per capita than any other society in the world. This first American gun culture emerged from a conjunction of the Indian desire for firearms with an acceleration of the contest among the European powers for control of North America. Of course the fact that the Indians did not have armies as such meant the widespread ownership of firearms in that nearly all males were warriors. Unlike European societies, arms ownership was not restricted to the state and the elite.

Despite their adherence to the gun, Indians did not abandon any of their other weaponry, including bows, tomahawks, and fire. In the 1770s Daniel Trabue described an Indian attack as beginning with the "Dreadfullest screams and hollowing that could be immagined," as the Indians charged "with large fire brands or torc[h]es."[112]

The contrast between the Indians' gun culture and white attitudes is most evident in the latter's lack of enthusiasm for their militia. Nearly every male Indian was either a warrior or hoped to become one, bearing a gun as a symbol of that status. White communities had the opposite problem, having to persuade, wheedle, and coerce their men into serving in the militia even in peacetime. In time of conflict, when members of the militia might actually have to perform their duty, the situation often became hopeless, and in every instance Colonial legislatures had to turn to conscription. After every war the Colonial militias went into a period of quiescence, as governments begged officers to serve, and threatened communities into holding their annual militia musters. And then, with every new war scare, these colonies found that their militias had again atrophied. For instance, in 1683, just six years after the end of the most destructive war in New England's history, the Council of Plymouth found it necessary to appoint officers, since so few were volunteering to serve. When a new Indian war began in 1689, the colony discovered its militia had become inoperative, and the guns in the hands of its citizens, and in its own armory, were almost entirely rusted or broken. Plymouth had no recourse but to appeal to England for new guns.[113]

By 1711 Connecticut had essentially abandoned its militia system "for a military system [that] began to look more like Britain's, which had long since learned to use bounty money to induce poor men to perform dangerous military service." Military service simply did not appeal to the vast majority of Americans. By 1740 every Connecticut recruit received wages, food, clothing, and a gun, as well as a share of any booty, as the colony was "openly and happily paying poor men to go to war." But since these poor men almost never owned guns, the colony armed them by simply confiscating the arms of those militiamen who did. Most contemporary observers agreed that these volunteer forces were superior to the old militia, though the new forces included both blacks and Indians, groups excluded from the right to own guns and serve in the militia.[114]

Even with these new incentives in place, the northern colonies found it difficult to encourage sufficient numbers of soldiers to serve. In 1746, for instance, Connecticut, which had a population of approximately one hundred thousand people, could not raise its projected force of six hundred men for the invasion of Canada. The state assembly therefore offered an exemption from prosecution for debt and an additional £30 bounty for those who would join up—a large sum equal to a year's wages for a skilled artisan. The assembly was shocked to discover that they were being outdone by recruiters from Massachusetts and Rhode Island, which could offer more incentives to enlist in their militias. The assembly responded by increasing the bounty and then threatened to draft the poor if they did not join. By such methods Connecticut finally raised its six hundred troops, 57 percent of whom did not have guns.[115]

There was an exception to this generalization of dormant militia in the southern slave patrols, which kept the southern militia's pulse at a life-sustaining beat, if barely. These patrols also became just a bit too routine and lax during times of peace, more an excuse to spend the night drinking with friends rather than actively patrolling. Their weapon of choice was the whip or club, not the gun; their goal was to whip or beat, not to kill, those slaves they found without passes. As a consequence, even southern militias began each war in complete disorder. In 1755 the crisis came to a head as colony after colony discovered that they were ill prepared for war.

Chapter Five

Brown Bess
in the Wilderness

The bullet misses, the bayonet does not.

–Marshal Alexander Suvorov[1]

Slaughtering Scots

At the turn of the eighteenth century, England was still a secondary military power. Its army of fifteen thousand was one-eighth the size of the French and Dutch armies, one-fourth the size of the Spanish and Swedish armies, and smaller than it had been in the fifteenth century.[2] Obviously England was capable of sustaining a much larger force—Cromwell's New Model Army had numbered seventy thousand troops—but as yet there seemed no reason for a large military because the Royal Navy was thought sufficient defense. The government also found it far less expensive to rely on the navy and a small, professional army. But such calculations did not account for the logic of imperial expansion, an enthusiasm that seized the British government at mid-century and propelled the United Kingdom toward such international prominence that it may be called the first modern superpower.[3]

The American colonies shared England's basically nonmilitaristic perspective, as well as the fiscal benefits of small outlays on military necessities. By the 1740s the militias of most colonies were moribund and had been so for several decades. Occasional conflicts with Indians or imperial skirmishes with the French had been met with groups of volunteers, most effectively rangers, small companies of men familiar with wilderness campaigning. The disastrous siege of Cartagena in 1741 and the victory at Louisbourg in 1745 were the only significant commitments of Colonial troops in the first half of the eighteenth century. The vast majority of Americans seemed perfectly content to leave matters that way. But events in Scotland in 1745 changed everything for the British Empire in some rather unexpected ways.[4]

In 1745 Charles Edward Stuart, son of the would-be James III, landed in Scotland with a small force of mostly Irish supporters serving in the French army. He quickly raised a large force of enthusiastic Scots who won several victories over the English under the field command of the brilliant Lord George Murray. At Prestonpans regulars armed with muskets had fled before the screaming Scots waving their terrible claymore swords. Charles Stuart marched as far south as Derby, but in the face of two English armies retreated back to Scotland. The Duke of Cumberland, George II's twenty-five-year-old son, commanded the English forces that chased "Bonnie Prince Charlie" into the Highlands. The Highlanders routed one English army at Falkirk in January 1746, the rain soaking the English muskets so that they were useless, and even the cavalry ran before the Scottish claymores. At Culloden Moor, Stuart ignored Murray's advice and made his stand against the superior English army. It was a miscalculation with enormous repercussions.[5]

The English victory at Culloden produced three major effects on the British North American colonies. In its aftermath, Cumberland's troops swept through the Highlands, killing, pillaging, and raping, beginning a process of removal that, over the next thirty years, sent thousands of Scots to America. This great and bloody victory also elevated "Butcher" Cumberland to a position of great authority within the British government; and he used his authority to encourage a more militaristic imperial expansion that would produce the Seven Years' War and lead to his own downfall.[6] But the battle itself introduced a long-lasting change in the way all future battles would be fought by European troops, by demonstrating the terrible efficiency and killing power of the bayonet.

Musketeers in the seventeenth and early eighteenth centuries relied on pikemen to protect them while they reloaded. This necessity produced the giant Continental armies, as each company of musketeers needed at least an equal number of pikemen. But the English government sought to avoid the expense of a large army, as well as the dangers of training a great number of civilians in the use of any weapons, even pikes. The British ideal became a highly trained, well-armed professional army, but not a large one. The increased gun production of the 1720s proved essential to the contemporary buildup of the British military. In 1721 the

Gunmakers' Company proofed eighteen hundred muskets a month; a decade later they were proofing twenty-five hundred per month.[7] The British army's new Long Land Service musket accounted for the bulk of that increased production.

Known as the Brown Bess, because of the brown staining of its barrel, this new musket did not represent a substantial improvement over its predecessor. More than five feet long and weighing sixteen and a half pounds, the Brown Bess, like its predecessors, could not be aimed in any useful fashion. Illustrations in manuals never show the soldier aiming a musket; their heads remain erect while shooting. The Brown Bess, like almost all muskets, did not have a sight.[8] Military experts of the time understood that soldiers were shooting in tense situations, in the midst of noise, smoke, and bloodshed, and handling weapons with an effective accurate range of forty yards at most. So simply leveling the musket and firing volleys made perfect sense. General Humphrey Bland's *Treatise of Military Discipline,* the standard British training manual among the American colonists from its first publication in 1727 through the American Revolution, recommended twenty to thirty paces as the maximum range of musket fire—beyond that was just a waste of ammunition.[9] General Basil Hughes estimates that no more than one-half of one percent of all balls fired in a battlefield volley hit the enemy.[10] In 1779 a company of "excellent Norfolk Militia," who practiced often, tested their weapons under the best possible conditions, hitting their six-foot-high target at seventy yards 20 percent of the time. An English marksman of the same time hit a four-foot-square target at one hundred yards 57 percent of the time. A longbowman, firing at the same target from the same distance, hit with 74 percent of his shots.[11]

The Brown Bess also misfired as often as any other musket. In 1811 the English armaments expert William Muller determined that, at best, the contemporary musket had a one-in-four misfire rate and that only half of those balls that did leave the barrel of a musket could impart harm at one hundred yards. The joke of the period was that in order to kill a man it was necessary to fire seven times his weight in lead. At least in terms of accuracy and deadliness, there was little difference between a musket made in 1700 and one made in 1850.[12]

The Brown Bess did, however, come with a Land Pattern socket bayonet. The bayonet came into use at the beginning of the seventeenth century, carried by crossbowmen for protection after they had shot their bolt. Yet little effort was made through the next century to modify the bayonet for the musket, until the 1720s, when it was fitted around the muzzle of the Brown Bess, allowing British soldiers to protect themselves after firing. Several military observers discussed the ways in which the bayonet would change warfare, but it was not until Culloden that the Duke of Cumberland demonstrated its efficacy.

Some particularly aggressive troops, including the Scots, had adopted the American method of firing, then throwing aside the gun in order to charge with a sword or ax, not taking the time or risk of reloading. The socket bayonet eliminated the need to cast the weapon aside, for now the musket was also a pike. The Duke of Cumberland made it standard practice for British troops to hold their fire until the enemy came into effective firing range (about ten yards), fire once, and then use the bayonet against the enemy, stabbing at the man to the right, rather than against the one immediately in front, so as to catch the enemy under his lifted sword arm. The length of the bayonet alone made it terrifying, generally reaching out from the soldier's body six feet. As James Wolfe wrote after the battle of Culloden, " 'Twas for some time a dispute between the swords and the bayonets; but the bayonet was found by far the most destructible weapon." By the time the British perfected the bayonet charge during the American Revolution, transforming the bayonet from a defensive into an offensive weapon, most observers would come to agree with Wolfe.[13]

The battlefield at Culloden made the bayonet's superiority immediately apparent. Suffering only some fifty casualties, the English had killed nearly one thousand Scots. Cumberland's forces demonstrated another advantage of the bayonet after the battle ended, as they walked over the field bayoneting the wounded and executing nearly one thousand prisoners with a minimum expenditure of ammunition and no danger to themselves from misfires or exploding muskets. The deadly thrusts of the bayonet at Culloden were replicated in every major land battle at least through World War II, and probably to the Falklands War in 1982. Frederick II of Prussia simplified the lesson to an aphorism: "Fire as little as possible with the infantry in battle: charge with the bayonet."[14]

As did the American Indians, many European commanders looked to take advantage of the musket's shortcomings while the enemy was reloading. The bayonet simplified this effort. Thus Marshal Maurice Comte de Saxe and the Marquis de Quincy both held that their own troops should take the enemy's first volley, and then charge with their bayonets while the defenders reloaded.[15] Frederick II shifted this approach, insisting that his own troops hold their fire until they were within ten paces, and then "give the enemy a strong volley in the face. Immediately thereafter they should plunge the bayonet into the enemy's ribs, at the same time shouting at him to throw away his weapon and surrender."[16] The latter point seems a bit superfluous; but the former was echoed a hundred years later by Confederate General Stonewall Jackson: "My idea is that the best mode of fighting is to reserve your fire till the enemy get . . . to close quarters. Then deliver one deadly deliberate fire and charge."[17] These tactics proved all too effective.

While his troops continued bayoneting Scots, the Duke of Cumberland returned to England a great hero. Not only did his father's government reward him with vast sums of money, it also moved him ever closer to the center of power. The duke's voice became the decisive one in most government counsels, a voice that favored aggression above negotiation, expansion rather than stability, war over peace. In 1754 the Duke of Cumberland, commander-in-chief of all British forces, welcomed a small encounter in the Ohio River Valley as the opportunity to launch a general war against France. Before Cumberland's own humiliating defeat at Hastenbeck, Germany, and his surrender of Hanover to the French in 1757, he would appoint a string of remarkably incompetent officers to command the English forces in America.[18] Their failures would bring the French within striking distance of complete control of the frontier regions of North America. Such an outcome would have locked the English colonists along the coast for decades. Yet the defeats also led to the rise of one of England's greatest leaders, William Pitt, who would take the dramatic action of arming vast numbers of American militia to fight for the empire. That decision, in turn, would have dramatic, unintended consequences.

Imagined Militias

The expansion of the British Empire did not proceed unopposed. From the late 1690s until the early 1720s, radical "country" opponents of the dominant Whigs advanced a critique of the central government that focused particularly on corruption and the danger of a standing army. These critics, identified by historians as the Commonwealthmen, replicated in many ways the old bow-versus-gun debate in their effort to revive the militia. Unorganized and incohesive themselves, the Commonwealthmen feared standing armies as a danger to liberty and a force for imperial aggrandizement. These opposition writers proclaimed the militia the embodiment of the nation, and claimed it sufficient to preserve the strength and survival of England. Yet theirs was a nation of property owners only. They feared mercenary armies of the poor paid to commit violence for tyrants. To avoid that fate, arms and property must be in the same hands, and the militia must be organized on an entirely local basis, without any central control. The Commonwealthmen were also a bit vague on how England would preserve its empire with a militia, but then theirs was a backward-looking ideology that idealized the imagined "gothic constitutions" of the Middle Ages.[19]

This attractive ideal—a well-armed citizenry ready to rise up in defense of the nation—had no basis in reality. The English militia revived briefly during the Restoration, since its "only task was the maintenance of internal security and that was always what it did best." But the militia lapsed into desuetude again by 1668 because of the mass indifference of those called upon to serve, the suspicion of a government that feared common people trained in any kind of arms, and the potent hostility of Whigs who saw the militia as a threat to English liberties. This latter position is most telling in light of the arguments of the Commonwealthmen. Those who actually lived with an active militia in the 1660s did not see it as a bulwark of basic liberties. They understood instead that the militia existed primarily to enforce order on the government's terms. But with all but the elite disarmed, the government no longer needed the militia, and was thus willing to give in to that Whig demand. And there was one final consideration in the abandonment of the militia at the end of the 1660s: it was embarrassing. As J. R. Western summarized the situation, "The militia always looked ridiculous whenever it took the field."[20]

There were many different reasons for finding fault with Commonwealth ideas. In 1726 a North Carolina settler agreed that "A Militia in an Arbitrary & Tyrranical Government, may possibly be of some service to the Governing Power, but we learn from experience that in a free Country it is of little use." On the frontier, after all, the people must "work hard . . . to provide the Common necessaries of Life for their Families, so that they cannot spare a day's time without great loss to their Interest," so that the militia is therefore even "more burthensome to the poor people." This author offered one final, rather obvious observation: "But besides it may be questioned how far it would consist with good Policy to accustom all the able Men in the Colonies to be well exercised with Arms." Far wiser, then, to rely on regulars for defense than risk arming commoners.[21]

Opponents found the Commonwealth ideas a formula for anarchy, one guaranteed to reduce the empire to feudalism in a nonfeudal world. Adherents of the standing army accurately pointed out the need for well-trained professional soldiers if Britain hoped not simply to hold its own in international contests but to expand its empire, adding that a militia competed for scarce manpower with the army's recruiters. The Whigs insisted that a standing army was less of a threat to liberty than a localized militia, as Parliament, the true embodiment of the nation, retained strict control over the military. Even the militia's stated purpose, defense against invasion, was better and less expensively served by trained professionals and volunteers. But the most pointed and effective argument of proponents of the army was the obvious issue that property owners had much better things to do with their time than devoting several weeks a year to military training. The Whigs found it necessary to remind the Commonwealthmen that England had left the Saxon age several centuries earlier, and that their plans looked back "to barbarous anarchy, not forward to ordered liberty." The militia envisioned by the Commonwealthmen properly belonged to another time, one that had nothing to do with the world of trade and commerce that concerned England at the start of the eighteenth century.[22]

The Commonwealthmen lost this historic battle, the militia died, and the British army and navy prospered, accounting for 65 percent of the total government expenditures in the first half of the eighteenth century.[23] And yet a great number of scholars have chosen to concentrate on the losers in this debate, insisting that their ideas exerted enormous influence a half-century later on the leaders of the American revolutionary struggle.[24] Fortunately for the existence of the United States, at least George Washington seemed unimpressed with the arguments of the Commonwealthmen, and the policies of the new government would barely reflect the proposals of these long-dead English authors. Their impact within the British Empire was equally negligible, with no significant calls for militia reform until long after the Commonwealthmen passed from the political stage. Nonetheless, this idealization of the militia showed a peculiar recuperative quality, rising repeatedly at a later date in patriotic speeches in America in direct denial of the historic experience.[25]

It is nearly impossible to find the well-armed, resolute militia of such imaginings in the American militia records of the eighteenth century. The probate records give the impression that few people owned guns in

Colonial America. That perception is accurate. It does not mean, however, that there were very few guns in America. The British government had sent several thousand guns to America by 1754, and the proprietors of the various colonies had sent hundreds more. The majority of these arms rotted away in central storehouses.

The British ordnance office discovered that their Brown Bess, considered the finest military musket in Europe, had a life expectancy of eight years. After that time, it required complete rebuilding, a task that could be performed only by a qualified gunsmith. As a consequence, the British army recalled roughly one-tenth of its firearms every year.[26] Assuming for a moment that most of the two hundred thousand men eligible for service in the Colonial militias in 1750 owned a gun, and assuming they took as good care of their weapons as British soldiers who were ordered to do so, the Americans would still have needed to replace or rebuild roughly twenty thousand firearms a year—a number equal to 80 percent of the total production of Great Britain's gun manufacturers in 1750. But most of those Americans who owned firearms lacked the ability to repair and replace their guns; the colonists had to make due with their aging muskets. Meanwhile, the population of the American colonies kept increasing while the flow of armaments dried up. By 1754 there were enough guns for only a small percentage of the American population—at most one-sixth of those eligible for militia duty. But the majority of these guns were unusable without a complete refitting. The fable of the family musket kept above the mantel ready for use will just not pass muster.

The colonists relied on the Crown for their guns, but the Crown did not particularly care that their colonists needed guns. The essential insignificance of its colonies to Britain is indicated by the fact that the first naval base established in the North American colonies was at Halifax in 1749. As a consequence of this governmental disinterest, large shipments of arms usually came to North America only with British troops.

The British government had a very good reason for preferring to send few arms to America: the Americans were unreliable. The correspondence of imperial officials is full of complaints that the colonists did not take care of the firearms they were given, tended to lose far too many, and never kept track of what they received. They also stole a great many. Repeatedly the royal governors or commissioners of ordnance complained that munitions sent to America were neither maintained nor adequately recorded. In 1712 Governor Alexander Spotswood of Virginia attempted to determine what had happened to "the arms and ammunition sent hither by her Majesty, some years ago" and "distributed through the sev'll Countys, to be more ready for the service of the Militia upon any Emergency." But as a consequence of "the negligence or death of some of the Officers to whom [the guns] were entrusted, there has been great Embezlements made." Spotswood never discovered what happened to these arms, but he suspected that most were traded to the Indians. The phrase "great embezzlements" occurs in several letters, though under different spellings and with distinctive degrees of anger and frustration. By 1738 the Virginia legislature had given up its efforts to arm the militia, noting that all previous laws "have proved very ineffectual."[27] After such experiences, the British government became ever more hesitant to send arms across the Atlantic, and the arms they did send were not always of the highest quality. Thus one New Jersey militia company complained in 1747 that the Lords of Trade had sent "300 Guns, or Things in the Shape of Guns, which were condemned by the Gunsmiths at Albany as not the value of old Iron." But then, the author continued, "those very arms had been in Oliver Cromwell's Army." Of course the real point is that the members of the militia relied entirely on the British government for their arms, having few of their own.[28]

In May 1744, as England's latest war with France threatened to involve the New England colonies, Worcester County responded to the legislature's call for a militia muster. The county's twenty-one militia companies, consisting of 1,440 men, each filed a report on their firearms. Though Massachusetts was the best-armed colony with the most consistent policy of arms purchase and maintenance, only four of these companies reported that they were "Mostly Equip'd." Eight companies were "Intirely Deficient," and six were half-equipped. Ten of the companies, containing 577 men, offered an exact reporting of their armaments; they had 248 guns, or enough for 43 percent of the men in these companies.[29] Despite the various war scares and the defeat of Braddock's army, the situation had actually worsened by September 1756, when Timothy Paine informed the legislature that the 293 men of the two Worcester companies mustered but would not march until the government supplied them with guns. The reason was simple: only forty-five men (15 percent) owned their own guns, and the company had "Twenty Arms . . . that were left by some Officers" when they came through town in the spring. With enough arms for only 22 percent of the militia in Worcester, the legislature sent Colonel John Chandler with an additional 228 "Province Guns." Chandler was pleased to report that at least his regiment was now well armed. But the chair of the committee of war reminded him that these arms and accoutrements belonged to the king and had to be returned on demand.[30]

Other militia companies were even less well prepared in the early eighteenth century, and remained that way. The governor, council, and legislature of South Carolina issued a joint memorial to the king in 1734 declaring that slave patrols took precedence over any other militia duties, and requested more arms and British Regulars for the colony's defense. Four years later Lieutenant Governor William Bull reported that regular militia service was "Inconsistent with a Domestick or Country Life," and few of the settlers in his colony were interested in serving. In 1747 Governor Glen requested a new militia law, telling the assembly that his leading officers reported that the entire system was on the verge of collapse because the men were refusing to muster. The new act, which stayed in effect until 1778, placed stricter fines on nonattendance but seemingly did little to improve attendance at the musters. Governor William Henry Lyttleton's instructions stated that "You shall take care that all Planters, Inhabitants, and Christian Servants be well and fitly supplied with arms." His first report back to the board of trade on the militia stated that they were not prepared nor properly armed, several regiments having not mustered for three or more years. In 1756 Charles Pinckney reported to the board of trade that the colony's militia could not be relied on to perform any duty but keeping the slaves in order.[31] The Virginia militia in these years was reported to lack sufficient arms and ammunition even for that task. "Virginia is a country young in war," George Washington wrote to Lord Loudoun in 1757. Until "the breaking out of these disturbances [it] has remained in the most profound and tranquil peace; ne'er studying war nor warfare."[32]

Colonel Henry Bouquet found the southern settlers "Extremely pleased to have Soldiers," but they would not act in their own defense. Arriving to take over defenses in South Carolina, Bouquet reported to Lord Loudoun that "ever body appears well disposed to the common Defence of the Country (as far as it does not interfere with private Interest or Conveniences)." South Carolina's militia "amounts to about six thousand badly armed Men," but fewer than seventy agreed to serve in defense of the colony in 1757, and the legislature refused to compel compliance

Even worse, in Bouquet's eyes, the government of South Carolina had allowed the munitions just sent over from England to sit out in the weather, where they had already rotted beyond repair.[33]

Three colonies had no noticeable militia in these years: Maryland, Delaware, and Pennsylvania. The opposition of the Pennsylvania Quakers to a militia reveals one powerful countercurrent in the traditional image of a universal militia widely supported. The Quakers fought the creation of a militia not just because of their pacifism, but also because they saw it as a tool of the proprietor. Through the first half of the eighteenth century the Penn family had to rely on persuasion to exert their will in what they saw as their colony, except in 1742, when they hired a group of sailors to beat up political opponents. That latter act set a dangerous precedent in the eyes of the Quakers. A militia armed by the government could work its will unhindered, even to coercing those opposed to military service to join their ranks. The Quakers were always willing to pay volunteers to serve on specific military expeditions, but for them a militia was itself the equivalent of the standing army feared by so many— and they were against it.[34]

The *London Magazine* of July 1746 found no evidence of the heroic universal militia in North America. Its eyewitness account of the militia of Maryland, Virginia, and South Carolina may have muted some enthusiasm for relying on the militia for defense. The author observed that the locals loved military titles: "your Ears are constantly astonished at the Number of Colonels, Majors and Captains that you hear mentioned." But there was no matching reality. The plethora of military titles makes "the whole Country" appear "a Retreat of Heroes: but alas! to behold the Musters of their Militia, would induce a Man to nauseate a Sash and hold a Sword, forever in Derision. Diversity of Weapons and Dresses, . . . and Want of the least Grain of Discipline in their Officers or them, make the whole Scene little better than Dryden has expressed it— . . . 'Of seeming arms, they make a short essay, / Then hasten to get drunk, the bus'ness of the day.' "[35]

Many historians have blithely declared that the British colonies were, in an oft repeated phrase, "the most heavily armed society in the world." But they offer not a shred of evidence for this assertion.[36] And how a society lacking even a single gun manufacturer could be the best armed is never explained. After the nearly ceaseless wars of the seventeenth and early eighteenth centuries, every European nation had built up huge stockpiles of firearms that dwarfed the few thousand scattered through the British North American colonies. If we exclude the military from these calculations, then the equation changes, since every European nation rigorously enforced limits on gun ownership. Addressing only firearms in private hands still leaves the eastern woodlands Indians as the most heavily armed societies, followed by New England and then a few of the Italian city-states. But the only way the southern British colonies could be included on such a list is by refusing to count slaves as people. Even with a whites-only count of gun ownership, the southern colonies, which also worked to limit gun ownership by the poor, did not approach the New England colonies. Because of the structure of laws and fears, one cannot make sweeping generalizations about Colonial America's relationship with firearms.

With one exception: the American colonies (and later, states) were never prepared for war. Whenever there was a crisis on the frontier, settlers sent petitions to the provincial government requesting British Regulars and arms for the local militia.[37] Their governments generally did the same thing, frantically requesting troops and arms from the Crown. Until 1755 most Americans felt confident that the regulars could eventually deal with every military problem. In that year this cherished faith was shattered in the backwoods of Pennsylvania.

Wilderness Warfare

There are many scholars who perceive warfare in eighteenth-century North America as especially brutal and violent. A few contemporaries also noted a distinctive cruelty across the Atlantic. The Swiss soldier Henry Bouquet described American warfare as "a rigid contest where all is at stake, and mutual destruction the object."[38] On the other hand, the numbers of casualties in American battles paled into insignificance compared to European rates. At the Battle of Blenheim in 1704, there were 50,600 killed and wounded on both sides, the British losing one-fourth of their total force, the French 40 percent of theirs. In 1758 Frederick the Great won the Battle of Zorndorf, losing nearly 40 percent of his force of thirty-six thousand, while the Russians suffered a 50 percent casualty rate from their similarly large army.[39] No war in Colonial North America approached those numbers. The routine slaughter in Europe would have demoralized the Americans

Americans received their first real taste of European warfare on July 9,

1755. On that memorable day General Edward Braddock led his army of 1,450 men into a rather traditional Indian ambush just a few miles from Fort Duquesne. For the first time, two large forces—by American standards—were well armed, as nearly one thousand French and Indians set upon Braddock's troops. According to Benjamin Franklin, Braddock grossly underestimated his Indian opponent, just as had many Colonial commanders before him. "These Savages may indeed be a formidable Enemy to your raw American Militia," Braddock supposedly told Franklin, "but upon the King's regular and disciplin'd Troops, Sir, it is impossible they should make any impression."[40] The Indians made a deep impression on both.

The British method of firing a volley and then bringing their bayonets to bear proved ineffective against an enemy hiding behind trees, unless the troops were allowed to move among the trees themselves. Instead, Braddock refused to allow his troops to leave the road and disperse into the forest, where their bayonets would have proved most effective in single combat. In essence, Braddock would not let his troops fight back, ignoring the specific requests of George Croghan and George Washington that their soldiers be spread out among the trees. Lawrence Henry Gipson's marvelous understatement is even more to the point: "the British need of adequate Indian support became painfully apparent."[41] If Braddock had been accompanied by Indian allies—well, allies to whom he would listen—it is highly probable that the whole disaster could have been averted. Instead, Braddock turned aside the assistance of friendly Indians and allowed his troops to be picked apart. "The Wonder," as Francis Jennings wrote, "is not that the British finally panicked and fled, but how they held out longer than two hours" against this massacre in which they suffered 977 casualties to their enemy's 39—casualties inflicted in equal parts by firearms and arrows. The troops were superior to their commander, a "stupid brute of a man whose prime qualification for command was the political favor" of the Duke of Cumberland.[42]

The aftermath of Braddock's defeat provided Americans with a new vision of British Regulars. Colonel Thomas Dunbar took command of the remnants of this British army and retreated toward the coast, abandoning his artillery to the French. In Philadelphia he requested winter quarters, though it was only July. As Franklin wrote, Dunbar did not think "himself safe till he arriv'd at Philadelphia, where the Inhabitants could protect him. This whole transaction gave us Americans the first Suspicion that our exalted Ideas of the Prowess of British Regulars had not been well founded." William Pitt soon reached a similar conclusion, though with his anger focused at the idiot officer corps.[43]

But it was not clear who or what could take the regulars' place. "The neat plans laid in England," Francis Jennings has written, "assumed that American recruits generally would be good marksmen with experienced skill in woodland warfare." Instead they were "mostly plowboys and drifters, younger sons and recent immigrants who had never spent a night in the woods. In an ambush they panicked disastrously." Or, as John Shy put it, the American militia "were just as bewildered and even less effective in the forest than regulars."[44] Lord Loudoun, commander of British forces in North America in 1755 and 1757, discovered that most Americans, even those living in frontier regions, had little knowledge of the use of firearms or the nature of warfare. The New Englanders, the best trained of the lot, were "frightened out of their senses at the name of a Frenchman." Jeffrey Amherst thought many of the Colonial volunteers had "never fired a gun in their lives." Loudoun asked the governments of New England to give him eight thousand men in 1756, but was so unimpressed that he asked the following year for four thousand, with the stipulation that these be "good effective men," if the colonies had any.[45]

With Braddock having burned far too many bridges to the Indians, Loudoun turned to companies of rangers for knowledge of frontier warfare. But he found that few Americans were qualified to operate as rangers—no more than a few hundred—and many of these were Christian Indians. Even the rangers often proved a major disappointment, and the British commanders actually established programs to train them to shoot accurately with rifles, weapons with which most of them were unfamiliar. In 1756 one company of German settlers in the supposed gun-producing heartland of Pennsylvania was trained by British marksmen "to fire at Marks, and in order to qualify them for the Service of the Woods, they are to be taught to load and fire, lyeing on the Ground and kneeling." Two years later, General Amherst ordered that ten rifles should be issued to every battalion of American volunteers to train and equip companies of marksmen. In 1759, frustrated by the failure of these efforts, Amherst commanded that the rangers and other would-be marksmen receive more ammunition so that they could practice regularly. Nonetheless, many historians have clung to what military historian Stanley Pargellis has called the "fond delusion" that America was home to thousands of rugged Deerslayers with their guns always ready to kill Indians.[46]

The American colonies did produce some rather rugged fighters, but they tended to be workers rather than frontier settlers. In 1756 Massachusetts governor William Shirley hired several hundred bateaumen to take supplies to Fort Oswego, supplying the force under the command of the American colonel John Bradstreet with hatchets and British army muskets. Just nine miles short of Oswego, some seven hundred French and Indians ambushed Bradstreet's three hundred men. On Bradstreet's orders, his men charged with their hatchets, hacking to death twenty of the enemy before the French and Indians fled. Hence, the first significant American victory since the Indian wars of the seventeenth century was won with hatchets.[47]

It was quite some time before they enjoyed another victory. The early years of the Seven Years' War proved a triumph for the Indians over the Colonial militia, as well as over Braddock's regulars.[48] While it is difficult to generalize about the attitudes of Colonial Americans, as of any people, it seems safe to say that they showed little eagerness for participating in the war during its first three years. Even the frontier settlers contradicted modern expectations of their character. In 1755, after Braddock's defeat, the frontier county of Lancaster was not screaming for blood, as might be expected. Instead it elected an all-Quaker delegation to the legislature, even though there were "scarcely One Hundred of that Profession in The whole County," according to Speaker Isaac Norris.[49]

But then frontier settlers had always relied on British Regulars and coastal militia for security and arms. With both these forces in disarray, most people on the frontier felt themselves exposed to the expected ravages of Indians and frantically petitioned their assemblies for arms. Curiously, it was the Quaker-dominated Pennsylvania assembly that responded most quickly to these pleas that the frontier was "in the utmost disorder and confusion and in great want of Arms and Ammunition." The assembly spent £1,000 on firearms for these settlements, which evoked an angry censure from the governor, who thought they had infringed on executive authority. The assembly, acting in desperation, also organized Pennsylvania's first official militia.[50]

The commander of this new militia was the self-proclaimed colonel Benjamin Franklin. Some observers in Philadelphia greeted his parades with a degree of contempt, questioning the capacity of these "puffed up" officers and wondering "Whether between 6 and 700 Men and Boys, a great Part of whom had never appeared in any former Muster, can with any Propriety be called a well trained Regiment... ?"[51] In September

1756 this unseasoned militia surprised and burned the Delaware village of Kittanning.[52] But other than in such surprise attacks, the American militia generally failed in its missions and certainly did not win the admiration of European officers. In August 1756 the eighteen hundred poorly armed New York militia at Oswego surrendered after the first volley fired by the French. Commander Montcalm-Gozon expressed great disappointment that the Americans had capitulated so readily, hoping that a protracted siege would draw English forces to their relief.[53]

The New England governments responded quickly when Fort William Henry was threatened by the French under Montcalm in August 1757. They saw it as the first real threat to their borders so far that century, and within a week had successfully mobilized one-fourth of the region's militia, five thousand men, to march to the fort's relief. But the fort fell before the New England militia reached Albany, where the New York militia was demonstrating far less enthusiasm for the cause—Lieutenant Governor James De Lancey told the legislature that all but a few units had deserted. The French had no intention of advancing from Fort William Henry, but marched back to Fort Carillon (later to be renamed Ticonderoga by the English). The New England militia therefore returned home, at a total cost to the colonies of £15,000 for eighteen days' service, one-third the cost of maintaining the British forces in America for the year. It was the militia's most effective action; to the British government it confirmed the high cost of relying on such a force. The colonies discovered that such campaigns exhausted their resources as well, and after just two years of war most of the Colonial governments found themselves out of funds for further efforts.[54]

The skills of the militia were evident: self-defense. They were not good soldiers, and never showed the capacity for wilderness campaigning displayed by the Indians, the Quebecois, or even their own rangers. The one great victory by Colonial forces in the Seven Years' War, the defeat of the French at Lake George in September 1755, verified the abilities and limitations of the militia. As Harold Selesky has summarized, "The soldiers lost heavily in a morning ambush, demonstrating once again their lack of skill at Indian-style war, but in the afternoon they repulsed every French attack from behind the breastwork around their main camp."[55]

Though the militia did not win many laurels, a number of Americans did acquire military experience that proved valuable in the coming years. Over ten thousand colonists enlisted to serve with the British during the Seven Years' War, more than in any other war up until that time. In their musters, the Colonial militia and volunteer units now concentrated on developing massed musket fire. The single volley followed by the bayonet advance or defense was quickly becoming the centerpiece of all military manuals after Culloden. Humphrey Bland set the standard: "The Commanding Officer of every Battalion should march up close to the Enemy, before he suffers his Men to give their Fire; and if the Enemy have not given theirs, he should prevent their doing it, by falling upon them, with the Bayonets on the Muzzles the Instant they have fired, which may be done under the Cover of the Smoke."[56]

But there was just one problem with the Americans studying this method: they did not have sufficient guns for their militia or even for their volunteers. The officers of both Shirley's and Pepperrell's volunteer regiments reported a dangerous "insufficiency of Arms and Accoutrements." Of those arms they did have "the Locks [were] wore out and the Hammers so soft, that notwithstanding repeated repairs they are almost unfit for Service, particularly Sir William Pepperrell's Regiment being old Dutch Arms" (i.e., from the mid-seventeenth century). Peter Schuyler found the same situation in his regiment; their limited supply of five hundred muskets, which they had received from Virginia, "are so extreamly bad, as to be hardly fitt for Service," one-fourth completely unusable, and with the rest, "the Locks daily breaking in the common Exercise."[57] But with sufficient supplies from England the Colonial troops could perform rather well. Shirley wrote Henry Fox that the American militia was essentially unarmed and would need fifty thousand muskets; the government sent two thousand in 1755, and promised another ten thousand the following year.[58] By 1759 there was evidence that the Americans were learning British military methods. At the Battle of Niagara in July of that year, Captain James De Lancey led his American troops in a bayonet charge that broke the French resistance. It was a well-executed maneuver, worthy of any battlefield in Europe.[59]

The British and Americans learned from one another. In 1758 General Loudoun ordered British Regulars to be trained in forest warfare, most particularly in responding to ambushes. Troops were instructed to disperse among the trees and fight as individuals, an innovation in violation of the same manuals the Americans were just beginning to use. One officer noted that his troops had become American: "The Highlanders have put on breeches.... Swords and sashes are degraded, and many have taken up the Hatchet and wear Tomahawks." The image of the

American was to be found in the ax; the nature of American warfare was understood as single combat.[60]

This reliance on hand-to-hand combat over "marksmanship" in North American warfare is evidenced by the abatis. Both sides in the Seven Years' War came to rely on this construction of green branches to keep enemy forces at a distance. Troops could not march or charge through this mass of unburnable branches, and had to content themselves with firing at the enemy, a wasteful and largely ineffectual mode of warfare.[61]

Not that these experiences prevented the colonies from trying to arm their militia. As the war heated up, each Colonial government reported in turn their desperation for firearms and men; there was no surplus of arms in the northern colonies. In 1756 the Connecticut General Court found their militia dangerously under-armed, with no arms or ammunition available for sale in the colony or its neighbors. Those Massachusetts militia companies holding musters in 1755 and 1756 reported between 15 percent and 25 percent properly equipped with firearms.[62] During Virginia's emergency call-up of militia in 1756, the government discovered that only one-quarter of those responding had firearms. The legislature quickly passed two special taxes to raise money to buy guns, while militiamen lacking guns were to be given them by the colony. Despite these taxes, Colonel Washington reported on the militia to Governor Dinwiddie: "Many of them [are] unarmed, and *all* without ammunition or provision." In one company of more than seventy men, he reported, only twenty-five had any sort of firearms. Washington found such militia "incapacitated to defend themselves, much less to annoy the enemy."[63]

Most governments responded to the shortage of firearms by offering bounties to anyone who would supply the state with a gun, backing up the offer with the threat to impress any gun not offered for sale. Even these efforts proved insufficient. In 1758 Connecticut owned two hundred firearms and received sixteen hundred from the Crown, which made eighteen hundred guns for five thousand militia. The government set about buying and impressing every gun it could find, offering additional bounties to any volunteer who would bring his own gun. Surprisingly few people were in a position to take advantage of this offer of quick cash. In one company of eighty-five men, only seven showed up with their own guns. The records indicate that this figure of 8 percent was fairly typical throughout the colonies.[64]

For the first two years of war, as the British and their colonists suffered repeated defeats, the Colonial governments attempted to purchase firearms anywhere and everywhere, pursuing each individual gun that might be bought or confiscated. Every legislature frantically turned to the Crown for aid. It was at this point, in 1757, with the Duke of Cumberland's shameful retirement from politics after his loss of Hanover to the French, that a new first minister stepped forward to change all the equations within the British Empire.

William Pitt truly focused England's attention on North America for the first time. He not only expanded the army and navy and subsidized the Prussians to keep the French busy on the Continent, he also sent twenty-five thousand men to America in 1758, one-third of Great Britain's effective strength. Additionally, he offered to reimburse the Colonial governments for their expenditures and to hire Americans as soldiers. This latter promise saved the Colonial governments from financial ruin and motivated them to create volunteer forces and companies of rangers.[65] From that point on the Colonial governments used financial incentives to raise troops. As Harold Selesky has written, "the leaders rejected any attempt to use the militia ideal of universal service as a model for the expeditionary regiments long before they received the imperial subsidies that allowed them to come close to creating a colonial version of a professional army by 1762."[66]

But Pitt went even further, promising the governors of the American colonies that "The King is further pleased to furnish all the Men" who volunteer for service "with Arms, Ammunitions, and Tents, . . . in the same Proportion and Manner as is done to the rest of the King's Forces." Here was an offer they could not possibly resist. For the first time in more than a century, it now appeared possible that the American colonies would finally have sufficient firearms for their defense.[67]

Pitt's policies altered the nature of warfare in North America. His reasoning was to put an end once and for all to the constant wilderness struggles with the French and their Indian allies by casting the French off the continent permanently. And the best way to attain that end, Pitt understood, was to send huge armies against the centers of French authority in America: their major forts that served as trading centers and supply depots for the Indians, as well as Quebec and Montreal. By defeating France's armies and seizing its two cities, the British would quash French power while cutting off Indian supplies and support. Victory lay, then, not through the Americanization of the British army, but through the Europeanization of warfare in America. Attaining that end required the arming of the American militia. Pitt not only subsidized the Colonial war effort, he also promised—and delivered—the guns to carry on that war. In 1757 he wrote all the governors in North America, stating that thousands of firearms were on their way from England but would take some time to arrive. Until then, he enjoined the governors to impress "all the serviceable arms that can be found within your Govt."[68]

Several governors made this effort, with mixed results. Lieutenant Governor James De Lancey of New York was able to purchase 2,250 firearms at high prices, bringing the total for his forces up to 5,310 muskets. One thousand of those muskets belonged to New York City, which supplied the guns only after being promised one thousand of the new muskets arriving from England. But Ordnance Officer James Furnis had to hire every gunsmith in New York City to repair the older weapons, and of that 5,310, he was able to salvage 2,500 muskets.[69]

When General James Abercromby arrived in late 1757 to lead the expedition against Canada planned for the following year, he found his American forces still largely unarmed. Pitt assured his commander that the government would be sending over twelve thousand guns immediately; until they arrived, Pitt advised Abercromby to search the army's magazines for extra guns and to "in Concert with the several Governors, give the most pressing Orders, that all the Serviceable Arms [are] to be Collected in the respective Provinces, [and] forthwith put into the best Condition."[70] But Abercromby discovered that the army's surplus of arms had been distributed among the colonials the previous year "because their own governments had been unable to equip them," and many of those guns had fallen into French hands with the surrender of Fort William Henry. Abercromby sent a circular to all the governors asking them to repair broken muskets and to search vigorously through their colonies for more firearms. Certainly all those who owned firearms should be required to contribute them for service.[71]

Despite the promise that every gun furnished would be replaced with a new Brown Bess once they arrived, Abercromby encountered resistance. Governor Thomas Pownall of Massachusetts insisted that the provinces were not responsible for supplying firearms and could not do so. No record of provincial firearms had been kept for some time, and there was a great deal of "Confusion and Collusion" over the fate of those arms that had been supplied in 1757. The guns not lost at Fort William Henry had been "suffered to become Private Property," for many Americans saw militia service primarily as an opportunity to acquire a gun. All the colonies could provide was men, not muskets, which should always be "Provided by the Crown." Governor Fitch of Connecticut was a bit less wordy; he simply demanded to know where he was supposed to find firearms for his troops.[72]

Governor John Reading of New Jersey claimed that his province possessed no firearms of its own and that few members of the militia owned guns, most of these being inoperable. Abercromby threw back the familiar image of American gun ownership: he was not "Satisfied with a bare assertion that No Arms are to be found Within Your Province, When at the same time it is known, almost to every one, that few, if any, of the People of the Continent are Without Arms." Yet by the end of May, only one hundred of the one thousand members of the New Jersey Regiment had muskets.[73]

Abercromby thought he was seeing every gun in the northern colonies, which was close to the truth. Since local militia officers and constables could confiscate a musket not offered for sale, surely he had lured out of hiding every firearm with his offer of double its value no matter what the gun's condition. It was not an impressive showing—roughly eleven thousand guns. The southern colonies were even worse off. Abercromby admitted to Pitt that the governors seemed to be correct—there were just not that many guns in America after all.[74] The evidence was all too clear when he gave orders to purchase all workable guns offered for sale. Governor Pownall was able to purchase 1,450 firearms for military use, many firearms taken home from British service the previous year, while most of the rest were extremely old. Thomas Hancock, acting as buyer for Abercromby, was able to buy another two hundred over three months. Pownall tried every venue to garner just a few more guns, failing to obtain the four hundred muskets seized from the Acadians in Nova Scotia before their deportation, and acquiring fifty guns captured from privateers. Nonetheless, Pownall, who was certainly doing his best to arm his militia, reported that just half of the province's seven thousand troops were now armed from all sources, including the twelve hundred (17 percent) carrying their own guns.[75] As it was, Pownall had to delay the movement of his troops until these various arms could be repaired. And that half of the Massachusetts force that still did not have guns were hardly pleased to be marching unarmed through territory subject to Indian attacks. Surely if they had owned guns, they would not have sacrificed their safety in this way just to prevent having to sell their musket to the British at a good price.[76]

Abercromby informed Pitt that the arms shortage in America crippled his effort to mobilize against the French: "I am sorry to tell you that I am under the greatest Difficulties imaginable for want of Arms; not only by Reason of the real Want, of them, but because the Provinces, knowing my Distress make a Handle of it, to retard their Troops from joining me, alledging that Men without Arms can be of no Service." He added that the guns "we have been able to get by Purchase at Boston & New York amount to a very inconsiderable Number." But then the British government had consistently discouraged the building of gun manufactories in America. Pitt responded to these arms shortages, which he discovered held in all the colonies, by rushing another eight thousand muskets to America the following year, more than had been sent in the entire last half of the seventeenth century.[77]

When Abercromby's forces finally began their march toward Canada, they moved reluctantly and slowly. It became evident not only that most of them did not own firearms, but also that many had never held one before. The records of several regiments indicate that their officers were still hunting furiously for muskets for troops even while they were marching to do battle with the French. Seventy of the hundred men from Middleton, Massachusetts, for instance, received their guns on the road.[78] As one historian noted, "Many provincials demonstrated complete ignorance concerning the handling of muskets as emphasized by the frequent firearms accidents recorded by observers." Even the better-trained Massachusetts militia units recorded incidents of soldiers shooting themselves, their officers, and "a girl milking" during target practice.[79] Amos Richardson of the Massachusetts Regiment reported that he had his first and only musket practice on July 4, 1758. "Tuesday, the forth Day . . . in the afternoon we all Had Leave to Shout off all ouer Guns: and we did. And there was a fine fiering of them for a spael: and some of ouer men Did Shut one of the Reglers Throu the Head which killed hem Daed."[80]

This particular campaign ended disastrously for the joint British-American force of six thousand regulars and nine thousand colonials. Montcalm's French troops repelled Abercromby's attack on Fort Carillon; Abercromby lost 1,600 regulars and 334 colonials before retreating. Everyone immediately set about trying to fix blame, whether because of the slowness of the Colonial volunteers or Abercromby's insistence on a frontal attack.[81] But that same summer a dramatic amphibious landing by British Regulars, with a bayonet charge under General Wolfe repulsing the French forces on the beach, led to the fall of Louisbourg. Indian resistance in the North collapsed later that year following the shipwreck of *L'Aigle,* carrying hundreds of arms for the French forces. Thereafter, the French were unable to supply their Indian allies with arms and ammunition. In the view of Canada's governor, Pierre-François de Rigaud, the Marquis de Vaudreuil, the end for the French came with this shipwreck, as no further supply ships were able to break the British blockade and bring much-needed gunpowder.[82]

But it was still necessary to defeat the French in battle. In 1758 Pitt selected General John Forbes for a new campaign against Fort Duquesne. It was an inspired choice. Honest and focused on his goal, Forbes worked well with his Colonial forces. When he found the Pennsylvania regiment still grossly under-armed, he logically asked the legislature to arm it with the guns sent over by the Crown. But the legislature, still smarting from their previous encounter with the governor over their sending guns to the frontier, felt that Forbes should ask the governor. Forbes worked patiently to overcome such political squabbles, and his force was soon armed with sufficient Brown Bess muskets. Faced with this well-armed and well-led force, the French burned Fort Duquesne and retreated. The Americans enjoyed a great victory without combat.[83] The following year General James Wolfe, a cruel man who had learned his craft at Culloden with Butcher Cumberland, personally led his forces in a bayonet charge against the French at Quebec. Though Wolfe died on the Plains of Abraham, the British triumphed, putting an end to the French empire in North America.[84]

The Indians proved more difficult to defeat than had the French. In December 1759 Governor William Lyttelton of South Carolina tried to bribe the Cherokee into submission with some muskets and a huge supply of gunpowder. He acknowledged that he had no choice, since his own militia was "altogether unfit" to defend the province.[85] The Cherokee, despite their lack of munitions, attacked the English settlers. Thus began a vicious war that saw the Cherokee attacking isolated settlers while the South Carolina troops ruthlessly killed Indian hostages. With the militia crumbling before the Cherokee, Lyttelton appealed to General Amherst for British Regulars. Amherst sent thirteen hundred Scottish troops against the Cherokee. These regulars indicated that they had indeed learned American ways, as they burned Indian villages and crops.

But the Cherokee eluded the regulars and carefully prepared an ambush. The regulars did not respond as the American militia had, by fleeing; instead they returned a volley of massed musketry, and it was the Cherokee who fled. The whole campaign claimed seventeen British lives and about fifty Cherokee. The British declared victory and returned to the coast.[86]

This success was outweighed by the disaster at Fort Loudoun in the summer of 1760, where one hundred regulars and an equal number of South Carolina militia were besieged for two months by the Cherokee. The English negotiated a surrender that left the Cherokee with half a ton of gunpowder and the English with the right to march home with their guns. But the Cherokee attacked the garrison once the English were in the open, killing thirty people and taking the rest prisoner.[87]

The English responded to this violation of the terms of surrender by marching another army of twenty-eight hundred regulars through Cherokee lands, where it burned fifteen towns and some fourteen hundred acres of crops. The Cherokee, again out of gunpowder, offered almost no resistance. For three years they had fought the English with their traditional weapons. In December the Cherokee, exhausted from the war and on the verge of starvation, agreed to peace. But as a final indication of their captivity to a culture of guns, they rejected the usual presents of clothing offered by the British and begged instead for gunpowder.[88]

Preachers among the Delaware spread the message that the Master of Life had become angry over Indian dependence on European goods, including guns. These Delaware ministers insisted that they needed to return to traditional ways to regain spiritual purity. Some, like Papoonan, delivered pacifist messages; others, like Neolin, called for a war of liberation against the English.[89]

The efforts of these Delaware prophets coincided in some ways with official British policy. General Jeffrey Amherst, as commander of all British forces in North America at the end of the Seven Years' War, wanted to put an end to the Indians' dependence on European armaments, though for other than spiritual reasons. He hoped that with the French removed, Britain could finally completely control the flow of armaments to the Indians. He therefore ordered an end to guns and gunpowder as gifts to the Indians, and to the trade of these munitions.[90]

By 1763 many eastern Indians had grown weary of their people's dependence on the English and joined Pontiac in his war to reclaim

Indian culture. And yet Pontiac used European weapons against the Europeans, so far as he was able. His forces captured seven English forts in May and June by hiding weapons within their clothing. These quick victories also gained Pontiac valuable caches of arms and ammunition. But Pontiac failed to take the largest western outposts, most particularly Detroit and Fort Pitt, as he lacked both the element of surprise and artillery. Even with a fresh supply of captured muskets and gunpowder, guns were not sufficient to take a fort; cannon or an extended siege leading to starvation were required. It is ironic, given the initial impetus of Pontiac's War to break free of European dependence, that Pontiac should have found himself so limited by reliance on muskets for victory. Further irony is evident at the Battle of Bushy Run, where Colonel Bouquet's relief force, bound for Fort Pitt, effected the traditional Indian trick of a faked retreat, drawing the attacking Indians into a perfectly set trap. That trap was sprung not with musket fire but with a well-executed bayonet charge. The Indians abandoned the field before this maneuver and Bouquet raised the siege of Fort Pitt.[91]

The secret of wilderness fighting was that it worked on an individual basis: small units engaged in hand-to-hand combat among the forests of North America. But large-unit encounters were another matter. Montcalm's defeat at Quebec in 1759, like Braddock's at Duquesne, made that evident. As Francis Jennings described the former battle, Montcalm ordered his troops to charge forth from their defenses against the British Regulars: "His wilderness fighters rushed forward in motley formation, formidable as individuals, disorganized as a mass. The British waited until their volley could take maximum effect, fired into the screaming mass, . . . then fixed bayonets and countercharged in an implacable, inexorably advancing line." The British won in fifteen minutes.[92]

The Myth Begins

In 1756 William Pitt attempted to bring the British militia system back to life. His first effort was defeated in the House of Lords, which found his conception of the militia dangerously democratic. Pitt, insisting that the militia would relieve the army of the need to defend England from invasion, tried again in 1757 and succeeded. Pitt's revived militia had no relation to that imagined by the Commonwealthmen; he did not plan to arm the public, only to train some of them to confront a possible French invasion. Those called up would be the poor, not property owners. Far from universal, the revived English militia was more a tax on the time of the poor, calling up between 5 percent and 8 percent of the qualified males.[93]

Despite its modest ambitions, Pitt's militia met opposition not only from the lords, but also from those who were supposed to fill the ranks. There was never much public enthusiasm for the militia, with opposition running from avoidance to riots. The government had to send twenty regiments into the field to quash these uprisings, expending the very resources they were trying to husband by reviving the militia. The Duke of Newcastle was delighted to report to a friend "that the militia goes down in very few counties; so I hope we shall soon have an end of that chimera."[94] Newcastle saw the militia not as the savior of liberty, but as a dire threat, "the ruin of our Constitution."[95] Newcastle was far from alone, as is indicated by the defeat in 1760 of a bill to extend militia organization to Scotland.[96] The government did its best to keep guns out of the hands of common people and did little to enforce the militia act, though some training and preparation were thought necessary. By the end of the war, twenty-eight thousand had enlisted in the militia but were never "tested in battle against regular troops," and the militia was not organized even on paper in every county in England until 1778. It was, in John Brewer's words, intended as the final "(somewhat flimsy) bulwark against foreign invasion. As such, it was the least important component of Britain's military effort" and vanished completely after Waterloo.[97]

The British militia, unlike that in the American colonies, was not perceived by the government as a tool for the maintenance of public order—that was the task of the military. The greatest peacetime source of violence within Britain were gangs of smugglers. These criminals usually armed themselves with pistols and were known to use them. On one memorable occasion in December 1740, one such gang did battle with government officials, killing a customs official and wounding two soldiers. The affair was a national scandal and the army was called out to crush the smugglers. Likewise, urban and rural riots were both met with regulars, as in the antimilitia riots of 1757. In 1766, faced with price riots around the nation, the army occupied sixty-eight British towns. With cause, the government continued to fear the militia it hoped to revive, and to rely on its standing army for internal security as well as external defense. And that military did not hesitate to use its guns, killing twenty-one civilians at Hexham in 1759 and twelve at the St. George's Fields massacre of 1768. There were no casualties among the soldiers in these encounters.[98]

Though most American colonists shared a similar ideology that could justify crowd action, they just did not have the same experiences of the militia, of crowds springing up in several locations at once, or of soldiers opening fire on civilians. There were almost no riots in the British North American colonies in the eighteenth century before the Stamp Act crisis of 1765. The Colonial militia met in an irregular fashion but had few tasks outside the South, where there were always a few members of the militia on regular duty as slave patrollers. Otherwise the militia maintained its slumber despite the Seven Years' War.

Those who did the fighting in America's eighteenth-century wars rarely fit the ideal of the universal militia put forth by the Commonwealthmen. One of the most astute students of the Colonial militia, Harold Selesky, has summarized its nature perfectly: "Many militiamen fancied themselves as soldiers because they could play on the parade ground without the slightest danger of actually being called to fight." The volunteers who joined the British in the war against the French and Indians tended, as in every war in the European world at that time, to be drawn from the lowest orders, what General James Abercromby called "the rif-raf of the Continent." Even George Washington admitted that most American volunteers enlisted out of desperation for the small bounties, often doing so several times in their poverty-stricken lives. It was so difficult to find volunteers other than the poor that Governor Thomas Fitch of Connecticut recklessly proposed enlisting French prisoners of war.[99]

Meanwhile, those who stood forth as exemplars of the idealized universal militia often made a mockery of soldiering. For instance, in 1762, "while the real soldiers were joining the expeditionary regiments, militiamen in both North Haven and Stratford held a 'mock Indian fight' at their annual musters in May." It seemed irrelevant to these men that "no militiamen had been asked to fight Indians for forty years," and the two musters descended into tragic farce in no time, with one soldier killed in North Haven, and another shot in the leg at Stratford, thus emphasizing "the average militiaman's lack of military skill and experience."[100]

Some historians have suggested that manliness in the Colonial period was defined by proficiency with a gun. If that were the case, then the practical evidence from the militia records would indicate that very few Colonial men worried about appearing manly.[101] More likely this is another case of historians reading current values into the past, for nothing in the literature of the period indicates a concern for gun ownership. Instead, the sword remained as the symbol of manly honor through the eighteenth century and was especially favored among British military officers, often to the annoyance of the provincial Americans.[102] It is a fact, however, that with the advent of the Seven Years' War, commanders of American forces found the vast majority of their troops not only unarmed but also unfamiliar with firearms. British officials had no choice but to supply thousands of guns to the colonists and to rely more than they initially hoped upon British Regulars to win the war.

And yet, with the war's end, many American colonists, mostly those who had played no role in the military effort, started a campaign idealizing the militia. Educated Americans seemed to have picked up fears of a standing army from the Commonwealthmen. Though they knew full well that they needed the British army to defeat the French and Indians, American successors to the Commonwealthmen argued that the militia served best to protect a nation's liberty and security. As one anonymous 1758 pamphlet put it, a free government's best defense lay in its own citizens: "every Freeman and every Freeholder should be a Soldier." In reality, of course, few of these citizens actually wanted to be soldiers. But as an ideal it was a powerful proclamation of the superior virtue and abilities of the common property-owning man. The author of this pamphlet, like so many other supporters of the militia, seemed to believe that an annual muster combined with a sense of duty would make civilians better soldiers than trained and paid regulars. It was an ideal that would plague the new United States in its military efforts for fifty years.[103]

Others were not so impressed with the militia after the Seven Years' War. Opponents of the institution found it a waste of time, while even supporters, such as Timothy Pickering, called for reform. Pickering's objections to the militia were class-based. The militia was filled with "Children, Apprentices and Men of Low Rank . . . [as] everyone who could pay a small Fine, thought it beneath them to appear on Muster." Another friend of the militia thought that the fault lay at the other end of the social spectrum, with officers hindering the proper development of a military spirit. For many officers, "the only end of giving them commissions was that they might be addressed by the title of captain."[104]

Surely, though, matters must have been different on the frontier, where the militia is imagined in a constant struggle to the death with savage Indians. Colonel Henry Bouquet well expressed the reality of the frontier-fighter myth. In 1764 he wrote a letter condemning the vicious cowardice of the Paxton Boys in killing unarmed and unresisting Indians who were seeking protection at the Lancaster jail. "After all the noise and bustle of our young men on the Frontiers, Every body expected that they would have offered their Services, as soldiers or Volunteers, for the defence of their Country, as being the fittest men for an Expedition against Indians, as the best way to wipe off the Reproaches cast upon them for the violences committed, and offered to defenceless Indians." But instead, they only sought employment in civilian jobs that would earn them a good income in safety. "Will not People say that they have found it easier to kill Indians in a Gaol, than to fight them fairly in the Woods?" But the former was the preferred method of frontier warfare for most settlers.[105]

The myth of the mighty militia, of "a people numerous and armed" ready to spring to battle against any foe, began almost immediately after the Seven Years' War. In fact the American militia had proven itself incapable of defeating even a single Indian tribe unless the Indians were Christian pacifists or the colonists were accompanied by hundreds of British Regulars and armed by the English government. Not that reality mattered. The myth would inspire many Americans in the belief that they could defeat anyone, even the powerful British Empire, in a few months. So potent was American virtue, it seems, that not even a supply of firearms was required. Fortunately, however, the British had left thousands of guns behind in America.

In many ways the Seven Years' War was a classic Colonial conflict. Each of the two superpowers attempted to get indigenous forces to fight their imperial battles for them. For the French, that meant the Indians; for the British, the European settlers of the Eastern coastal regions. Ultimately, neither power succeeded, and the contest was decided by the superior British Regulars and navy. Nonetheless, this war represented the first concerted effort by the government to arm the common citizens of North America. Both France and England poured resources, including firearms, into North America. Most guns ended up in the hands of the English Colonial governments, though individual subjects and a great many French and Indians also came to own these guns. England's army in the Seven Years' War grew to ninety-two thousand, its navy to seventy-five thousand personnel, its expenditures reaching £1 million a year in

North America. And, remarkably, at the war's end, the Crown reimbursed the colonies for half of the £3 million they expended on the war effort. Along the way, England had provided some £200,000 worth of ammunition and twenty thousand firearms to the provincials at no charge. The government would attempt to reclaim these guns in 1763, and then again in 1775.[106]

Chapter Six

A People Numerous
and Unarmed

Using rifles in war is certainly savage and cruel, but
the Americans may alledge in their defence the law
of absolute necessity, . . . for they, undisciplined and
unused to arms, are compelled to make use of every
advantage Providence has put in their power.

–Lewis Nicola, *A Treatise of Military Exercise Calculated
for the Use of Americans* (Philadelphia, 1776)

The Guns of Lexington

At four in the morning of April 19,
1775, a group of 130 men gathered
on Lexington Green, Massachusetts. This was the town's militia, under
the command of Captain John Parker. For the past year these men had
expected some sort of clash with the British and had devoted more
and more time to training. The government of Massachusetts had also
thoughtfully provided them with ammunition and firearms for those in
the unit who did not own a gun. These munitions were stored in the
meetinghouse. On this particular morning, a Boston silversmith, Paul
Revere, alerted the militia that British Regulars were on the march.

The men of the Lexington militia were uncertain what was expected
of them. After a brief discussion, many went home while others settled in
Buckman's Tavern. But just half an hour later, at four-thirty in the morning, they were again aroused by a frantic drumming announcing that the
British had entered the town. Many men ran to the meetinghouse for
arms and ammunition—40 of the 110 militia were unarmed—others
milled around the green while Parker attempted to get his men in line.
Six companies of British infantry, under the command of Major John

Pitcairn, entered the other side of the green. These troops settled into their formidable ranks, recently cleaned Brown Besses fixed with long bayonets at the ready. The two sides faced each other across an open field, much as military units in Europe would have done. Pitcairn called out: "Lay down your arms, you damned rebels, and disperse!" Staring at those two hundred bayonets just thirty feet away, Parker thought the dispersal part of the command a very good idea, and ordered his men to fall out.[1]

But Pitcairn wanted their guns. Someone fired that famous first shot, and then a British officer ordered his men to fire. Two platoons emptied their muskets at ten yards' distance, then charged with their bayonets, killing eight and wounding ten. Jonas Parker was the sole member of the militia to stand his ground and shoot; he was bayoneted and killed while reloading. Only six other Americans pulled their triggers while falling back; a British private was grazed by a bullet. The battle was over. The war had begun.[2]

The British government understood that the central weakness of America lay in its lack of armaments. This war's first battle came in response to General Thomas Gage's effort to seize the stockpiles of arms and ammunition scattered in various towns surrounding occupied Boston.[3] At one of these towns, Concord, Colonel Francis Smith's troops got their first taste of the American ability to fight back. Initially all the militia in Concord retreated before the regulars, but while searching the houses for munitions, some soldiers set fire, perhaps accidentally, to the courthouse and blacksmith shop. Convinced that the British were burning their town, the four hundred militiamen gathered from several towns moved toward North Bridge, where several companies of regulars stood at ease. Though not in formation, the British fired at the Americans, killing two. The militia was stunned. "God damn it!" someone shouted, "They're firing ball!" This shooting was entirely unexpected, and scores of Americans opened fire at some twenty feet, killing three and wounding nine British soldiers.[4]

Even at very close range, few of these shots hit the enemy, which was the norm in eighteenth-century warfare. Though British casualties were light, it was now the turn of the regulars to be stunned. The colonists had shot back! This was an unprecedented turn of events. In not so much a retreat as a panic, the British left Concord in a hurry, their officers trying to bring them into order. The militia stood around talking, wondering what it all meant.[5]

But other militia units lined the road back to Boston. Neither side in this long battle fought very well. Occasionally a unit of the British would trap some Americans and charge with their bayonets; at other times some rebels got off an effective volley and then retreated into the woods. But for the most part the British retreat was just a constant barrage of individual shots from each side, most missing, but enough hitting to disorganize the British command. One group of Americans hiding near the road fired a volley at Major Pitcairn from ten yards. All missed. They did, however, frighten Pitcairn's horse, which ran off, leaving the rider unhurt, though shaken, on the ground. One of the English soldiers wrote in his diary that "we were totally surrounded with such an incessant fire as it's impossible to conceive, our ammunition was likewise near expended."[6]

As Allen French wrote in 1925, "Every narrative of the fighting [at Lexington and Concord] speaks of the superior shooting of the provincials, with the easy assumption that as a body they were marksmen." Yet as French's careful study of the casualties suffered by the British on their retreat from Concord demonstrates, "superior as they may have been to the British, marksmen they were not." A total of 3,763 Americans are known to have participated in this long day of battle. Not all of them held guns, and not all fired, but among them they hit 273 British. Expert marksmanship requires training, good equipment, and a regular supply of ammunition for practice. These farmers rarely practiced, generally had no ammunition, and owned old muskets, not rifles, if they owned a gun at all. Guns were in such short supply that in the months before Lexington a number of efforts had been made to buy or steal muskets from British soldiers.[7]

At Lexington, General Hugh Percy waited with a thousand regulars and artillery, saving the troops under Colonel Francis Smith from complete disaster as the Americans moved back after a round from the cannon. At Menotomy, Massachusetts, the Americans fell on the British with a vengeance; the combat was almost entirely hand-to-hand, axes against bayonets. Regulars attacked unarmed civilians and looted houses; the retreat turned into a rampage. Most of the casualties occurred in this last encounter, before Percy was able to disengage and get his troops to safety behind British lines. The affair had been a disaster for the British, not only because they had suffered 273 casualties compared to 95 for the Americans, but also because a great many Americans now believed that common people could defeat British Regulars.[8] On occasion in the long war that followed, that assumption would prove correct, but generally only if those common people were well trained and well armed. The myth of a universally armed militia of marksmen, just crafted in the aftermath of the Seven Years' War, would take a terrible beating over the ensuing eight years.

The Path to Violence

In the decade from the Stamp Act crisis of 1765 until the confrontation at Lexington Green, Americans had many opportunities to exercise a violent spirit. White Americans had long demonstrated a capacity for violence against Indians and blacks, but, at least in the Colonial period, indicated a remarkable hesitance to kill one another. Individual acts of murder were almost unheard of; even the infamous southern duel appeared only after the Revolution. Political and social conflicts among whites almost never involved violence—until 1768. In that year English colonists exchanged deadly gunfire with other colonists for the first time. This alteration in cultural values may have resulted from the removal of the French threat that had long unified the English settlers, or from the presence of more guns left over from the Seven Years' War, or perhaps even from the increased Scots migration to the backcountry of the South, as some historians have suggested. But for whatever reason, the Regulator movement stands out as a unique event in Colonial America.

The South Carolina Regulators were mostly harmless. They hoped to reform the political and legal systems with an aim toward increasing law enforcement on the frontier. Their only confrontation with progovernment forces came on March 25, 1769, at the Musgrove Plantation on the Saluda River. Both sides refused to fight, and the battle was canceled with the agreement that "the name of Regulators should be abolished, and that, for the future, the law should take its course without opposition." If these were protorevolutionaries, as some scholars have maintained, they were awfully polite ones.[9]

The North Carolina Regulator movement came a lot closer to being a serious affair. The western part of the state was generally agreed to be rather lawless after the end of the Seven Years' War. Moravian bishop August Spangenberg stated that the region was held in thrall by "fist law," with criminals going unpunished and authority devolving to the strongest. The Regulators moved, by their lights, to bring order to the region when the government would not act. They particularly objected to the payment of taxes in specie, which they did not have. On April 8, 1768, in Orange County, Sheriff Tyree Harris seized a horse from a farmer who would not pay his taxes. A crowd of one hundred came to the county seat in Hillsborough to reclaim the horse, which they did, firing on the house of Edmund Fanning, a local official, in the process. Fanning called out the militia, but they refused to come.

Unlike the brutal Paxton Boys in Pennsylvania, the North Carolina Regulators were hardly intent on violence. In fact their most prominent leader, Herman Husband, was a pacifist who relied entirely on nonviolent methods of protest. When the local sheriff arrested Husband and another leader in the time-honored fashion of public dissent, a crowd of some seven hundred people surrounded the jail in Hillsborough. The sheriff also sought to avoid violence, and so released his prisoners. Governor Sir William Tryon responded to this outrage by calling out the province's eastern militia and marching on Hillsborough with this force of fourteen hundred to protect the superior court. They were met by thirty-seven hundred Regulators, who also sought to insure justice. The two groups waited patiently while negotiation resolved the various court cases to the satisfaction of both parties. Then the governor declared that order had been restored and sent the militia home.

The next spring Tryon marched west with a large force of coastal militia to crush the Regulators once and for all. Blocked at Salisbury, he retreated, again avoiding battle. Tryon was encouraged in this policy by the discovery that most of his gunpowder had been destroyed by a group of Regulators disguised as slaves.

But Tryon pressed on, confident that his forces were still better armed and organized—and they were certainly the former, having several cannon. On May 15 some Regulators beat two militia officers loyal to Tryon. The governor resolved to do battle and terminate this threat, confronting the Regulators near the Alamance River. Tryon's militia refused his order to fire several times, but once Tryon convinced them to start, it was difficult to get them to stop. For two hours the coastal troops and artillery exchanged fire with the Regulators, with little effect. Finally Tryon ordered a charge and chased the Regulators off, his forces then setting the nearby woods on fire, the flames claiming several lives. The coastal militia suffered ten deaths, the Regulators nine. Here was, by far, the single bloodiest fight between Colonial whites. Tryon did not want it repeated, and offered rewards for any guns captured from the Regulators. Many observers recognized that something changed at Alamance: white Americans now demonstrated a dangerous disposition to fire on one another. If the government supplied sufficient guns and powder, they would keep on firing until their ammunition was exhausted. There was more evidence of this attitude in the years ahead.[10]

Americans took to the streets often between 1765 and 1775, and showed themselves willing to commit acts of mob violence starting in 1770. Yet only in North Carolina did members of the crowd use firearms on their opponents. The American crowds, rural and urban, were capable of great cruelty—humiliating, beating, tarring and feathering their enemies—but they did not kill their white victims. In a series of violent street battles in New York between soldiers and artisans, many suffered contusions and bruises, but no one, soldier or civilian, thought to use a gun in these bitter struggles. In Boston, customs collector John Robinson beat patriot leader James Otis unconscious with a cane. The only incidence of gunfire in the long decade leading up to rebellion came in Boston in 1770, when British soldiers opened fire on an angry crowd and killed five men. The crowd did not return fire, no guns were produced, there were no lynch mobs, and the soldiers were brought before a court of law, defended by John Adams, and found innocent. The rule of law held in Colonial America until the very end, with those owning guns clearly hesitant to use them.[11]

There were traditional ways by which communities expressed their dissatisfaction with government policies, and traditional governmental responses to such protests. The Stamp Act crisis had been the perfect expression of that form of time-honored protest, with people gathering in large meetings, petitioning Parliament, even intimidating officials. None of that was new. Even the Boston Tea Party could be seen as just a more extravagant form of customary protest, though this destruction of property demonstrated greater flair than the norm. In England and America the next step tended to be a show of force, and occasionally the trial and execution of a few obvious and obnoxious leaders. But the British government feared that the distance was so great and the Americans so out of control that the normal political discourse had collapsed.[12] Parliament therefore did its best to limit the ability of the American colonies to move beyond the traditional forms of nonviolent protest by ordering an embargo on all firearms, lead, gunpowder, component parts, and accessories in October 1774. America was to remain safely unarmed.[13]

Nonetheless, as the likelihood of war with Great Britain increased in 1774, Americans took to reassuring themselves with stories of their military prowess. Critics such as Timothy Pickering Jr., commander of the

Salem, Massachusetts, militia, heaped scorn on the militia as a useless excuse to hold a party.[14] But Pickering and the other Cassandras were ignored; most white Americans saw the capability of their militia grow daily, while patriots told one another that they were all geniuses with fire-arms, even if they personally did not own one. In October 1774 John Andrews, a dapper Boston merchant of no known military experience, wrote a friend about a man in the town who hit a target three times after an entire company of regulars had missed. The man then bragged to an officer that "I have got a boy at home that will toss up an apple and shoot out all the seeds as its coming down." Andrews then reported of another "countryman" who was "near eight feet high" and the smallest in his fam-ily. One is free to believe both stories.[15]

It became almost a fad in the last year before the war to make outra-geous claims of shooting prowess, usually in reference to some unspecified frontiersmen. Richard Henry Lee boasted to his brother in February 1775 that he was unconcerned at the prospect of war, as the western part of Vir-ginia could furnish six thousand "Rifle Men that for their number make [the] most formidable light Infantry in the World." He insisted that every one of these men could hit an orange at two hundred yards, and "Every shot is Fatal." For some reason these six thousand marksmen did not materialize during the war. Just a few months earlier, Governor William Bull of South Carolina stated that his province's militia was interested solely in their uniforms and drinking in taverns.[16]

Even sensible people, like the young James Madison, were swept up by the mythology of shooting skill. Madison, a little man who devoted most of his time to reading, wrote his friend William Bradford that news of Lexington and Concord had excited an enthusiastic "Military Ardor" in Virginia, and he had himself taken to firing a gun. "The strength of this Colony," he wrote, "will lie chiefly in the rifle-men of the Upland Coun-ties. . . . You would be astonished at the perfection this art [of shooting] is brought to. The most inexpert hands rec[k]on it an indifferent shot to miss the bigness of a man's face at the distance of 100 Yards." Certainly shooting at faces was more practical than oranges, but Madison went on to claim that enemy troops would be mowed down at two hundred yards. His own excitement building, Madison added that officers could be hit at 250 yards. Within a few years, Madison would be sitting on the Virginia Council of State receiving petitions from unarmed frontiersmen begging for government arms and troops while frantically trying to find guns for "raw Militia ill armed, half Clad, ignorant of Disipline, & of every thing requisite," even for guarding prisoners of war.[17]

The experience of conducting the war destroyed the myth of the universal militia for Madison, as for most revolutionary leaders. In the aftermath of Concord, during the *"rage militaire,"* as Charles Royster has so aptly named it, thousands of Americans imagined that their virtue and the militia would crush the British and bring peace on American terms. This vision of "a people numerous and armed" has haunted the United States ever since, as many Americans still believe that throughout the colonies brave men took down their trusty rifles and rushed to fight the redcoats. Probably the major reason why the American Revolution lasted eight years, longer than any war in American history before Vietnam, was that when that brave patriot reached above the mantel, he pulled down a rusty, decaying, unusable musket (not a rifle), or found no gun there at all. The enthusiasm for the struggle was certainly there, but the guns were not. All efforts to require the militia to arm themselves flew in the face of reality. As one Pennsylvania militia colonel wrote the state's executive council, if they wanted his regiment to fulfill "their Duty in that part of the Law which orders them 'to provide Arms, &c.,'" then the state must send them guns.[18]

In that initial rush of enthusiasm, Timothy Pickering Jr. wrote the first American military manual. It is curious that a supposedly violent society in which all adult males owned and used firearms and belonged to the militia should not produce a manual of military procedures or a guide to gun use in its first 170 years. It is appropriate that this manual should have been written by a critic of the militia. Pickering's *Easy Plan of Discipline for a Militia* drew upon English models, but without the excess formality, or what he called the "trappings (as well as tricks) of the parade," and the brutality of European punishments. Pickering's error, as Royster has pointed out, was in calling his plan "Easy." There was nothing easy about training men unused to combat or firearms in the discipline required for war.[19]

Some governments made an effort to back their enthusiasm for the approaching war with the armaments necessary to fight it; most waited until the war had started. Militia records indicate that the colonies did not possess sufficient arms for any sort of sustained conflict, as the more astute patriot leaders recognized.[20] Maryland's 1768 inventory of arms counted 200 muskets, 86 carbines, and 35 pistols in usable condition; 442 muskets "very rusty" with broken or no locks; 104 carbines "mostly without locks, and not worth repairing"; 9 pistols with broken locks; and 262 swords. The Colonial government collected these arms and stored them above the conference chamber to prevent further decay.[21] In 1775 the Virginia powder magazine in Williamsburg, which contained most of the guns in the province, held 108 new muskets without locks; 157 trading guns; 527 "old muskets in various states of disrepair"; 1,500 cutlasses; 150 old pistols, "some without locks"; and "a lot of gunpowder in poor condition." The state armorer was able to repair 342 of these muskets.[22] With such armaments did the Americans plan to face the most powerful nation in the world. It was no wonder that in April 1775 John Murray, the Earl of Dunmore, Virginia's governor, thought he could incapacitate the Virginia militia simply by removing those muskets and the powder from the Williamsburg arsenal to a British ship, the *Fowey*. Dunmore at least appreciated that the militia depended on government arms.[23]

There was a militia revival in the year before the beginning of the war, but it was inconsistent, unfocused, and largely confined to New England.[24] In 1772 half the registered members of the North Carolina militia did not appear for muster; the government did not try again until 1775.[25] South Carolina's government, which had not ordered a muster since 1771, recommended in January 1775 that all those eligible for militia service should learn how to use guns, and meet with their local companies once a month. It was a startling admission that at least a large number of the province's citizens were unfamiliar with firearms. But when a member of the legislature proposed that the government purchase "a large quantity of stands of arms to be distributed among the poor people throughout this colony," the measure was tabled without discussion.[26]

With British troops actually in their midst, the New England colonies began preparing for a military showdown as early as October 1774. That month the Massachusetts Provincial Congress voted to purchase £20,000 worth of guns and ammunition, as well as to reorganize their militia for regular service.[27] In December 1774 John Sullivan led a raid on Fort William Mary at New Castle, New Hampshire, seizing its entire supply of arms and gunpowder. (This would be the same gunpowder used at Bunker Hill six months later, and there would not be enough.) The Massachusetts Provincial Congress authorized the seizure of all British munitions in the colony, and, recognizing their shortage of firearms, "do recommend the making of gun-locks." Many towns followed the example of Westboro, where the town meeting voted to appoint a committee to acquire ten half-barrels of powder and "12 good fire arms with bayonets and Sixty Cartridge Boxes & 60 hatchets" for use by the town militia "as soon as possible." Towns drew up lists of who was to receive a gun from the town stores and how much powder and bullets in case of alarm.[28] Massachusetts conducted a very thorough census of arms, finding that there were 21,549 guns in the province of some 250,000 people. General Gage succeeded in capturing or expropriating 1,778 of these in the immediate aftermath of the Concord campaign. The colony went to war against the British Empire with 19,771 guns.[29]

The Connecticut assembly hoped to improve the quality of their militia by ordering every company to inspect and repair all firearms and to hold twelve half-day training musters before May 1775.[30] Some citizens were more enthusiastic about these preparations than others, and most companies held only one or two musters by April. One witness to the Marblehead muster at the beginning of 1775 reported that "the regiment did not fire a single volley, nor waste a kernel of powder." British ensign Henry De Berniere witnessed one of these musters in Framingham, describing a speech by their commander, which followed the military wisdom of the day in recommending "to charge us cooly, and wait for our fire." But they did not practice such things. They only marched about for a few minutes, "drank until nine o'clock, and then returned to their respective homes full of pot-valour."[31]

When news of Lexington reached New Haven, Benedict Arnold inspected his troops and found them largely unarmed. He threatened to break into the town arsenal in order to arm his men, but the town's selectmen relented and opened the doors to his militia, with Arnold supervising the distribution of Brown Besses. Of Connecticut's twenty-six thousand militia, four thousand (15 percent) responded to the Lexington alarm. Most observers considered this an impressive display of enthusiasm. Half these men served less than a week.[32]

Connecticut and Massachusetts were the colonies best prepared for the conflict, having carefully stored their guns after the Seven Years' War. Yet, as Arnold's experience demonstrated, even these colonies faced a shortage of firearms from the very first day of the conflict. Most of the new states followed the practice from the Seven Years' War of awarding ten shillings to any volunteer who brought his own gun, threatening to confiscate those guns that were not offered up for service. And just as in the Seven Years' War, the various governments quickly discovered that most members of their militias did not own guns.[33]

The equipment lists of individual companies reveal this shortage. Some towns were rather well-off. For instance, after its recent purchases, Westboro, Massachusetts, owned sufficient arms for 80 percent of its militia. The norm, even in New England, was a far lower percentage. At the beginning of the war the seventy-two men of the Charlestown, New Hampshire, militia owned thirty guns of various kinds, but only ten ramrods, an absolute necessity for loading a musket. They also owned four swords and nine bayonets. Only seventeen of their number owned a flint, twenty-four owned some gunpowder, and eighteen had some bullets. Put another way, there were enough guns for 42 percent of the Charlestown militia, but less than one-fourth had everything needed to actually fire a gun.[34]

There was a status component to gun ownership, in that officers almost always owned guns, while enlisted men were less likely to hold a gun, from whatever source. In the ten companies of Colonel Ebenezar Learned's Massachusetts regiment "at the end of the campaign of 1775," eleven of the thirty-one officers (35 percent) and 127 of the 494 enlisted men (26 percent) possessed guns.[35]

These limitations in American armaments became evident at the heroic stand on Breed's Hill in June 1775. American volunteers lived up to the best image of the militia as they withstood two assaults by British Regulars, firing rough volleys at close range, and giving way to British bayonets only on the third attack, after they had run out of ammunition. Even the vain Lord Percy had to admit that the Americans provided the British "a very obstinate engagement," inflicting such casualties that "our army is [now] so small that we cannot even afford a victory."[36] Americans looked at the battle and saw that their militia was not that bad after all. Thomas Jefferson voiced what later became the standard view when he ascribed the victory "to our superiority in taking aim when we fire; every soldier in our army having been intimate with his gun from infancy." He proclaimed that a "want of discipline" was irrelevant beside "native courage and a cordial tho' governable animation in the cause." Those who actually knew something of warfare were not so certain.[37]

Many knowledgeable British officials knew that the American colonies did not have the resources to resist the British army, and they acted on that reasonable perspective. The British thought themselves justified in operating in the traditional manner by responding to accelerating resistance with military force. Even after the Battle of Bunker Hill, General John Burgoyne wrote that "I believe in most states of the world as well as in our own, that respect, and control, and subordination of government . . . depend in great measure upon the idea that trained troops are invincible against any numbers of any position of undisciplined rabble; and this idea was a little in suspense since the 19th of April." Between this ideological commitment and the poor showing of Colonial militia in the Seven Years' War, it is little wonder that General Thomas Gage should have felt such shock in the summer of 1775: "These People Shew a Spirit and Conduct against us, they never shewed against the French, and every body had Judged of them from their former Appearance, and behaviour . . . which has led many into great mistakes."[38]

It is certainly true that thousands of Americans rushed forth to confront the British Empire in 1775, but they showed up for service largely empty-handed. Not surprisingly, volunteers expected the new government of the United Colonies to supply them with firearms, as was the norm, then and now. Over the next eight years, virtually every militia muster and every officer's report on the question of armaments presented the same complaint: their soldiers needed guns and training in their use. Congress filled the gap by turning to Europe, either by buying firearms from the French and Dutch, or by capturing them from British troops. George Washington and the other leaders of the Revolutionary struggle learned a valuable lesson from the simple fact that 90 percent of the firearms used by the Americans in the Revolution came from Europe during the years of war.

Arming the Revolution

The American colonies began the Revolution with more weapons than they had possessed at any time in their history. Most of the guns in private and public hands came from the twenty thousand Brown Besses supplied by the British government during the Seven Years' War. In addition, some of the wealthier Americans, intent on acting the part of English gentlemen, purchased finely made firearms directly from Europe. For instance, in 1767 George Washington ordered a "Handsome fowling piece" for his stepson from the London gunsmith John Brazier. This was a gun fit for the country gentry, having "fine silver Mountg, with . . . Walnut Stock, barrel blewed with a Silver Sight, . . . sliding bolts," and an attractive carrying case; all for £8, 8s—the equivalent of two years' wages for an artisan.[39]

The early 1770s also witnessed a sudden influx of trained gunsmiths, including several from Germany, who hoped to find a market for their skills. The number of gunsmiths in America doubled in the decade prior to the Revolution, convincing some leaders that these gunmakers could supply all the weapons needed in the conflict with Great Britain. But such judgments seriously miscalculated the productivity of individual gun-smiths who were unable to make locks, which continued to be imported from England.[40]

Initially Americans acted on their own publicity, putting faith in American gunmakers. In March 1776 the Pennsylvania Committee of Safety commissioned William Henry to arrange for the production of two hundred muskets in supposedly gun-rich Lancaster County, which one historian has labeled "the Arsenal of America." Though Lancaster County had more gunsmiths than any area in the United States, it took eighteen months to produce those two hundred muskets. Just as Henry, now the commissary of Lancaster County, was finishing this order, Richard Henry Lee wrote to request that he "collect" five hundred mus-kets for the Virginia militia, which were largely unarmed in 1777. "As these are good men, they ought to have good arms." But Henry could do nothing to help Virginia. All local supplies were exhausted.[41]

Ethan Allen had an easy answer to the problem of acquiring guns: take them. Allen was the leader of a group of frontier farmers calling themselves the Green Mountain Boys who contested New York's claim to their land. Owning few guns, and having almost no access to gunpowder, they had maintained their struggle for seven years through bluff and double-talk. But with the news of Lexington, they understood that they faced a far more formidable foe in the British army, as well as a major opportunity at Fort Ticonderoga. On the morning of May 10, 1775, Allen led eighty-five of his Green Mountain Boys across Lake Champlain, hop-ing to take the fort by surprise. With only twenty muskets among his troops, it was his only chance. But the British garrison did not know that there was a war on, and Allen's forces rushed in, seized the neatly stacked muskets of the regulars, and demanded the surrender of the shocked and confused commander. The Green Mountain Boys found themselves in possession of one hundred cannon and several hundred muskets. It was like Christmas for Revolutionaries.[42]

The amazing sequel to this sudden arming of the settlers of the north-ern frontier was that Congress wanted Ethan Allen to give it all back. They sent an official apology to the Canadian people, regretting this hasty attack on Ticonderoga, promising that the United Colonies had no intention of troubling Canada, and ordered Allen to move all the military stores to a safe repository in expectation of a peaceful settlement of their spat with Britain. Allen thought Congress collectively insane. Rejecting these orders, he warned that "it is bad policy to fear the resentment of an enemy." Americans were now at war with Great Britain, and they needed these guns. Congress wisely let the issue die.[43]

Though Congress initially hesitated, most colonies followed Allen's example, seizing whatever British arms and ammunition they could.[44] As the conflict with England escalated, leaders at every level realized just how unprepared the United Colonies were for war. All the legislatures and conventions made the effort to support local gun and gunpowder production, granting every sort of incentive and subsidy available to them, pursuing every path, no matter how trivial, in acquiring weapons for their troops. Searches were made of all possible locations where even a single gun or container of powder may have been stored. And Revolutionary agents scoured the countryside, seeking guns in any condition for repair. These efforts were born of desperation, as soldiers were sent off to war without weapons. Nearly every page of the military records of Virginia contains some reference to the colony purchasing or renting a single gun, or even purchasing individual parts such as gun locks. There was the occasional windfall, as when Captain John Manly captured the British ship *Nancy* with more than two thousand stands of arms aboard in November 1775. But, as the account of stores kept by Washington's new Continental army outside Boston confirms, the Americans had to rely on dozens of shipments of individual guns and half-barrels of powder for use by the army, including a small chest of powder from Ezra Ripley, "Colledge Student." It was an amazing amount of trouble to go to, locating and buying these guns and parts one by one, but the state had no choice. After two years of effort, Virginia collected 3,325 muskets and 2,098 rifles, almost all of which required immediate repair.[45]

Faced with the need to fix nearly every gun they acquired, the legislatures brought their coercive power to bear in support of gun repair and production. They expropriated the labor of every type of smith, setting prices and requiring their acceptance as a patriotic duty. Connecticut flatly declared its authority to require "any and every such gun smith . . . to make arms for this State," while ordering all apprentices and journeymen smiths to continue with their masters for the war's duration, forbidding them from enlisting in the army, so vital was their undeveloped skill.

The Pennsylvania legislature threatened to blacklist gunsmiths who refused state contracts "as enemies to their country," and to seize their tools. Congress even specified the nature of the gunsmith's work, instructing them to concentrate their efforts on muskets and not waste their time making the more expensive rifles that soldiers found difficult to use.[46]

Individual commanders often excercised the same authority. In 1777 a company of Virginia soldiers under Captain John Henry "marched with their arms" into the house of gunsmith Johann Messerschmidt in Lancaster and ordered him to repair their guns, none of which was fit for service. For the next three weeks Messerschmidt "repaired all the arms of the Virginia Company," which kept "a guard . . . around the House and Gunshop" to insure that the gunsmith did not run off. The Pennsylvania government drafted fifty artisans from clockmakers to goldsmiths to work as gunsmiths for the state. One of these, blacksmith Jonathan Carson, received all 250 rifles from the public stores for repair to "arm all the Rangers that will be got—from what I can learn there is about sixty of them Enlisted." Carson reported that these rifles were "in very bad order, most of them wants Locks, & a great many Stocks & Locks." Like so many other gunsmiths, he did the best he could under difficult circumstances, but there were too few parts, tools, and qualified workers available, and the end product was often dreadful. For instance, in February 1776 Maryland's inspector tested seventy-two muskets from the shop of Baltimore's leading gunsmith, Peter Lydig. Eight of them promptly burst. In May the inspector tested twenty-eight muskets acquired from a local gunsmith and declared them "vile trash." Only eight "can be made use of," he reported, "and it is quite out of my power to repair or make these arms fit for use." He thought the gunsmith was "culpable" of fraud.[47]

The frontier regions were worst hit by this scarcity of firearms. In 1779 Colonel Archibald Lochry reported that there were 239 guns in Westmoreland County, Pennsylvania, only 27 of which were privately owned. There were also some "Old English muskets . . . belonging to this State . . . [that] are all Unfit for Service." Militia commanders in the other frontier counties reported similar crises: fifty or sixty muskets at most in Bordenstown; half the militia unarmed and no flints at Fort Augusta; one hundred privately owned and fourteen public arms at Allentown; the six hundred men of Chester County had fifty public arms and twenty privately owned guns "much out of repair"; the company at Pittsburgh had guns, "but those we have are the [refuse] of the Military Store at fort Pitt." A year later Colonel Lochry wrote again to inform the governor that

"What few arms we have still left are so out of repair that they are almost useless, and it is out of my power to get them repaired in this quarter." As Lochry observed, the frontier was not home to gunsmiths, most of whom found that only the few American cities provided sufficient custom to keep them in business. Bedford County in western Pennsylvania had only a single gunsmith, Jacob Saylor, during the Revolution, and he had no assistant. The Committee of Safety for northwestern Virginia met at Catfish Camp in 1777 to recruit a smith "for the purpose of Repairing Guns, Makeing Tommehocks, Scalping Knives, &c."[48]

These shortages naturally had an impact on military events. Benedict Arnold held up his attack on Quebec until Captain Hanchet and his six blacksmiths could make more pikes. A council of officers ordered that the attack be launched "as soon as the men are well equip'd with good arms, Spears, hatchets, . . . &c." The delay cost seven weeks, time enough for the British to strengthen their defenses.[49] In 1777 Washington, longing to strike at the British army marching toward Philadelphia, had to postpone his attack several times as his troops' arms "were much impaired" and their ammunition "intirely ruined" by incompetent storage. Reluctantly Washington withdrew "the Army to some place of security untill the Arms could be repaired and the Ammunition recruited."[50]

The shortage of arms led to a competition for elusive supplies between the army and the various state governments. Maryland in 1776 tried to handle both through an equitable division of scarce resources. The militia expected the state to supply arms; thus the Maryland Council of Safety issued forty-five guns to a company of sixty-six men, "which is all we can engage for" as they also had a commitment to arm the state's Continental brigade. More typical was the experience of the Pennsylvanian lieutenant Enos Reeves, whose company had only ten guns for thirty-three men in 1782. Reeves "apply'd to Gov. Burke [of North Carolina] for arms, who denied me, giving as a reason that the arms belonged to the state, therefore he could not give them to Continental Troops, rather letting me and my men run the chance of being captured."[51]

Those who served in the American cause made use of every kind of weapon they could obtain. In July 1775 the Pennsylvania Committee of Safety instructed their president, Benjamin Franklin, who promoted bows as far superior to muskets, "to procure a model of a pike" for use by their troops. The committee noted that "It has been regretted by some great soldiers, particularly by Marshal Saxe, that the use of pikes was ever laid aside, and many of the experienced officers of the present time agree with him . . . that it would be very advantageous in our modern wars to resume that weapon." Among the advantages of the pike, they noted, was that "its length reaching beyond the bayonet" negated the charge of any other forces. But the real issue was a lack of an alternative because of the shortage of guns: "At this time therefore when the spirit of our people supplies more men than we can furnish with firearms, a deficiency which all the industry of our ingenious gunsmiths cannot suddenly supply, and our enemies having, at the same time they were about to send regular armies against undisciplined and half armed farmers and tradesmen . . . prevailed on the other powers of Europe not to sell us any arms or ammunition." Thus the perceived need for pikes, which, in the committee's words, "Every smith can make."[52]

By 1776 smiths of every kind were swamped with work, and could not even meet the demands for spears and pikes. In September of that year, Maryland ordered 1,000 pikes for use by its troops but rated only 50 of the first 335 they received "pretty good," while 250 "are good for nothing." Virginia emptied out every storehouse in the state, issuing its last guns, swords, and spears—many of each from the seventeenth century—and still found a large proportion of its force unarmed. Massachusetts ordered its blacksmiths "to work on the sabbath" making spears. Washington complained that the spears being made for his troops were "ridiculously short and light, and can answer no sort of purpose," demanding longer and heavier ones. Washington was particularly insistent that his officers carry pikes or spears, as "firearms, when made use of, withdrawing their attention too much from their men . . . has a very awkward and unofficer-like appearance."[53] Wanting alternatives, Americans turned to polearms to, in Washington's words, "supply the defect of arms" right through the end of the war.[54]

Washington wrote John Hancock in early 1776 that "I have tried every Method I Coud think of to procure Arms for our Men, they realy are not to be had in these Governments." That same day he sent another letter to Hancock adding that when he did get guns for the militia, they proved "careless of their Arms."[55] So many of the guns the army received were in such poor shape as to be useless, and there were too few smiths to aid in their repair. The Continental forces in New York found that there was "not a sufficient number of Armourers at Albany to repair" their guns. Enormously frustrated, Washington worked patiently with every possible source, pursuing every avenue in his search for guns. These extensive endeavors did pay off, in the short run, as enough guns were discovered or seized to arm three-quarters of Washington's troops by the summer of 1776, a 50 percent increase in just six months. Of course that meant that one-fourth of those serving in the Continental army still lacked guns.[56]

Even before declaring independence, Congress acknowledged that its "first priority was the importation and manufacture of arms and ammunition." As Massachusetts representative Robert Treat Paine declared, "Salt petre, Sulphur, lead, cannon, musketts, like our dayly bread should never be out of our attention."[57] And yet, congressional efforts were, as Wayne Carp has noted, "notably disorganized." The several states were responsible for supplying most of the necessities of the Continental army, but not guns, for Congress understood that they had no way of getting any. Congress essentially authorized any merchant and any state to go hunting for firearms, but could find no way to alter the basic equation of the United States' need to import most of its munitions from overseas.[58]

Domestic production of firearms remained almost nonexistent, though gunpowder production increased to one-third of all that used by American forces by 1777—a year of terrible shortages in powder. There was no powder mill in the colonies until 1675, when Massachusetts established an experimental one under the management of Walter Everenden. This mill had done fairly well, and it was the only powder mill to prosper in Colonial America. But it ceased production in 1750, leaving the colonies entirely dependent on Europe for gunpowder.[59] From the first year of the Revolution, Americans struggled to make their own gunpowder. Instruction books appeared and state governments offered major incentives. Several of these efforts succeeded, especially in Pennsylvania. By the end of the war, an estimated two hundred thousand pounds of gunpowder had been produced in the United States, compared with 1.5 million pounds imported from France and the Netherlands. But much of what the Americans made was terrible, and Congress launched an investigation into the inferior powder purchased from Oswell Eve, which had endangered the lives of many Americans. The fact that Americans went from producing nearly zero to fifty thousand pounds of powder per year represents a remarkable accomplishment. The colonies enjoyed no such luck with firearms.[60]

A big part of the problem was resources. Despite the constant efforts of Colonial governments to build iron foundries, iron was mostly imported from England. Only fifteen hundred tons of iron had been produced in seventeenth-century English North America. Despite the Iron

Act of 1750, by which Parliament sought to stifle the development of all metal trades in America, production levels increased considerably in the decade before the Revolution, but it was hardly sufficient for a large gun manufactory. It was only after the Revolution that enough iron would be produced to sustain such an endeavor.[61]

Putting aside the lack of iron and gunsmiths able to make gun locks, several states pursued arms manufacture during the Revolution. Even though their goals were modest, most of these efforts collapsed within a year. Pennsylvania's target for 1776 would have produced 7,716 muskets, which M. L. Brown labels "a singularly unimpressive figure."[62] But the state gunsmiths never came anywhere near that target, making less than one thousand guns per year. James Pollock and Samuel Laird of Carlisle, Pennsylvania, wrote Franklin in 1776 that they were having trouble finding gun locks, "which are not to be purchased at any rate." The state abandoned its Philadelphia gun factory at the end of 1778, shifting its efforts to its gun repair shops in Allentown, Carlisle, and Reading. Other efforts to establish gunshops failed as the state concentrated on repairs and banned the sale of armaments beyond its borders in an effort to reserve firearms for the militia.[63]

Massachusetts was somewhat more successful. In June 1775 a special committee of the Provincial Congress reported that there were thirteen smiths and armorers in the state capable of repairing firearms, which they thought "sufficient" for current needs. But they added two significant caveats: all of these smiths are "in want of tools and stock," and all but one "are very imperfect in the business they profess." The exception, Richard Falley, "is a complete master," and the committee recommended his appointment as official state armorer. The Provincial Congress ignored that recommendation, but it did order that each state regiment appoint an armorer, no matter how "imperfect in the business they profess." Within a few months the Committee of Safety was complaining "that the armorers frequently deliver the arms out of their shops unfit for service, and delay the work unnecessarily; in order to prevent occasion for such complaints in future." Falley became armorer for Massachusetts's 18th Regiment and did quite well, advising the council on the musket standards set in November 1775. But Falley and the other smiths attempted only to repair firearms. They did not actually make any.[64]

In July 1775 the Virginia legislature licensed the Virginia State Gun Factory. The director was Washington's brother-in-law, Fielding Lewis. A year later, when Lewis wrote Washington that "Our Manufactory has not yet made one Musquet, the Hands have been imployed in repairing the old Gunns from the Magazeen . . . and repairing the Gunns belonging to the several Companys that have passed thro' this Town," the Virginia council requested that the Hunter Iron Works (right across the river from the Virginia State Gun Factory) enter the gunmaking business. Production from both sources remained minor, the Hunter works delivering eighty muskets to the Continental forces, and both shops had enormous trouble finding trained workers. James Hunter wrote Governor Jefferson at the beginning of 1781 that "it is not in my power to repair any of the arms sent me" by the state, as "my workmen in that branch having all left me, and the manufactory of small arms being, of consequence, discontinued." At its peak in 1782, the Virginia State Gun Factory employed nineteen workers, all of whom repaired firearms. Virginia's commissioner of war thought "the great expence the state has been run to and the small advantage we receive from the factory" justified reconsidering its continued operation. The governor's council agreed and closed the factory in 1783.[65]

Stymied at establishing their own gunshops, the state governments entered into contracts with individual gunsmiths, offering subsidies to artisans who would shift over to arms production. The Rhode Island legislature, not wanting to give money directly to anyone, voted to allow Jeremiah Hopkins to conduct a lottery to raise the $200 he needed to buy gunsmith's tools. Gilbert Forbes took one such advance from the New York Council of Safety, and then disappeared. Richard Smith of Salisbury, Connecticut, played the same scurvy trick on his legislature and was tried for treason. Henry Watkeys appears to have been entirely sincere when he took New York's money in June 1775, but discovered that making guns was much harder than he had initially suspected. Sixteen months later, after producing only six inferior gun barrels, he informed the New York legislature he was "poor and now removed to Brunswick in Jersey."[66]

Learning caution from such incidents, other states offered bounties to gunsmiths who met repair or production goals, safe in the knowledge that they almost never had to pay out these public funds. Most efforts to encourage gunmaking ended like those in Virginia, with the gunsmiths lacking the correct tools, unable to purchase locks—which they could not make themselves—or to find qualified workers, and finally begging the legislature for more money in order to get started. In desperate efforts to encourage arms production, state governments threw good money after bad, and they even agreed to locate and supply all the parts necessary for the manufacture of guns, often to no effect. Maryland found the materials for 110 muskets to be made by Nicholas White and Christopher Edelin of Frederick but never saw the finished product. Virginia had better luck with Peter Light, who received a contract and advance for two hundred muskets in 1776. Three years later he turned over thirty guns to the state.[67]

State officials were surprised to learn that few gunsmiths owned all the tools needed to make a complete musket and usually had knowledge of only one specific aspect of gun repair. In 1781 a frustrated Governor Thomas Jefferson ordered that "a proper person" be sent "out to collect gunsmiths," while New York's legislature sent an agent to England to recruit gunsmiths, though neither effort had any known success. Virginia's congressional delegation made concerted efforts to locate experienced gunsmiths to repair their state's firearms, only to find themselves competing with similar efforts from their colleagues. Other states came to terms with the reality of the gun trade and entered into deals such as that Maryland made with Richard Bond, whose "Gun Factory" made gun barrels—and nothing else.[68]

While state support was forthcoming, there were very few successful gunmakers. The only southern example was the team of Adam Stephen and Anthony Noble, who ran a factory in Martinsburg, Virginia, employing thirty men and capable of making as many as eighteen muskets in a single week. If they maintained that rate, they could have armed the Virginia militia in twenty-one years, assuming no gun loss or population growth. More typical were the gunsmiths who never made a single musket, like Francis Gideon of Virginia, who ended the war with "a number of public Arms" in his house still waiting to be repaired after more than a year. North Carolina established the Public Gun Factory on Black River, which produced one hundred rifles during the war and then closed shop. Maryland's gun factory never even began operation, and the legislature was reduced to buying ten rifles from a Fredericksburg riflesmith, who took five years to deliver. New Jersey's State Gun Factory closed in December 1776, a few weeks after its completion. All these frantic efforts to make guns were abandoned with the Treaty of Paris in 1783.[69]

Every contemporary knew that the Americans of 1775 were "half armed farmers and tradesmen." Every legislative body in North America entered a desperate search for any and all forms of weapons, including guns. Congress and most of the states disarmed all "disaffected persons" without recompense, and gave their arms to the Continental army.[70] But there were not enough guns among the disaffected persons, or loyalists, as they called themselves. Faced with fielding forces armed mostly with spears, clubs, and old muskets, Congress finally acted in early 1776, and sent first Silas Deane, and then Benjamin Franklin and Arthur Lee, to Paris to begin arranging the purchase of firearms from France and the Netherlands. Thanks to their efforts, the new United States received one hundred thousand French and Dutch muskets during the War for Independence. The first shipment of twelve thousand Charleville Model 1763 muskets arrived in Portsmouth, New Hampshire, in March 1777. Shortly after that eleven thousand muskets arrived in Philadelphia. These guns came just in time, as the Continental army was "exceedingly deficient" in guns, and state after state discovered at the beginning of 1777 that there were no guns left to distribute to their troops. Nathanael Greene told Washington that "Nothing could have happened more seasonable" than the arrival of these muskets, "as the Congress have none in Store."[71]

Having acquired the necessary arms, the next question was, Who was to bear them? Many leaders believed their own prewar rhetoric that the militia could win the war; others found that notion laughable.[72] Drawing from their experience of the first three years of the war, the majority of those who served in Congress joined Washington in favoring a well-armed professional army, trained in the use of firearms and willing and able to use them—though Congress rarely backed words with money. Even when the nation's very security was at stake, the militia just did not turn out when ordered. One Pennsylvania statute recognized the problem: "And whereas many militia men by removing from one battalion or company to another, find means to escape their tour of duty. . . ." Even late in the war, after long experience with many humiliations, the militia remained largely an abstraction. And even its strongest proponent, General Charles Lee, rejected the idea of the militia fighting British Regulars in any but partisan actions. One junior officer in the Continental army described the North Carolina militia in 1782 as "under no kind of order, they may appear or let it alone." That was one of the nicest things said about the militia.[73]

And if the militia did turn up, they were, in the opinion of the best-informed sources, largely useless. In 1776 Richard Henry Lee—the same man who had bragged of those unconquerable six thousand frontier riflemen a year earlier—wrote that the Continental army was repeatedly crippled by the "large frequent desertions of the militia." Washington, in Dec

Higginbotham's words, had long appreciated that "Militia training had always fluctuated between being haphazard and being nonexistent."[74] In his first evaluation of the militia during the war, Washington wrote John Hancock "that no Dependence can be put on the Militia for a continuance in Camp, or Regularity and Discipline during the short time they may stay." The job of the American, like the English, militia must be the maintenance of internal security, not the protection of the state.[75] Washington was pleasantly surprised when the New England assemblies, embarrassed by the unreliability of their militia, redoubled their efforts to supply troops for the Continental army. But even then, he found little to recommend the militia, writing the New England governors that the militia were good for only "a few days, as they soon get tired, grow impatient, ungovernable, and of course leave the Service." Washington asked the obvious question: "What will be the consequence, then, If the greatest part of the Army is to be composed of such men?"[76]

Washington discovered the answer to that question in 1776, as his army melted away. He blamed the militia, whose "example has Infected" the rest of the army. By the time of the Long Island campaign, Washington was writing Hancock that "the Militia instead of calling forth their utmost efforts to a brave & manly opposition . . . are dismayed, Intractable, and Impatient to return. Great numbers of them have gone off; in some Instances, almost by whole Regiments."[77] His opinion of the militia sank with each passing year. By October 1780, at the very crisis point of the war, Washington issued a "circular to the states" criticizing the idea of "carrying on a War with Militia." His conclusion demonstrated the lessons of the previous five years: "The Idea is chimerical, and that we have so long persisted in it is a reflection on the judgment of a Nation so enlightened as we are, as well as a strong proof of the empire of prejudice over reason." Washington bluntly stated that " 'Tis time we should get rid of an error which the experience of all mankind has exploded, and which our own experience had dearly taught us to reject." And yet, he continued, there were those who still promoted the militia: "We have frequently heard the behavior of the Militia extolled . . . by visionary Men whose credulity easily swallowed every vague story in support of a favorite Hypothesis." Pursuing this "infatuation" with the militia would produce a deserved defeat, as "America has been almost amused out of her liberties." Washington concluded, "I solemnly declare I never was witness to a single instance that can countenance an opinion of Militia or raw troops being fit for the real business of fighting." Here then was a stunning vote of no-confidence from the one man who knew best the capabilities of the militia. Everything he had seen convinced him that a reliance on the militia would lead to ultimate disaster for America.[78]

The militia's performance in battle generally validated Washington's opinion of that institution's utility. Despite the efforts of the early 1770s to increase the number of musters and improve the drills, the militia entered the Revolution largely untrained in the use of guns. And as in the Seven Years' War, that ignorance of firearms was reflected in accidental shootings from the first encampment outside Boston until musters at war's end. There was also the traditional problem of the common American soldier's inability to care for his gun. In 1779 President Joseph Reed of Pennsylvania complained that state arms that had been lent "out [for] only a few Muster Days" had been returned "in such a Condition as to take considerable sums to repair them."[79] And also as in earlier wars, after the initial rush of enthusiasm, members of the militia showed little interest in serving. As a consequence, legislatures had to offer ever larger monetary inducements; for instance, the daily pay in North Carolina increased fourfold from two shillings a day in 1774 to eight shillings in 1778. Similarly, officers had to make concessions and deals with the militia to gain their service. And even with every possible inducement, including free guns, "The Militia," in Nathanael Greene's words, "have refused to turn out when there has been the greatest want of their Assistance." Greene simply had to point to the campaign of 1776 for evidence. As the British advanced up the Hudson River and Washington called for the local militia to join with him in defending the region, many companies simply refused to muster. Colonel A. Hawkes Hay reported that only eleven men from his entire regiment showed up for duty. Daniel Morgan advised Greene that the best way to deal with the militia was to put them in the center of the line, "with some picked troops in their rear, with orders to shoot down the first man that runs."[80]

After their courage at resisting the British attack at Bunker Hill, the militia suffered an almost instant demise in their reputation, which the brilliance of General John Stark's volunteers at the Battle of Bennington in 1777 only partially salvaged. Far more typical was their inglorious retreat at Kip's Bay, where, in the words of eyewitness Nathanael Greene, the militia ran "at the appearance of the Enemies advance Guard." But they did not limit their damage to leaving only their part of the line: "They struck a pannick into the Troops in the Rear, and Fellows and Parsons['] Brigade run away from about fifty men," leaving half of

Washington's artillery, sixty-seven cannon, in British hands. In contrast, the Continentals forced one thousand regulars to retreat after a vigorous attack. It was no wonder that Greene, one of the most insightful military commanders of the war, thought the militia completely inappropriate for warfare. After a close observation, he wrote that "the Jersey Militia behaves scurvily and, I fear, are not deserving the freedom we are contending for."[81]

The Battle of Camden brought home the danger of placing any reliance on the militia. After five years of attempting to arm and train the militia, they "did not squeeze their triggers but threw down their loaded muskets and ran." As General Otho Williams described it, "fixed bayonets put an end to the contest," as the militia fled at the very sight of those glittering blades. Then, Williams wrote, "the torrent of unarmed militia bore" most of the rest away, preventing the reserve from coming to the rescue of General Johann DeKalb's Continentals, who had twice repulsed the British. As Robert Middlekauff has dryly written, "The Americans did not withdraw from the battlefield in a manner recommended by military manuals." Instead they ran in terror, leaving the Continentals to be overwhelmed by the British, DeKalb to his death, and their guns— which had taken so much trouble to acquire—on the field, still loaded for battle.[82]

The militia was plagued not simply by a lack of training and experience, but also by a shortage of firearms, even late in the war. In 1781 General Friedrich von Steuben, Washington's brilliant inspector general, reported to Governor Thomas Jefferson that, of the thousand militia who responded to Benedict Arnold's raid on Virginia, only four hundred were armed and that not a single shot had been fired in an effort to halt the British advance. Colonel Richard Elliott informed Jefferson that only 15 of the 225 men in his Brunswick County regiment owned guns. The state had to supply the rest. Nathanael Greene stated the case with his usual precision when he wrote that "the Militia are such a constant drain upon our Provisions and military Stores of all kinds that our Magazines and Arsenals are all together inadequate to our consumption." The states could not "provide arms for a numerous militia," which meant that they turned to the Continental army for those guns. But the army could not afford to arm "thousands of men that scarsely render the least shadow of advantage to the cause; these men are consuming our provisions, wasting our Arms and Ammunition, increasing our expenditures of every kind, draining our funds." Greene felt that the army would be far better off, and better armed, if they avoided calling upon the militia for assistance. By 1779 Congress largely agreed and "wish to avoid calling out the militia, which is attended with great loss and expence."[83]

On some occasions, it is true that the militia did demonstrate remarkable courage, despite being poorly armed. In September 1781, when the renegade Benedict Arnold's British forces attacked Fort Griswold in Connecticut, the defending militia was armed with a wide variety of weapons. "Those defending the fort," wrote one participant, "fought desperately with spears or pikes fifteen or sixteen feet in length, with which they did good execution." The commander of the American volunteers, Lieutenant Colonel William Ledyard, knew that the militia had already abandoned Fort Trumbull and its cannon after firing a volley. Ledyard, with few guns and little ammunition, waited until the British were within a few yards of the fort before firing his one cannon double-loaded with grapeshot. Twenty British fell from that single shot, including their commander, Colonel Edmund Eyre. His place was taken by Major Montgomery, who was run through with a pike as he topped the fortification. Arnold reported that his forces attacked with bayonets and were "opposed with great obstanacy by the garrison with long spears." What he left out was that after the Americans' surrender, Arnold's forces slaughtered most of the garrison. Only six Americans had been killed up to the point that Ledyard handed over his sword, with which he was immediately stabbed. Within half an hour, the British had killed another 80 Americans with their bayonets; only 27 of the 140 members of the garrison escaped serious injury or death.[84]

The Battle of Cowpens in 1781 offered further evidence that it was still possible for the militia to fulfill their vaunted role. But that victory was the consequence of Daniel Morgan's careful planning in placing the militia in front of his Continental units, and his working out a deal with the militia whereby they agreed to fire a volley and then leave the field. Even then, Morgan repeatedly had to cajole and even beg the militia to keep their part of the bargain in the face of Banastre "Butcher" Tarleton's English forces, and most of the militia initially made to flee as soon as the English started to leave the field. It seemed as though the militia understood any movement as full-scale retreat, and Morgan and Colonel Andrew Pickens had to place themselves between the militia and their horses, waving their swords threateningly in order to keep them from turning victory into rout. The militia kept blundering around the field, convincing the British that the Americans were in flight. At that very moment when the British confidently charged, Morgan had Lieutenant Colonel John Howard's Continentals perform a perfect change of direction, fire a withering musket volley at ten yards, and then charge the British with fixed bayonets. Tarleton's forces collapsed before the American bayonets, and the militia, which had to fire only that single volley, managed to hold on to their guns this time.[85]

Most members of the militia who gained a knowledge of firearms did so through Continental service. But that knowledge required that they actually have a gun to hold. At the very least, the officers of the Continental army appreciated the value of firearms, based on their shortage. They understood that a lost or broken gun might not be replaced until after the next battle, if then. As a result, whenever soldiers broke ranks on the march, for whatever reason, "they are obliged to leave their Arms with the Battalion." The leaders feared that such soldiers might desert, taking their muskets with them. Washington reminded his troops on several occasions that they needed every gun, and thus extreme care must be taken to preserve them. He personally ordered the severe punishment of anyone who lost or sold a gun. General Putnam tried to solve this problem by ordering all guns to be branded. The brand was kept at headquarters, from which it was stolen within the month.[86]

The Continental army did its best to track every gun in its possession, noting when even a single firearm was "Carried off By Deserters." If a soldier became sick, his gun, unless it was his personal possession, was transferred to someone well enough to use it. Medical records at hospitals recorded whenever a soldier arrived with a gun, which was unusual. In December 1781 the New Wine Hospital admitted 167 men, only 2 of whom had guns, each his private property.[87] General Nathanael Greene issued strict orders in November 1775 that "No guns are to be permitted to be carried away from the army on any Condition. If any has guns here of their own private property and are fit for service they will be paid for them by the Continental Congress." It is notable not only that all guns were considered the property of the nation, but also that the idea of a privately owned gun was treated as unusual. Greene regretted seizing private property, "but the Army cannot be provided for any other way and those we retain are very indifferent, generally without Bayonets and of different Sizd Bores. . . . I wish our Troops were better furnisht. The Enimy has a great Advantage over us."[88]

Repairing these "indifferent" guns became a major struggle for the Continental army, as there were just not enough smiths familiar with firearms. Continental officers constantly sought anyone with a knowledge of guns to help in repairing them. Greene had far more luck finding arms by personally inspecting battlefields after the armies had moved on. On one occasion he found three hundred muskets "out of repair" abandoned by his own troops after they retreated from Harlem Heights.[89] Americans tended to lose their guns as freely as the British—though the British had more to lose. When the British took Fort Lee in November 1776 they captured twenty-eight hundred muskets, roughly one-third of Washington's total store.[90]

And of course there was the continued problem of acquiring powder and other accoutrements. When Washington and his staff reviewed their new army before Boston in 1776 they were "astonished" to learn that the army had only 9,937 pounds of powder, "enough to furnish half a pound a man." General John Sullivan reported that Washington was so stunned "that he did not utter a word for half an hour." The shortage was so severe that militia companies could not afford to waste this valuable resource on shooting practice; most drills culminated with the militia firing their muskets without powder, settling for a dull click rather than a bang. Washington found it necessary in May 1776 to forbid "Firing of Guns upon any pretense Whatsoever" in order to save ammunition. The low supply of flints, most of which came from Europe, often reached crisis proportions. In European armies, ten flints per soldier was a normal supply; prior to 1782, a Continental regiment usually did not have one flint per man; by end of the war, most had three flints per soldier, enough for one hundred shots under perfect conditions.[91] The shortage reached such levels in mid-1776 that General Greene ordered that "Any one snapping his lock without orders to be confined for two days on bread and water."[92]

England also suffered from a shortage of firearms. English arms manufacturing could not keep up with the needs of the expanded English army, the government arming most of its German troops with guns from the Netherlands. Gun manufacturers there freely sold to both sides until their country entered the war on the American side in late 1780.[93] The British government had swallowed the recent publicity about American knowledge of firearms, and thus were deeply shocked when they discovered that loyalist units lacked firearms. Most volunteers did not own a gun, and those who did generally had rusting old muskets—just like the other Americans. Like the patriot militia, loyalist units competed for available firearms. Colonel Ambrose Mills arrived at Camden, South Carolina, in October 1780 needing nearly two hundred guns; Lord

Rawdon's Irish Volunteers needed roughly the same number. Cornwallis made two hundred old French muskets captured from the Americans available to these units. There was plenty of ammunition, but Mills received just sixty-one muskets for his troops. The shortage was so extreme that Cornwallis ordered a halt to further loyalist recruitment. In New York City, General Henry Clinton put a stop to the firing of salutes and the firing of muskets during drill because of a shortage of gunpowder. The mighty British Empire had reached the limits of its armaments.[94]

Both sides burned up resources in efforts to arm their American supporters. Reports from the American inspector general indicate that problems persisted despite the European guns. In May 1779, for instance, Colonel William Richardson, commanding the 5th Maryland Regiment, reported that 220 of his men had bayonets that did not fit their muskets, while Colonel John Grumby of the 7th Maryland Regiment found that 26 percent of his men did not have firearms. The New York brigade had arms sufficient for 37 percent of its troops, as "a great number of Arms were either lost or ruined for want of care, those which remain are in Extreme bad order." The brigade's inspector stated that only the 3rd Regiment showed any ability to take care of its arms, and he was particularly concerned that there were bayonets to supply only one-third of the brigade. Inspectors from several Virginia regiments expressed a similar anxiety over the lack of bayonets—having enough for only 52 percent of the Virginia line—which they held more important in battle than gunpowder. They also faced continuing shortages of firearms. The best-armed unit was Daniel Morgan's, which still needed rifles for 10 percent of its marksmen. These were regiments of the Continental army; conditions were far worse among the volunteer state militia serving with the army. Colonel William Brink of the 2nd Virginia State Regiment admitted that his regiment's arms "are in bad order," most "want repair and almost the whole without Bayts." The same held in nearly every regiment.[95]

Washington understood that he could not hope to field units in which a quarter of the soldiers did not have a gun, and his staff worked through the summer of 1779 supplying French guns to these regiments. But unusual problems appeared. After the inspector general thought he had given enough arms for the entire Pennsylvania line, he discovered that they were still one-tenth short, as some soldiers had never used firearms before and had therefore not bothered to mention that they needed a gun. Other regiments had not bothered to mention in their returns arms "which could not be repaired," often because they did not realize that a gun was broken. It is understandable that the inspector general expressed frustration with this ignorance and lack of thoroughness. An inspection of the Connecticut line ended with the comment that "The Arms of these two Brigades are in a worse Condition than in any other part of the Army." Their "Arms [are] in a very bad Condition for want of care," and 45 percent had no guns at all. Many units competed for the title of "the worst in the army." Among the returns, one stands out as exceptional. The April 1780 review of Colonel Hazen's regiment of foot concludes: "This Regiment in good Order the Arms and Accouterments well taken care of a few wanting." There is no other report quite like that one.[96]

A persistent problem for the officer corps was the common soldier's failure to care for his weapon. After an inspection of the Pennsylvania Regiment of Foot in July 1777, Washington "was surprised this day to see the bad condition of many arms, they being not only unfit for fire, but very rusty, which latter is in the power of every man to prevent, and the neglect of it may arise from an inexcusable inattention of the orders."[97] On another occasion that same year, Washington, after an inspection of arms throughout his command, condemned "the bad condition of many Arms, they being not only unfit for fire but very rusty." This time he faulted "an inexcusable inattention of the Officers."[98]

Washington became nearly obsessed with the cleanliness of his troops' firearms, realizing full well that a fouled gun was useless if not dangerous. The orderly books of the Continental army are full of his orders that guns be cleaned regularly, weekly if possible. Efforts by some troops to comply demonstrated their complete ignorance of firearms. After a round of stringent orders from Washington on the need to clean guns in June 1777, officers began reporting that many soldiers thought that they could clean their guns by firing them—a completely erroneous notion. In response, Washington ordered that "The frequent discharging of pieces in order to clean them, and keep them in order, occasions so great a waste of ammunition that the Genl orders in very pointed and Positive terms that no Musquet be loaded with Cartridge until we are close to the enemy." Washington further commanded that this order be read weekly and that only guards were to be supplied with "a small quantity of powder ball and wadding."[99] Unlike the British army, the Continental army was caught in an almost impossible bind: desperately needing to train troops mostly unfamiliar with the use of firearms, yet lacking sufficient ammunition to train them properly. Washington's solution was to give his limited supply of guns to those "fitest for duty," with spears and pikes for the rest; or as General Israel Putnam put it in 1777, what arms exist "will be put in the Hands of the best Men."[100]

Unit after unit of the Continental army remained dangerously under-armed through most of the war, with the phrase "unable to serve for lack of proper equipment" frequently noted in the records. And the arms they did have, they did not care for adequately. The records indicate that hundreds of soldiers, as many as one-half the total (it is difficult to be certain of the meaning of many entries), had never used a gun before, and often remained ignorant of their use for months after they joined the service. As late as January 1782, after thĕ army had gained a windfall of thousands of British arms from Yorktown, some regiments continued to report significant shortages, often as a result of carelessness on the part of the soldiers. In that month General John Patterson found 37 percent of his 2nd Massachusetts Brigade of Foot lacking firearms; Colonel Henry Jackson reported that 53 percent of his 3rd Massachusetts Regiment were not fully armed; and Colonel Rufus Putnam discovered that an astounding 56 percent of his 5th Massachusetts Regiment were unarmed. Given that units of the Continental army could field only one-third to one-half of those able to serve because of a shortage of firearms, it is quite amazing that Washington's forces triumphed.[101]

But what of that famous marksman able to hit an orange at one hundred yards? Washington cleverly took advantage of the popular image, telling his men that he "earnestly encourages the use of Hunting Shirts" as very practical. "Besides," Washington added, "it is a dress justly supposed to carry no small terror to the enemy, who think every such person a complete Marksman."[102] As in the British army, there were some companies of select marksmen using the slower but more accurate rifles. In fact, it was the British who worked hardest at developing marksmen, having the guns and ammunition for regular practice—though they did ignore the remarkable innovation of Major Patrick Ferguson, who designed a breech-loading rifle.[103]

Americans started the war largely ignorant of rifles. John Adams wrote his wife Abigail that he had just seen "a peculiar kind of musket, called a rifle." It was amazingly accurate for a gun, but slow to load. Daniel Morgan's riflemen spread the fame of that weapon, all of which were provided by the government. Morgan's men performed brilliantly at the two Saratoga battles and demonstrated the value of the rifle's greater accuracy.[104] But that advantage diminished in large-scale battles, where smoke obscured the enemy. In such a situation it was the volume of fire that mattered, and the musket could be loaded three times as fast. It was also quickly discovered that American rifles tended to be poorly made in contrast to the European musket. Not only did they fail to stand up to the stresses of common usage in the military, but as there was no standard caliber, ammunition was difficult for a quartermaster to supply. The Congressional Board of War made this opinion explicit by explaining in 1776 why they issued any rifles at all: "Were it in the power of Congress to supply musketts, they would speedily reduce the number of rifles and replace them with the former, as they are more easily kept in order, can be fired oftener and have the advantage of Bayonets." Washington worried especially about the latter point, wondering how a rifleman could possibly protect himself after firing. For that reason, he ordered Morgan to arm his men with spears. The soldier had to be able to defend himself after firing, and in the absence of bayonets axes would do (the list of "military stores" in the Carlisle, Pennsylvania, armory after the war included two thousand tomahawks). General Wayne was even more succinct, stating that he hoped never to see another rifle.[105]

But other than the specially trained and equipped units, the vast majority of those in the Continental army showed no special facility for shooting. Every observer agreed on this point, and the army acted upon it. There was nothing different in this regard from any European army. "Shooting is efficient only if one hits the target. And that was exactly what eighteenth-century infantry did not do. Aiming, strange as it may seem, was strictly forbidden."[106] Everyone acknowledged this fact, thus the colorful uniforms, as though mocking the other side to try to hit these obvious targets. The Continental army was no different, even if its blue uniforms were more muted than British red. General Steuben's regulations differed from most European manuals in only one telling particular: Steuben mentions musket fire twice. "The officers must . . . observe that the soldiers . . . level their pieces at a proper height; for which purpose they must be accustomed always to take sight at some object." That statement could be from any English guide. But then comes the clincher: "in these exercises, the men will use a piece of wood, instead of a flint." No ammunition or flints were to be wasted, the purpose being to practice not aiming, but pulling the trigger. If the officer chose to use ammunition in order to provide a sense of musket fire, "the officers must carefully inspect the arms and cartridge boxes, and take away all the cartridges with ball." Again, the soldier was not actually to fire anything at a target, but to learn to fire in volleys as in Europe, though the shortage of ammunition prevented the actual replication of the experience of firing. Steuben devotes far more space to reminding officers to verify that the soldiers are cleaning their guns; only constant inspections—Steuben recommended daily—would insure the average soldier's attention. The army acted upon this advice.[107]

For Steuben, as for nearly every other military officer in the Western world at this time, it was the bayonet that mattered. As General Sir William Howe told his troops on Long Island in September 1776, the bayonet defeated the Americans "even in woods where they thought themselves invincible." Therefore he counseled that they place "an entire dependence on their bayonets." Lord Percy attributed British success on Long Island "intirely . . . to our Men attacking them [the Americans] the proper Way. The moment the Rebels fired our Men rushed on them with their Bayonets & never gave them Time to Load again."[108]

Certainly the British victory at Long Island demonstrated the wisdom of that reliance, as did the even more notorious battle at Paoli the following year, where the British attacked with muskets from which the flints had been removed, using their bayonets to decimate the Americans before they had a chance to load their weapons. Of course bayonets also had their failures; after all, General John Burgoyne's general orders at the start of his invasion from Canada stated that his troops should place "reliance on the bayonet," as "even a coward may be their match in firing. But the bayonet in the hands of the valiant is irresistible." The bayonet and his men's valor could not overcome Burgoyne's incompetence. Nonetheless, British bayonet charges repeatedly stopped American attacks, and proved particularly terrifying to militia units.[109] For instance, in January 1781 Cornwallis's forces came under heavy fire while fording the Catabwa. Sergeant Roger Lamb wrote that while they were wading the river, weighed down by "their knapsacks . . . [and] 60 or 70 rounds of powder and ball in each pouch tied at the pole of their necks, their firelocks with bayonets, fixed on their shoulders, 300 of their enemies (accounted the best marksmen in the world) placed on a hill as it were over their heads, keeping a continued and very heavy fire upon them." And yet somehow those "best marksmen in the world" were unable to do much damage to the British troops, who emerged from the river with their bayonets leveled, the Americans fleeing before this soggy charge.[110] Anthony Wayne, who lost more than two hundred men at Paoli, followed the British example in his brilliant victory at Stony Point, New York, on July 7, 1779, his troops taking the fortress with unloaded muskets.[111]

Most Continental officers placed little confidence in the ability of their troops to fire their muskets safely until after they had been well trained. In 1777 General John Peter Gabriel Muhlenberg ordered his entire division to "practice by actual fire," but with blank cartridges and no balls. They were to use powder, in order to get used to the noise, smoke, and kick, but only the sentries, who patrolled with fully charged muskets, were to discharge their weapons at the end of their shift in order to remove the balls—and even then only with the permission of an officer. The orderly books indicate that, outside of battle, the average soldier went several months without actually firing a musket more than once or twice; for the first several months, he did not use a fully loaded weapon. In that context it is not too surprising that General Israel Putnam twice held courts-martial of soldiers who intended to kill fellow soldiers but missed at close range—he seemed as angry with the failure as with the attempt.[112]

The main mission of the Continental army was to teach Americans to fight according to European standards. That meant not only learning the use of the bayonet, but also the need to hold one's fire until the enemy was within effective range. It is an obvious but critical point that Colonel William Prescott's famous command, "Don't fire until you see the whites of their eyes," was a necessary instruction that American officers issued repeatedly. All European armies trained their troops to hold their fire until the enemy was near; the Americans did the same. Washington told his officers that they must take "particular care" with their men so as "to prevent their firing at too great a distance, as one Fire well aim'd [a volley] does more execution than a dozen at long-shot." There was solid evidence during the campaigns of 1777 that these exercises were taking hold. At the Battle of Red Bank the Americans under Colonel Christopher Greene held their fire until the German troops were atop the fort's walls, and then delivered a volley followed by a bayonet charge that cost the enemy nearly four hundred casualties against thirty-seven American dead and wounded. And on several occasions American forces stopped advancing British troops dead in their tracks with such standard methods.[113]

But when it came to fighting the Indians, Washington showed not the slightest interest in European forms of warfare. As he succinctly stated in his instructions to General John Sullivan for the campaign against the

Iroquois in 1779 (in sentences that could have been penned by John Smith in 1609): "The immediate objects are the total destruction and devestation of their settlements. . . . It will be essential to ruin their crops now in the ground and prevent them planting more." Washington added that "It should be . . . impressed upon the minds of the men when ever they have an opportunity, to rush on with the war hoop and fixed bayonet. Nothing will disconcert and terrify the indians more than this." Most American commanders employed traditional methods of starvation and slaughter against the Indians. As in the seventeenth century, it was fire and blades, not guns, that were the weapons of choice in these campaigns of grotesque cruelty but little outright killing; most lives were claimed by starvation and disease. General John Sullivan's notorious operations against the Iroquois followed Washington's advice, destroying an estimated 160,000 bushels of corn and driving the Iroquois to the verge of extinction through starvation. Every "battle" against Indians sounds the same, as when Evan Shelby drove the Cherokee from their homes and burned their crops. Thomas Jefferson wrote of this 1779 campaign that Shelby's men succeeded in "killing about half a dozen men, burning 11 towns, 20,000 bushels of corn . . . and taking as many goods as sold for twenty-five thousand pounds."[114]

This crusade against the Indians was an excuse to loot. In 1781 Andrew Pickens took a break from battling British Regulars and led his South Carolina troops against the Cherokee. Using special short swords made for the purpose, these American Revolutionaries hacked to death the unarmed inhabitants of a village they caught by surprise. The Cherokee could not understand these "madmen" who burned their fields and killed women and children. Two years later it was the turn of the Moravian Delaware to be completely baffled, as militia units beat to death ninety-six Christian Indians. As Colin Calloway summarized the war on the frontier, "In the Revolution, American armies waged war against Indian cornfields."[115]

Year after year, Congress, the states, and the Continental army struggled to arm the American troops. Their long efforts paid off, when they were no longer needed. The trend toward the complete arming of the Continental army received a huge boost with the American victory at Yorktown in October 1781. Thousands of British arms complemented the thousands already received. At its peak strength in the winter of 1782, General Heath's army of New Englanders had 6,389 effectives, and exactly five thousand muskets (no rifles), enough for 78 percent of the men. The French, in contrast, actually had a surplus of arms. In October 1783 the Massachusetts line found that, for the first time, it had a gun for every soldier in their regiments. As Wayne Carp wrote, "After seven and a half years, Washington finally had an army ready to fight." Five weeks later Congress received the signed copies of the peace treaty ending the war.[116]

Republican ideology had not won the Revolution. The militia, Jefferson's repository of courage and virtue, had not come through in times of ultimate crisis; the Continental army, the professional soldiers, had. And it was not the independent property owners who had rushed to serve out of a sense of duty, but the poorest elements of white society who had been lured into the Continental army by bounties and promises of land. These facts troubled many American leaders. They were faced with a choice between abandoning their mythology or their knowledge. A great many Americans chose the latter course, and set to work rewriting the history of the American Revolution. As Charles Royster concluded, "Americans reclaimed the war from the army to whom they had tried to entrust it. . . . The future security of American independence would rest not on a military establishment but on public virtue. To believe that public virtue had the strength to sustain independence, Americans wanted to believe that public virtue had won it." Thus "civilians could portray themselves as the rescuers of the army at Valley Forge rather than the main cause of the army's hardship."[117] In this republican version of events, still evident in standard textbooks though long abandoned by historians of the period, the heroic militia rushed to arms and picked off the British with excellent marksmanship from behind trees. That such a version is not validated by these sources, or by logic, is irrelevant. Far too many people in the new nation required an idealized version of events to be troubled by the facts. Yet the ambiguity remained. even while proclaiming that their militia had won American freedom, the vast majority of American males showed not the slightest desire to serve in the militia. Professionals like George Washington took this conduct as another reason for supporting a standing army; amateurs like Thomas Jefferson took it as another reason to live by the dream rather than the reality. The bill for this self-delusion would come due—again—in 1812.

Chapter Seven

Government Promotion
of Gun Production

Since the invention of gunpowder has armed the
weak as well as the strong with missile death, bodily
strength, like beauty, good humor, politeness and
other accomplishments, has become but an auxiliary
ground of distinction.

—Thomas Jefferson[1]

The Constitution and Guns

The Revolution presented the first opportunity to establish a gun culture among the whites in North America. Thousands of males had been trained in the use of firearms, and the war had brought tens of thousands of muskets from Europe to America. It seemed as though the United States had a limitless supply of armaments for its rapidly shrinking army. There certainly appeared to be no reason to bother making new weapons. As Henry Knox wrote Congress, he was "filled with rapture" when he examined all the arms "wrested by the hand of virtue from the arm outstretched to oppress it."[2]

However, the new state governments hesitated to promote the ownership and use of firearms by all of the inhabitants of the United States, and, more important, even those who had been trained in the proper care and maintenance of firearms demonstrated a surprising lack of interest in transferring that knowledge to peacetime activities. In fact, most veterans turned their back on their guns, walking away from their encampments without their heavy muskets, even when the government offered them for sale at low rates. In the years after the war's end, these veterans, like most males, showed not the least noticeable enthusiasm for continuing military exercises in the militia, which died a slow, embarrassing death as a national institution.

As troops were decommissioned, their arms were "stacked like cord-wood" in whatever building was at hand. The arms of the last troops discharged in 1783 at West Point were stored in wooden shacks near the Hudson—hardly the best storage site.[3] Knox noted the inferior condition of these makeshift arsenals and warned Congress that these weapons were "too valuable to remain neglected." He drew their attention to the great number of arms they now had and invited Congress to compare them to the "scanty" supply they had in 1775. He asked for twenty armorers to clean and repair the guns, promising that "the many defective arms . . . do not want much labor to put them in perfect order."[4]

Congress felt the nation was too close to bankruptcy to afford such repairs and allowed this vast stockpile of arms and ammunition to rust away. Captain John Doughty, commanding at West Point, continually requested funding to repair the arms in his care and repack the gunpowder before it decayed. "The war office has favored me with four promises but no performance," he reported.[5] Knox and other officers kept requesting action; Congress kept deferring until some later, more prosperous day. When Congress finally acted in 1794 and voted to build the arsenal at Springfield, Massachusetts, the purpose was not storage but the manufacture of new weapons to replace those that had rotted over the past decade.

Those who led the Continental army to victory understood, even before the war was over, that the United States put itself in a precarious diplomatic and defensive position by depending on France as the source of its firearms. They also appreciated that the thousands of French and British guns in American hands would quickly decay and rot if not collected and maintained in government arsenals. They knew full well that no reliance could be placed on the militia to provide for the new nation's security, internal or external. The efforts of these nationalists to find and then create a stable source of firearms for the United States began a long process on the part of the federal government to arm its white male citizens. It would prove an extremely difficult and frustrating task that took seventy years.[6]

The first men to address this issue of the future of the gun in the United States were George Washington and Alexander Hamilton. Before the Revolution was even over, Washington wrote Hamilton, who was chair of a congressional committee looking toward peacetime defense, that the government should provide the militia with all its arms, ensuring that they were of a uniform quality.[7] The very next month, in June of 1783, Hamilton submitted a "Report on a Military Peace Establishment" to the Continental Congress. Hamilton advised Congress that the country should always have in storage arms for thirty thousand soldiers. Current sources were insufficient to attain that level; "a more systematic" means of provisioning the army with guns other than "by the states separately" required that Congress move quickly "to establish foundries, manufactories of arms, powder &c." A job so vital to the nation's defense should not be delayed because of a lack of trained gunsmiths; using troops as workers would enable the country to acquire arms "on better and cheaper terms than by importation." Hamilton perceived self-sufficiency in gunmaking as a national necessity, for "every country ought to endeavour to have within itself all the means essential to its own preservation, as to depend on the casualties of foreign supplies is to render its own security precarious." Congress had "a constitutional duty" to create "a well regulated militia." Attaining that end required that they supply the militia with arms that would become the militiaman's "property at the end of his time of duty." Hamilton repeated these arguments several times over the next twenty years.[8]

Hamilton hoped for action from Congress, which proved a rather vain expectation. Congress had no intention of regulating the militia, nor did it want to improve the armaments of the Continental army—it just wanted these heroic soldiers who had won American independence to go home. Within a few years of the war's end, the U.S. military establishment numbered less than a thousand men. For that crucial period between the end of the Revolution in 1783 and the inauguration of George Washington as president in 1789, the security of the nation did indeed depend on the militia. It was a close call.

The early national period witnessed a tension between federal efforts to arm white male Americans and elite fears that poor whites might put such weapons to an incorrect, class-based use. Senator Rufus King warned his colleagues in 1790 that "it was dangerous to put Arms into the hands of the Frontier People for their defense, least they should Use them against the United States."[9] The clear implication was that if the government did not arm them, they would not have guns. Nationalists found ample justification for their fears in Shays's Rebellion.

Shays's Rebellion was an obvious indicator of the dangers facing the country. The Shaysites themselves kept insisting that their political protest followed Revolutionary traditions. Facing serious economic adversity and an unresponsive state government using the courts to pursue aggressively those who could not meet their debts, hundreds of poor farmers in western Massachusetts acted as crowds often had in the Colonial period to close down the courts and harass tax collectors.[10] They considered their protests legitimate, presenting petitions to the general court and holding county conventions when these petitions failed to receive a response. For the Shaysites it was 1774 all over again, and they turned to insurrection only in the absence of an alternative, when their government demonstrated its indifference to their interests and needs. Daniel Shays felt that the "virtue which truly characterizes the citizens of a republican government, hath hitherto marked our paths with a degree of innocence."[11]

The state government felt differently, acting with energy in crushing what they saw as a rebellion, a challenge to legitimate authority. As during many Colonial conflicts, the Shaysite crowd was the militia, limiting the state's ability to call on those forces for support. Uninterested in compromise or negotiation, the Massachusetts senate declared the uprising an "open, unnatural, unprovoked, and wicked rebellion." The general court suspended habeas corpus, gave the governor emergency powers, and raised what amounted to a private army through contributions from Boston's merchants to "establish the just authority and dignity" of government. The first clash came at the Springfield arsenal, where Shays's followers, many of them veterans who had foolishly not brought away their Continental arms, hoped to acquire the guns they needed to resist effectively the state's army. The arsenal held seven thousand muskets and bayonets, as well as more than one thousand barrels of powder. Some fifteen hundred Shaysites, armed with an assortment of clubs, farm implements, old muskets, and fowling pieces, moved through the snow on January 25, 1787, against the one thousand state troops protecting the arsenal. The state's forces were well armed from the arsenal's stores, which included cannon. The only shots fired were fifteen rounds of grape from that artillery, which killed four of the farmers, wounded an additional twenty, and sent Shays's forces fleeing in terror. The state's troops suffered no casualties. A week later, General Benjamin Lincoln routed the remaining insurgents without firing a shot, effectively ending Shays's Rebellion.[12]

Though the rebels had not exactly distinguished themselves in the martial arts, their uprising had far-reaching consequences. George Washington wrote to James Madison that "We are fast verging to anarchy and confusion." The crisis in Massachusetts was but a local variant of a national problem requiring a federal solution.[13] Most of the new nation's would-be leaders found the Shaysites dangerous levelers who could easily link up with other supporters of excessive democracy, unless, as Secretary of War Henry Knox recommended, federal troops were sent against them. Even Samuel Adams, one of America's leading democrats, rejected pardon for the Shaysites: "The man who dares to rebel against the laws of a republic ought to die."[14]

Washington displayed more skepticism, attempting to learn if the rebels had "real grievances" and why the government of Massachusetts did not address these problems. But if the Shaysites lacked some substantive complaint against their government, then Washington agreed with Knox that the states must move to defend their interests or witness the dissolution of government.[15]

Shays's Rebellion was one of several key factors responsible for the calling of the Constitutional Convention in Philadelphia in 1787. To those favoring a stronger national government, the Revolution had clearly demonstrated the flaws in the militia when faced with a foreign invader, while the insurrection in Massachusetts indicated the unreliability of the militia when confronted with internal disorder. From Edmund Randolph's opening speech, the convention would return repeatedly to the reform of the militia, as the majority of those present hoped that the Constitution they were writing would prevent further disorder by bringing the militia under more direct federal control.

In listing the reasons for writing an entirely new government compact to supercede the Articles of Confederation, Randolph gave as his first reason: "1. that the Confederation produced no security agai[nst] foreign invasion; . . . and that neither militia nor draughts being fit for defence on such occasions, enlistments only could be successful." The "common defence" required some sort of national army. The Revolution demonstrated that "*Volunteers* [are] not to be depended on" in case of war; while "*Militia* [are] difficult to be collected and almost impossible to be kept in the field. . . . Nothing short of a regular military force will answer." None of this was to be taken as an effort to terminate the militia; rather, in Alexander Hamilton's words, "the Militia of all the States [are] to be under the sole and exclusive direction of the United States."[16]

Several speakers expressed concerns that the states would lose their sovereignty if the militia came under federal control, and Rufus King and Gouverneur Morris feared that free state militia would be called upon to put down slave insurrections. General Charles Pinckney, who held that "Uniformity was essential" as "the States would never keep up a proper discipline of their militia," dismissed all these objections as pointless "distrust of the Genl Govt." John Langdon agreed, seeing "no more reason to be afraid of the Genl. Govt than of the State Govts." The overriding sense of the convention was that the militia could not be expected to, as Randolph put it, "suppress domestic commotions" and required federal supervision. The alternative was disorder.[17]

Historians have amply demonstrated the difficulty of ascribing to the framers of the Constitution a consensus on the original intention of many of its clauses. The Constitutional Convention hammered out a document full of compromises and barely obtained concessions.[18] On one point at least there was no disagreement: Congress should arm the militia. Some speakers felt that the states could organize and discipline the militia, but none held that any state could keep its militia well armed and all agreed with the need for federal guidance. As Luther Martin, a member of the Philadelphia convention who became an Anti-Federalist, told the Maryland assembly later that year, "As to *giving such a power* [to regulate the militia], there was no objection; but it was thought by some, that this power *ought* to be given with certain *restrictions*." Most particularly, Martin had hoped for a limitation on the president's power to order a militia beyond the borders of its home state.[19] The majority of the convention brushed aside this latter fear and agreed with James Madison that the whole purpose of federal regulation "is to secure an effectual discipline of the Militia." The states had repeatedly proven their inability to arm, discipline, and deliver their militia when called upon. "The States neglect their Militia now," Madison went on, "and the more they are consolidated into one nation, the less each will rely on its own interior provisions for its safety. . . . The Discipline of the Militia is evidently a *National* concern, and ought to be provided for in the *National* Constitution."[20]

Madison had his way, as article 1, section 8 of the Constitution granted Congress the authority to call "forth the Militia to execute the Laws of the Union, suppress Insurrections and repel Invasions." Some modern observers argue that the framers perceived the militia as a check on governmental power; yet the Constitution accomplishes the exact opposite, making the militia a potential tool of the central government for the repression of any challenge to federal authority. Toward that end, the Constitution made Congress responsible for "organizing, arming, and disciplining, the Militia."[21]

As early as 1787 a counterfactual faith in the militia had become a core American belief. More difficult to determine is the relationship between this notion of the militia as a prop of the state and the ownership of firearms. The question is significant, as so many modern observers hold that there was an exact correlation between the individual ownership of firearms and the militia, a relationship that informed the Second Amendment.[22] A careful reading of the historical context of that amendment—the point of this chapter—indicates that the state and federal governments continued the legal British tradition of controlling the supply of and access to firearms.[23]

As previously discussed, the Colonial governments had followed the British precedent in maintaining authority over firearms. Guns were used and owned at sufferance, the state reserving the right to limit, regulate, or impress those arms at its discretion. Under common law this "reserved right of the sovereign" differed from eminent domain. It lacked a requirement for just compensation, since firearms were always seen as in the service of the monarch, and it did not require a special act of Parliament. The American Revolution did not change that English heritage, as the loyalists discovered when their firearms were confiscated.[24] State legislatures needed no further argument than public safety, or in constitutional terms, the state's police powers, to justify gun regulation. In this regard they adhered to the English common law heritage and the practice of every European nation. As Edmund Burke held, the state's primary justification is, after all, public safety, and therefore the legislature has a legitimate interest in passing acts to secure that end. These measures aroused amazingly little debate—other than accusations that they were not stringent enough or rigorously enforced.[25]

The Massachusetts Constitution of 1780 declared that "The people have a right to keep and to bear arms for the common defence." That right did not place the individual beyond the discipline of the state, for the next sentence stated that, "And as in time of peace armies are dangerous to liberty, they ought not to be maintained without the consent of the Legislature; and the military power shall always be held in exact subordination to the civil authority, and be governed by it." The people bear arms for the common defense out of an inherent suspicion of the military, despite the experience of the Revolution. But the Massachusetts Constitution did not end there; article 4, section 1 grants the legislature authority to pass laws for the support and regulation of the state's militia, while article 12 required all militia officers to report to the governor every three months on the number of arms held by the state.[26]

Even the most seemingly individualist renderings of gun rights must be matched against the actions of those responsible for these statements. For instance the 1776 Pennsylvania Constitution declared that "The people have a right to bear arms for the defense [of] themselves and the State; and as standing armies in time of peace are dangerous to liberty, they ought not to be kept up. And the military should be kept under strict subordination to, and governed by the civil power." Again, it is the state's authority that stands out in this declaration, and the state of Pennsylvania did not hesitate to exercise that authority, disarming loyalists and any others who refused to take an oath of allegiance to their government. Gun ownership in Pennsylvania, as in every other state, was premised on the notion that the individual would use that weapon in the state's defense when called upon to do so; to make the point completely clear, the state required an oath to that effect. The Test Act called for the disarming of those who would not take the oath of allegiance.[27] As Don Higginbotham pointed out, "In all the discussions and debates from the Revolution to the eve of the Civil War, there is precious little evidence that advocates of local control of the militia showed an equal or even a secondary concern for gun ownership as a personal right."[28]

The Constitution's treatment of the militia was in keeping with various state constitutions that aimed to craft a workable militia structure. As the Virginia Declaration of Rights of 1776 stated, "a well-regulated militia, composed of the body of the people trained to arms, is the proper, natural and safe defence of a free state . . . and that in all cases, the military should be under strict subordination to, and governed by, the civil power." It is hard to miss those opening words, in which Virginia declares its faith in a trained militia. But convincing citizens to submit to that training—there lay the rub.[29]

The militia provisions of the Constitution outraged the Anti-Federalists, who insisted on state control. The Anti-Federalists sought limits on the powers of the central government rather than enhancement of individual rights. After the Philadelphia convention, Luther Martin and other Anti-Federalists imagined every possible scenario of federal tyranny rendering the states impotent. Under the Constitution, Martin charged, Congress could decide not to arm the militia, with the result that the militia would have few if any guns. Patrick Henry picked up on this

reasoning and suggested that Congress could render the states undefended—an issue of real concern in states that actively repressed and
enslaved a large minority—or, in South Carolina, a majority—of their
population. "Of what service would militia be to you," Henry asked,
"when most probably you will not have a single musket in the State; for as
arms are to be provided by Congress, they may or may not furnish them?"
Apparently Martin and Henry believed the people incapable of acquiring
their own firearms. Henry feared what Congress would not do, and others suspected that the federal government would use its control over the
militia to oppress the states.[30]

This fear that the central government would either send the militia
into one state at a time to attain supremacy or disarm the militia through
inaction struck many Federalists as absurd. After all, it was Congress,
with representatives drawn from those very states, that would pass the
necessary legislation. In his reply to Martin, Oliver Ellsworth charged
that "one hour you sported the opinion that Congress, afraid of the militia
resisting their measures, would neither arm nor organize them, and the
next, as if men required no time to breathe between such contradictions,
that they would harass them by long and unnecessary marches." The
Anti-Federalists wanted both sides of the argument, that the federal government would both arm and fail to arm the militia.[31]

The Federalists also pointed out another obvious flaw in Anti-
Federalist logic: the militia remained under the direct control of the states
when not in national service. The states "would be free to increase their
arms and their training as they saw fit." And as Edmund Randolph observed, their officers were all appointed by the state governments and
were therefore hardly likely to act contrary to that state's interest.[32] For
the Federalists, the Constitution's militia clauses operated within their
understanding of concurrent power. State and federal governments
shared authority over the militia. The Constitution made Congress responsible for organizing and arming the militia, but nothing in that
wording contradicted the states' ability to use their militia as they saw fit
when not in active federal service. If an individual state found the militia
poorly organized or under-armed, there was no limitation on its right to
correct these faults. In this way the militia would neither be so strong as to
become a standing army, nor so weak as to be ineffectual against domestic
insurrection.[33] Most Federalists followed the lead of Madison and Randolph at the Virginia ratifying convention in maintaining that a federally
regulated militia was the best way of avoiding a standing army.[34]

To a degree, this argument that a well-regulated militia would allow the United States to avoid a standing army was disingenuous. Most Federalists had every expectation that the nation would build a more powerful army with the new Constitutional government. Certainly most Federalists would have agreed with Gouverneur Morris's later assessment that "An overweening vanity leads the many, each man against the conviction of his own heart, to believe or affect to believe, that militia can beat veteran troops in the open field." At the Constitutional Convention, "This idle notion, fed by vaunting demagogues, alarmed us" into giving support to the militia. Those present, Morris argued, should have recalled better the Revolution, which taught that "to rely on militia was to lean on a broken reed." Alexander Hamilton was more succinct in *Federalist* No. 25: "I expect to be told that the militia of the country is its natural bulwark, and would be at all times equal to the national defence. This doctrine, in substance, had like to have lost us our independence. . . . The facts which, from our own experience, forbid a reliance of this kind, are too recent to permit us to be dupes of such a suggestion."[35]

Though the Anti-Federalists' arguments lacked cogency, James Madison had promised during the ratification process to consider amendments to the Constitution. Madison kept his word. He even turned his attention to those proposals that addressed the structure of the militia. Among the changes recommended were limitations on the number of militia under federal control, their training, the nature and duration of martial law, the use of militia beyond a state's borders, the status of conscientious objectors, and the degree of state control over the militia. None became part of the Second Amendment, as Madison preferred simplicity and clarity in all of the amendments he put before Congress.[36]

While considering the first amendments that would become the Bill of Rights, Madison rejected all changes to the Constitution that would weaken the federal government, including its control over the militia. As he rhetorically asked, "For whose benefit is the militia organized, armed and disciplined? for the benefit of the United States."[37] The result was a single sentence with a clarifying preamble: "A well regulated Militia, being necessary to the security of a free State, the right of the people to keep and bear Arms, shall not be infringed."

Madison stated his own understanding of the Second Amendment when he presented it to the House of Representatives. "In our government it is, perhaps, less necessary to guard against the abuse in the executive department than any other, because it is not the stronger branch of the system, but the weaker." The people need not fear their national government, which had few means by which it could exert its authority; the real danger lay closer to home, in a tyrannical majority lacking checks on its democratic power. "I confess," Madison continued, "that I do conceive, that in a government modified like this of the United States, the great danger lies rather in the abuse of the community than in the legislative body. The prescriptions in favor of liberty, ought to be levelled against that quarter where the greatest danger lies, namely, that which possesses the highest prerogative of power: But this [is] not found in either the executive or legislative departments of government, but in the body of the people, operating by the majority against the minority." For Madison, it was an unrestrained citizenry that was to be most feared, and the Bill of Rights, he thought, should protect the minority against the majority's transgressions.[38]

The Second Amendment's purpose is fairly indicated by the ensuing debate and legislation. The House debate focused on two issues: the "use of the militia" in preventing "the establishment of a standing army," and the wisdom of allowing religious exemptions for service in the militia.[39] The legislation that resulted uniformly sought to regulate the militia, starting with the first national militia act of 1792, while legislatures in every state further revealed their intentions in the limitations they imposed on gun ownership, whether in denying that right to blacks, Catholics, Indians, or the foreign born.[40]

There were those who, after the American Revolution, imagined a future of universal ownership of guns, and thus a universal militia. For instance, Joel Barlow wrote that "The people will be universally armed; they will assume those weapons for security, which the art of war has invented for destruction." As a consequence, the militia would include all free citizens in the defense of the state. John Taylor went even further in his call for a constitutional amendment *requiring* all citizens to own guns. After all, he wrote, a "naked permission to keep and bear arms" was insufficient for national defense. Only a "real militia," one that actually trained in the use of arms, could protect the country from its enemies. But those with experience of the realities of government, war, and gun production knew that such visions were fantasies. The leaders of the new nation followed Washington's lead in calling for a standing army backed by a smaller, more organized, and better-armed militia. The Constitution provided the framework for such a structure. The first federal Congress set about giving it shape.[41]

A Proper Defense

George Washington had little cause for satisfaction with the army he commanded as president under the Constitution. Disaster followed disaster, as the minuscule U.S. Army met defeat on the frontier at the hands of Indians using axes and guns. In October 1790 General Josiah Harmar's force of 320 regulars and 1,130 poorly armed frontier militia fought three quick battles with the Maumee Indians near Fort Wayne, Indiana. In each of these battles the militia fled, leaving the regulars to be annihilated. A year later, General Arthur St. Clair took the field with the entire army of the United States—all six hundred of them—supported by fifteen hundred militia. On the banks of the Wabash River, Indians surprised St. Clair's force; the militia fled, the regulars were slaughtered. After these humiliating defeats, Congress authorized a new, larger army under the command of Anthony Wayne. Wayne spent two years preparing his forces in what has been called "possibly the best-trained command in the history of the United States Army." At the Battle of Fallen Timbers in August 1792, Wayne repeated his tactic of Stony Point of relying on the bayonet. His thirty-five hundred regulars destroyed the Maumee force and restored some honor to the army.[42]

The frontier militia themselves could not fight the Indians with any hope of success, so they consistently lured in the army with promises that they would help, and then requested arms in order to provide that assistance. When General St. Clair responded to calls for assistance from western Pennsylvania in 1790, local militia commanders told St. Clair that most of the settlers lacked arms. Secretary of War Knox supplied federal arms to the militia.[43] Major Ebenezer Denny, serving with St. Clair, recorded in his diary that Kentucky militia were arriving, but "They appear to be raw and unused to the gun or the woods; indeed, many are without guns, and many of those they have want repairing."[44] Four years later, one militia commander from "the frontier of the State of New York" wrote Knox that as "this part of the country . . . [is] destitute of Arms and ammunition the scattered Inhabitants of this remote Wilderness would fall an easy prey to their savage neighbours should they think proper to attack them." Knox sent several thousand muskets west for use by frontier militia.[45]

The Indians themselves got most of their arms from the same source, as militia and federal troops tended to lose their muskets at an astounding rate. St. Clair's retreating troops abandoned their weapons in order to run faster. As St. Clair's adjutant general, Winthrop Sargent, wrote immediately after the battle, "The conduct of the army after quitting the ground was in a most supreme degree disgraceful. Arms, ammunition and accoutrements were almost all thrown away. . . . The road for miles was covered with firelocks, cartridge boxes and regimentals." Only a bayonet charge by the 2nd Regiment saved the army from total destruction. St. Clair estimated the total loss at twelve hundred muskets.[46]

Most scholars of St. Clair's defeat agree that his forces were completely inexperienced in the use of firearms. William Guthman wrote that "Many of the Federal recruits had never owned guns prior to their enlistment in the corps and their lack of care and misuse rendered hundreds of muskets unserviceable." St. Clair noted that some volunteers brought their own guns, almost all in need of repair, but that most had little experience with firearms, "and many never fired a gun" before. The shortage of gunpowder on the frontier made target practice or even the general firing of muskets in practice volleys extremely rare.[47] Major John Francis Hamtramck wrote General Josiah Harmar, "if you thought proper to allow me some ammunition for the purpose of practicing the artillery and infantry I am well persuaded that it would be of great service, for the men appear to me to be unacquainted with firing." When powder was issued for practice, it was of the poorest quality. Thus Harmar wrote back to Hamtramck that "Bradford took with him a barrel of damaged powder which will answer the purpose of practicing."[48] Pennsylvania even passed a law requiring every county to supply each militiaman with the necessary ammunition to practice firing on the annual muster day. At least one day a year they would fire a gun.[49]

For Federalists, the Whiskey Rebellion of 1794 simply drove home the point that little or no reliance was to be placed in the militia. President Washington issued a call for thirteen thousand militia from Pennsylvania, Maryland, Virginia, and New Jersey. Many common members of the militia refused to turn out to preserve order while officers resigned their commissions. As in Shays's Rebellion, some militia companies were themselves the rebels. Those who did show up for service brought few guns. Governor Henry Lee of Virginia discovered that his troops were largely unarmed and called on the federal government to arm the state militia. Lee called up thirty-three hundred militia, two thousand (61 percent) of whom were issued guns from the state arsenal. The officers of the Georgetown, Maryland, militia reported that they needed 370 muskets for their 390 men. They promised to return the weapons whenever the governor requested. Maryland's Governor Thomas Lee wrote to Secretary of War Knox arguing that the federal government bore complete responsibility for the militia; the states simply facilitated organization. The federal law required each man to arm himself, but lacked any enforcement mechanism, while Maryland law carried a fine of four cents for failure to arm oneself, which Lee labeled an "imbecility." In the face of Knox's refusal to send arms to Maryland, Lee proposed a deal, whereby Maryland would supply as many troops as possible from its Frederick arsenal, with the federal government supplying all other military needs. In Pennsylvania, Governor Thomas Mifflin's chief concern was keeping firearms out of the hands of the western militia.[50]

These problems aside, Washington did get his army. He opened the federal repositories to arm the troops he led into the field against the Whiskey Rebels; his force was larger than any he had commanded in the Revolution. The rebellion simply evaporated before such a show of force; the only deaths came from a pistol going off accidentally and a drunken brawl that ended with a fatal bayonet wound.[51] One can only speculate whether the Whiskey Rebels would have behaved differently had they known just how ignorant of firearms were most of Washington's troops. Hardly a disciplined force, the government militia looted, drank heavily, and beat civilians randomly. It was neither well trained nor well armed. General Samuel Smith, commander of the Maryland militia, reported to the House of Representatives that the majority of the Virginia and Maryland troops were ignorant of the use of arms. Many did not know how to load a musket, and others had never carried one in their lives.[52]

The failure of the militia in the Whiskey Rebellion led to renewed calls for a select militia and a stronger standing army. "The militia," Lawrence Delbert Cress has written, "had only reluctantly taken up arms, and then only after the infusion of a large number of substitutes and volunteers." Even many of the administration's opponents, soon to be known as Democratic-Republicans, now doubted the worth of the militia; and even former Anti-Federalists joined in supporting the disarming of the Whiskey Rebels, despite the Second Amendment.[53] One of these men, William Findley, who had sympathized with the rebels, was appalled by the militia's conduct. The first necessity of any republic had to be public order; if the militia could not handle it, Findley stated, then a standing army would. Federalists and Republicans agreed that the task of the militia was to enforce social order, and that the militia could do a lot better. Federalists wanted to centralize militia administration to ensure greater efficiency, a goal that aroused the suspicion of Republicans who saw militia reform as code for a standing army.[54]

Washington and Knox had used the Whiskey Rebellion as well as Harmar's and St. Clair's defeats on the Western frontier to keep the army fully supplied. The army, however, had to content itself with weapons from the Revolution cleaned and repaired at West Point, a situation that Washington knew could not long prove adequate.[55] Two problems therefore faced the American defensive establishment in the 1790s: the unorganized and untrained condition of the militia, and the impending shortage of usable firearms. The Federalists proposed two obvious solutions: a select militia and federal support for a domestic firearms industry.

In the long, carefully considered debates over the Militia Act in the first federal Congress, which descended even to the exact bore of the muskets to be required of the militia, the speakers returned repeatedly to just how much authority the federal government should have in exercising its constitutional mandate of regulating the militia. Several representatives noted that every increase in federal power came at the expense of the states. Thomas Fitzsimmons rejected the need for militia training as "a great tax on the community, productive of little instruction or edification, either in regard to military tactics, or the morals of a civilized nation." Most members, however, agreed with Roger Sherman of Connecticut that "the different states had certainly an inherent right to arm and protect the lives and property of the citizens." But to "more effectively . . . exercise this right" the states needed "to give up to the general government the power of fixing what arms the militia should use, by what discipline they should be regulated," and various other forms of precisely ordering the nature of the militia. The only power left to the states in this formulation was "the right to say what descriptions of persons should compose the militia, and to appoint the officers that were to command it." Joshua Seney of Maryland thought even this latter qualification would grant the states too much power, which they could easily abuse.[56] In response to the Whiskey Rebellion, Congress passed "An Act to provide for calling forth the militia to execute the Laws of the Union," placing the militia directly under presidential authority in case of invasion or insurrection. They also increased funding for the army.[57]

While Congress was quite willing to grant the president control over the militia, it did not support his pet plan for a select militia. Washington agreed completely with Friedrich von Steuben's dismissal of the "flattering but . . . mistaken idea—that every Citizen should be a Soldier." The Revolution had made clear that "the use of arms is as [much] a trade as shoe or boot making." Washington favored some sort of apprenticeship program for the military arts, first proposing a select, volunteer militia in 1783. Three years later Henry Knox presented the first of his many plans for a national militia to the Continental Congress; it was completely ignored. With the war over, few members of that Congress found any reason to pay any further attention to military matters.[58] With the Constitution in place, Knox, with Washington's support, tried again in 1790 and 1791. Knox proposed to Congress that they create an active, highly trained (ten to thirty days per year), and well-armed reserve that could be called into service by a state or the federal government. As in all of these proposals, the federal government would supply guns to those serving in the select militia. The "universal militia" would become nothing more than a way of registering all those eligible to carry arms in time of war.[59]

Knox's proposal was logical, legal, and necessary, and would have aided the nation enormously in a range of future crises. Congress would have nothing to do with it. The people's representatives may have shared the view of former Anti-Federalist John Smilie of Pennsylvania, who warned that "when a select militia is formed; the people in general may be disarmed."[60] But Smilie, like most Anti-Federalists, had no problem granting the state the authority to decide who should be allowed to serve in the militia, or to limit those ineligible from owning guns. Nor did most Anti-Federalists want to see the propertyless carrying arms in or out of the militia.[61] Other members of Congress opposed anything smacking of a standing army. Senator William Maclay complained that Congress's first error had been allowing the appointment of a secretary of war in time of peace; now they needed to supply "an Army for fear the department of War should lack employment . . . give Knox an Army, and he will soon have a War on hand."[62]

The debate over the future of the militia demonstrated an ideological fissure in America. Federalists looked to Europe and saw that warfare was changing fast, with massive armies and well-trained corps of light infantry sweeping away the last remnants of medieval warfare. Harrison Gray Otis was not alone in thinking that in the United States the "art of war is least understood." He insisted that at least a few men must be trained in modern methods of warfare, if only to be on hand to advise the militia when war came. Otis and most Federalists pointed to the experience of the American Revolution and asked whether the United States was in a better condition for war now than in 1775. Their answer was a ringing negative. To prevent disaster, the country needed a larger army staffed by professional soldiers and a centralized select militia subject to extended training. Federalist support for volunteer militia companies appeared to Republicans an obvious assault on the ideal of a universal militia. The fact that the universal militia had never existed and that the current militia showed no signs of life remained irrelevant to this ideological absolute.[63]

A curious side effect of these heated debates over the militia was a brief militia revival; a resurgence born of political fears. Late 1798 and early 1799 witnessed the threat of war with France, Federalist calls for a stronger army and more centralized militia, and a number of wild rumors, including that Republicans were hoarding arms and that Hamilton was going to lead the army against domestic opponents. John Nicholas published a letter accusing the Virginia legislature of storing arms in the capitol for use in a rebellion against the federal government. Evidence was found in the legislature's recent reorganization of the militia and its appropriation of funds to buy arms for the militia and build an armory in Richmond.[64] Federalists in Richmond and Petersburg, Virginia, responded by organizing the first private militia companies.[65] Shortly thereafter Republicans in Philadelphia organized the Republican Blues, a private militia company, "in order to defend the country against foreign and domestic enemies and [to] support the laws."[66] Pressured by the states, Congress passed a new militia act, but Maryland's Governor Stone refused to cooperate until the federal government reimbursed the state for the arms it lost during the Whiskey Rebellion. Along with the threat, he sent a request for new arms for the militia, reporting that the state was dangerously underequipped. The next governor repeated these entreaties and was equally ignored.[67]

The private, volunteer companies were generally better-armed and far more enthusiastic than their state-sponsored counterparts. For instance, the Washington Artillery of Washington, D.C., which started in the 1790s, maintained its exclusivity through a required election for all new members. Recruits were expected to supply their complete uniform as a sign of seriousness, but guns came from the company's private supply, which was sufficient for the entire troop. A new member of the company did not have to own a gun, but he did need a tailor.[68] In contrast, during the war scare in 1798, when the Quasi War with France seemed likely to expand, the nearby Alexandria militia regiment, only 18 percent of whom bore arms, frantically turned to the Virginia government for an additional five hundred muskets. The governor offered 250, noting that requests for arms were coming in from militia companies all over Virginia. The Fairfax County militia was in slightly better shape, needing only 250 guns to finish arming their 563 militia.[69]

The most active state militia, and the one best prepared for war, was in Massachusetts. Back in 1781 that state had created two kinds of militia: the Train Band and the Alarm List. The former, some five thousand volunteers, met and drilled regularly. The Alarm List was just that—a list of all fit males aged sixteen to sixty-five—who were required to keep arms and equipment and appear with them once a year at muster. The state saw to the arming of the Train Band while the towns were responsible for the Alarm List. The result was predictable: the Train Band generally met once a year and took such poor care of their equipment that the state employed gunsmiths to keep the guns in good repair; the Alarm Band atrophied. Some elite outfits, such as the Worcester County Regiment of Cavalry, simply disbanded; others looked for any excuse to cancel their annual musters: poor weather, inconvenient location, disagreements over the election of officers. And those were the volunteers. Levi Lincoln of the Worcester Light Infantry wrote that "the Militia of the Town of Worcester has long been in an undisciplined, ununiformed & unsoldierible situation." A militia could not function with so many "individuals thus transiently coming and going, not intending a permanent abode in the Town, find[ing] no inducement properly to equip & uniform themselves." Lincoln reported that the common soldiery was entirely "indifferent" to the state of the militia, and "gentlemen" found no incentive to purchase arms and equipment. Lincoln and several others therefore sought to organize a more exclusive militia company with membership based on election. The general court approved this request.[70]

In southeast Pennsylvania, those outraged by the new direct federal tax on houses, lands, and slaves, as well as by the Alien and Sedition Acts, launched what is known as the Fries Rebellion. In the first months of 1799 the rebels, most members of the militia, threatened tax assessors, one with being made to "dance around" a liberty pole, another with being "committed to an old stable and . . . fed rotten corn." Otherwise their only violence came with the beating of an assessor in a tavern, but their greatest crime came when John Fries, a local militia commander, led more than one hundred men armed with swords, clubs, and rifles to free some prisoners. No shots were fired, the point being a traditional effort to protest corrupt authority in what Fries's attorney Alexander Dallas called a "system of intimidation." To President John Adams, this system was treasonous, and he ordered five hundred federal troops under General William MacPherson to put down the uprising. There was no resistance, no violence, as this little army rounded up the leaders of the "rebellion" at a cost to the government of $80,000. Fries and two others were arrested, tried, convicted, and pardoned, and that was the end of it.[71]

Alexander Hamilton understood well the danger of "magnifying a riot into an insurrection, by employing in the first instance an inadequate Force." He advised Secretary of War James McHenry that "Whenever the Government appears in arms it ought to appear a *Hercules,* and inspire respect by the display of strength." Apparently five hundred well-armed troops were enough to overawe the poorly armed rebels. As with the Whiskey Rebellion, the insurgents found little support once the government acted. Even ardent Jeffersonians, while objecting to the use of federal troops instead of the state militia, agreed that anyone challenging federal authority should be brought to justice.[72]

As rumors spread that the Federalists might prevent Thomas Jefferson from taking office in 1801, Republican John Beckley of Pennsylvania charged that Federalists had removed "several hundred stand of arms and 18 pieces of cannon, heretofor in the hands of the Militia, . . . into the public arsenals of the U.S."[73] Fearing a showdown, Governor Monroe of Virginia planned for the Virginia militia to block any effort by federal troops to remove the federal arms stored in Virginia—which would have meant seizing them for state use.[74] Monroe even sent a spy, a militia officer, to check out the quality of these arms. Major T. M. Randolph reported that these "4000 excellent muskets and bayonets" had been seized from the British at Yorktown.[75] Governor Thomas McKean of Pennsylvania was even more emphatic in his preparations, informing Jefferson that "arms for upwards to twenty thousand were secured" by his government for the militia in case their service was required. He did not expect them to bring their own arms but planned to supply the militia with state arms.[76]

The militia debate at the turn of the century contained a powerful, and seemingly contradictory, political quality. The Republicans, though giving greater rhetorical support to the militia, would not back up that endorsement with financial or legal support. They tended to oppose any legislative coercion of militia duty. In contrast, the Federalists, supporters of a standing army and consistently contemptuous of the militia, worked hardest to arm and train the militia, and so sought laws mandating militia service. The Federalists ridiculed the untrained and buffoonish militia in Republican-controlled states, which generally did not allow enough money to train and arm their companies. "What could Pennsylvania do aided by Virginia," a Federalist paper asked of two Republican states, "the militia of the latter untrained and farcically performing the manual exercise with cornstalks instead of muskets?"[77] But as the crisis passed with the temporary resolution of the conflict with France and the peaceful inauguration of Thomas Jefferson, military enthusiasm waned, and militia companies throughout the country held ever fewer musters.[78]

The Search for Guns

In some ways the militia debates of the 1790s skirted a far more important issue. Real political independence required military independence, which in turn necessitated a domestic arms industry. Washington raised this question in his first annual message to Congress in 1790, clearly stating the lessons he had learned in the war: "A free people ought not only be armed, but disciplined; . . . and their safety and interest require that they should promote such manufactories as tend to rend them independent of others for essential, particularly military, supplies."[79] In late 1791 Secretary of the Treasury Alexander Hamilton attempted to bring system to this effort with his "Report on the Subject of Manufactures." Central to Hamilton's study of industry in the United States was the perceived necessity of developing those enterprises most essential to the nation's defense. The opening paragraph echoed Washington's message to Congress, which had in turn recapitulated Hamilton's 1783 report to Congress: "The Secretary of the Treasury . . . has applied his attention . . . to the subject of Manufactures; and particularly to the means of promoting such as will tend to render the United States, independent [of] foreign nations, for military and other essential supplies." This linking of independence and gunmaking was a constant theme for Hamilton as "Not only the wealth; but the independence and security of a Country, appear to be materially connected with the prosperity of manufactures." Hamilton defended the need for government support of domestic industries by arguing that an independent nation must be self-sufficient in "the means of Subsistence habitation clothing and defence. The possession of these is necessary to the perfection of the body politic, to the safety as well as to the welfare of the society; the want of either, is the want of an important organ of political life and Motion; and in the various crises which await a state, it must severely feel the effects of any such deficiency."

Hamilton's audience understood full well the context for these remarks: the Revolution. And in case they forgot, Hamilton reminded them: "The extreme embarrassments of the United States during the late War, from an incapacity of supplying themselves, are still matter of keen reflection." This was no abstract historical debate, for "A future war might be expected again to exemplify the mischiefs and dangers of a situation, to which that incapacity is still in too great a degree applicable, unless changed by timely and vigorous exertion." Now that the Constitution was in place, it was time to turn attention to building up an armaments industry: " 'tis the next great work to be accomplished."[80]

But these industries would not develop on their own. In Hamilton's New York City, for instance, the largest producer and dealer of guns in the final quarter of the eighteenth century was Gilbert Forbes, who never had more than fifty guns in stock. A study of thirty-six New York newspapers published between 1777 and 1799 found only nine gunsmiths advertising. Except for Forbes, none of these gunmakers did very well for themselves. Dozens of artisans throughout America had entered the gun cleaning and repairing trade during the Revolution, but as business quickly ebbed with peace, they returned to their previous crafts. Typical was William Allen, who made and repaired guns, "coffee-mills, mill saws, and . . . all kinds of jobbing in his branch of business," in the flea market from 1780 until 1807. By the end of the century, New York had two other gunmakers, Robert Corbett and John Dobson, who specialized in selling and repairing English guns, as did James Slater, who advertised that he also sold vegetables.[81]

Nothing had changed from the Colonial period, with all sorts of artisans, from ironworkers to jewelers, taking a hand in gun repair. Guns in this period were popularly perceived as luxury items; individual pistols and muskets advertised for sale generally dwelled on their style and, ironically, their English quality. Thus an advertisement offering "A Pair of silver-mounted Pistols, the property of an Officer of distinction. The locks are excellent, made by the famous Columbell" of London.[82] There is little evidence of a market for guns among the public. One study of the twenty-four newspapers published in Philadelphia, Maryland, and South Carolina from 1786 to 1800 reveals not a single advertisement for a gunsmith or gun repairs. An examination of the *Pittsburgh Gazette* in the same years discovers George McGunnigle, who advertised that he "makes locks, keys, hinges of all sorts, pipe tomahawks, scalping knives, . . . [and] all kinds of iron work for a kitchen." At the end of his long text, he adds that he "cleans and polishes guns and pistols."[83]

Hamilton understood that current production could not even approximate the most minimal needs of the United States. He therefore assured Congress that America's gunmakers "require the stimulus of a certain demand to render them adequate to the supply of the United States." The source of that stimulus seemed obvious to Hamilton: government subsidies and government patronage. Congress should appropriate funds not only to purchase firearms as a prod to gunmakers, but also to aid in the capital development of these manufactories. Hamilton advised that "provision should be made for an annual purchase of military weapons, of home manufacture" and for "the formation of Arsenals." He went even further, suggesting that private companies would not be sufficient. Congress needed to consider "whether manufactories of all the necessary weapons of war ought not to be established, on account of the Government itself." Hamilton admitted that, "As a general rule, [government] manufactories . . . are to be avoided." Gunmaking was the great exception to this rule. Hamilton insisted that the ideas he was advancing were hardly radical, as "Such establishments are agreeable to the usual practice of Nations and that practice seems founded on sufficient reason." It made no sense to leave "these essential instruments of national defence to the casual speculations of individual adventure." He then presented his clinching argument: guns are not "objects of ordinary and indispensable private consumption or use."[84]

Hamilton, Washington, and every member of Congress who had participated in the American Revolution knew that most Americans did not own guns and had no interest in buying them. As Hamilton said, guns were not "objects of ordinary and indispensable private consumption or use." Guns were most important as military weapons, and domestic production should be encouraged by the government precisely for that reason and because private demand would never lead to a sufficient supply for the military. Modern experts agree with the judgment of eighteenth-century specialists that firearms used by professionals, soldiers, and hunters had a life expectancy of five years. At that point they would need serious maintenance and repair, or to be replaced. The British army, which required the regular cleaning and inspection of all its guns, replaced roughly one-tenth of its well-made Brown Besses every year before the Napoleonic Wars. Using the army's replacement rate, and taking no account of population growth, means that Americans, if indeed every adult white male used a gun regularly to hunt, would have needed to purchase some fifty thousand guns a year by 1800. Where were they to find this many guns?

The problems inherent in any effort to arm the militia or even the U.S. Army were amply demonstrated in 1792. Congress, trying to keep the militia alive and to meet its constitutional mandate to regulate the militia, passed "An Act More effectually to provide for the National Defence." This act declared that "every free able bodied white male citizen of the respective States" between the ages of eighteen and forty-five should be enrolled in the militia and must appear "when called out to exercise." Further, "every citizen so enrolled, shall . . . be constantly provided with a good musket or firelock, a sufficient bayonet and belt, two spare flints," and other accoutrements. Congress took upon itself the responsibility of providing those guns, and specified that within five years all muskets "shall be of bores sufficient for balls of the eighteenth part of a pound." All arms and ammunition intended for militia use remained exempt from attachment in any civil suit. To keep track of its arms, each company was to make regular returns of arms and ammunition to each state's adjutant general, who in turn reported directly to the president.[85] To begin this process, Congress ordered the purchase of seven thousand muskets. Over the next two years the government was able to purchase only 480 "rifle guns."[86]

In 1793 Secretary Knox reported to the Senate that efforts to organize and arm the militia faced failure. Admitting that domestically produced guns were more expensive than European firearms, Knox insisted that considerations of cost must be irrelevant "compared with the solid advantages which would result from extending and perfecting the means upon which our safety may ultimately depend." Knox succinctly recommended that the federal government take over the production of firearms.[87]

Though some members of Congress thought that Washington and Knox exaggerated the problem, the experience of individual states matched warnings from the executive branch. Late in 1792, during a brief conflict with the Creek Indians, Charles Pickney reported to the South Carolina assembly that the frontier militia was dangerously under-armed. The western counties, "if properly supplied by Government with the means, [are] well disposed to exert themselves in defence of their possessions," but the state lacked sufficient stores to arm them. Governor Moultrie added his voice in alarm over "the defenceless Situation of the Frontier Inhabitants for want of Arms and Ammunition."[88] The legislature sent the two hundred stands of arms stored in the state house west and authorized the governor to purchase six hundred more muskets for public use. It took a year to acquire these guns, by which time the state government determined that it needed even more guns, which it frantically tried to acquire in Philadelphia. To see that these state guns were better cared for, the legislature ordered an arsenal capable of holding arms for five thousand men to be built at Abbeville. This arsenal was finished in December 1793 and the state then tried, unsuccessfully, to get the national government to pay for it. The experience of South Carolina in 1792 and 1793 demonstrates that whenever even a limited frontier war broke out, state governments had to request the aid of other states and the federal government, empty the public storehouses of guns for the frontier, and seek to purchase ever more arms.[89]

Most state governments appreciated that they could not possibly arm their militia without federal help. The 1792 national militia act had not clarified matters, since the most important issues—where the states would acquire guns and who would pay for them—had not been resolved. Maryland took the unique path of allowing its militia system to collapse; the legislature simply allowed the old militia law to expire, while it waited to see what the federal government would do.[90]

Henry Knox, hoping to federalize arms production, played on this knowledge of the states' inability to meet military crises. In 1794 Knox reported to Congress on the condition of the American militia. The greatest problem was that the "militia are requested to arm and equip themselves, at their own expense; but there is no penalty to enforce the injunction of law." The Whiskey Rebellion highlighted the defensive crisis facing the nation. "The deficiency of arms cannot be more forcibly exemplified," Knox wrote, "than that, to arm the militia lately called into service, estimated at fifteen thousand, the number of ten thousand arms have been issued from public arsenals. Loss and injury must be expected to arise upon the articles issued." In other words, only one-third of the militia called up to respond to the rebellion bore arms. The rest had to be supplied from federal stockpiles. By Knox's estimate, the nation could field 450,000 militia, of whom no more than 100,000 either owned or could be supplied with guns. The remaining 350,000 muskets, plus replacements for unusable weapons among the remaining 100,000, could not be met by buying guns in Europe, given the war there, nor by American gunmakers. Knox saw only one choice: government arsenals. "The only solid resource to obtain a supply," he said, "is the establishment of manufactories within each state."[91]

Despite initial fears of granting the central government too much power, Congress eventually agreed with Washington and his cabinet on the importance of arming the militia and army. If war broke out against a European power, the United States would be in no position to offer an adequate defense, and it could no longer expect to receive arms from France, as it had during the Revolution. America had to create domestic sources of firearms. Congress therefore appropriated the funds necessary to purchase fourteen thousand muskets and to build three armories to make firearms. The first of these national armories was built at Springfield, Massachusetts, the second at Harpers Ferry, Virginia; the third was never built. The United States government was now in the gunmaking business, an enterprise it would dominate and direct through the 1860s.[92]

Congress knew from the start that American gunmakers could not collectively produce in a reasonable period the fourteen thousand arms they hoped to buy. They did seek to confine the market by forbidding the export of American-made arms, the idea being that the government needed all the guns produced in the United States—not that there was any market for these inferior and more expensive guns abroad. In return for that limitation on production, Congress was basically promising to buy whatever American gunsmiths could make. Based on Hamilton's and Knox's estimates, they expected that production level to be seven thousand muskets in two years. Congress therefore appropriated $100,000 to the American minister in London to buy additional British firearms, while the British firm of Ketland garnered a contract to make the locks for the American-made muskets and rifles, a trade they maintained until 1812. Thus it was that the U.S. government's first large purchase of firearms after the winning of independence came from England, and that U.S. gunmakers could hope to reach the modest target of thirty-five hundred guns per year only by being supplied with English-made locks.[93]

Nonetheless, American gunmakers had troubles producing their seven thousand firearms. As delays persisted, the new secretary of war, Timothy Pickering, admitted that buying American-made guns was not only more expensive, but also less efficient. Regardless, he insisted to the Senate that the long-term advantages of patronizing American gunmakers far outweighed the disadvantages, especially as these gunmakers would certainly go out of business without government contracts. On Washington's orders, Pickering encouraged domestic production by ordering an additional nine thousand muskets "after the model of the French arms, which compose, by far, the greatest part of those in our magazines." He issued further advances even though the previous orders had not yet been met, and distributed gun locks purchased from England among these gunsmiths. They were all in serious denial about the capabilities of American gunsmiths.[94]

In 1795 a lone entrepreneur, Eli Whitney, decided to take advantage of these delays—and of personal connections—to win government funding. Whitney, already famous as the inventor of the cotton gin, entered the gunmaking business for a simple reason: to avoid bankruptcy. He did not in fact know anything about making firearms, but he hoped to use government advances to save his cotton gin business.[95] Secretary of the Treasury Oliver Wolcott Jr. was only too happy to believe Whitney's optimistic predictions, signing a contract for ten thousand muskets and bayonets modeled on the French Charleville Model 1763, still the most common musket in America. The government agreed to provide a $15,000 advance in three payments, all the gun stocks, and to pay all inspection costs. In return, Whitney promised to deliver four thousand muskets by September 1799, with the remainder handed over within the following year. Wolcott also signed contracts with twenty-six other gunmakers to purchase an additional thirty thousand muskets. Wolcott's expectations appear hopelessly optimistic, given that even the U.S. armory at Springfield (Harpers Ferry began production in 1801) could make only two thousand muskets a year.[96]

Within a year Whitney recognized the basic problem with large-scale arms production in the United States: there were not enough trained gunsmiths. In order to win more time from the government, Whitney invented the idea that he was developing interchangeable parts, which would transfer ever more of the labor to machines.[97] Whitney failed miserably in his effort to move beyond handmade firearms. He did succeed, however, in convincing government officials that he was about to make an important technological breakthrough. In his famous demonstration before John Adams and Thomas Jefferson in January 1801, Whitney fitted the parts from ten different gun locks to one musket using only a screwdriver. Jefferson, in his letter to James Monroe, expanded that number of locks tenfold in claiming that Whitney "has invented moulds and machines for making all the pieces of his locks so exactly equal, that take 100 locks to pieces and mingle their parts and the hundred locks may be put together" in any order.[98] But Whitney actually engaged in a shell game. His gun parts carried individual identification marks so that they could be fitted to one another, and each had been carefully hand-filed to insure that fit. The ten locks he used in Washington, D.C., in 1801 had been especially prepared for the purpose of deceiving the president-elect. From that day forth Whitney found it easy to persuade government officials that he was just about to make interchangeable parts for firearms in the absence of any real evidence to that effect.[99]

Whitney succeeded with his little fraud largely because most people, including many gunsmiths, remained uncertain of the very nature of their product. An 1803 article in a scientific encyclopedia admitted that the science of guns was beyond contemporary understanding. Certainly "the art" of gunnery "depends upon mathematical knowledge," but what exactly made guns work was open to debate. The "excessive power" of gunpowder "appears to proceed from the sudden generation of carbonic, hydrogen, and nitrogen gases." Gunmaking retained the alchemical aura of the mysterious, and the author noted that a white gunpowder that made no noise "has been talked of . . . but no powder answering this description has ever been seen." Whitney played on these fantasies.[100]

Granted, there is a solid myth, very hard to shake, that Eli Whitney developed the production of interchangeable parts. In fact, his guns never had interchangeable parts; the process eluded him and every other private gunmaker in America, including Samuel Colt fifty years later.[101] The U.S. Ordnance Department developed this essential characteristic of "the American system" at its Springfield armory with its model 1842 musket. No private manufacturer had sufficient capital to undertake such an enterprise. As the leading historian of arms production in the United States, Merritt Roe Smith, has observed, "Since precision production was expensive, . . . only the government could afford the luxury of complete interchangeability."[102] The rest was promotion and advertising.

Far from demonstrating how easy it was to build guns with interchangeable parts, Whitney had a great deal of difficulty in making any guns at all. He could not locate sufficient iron or workers who knew the trade, and had enormous trouble organizing those workers he could find. Under Whitney's authoritarian management style, his Mill Rock armory was reputed to have the highest turnover rate in the arms trade. By 1799 he had not yet delivered a single musket, but received another $10,000 advance from Wolcott to keep trying. By the end of 1800, when Wolcott resigned from the treasury, Whitney had still not handed over a single firearm.[103]

Throughout this process, Whitney and all independent observers understood the necessity of government support for building up America's gun industry. Colonel Decius Wadsworth, chief of the Ordnance Department and Whitney's close friend, wrote the secretary of the treasury in 1800 supporting further funding for Whitney's efforts. Though Whitney had yet to make a gun, Wadsworth explained that the reason was that he was trying to make what no American ever had in any number, "the most difficult part" of gun production—the lock. Wadsworth was confident of Whitney's "eventual complete success, provided he receives suitable support and encouragement from the government." Prompted by Wadsworth's enthusiasm, the government agreed to another $10,000 advance.[104] At one point the government even lost track of how much it had paid Whitney, who received $134,000 from this contract, all but $2,400 before its completion.[105]

These advances were interest-free and unrelated to results. Simeon North of Connecticut contracted to make the first five hundred pistols for the government in 1799. The following year, though North still had not delivered the first shipment, the Ordnance Department agreed to another fifteen hundred pistols with an advance of $6,000.[106] It never seemed to occur to any contemporary that gun manufacturing should be left to the vagaries of the free market, perhaps because they all knew that the public was not sufficiently interested in guns.

There is evidence that the number of private gunmakers in the United States actually decreased in the first decade of the nineteenth century. Between 1800 and 1804 only six gunsmiths advertised in New York's eighteen newspapers. Those who did so continued to appeal to the elite market. Thus William Allen announced that he specialized in English guns, while Benjamin & J. Cooper from Birmingham "invite gentlemen sportsmen to call at their shop" to inspect their fine selection of English guns. Others, from a whipmaker to a plate-ware dealer, announced that they had English guns for sale, and most merchants dealing in imported goods generally carried a few English guns. No one seemed to want to admit that they carried American-made firearms. There were several notices, however, asking customers to pick up guns left to be repaired, notices that often ran for months. As during the Revolution, those repairing guns practiced many trades, from blacksmith to trussmaker.[107]

The shortage of gunmakers in the early republic is clearly illustrated in the history of Virginia's effort to establish an armory. In 1797 Governor James Wood informed the legislature that his government had searched the state to find anyone who could make arms for the militia, without success. Wood therefore contracted to purchase four thousand stands of arms from England and another four thousand muskets from the Globe Mills in Pennsylvania. The latter source made just 925 arms over the next five years and then went bankrupt. It was at this point that the Virginia government agreed with a plan that John Clarke had been promoting for several years to build an armory in Virginia to make guns for state use. In creating the Virginia Manufactory of Arms at Richmond, Clarke found it necessary to buy all his tools in England. More frustrating, he quickly discovered that there were only a few gunsmiths in Virginia and they all did exclusively repair work. Clarke ended up hiring sixty-eight workers, all of them from outside Virginia and a dozen brought over from Ireland. For the rest of its brief history this need to find skilled gunsmiths prevented the armory from ever producing many arms. Virginia's was the only state armory in antebellum America, averaging 2,130 muskets per year, or twenty-six guns per worker.[108]

Lancaster, Pennsylvania, an historic gunmaking district, contained ten gunmakers in 1803, and they worried that their craft was dying out.[109] In a petition to Congress they complained that a recent act exempting "arms manufactured in foreign countries" from export duties would "crush this manufacture in its infant establishment." Pointing out the obvious, they wrote that there were currently too few arms manufactured in the United States and too few people capable of repairing those necessary for national defense. With proper government "patronage and encouragement," and high import duties, they predicted that they would soon be making twenty thousand stands of arms a year in Pennsylvania. They admitted that they had already received government support, but transformed that largesse into an entitlement. "Allured" by government contracts, "they have increased their establishments, taken in and instructed apprentices, and excited, by their undertakings, a competition—a spirit of enterprise, among their fellow citizens, in this manufacture, so essential to national safety, national independence, and national reputation." Free trade would crush this enterprise, with the government to blame. The Lancaster gunmakers had become dependent on government contracts and funding; every year they received orders for twenty-five to one hundred guns, which they divided among themselves, each making a few of the guns. They concluded their plea with a striking question that reminded Congress how few gunsmiths the nation could call upon: "Arms may be imported, but who will keep them in repair?"[110]

Congress did not abandon its gunmakers, retaining a duty on foreign firearms. The government's continuing financial support of private gunmakers flew in the face of results. Just under one thousand had been delivered by September 30, 1800, the date on which the government was supposed to have received the forty thousand muskets commissioned from twenty-seven gunmakers. Many gun factories turned out to be flash-in-the-pan operations, taking advantage of government contracts and then vanishing. Others delivered just a few guns and then abandoned the business.[111]

Eli Whitney proudly turned over his first five hundred muskets one year later—after spending $30,000 in government funds—making these among the most expensive muskets available in the United States at that time. The government promptly provided another $5,000 to encourage further production. By the end of 1801 Whitney delivered five hundred more muskets, while the other gunmakers finished 646 muskets between them. Whitney's thousand muskets raised the hopes of Secretary of War Henry Dearborn, but without cause, as Whitney kept asking for further extensions on delivery deadlines. Whitney did not fulfill his contract until late in 1809, nine years behind schedule. The other twenty-six gunmakers produced just two thousand muskets—twenty-eight thousand (93 percent) short of their goal—only one of them fulfilling his contract with the government, and that five years late.[112]

At peak production, Whitney's force of fifty workers made fifteen hundred muskets in a single year. This rate of thirty muskets per worker per year was 50 percent higher than the average that a single gunmaker aided only by an apprentice could hope to make. Yet it was still not a significant economy of scale, and was still a long way from meeting government demands. These production levels were particularly unimpressive because Whitney continued to purchase finished gun stocks and barrels from other gunmakers until the mid-1820s. Whitney saw his armory not so much as a manufactory than as an assembly shop where guns were fitted together, with the hand-filing of parts the most common task. Files were the most common tool in Whitney's shop, as in any gunsmith shop in America. Whitney's one great innovation came not in technology but in management. He was able to calculate his costs with far greater accuracy than any gunmaker in the United States, even figuring interest and insurance into his overhead. In this fashion he insured a sound profit at every turn, while other armsmakers guessed at costs and added what seemed a fair profit to that figure.[113]

There was just one further problem: Whitney's guns were dreadful. The U.S. government accepted them but did not test them until 1808. In that year Secretary Dearborn was boasting of Whitney's muskets to a guest, who asked to inspect one. When they examined the musket, they found its brass pan did not close, the ramrod bent at its first use, and the breech plate was, well, substandard. Dearborn was livid, entering into a long dispute with Whitney.[114]

The government had better luck with its own armories. Dissatisfied not only with the slow rate of production on the part of private gunmakers, but also with the inconsistent quality of the finished product, the government armories accelerated the production of muskets, rifles, and, starting in 1805, pistols.[115] But Harpers Ferry and Springfield remained partially dependent on Europe. The Department of War insisted that its guns meet European standards; thus the two armories produced muskets based on French designs with an emphasis on high-quality bayonets. Their raw materials also came largely from Europe. Of the twenty-two thousand pounds of steel purchased by Springfield Armory between 1798 and 1800, only five hundred pounds came from the United States.[116]

Even with high levels of government support, it took far longer than expected for the armories to reach levels considered satisfactory. Springfield Armory, which aimed to produce 4,200 muskets per year between 1795 and 1799, manufactured 7,750 in its first five years, 37 percent of its goal. In the first decade of the nineteenth century, Springfield Armory averaged just over five thousand guns of all kinds per year. Harpers Ferry could not meet that standard. As Merritt Roe Smith has written, "Productivity at Harpers Ferry between 1801 and 1806 revealed few signs of growth," with an annual output of seventeen hundred arms a year.[117]

The federal government could do only so much to overcome two centuries of reliance on Europe for firearms. In 1810, after fifteen years of government support, Secretary of the Treasury Albert Gallatin issued a report on manufactures. Gallatin listed guns under "manufactures of iron," which "consist principally of agricultural implements," adding that "all of the finer species" of such work was imported from Britain. The two government arsenals reached a high of nineteen thousand muskets that year, with another twenty thousand guns made by private manufacturers nationwide—thirty-nine thousand guns for a population of 7,202,014, more than 1 million of whom were supposed to be in the militia (or, enough guns for less than 4 percent of the militia). Gallatin also noted that "The manufacture of gunpowder is nearly . . . adequate to the consumption," with the country importing 200,000 pounds a year while exporting 100,000 pounds. More gunpowder could easily be produced, "if there was a demand for it."[118] The government still had a long way to go if it hoped to meet the Constitution's mandate in article 1, section 8, "To provide for organizing, arming, and disciplining, the Militia."

Arming the Militia

American gun production at the beginning of the nineteenth century was minuscule. A gunsmith who made twenty guns a year did very well for himself. Washington, Hamilton, Knox, Adams, and even Thomas Jefferson—otherwise a naïf on military matters—understood well the shortage of firearms in the United States; their continued dependence on European manufacturers grated on their patriotism. Lacking even one gun manufactory in the entire country, Congress ordered the establishment of federal armories and arsenals under government control. In 1808 Congress passed its single most important piece of legislation promoting the development of a domestic gun industry. The 1808 Militia Act appropriated $200,000 a year "for the purpose of providing arms and military equipment for the whole body of the militia of the United States, either by purchase or manufacture." The act further authorized the president to purchase sites for and erect arsenals and arms manufactories "as he may deem expedient." "All the arms procured in virtue of this act, shall be transmitted to the several states . . . in proportion to the number of the effective militia in each state and territory."[119] From that date until 1865, the federal government pursued a policy aimed at making the United States self-sufficient in firearms and of arming the nation's adult white male population. Neither task proved easy, and the first would be accomplished long before the second.

A largely unarmed United States faced an angry world in 1808. Though the great powers of Europe seemed primarily concerned with tearing one another apart, they also appeared intent on dragging America into the Napoleonic Wars, either through inducement or by bullying.

Congress had real cause to fear that war with either Britain or France was imminent, and Thomas Jefferson pursued both a pacific embargo of trade with Europe and a halfhearted effort to arm the nation for defense. Jefferson held a generally ambiguous attitude toward a standing army: he did not want one, but understood its necessity. He sought evidence that his faith in the ability of the militia to protect the nation was well placed, but without much luck. As he formulated his position in his first inaugural address, "a well-disciplined militia, [is] our best reliance in peace, and for the first moments of war, till regulars may relieve them." But when matters became serious he needed both a "well-disciplined militia" and a standing army to replace them. Thus Jefferson found himself trying to do the same as Washington, only by spending less money.[120]

Most of Jefferson's followers shared his esteem for the militia. During an 1803 congressional debate on whether Washington, D.C., should have a militia, William Eustis (a future secretary of war) proclaimed that the militia was necessary for the defense of government, a point made by most of the other speakers. Though a rather unrealistic perspective, as would become apparent in 1812, this ideological reliance on the militia persisted. The Jeffersonians hoped to arm the people and not the army, an unrealizable goal. Nor would Congress accept any effort to reactivate the militia, rejecting Jefferson's modest reform efforts, as they would those of President Madison in 1809 and 1810, for their excess of centralization. Adhering to their ideology rather than the Constitution, Republicans insisted that the states must decide on the organization of their militia. Finding that the states would do nothing on their own, Jefferson again shifted his ground. It was only "when Jefferson failed to realize any of his utopias," Russell F. Weigley has written, that "he habitually made a flexible adjustment to the world as he found it." In this case, Jefferson perceived that America's citizens were largely unarmed and uninterested in militia duty, so the country "would have to settle for a standing army."[121]

Not everyone agreed with this notion that the government should arm the people. New York's Governor Daniel Tompkins thought it improper for the state to arm the people, telling a delegation of citizens from Ontario County who were requesting arms in 1807 that every freeman should take pride in gun ownership and not depend on the state arsenal. Tompkins noted that the legislature had acted on this assumption, and thus had purchased few arms for the militia. The result, Tompkins admitted, was that every militia company in the state was deficient in arms. The following year, a group of citizens from frontier Jefferson County, New York, wrote to President Jefferson begging the federal government to provide arms, as they feared the outbreak of an Indian war. The petition stated that there were three thousand men capable of bearing arms, yet that no more than four hundred guns were available in the whole county because the people were "extremely poor."[122]

Jefferson hoped to find evidence that he could avoid these expenses. In 1803 he therefore instructed Secretary of War Henry Dearborn to conduct a careful census of firearms in America, with the intention of demonstrating that the American militia owned sufficient firearms. The results disappointed Jefferson. In a country with 524,086 official militia, Dearborn found 183,070 muskets, 39,648 rifles, and 13,113 other firearms, for a total of 235,831 guns (there were also 11,882 sabers). That was enough guns for 45 percent of the militia, one-fifth of the white male population, and just 4.9 percent of the nation's total population. Half of all these guns were in the hands of the federal government, with about one-quarter in state arsenals. The remainder were privately owned.[123] Dearborn's study was much more thorough than Henry Knox's 1793 effort, and was disturbing enough for him to make an additional meticulous count of all federal firearms in 1806. That second count caused even greater concern, with 113,501 muskets, 3,666 rifles, 1,938 pistols, and 980 carbines and fusees.[124] Dearborn concluded that if the United States continued to rely on the militia for its defense, and if the people would not arm themselves, then the federal government would have to do so. On this point at least, Jeffersonians and Federalists agreed. Though they still disagreed over who in the militia should get the arms—the Federalists still calling for a select militia—they did not dispute that the militia needed guns. Dearborn's numbers convinced a unified Congress to pass the 1808 Militia Act.[125]

As an immediate step, while waiting for America's gunmakers to kick into high gear, Jefferson's government offered public arms to the states at the rock-bottom price of $10 per stand. Only three states took them up on this offer: Maryland purchased 7,600 guns, Georgia 4,000, and Delaware 650. The other states held out, preferring to wait for the government to give them guns free. They would have a long wait.[126]

The government armories at Springfield and Harpers Ferry were doing fairly well, producing between five thousand and ten thousand guns every year between them. But that was barely enough to keep the army in working firearms. The experience of 1798 indicated that no gun-maker in America could produce more than a hundred muskets a year, except Eli Whitney, whose reliability even Jefferson came to question. Congress hoped that a concerted effort by the federal government to arm the militia would encourage gunmakers to expand their operations. Jefferson appointed Tench Coxe, purveyor of public supplies, to handle the procurements. In June 1808 Coxe took the unusual step of placing advertisements in most of the major newspapers in the country, calling for bids. Over the next five months Coxe signed contracts with almost everyone who replied to his advertisement.[127] These nineteen gunmakers agreed to deliver a total of eighty-five thousand muskets over the next five years. The single largest contract was for ten thousand muskets with Pennsylvania's Henry family, in their third generation of gunmaking. The government advanced nearly $100,000 to aid these gunmakers, not a single one of whom met his schedule. After two years, by which time seventeen thousand muskets were due, only three thousand had been delivered. By the end of 1813, the government was to have spent one million dollars and acquired at least 85,000 muskets; they had spent half that amount and received 34,477 guns (40 percent). Several gunmakers wanted to give up and get out of their contracts; even the Henry family bailed out after delivering 4,246 of the 10,000 guns they had promised to make. The new commissary general of purchases, Callender Irvine, willingly agreed to terminate these contracts, especially after his inspection convinced him that those guns delivered had little value beyond what they would fetch as scrap.[128]

In short, gun production outside of the two national armories continued to be a matter of small-scale operations. Tench Coxe's report of American manufactures in June 1813 listed a total of 154 gunmakers in eleven states, 115 of them in Pennsylvania. He placed the total value of these enterprises at $593,993, an average capitalization of $5,165, but a mean of just over $1,000. Coxe did not discuss the manufacturing capabilities of America's gunmakers, even though there was a war on. Instead the poor quality of these guns captured his attention, leading him to suggest that it was about time for the government to establish adequate testing facilities.[129]

At this very time that many Jeffersonians began questioning the capacity and ability of American gunmakers, others started wondering whether Washington had not in fact been right about the militia. In 1809

Connecticut's Benjamin Tallmadge, a member of the House of Representative's Committee on the Militia, issued the usual insistence on the value of the militia. In response, General Ebenezer Huntington, Revolutionary War veteran and past commander of the Connecticut militia, stated roughly that "as soldiers [the militia] are not worth their rations." He did not believe that the government should waste its time arming the militia, as they did not take care of their arms, which are soon "destroyed with rust," and "I have no doubt might be considered a total loss in five years." Huntington returned to Knox's older idea of volunteer units, smaller and better trained, and committed to taking care of their arms. Without such reform, the militia would be little better than "food for powder on the day of battle."[130]

Republicans slowly came to the realization that their ideology of a well-armed universal militia had no relation to reality. Prominent Republicans like Joseph Priestly and John Taylor of Caroline wrote in favor of a professional army, dismissing traditional fears of a standing army as irrelevant. National survival had to take precedence over ideological purity. Maximillian Godefroy, a French veteran living in Maryland, published a pamphlet in 1807 arguing that the American resistance to all military skills, from shooting to marching, left the country no alternative but to turn to a professional army. In America, Godefroy wrote, "military talents are repulsed, and military ideas rejected as useless." While Europe was developing a whole range of new military techniques, the United States clung to vain hopes that the militia would somehow save the nation. Many in Congress agreed with Representative Harmanus Bleecker of New York, that "the militiaman is best employed at his plough."[131]

David Humphreys had stated the case plainly in 1803 when he observed that military skills are "not so simple and easy as to come instinctively without practice."[132] The most ardent Republicans came to understand that the militia needed guns in order to learn how to use them. In state after state, officials complained that they were not yet receiving the free arms promised under the 1808 Militia Act. In 1809 Joseph Bloomfield of New Jersey began an angry letter to Congress by quoting the Constitution as requiring Congress to arm the militia. He then added pointedly, "They have not done it. The National Legislature have neglected what they ought have done the moment it was in their power" to arm the militia. He lambasted the idiocy of expecting individuals to arm themselves, a highly unlikely prospect. In no state, Bloomfield declared, had even one-sixth of the militia succeeded in arming itself appropriately. He laid the responsibility for the nation's undefended state squarely on Congress, which he believed had shirked its most fundamental duty.[133]

The separate states had not done much better. Massachusetts and Virginia were the best-armed states with just over thirty thousand muskets each. The majority of these arms had been purchased in Europe; despite its armory, Virginia continued to import arms until 1812. Only five other states made any significant purchases in the first twenty years of the republic: Maryland and Georgia, which had purchased guns from the federal government; Pennsylvania, which bought one thousand guns from several sources in the 1790s; and Connecticut and New York, which each purchased more than one thousand guns from 1800 to 1810. Massachusetts took a different path, attempting to regulate the manufacture of firearms within its borders, and spending tens of thousands of dollars to repair preexisting firearms rather than acquiring new ones. As the crisis with France and Britain heated up after 1808, several states attempted to fill the gap by helping their own gunmakers by granting contracts for militia arms. Only New York saw its contract fulfilled, though in twice the time allotted. That successful gunmaker was Eli Whitney, who had been left out of this round of federal largesse.[134]

In the crisis of war in 1812, the government turned to anyone who could make firearms, no matter how unsatisfactory earlier experiences. As a consequence, even Whitney received a contract for fifteen thousand muskets. Whitney was supposed to deliver the first few thousand by May 1813. It was August 1814 before the first five hundred were ready for inspection. It was not a happy inspection. Callender Irvine took his duties seriously and had little patience for Whitney's excuses. Irvine discovered that Whitney's bayonet was two inches shorter than specified and could be bent by hand. Irvine also found fault with the poor construction of the stock and the lock, while the breech was not watertight. But worst of all, the barrel was crooked. And this particular musket was the one that Whitney had selected as best exemplifying the quality of his production. Irvine was furious, telling Whitney that not a penny more would be paid for such defective weapons.[135]

Whitney responded with an amazing countercharge. Playing the aggrieved party, Whitney stated that he had contracted to duplicate the muskets he had made for New York, defects and all. The contract stated that he should make guns "in all respects conformable to the Model of the muskets which the said Whitney hath heretofore manufactured for the

State of New York." Given that wording, Whitney wrote, "From this standard I consider myself as having no right to deviate without the consent of the government and I humbly conceive that government have no right to *require* a deviation without my consent." The muskets he made for New York and the United States shared exactly the same problems. The idea that the government could find quality muskets at the prices they offered was, in Whitney's view, simply ludicrous: "it is an expectation which can never be realized." The government was offering $13 per gun, and Whitney valued the model Irvine rejected as equivalent to a $40 gun. "I am well aware," he told Irvine, that a superior "workman" might make "a small number of muskets . . . stocked with all that nice precision and exactness which is observed in stocking a Sporting gun which is sold for twenty guineas." But attaining such quality, equal to the best guns made in Europe, would require much more money. As it was, Whitney's production levels had dropped to ten guns per worker per year. Whitney reminded Irvine that "I have had more practical experience in Musket making than any other man in America, having been longer employed in that business and manufactured a greater number of Muskets than any other individual in the U. States." Clearly, to Whitney, Irvine was being quite unreasonable.[136]

Irvine was not impressed. As desperate as the nation was for any firearms, it still needed guns that worked. He reminded Whitney that his opinions were meaningless, as "you are not a practical Gun Smith." He was a businessman seeking his own interest, in this case to the detriment of the nation's defense. "But I have neither leisure or time to spare for an Epistolary controversy with you," he angrily told Whitney. "You have failed to execute your engagements to the manifest injury of the Service. . . . It is therefore my duty to require of you to refund promptly, the money with interest which had been advanced to you by the United States."[137]

Irvine underestimated Whitney. He may not have been "a practical Gun Smith," but he certainly understood the connection between politics and arms production. While Irvine attempted to bring suit against Whitney for the money the government had already given him, Whitney was meeting privately with the secretaries of state, war, and the treasury, as well as with President Madison. The upshot of these efforts was that the Ordnance Department found itself purchasing a total of fifteen thousand Whitney muskets. The first one thousand arrived in time for the end of the war, the remainder being delivered between 1815 and 1822. Whitney emerged from the War of 1812 the most prominent gunmaker in the United States. It was a status he did not deserve, as even he admitted that his guns did not work very well.[138]

Simeon North should have captured the public's attention, as he made some of the finest guns in America. But he lacked Whitney's flair for self-promotion and politics, and Whitney's willingness to prevaricate.[139] Like Whitney, North needed a steady fix of federal funds in order to stay afloat. For instance, in 1813 the government supplied North with a $20,000 advance toward the production of twenty thousand pistols. In 1816 he altered the design of these pistols and received an extra $1 per gun and another $25,000 advance. Three years later, the government made a $20,000 advance for another twenty thousand pistols. North eventually delivered these forty thousand pistols, though it took eight years. Other gunmakers simply went under when the war ended.[140]

The Militia in Peace and War

The first great test of the southern militia under the Constitution came in Virginia in 1800. The southern militia's primary purpose was the preservation of white supremacy. The slave patrols, whose members were drawn from the militia rosters, handled routine policing. But slave insurrections pushed the militia to its limits, demonstrating that not even the fear of slave uprisings sufficed to motivate the majority of whites to own guns and practice their use. In the first year of that new century, an African American named Gabriel rattled the south to its core with a vivid anticipation of the danger facing southern whites. Gabriel's Rebellion also revealed a core paradox in the question of arms in the South: the need of the state to hold guns that would be easily accessible to the militia, but not to the slaves. These stored arms became the most tempting target for any revolutionary force. Thus Gabriel's first goal was to capture the militia arms stored in the Richmond capitol. Gabriel understood that his forces would initially be armed only with swords, knives, pikes, and what few muskets he could seize from the white planters.[141]

A further weakness in the southern militia was their reliance on slave workers to maintain and even guard their armories. At the heart of Gabriel's plan to seize the government's arms was Cowley, the door-keeper of the capitol since the Revolution, who held all the keys in his possession. Even the most trusted slave might be enticed to join in an effort to win freedom. Cowley intended to hand over the keys to the armory as soon as Gabriel showed up with his forces.[142]

Gabriel appreciated the need for weapons and sought out any slave who had access to either a sword or a musket. He recruited a slave named Gilbert by asking if Gilbert "had a Sword." Gilbert "replied that his Master had one hanging up in the house, which he would get." Other slaves told Gabriel that they would join him only if he could supply them with arms.[143] They understood that arms were not readily available, and that a sword was as good as a gun in a surprise attack. At the beginning of his rebellion, Gabriel had access to only six guns, but he was a blacksmith and he ingeniously manufactured a great many swords by splitting farm scythes in two. When Gabriel learned that a local tavern owner stored several firearms, he immediately made that tavern his first stop on the road to Richmond, while a second group would head to the unfinished penitentiary, where powder was stored.[144]

As soon as Governor James Monroe heard the rumors of the planned uprising, he ordered all the "publick arms" moved from the capitol to the penitentiary under a guard of thirteen armed militia—a surprisingly small force, but all that was available at the time. The problem then became to issue some of these arms to the militia units called up by Monroe. One of the curious aspects of the rebellion was Monroe's hesitance to call out the militia because of its expense. As Monroe discovered, militiamen, even in the face of a slave rebellion, extracted every possible penny from the state for their service. They did not rush to service when called; they had to be cajoled, and the prime incentive was pay. The cost of suppressing Gabriel's Rebellion ultimately absorbed a tenth of Virginia's annual budget.[145]

A general panic spread through much of Virginia at the start of Gabriel's uprising, and whites demanded immediate militia protection. The Suffolk militia found, however, that they had too few guns to provide an effective defense, and appealed to the governor for aid. Monroe promised to supply arms, but then discovered that the state had insufficient guns even for the five hundred militia so far ordered into action. The militia officers appealed repeatedly for aid, without success, finally arming their troops with whatever they could lay their hands on, mostly bladed weapons.[146]

Most observers, including John Randolph, felt that only heavy rains and the early discovery of the uprising prevented a successful slave rebellion. As James Callender wrote Thomas Jefferson, the insurrection "could hardly have failed of success, . . . for after all, we could only muster four or five hundred men of whom no more than thirty had Muskets."[147] Norfolk mayor Thomas Newton was delighted to hear that the militia had been called out, but complained that "they have not arms, and are on that account only equal to the slaves except in numbers." Mayor Newton insisted that it was the state's job to see that the militia was properly armed. Mayor John Bracken of Williamsburg felt the same, and frantically requested "the loan of 25 Stand of Arms & the necessary Accoutrements" from Governor Monroe. Williamsburg received nothing from the state, its stores already exhausted. Their opponents were not much better armed. The militia searched every slave quarters in the area for weapons. On the Prosser plantation, Gabriel's home, they found "a number of rude arms," and not much more.[148]

During the slave insurrection scare of 1802, Monroe reserved most of the state's arms for the 19th Regiment of Richmond, charged with protecting the capital. That unit was fully armed with "four hundred and twelve stands of public Arms." Monroe felt that he had learned his lesson from Gabriel's Rebellion, and that with the vast majority of his citizens "unarmed . . . they may become a prey to a very small force." He therefore sought to ensure that the slave patrols were better armed and far more intrusive.[149] The terror aroused in the white breast by Gabriel's Rebellion saw an increase in the purchase and carrying of firearms. Like many other of the planter class, Benjamin Howard started carrying a pistol with him wherever he went, even "a courting." Still, it is difficult to imagine how much good a single-shot flintlock would have done Howard in the face of a slave insurrection. More significant was the almost immediate dormancy of the Virginia militia. When the terror passed, most white males lost interest in military matters and returned to their fields and their crafts.[150]

Almost immediately after Gabriel's Rebellion, militia companies throughout the South had difficulty finding officers. Elections were followed by immediate resignations. State governments responded by appointing officers, with penalties for noncompliance. Officers who did serve discovered that many of the men issued muskets for use on muster day failed to show up. Charles Little, appointed commander of the Alexandria militia against his will, asked the governor how to recover such arms, and was told just to go get them—something he was loath to do. Most commanders dealt with this problem, which persisted until the state built centralized arsenals in the 1870s, by keeping their guns in their houses and issuing them only on muster days.[151]

Curiously, the city volunteer militia companies continued to flourish when all others dried up. Washington's Artillery Company prospered, as did the artillery company in New York City, founded in 1806. Linked to the Masons, this volunteer company became the favorite at parades in the early republic, whether in Fourth of July celebrations or at funerals of prominent figures. Like other volunteer companies, the emphasis was on uniforms, with the company storing and supplying muskets for parade use. This company, which attracted some of the most respectable young men in the city, was also the most successful. In 1807 it grew to four companies totaling 129 men and eleven officers, and eventually became the 7th Regiment, the most prominent militia company in the state. But that development came well after the War of 1812.[152]

The public militia companies did not enjoy similar fortune. In the midst of the Embargo crisis of 1807, the Delaware adjutant general received returns that caused him to despair. In the 2d Regiment, the sixty-nine men of the third company had twenty-six guns of different caliber, not one of which was deemed serviceable; the eighty-five men of the fourth company had twenty fowling pieces, not one fit for service; while the fifth company had eighty-five men with thirty-five useless guns. No wonder Governor Mitchell told the legislature that the militia was effectively unarmed and that it was ridiculous to expect the people to arm themselves.[153]

One can examine the records kept by any public official associated with the militia in the early nineteenth century and find similar complaints of the lack of firearms and the general failure of the system. Two examples, one urban and the other frontier, should give a sense of this crisis. W. C. C. Claiborne served as governor of the Mississippi Territory between 1801 and 1803, and Jefferson appointed him the first governor of Orleans Territory in 1812. His letters from these posts evidence well his frustration with what he called the most "unpleasant & difficult undertaking" of organizing the militia. He complained to Secretary of State Madison in the beginning of 1802 that his efforts "to organize the Militia" of Mississippi had met "many obstacles . . . the greatest of which are the want of arms and the means of obtaining a supply." The government helped by sending 163 rifles and one hundred muskets to be stored for the militia's use, increasing the number of guns in the territory by 47 percent to 820, enough for 31.7 percent of the registered militia.[154] Claiborne faced roughly the same difficulties in Louisiana. The militia system there "is greatly defective." Men were not showing up or not obeying orders; the best-disciplined group was the free black regiment; one battalion, the Blues, simply dissolved itself so as to not bother with musters; and "the muskets of several Company's . . . have been reported to be as totally unfit for use, and I am solicited to furnish arms, which would enable them to render service if the occasion should require." He suggested to the local army commander that they exchange defective, privately owned muskets for good army guns. The army agreed to supply three hundred muskets; yet within two years Claiborne was again complaining to the legislature that the militia "must to armed and disciplined." Two years after that, in 1811, he again "renew[ed] my entreaties for a more energetic Militia System."[155]

The militia companies of Washington, D.C., so close to the center of national power, demonstrate the same problems. The public's general attitude is easily revealed by the passage of an act in 1803 making it illegal to heckle the Washington militia at muster. The voters of Alexandria indicated their attitude that same year when they passed an ordinance forbidding the firing of firearms within town boundaries, requiring the militia either to meet outside of town or to refrain from discharging their arms during musters.[156] An effort by the D.C.-area militia to celebrate Independence Day with a parade was canceled for lack of interest. A city effort, lacking militia involvement, went ahead. Ironically one of the toasts at the celebration was to the militia as "the surest safeguard of republican governments." The country may have been in trouble.[157]

Of all the companies listed in the District of Columbia, only the volunteer Artillery Company held musters between 1803 and 1807. On July 4 of that latter year the D.C.-area militia brigade held its first full muster, with the Alexandria militia receiving, without benefit of enabling legislation, sufficient federal arms for half their membership. Nonetheless, during the war scare later that summer, a delegation from Alexandria called on President Jefferson himself to request that the remaining units be armed by the federal government. He promised to keep some arms in readiness should they be attacked.[158]

The first captain of the newly organized Columbian Dragoons proved more resourceful. William Brent also went straight to the top, requesting that the president supply arms for those who could not afford them. In the most grandiose terms, Brent told Jefferson that "as the happiness also of millions depends on the safety of the Government, we flatter ourselves that a supply of sabres, Pistols & Carbines will not be deemed an indelicate or unreasonable request." Jefferson ignored Brent as he did Senator Samuel Smith, who requested a loan of arms for the Baltimore militia. Jefferson insisted that only militia in the field or about to take the field would receive federal arms. Smith gave up; Brent turned to the secretary of war, who allowed General Mason, commander of the D.C. militia, to request surplus arms from the navy, which was replacing some of their arms with new muskets from Harpers Ferry. Thus the Dragoons "borrowed" seventy-five old navy muskets. Such was the path of militia armaments.[159] A final indicator of the dependence of local militia companies on federal arms is offered by a group of young Washingtonians, who formed themselves into a volunteer company, only to disband a few days later when the War Department rejected their request for guns.[160]

The 1808 Militia Act intended to prevent militia companies from collapsing by promising a steady flow of government arms. But, as discussed above, the reality proved a different matter, with domestic gun production unable to meet even the modest contracts of the U.S. government. With the renewed war scare in 1810, several governors reported with alarm the inadequacy of their militia's armaments. The federal government responded by attempting to prod the gunmakers into rejuvenated efforts.[161] In 1810 William Henry Harrison observed in the leading Republican newspaper that nothing but empty words backed up the universal militia ideal: "There is no political axiom more generally diffused amongst the people of the United States, than that which declares a militia to be the only proper defence of a republic." Yet training and government support for armaments were minimal.[162]

In December 1811 a special House committee on munitions reported confidently that "the manufacture of cannon and small arms, and the stock and resources of all the necessary munitions are adequate to emergencies." Reassuring themselves, the committee noted the "flourishing state of the foundries" that "have arrived at perfection." Looking over the lists of munitions owned by the U.S. government, they found some slight cause for concern. The government owned 224,402 stands of arms, onetenth of which were unusable. On paper this certainly looked like more than enough firearms for a war, but there were less than another one hundred thousand guns in the whole country, enough in total for just half the militia. The committee therefore urged that "a further provision of all the munitions of war be forthwith made."[163]

The governor and legislature of Kentucky disagreed emphatically with the congressional assertion that America was well armed. In a March 1812 petition to Congress, they drew attention to the difficulty of "hunting up arms" in time of emergency, called for immediate militia reform, and requested funding to erect a manufactory of arms in Louisville in order to bring a steady supply of arms to the western regions of the United States.[164] Though war with Great Britain appeared imminent, the country's leadership made no effort to prepare for the conflict; in fact they were certain that no preparations were necessary. The House committee responding to Kentucky's petition asserted that the United States did not need to worry about producing more arms. Though government contracts for arms had not yet been met, the committee reported that a total of 33,821 guns had been manufactured in the United States in 1811. The committee did note in passing that the federal armories at Springfield and Harpers Ferry accounted for 22,020 (65 percent) of these firearms, meaning that private gunmakers had, with every possible government incentive, produced only 11,801 guns. But not to worry, they said, as that should be enough to supply the needs of what would surely be a quick and painless war.

The committee added one more reason for not building a new armory: Congress had already tried doing so. In 1803 the government had ordered a "manufactory of arms" at Rocky Mount, South Carolina. At great expense "buildings [were] erected for that purpose," but the effort was abandoned because of "the difficulty of obtaining suitable workmen" to make firearms. The buildings were "converted into Arsenals and store houses for the safe keeping" of arms. The committee exposed a curious contradiction in their optimism; on the one hand they were certain that the United States had the manufacturing capability to make enough arms, yet they refused to build a western armory because of a lack of trained workers. Within a few months the country would begin paying a heavy price for this irrational faith.[165]

Optimism and government funds intended to promote domestic arms production failed to arm the militia, and the United States entered the War of 1812 grotesquely unprepared for a sustained conflict. Jefferson had allowed the army's total strength to fall to twenty-four hundred men in 1807. As the war approached, Congress authorized an army of ten thousand, but recruiters had little luck finding that many men in America willing to serve. Incredibly few Americans had ever served in the military; those who had suffered grievously, as the army mistreated its rank-

and-file horrendously. There is no evidence of any romanticization of military life in the decade prior to the War of 1812; there was no cultural incentive to sign up. When Congress declared war in June, the U.S. Army consisted of 6,750 men. Wellington commanded 46,000 men at the Battle of Salamanca the next month, while Napoleon led an army of 450,000 into Poland.[166]

It quickly became evident that the House committee of 1811 had been grossly misled, or were themselves lying, when they stated that one-tenth of the government's quarter-million guns were nonfunctioning. In October of 1812 William King, the assistant inspector general of the U.S. Army, found the percentage much higher. For instance, the arms of the 14th Regiment "are in infamously bad order. They appear to be old muskets that have probably been bought up at reduced prices by the contractors . . . and are now placed in the hands of men who are almost within gunshot of the enemy . . . at least one-fifth of them are unfit for service; and . . . were they to undergo a critical inspection, a much larger proportion of them would be condemned." The ammunition was "very bad; some of the cartridges are said to have been made up in 1794. There is a scarcity of flints." Captain William King, inspecting the 12th Regiment at Buffalo that same month, reported many of the muskets out of repair and that each soldier had only a few flints and cartridges, "and many of them very bad, . . . and there is no ammunition in store at this place."[167]

Matters were much worse among the militia. With his preliminary war message in April 1812, President Madison, the man who wrote the Second Amendment, called upon "the several states, to take effectual measures to organize, arm, and equip, according to law" their militia. The states were in desperate need of help, with nearly every militia in the country appealing for arms and ammunition.[168] Pennsylvania's adjutant general reported that his state's 99,414 men could take the field with 30,366 guns, both publicly and privately owned. In July 1813 the House Committee on Military Affairs stated the obvious: "the war found the militia badly armed." Four states—North Carolina, Maryland, Delaware, and Tennessee—did not even have adjutants general for their militia. General William Lenoir informed North Carolina's governor that "a considerable part of" the seven thousand militiamen who reported for service were "unarmed." He had no idea "how they are to be furnished with arms." The situation was worse in Vermont, Rhode Island, and New York. The last state's Senator Obadiah German felt that "the evils attending upon calling a large portion of the militia into actual service for any considerable time, is almost incalculable." He correctly prophesied that the event "will teach you the impropriety of relying on them for carrying on the war."[169] The historian Lawrence Delbert Cress has offered a more biting conclusion: "Ironically, the ideological tenets that had informed Republican critiques of Federalist policy over the previous decade would render the republic in the years preceding the War of 1812 virtually defenseless—this despite a clearly discernible sense that the nation's peacetime forces required significant reform."[170]

The federal government did its best to make up for its previous complacency, rushing to supply modern, usable muskets to the army, and any kind of guns to the militia. The War Department gave priority to those militia it thought most likely to see battle, sending five thousand muskets to Connecticut, two thousand to New York, and fifteen hundred to Louisiana in the first year of the war. The secretary of war was particularly concerned with the militia in the area of Washington itself, which would be called upon should the British attack the nation's capital. The Maryland militia therefore received fifteen hundred guns and the D.C. militia twenty-two hundred as an indefinite loan; old arms in their possession were recalled for repair. Each militia member who received a gun took it into his personal possession on promising to care for it and return it when required. Repeatedly militia officers reported that many of those receiving firearms appeared to have never handled one before.[171]

The concerns of the War Department were well founded, for when the British did attack Washington, D.C., in August 1814 the militia crumbled. The British expeditionary force was tiny by European standards— a mixed force of 4,370 infantry, marines, and sailors, with just three artillery pieces. In theory they faced an aroused populace able to field some fifty thousand militia within a day's march of the capital. There were certainly enough registered members of the militia, but these had rarely mustered, let alone trained, and most were unarmed. The Virginia militia had no supply of flints, a necessity for actually firing a gun, while the governor of Pennsylvania could not call out the militia to protect Washington because the legislature had failed to pass a new militia law. Those who did show up did everything wrong, even reversing the famous mythology by forming themselves into neat ranks in open fields while the British fired at them from behind the cover of trees. Admiral Alexander Cochrane's forces easily defeated the nearly twelve thousand U.S. regulars and militia he encountered, including General John Stricker's beautifully uniformed Baltimore regiment of three thousand men. Thousands of Americans quietly slipped away for home without ever firing a shot in defense of their nation's liberty. It was a sorry show, as smoke rose from the burning White House, and British sailors cavorted in the Capitol.[172]

Many contemporaries thought the local militia units simply cowardly, but at least one regiment had a sound reason for not acting in defense of the capital city: they had almost no guns. In October 1814 Colonel George Minor testified before Richard M. Johnson's House committee that was investigating the fall of Washington, D.C. Minor, in command of Virginia's 60th Regiment, arrived at Washington with six hundred infantry and one hundred cavalry. He found his troops grievously short of arms, reporting personally to President Madison "as to the want of arms, ammunition &c." Madison sent him to General Armstrong, who told him that "arms, &c. could not be had that night, and directed me to report myself next morning to Colonel Carbery, who would furnish me with arms, &c.; which gentleman, From early next morning, I diligently sought for, until a late hour in the forenoon, without being able to find him, and then went in search of General [William] Winder." He found Winder and was told to wait. As a consequence, this regiment, described by General Winder as "wholly unarmed," never saw battle.[173]

The experience of the best-armed state militia, that of Massachusetts, is instructive. There were a total of just under forty-nine thousand privately owned guns of all kinds, exactly 3,700 public arms held by members of the militia, and reserves consisting of "177 spears, 5 casks of flints, 2 cases of gun locks, 12 powder horns, 35 muskets 'out of repair,' and 124 firearms, good"—enough for 76 percent of its 69,553 registered militiamen (180,000 were eligible for militia service). In contrast, New York had 46,270 guns for 92,554 militia (50 percent) and Virginia 18,697 for 80,863 militia (23.1 percent).[174] Allotted 5,688 muskets by the federal government, Massachusetts had received none by 1813, despite the fact that, as the adjutant general complained, the Springfield Armory was within its borders. (He ignored the fact that all the guns produced at the armories were earmarked for the army.) The state government therefore withheld federal taxes, using the money to purchase guns from state gun manufacturers. Fortunately this extortion worked, since the total output of Massachusetts gunmakers, excepting the Springfield Armory, was only a few hundred guns per year. But the federal government caved in and sent the first of five shipments of federal firearms totaling twenty-three hundred muskets. In addition Massachusetts purchased 2,178 guns from various sources, allowing it to arm an additional 4,478 men. The legislature ordered these guns issued to every town, with all military equipment to be returned to the state at war's end. It took the quartermaster general two years to get most of these muskets back; several hundred just vanished.[175]

Much of Massachusetts's war effort consisted of cleaning and repairing firearms. Militia musters indicated that most of those forty-nine thousand guns in private hands needed immediate attention. Militia officers were consistently amazed to discover that French muskets from the Revolution were the most common weapon among their troops. The lack of uniformity made repair very time-consuming, as well as producing "great confusion . . . in the distribution of cartridges," in Quartermaster General Amasa Davis's words.[176]

Massachusetts, like every other state, encouraged the organization of volunteer militia companies. These efforts met with mixed results at best. For instance, the Boston Rifle Corps, founded in March 1814, required each member to supply his own arms, but they quickly discovered that only seven of their forty-seven members had guns of any kind. A committee set out to locate the forty rifles they needed. They visited General Dearborn and asked if he had any to lend. He answered that he did, but only if they agreed to join the army. Unwilling to go quite that far, the rifle corps drilled with their seven rifles, taking turns firing them for practice. In November Adjutant General Davis agreed to provide the needed rifles, and the company held its first fully armed drill the next day, agreeing to store all their arms at their captain's house. Within four months of the war's end the rifle corps was no longer able to get enough members together to hold a meeting; by June 1815, when Massachusetts demanded the return of the forty rifles, the company dissolved. It had lasted just fifteen months.[177]

Matters were no better with frontier militia units, which also lacked arms and experience with their use. Frontier governments panicked when regulars moved out of their territory, insisting that the unarmed state of the settlers left them defenseless without the army. Thus Governor Claiborne of Louisiana wrote the Senate that any diminishment of the government forces stationed there endangered "the safety of the state," for the "militia are not & cannot for some time be made efficient [as] the Want of Arms & munitions of War, are sources of great embarrassment." He begged them to loan the state at least thirty-four hundred muskets and four hundred sabers. Or, as he put it to the local army commander, "the militia of Louisiana, is for the present in a state of Great Derangement."[178]

The militia proved even more of a detriment when it actually went to war, eating up the resources of the army while giving a false sense of strength in numbers. In September 1812 General Stephen Van Rensselaer arrived at the Niagara frontier with a force of seven hundred militia intent on invading Canada. As he wrote to Secretary of War Dearborn, his troops were not "in that condition which the approaching crisis will require," being short of every article of war and lacking arms and ammunition. He had enough powder for ten rounds per man, but lacked "lead to make cartridges." To Governor Tompkins he wrote, "I lament when I tell you, that neither arms, nor ammunition are provided for those brave men; no, not one musket to six men. . . . [We] are destitute of arms and ammunition; they are neither of them to be purchased in the country." The War Department sent arms, which Van Rensselaer thought inferior, "not fit for use. The armourers are here, busily engaged" repairing guns.[179] Van Rensselaer's campaign ended in complete disaster as his militia refused to cross into Canada to save the regulars who were being overwhelmed by the British, and "dissolved into a crowd of spectators, watching the distant battle as if it were waged solely for their entertainment." Winfield Scott angrily reported that a group of five hundred militia surrendered without firing a shot. A year later, after a similar disaster on the Niagara frontier, General George McClure of the Albany Volunteers summed up the attitude of many of its own officers when he wrote Secretary of War John Armstrong that the militia are "very little better than an infuriated mob."[180]

While a lack of proper armaments is a classic military excuse for not attacking, several frontier campaigns were hampered and even abandoned for lack of munitions. In October 1812 General Tupper reported that his 960 men had only three rounds per man. General James Winchester commanding the Kentucky Volunteers reported himself in the same position. They both received replies from the quartermaster that there was no ammunition to be had. When ordered nevertheless to march against the enemy, only two hundred of Tupper's men agreed to do so. The campaign was abandoned, as was another effort the following year.[181]

One could go on and on with examples of inept, poorly armed, and horribly disciplined militia almost losing the War of 1812 for the United States. Mostly the militia just did not show up.[182] And yet, even in the midst of a disastrous war, Congress rejected militia reform, leaving the government to rely on volunteers and several states contemplating the formation of their own armies. The primary objection to any alteration in the militia structure remained a fear of centralization.[183]

But there was one bright moment for the frontier militia—the Battle of New Orleans. Some contemporaries thought it appropriate that the militia finally drew itself together after the war had ended, but there is little doubt that it performed well at New Orleans. It is the nature of that performance that is widely misunderstood. The classic vision is of frontier riflemen mowing down British Regulars with brilliant marksmanship. But as in the Revolution, there is little evidence of such skill in the handling of firearms.[184]

Andrew Jackson himself was less than complimentary. Writing to James Monroe the day after the battle, Jackson doubted the militia's usefulness. The Louisiana militia had abandoned every post before the British advance, not even putting up a token resistance as they fled to the safety of the city's defenses. During a preliminary engagement with the British on December 23, 1814, the militia had fired wildly the moment they sighted the British, inflicting almost no casualties, and then disengaged, leaving the fighting to Jackson's marines. His retreat was saved by the attack of Colonel John Coffee's mounted riflemen, who fought a ferocious hand-to-hand battle with the British. Coffee's rifles did not have bayonets. His men fought with knives and clubbed rifles against the British bayonets.[185]

Jackson could not "impede these operations," as the British slowly tightened their hold on the outskirts of New Orleans. "The nature of the troops under my command, mostly militia, rendered it too hazardous to attempt extensive offensive movements in an open country, against a numerous and well-disciplined army. Although my forces, as to number, had been increased by the arrival of the Kentucky division, my strength had received very little addition; a small portion only of that detachment being provided with arms." He thus had no choice but "to wait the attack of the enemy." Fortunately for Jackson, they did so, right in front of his artillery.[186]

Cannon, not firearms, won the Battle of New Orleans. The myth, and the old song, give all credit to the Kentucky riflemen. Every military historian knows, as John Ward so concisely put it, that "it can be flatly asserted that Jackson's overwhelming victory can in no way be attributed to the sharpshooting skill of the American frontiersman." This was a "fact . . . recognized by those who took part in the battle and also in the immediate newspaper accounts of the battle." The Kentucky militia, which consisted of 2,368 men, had just seven hundred firearms among them, "and the arms they have are not fit for use," according to Andrew Jackson. Governor Claiborne of Louisiana complained to Secretary of War Monroe of this "scarcity of arms" among the arriving militia, who added nothing to the city's defense. While the New Orleans volunteer militia was well armed, "The militia in the Interior of the State are almost wholly destitute of arms." The long-promised federal guns arrived after the battle. Fortunately Jackson's troops received several hundred muskets and ammunition from U.S. naval gunboats for use in the land battle.[187]

Jackson arranged his forces carefully, placing unarmed men with the armed to bulk the appearance of his force, and to use the guns of any soldiers wounded during battle. He kept one thousand unarmed Kentuckians in reserve. Coffee's riflemen were on the far left flank and played little role in the battle. The British marched straight into the American artillery. They then, amazingly, stood around waiting for their fascines and scaling ladders, which had been stupidly placed at the rear of the army, to work their way forward. During that wait, the American artillery tore into them, killing scores of regulars before they even came into musket range. The Americans fired their muskets amid the thick smoke of battle at near point-blank range, and the British attack collapsed, leaving 291 dead and more than a thousand wounded.[188] The *Kentucky Palladium* reported that "Our artillery was fired upon their whole columns, about an hour and a half, within good striking distance, whilst advancing and retreating, with grape & cannister; and the slaughter must have been great." Andrew Jackson's own description of the battle credited the cannon manned by members of the U.S. Navy and Army and some of the Barratarian pirates, with the victory.[189]

But the myth of Kentucky riflemen picking which eye of British officers to shoot out fulfilled some deep national yearning. An imagined American equality seemed to demand that every man could be the equal of the best-trained troops in the world—at least in popular songs and tall tales. Just as after the American Revolution, the militia received undeserved credit for that great triumph, so now, after the disasters of the War of 1812, common Americans could be credited with moving directly from their plows to the defense of liberty. It hardly mattered that such a vision of the war flew in the face of all known facts of the militia's conduct. In battle after battle the militia had performed terribly, if at all. The only view that most regular troops had of the militia in the midst of battle was of their backs as these "citizen-soldiers" fled in terror. At least at the Battle of New Orleans they had stayed in their positions behind the barricades. That was good enough for constructing a myth of democratic heroism.[190]

There is one final blow to the popular image of the frontier rifleman worthy of mention. After the battle, Coffee's Tennessee Volunteers challenged Beale's Rifle Company to a shooting match. Beale's volunteer company consisted of the "leading merchants and professional characters of the city" of New Orleans. As John Ward wrote, "It is almost too happy for present purposes," that Beale's urbanites won a complete victory over the frontier riflemen. In shooting, as in other sports and most other activities, practice wins out over an imagined innate genius every time. Contrary to one of the most cherished fictions in American culture, simply living on the frontier did not make one an excellent shot.[191]

Chapter Eight

From Indifference
to Disdain

The right of the citizens to keep and bear arms has
justly been considered as the palladium of the
liberties of a republic. . . . And yet, though this truth
would seem so clear, and the importance of a
well-regulated militia would seem so undeniable,
it cannot be disguised that, among the American
people, there is a growing indifference to any system
of militia discipline, and a strong disposition, from a
sense of its burdens, to be rid of all regulations. How
it is practicable to keep the people duly armed
without some organization it is difficult to see.

—Joseph Story, 1833[1]

The Distribution of Firearms
in the Early Republic

The War of 1812 indicated, with an
accuracy that terrified the country's
political elite, that most Americans did not own guns, did not know how
to use guns, and did not particularly care if they ever carried a gun for any
purpose. Reliance on the myth of an armed and vigorous militia had
almost cost the United States the war. As it was, the nation emerged
humiliated and chastened. Though the militia myth would be reborn in
the stories of the Battle of New Orleans, the militia itself would suffer an
ignoble demise from which it never recovered.

The country's reliance on the militia required the government to
know exactly how well armed were its citizen soldiers. It was relatively
easy to keep track of the number of arms in the hands of the U.S. Army,

but not so with the militia. In theory every member of the militia supplied his own gun, as the Militia Act of 1792 required. In practice, nothing of the sort happened. As the House Committee on the Militia observed in 1827, "the experience of many years proves the law to be useless and unavailing. As well might Congress require the Militia to furnish their own subsistence" as their own guns. Almost from the start, every state realized the futility of such an effort, offering rewards of various kinds to those who owned a gun, but otherwise attempting to supply state firearms to individual militiamen.[2]

But the states needed to have some idea how many guns they needed, which pushed them to track the private ownership of firearms, as well as the number of public arms stored for use by the militia. Though not uniform in procedure, these censuses of firearms were conducted by militia officers and constables going house-to-house in their districts, counting the number of firearms, and occasionally determining their condition. Interestingly, there is no record of any opposition to or even complaint against these gun censuses. They were as much an accepted responsibility of the government as any other form of information gathering.[3]

Inevitably there are problems attached to the use of statistics in history. Unarguably we can never be certain how accurate or thorough are any of the records upon which we draw, no matter what the agency or its province and level of authority. Clumsiness and corruption, public resistance and noncompliance, laziness and vague categories, the changing meaning of words and mathematical incompetence on the part of the original collectors of information—all impair our ability to claim statistical accuracy. Yet the most thoughtful critics of quantitative methods agree that there is no real alternative to employing these records, with the proper caveats inserted. Without such efforts at quantification, we are left to repeat the unverifiable assertions of other historians, or to descend into a pointless game of dueling quotations—matching one literary allusion against another. Far better to match an entire collection of documents with other primary materials; for instance, probate and militia records. If historians can use a diversity of sources to produce a range of quantifiable data tending to confirm the same or at least a similar portrait of the past, then we may gain some degree of confidence that we are at least proceeding on the right track. In other words, the aggregate matters.[4]

In 1803 Secretary of War Henry Dearborn conducted the first significant census of the militia and its arms, both privately and publicly owned. Dearborn discovered that 45 percent of the militia bore arms. His census

of weapons, which was certainly incomplete, indicated that just 4.9 percent of America's population was armed, or 23.7 percent of its white adult
males. In 1810 Secretary of War William Eustis, in what was probably the
most thorough and exact of all the studies, found that almost nothing had
changed: 45.4 percent of the militia bore arms; the total number of guns
recorded was sufficient for 4.3 percent of the American population, or
20.9 percent of the white adult males. Though the population of the country had increased by 50.2 percent in those years, the militia had grown by
29.3 percent, and the number of available guns by 30.7 percent. Ten years
later, John C. Calhoun found some slight improvement, with 47.8 percent
of the militia bearing arms, and enough guns for 4.7 percent of the American population, or 19.9 percent of the white adult males (down a point).
But Calhoun found it rather disturbing that several states had simply
ceased bothering to issue militia returns or to keep track of firearms; it
appeared that these governments no longer cared whether the militia carried guns or not. By 1830 just 31 percent of America's militia bore arms.
Though the population had increased 152 percent since the 1803 gun census, and the number of militia by 115 percent, the number of available
guns had increased by just 48 percent in those twenty-seven years. The
United States thus had enough arms for 12.5 percent of the adult white
males, or 3 percent of the total population.[5]

These censuses also indicate a curious regional variation in gun ownership. The region suffering from the gravest shortage in firearms was the
South. In 1803 there were enough arms in the Northeast for 52 percent of
the militia, in the West for 51.6 percent of the militia, but in the South for
just 29 percent. As white Americans moved into the Southwest, the percentage of western militia with access to arms decreased to 42.2 percent in
1810. In contrast the Northeast increased to 56.2 percent, while the Southeast remained roughly unchanged at 29.8 percent. In the years after the
War of 1812, the southeastern states made concerted efforts to arm their
militia, storing the weapons in guarded armories, raising the number of
militia with access to arms to 51.9 percent. The West fell to 38.4 percent,
while the Northeast declined slightly to 51.9 percent. The 1830 census,
though not completely reliable, indicated the impact of extensive population growth in the Northeast, as the number of arms the militia could
draw upon decreased to sufficient for 36.1 percent of the registered members. The Southeast returned to its former low level of 28 percent, while
the West dropped further, to 23.2 percent. Given the mythology of universal gun ownership, these statistics are rather surprising.[6]

One state that made concerted efforts to determine the level of gun ownership was Massachusetts. On several occasions the state government counted all privately owned guns. As their findings indicate, at no point prior to 1840, when there were 21,760 privately owned guns in the state, did more than 11 percent of that state's citizens own firearms (30 percent of the adult white males). In addition, the state had received 11,657 muskets and 1,260 rifles from the federal government over the years from 1813 to 1842. And still the adjutant general felt that the militia remained so poorly armed that in 1822 he purchased a few hundred condemned British military carbines (forty-three of these carbines were still in the Bangor State Arsenal in 1874). And yet Massachusetts was, along with Connecticut, the center of arms production in the United States.[7]

In 1812 a similar census in Pennsylvania found 30,366 guns, both publicly and privately owned, for the 99,414 men in the militia (30.5 percent; or 3.7 percent of the population). In 1837 another census in New York revealed that of 84,122 state troops, 30,388 (36.1 percent) had neither private nor public arms in their possession, and 15,500 (18.4 percent) of those who had guns had no flints. Even in the heavily armed—and deeply paranoid—state of South Carolina, militia officers continually expressed shock over the shortage of firearms. In 1825 General Robert Y. Hayne reviewed Charleston's 2,060 troops, finding that 509 had no arms at all. Of those who had guns of some kind, the majority bore muskets "in bad order." The following year, one militia company rejected a shipment of arms from the government as inadequate; its commander wrote to the governor, "I have taken the sense of my company and they refuse to make use of such arms." In 1837 the adjutant general reported that South Carolina's arsenals held 7,091 muskets and 962 rifles, most of which were "wholly unfit . . . for actual service."[8]

These returns give little indication of the condition of these firearms or of the citizenry's ability to employ them. Practically every adjutant general and militia commander in the United States in the antebellum period complained of the indifference with which Americans treated their weapons, and many state governments discovered that their armories were full of useless firearms. In 1843 Massachusetts determined that 6,649 (47.5 percent) of the 13,994 muskets in the Cambridge Armory were useless and sold them over the next several years for less than $3 each.[9]

Unlike today's glistening beauties, firearms in the eighteenth and nineteenth centuries were made of iron, and as a consequence required constant attention to save them from rusting. Most people who owned

guns brought them forth but once a year, on muster day; so it is little wonder that those who did not have servants tended to let their weapons rot.
In 1817 Virginia's adjutant general, G. W. Gooch, warned that the state's
militia companies did not keep their arms "in good order—indeed, I
might say, [not even] to preserve them from ruin." Gooch tried ordering
greater attention to the care and maintenance of the militia's weapons, but
he found such efforts worthless; he finally ordered that all public arms be
collected and stored in a single location.[10] Fifteen years later the federal
government considered building an arsenal in Florida because the arms
sent for their militia "were soon lost or destroyed, by reason of there being
no suitable persons to take care of them, and no proper place of deposit."[11]

It is no wonder that Winfield Scott's *Infantry Tactics,* published in 1825
and used by the army through the Civil War, declared the preservation of
firearms a military priority too important to be entrusted to the common
soldier. Article 31 stated that "Fire-arms are very liable to be damaged, or
rendered unfit for service," as a consequence of normal military routines.
To prevent such damage "not a screw nor a pipe will be moved by the soldier, without express permission from the proper authority," with the
tools for such tasks kept by the sergeants. "If there be an armorer present,
he alone will be entrusted" to repair weapons, no matter how minor the
task. All "vicious practices" that threatened to damage any part of the gun
were strictly forbidden, with the guns to be cleaned after rain or even if
left out in a morning dew. Scott insisted that the guns not be left in the
care of privates, but collected and stored under guard every night.[12]

Scott's plans changed the behavior of the army, but not of the state
militia. Out on the frontier in 1841, Michigan's new quartermaster general asked his predecessor to call in all the public arms. The latter stated
that there were none. The new quartermaster assumed that all the federal
arms Michigan had received must have been distributed to the militia, but
he quickly discovered that no records of these disbursements had been
kept, and his personal inspection of every company revealed only four
hundred guns in the whole territory. Fifteen years later a different adjutant general was still complaining of the lack of care for guns issued to
volunteer militia companies. Many guns were "exposed to the weather,
with no one willing to interest themselves in their protection or safe keeping." The state lacked proper storage facilities and many of the state's
arms had been stored in damp cellars for years and rendered useless. He
noted that one company, celebrating a political victory at the state capitol
itself, had thrown guns and even their cannon into the river.[13]

An awareness of the public's lack of enthusiasm for firearms led a House Committee on the Militia, chaired by William Henry Harrison, to propose in 1818 that the government keep its arms in armories under federal control and maintenance rather than giving them directly to the people. The committee felt that the nation's guns, so grossly abused by its citizens, should be left in the care of experts who could keep them operational. This recommendation was tabled, only to be repeated time and again over the next twenty years. (Completely ignored was Harrison's proposed constitutional amendment to teach the military arts, especially the handling of firearms, to all boys in primary school.) In the absence of such legislation, no militia could expect that its arms would be ready, or even present, when needed. The Pennsylvania adjutant general found only 28,465 of the 44,831 guns supposedly stored in its armories in 1821. Since the number of firearms in private hands had not changed to a notable degree, the adjutant general concluded that the missing weapons had been used for scrap, the metal ending up as part of a plow.[14] In 1838 Secretary of War Joel Poinsett complained to Congress that military expenses were nearly four times what they should be largely because the militia seemed incapable of caring for their arms. The following year he reported that "when mustered, a majority of [the militia] are armed with walking canes, fowling pieces, or unserviceable muskets." Nothing had changed since the end of the War of 1812.[15]

Probate records provide a useful corroboration of these militia and census figures. These transcripts of a deceased male's possessions are not a perfect source, and there has been a long, instructive debate on their reliability as historical sources.[16] Nonetheless, probate records do open a window on common household objects. Some inventories are more meticulous than others, though they all reported each and every object, piece of property, debt, and credit belonging to the deceased. Some regions, particularly the South, had a bias in the inventories toward property owners; apparently many poor whites did not leave enough effects behind to bother recording. A region of high literacy and property ownership was thus likely to leave the most accurate records, especially as these inventories tended to note the condition of the goods, from bent spoons to rusted plows. In this context it is significant that only 14 percent of the twelve hundred probate records studied from the frontiers of northern New England and western Pennsylvania during the years 1765 to 1790 included firearms. The same regions in 1819 to 1821 reveal only a slight increase in ownership, to 16.2 percent. The inventories reported just over half (53 percent) of these guns in the first period as either broken or in some sense dysfunctional, decreasing to 31 percent in the second survey period. In either time, a musket or rifle in good condition was subject to some comment in the probate inventories and earned that piece a high valuation. Obviously guns could have been passed on to heirs before the death of the original owner. Yet the wills, which generally list such bequests no matter how minor the item, contained only a handful of firearms, producing only an insignificant alteration in the total figure of gun ownership. Stated briefly, the probate inventories reveal that privately owned guns were slightly more common in the South and urban centers than in the countryside or on the frontier, and that gun ownership remained rather constant until the 1830s, increasing by half again over the next twenty years. By 1849–50, guns appeared in nearly one-third of all probate inventories (though by that date the records for cities become less reliable).[17]

Almost all of these probate inventories are for white males. Most states had laws forbidding blacks from owning guns, and none of the very few women's inventories lists a gun. The inventories, therefore, are from the people most likely to own guns—less than a quarter of the total population (white males over the age of fifteen made up 23.8 percent of the 1820 census). The figures indicate that few people actually had guns in their possession, at least at the time of death. If we dare to include women and blacks in our definition of Americans, it would appear that at no time prior to 1850 did more than a tenth of the people own guns.

The low levels of gun production insured that no more than one-tenth could possibly own guns. Outside of the national armories, gun production showed few signs of life. The War of 1812, like the American Revolution before it, inspired a whole new group of artisans to try their luck as gunsmiths. Few survived more than a few years after the war ended, the economic panic of 1819 putting a finish to most of these enterprises.[18] Even the Richmond Armory closed shop in 1821, as the Virginia legislature saw no reason to bother to make more firearms; within a year the building was a decaying ruin. Harpers Ferry and Springfield together made twenty-five thousand guns a year by 1818, while private gunmakers produced eight thousand guns a year for the government.[19] And then, in 1823, Washington stopped granting advances while also requiring, for the first time, that guns pass a number of proof tests. These changes limited enormously the attractions of making guns for the government and further undermined the growth of a domestic gun industry.[20]

The 1820 Census of Industry, which was the most careful effort yet to determine the productive capacity of America, discovered only fourteen private gun manufactories capitalized at more than $500. There are, of course, many problems with these statistics as well; a great deal of information is missing, and the eastern states generally omitted the smaller gunsmiths from their compilations. Nonetheless, this census is one of the few indices on gunmaking nationwide. Excluding the national armories leaves a total of sixty-four gunmakers employing 311 workers (the one certainly accurate figure) with a recorded capitalization of $223,000 and a market value of goods produced of $170,660. Given that most gunmakers devoted much of their labor to gun repair, and rating guns at their lowest possible evaluation of $15 each, that market valuation of goods produced equals 9,510 guns from these sixty-four gunmakers. Ohio and Tennessee made the most exact count, seemingly including every gunsmith in their states, even those who owned just "a set of tools." The census found seven gunsmiths in Ohio, capitalized at $18,908, employing nineteen workers, and producing $10,150 worth of goods and services. Tennessee had many more gunsmiths, twenty-seven shops employing sixty workers, but a much lower capital base of just $4,677, yet a higher market value of goods at $20,074. Again, based on the assumption that every penny of that market value represented a gun of the lowest cost, it seems that Ohio's gunmakers produced, at most, 677 guns, while Tennessee's made 1,338 guns. It should finally be noted that several entries made note of the fact that the shops had laid off workers because of the depression, which indicates a possible decline in total gun production. But overall these findings matched fairly closely other studies by the federal government of America's gunmaking capacity, which was uniformly rated as undeveloped.[21]

Most communities lacked gunsmiths and had to rely on blacksmiths to make the necessary repairs to guns—and they did not always know what they were doing. Even qualified gunsmiths often found far more work available in general smithing. For instance, David Reese, the first gunsmith in Buffalo, New York, had a sign in the shape of a large ax and took pride in his axmaking skills. Reese did repair several firearms, but he made no guns from 1800 to 1825. It is striking that there did not seem to be much of a market for guns in this frontier town. In 1817 M. D. Mann arrived in Buffalo, announcing that he would commence making and repairing guns. In 1819 he declared bankruptcy and closed his shop. The same fate awaited Peter Allison, who opened his gunshop in May 1825 and was gone by the end of the year. Primarily poor farmers, frontier settlers needed to spend what little surplus capital they had on farm equipment, not expensive luxury items like firearms.[22]

Guns of any quality tended to be either rugged rifles made to order for those who made their living from hunting, or beautifully crafted to grace the study and, on special occasions, the hands of a member of the elite. The overwhelming majority of guns in circulation were poorly cared for and passed on from generation to generation as family heirlooms, and not kept in operational order. The consequence was that most states made frantic efforts at the beginning of military campaigns to get their militia's guns into working order. And then, the militia vanished.[23]

Collapse of the Militia

In his first inaugural address in 1809, James Madison reminded his fellow Americans to "always remember that an armed and trained militia is the firmest bulwark of republics—that without standing armies their liberty can never be in danger." In February 1815 a very different James Madison told both houses of Congress that recent "experience has taught us that . . . the pacific dispositions of the American people" afforded insufficient protection against the violence that appeared to be "the ordinary lot of nations." The events of recent years had demonstrated "that a certain degree of preparation for war is not only indispensable to avert disasters in the onset, but affords also the best security for the continuance of peace. The wisdom of Congress will therefore, I am confident, provide for the maintenance of an adequate regular force, . . . and for cultivating the military art in its essential branches, under the liberal patronage of Government." As John Dederer pithily summarized this change of mind, "Apparently, the burning of the presidential mansion by British regulars in 1814 altered his opinion."[24]

Congress also smelled the smoke from the burning government buildings. At war's end, Congress increased the army to 12,700 men, the largest to date. The following year the Republican Congress funded a major program of coastal defense and naval expansion. Such a rejection of the Jeffersonian notions of economy and a reliance on the militia appalled such "Old Republicans" as John Randolph, who felt that the new system "out-Hamiltons Alexander Hamilton."[25] Some, including the future champion of states' rights, John C. Calhoun, saw clearly the lesson of the War of 1812. As secretary of war, Calhoun attempted the centralization of the militia and the expansion of the army, but was defeated at every turn.[26] With the public having lost all interest in the militia, neither Congress nor President Monroe showed the slightest interest in reforming the militia.[27]

The militia ideal seemed clear enough: every man should own a gun and appear for militia service when called. Adjutant General William H. Sumner of Massachusetts had stated this noble goal clearly: "Under the Constitution, the Militia must ever be estimated the bulwark of civil and individual liberty. Directed by public sentiment, it will guard us from the oppression of power; regulated by wisdom, and patronized by the Government, it will secure us from anarchy; officered, trained and supported by the States, it is the guarantee of their sovereignty and union; and properly armed and disciplined, . . . it forms an impenetrable barrier to the invader." But the War of 1812 convinced many Americans that the militia was a burden to a free people.[28]

During the war, the government had fined nearly ten thousand militiamen for failure to respond when called into service. Collecting these fines proved a near impossibility, as local officials refused to aid this effort.[29] A congressional select committee reported in 1822 that "not one cent of that amount has yet reached the Treasury of the United States. Instead of receiving any money from this source, the United States have paid the sum of $24,241.08 out of the public Treasury towards defraying the expenses of the courts-martial by which those very fines were assessed." That amount would rise to $97,000 in the face of much popular opposition, with officials often facing countersuits in response to their efforts to punish those who violated the militia ideal. As Leonard White has written, "no one had ever foreseen thousands of militiamen would be fined nearly half a million dollars under the terms of an act passed in 1792 to deal with the occasional individual case." As a consequence, "no one in the executive branch cared to press the law to its conclusion."[30]

Having failed to demonstrate its usefulness in the War of 1812, the militia lost its central role in national defense plans.[31] Though the federal government continued halfhearted efforts to arm the militia, most states lost interest in the institution. At the same time, urbanization accelerated the movement away from community-based militia companies. The anonymity of the cities made it both easier to avoid militia duty and harder to find others of a like mind. As Alexis de Tocqueville noted in the 1830s, the nature of American associations had shifted significantly. Starting in the 1810s Americans no longer based their adherence on locale as much as on career, politics, or some other special interest. Militia companies now formed on the basis of profession rather than community; the earliest such instance may have been the butchers of New York City, who formed their own militia company in 1814. Such working-class units did not last very long, unlike upper-class units devoted to fancy uniforms and shiny equipment.[32]

These elite volunteer companies earned the name of "uniform companies," because they supplied and were obsessed with their own uniforms. The costliness of their livery served as an effective class barrier. The New Haven Light Infantry prided itself on its cap, which cost $6, more than a standard day's wages. Privates' uniforms in some companies cost as much as $120, with officers needing $150 for theirs. Obviously most workers could not possibly afford such uniforms, let alone the elegant guns favored by these volunteer units. By the 1820s, local elites had deserted their commitment to the town's standing militia, helping to undermine the communal identification of that organization.[33]

These new volunteer companies were far from militarist. The official historian of New York's 7th Regiment, Emmons Clark, has admirably described the typical officer in these years: Major John Telfair, elected every year from 1823 until his retirement in 1836, was "not a strict disciplinarian nor fond of the details of drill. . . . He belonged to that school of officers who love the militia service for its society, its display, and its parades, rather than its drills and military tactics." The first colonel of the regiment was twenty-eight-year-old Prosper Wetmore, who preferred writing poetry to studying war, and whose men admired him for his generosity in buying drinks.[34] This regiment spent far more time in the Shakespeare Tavern than on the muster field—a lot more time. For eleven years these young men debated their uniform before settling on one based, appropriately enough, on a gray business suit. Their rule book devoted several pages to the "Bill of Dress," with its careful and precise description of every aspect of their uniforms, but only a single sentence to firearms: "Musket according to law." Debates persisted over the details of the uniform, even on the style of a white plume in the cap, but the only discussion of guns came in 1839, when Captain Henry Shumway moved to change to a black leather gunsling. This radical notion was defeated, though it finally won over the troops in 1849. As Clark writes, "During the whole history of the Regiment no subject . . . ever provoked so fierce and bitter a controversy as the proposed change in the uniform hat" in

1842. But then their only official tasks were the Fourth of July parade and escorting prisoners to their place of execution. The New York *Commercial Advertiser* described the regiment during one of the July 4th parades as "All plumed, like ostriches," and "Wanton as youthful goats, wild as young colts."[35]

Even those who owned guns and attended militia musters lacked experience in their use. Musters were, after all, usually held but once a year; parading, drinking, and partying clearly took priority over target practice. Those drills that did occur involved marching, not shooting, as any muster book reveals, and the individual soldier often had to be reminded how to load a musket, if such an action proved necessary at all.[36] In 1819 Charles K. Gardner wrote an instruction manual for use by militia companies after discovering during the War of 1812 that "so many militia-men . . . are not skilled in the use of the Rifle or Musket." But guns did not inspire passions—clothing did. The militia records of Oxford, Massachusetts, which begin in 1755, devote more space to uniforms than any other subject. The company argued over the color of their pantaloons (white or blue) from just after the Revolution until 1823, and plumes (white or black) until 1824. They spent a year debating whether to require each member to powder his beard when appearing at muster, voting in May 1821 to so require, then repealing that act in October. There were also instances of companies disbanding because of a change in uniform. The Oxford militia voted for the first time in May 1819 to meet once a year "for the purpose of fireing at a mark." In 1823 they voted 35–5 to stop this annual target practice in order to avoid public humiliation.[37]

Target-shooting contests often proved a major embarrassment for all concerned. When the 2nd Company of New York's 7th Regiment held their first target-shooting contest in 1825, it was "not a very brilliant exhibition of sharp shooting." But then very few members had ever fired a musket before. Their performance was so poor that the majority of the regiment never participated in another such contest.[38] The regiment's colonel, William M. Stone, editor of the *Commercial Advertiser,* described his match against Major Mordecai M. Noah as a less-than-epic battle. The two men "took a shot—not at each other, but at the target—at the usual distance" of twenty yards. "The major . . . began his preparations for the conflict by deliberately [finishing] off a bottle of claret. He then grasped the musket, which he held tolerably steady, shut up the wrong eye in taking sight, and blazed away. The judges, seeing the point toward which the muzzle was directed, stepped a few yards farther back; but, after the smoke had cleared away, they were all found safe, and reported that he had made a good shot." Stone admitted, however, that "neither of us had hit the target, the major's shot striking the ground at a distance of about eight feet from the tree" to which the target was attached, while Stone hit the tree below the target. Stone was declared the winner, and "the officers, invited guests, and the troops sat down to a well-spread table." The following year, Colonel Stone was shooting when a fellow officer, standing some ten feet from the target, fell to the ground. It turned out to be a practical joke, but Stone felt such an outcome far too likely and he "abjured target-firing . . . from that day forward."[39]

When the prestigious New Haven Grays held their first target-shooting contest in 1822, forty-three men fired 172 shots at a target six feet high by twenty inches wide at one hundred yards. Only twenty shots (11 percent) hit any part of the target. The winner, Frederick T. Stanley, admitted that he had "but little experience in the use of firearms, and have neither before or since owned a pistol, rifle, musket, or fowling piece." His gun was on loan from the state arsenal. In 1826 the Grays shortened the distance to one hundred feet, which improved their ratio to sixty-five hits out of 198 shots fired (33 percent). Shortening the distance again over the next several years raised their percentage of successful shots as high as 48 percent in 1827. As a Pennsylvania newspaper so unkindly said of one company's effort at target shooting: "The size of the target is known accurately having been carefully measured. It was precisely the size and shape of a barn door." The prize went to the man "who came nearest to hitting the target."[40]

With manliness so often linked with proficiency with firearms, we must wonder what it means that American men were generally such terrible shots.[41] There are instances of militia units shooting their officers, bystanders, and one another during target practice. Even that man's man, Robert E. Lee, could bag but four birds in a pigeon shoot (in which a captured pigeon is placed in a black box, shaken, and released, whereupon the shooter raises his gun and hopes to blow the bird away) that lasted all afternoon, and Lee was outshot by his British opponent.[42]

The records of any militia company in the twenty years after 1815 replicate the tension between an interested few struggling to uphold the law and the indifferent majority. For instance, in 1818 thirty-two members of the Uxbridge, Massachusetts, militia petitioned the governor to disband their unit in order "to increase the dignity and respectability of our Militia." The company's membership had fallen to just forty men, only seventeen of whom owned a gun. They hoped to reform as a properly armed volunteer company "and excite in others a laudable spirit of exertion to qualify themselves for a correct and honourable discharge of the duties imposed upon them by the militia laws." The governor approved their petition, allowing the all-volunteer Uxbridge Grenadier Company to replace the town militia.

The first task of the company was to find guns for its twenty-three unarmed members. The company's commander went into Boston to order these guns from dealers there, paying with funds provided by the town. The guns were accepted on the condition, as article 8 of their constitution stated, that "Every member . . . shall keep his gun in a clean, neat, soldierlike manner." Fines were extracted for allowing a gun to become rusty. Such efficient management led to the rapid increase in the company's membership to forty-five men. But by 1820 enthusiasm began to wane, and by 1827 sixteen of these men had been discharged at their own request. New additions, generally the sons of older members, led to a fluctuating membership, which rose as high as fifty men in the early 1820s. But given that the town was supposed to field an active militia of 140 men, this number was hardly impressive. And like other militia companies, the Uxbridge Grenadiers devoted more energy to their uniforms than any other task. Like other companies, they tried target shooting but gave it up as too humiliating. On May 3, 1831, just sixteen men appeared for muster. The records end there.[43]

In the years after the War of 1812, avoidance of militia duty reached epidemic levels. Much of it was perfectly legal, as state laws exempted ever more citizens from the need to serve—Secretary of War James Barbour estimated in 1826 that exemptions from militia duty in some of the states "are equal to one-half of the whole number" eligible to serve. That same year Congress excused all clerks in the departments of war, state, navy, and treasury from militia duty, eliminating in one stroke one-tenth of the District of Columbia's militia strength. The South Carolina Militia Act of 1833 excluded from militia duty most government officials, clergymen, teachers, students, doctors, pilots, ferrymen, sheriffs, and jailers; toll bridge, grist mill, and forge operators; canal, railroad, bank, and lunatic-asylum employees; arsenal and lock keepers; toll collectors; all federal officials; and, most significant, all members of volunteer fire companies. In South Carolina, as in nearly every other state, fire departments proved the premier method of avoidance, indicating that antebellum American males would rather carry hoses than guns.[44]

Generally individuals were saved the trouble of fabricating excuses to avoid militia duty, as state governments themselves undermined the entire militia structure. Several states followed the lead of Delaware, which passed "An Act to Repeal Military fines for non-attendance on days of parades" in 1816. With the state then lacking any coercive power to enforce attendance, scores of militia companies vanished within a few years, leaving the militia effectively dormant in Delaware. The state guaranteed this inactivity by refusing to replace those officers who resigned in protest.[45] In 1827 the legislature attempted to reverse direction by enacting a new militia law that carried heavy fines for nonattendance. The public response was immediate: they turned out most of the old legislature and voted in a new governor, Charles Polk, who led the drive to repeal the offending act. In 1829 the legislature repealed all fines and penalties, and the state issued no new commissions for the next seventeen years. Delaware's militia ceased to exist, leaving only a few scattered private volunteer companies. In 1846 Delaware was unable to respond to President James K. Polk's call for militia to fight Mexico. Fifteen years later Governor William Burton responded to yet another presidential call for a regiment of militia by stating that Delaware did not have one.[46]

Very few American males indicated any interest in militia membership during the 1820s and 1830s. They preferred to join fraternal organizations with secret handshakes or volunteer fire companies. These institutions were lively and respected, while the militia carried a reputation for absurd conduct. Massachusetts Adjutant General William H. Sumner reported that "in some towns, the Fire Department enrolls more members" than the state militia "exhibits in the field"—but then fire departments responded to real threats, not imagined dangers, as was the case with the militia. In addition, the "better class of citizens" had long avoided service in the militia, hiring substitutes from the ranks of the young and often unemployed, when they did not ignore it entirely, lending the militia a further air of sitting on the bottom social rung. Outside the South, few men desired to serve as an officer. In Lee, Massachusetts, the company held ballot after ballot to select a new commander, but each winner refused to serve. One declared, "I don't thank you, and I won't serve you." The company gave up. More common was the problem of officers serving just a single year, which freed one from all further militia duty. New York's adjutant general complained in 1843 that "resignations are becoming more & more frequent and it would seem that many who receive Commissions desire to hold them only so long as the law requires they should in order to exempt them from further duty."[47]

Many people opposed the very institution of the militia. Temperance proponents objected to the excessive drinking that accompanied musters; peace advocates hated the militarism, no matter how pathetic; merchants and farmers resented the lost time and taxes; labor groups resented the expense of buying guns, flints, and ammunition; others found no utility in the institution now that the United States was not threatened by any external foe. Even in the absence of foreign enemies, some opponents feared that the existence of the militia could encourage a democratic government to declare an unnecessary war.[48] But most critics found the militia simply anachronistic. In 1834 the New Haven, Connecticut, *Daily Herald* wrote after a muster that "This relic of antiquity . . . is now distinguished only by its absurdity and its gross deflection of public morals. . . . [It] is worse than useless. . . . We hope that our Legislature will soon put an end to this ridiculous farce."[49]

The muster became a particular object of ridicule in the 1820s. *Brother Jonathan,* a popular northern news magazine, described a militia muster as "useless and unseemly," its members "obstructions of humanity" and "extraordinary looking individuals, with . . . rusty muskets dangling at the end of their arms . . . waiting with an indifference certainly highly praiseworthy in professional soldiers." This journal, at least, felt that "this shamefully ridiculous practice has continued too long already, and should be abolished forthwith. What is the object—what the utility of it?" T. L. Hagood, a company commander, described the militia to New York's governor William Bouck as "mere *mobs* of half-drunken men." Senator James F. Simmons told the Rhode Island constitutional convention of 1842 that "For fifteen or twenty years, the militia trainings have been mostly a farce, nothing but an exhibition of rags, caps, and broomsticks. And with the exception of a few . . . volunteer companies, the militia [are] not to be relied on." Even children's books derided the militia. In one from the mid-1820s, a boy observed a militia muster: "I saw many drunken men. One was crawling on his hands and feet like a dog, being too much intoxicated to walk upright. Two of them were fighting; the blood ran down their faces, and they looked like furies." Not much of a role model for young men and patriots.[50]

Such descriptions of poorly armed, buffoonish musters filled the popular press. Such ill-armed troops came to be called "cornstalk militia," a more polite phrase than several employed. An observer of an 1830 muster in York, Maine, described it as "a curious spectacle:—fantastic companies in rag-tag-and-bob-tail uniforms,—no two alike,—with arquebuses, blunderbuses, firelocks, guns, muskets and Queen's arms of every conceivable shape and form, except the right one; and not one in a hundred would be of the least practical use, except as bludgeons or shillalays in a single combat or hand-to-hand fight." A Reading, Pennsylvania, muster featured "young men in line carrying broomsticks, unless one happened to be the proud owner of a gun of some sort." General J. Watts dePeyster, the commander of New York's militia and the institution's leading proponent for over thirty years, said that "We always associate the term militia with the rag-tag and bob-tail assemblages armed with broomsticks, cornstalks and umbrellas"; but he offered no evidence that this portrait lacked accuracy. Even Secretary of War Joel Poinsett complained to Congress in 1839 of the militia, "when mustered, a majority of them are armed with walking canes, fowling pieces, or unserviceable muskets."[51]

Militia companies reflected this public sentiment as many made a deliberate mockery of the whole enterprise. As a sign of opposition to the system, soldiers often nominated and elected fictitious characters or the most unlikely and inappropriate officers as a way of bringing the militia into disrepute. Abraham Lincoln told how the Springfield militia elected "old Tim Langwell, the greatest drunkard and blackguard, for Colonel." Many officers were elected specifically on their promise that they would not call musters. Jean Baptiste Beaubien was elected colonel of Chicago's militia every year from 1834 to 1847, calling only one muster during that entire period. The ever-pained William H. Sumner, adjutant general of Massachusetts, complained in 1834 that "The records of my office are disgraced with returns of persons of infamous character to honorable places,—of town paupers, idlers, vagrants, foreigners, itinerants, drunkards and the outcasts of society" elected militia officers. "Sometimes the returns are of persons wanting *mental capacity,* and at others the *physical ability* to perform the duties of their stations." In 1824 Pennsylvania's 84th Regiment elected as colonel a man who had at least the physical ability in John Pluck, a professional wrestler. A board of officers declared his election invalid, but the soldiery reelected Pluck. In a speech to the troops, Colonel Pluck "defended the election by claiming that at least he was not afraid to fight, which was more than could be said for most officers." Often militia companies killed themselves off by not electing officers, for only officers could call musters. In 1827 North Carolina's Adjutant

General Beverly Daniel stated that "nearly one-half of the companies are without officers to command them."[52]

When the members of a militia did not mock themselves, the crowds would. Davy Crockett observed that there were always more men in the crowd watching the militia than in the militia itself. Locals, including many who should have been taking part in the exercises, often gathered to make fun of the militia. The crowd's favorite target was the poor marksmanship of the militia. In Connecticut, a Waterbury social group called the Fantastics burlesqued the militia with their deliberately comical musters and pretenses of shooting one another by accident. The state responded with a law against such mockery. Even the famously heroic Concord militia company earned the nickname "the shad company" after their captain forgot about the muster and went into town to sell fish. Some state legislatures attempted to outlaw heckling the militia; for instance, in 1835 South Carolina passed a law fining any person who heckled or disrupted a militia muster $50. In 1841 the legislature reinforced the fine with a five-day jail sentence. In 1834 New Hampshire threatened arrest and fines to anyone who by "appearing in a grotesque or unusual dress, or by affected awkwardness . . . attempt[s] to disturb the order of parade and to bring ridicule" upon the militia. Four other states passed similar laws.[53]

Labor unions made the persistence of militia musters a prime grievance that fell disproportionately on the workers. Guns were still expensive, equal to several months' wages for a skilled laborer. Even William Sumner felt that it was ridiculous to expect a worker to buy his own gun. In 1835 Secretary of War Lewis Cass bluntly told Congress that "it is vain to expect that the whole adult male population of the country can or will furnish themselves" with guns. Five years later Representative Philip Triplett of Kentucky told Congress that not one-fourth of the men in the country could afford to buy a gun "without selling some article of property necessary to the support of themselves or families."[54]

In the face of such widespread contempt, the highest officials in several states, including adjutants general, came to oppose the militia. The governor of Indiana, James Brown Ray, told the assembly that it was useless to repeat "so frequently and unsuccessfully, attempt upon attempt, to instruct the great mass of people in the art of war" when they clearly were not in the least interested. These are but "efforts to perform impossibilities. Our existing militia laws, commit violence upon the rights of conscience, as well as impose penalties on poverty, by exacting equipments

and services which many of the people are not able to perform." To expect
the majority of people to own arms "is as hopeless as it would be a waste of
treasure." With the public uninterested in the militia, there was no reason
to continue its operation. Ray's successor, Noah Noble, agreed that the
militia system, "which has no hold upon the affections of our citizens,"
was "a severe tax upon their time" for no visible purpose. The state lost
150,000 man-days of labor every year because of militia activities—but no
more. From 1832 to 1844 only volunteer groups mustered in Indiana, and
the state's adjutant general did not issue a single annual report during that
period.[55] Little wonder, given such inattention and hostility, that the militia system withered and died in the United States.

By 1830 it was basically impossible to determine how many people
considered themselves part of the militia. The last nearly accurate return
was in 1820; from then until 1860 most states simply made up a number.
In his 1828 returns, the adjutant general of Alabama reported that "No
doubt the militia of this State is 30,000 strong," though the manuscript
returns listed just under twenty-three thousand. The adjutant general of
Indiana also simply added seven thousand men to his total, while the
adjutant general of Missouri maintained that his militia, listed as 3,824,
actually exceeded twelve thousand. Vermont had no adjutant general
from 1825 to 1837 and made only a single return between 1820 and 1840.
Mississippi and Delaware simply stopped sending in returns in 1814;
many other states followed suit.[56]

South Carolina was one of the few states to attempt to keep its militia
alive. It did so by repeatedly turning to the federal government for aid. In
1830, in the midst of the Nullification crisis, the legislature petitioned
Congress for redress of its expenses during the War of 1812. With its militia grossly under-armed at the beginning of war and "the national government being unable . . . to put muskets into the hands of the militia,"
the state had no choice but to act in the stead of the federal government in
arming its citizens, spending $200,000. Feeling a keen sense of entitle-
ment at the same time that they were nullifying federal legislation, the
legislature of South Carolina expected the central government to reimburse all their expenses toward the purchase of these 4,017 muskets (the
federal count was 3,267). Though "the State . . . stood greatly in need" of
these guns at the time, it "has now no use for them whatever." The federal
ordnance department made the silly offer to repay South Carolina in guns
rather than money. The legislature wanted the money. The Congressional Committee of Claims felt little sympathy, not simply because other

states had tried to arm their militia without expectation of restitution, but also because many of the guns in question had been lost or damaged beyond repair.[57]

Even in South Carolina many citizens saw the militia as a nuisance, completely superfluous in times of peace. Many militia officers thought that the system should be entirely voluntary, while common soldiers felt they should be better paid when they had to serve on slave patrols. In fact, if not for the terror of slave rebellion, the militia would have vanished from sight in South Carolina and every other southern state. However, even that fear could not generate much enthusiasm among most whites, and the South Carolina legislature tried desperately to make the militia work, reforming the whole system ten times between 1815 and 1846. Yet the legislature continually avoided deep, substantive changes. With the dread of slave insurrection always lurking just beneath the surface, the state's leadership feared the consequences of too radical an alteration in a system which, if not very good, at least seemed to work.[58] Similar concerns persuaded the Virginia council, in 1829, to arm any volunteer militia companies organized "where from the number of slaves, danger of insurrection may by apprehended." They defined that area as anywhere slaves lived and worked.[59]

Those states that attempted to maintain their militia in the 1830s tried to minimize the degree to which membership interfered with daily life. In 1831 the Missouri legislature, like so many others, passed a law limiting the militia to a single muster a year, and then solely for "roll call and inspection."[60] The Connecticut legislature was even more congenial, attempting to save its militia by holding only a single muster a year, exempting those who appeared at that muster from the poll tax, and granting a lifetime exemption to any citizen who showed up for ten years in succession with his own gun. It was a running battle between the will of the legislature and the general public over the very existence of the militia. In 1847, with only three thousand men enrolled in the militia (less than 5 percent of the adult males), Connecticut gave up, shifting government financial and material support to volunteer militia companies. The complete absence of public debate over these dramatic changes provides a certain barometer of collective indifference. As Stewart L. Gates observed, the legislature received far more commentary on the price of fireworks than the future of the militia.[61]

Even in Massachusetts, the most militarist state, the militia simply unraveled in 1830 when the legislature extended militia exemptions to everyone over the age of thirty. Scores of companies simply ceased to exist, others found themselves without officers, most suffered the loss of half their membership. Even staunch supporters of the militia acknowledged that the legislature's act accurately reflected public sentiment. General Avery wrote that "a large portion of the community" was "opposed to the Militia system" and would settle for "nothing short of its total annihilation." The public heaped upon the militia "disrepute, contempt, and ridicule!" Now "reputable men are ashamed to be seen in the ranks." Only a few volunteer companies survived, which the adjutant general H. A. S. Dearborn attempted to keep alive through "greater inducements," such as direct gifts of firearms. Despite such consideration, by 1836 Dearborn sadly reported that even these volunteer companies paid almost no attention to the maintenance of their weapons, and the need for repeated gun repairs cost the state a great deal of money.[62]

Several states responded to the growth of antimilitia sentiment by abandoning the universal militia ideal entirely and turning to a volunteer system. Massachusetts switched to a volunteer system in 1840 as, in the words of its adjutant general, "the voluntary System is more in accordance with the temper of the times." A few states enjoyed some success with volunteer companies; others could not find any enthusiasts. In 1824 Pennsylvania had 20,594 guns for 158,512 official and 23,736 volunteer militia. The government initially decided to share the weapons it received from the federal government between the two groups, but soon realized that those given to the official militia were never cleaned and quickly became useless. So in 1832 the state determined to supply guns only to the volunteers, and in 1849 it ended the official militia entirely. Vermont stopped its general musters in 1832, switching to a volunteer system. In 1844 it gave up and terminated the state's militia system entirely, as did Maine and Ohio that same year, and Rhode Island the year before. Michigan, Missouri, Louisiana, New York, Connecticut, and New Hampshire all abandoned their militia systems between 1846 and 1850, while Kentucky's 1850 constitution did not even bother to mention a militia organization. When New York ended its militia musters, *Niles' National Register* wrote, "We congratulate the people of this commonwealth warmly and heartily upon their emancipation from mock military duty."[63]

The militia of some of the new states, such as Mississippi and Florida, never got off the ground. Florida issued its first call for the militia in 1823, but no one showed up. John Rodman, the federal customs collector at St

Augustine, reported to his superiors in 1826 that there was no militia in the city and neither the governor nor the appointed militia officers were making any effort to organize a company. The government did place some advertisements in the newspapers warning eligible males to obey the law, but the public responded with indifference. The *Pensacola Gazette* joined Rodman in blaming the government for not enforcing the law, observing that its only result so far was to produce some officers with fancy titles, no actual militia. Governor William P. Duval insisted that any effort to enforce the militia law would lead to the mass resignation of the state's officers, persuading the legislature to encourage volunteer companies. But only a few of the volunteers owned firearms. Duval wrote Secretary of War Calhoun begging for arms, and received one hundred muskets. These were immediately distributed, and Duval pointed out to Calhoun's successor, James Barbour, that he needed three hundred more for his volunteers. Duval added that there was no place in Florida to buy guns.[64]

The Florida legislature attempted to respond to these realities by ordering only a single muster a year and changing the law requiring guns for militia service to recommending them. The legislature, which passed eight militia acts between 1822 and 1833, even granted free passage on all ferries and bridges to those going to and from militia musters. Nothing seemed to work. In 1829, in response to Indian attacks, Alachua County tried to form a militia company, but found that only 10 percent of those who showed up to serve owned guns. There is something rather poignant about a frontier governor, supported by a petition from the legislature, writing the secretary of war pleading for sixty-five rifles for a volunteer militia company in Tallahassee. Not only does it call much of the frontier mythology into question, it also indicates just how few guns were available when two prominent public officials devoted energy to sixty-five guns. In 1831 Florida finally held a militia muster, with 827 officers and men out of 4,000 eligible. With that showing, the state earned nine muskets from the federal government, ten in 1832. It is little wonder that Duval stated bluntly that the Florida militia could not protect the state because of a lack of arms and ammunition.[65] A careful student of the Florida militia observed that not only were state and federal laws mandating every man to supply his own arms ignored, but "It appears that the frontiersmen did not take the minimum steps necessary for self-defense."[66]

The indifference of both individual militiamen and state officials to their armaments was cause for continual federal concern from 1815 to 1840. The Supreme Court did its part to prop up the militia, though their rulings had little impact. In *Houston v. Moore* (1820) the Court ruled that a militiaman who refused to respond to a federal militia call-up was in violation of national law; while Justice Story spoke for a unanimous Court in *Martin v. Mott* (1827) in upholding the Calling Forth Act of 1795, placing each individual militiaman under the direct control of the president. These decisions did little to halt the public's growing impatience with the militia.[67]

The most persistent nags were the House Committee on Military Affairs, the secretary of war, and the chief of ordnance for the War Department—Colonel George Bomford for most of this period. Year after year Bomford and the secretary of war reported on the poor condition of public arms; year after year the House committee proposed laws requiring the states to store the arms supplied by the federal government; year after year Congress refused to act. In 1824 Bomford identified the basic problem: "When the arms are delivered, they become the property of the State, and the officers of the General Government no longer exercise any control over them." From then on, the guns were essentially lost to future use. Most of the states simply turned the guns over to unarmed members of the militia, with no effort at guaranteeing maintenance. As a consequence, the guns would "in the course of a few years, be greatly injured, if not irreparably damaged and lost." At the same time, this procedure ensured that "few individuals will provide arms, at their own expense, when the State will furnish them gratis." Bomford made a telling observation in noting that, despite the direct gift of guns that had armed one-tenth of the militia since 1816, in times of crisis "sole reliance must be placed upon the arms deposited in the public depots," for on every occasion privately held arms were found to be almost entirely unusable. He "confidently" predicted that in future crises, those states that had distributed arms to individuals would find their militia largely unarmed. Guns, Bomford concluded, should be kept in arsenals and distributed only in an emergency.[68]

It probably did not matter much that these arsenals were never constructed, for the existing arsenals did not inspire much confidence. Only in Massachusetts were arsenals maintained and guarded with any degree of competence. Sometime in 1838—authorities had no idea when—thieves entered New York's Watertown arsenal on several occasions, stealing at least 330 stands of arms and two thousand pounds of powder,

Later the same year robbers made off with an estimated one thousand muskets and bayonets from the Elizabethtown arsenal. The state was in an uproar over the loss of these public arms. Neither arsenal had a guard, only a single keeper who made $25 a year to keep an eye on things. Governor W. L. Marcy defended the state by telling the Assembly "that the state arsenals . . . are not, nor are they designed to be, places of strength. They are merely deposites for arms and munitions of war." Security did not seem necessary as "it was anticipated that there would be, at all times and under all circumstances, a general disposition among our citizens . . . to defend [the arsenals] whenever they should be threatened with an attack or exposed to be pillaged." Marcy compounded this idiotic statement by noting that some twenty artillery pieces belonging to the state may have been stolen, no one was certain. Probably, the governor thought, these weapons were intended for the rebels in Canada. In response the assembly demanded to know how the governor planned to prevent "armed assemblages of the citizens of this state." The governor suggested the U.S. Army would be necessary for such an emergency, since the militia would now be almost entirely unarmed.[69]

Curiously, New York did nothing to secure their remaining arms, or to protect those that continued to be delivered by the federal government. In 1840 the state's commissary general found all the state's arsenals in grievous disrepair. The Albany arsenal had a leaky roof, which had led to the rusting of all its weapons, while the New York City arsenal had cracked beams, a sinking first floor, and walls close to collapse. The backyard of this latter structure, enclosed only by a wooden fence, contained open sheds full of ordnance, all of which was exposed to "wind, weather, fire, and mobs." Governor William Seward ordered a brick wall built around the backyard and a series of fireproof gun houses for the artillery.[70]

New York was not exceptional. Other than Massachusetts, the New England states turned their guns over to the towns, making the selectmen responsible for maintaining a magazine; in reality the guns and munitions usually ended up in a closet in the meetinghouse. South Carolina established two arsenals: one a very well built structure at the Citadel in Charleston, the other in Columbia in the basement of the capitol. Security at the latter site was lax, with the doors left open and no locks on the windows. In the 1850s California issued its guns directly to the individual militia units for storage in their meeting rooms—several of these meeting rooms blew up.[71]

While the states were losing interest, Congress maintained at least an official concern for the future of the militia. The federal government provided the several states with 93,271 muskets, 11,562 rifles, 17,529 pistols, and 12,832 swords between 1816 and 1830.[72] The House Committee on Militia made an obvious point in 1829 when it noted that "An indispensible requisite in forming an efficient militia is a knowledge of the correct theory and practice of the use of fire-arms, as well as the certain means of acquiring them." Observing that none of these criteria had yet been met, the committee recommended doing away with any still-existing requirements "compelling individuals enrolled for militia service to furnish arms." While holding up the goal of a nation of "citizen soldiers" ever ready for war, the committee insisted that the people could not be expected to learn the use of firearms and military discipline without federal aid. The appropriation for arming the militia should therefore be increased to a point where the government would supply all members of the militia with a gun. The committee added that these efforts would be meaningless unless Congress could offer some system of incentive to encourage more practice in the use of firearms. The committee cast around for someone to blame for allowing the militia "to degenerate into inefficiency and insignificance," and settled on the executive branch.[73]

More constructive was the effort by Secretary of War James Barbour in 1826 to launch a national reform of the militia system. Barbour can hardly be labeled a fan of the militia system. He told President Adams that he favored some form of reorganization "by which at least a million and a half of our most useful citizens would be relieved from the unprofitable pagentry of military parade for five or six days in the year, constituting so injurious a draft on their industry." But at least the secretary of war took his job seriously.[74]

Barbour began by contacting every state government and a number of military experts. Some fifty officials from twenty states responded, nearly all of whom castigated the militia while endorsing a shift to volunteer companies. Taken together, the letters form a staggering indictment of the militia system by its main promoters, and a concise indication of the shortage of firearms in the United States at this time. It is worth taking a close look at this exchange among exactly those men who knew most about gun use and ownership in America, for it offers a portrait at complete variance with the current mythology.[75]

Had the United States actually needed to rely on the militia for the defense of its liberty, personal or national, the letters to Barbour would have been chilling. Richard Harwood, adjutant general of Maryland, had no idea how many men served in the militia in his state and did not want to see any changes made. His state eschewed musters as "disadvantageous to the militia. They tend to corrupt the morals of the people." General J. B. Harvie agreed, calling musters "injurious." Governor Edward Coles of Illinois found no reason in this time of peace to devote any more energy to the militia. "Frequent musters," he wrote, "are injurious to society and are productive of little benefit to the militia. But little military information is gained, bad moral habits are acquired, and much time is lost." William Murphy of Ohio rejected militia musters in peacetime as "useless." "Worse than useless," was the preferred evaluation of General T. Cadwalader of Pennsylvania, who insisted that "No correct instruction is received at such musters, and their effect on the morals of the people is positively injurious."[76]

These were mild sentiments. General Jonathan Watmough of the Pennsylvania militia held that "nothing can be more entirely inefficient than the militia under the existing organization." He offered a graphic denunciation of the militia muster: "Without arms, in nine cases out of ten badly officered, they merely comply with the letter of the law, and repair to their colors, not from the elevated feeling of duty to their country, . . . [but] to avail themselves of an indulgence, without restraint, in all the immoralities of legalized misrule." Watmough invited Barbour to "attend a militia muster, under its most favorable circumstances, in a retired country situation, and these evils are presented to your sight in all their enormity. Riot, drunkenness, and every species of immorality, are the order of the day, which the pageant boobies, called officers, have neither intelligence to anticipate nor intellect sufficient to prevent." General H. I. Williams, another militia officer, reported that "All the musters at which I have been present . . . were always scenes of the lowest and most destructive dissipation, where nothing was to be acquired but the most pernicious habits. . . . Anything would be an improvement which diminished the numbers assembled on these occasions." An anonymous Kentuckian proclaimed musters a waste of time and money: "They see nothing, they hear nothing, and they know nothing." On this one point, at least, the writers were almost unanimous—that musters were at best a waste of time and money, at worst an assault upon public morality.[77]

The experts found less agreement on the value of volunteer companies. Bernard Peyton, adjutant general of Virginia, thought that volunteer corps, which accounted for 23.8 percent of his militia, "are generally composed of the most ardent and patriotic young men."[78] General John H. Cocke of Virginia found advantage in the volunteer companies "filled with a better class." It was exactly that characteristic that led Colonel John R. Wallace, also of Virginia, to state his preference for the regular militia composed "of the hardy laborers of the country, while volunteer companies are formed by the sons of richer individuals," and as such were more interested in luxuries than military duty. General Amariah Kibbe of Connecticut also failed to see the advantage of volunteer companies, which consisted of "young men possessing wealth, intelligence, and martial spirit, which leads them to excell mostly in their equipment." Almost alone, Kibbe favored more musters, so that the militia could become "habituated to arms. . . . Unless arms and equipments are often inspected, they will become impaired and useless; unless the troops are often reviewed, they will not be ambitious to excel in arms." While Governor H. Johnson of Louisiana agreed with Kibbe in finding the volunteers, whom his state supplied with guns, arrogant and a drag on the regular militia, he held that "frequent musters . . . are detrimental," and was confident that in an emergency there would be plenty of time to learn military skills.[79]

In their defense, several commentators noted that the volunteer companies always possessed superior arms and equipment, and actually took care of them. Joseph Sewall, judge advocate of Maine, agreed with this judgment, but worried that the volunteers drew off the best and most ambitious members of the regular militia. Musters he dismissed as stupid, involving little more than "a review, and a few evolutions of the line." There are often "more spectators than troops; and the time, in many instances, is unfortunately spent in indulgences that are prejudicial to the morals of the community." So the point was to keep the regular militia, but not have it do anything. James Appleton noted that volunteers exist only to avoid the regular militia service and these embarrassing musters: "Were there no regular militia, it is questionable whether you would have any considerable number of volunteers." North Carolina's Adjutant General Beverly Daniel offered a distinctive view in suggesting that volunteer companies, which constituted only 5 percent of the total in his state, be confined to towns, as those in the countryside proved fleeting and ill equipped. The regular militia could simply be forgotten. "The discipline of the great body of the militia," Daniel wrote, "can sustain no injury by any change in this respect [musters], as they acquire none [discipline] under the present mode of training."[80]

Division Inspector P. A. Browne of Philadelphia did not think that the current militia should simply be abandoned. He observed that most men joined volunteer companies for the uniforms; perhaps the government should supply fancy uniforms to the regular militia—a suggestion made also by General Theodore Sill of New York. Browne declared musters "time thrown away." A few days' training "can never make a soldier, but it may make a drunkard or an idler. It ought to be entirely abolished." He did not specify on what occasion the uniforms would be worn if musters ended.[81]

Torn between continuing the militia or scrapping the system entirely, Barbour's experts agreed on one point: that any reform must originate in Congress. North and South, they all insisted that there was simply no way that the states could handle the problems facing the militia, especially on the issue of armaments. General John M. McCalla of Kentucky declared, "Our laws are little better than an order to disband the militia altogether. We have in consequence looked to Congress for some redeeming act which will place the system on a respectable footing." Kentucky law exempts "a militiaman from parading with a gun if *he does not actually own one*." McCalla has seen "regiments parade in which not more than one in forty or fifty have a gun at all." His own regiment "which enrolls upwards of 1,000 men, parade less than 110."[82] Another Kentuckian felt the government's policy of arms distribution the gravest issue. The governor of Kentucky distributed federal arms to individuals; the guns were then "scattered over the State in every direction, many of them destroyed, many become injured and useless without having seen the slightest service." The men were not required to care for them and collecting them in an emergency would prove fruitless. He reminded the secretary of war "how near New Orleans was being lost for the want of a few muskets." The government must hold on to the firearms in arsenals as "should our present system be pursued, in future wars we shall be wholly unable to act either offensively or defensively for want of arms; for I venture to assert that, within fifteen years' time after the distribution of those arms, three-fourths" will have vanished.[83]

Only Governor Oliver Wolcott of Connecticut maintained that there was no problem with firearms distribution. His militia, he told Barbour, was well armed. The state's longtime adjutant general, Ebenezer Huntington, disagreed. The cavalry was armed only with swords and pistols, which made them a largely ineffective force, while the infantry found the idea of owning a gun "irksome." Huntington declared musters "of very little use . . . merely affording a red-letter day, or day of dissipation to the vicinity of the parade ground."[84]

Every other state reported a similar lack of firearms and of enthusiasm for owning them. Daniel Elmer of New Jersey blamed pacifism for killing the militia. "Notwithstanding the law of the United States and the law of this State—both require the militia man should arm himself—few are armed." His brigade had two thousand members, and only 375 stands of arms, 225 of which belonged to the state—only 7.5 percent of his troops owned guns. J. G. Swift of New York insisted that the militia would remain useless until it was properly armed: "It would require nearly a century to arm the present militia by the existing means." If nothing else, the government should sponsor musters of several days where troops would learn how to fire, clean, and care for their arms. He added that most of the current schoolbooks taught a contempt for the militia.[85]

Missouri's Adjutant General John O'Fallon offered an amazing reversal of the common modern perception of frontier attitudes. O'Fallon wrote that "The condition of the militia of this State must necessarily make this communication short and unsatisfactory." Only a few companies bothered to muster, and there were no volunteer companies in Missouri despite official efforts to encourage them. So long as the people were intent on the necessities of settlement, no one could expect them to demonstrate "a proper military spirit." Perhaps, O'Fallon added, when the state is a little wealthier the people will have the time for such matters as training in the use of arms. He concluded by suggesting that the government send him some rifles so that he could attempt to put together a company of volunteer riflemen.[86]

Summarizing well the opinion of many experts, General Jonathan B. O'Neall of South Carolina stated that the real issue before the country was the militia's lack of arms. Every writer who addressed the subject told Barbour that there was no way that the militia could ever arm itself. "Muskets and bayonets cannot be procured," O'Neall said, "and if they could, the citizens would very unwillingly submit to the expense." The guns at musters come in "all sizes and fashions, and generally [are] so badly constructed as to be of no value for any service." He warned that the militia could never be properly armed "until the government places arms in the hands of the citizen soldiery." Until such time, the militia and its "musters are of no value." Governor James Brown Ray of Indiana seconded this position. Given the shortage of firearms, it is not surprising that another writer favored requiring drills with wooden arms.[87]

However, Timothy Pickering of Massachusetts, like many others, but more forcefully, thought this idea of arming the whole militia positively "evil." There was no threat of invasion; it was internal insurrection that should concern them. Pickering favored the volunteer companies, but thought it necessary to offer the volunteers "instruction in loading, taking aim, and firing." Several others spoke to this need to teach the militia to shoot properly.[88]

John H. Hall, the leading innovator in armaments in the United States, wrote from Harpers Ferry that the real need of the militia was to learn how to shoot. With heavy emphasis Hall recommended "*The establishment of prize-firing as a part of the exercise of our militia.*" Not only would it encourage the militia to practice firing, but also to take care of their guns. Population increase outstripped the ability of the national armories and private gunmakers to arm the militia. Hall referred to the examples of Bunker Hill and New Orleans to show the capacity of the militia, though at these battles the militia "labored under serious disadvantages, both from the quality and quantity of their arms," a problem that would recur in another national emergency if the government did not expand gun production. "It is therefore not a question of whether they shall be armed at the public expense, or at their individual expense, but whether they shall be armed at all."[89]

Barbour passed these letters on to a board of officers chaired by General Winfield Scott. The board's lengthy recommendations with all the letters were sent to Congress and lost to sight. The House Committee on the Militia did issue a report that found that "the experience of many years proves the law [requiring the militia to arm themselves] to be useless and unavailing." The committee agreed with the experts that it is "unjust" to expect the militia to supply its own arms, though it was reasonable to require such of the volunteer companies, as they had the "*ability* to procure the requisite arms." They further agreed "that the arming and equipping of the militia, to the extent that it may appear to be expedient, is one of the duties devolving on Congress by express constitutional provision; that a resort can only be made to the national treasury for that purpose; and, if the annual appropriation is not sufficient, that it ought to be increased until it shall be commensurate to the object." Their calculations showed that "if the present number of enrolled militia were to *remain stationary,* the existing annual appropriation would not supply them with arms in less than *seventy-five years*." For that very reason the committee recommended that the country rely on volunteers in the future and limit the size of the militia. It was a recipe to do nothing, which is precisely what Congress did.[90]

For the next ten years every session of Congress witnessed efforts, minor and major, to reform the militia. Several state governments petitioned Congress to take on this task, arguing, in the words of New Hampshire's petition, that "the organization of the militia . . . [is] entrusted by the Constitution to the general government, . . . and can be only and efficiently and satisfactorily done by that government." Or as the New York legislature put it, "The defects in the established militia system . . . are wholly beyond the reach of the legislative authority of the State." In response, the Twentieth Congress saw two competing uniform militia bills, one from Senator John Chandler of Maine, the other from Representative Hedge Thompson of New Jersey. Both were tabled, as were Thompson's next two efforts in the Twenty-first Congress, and the efforts of Representatives Daniel Barringer (North Carolina) in the Twenty-second, Henry Hubbard (New Hampshire) in the Twenty-third, Thomas Glascock (Georgia) in the Twenty-fourth, and David Wagener (Pennsylvania) in the Twenty-fifth Congress in 1839. The last major effort at federal reform prior to the 1880s came in 1839 from Secretary of War Joel R. Poinsett. Responding to a request from the House of Representatives to determine the relative expense of employing militia as compared to regular troops, Poinsett declared the militia almost four times as expensive. Paymaster General Towson's analysis found that the chief expenses would be incurred in arming a mostly unarmed militia and covering the enormous losses of material sustained by a people who seemed incapable of caring for their arms. Poinsett recommended arming and training a select number of volunteers.[91]

Democrat Poinsett's plan became a major issue in the 1840 election. The Whigs, whose candidate was the militarist William Henry Harrison, portrayed President Martin Van Buren as a warmonger seeking to establish a military dictatorship. But what, the Democrats demanded, could be wrong with the government arming the people? Speaking in Brooklyn, Silas Wright asked how the Whigs could fear "200,000 men like yourselves, who are to be permitted to have arms, and to learn the use of arms?" But then that was precisely what the Whigs feared: 200,000 armed workers.[92]

The Whigs found all of this talk of militia reform entirely needless. As Representative Triplett put it: "We do not believe that our soil might be polluted by the foot of the invader, our cities taken and sacked, and our forts occupied before our armed citizens could be taught the elements of tactics or the simple use of the firelock." Nor did Triplett anticipate that the United States might itself be the invader of another country. With the Whig victory in 1840, all efforts at national reform of the militia were abandoned. As Representative George Keim, chair of the House Committee on the Militia, admitted, the militia had "sunk under the weight of public opinion."[93]

The Whigs won and Poinsett's plans were shelved. But the most compelling argument against these efforts to arm the militia came, oddly, from the adjutant general of the United States, who "estimated" that it would cost precisely $335,269.04 a year to arm just the active part of the militia. And even then they could not hope to succeed, for the government armories were producing only 14,200 muskets a year. Since 300,000 of the 500,000 men (60 percent) in the active militia—active in terms of having registered—had no firearms, the government would need twenty-one years to arm those in need of guns, putting aside population growth. On paper, at least, militia membership increased annually at double the rate of national arms production. Since, in the adjutant general's view, the private sector could not respond to this increased demand, the choice was either to buy guns in Europe or spend the money to expand the government arsenals. Congress chose to do neither.[94]

Sometimes, though not often, this inaction aroused the anger of those devoted to the improvement of the militia—a small number.[95] In 1831 a group of Massachusetts militia officers petitioned the government for a national, uniform militia system based on a small, well-armed, active militia. Just as their goal harkened back to George Washington's proposals, so did their justifications. The Massachusetts officers pointed out that the Constitution made "the national government" responsible for the "organization, and of providing the mode of arming the militia." Congress talked every year of reforming the militia, yet no bill had passed. Those willing to contribute their time should be rewarded with a usable gun, rather than having to buy their own. "The present appropriation for arming the militia, which would require seventy years for the accomplishment of its purpose, is so entirely inadequate that any suggestion from us for its extension becomes unnecessary." These officers noted that they were seconding the recommendations of the 1826 board of officers appointed by Barbour; in 1832 a "Convention of Militia Officers of Pennsylvania" would in its turn support the Massachusetts report. All attacked as meaningless the ideal of a universal militia, finding it "inexpedient for the government to attempt to arm and instruct the whole body" of men. All were ignored.[96]

Improperly armed, the militia could not do its duty. During Nat Turner's Rebellion in Southampton County, Virginia, in 1831, newspapers reported that the local militia were "very deficient in proper arms, accoutrements and ammunition." Governor John Floyd spent weeks trying to acquire arms and ammunition to supply these units, and he continued to do so even after the rebellion had been repressed. "I am daily sending them a portion of arms though I know there is no danger." Similarly, militia units on both sides of the Dorr Rebellion in Rhode Island in 1842 lacked sufficient arms to assert their political will effectively. Given that the supposed purpose of the militia was to protect American liberty and order, it is ironic that neither the state nor the rebels were well armed. The Rhode Island government had turned to Massachusetts for arms to repress Dorr's forces, but was rebuffed. The adjutant general of Massachusetts, Henry A. S. Dearborn, acted on his own to supply these weapons from the Cambridge Arsenal, for which he was removed from office in 1843.[97]

The performance of the militia in the few Indian wars between 1815 and 1846 demonstrated that the common white male had not yet found sufficient interest in firearms to actually learn how to use one. The Black Hawk War of 1832 got off to a poor start, as the Illinois and Michigan militia appealed for federal arms and the support of regular troops. Michigan had no shortage of volunteers, but half of these frontier settlers who showed up to fight the Indians did not own a gun—and these were the volunteers who expected to do battle. Philip St. George Cooke described the Illinois militia as "An irregular, ill-armed force," while General John R. Williams reported that one frontier community of one hundred families had fifty guns among them.[98]

The Seminole War on the Florida frontier proved even more embarrassing. In the early 1830s white settlers moved ever closer to the land of the Seminole, a congregation of the survivors of many different Indian tribes as well as runaway slaves and their descendants. The state government actually tried to limit these movements, appreciating the vulnerability of the white settlers and their militia to Indian attacks. In 1832 General Richard Call of the state militia warned Secretary of War Lewis Cass that Florida was almost devoid of arms and had no arsenal. There were only enough guns in both private and public hands for one-quarter of the militia at most. Governor Duval followed up with a request for 240 muskets and 250 rifles, noting that Florida had so far received only 198 firearms from the federal government. These letters were filed, and Florida did not receive any guns until 1835, when the U.S. Army issued 120 muskets to the state militia. But they failed to issue any cartridges or powder, and General Joseph Hernandez stated that none were to be had in Florida.[99]

In the first week of December 1835, the combined grand juries of Alachua and Hillsborough Counties warned that an Indian war was imminent, and yet there was no militia in either county, few arms, and no access to arms. There was not even a gunsmith in the whole state who could repair the older guns in private hands. Militia Colonel John Warren, predicting imminent war, issued orders to seize every privately owned gun that his officers could find. These predictions of disaster proved prescient. Just two weeks later a group of 180 Seminole surprised Captain Francis Dade's 107th Infantry on their way to Fort King, killing all but three men. The Indians, mostly armed with muskets, had risen suddenly from the thick underbrush, firing at point-blank range. Roughly half of Dade's command were hit in this first volley; those soldiers who carried loaded firearms appear to have fired them straight into the air in their shock while the rest of the survivors struggled to load their weapons. Even the cannon was fired without aiming. The Seminole employed the old trick of dropping to the ground at the moment it looked like the soldiers would fire, and then moved in for the kill with their tomahawks and clubs. The American regulars were well armed with new muskets and rifles, all of which fell into the hands of the Seminole.[100]

Panic ensued throughout Florida. Many militia companies refused to muster, insisting that their unarmed condition made such an exercise pointless. Those units that did muster were nearly unarmed, and what guns they had were described as pathetic. Sergeant James Ormond reported that his own company of militia was "an undisciplined rabble . . . not a man had ever before seen a gun fired in anger." Every observer, from Governor John Eaton to General Winfield Scott, reported that there were few guns in Florida and that the militia was largely unarmed.[101] Scott discovered that even those troops arriving from Georgia and Alabama with guns—one-third of the total—had absolutely no accoutrements, cartridges, or flints. General J. W. A. Sanford, commander of the Georgia militia, validated that calculation, reporting that of his thirty-five hundred volunteers "*less* than one-third were armed, and those variously and indifferently. . . . Our miserable deficiency in this respect was most strikingly displayed to my view when, upon the occasion of an alarm, and it was expected that the enemy would be upon us in full force, I had the mortification of beholding ... fifteen or sixteen hundred men with no weapons of defence beyond their side-arms, clubs, and club-axes." Scott pointedly asked the southern governors to send only "*armed men*" in the future.[102]

In desperation Governor Eaton appealed for arms from the other southern states. Georgia sent six hundred muskets from its Augusta arsenal. General Call purchased all the guns locally available, which were mostly small-bore shotguns. The citizens of Key West bought guns for their militia in Havana. These efforts continued over the six years of this war.[103] In 1837 the grand juries of Alachua, Columbia, and Hillsborough Counties made clear the attitude of most frontier settlers when they voted that the United States government was responsible for the defense of Florida against the Seminole. Judge Robert R. Reid, a future governor, approved this finding.[104]

In fact the federal government was arming the militia to fight the Seminole, though in odd ways. The governors of Georgia, Alabama, and Florida drained the federal arsenals in search of weapons, taking guns belonging to the U.S. Army. The commander of the Mount Vernon Arsenal wrote General Scott that the secretary of war had granted these governors the authority to empty his arsenal, to the detriment of the army. Just four days earlier, Scott had written General Thomas S. Jesup that "we shall be much delayed in taking the field on this side by the non-arrival of our most essential supplies—muskets, rifles, musket accoutrements, ammunition, &c." He desperately needed guns in order to take the field and now learned that those guns had gone to the militia, who would not take the field. Until federal arms arrived, Scott concluded, "there were not armed men in sufficient numbers ... even to guard the important points on the Chattahoochee." Astounded by the ignorance of firearms demonstrated by the volunteers, Scott issued orders almost identical to those by Washington sixty years earlier on the need to clean and care for the guns and to avoid firing them needlessly.[105]

As the Seminole War demonstrates, the armed frontier was created by the federal government, years after American citizens had moved into the area. In 1841 the federal government aided the establishment of armed settlements along the border of Seminole lands.[106] Despite federal support, the government of Florida continued to feel that it lacked sufficient arms for its own defense. Throughout the 1840s and 1850s the state pestered a succession of secretaries of war with requests for more arms.

Governor William D. Moseley went so far as to make up a giant militia of more than twelve thousand men in order to get at least a few more guns out of the government. Unfortunately, he had not coordinated his efforts with the state's adjutant general, who reported that there was no militia organization in the state. The secretary of war told the governor that Florida's account was overdrawn by 153 muskets from the last war, and it would simply have to wait its turn behind the other states. In 1851 Florida received eighty-six muskets, which, according to the state's quartermaster general, meant that the entire state militia, which did not exist, now possessed 259 muskets, 121 rifles, and 348 pistols. But the state armory had blown over in a storm, and sixty-one of those muskets had been seriously damaged. As an added insult, Colonel A. L. Craig of the U.S. Ordnance Department informed Governor James Broome that Florida should not expect any more federal requisitions until 1869. Somehow Florida survived the antebellum years without an organized militia or an armed citizenry.[107]

While the years from 1815 to 1846 were notably peaceful ones for the United States, the lack of enthusiasm for free guns during this period remains surprising. The federal government continued to give away guns under the 1808 Militia Act, still spending $200,000 a year attempting to arm the state militia. Yet the governors of most states made only a minimal effort, or none at all, to acquire these guns—an accurate reflection of their constituents' lack of interest in military matters. These free guns were granted on the basis of militia returns; after 1830 most states just made up some numbers, while several states did not even bother to file any returns, and by 1840 most militia companies did not even bother to muster. In 1851 the U.S. Army Ordnance Office informed Congress that only seven states had made militia returns in 1850, while seven other states and the District of Columbia had not made a return for the previous decade. The federal government could not give away its guns.[108]

There was one major, ironic exception to this massive disdain for free guns: the Quaker state. The Pennsylvania government took advantage of the lack of interest of the others to maximize its armaments by paying a penny for each name enrolled on the militia lists, resulting in the largest militia returns in the nation. As the New York Senate complained, even though Pennsylvania's "population is less by at least one million than our own," that state continually reported more militia to the federal government and received more arms.[109]

Incredibly, even when states took federal arms, they rarely expended any money for their maintenance, and Congress made no provision for the verification of numbers or for the storage of weapons. States were thus entirely free to do what they would with the weapons, perhaps most commonly just letting them rot in inadequate storage facilities. State militias almost never repaired broken weapons, rarely discarded obsolete ones, and simply stored the vast majority of weapons without regular servicing in the most inappropriate locations. Certainly this official lack of interest reflected the general population's inattention to firearms and military matters.[110]

The old myth of the military effectiveness of the militia has taken a battering over the last twenty years as historians have studied its performance more carefully. Military historians have debated the utility and commitment of the militia, and they generally doubt both. Those scholars have noted the absence of a well-armed and efficient militia in the period from the French and Indian War through the War of 1812.[111] Those findings are strongly supported by the extant military records, though the period of militia ineffectiveness should be extended into the 1850s. The militia records from the first half of the nineteenth century are packed with complaints of the shortage of weapons, the poor quality of those available, and the routine failure of their rank and file to care for the weapons they did possess. Regular army officers also commented often on the recruits' unfamiliarity with guns. One simple fact stands out from these records: in the early nineteenth century, the majority of American men did not care about guns. They were indifferent to owning guns, and they had no apparent interest in learning how to use them. In order to avoid paying for a standing army, Congress had hoped to change their constituents' minds by supplying the guns for militia use. But the public as a whole was hostile to the militia and disdainful of the man who felt the need to use a gun.

The Literary View of Guns

Judging from the popular literature of the day, the public seemed completely uninterested in firearms. The first book of any kind to lavish attention on the details of gun production was part of the Marco Paul children's series from the early 1840s. The author, Jacob Abbott, has two boys visit the Springfield Armory, where they are amazed by all that modern science can accomplish and explain. When the two boys go into

the arsenal itself "They were both struck with astonishment at the imposing spectacle which was presented to their view. . . . The dark and glossy
brown color of the stocks, with the highly polished lustre of the bayonets,
and other metallic parts, gave to each individual gun a very beautiful
appearance." The narrator observes that though these muskets are stored
in the best possible conditions, they must still be oiled "every few years" to
prevent rusting.[112]

Despite the obvious appreciation for the art inherent in gun production, the author questions the wisdom of all these weapons even existing.
Marco believes that "it is a good plan to make all these muskets," so that
"when the enemy comes to fight us, we shall be ready for them." His
cousin Forester is less certain. "It generally makes men quarrelsome to go
armed . . . and I didn't know but that it might possibly have the same
effect among nations. In some countries," though not apparently the
United States, "it is the custom for almost every gentleman to carry some
deadly weapon about him—as a little dirk or dagger, or a pistol; and in
such countries, quarrels, and murders, and assassinations are generally
very frequent."

The book closes with a long condemnation of the gun, many aspects of
which are relevant to the end of the twentieth century. Carrying weapons
makes men "fierce in spirit, boastful, and revengeful." Marco suggests
that the opposite should be the case, offering the earliest known version of
the popular phrase that "an armed society is a polite society." Surely,
Marco says, if people "know that everybody is armed, . . . I should think
that that would make them keep civil." Forester counters that men with
guns are like little boys with sticks, bound to hit each other with them.
Every man, he wrote, "has an exaggerated idea of his own skill and
power, and thinks that, in a fight, he should come off conqueror." In
a surprisingly astute observation, Abbott has his young hero refer to a
recent technological breakthrough: "When a man gets a new patent revolving pistol, which will discharge six bullets in as many seconds, the
possession of it awakens a sort of desire to try it. 'There,' says he to himself, 'I should like to see a robber attack me now'; or 'if anybody wants to
insult me now, let him come on.' Thus his mind assumes a belligerent
attitude, ready to take offense at any provocation."[113]

When Marco counters that one should certainly carry a gun in a heavily armed place, such as New Orleans, Forester states that he would be
less safe for being armed. Being unused to fighting or firing a gun, "you
would feel a kind of excitement and trepidation, and would not act cooly

enough." A prospective "robber, seeing that you were going to try to shoot him, would shoot you, . . . whereas, if you had offered no resistance, he would probably only have robbed you, without taking your life." And even if Marco succeeded in murdering a robber, it would haunt his thoughts forever. "The indignation and anger which you felt when you shot at him, would be changed into pity and compassion. . . . You would begin to imagine excuses for him. You would think that perhaps he had been neglected as a boy." Should Marco feel no "sense of his guilt" for shooting the robber, "satisfied that he deserved to die, you would wish that you had left it to somebody else to be his executioner." Marco comes to think that "between the two evils of suffering a robbery or committing a homicide, it would be best . . . to submit to the former." Forester in turn is willing to concede to Marco's point that perhaps countries should go armed, as individuals are protected by the laws of their nation and thus do not really need weapons.[114]

A Kiss for a Blow also makes a journey to the Springfield Armory. Overwhelmed by the thousands of muskets he sees there, the narrator asks one of the workers "what object they had in view in making these deadly weapons. They admitted that they made them to furnish men with the means of mutual slaughter." The young man then wants to know what the workers would think if he earned his living making weapons for his five brothers and six sisters to kill one another. "That you would be a most unnatural and bloody-minded brother." Having further evoked parental disapproval from the workers, the author suggests that their own logic required them to quit their jobs. At the very least they should inscribe "Love your enemies" and "Thou shalt not kill" on the side of the guns they make. The workers of course dismiss this idea, and that of quitting, for guns are tools of "Hatred and Revenge" and would appear silly with biblical injunctions on them. It is striking that the narrator makes no effort to speak to management, perhaps because Springfield was run by the U.S. government.[115]

Incredibly, children's books and adult magazines went even further, questioning the necessity for violence at all, even in the American Revolution. In 1842 the Unitarian minister Sylvester Judd delivered a sermon, later issued as a pamphlet, summarizing the arguments demonstrating that the Revolution was immoral and unnecessary. Judd held that a free people should practice only nonviolent resistance, as it violates any definition of democracy to take the life of a common soldier in order to win a political point. These were very radical ideas for any society in the nineteenth century, anticipating not simply Henry David Thoreau's 1849 essay on civil disobedience, but also the ideas of Gandhi.[116]

The same year that Thoreau published his pacifist manifesto, Joseph Alden brought out a children's book, *An Old Revolutionary Soldier,* questioning the heroic qualities of the American Revolution. Foster, the old Revolutionary soldier of the book's title, joined the Continental army as a teenage boy. His descriptions of battles anticipate the celebrated research of General S. L. A. Marshall in World War II, which indicated that most soldiers never knowingly fired on the enemy. Alden's description of eighteenth-century warfare is among the most accurate in American literature up to that date. On the American side "the soldiers were undisciplined and poorly armed." Battles involved a great deal of maneuvering and running around, and not a great deal of shooting. And Foster reports that he and his comrades never aimed at the enemy, but instead "held our guns about breast high, and pointed them towards the enemy's ranks." After that first volley "the smoke was so thick that we could see nothing. We could only point our guns towards the place where we supposed the enemy were." But most of the soldiers never reloaded. The British, though better armed and trained, also found their guns largely useless: "They wasted a good deal of the King's powder and ball in ploughing up the earth there." A neighbor boy asks, "Did you ever shoot any of the British?" Foster responds, "I hope not."[117]

His audience of teenage boys cannot believe their ears. Where is the heroism, where the glory of war? But the old soldier answers only that war is nothing but murder by a more acceptable name. Alden could not quite bring himself to declare the Revolution unjust, and had Foster say that "I believe the war of the Revolution was the most just war that was ever entered into on political grounds." Nonetheless, he can find nothing to recommend the experience of fighting that war. The soldiers themselves came "to delight in destruction and mischief for their own sake." These Americans were no heroes, but looters and sinners who beat small children after stealing the food out of a sick mother's mouth. The only bright memory for Foster came when he befriended a British soldier stuck on early morning sentry duty in the lines opposite. One boy protests, "I never supposed that soldiers, who were fighting for liberty, would be guilty of such things as you have told me." Foster deflates that balloon immediately: "My dear young friend, we didn't think much about liberty."[118]

These boys had thought the American Revolution glorious; now their enthusiasm for all war wanes. As one boy summarizes, "a soldier's life made the soldiers . . . bad." His father agrees and warns him that "The more you know about war, the less you will like it." This father then launches into the standard pacifist line of the day about war draining a nation's resources, creating poverty, killing people to no purpose, and, worst of all, loosening public morality. Wars begin so that a few, particularly the munitions makers, may profit. Like most children's stories of the day, and so unlike what our children now see daily on television and in their video games, guns are never portrayed in a positive light. In the antebellum period, children were not presented playing with guns or involved in games of cowboys and Indians, cops and robbers, mass murderers and serial killers. Perhaps these authors missed the inherent evil of young children, and perhaps they did not see the ruthless quality of children's games, but they certainly never recommended brutality or slaughter to America's children. It would take a more advanced civilization to reach that stage of development.[119]

The militia provided an unfailing target for ridicule in popular literature, even in the South. In fact, the most biting portraits of the militia in the antebellum period came from the pens of two of the South's most popular authors, Johnson Jones Hooper and Augustus Baldwin Longstreet. Militia officers were continually parodied for incompetence, laziness, drunkenness, and military pretension and ignorance. Hooper's Simon Suggs was even worse. In 1836 an Alabama town goes into hysterics over news of an approaching Indian attack and Simon Suggs sees his chance. Since militia officers are elected, Suggs determines to appeal to the people's worst passions. "Not that Suggs is particularly fond of danger," Hooper wrote, "but because he delighted in the noise and confusion, the fun and the free drinking, incident to such occasions." And since he "knew there was no danger" of an actual attack, Suggs "magnified the danger, and endeavoured to impress upon the minds of the miscellaneous crowd . . . that he, Simon Suggs, was the only man at whose hands they could expect a deliverance from the imminent peril which impended." Suggs is elected captain of the militia, declares a state of emergency, and uses the occasion to confiscate all the alcohol in town, "court martial" a woman who annoys him, keep the fines he imposes, and get uproariously drunk. Longstreet's Georgia militia was only slightly more dignified. He reports a muster at which twenty-four men are present and forty absent. Their equipage is far from formidable: "guns, 14; gunlocks, 12; . . . bayonets, none; belts, none; spare flints, none; cartridges, none; horse-whips, walking canes, and umbrellas, 10." The attempt to get them to wheel about produces "Bedlam," and the narrator gratefully abandons the scene.[120]

Pacifist journals such as the *Advocate of Peace* and the *Non-Resistant* gleefully published examples of the failed or nonexistent militia system. Often these journals simply needed to quote the adjutants general of the several states. Thus in 1839 the *Non-Resistant* quoted from Dearborn's report on the Massachusetts militia, which noted that thousands of men did not participate in the annual militia muster, and that 230 of 490 companies in the state did not even meet, while most of the rest "exhibit much indifference and incompetency on the part of many of the officers, and a reckless and un-soldier-like spirit in a large portion of the non-commissioned officers and privates." Pacifists found evidence of civilization in the fact that there were five hundred vacancies among the officer corps, and that "many of the companies . . . positively refuse or neglect to choose suitable persons to office."[121] Even mainstream presses like New York's *Journal of Commerce* took pleasure in deriding the absurdities of the whole militia system. In their more sober moments, these articles questioned the very purpose of the militia system, which seemed aimed at teaching "murder by the wholesale." And these critiques often spilled over into condemnations of guns themselves, which were seen as no different than the "tomahawk and scalping-knife" in their barbarity.[122]

There was a surge of pacifism in the 1830s and early 1840s. The Peace Convention held in Boston in September 1838 went so far as to insist that "we deem it unlawful to bear arms." They made this bold proclamation on Christian principles. Their reading of the Bible led them to believe that "there is great security in being gentle . . . and abundant in mercy; that it is only the meek who shall inherit the earth, for the violent who resort to the sword are destined to perish by the sword." On this basis they took the unusual position of condemning those who made firearms: "If, then, the time is predicted, when swords shall be beaten into plough-shares, . . . and men shall not learn the art of war any more, it follows that all who manufacture, sell, or wield those deadly weapons, do thus array themselves against the peaceful dominion of the Son of God."[123]

This antimilitarism spread well beyond pacifist circles, as is indicated by the closing down of the militia in most states. Also notable in this regard were the repeated calls to close West Point military academy. As the Ohio legislature told Congress in 1834, an academy that taught the art of war was "wholly inconsistent with the spirit and genius of our liberal institutions." The legislatures of three other states—Tennessee, Connecticut, and New Hampshire—also passed resolutions calling on Congress to shut down West Point, and no less than the frontier hero Davy Crockett introduced one such resolution in the House of Representatives in 1830 condemning militarism as contrary to the genius of a free people. In 1844 the House came within a single vote of cutting off the academy's appropriation. A great many Americans in the age of Jackson saw everything military and violent as a direct contradiction of democracy.[124]

Even among those who gave little thought to pacifism, the gun often appeared to be an exotic weapon, remote from the needs of civilization. From James Fenimore Cooper to Catherine Maria Sedgwick, much American literature in the period from 1820 to 1850 glorified the frontier, and even offered dramatic accounts of violence. But in these romantic visions, there was a sense in which possession of a gun separated one from civilization. And it was only in the very first stages of the white man's encounter with a specific frontier that there was any room for the gun. In his glorious isolation the frontiersman had as his only "companions, his rifle and his dogs, to keep alive his warm affections." But far too soon "He hears the axe of industry," and then "the substitution of plough shares for hunting knives, and pitch forks for the sturdy old rifles of former days." Likewise, the "officers of our army . . . on distant outposts in the west, far beyond the utmost limit of civilized life," have only a "good rifle, or bird gun, with a setter or a leash of grey hounds" to offer relief from this "alienation and banishment from their family and friends."[125] And when violence occurred on these frontiers, it was the knife that was favored and most often used, not the unreliable gun.[126]

In brief, then, guns just did not fit into most Americans' views of themselves as a people in the 1830s. Even illustrations in newspapers, journals, and books attest to this lack of interest. Pictures of soldiers almost always portrayed them carrying swords rather than guns, rural scenes had farmers with plows, not guns, and even hunting illustrations featured dogs, not guns. This statement may appear impressionistic, but it rests on an examination of a large body of artwork. Nonetheless, a cultural value is clearly expressed when almost every illustration in a military magazine, *Army and Navy Chronicle,* portrays soldiers with swords, lances, and pikes rather than guns. At the very least it seems safe to say that the romantic association of combat with bladed weapons in the age of

Walter Scott extended even to those most committed to the development of the military in the United States.[127]

In 1840 the militia appeared a dead institution, and the public demonstrated little veneration for the gun. Yet there were those in the United States intent on promoting firearms for a number of different reasons. Aided by forces well beyond their control, they converted America into a gun culture in a single generation.

Chapter Nine

Creation of a
Gun Subculture

No pleasure, nor pastime, that's under the sun,
Is equal to mine with my dogs and my gun.

—*American Turf Register and Sporting Magazine,* 1830[1]

Travelers' Tales

When American historian Frederick Jackson Turner set out in 1893
to distinguish the United States from the rest of the world, he looked to its
frontier experience. Here was the root of American exceptionalism, and
of American democracy. Turner perceived only good growing from the
frontier. Even frontier violence served the nation well. Turner saw violence directed solely at the Indians, and therefore found it acceptable:
"The Indian was a common danger, demanding united action." The
frontier served "as a military training school, keeping alive the power of
resistance to aggression, and developing the stalwart and rugged qualities
of the frontieroman." But Turner never thought that violence had been
one of the distinguishing characteristics of the frontier. Warfare was far
from the primary task of the pioneer; clearing the land, tilling the soil,
building institutions—these demanded the energy of western settlers,
who were known for their enterprise rather than their violence.[2]

Turner devoted most of his research to demonstrating that the frontier
was about settlement, enterprise, and innovation. Therein lies the great
tension in accounts of the American frontier for historians: contemporary
sources speak overwhelmingly of the energy and ambition of the Americans, or their greed and materialism in hostile accounts; what is seldom

addressed is violence. Certainly violence was there, in state-sponsored and state-supervised warfare against the Indians and, briefly, Mexico. But historians want more, they want shoot-outs and vigilantes, stagecoach robbers killing everyone in sight, and barroom brawls that descend into gunplay that takes a dozen lives. Streets littered with bodies—that is the expected scene. And again, some of these scenes can be found in isolated moments, though almost always after the Civil War.

To support the image of the United States as a heavily armed and violent society, writers have picked up on a very few quotations and recycled them widely.[3] Accuracy requires a more careful reading of these quotations in their full context. Generally stated, an examination of eighty travel accounts written in America from 1750 to 1860 indicates that the travelers did not notice that they were surrounded by guns and violence. Only a few accounts written in the 1850s express shock at the level of violence in the United States, though again without emphasis on gun use.[4] That absence of discussion about guns in travelers' accounts is intriguing because most of these writers noted any and all differences, large and small, from their homes, whether Europe or the eastern United States or Japan.[5] Even the most critical observers who raised every flaw for ridicule failed to mention gun ownership and violence as distinguishing faults of America. For instance, Frances Trollope, who despised everything about the western United States she visited in the 1820s, most particularly the Americans' lack of manners, somehow never noticed their violent character or predilection to carry firearms.

The few authors who observed violence as in some way unusual in America fall into two categories: those repeating stories they had heard of particularly brutal fighting techniques, and those who visited the South and were sensitive to the brutality of slavery. In the former case, the travelers never actually saw these fights; they only repeated the tales others told. In 1839 Charles A. Murray wrote the famous line: "as is well known, they tear one another's hair, bite off noses and ears, gouge out eyes, and, in short, endeavour to destroy or mutilate each other." He never witnessed such an event himself, but still claimed that it "is well known." By the end of his trip Murray concluded that there was no more crime in America than England, and that though the frontier contained "in proportion to their size as profligate, turbulent, and abandoned a population as any in the world, theft is unknown." The only explanation Murray could offer for this lack of civility and of crime was that "So easily are money and food here obtained by labour, that it seems scarcely worth a man's while to steal." The biggest problem in the United States was that "of comfort, quiet, and privacy, they know but little."[6]

Unintended evidence offers few examples of the gouging, biting, and general mayhem so popular in stories of the frontier. There the stories matched the casual evidence—the runaway slave ads alone are filled with graphic descriptions of the scars left by white violence—but guns almost never figure in these tales. Those visitors who described the violence of slavery—nearly all of whom came to despise the institution—noted the brutality of the beatings inflicted, not the presence of guns as a necessity of control.[7]

Frances Trollope, Thomas Hamilton, Frederick Marryat—these were people who *hated* the United States. They despised its notions of equality, its obsession with money, its religious hypocrisy. Surely if most Americans had been carrying guns they would have commented on it—later critics certainly did.[8] Negative evidence is difficult to marshal; one cannot move from book to book, saying, "no guns here." But the nature of the contempt in which some visitors held the Americans reveals striking differences between current perceptions of early America and those of contemporaries attuned to any difference from the European norm. Thus Marryat sneered in 1837 that the "unwillingness to take away life is a very remarkable feature in America, and were it not carried to such an extreme length, would be a very commendable one." He was speaking of the American hesitance to use capital punishment compared to the more strenuous justice system of England. But Marryat attributed a general squeamishness and even feebleness to Americans based on their faith in equality: they did not want to commit murder, even legal murder, for fear of violating the notion that one person is as good as another.[9]

When foreign visitors spoke of American violence, it tended to be, in Thomas Hamilton's words, "the violence of the press." Few foreign visitors contested the absence of good manners in the United States; but they found evidence of this crudity in the American "barbarisms in language," not in any freewheeling use of firearms. A self-confessed snob, Hamilton was prepared for the worst in America. He had heard that if two Americans disagreed about anything, that "the rifle settles the dispute. One or the other becomes food for the vultures." Yet the reality he found was so different as to be boring: "A traveller on the Mississippi has little to record in the way of incident." Twelve years earlier, in 1808, Christian Schultz was slightly disappointed with notoriously violent Natchez, for nothing of interest happened while he was there. Finally, just as he was leaving town, he overheard two drunken flatboat men arguing over "a Choctaw lady." But their argument consisted of "curious slang," such as "I am a man; I am a horse; I am a team. I can whip any man in all Kentucky, by God." To which the other replied, "I am an alligator; half man, half horse; can whip any on the Mississippi by God." They went on like this for half an hour. Charles J. Latrobe wrote in 1836 that "though I saw many boisterous doings, and many an amusing specimen of rough manners, I never saw any one stabbed or gouged." George W. Featherstonhaugh described an amazing encounter between the most "unblushing, low, degraded scoundrels" he had yet met, which ended with the two men admiring one another's knives.[10]

Those who saw American mobs, such as Harriet Martineau, found them less destructive than in Europe for the simple reason that "the mobs of America are composed of high churchmen, (of whatever denomination,) merchants and planters, and lawyers." These relatively well-behaved crowds occasionally killed someone, especially in the South, but they paled beside the homicidal passion of European mobs. Frederick Marryat made a similar comparison when he attended a militia parade. In contrast to Europe, "The crowds assembled were, as American crowds usually are, quiet and well behaved." It was the militia that was disorderly. Marryat held the Americans to be the least militaristic people he had ever encountered—another sign of weakness in his eyes.[11]

The historian Ray Allen Billington, speaking of post–Civil War travel accounts, held that "Travelers were prone to exaggerate tales of frontier violence because they saw what they wanted to see. Those with anti-American prejudices saw a savage land; those with opposite views painted a picture of peace and prosperity." After the Civil War visitors expected frontier lawlessness and emphasized every example while ignoring the typical settlers quietly farming their land or working long hours in the mines. Several travelers noted this distortion, blaming it on the dime novels that became so popular after the war.[12] Before the war, it was the knife that aroused outrage. Charles A. Murray had heard much of "the cowardly and almost universal practice of carrying a dirk-knife," a small knife "only fit for the hand of an assassin." He had himself seen "several well-dressed Kentuckians, who would probably think themselves much injured if they were not considered gentlemen of the first grade, picking their teeth with these elegant pocket-companions, in public." Murray did not see the dirk used for violent purpose himself, beyond the picking of teeth, but he held man "sufficiently irascible, and when angry, prone enough to inflict injury on his fellow-creature, without deliberately furnishing himself with a weapon calculated to occasion death, or permanent mutilation." At least a few states agreed with Murray, and outlawed the dirk as a dangerous weapon.[13]

Europeans definitely noticed that America was different. If they admired the Americans, they noted their drive; if they did not care for the United States, they noticed greed. Thus Thomas Moore wrote in 1804 of the American desire for money:

> Long has it palsied every grasping hand
> And greedy spirit through this bartered land.

Charles J. Latrobe thought Americans "as busy as wasps in a sugarcask. . . . They have apparently no thought, no reading, no information, no speculation but about their gains—dollar is the word most frequently in their mouths." Alexis de Tocqueville may have been more eloquent when he wrote, "I know of no country, indeed, where the love of money has taken stronger hold on the affections of men."[14]

Travelers saw wastefulness, the lack of hierarchy, materialism, selfrighteousness, ambition, mobility, cultural crudeness, restlessness, and many other traits, but somehow they just did not see the guns that were supposedly all around them. They especially did not notice all those young children learning to use a gun from infancy. One would think that such astute observers as Tocqueville would have noticed such things. Yet the only references to firearms tend to appear in the accounts of those who came specifically to the United States to hunt. They noticed guns, and they observed the inferiority of the American firearm.

One of the first Europeans to make the journey to America specifically to hunt was John Josselyn in 1670. At Cape Ann, Massachusetts, he met Michael Mitton, a professional hunter who specialized in duck and geese. Mitton impressed Josselyn with the efficiency of catching birds with nets rather than using fowling pieces. But Josselyn found the Indians less savage and better bred than the English settlers. He acknowledged that "there are many sincere and religious people amongst" the settlers, but most seemed "rigid" in their faith, "great Syndics, or censors, or controllers of other mens manners, and savagely factious amongst themselves." Further, they seemed to Josselyn unnaturally concerned with money in its most trivial details.[15]

One hundred and sixty years later Charles Augustus Murray followed

Josselyn's path to America, and reached roughly the same conclusions. Murray hunted with both whites and Indians, and thought the bow superior for many kinds of hunting, as it could be fired more quickly than a flintlock and could be reloaded on horseback. He also found that hunting buffalo was not as simple as he had been told; it took three or four shots from his rifle to finish off a bison. Murray's hunting stories, like most others published in the first half of the nineteenth century, are full of missed shots, absurd errors like leaving one's rifle in camp or putting too little powder in the barrel, dull hunts, and the failure to shoot anything—leading the hunters to buy venison from the Indians. Murray moved among those who cared most about the utility of their firearms, the professional hunters who made a living from killing animals in order to sell their hides and trade their meat with frontier settlers. On one occasion he joined in with some frontier hunters and "amused ourselves with shooting at a mark for small wagers." Murray thus "witnessed the skill of most of the professional hunters" in the Allegheny Mountains and farther west. He concluded that "at a short distance (from twenty-five to fifty yards) they shot with much precision; but, although their rifles are so long and heavy in metal, their performance" at the longer distances "was very inferior to that of many sportsmen whom I could name in Britain." At first the American hunters tended "to jeer at my light short rifle." But—and Murray insisted that he was not a good shot by British standards—"after a few days in the woods, when they found that I could frequently hit a running deer, (a shot which they rarely attempted,) their disrespect for my weapon was much diminished."[16]

One of the few foreign travelers to comment specifically on the nature of American-made guns, Murray found them inferior to anything made in Europe. The Englishman William Oliver, writing in 1843, found American guns "coarse in material as well as workmanship; and notwithstanding their great thickness, they not unfrequently burst." The latter quality baffled him until he took apart an American-made rifle and discovered it was made of the most inferior metal welded together rather than properly bored from a single bar of iron. The locks were of the poorest quality—English rejects it seemed—productive of constant misfiring: "I have seen a fellow snap five times in succession with the most imperturbable coolness," so used was he to misfires. Oliver came to doubt that Americans knew anything about guns or their use; they certainly had grown accustomed to using a sort of inferior and even dangerous firearm that no respectable British shooter would ever accept.[17]

Hunting in America disappointed Murray. He had expected more gentlemen hunters, but only army officers on frontier posts seemed to fit that description. Fortescue Cuming, traveling in Kentucky in 1808, had a similar response. Initially startled at seeing two ill-dressed men sitting in the doorway of a frontier cabin holding rifles, Cuming soon discovered that they were professional hunters, but hardly the gentlemen he expected. In the 1840s an anonymous English traveler mocked the hunting skill of backwoods Americans. He described a party of thirty hunters getting lost while tracking wolves, leveling ten guns at a wolf and all missing, and accidentally shooting one of their own number.[18]

Many foreign visitors expressed disappointment that the game was often not quite so plentiful as had been reported. Charles Murray wrote that "I had been so often 'taken in,' since I came to this country, that I was rather cautious in giving credit to the stories of the abundance of game with which settlers in the western world amuse strangers." Repeatedly he was told that a certain area was so rich in animals that he had but to level his gun and fire, and the deer would fall like leaves. Whenever he hunted such an area and found, after several days, that he fired only once or twice, he was always assured that fifty deer appeared as soon as he left. "In fact, this amplication forms a prominent feature of their character," Murray wrote. Americans just could not be "content with the extent and fertility of their territory, the magnificence of their rivers and forests, all of which are unequalled in the civilized world, they will claim credit for themselves a similar pre-eminence in cases where it is so evidently undeserved, that a traveller feels an inclination to discredit all alike." Murray cautioned patience: "although the American geese are not swans, they are very good geese."[19]

In 1837, a few years after Murray left, a truly serious hunter came to the United States. The German Friedrich Gerstacker spent six years in America, most of his time devoted to hunting. Unlike Murray, Gerstacker came to like most Americans but, oddly, not the hunters, too many of whom were "making constant love to the whiskey-bottle," and got more excited about the idea of hunting the drunker they became, until they passed out. Though his book is full of rather tame hunts, Gerstacker noted that the modern "American hunter spares nothing, . . . a war of extermination has been waged against the poor stags and bears" that would lead within five years, he predicted, to the destruction of all the game east of the Rocky Mountains. And amazingly, it was a very small number of men committing this slaughter; not sportsmen, in Gerstacker's eyes, but butchers focused on the market value of the animals. Gerstacker was certain they were making a mistake by overhunting; on several hunts with experienced local hunters along the Mississippi, they found nothing to kill and often returned from their hunts "hungry and tired, without having seen a single head of American game." Gerstacker tried to make a living as a professional hunter, but needed to devote long stretches to working for farmers. Hunting just could not be relied upon for a steady supply of food, and Gerstacker and the other hunters were often reduced to eating acorns and berries.[20]

Friedrich Gerstacker loved to hunt, but he was no romantic. He did not offer stories of great shots or heroic exploits on the trail; the hunts he describes are workmanlike, methodical, the product of a great deal of labor and preparation, especially in the cleaning of guns. Gerstacker offers a guide to the reality of hunting in the 1840s. He and his partners almost always shot just one animal to eat or to sell for food—after all, it was difficult to carry more than one carcass over the great distances these hunters covered. Since it generally took at least two shots to bring down any game, Gerstacker often ended up battling his prey with a knife or with the aid of his dogs, for there was not time to reload. Dogs were the one real necessity for hunting, even more than a gun, for traps can easily replace a gun. Dogs were capable of running animals "to a tree, so that they could be more easily shot," and were useful when an animal was wounded by the hunter's shot, the most common occurrence. Gerstacker thought "turkey hunting with dogs is one of the most amusing and convenient sports in the world"—convenient because one did not have to be a crack marksman when shooting at animals in a tree above one's head. Missed shots startled the turkey so that it plummeted to the ground, and "his heavy weight will infallibly kill him in his fall."[21]

In Gerstacker's experience, hunting involved errors and humor. He knew of hunters forgetting their guns and "hunting with an unloaded gun." A fellow hunter told of aiming at some ducks and pulling the trigger, but the musket "only snapped, the expected recoil failed, and I fell head over heels into the lake. I . . . never saw ducks or musket again." Another hunter calmly accepted the fact that his old gun misfired twice for every shot it got off. It took a lot more time that way, but he was in no hurry.[22] Hunting involved little shooting; Gerstacker and his companions could not afford to waste their limited supplies of gunpowder. Gerstacker recorded many days' hunts when no one fired a musket or rifle: "Lucky was it that we took provisions, for not a shot we fired. Next day was almost as bad, and if Conwell had not knocked over a turkey, we should have been reduced to chew sassafras." After several days of fruitless hunting, Gerstacker and his partner refused to head home despite their lack of food because "people would believe that we had lost the power of shooting a deer." They were saved from hunger and dishonor by a group of Cherokee and Choctaw, who fed them and helped them track down a suitable deer.[23]

Like most hunters, Gerstacker did not enjoy hunting alone: "My long solitude, had considerably cooled my shooting propensities, and I resolved to seek human society." When he stumbled upon another lone hunter, "We greeted each other heartily, and were mutually delighted at the chance meeting." Hunting was a social activity, and Gerstacker once came upon a grim reminder of the danger of solo hunting: the skeleton of an Indian with a rusty rifle and a knife by his side, and the skeleton of a bear nearby.[24]

The American hunters Gerstacker met were not walking out from their farm on an afternoon for a quick kill in time for dinner; they were professionals like those Murray knew. The local farmers were amazingly hospitable and willingly provided him with lodgings for weeks on end, but they had no time for such frivolities as hunting, as they were too intent on their farming, too dedicated to getting ahead. That aspect of the American character amazed Gerstacker, as it did most visitors. Of greatest interest to the frontier settlers with whom Gerstacker spent the most time were the weekly debates at the local schoolhouses, held every Friday night and regularly attracting people from miles around. Not that these frontierspeople were intellectuals. Gerstacker felt their most notable skills were those related to farming. He noted that they were very "expert" at the use of axes, "which they begin to wield as soon as their arms are strong enough to use them," adding that axes made very good weapons.[25]

The only romance in Gerstacker's book appears with his descriptions of the scenery. He certainly had no romantic attachment to his gun, which he often threw aside when chasing injured game with his knife, returning to find his rifle later. After he traded his rifle for food, he twice borrowed a gun for a hunting trip, a commonplace occurrence.[26] None of the hunters stood out as a better shot, except the Indians with their arrows, and the knife was the most reliable weapon.[27] And most nonprofessional hunters earned Gerstacker's contempt. For instance, a group of North Carolina planters kept a tame bear that occasionally they released, chased around vigorously until treed, and then dragged home. Once they all threw themselves on the poor bear and wrestled it into submission: "Not wishing to kill him, no one brought a rifle." Another time they used an ax to cut down a tree when the beer would not come down on his own. Eventually the planters tired of the game and unceremoniously slaughtered and ate the bear.[28]

On one memorable hunting trip, Gerstacker and two friends left their large hunting party and headed off with one rifle between them, "but each had his large hunting-knife." They tracked a bear to its cave, and Gerstacker wrote, "I examined my rifle closely to see that all was right, . . . the elder Conwell warned me to make sure of my shot, adding dryly, by way of comfort, that it would be all the better for me; for if I missed I should be the first to suffer the animal's fury." Even at close range, hitting a bear was not a sure thing, as too many things could go wrong with the gun. Gerstacker crawled to within six yards of the sleeping bear, concerned about the accuracy of his aim, and still "I pulled the trigger too soon. The cave was filled with smoke; a fearful groan announced that the beast was wounded." Crawling out of the cave to reload, pursued by the bear, "I had dropped my rifle, as it very much hindered my retreat." The hunters then set a large fire in front of the cave to trap the bear, while one of the men dispatched the two cubs by dashing their heads against the rocks. The mother bear retreated and Gerstacker regained his rifle, "covered with blood and slime." He reloaded and pressed on to a new attack, shooting the bear from eight feet away, this time killing it.[29]

A modern reader may be most amazed that Gerstacker survived, as he walked throughout frontier America for six years, often alone. On a few occasions, when he was desperately hungry, his hands shook so much from the cold that he missed the easiest shots. He often wandered off without his rifle, once even encountering a wolf along the way—fortunately the wolf just strolled off. He knew that the frontier had a reputation for being "overrun . . . with a number of bad characters," and many people back East and in Europe "thought all its inhabitants went about armed to the teeth with pistols and bowie-knives." But Gerstacker did not see these banditti or hear about any outlaws, even in Arkansas, where "I have traversed the State in all directions, and met with as honest and upright people as are to be found in any other part of the Union." Gerstacker's one fight occurred when a ship's captain became angry because the German gave food to a poor woman. Gerstacker did not rely on his gun, but hit the captain and then attempted to throw him overboard. He hunted with Indians and with frontier wildmen without incident. The mosquitoes were generally more dangerous than the Indians, and the only real danger came from nature, as was revealed by his last hunt, when his friend Erskine was killed by a bear after a missed rifle shot from a distance of five feet.[30]

Erskine's death ended Gerstacker's enthusiasm for hunting. He refused further offers of hunts, "intending to give up shooting," and returned to Germany.[31] Gerstacker had expected to see violence in America, and he did, but only in the slave states.[32] The two contemporary symbols of that violence were the knife and the whip. Descriptions of violence routinely depict fisticuffs, the true measure of manhood in the early nineteenth century, and the threat of a knife; firearms are rarely mentioned. The Kentucky legislature famously found it necessary in 1798 to pass special penalties for slitting a nose or ear, or putting out an eye while fighting.[33] One traveler in the 1830s reported that there were three people in the Nashville jail, one for stabbing, one for gouging, one for nose-biting. By the 1840s most travelers in the Southwest commented on the bowie knife as the most obvious accoutrement; they rarely mentioned guns in this context until the 1850s. Fortescue Cuming, who had little good to say about the people of Kentucky, wrote, "Their hands, teeth, knees, head and feet are their weapons." Though he did not think they fought as well as "the lower classes in the seaports of either the United States, or the British islands," he heard that—but did not see himself—Kentuckians quickly descended to "kicking, scratchings, biting, [and] gouging each others eyes out." In contrast, an 1818 guidebook said of Kentucky: "No where in America has the almost instantaneous change, from an uncivilized waste to the elegances of civilization been so striking."[34]

The point is that the United States did not strike any of its visitors as distinctive in terms of guns, nor was the antebellum frontier different from the more settled East. Any frontier is home to many myths, as it is a place where people can reinvent themselves. In an arrangement that could have inspired Mark Twain, two new arrivals in Kansas agreed to address each other as "General" and "Colonel." It appears that no one ever asked for the source of these honorifics, but each man became prominent in the community, one as a senator. As Timothy Flint wrote, the frontier was "a paradise of puffers."[35] At every turn people boasted of heroic deeds that did not bear up to much examination. Self-proclaimed colonels bragged of the dozens of Indians they slaughtered, while "alligator horses," workers who took pride in extravagant boasting, loudly asserted their ability to best any ten men in a fair fight. It was all just nonsense, but many eastern reporters took the stories as true, or at least pretended that they did, and made a fair living transcribing the absurdities of braggarts, creating a legendary Wild West.[36]

These legends are often accepted because modern readers, in a form of self-projection, feel that a less advanced society must have been more violent than their own. As Ray Allen Billington astutely observed of another supposed frontier quality, "the legend of frontier individualism rested on what people thought should be true, rather than what was true." Billington dismissed individualism as a completely inaccurate portrayal of frontier reality, migrants and settlers having no real choice but to cooperate.[37] More than any other need, self-defense born from shared needs commanded a unified response. The threat to the western settlements of the United States came from the Indians whose land the settlers crossed or expropriated, not from one another—yet. So they acted in the common defense, organizing what Billington called "walking republics" on the overland trail, making certain to maintain security, internal as well as external, sharing what guns they had, and calling on the U.S. Army at every turn. As the work of John Phillip Reid so clearly demonstrates, the migrants upheld the highest standards of law on the trails.[38] They were far from the libertarians or anarchists generally portrayed in many modern novels and films. In fact most western communities demonstrated little tolerance for social deviance. The Ohio legislature in 1816 placed heavy fines on swearing, firing guns across a stream, and running horses through towns, among other transgressions upon which they frowned. And when they arrived in their new homes, settlers generally acted together to arrange a safe and ordered extension of eastern society. John D. Borthwick, a Scottish traveler to the gold-mining operations of California, felt that "the Americans have a very great advantage, for . . . they are certainly of all people in the world the most prompt to organize and combine to carry out a common object." One migrant in a later period noted that "Their common security locked them in amity."[39]

With the exception of such transient events as the gold rush, the antebellum American frontier consisted largely of farmers and small merchants striving to re-create the world they knew. Many travelers noted that frontier settlements looked like miniature versions of eastern towns, and the settlers saw themselves as the bearers of civilization. As Henry Ward Beecher wrote, "They drove school along with them as shepherds drive flocks. They have herds of churches, academies, lyceums." Even those "not especially controlled by the influences that school-house and churches create" wanted these symbols of civilization for their communities.[40] Describing her experiences of the post–Civil War Kansas frontier, Elise D. Isely offered the perfect summation: "I have read in books that the people of the frontier kept moving ever westward to escape civilization. But if my experience counts for anything, such people were the exceptions. So eager were we to keep in touch with civilization that even when we could not afford a shotgun and ammunition to kill rabbits, we subscribed to newspapers and periodicals and bought books." Or, as Tocqueville stated, the "pioneer" may appear "primitive and wild" because of the poverty of his house, "but he wears the dress and speaks the language of the cities; he is acquainted with the past, curious about the future, and ready for argument about the present; he is, in short, a highly civilized being, who consents for a time to inhabit the backwoods, and who penetrates into the wilds of the New World with the Bible, an axe, and some newspapers."[41]

Pick any town, and it will look roughly the same. Education mattered most, even on the southern frontier. And, bizarrely, these frontier schools maintained the classical curriculum, including the study of Greek and Latin.[42] After just three years of settlement, New Salem, Illinois, Abraham Lincoln's hometown, had less than 150 inhabitants, yet boasted a school, a debating society, and a nonsectarian Sunday school.[43] The people of Canandaigua, New York, "then a hamlet on a raw frontier," were so enthusiastic for a bookstore that in 1804 "they physically detained [James Bemis] until he agreed to open his shop in that village." In 1788 there were five hundred people in Lexington, Kentucky, and six book dealers—but no gunsmith. In 1796 Cincinnati had five hundred people and two bookstores; in Iowa, Davenport's first bookstore opened just three years after the town was settled—neither town yet had a gunsmith. One book dealer catered to the miners of the California gold rush with "the works of Shakespeare, Byron, Milton, Gray, Campbell and other distinguished poets."[44] Dayton, Ohio, opened its first library in 1805, its one hundred citizens drawing lots to see who would get first choice when the books arrived. The inhabitants of Lexington in the 1790s raised $500 to buy books; Cleveland did the same in 1811 when there were sixty-four people in town; the first twenty-four male settlers of Madison, Indiana, each contributed $5 toward the purchase of a town library. In town after town, citizens proved more willing to raise money for books than for guns. Guns were for special occasions, books for every day.[45]

Foreign visitors were often pleasantly surprised to note the presence of a great many books in even humble frontier homes, as well as a tradition of sharing these books widely. Francois A. Michaux, traveling through Kentucky in the first years of the nineteenth century, wrote that "literature was most commonly the topic of conversation." A New Englander's comments were typical of this positive view of the frontier settler: "In travelling through the country" of frontier Illinois, "one will meet with a well thumbed and select library in the log cabin, and listen to discourse on any topic in that rude home which would give spirit and life to an assemblage in a Boston drawing-room." Of course the critics like Frances Trollope denigrated the conversation in a Boston drawing-room as not of the highest value anyway.[46]

Many towns called themselves the "Athens of the West," a silly pretension demonstrating the goal of many settlements to be recognized for their civilized attributes. Lexington, Kentucky, proclaimed itself such an Athens in 1810, when it had four thousand people, two bookstores, three academies, and Transylvania University. Within a few more years the town had a theater, a natural history museum, reading rooms, the magazine *Western Review,* Matthew Houett's painting school, and, in 1817, the first performance of a Beethoven symphony in the United States. Can any modern town of comparable size claim the list of cultural events noted with annoyance by one Cincinnati resident of his "Athens of the West"? "Discourses on Theology—Private assemblies—state Cotillion parties—Saturday Night Clubs, and chemical lectures . . . like the fever and the ague, return every day with distressing regularity." The same held true for new towns farther west. Virginia City, Nevada, one of the more notorious western towns in America's collective imagination, claimed by its second year schools for one thousand children, three theaters, and a two-thousand-seat opera house where Italian operas were favored. A similar pattern held in early Denver and Leadville, Colorado. And what was one to make of William Chapman's floating Shakespeare festival, which from 1831 traveled down the Mississippi every fall, drawing thousands of customers? Visitors from the East Coast and England commonly commented on the middle-class appearance of many western towns, often with disappointment.[47]

Many efforts at cultural enrichment failed, proved little more than short-lived intellectual fads, or succumbed to complaints of too much civilization. In the 1830s one settler confessed to being "heartily tired of the endless imitations of Scott, Byron, and Moore, and the rest of them, and stand ready to welcome something new, even though it should smack of

the 'Horse,' contain a touch of the 'Alligator,' and betray a small sprin-
kling of the 'Steamboat.'"[48] Others wanted to cut straight to the necessities. One student told his teacher that "Daddy says he doesn't see no use in
the high larn'd things—and he wants me to larn Inglish only, and book
keepin, and surveyin, so as to tend store and run a line." It was such attitudes, and religious revivals, that the less generous foreign visitors commonly mocked.[49] They certainly would have addressed the widespread
use of firearms had they observed such, especially as many travelers'
accounts record the tendency of Americans to use militia titles with no
evidence of any actual military service. English visitors seemed particularly amused by this practice, probably because of their heightened class
consciousness.[50]

The town histories are packed with struggles to clear the land, political battles between Whigs and Democrats, conflicts over funding schools
and libraries, attacks of diseases that claimed young lives—the verbs may
be violent, and the stories may be less dramatic than a shoot-out, but guns
do not appear. Likewise, the city directories have bookshops, music stores,
restaurants, and schools, but seldom a gunshop.[51] As Turner noted, westerners "saw in the steamboat a symbol of their own development." The
Western Monthly Review picked up on an early discontinuity between the
perception and reality of western society. Noting that Easterners generally thought of frontier settlers as barbarians, the magazine (probably its
editor Timothy Flint) offered the opinion that "An Atlantic cit [citizen],
who talks of us under the name of backwoodsman, would not believe,
that such fairy structures of oriental gorgeousness and splendor" as the
steamboat were "actually in existence, rushing down the Mississippi . . .
bearing speculators, merchants, dandies, fine ladies, every thing real, and
every thing affected, in the form of humanity, with pianos, and stocks of
novels, and cards, and dice, and flirting, and love-making, and drinking,
and champaigne. . . . A steamboat, coming from New Orleans, brings to
the remotest villages of our streams, and the very doors of the cabins, a
little Paris, a section of Broadway, or a slice of Philadelphia, to ferment in
the minds of our young people, the innate propensity for fashions and fin-
ery." This is hardly the vision of the barbarous West presented in the typical Western.[52]

The steamboat raises another significant difference between the modern image and the contemporary reality of the frontier: the source of violent death. Many observers who traveled through America's western
frontier between 1830 and 1860 identified the steamboat as the greatest

danger facing any traveler. Charles Latrobe felt that the "history of steamboat disaster is one of the most terrible and revolting imaginable; and the disregard of human life" evident in these accidents "which is as yet, generally speaking, a feature of the West, is a sure proof that the standard of moral feeling is low." The statistical record supports his observation, in that industrial accidents consistently claimed more lives in a single year than were murdered in any state in the entire nineteenth century.[53]

Even on the frontier that preceded the town, visitors saw enterprise, not gunfire. Lambert Lilly spoke of that trading spirit that usually led to "copartnerships [which] is carried on with great good-will, and no little merriment. But at other times, quarrels arise." But these usually "fall short of blows and bloodshed," and "the aggrieved or offended party loosen" their boat "from its troublesome neighbor, with a volley of abuse" and leave. Daniel Boone read *Gulliver's Travels* around the fire with his fellow hunters and named sites after places in Swift's book. Likewise, one early trapper recalled reading Byron, Shakespeare, Scott, Clark's commentaries on the Bible, and "other small works in Geology, chemistry and philosophy" during his winter camp. It is unlikely that many modern campers in our state parks are reading works of such quality and intellectual caliber. Another referred to winter camp as their "Rocky Mountain College." Even illiterates like Jim Bridger enjoyed listening to others read Shakespeare aloud. Perhaps there is a degree of exaggeration or poor memory in these accounts of literate mountain men, but at the very least one can safely say that movement and making money, not violence, marked the frontier, and the rest of America.[54]

One Scottish traveler from 1822 is particularly interesting, as he is the only one of those studied who mentioned that he had heard how attached were Americans to their guns. He had been told that "Not only in general do they make the musket their amusement throughout the states . . . [but] in every house it may be found ready loaded for action." Yet he found no evidence to support this assertion. When he viewed a Connecticut militia company in action, he rejected as mythology any tales of a close relation between Americans and their guns: "Their implements of war, long brass clasped german firelocks, rusty fowling pieces, fusees, and musketoons . . . would have equipped the much famed troops of Falstaff." This visitor could barely believe the degree to which the militia lampooned themselves: "They marched along, some supporting [arms] others presenting weapons on the ground. They never designed to be all one way or going the same road. Some straggling behind a dozen of yards apart, were locked in each others arms, and on tiptoe were acting the fool, or dandy. Another party bustling along, were humorously kicking the breeches of those before them with their knees. . . . The Captains raved and they laughed, and ended the whole in good humor."[55]

The first historians of the United States also seem to have overlooked not only the centrality of guns, but also the country's violent nature. Even the frontier seems free of unusual levels of personal conflict, according to their accounts. George Bancroft, Richard Hildreth, John Bach McMaster, and the other members of this first generation of American historians all spoke of the distinctive opportunities of the frontier, paying homage to the Jacksonian ideology of the "free lands" of the West creating free men. The Whigs and Republicans among them noted the price paid by the Indians for this progress, and correctly observed that it was the U.S. Army that dealt out most of the violence against the indigenous population of the West. But they remained silent on the universality of gun ownership.[56]

Even western magazines showed a decided coolness toward hunting and militarism, with occasional opposition to both. The *Western Monthly Magazine* of Cincinnati stated that "We aspire to be useful." Yet it found no need to publish anything on guns, hunting, the military, or militia, being much more concerned with education. In its first three years, 1834 to 1836, this magazine published thirty-six issues and 356 articles; there was one article on hunting, one on a shooting match, and four on Indian wars—and not a single other article on any gun-related theme. Likewise, the *Western Miscellany* published three hundred articles in its first year, 1849, offering only two hunting articles. "On Western Character," an article in *Western Miscellany,* described westerners as marked primarily by autodidacticism and ingenuity, insisting that respect for the law and the avoidance of violence were far more notable in the West than the East. While these magazines were, in part, promoting the West, their observations that eastern and European cities were more violent are valid. On the few occasions when guns were mentioned in articles, usually as part of a story on combat, they were discussed as being surprisingly ineffective. Again and again in these and other magazines, hunters and soldiers fired and missed. After the first errant shots, which were "without much effect" because of distance and intervening trees, battle descended to tomahawks and knives, the real weapons of frontier combat. Sometimes the descriptions bordered on the comic, as in one historical account of the siege of Fort McIntosh, Ohio, in 1782. Volley after volley was exchanged without a casualty. Finally a relief column appeared, the Indians ran away, and the "battle" was over.[57]

The literature of the frontier, where American realism was born, repeated many of these themes. Writers like Augustus Baldwin Longstreet, Joseph G. Baldwin, and Johnson J. Hooper focused on the sports, the con artists, and the eccentricities of the frontier, but without much discussion of firearms. These books made the frontier appear even less violent than the reality, since they rarely mention the Indian wars.[58]

The most famous novel of the early frontier is probably James Fenimore Cooper's *The Pioneers,* first published in 1823. This book begins with an unusual meeting between Cooper's representative of frontier mores, Leatherstocking, and of the cultivated elite, Judge Temple. The judge, shooting his fowling-piece from the seat of his carriage, believes he has hit a deer, which Natty Bumppo claims for himself and his protégé, Oliver Effingham. Bumppo contemptuously rejects the judge's "pop-gun" as a toy rather than a tool. The reader soon learns that Judge Temple has actually shot Effingham, while it was the frontiersman with his plain but utilitarian long rifle who has hit the deer. Of the two archetypes of frontier gun owners, the gentleman and the hunter, only one knows what he is doing, only one really deserves to carry a gun.[59] But in the years following the appearance of Cooper's first Leatherstocking novel, a group of eastern gentlemen elevated hunting in America to a noble art fit for the elite.

Hunting in Early America

The twenty-five years after the end of the War of 1812 witnessed a growing popular contempt for guns as attributes of a more barbarous age, and disdain for the militarists who demanded renewed public commitment to arming the nation. Firearms did not appear in popular culture as essential to the pursuit of happiness until the mid-1830s, when a hunting subculture emerged among the elite who sought to emulate the idealized British gentlemen and hoped to preserve their sport from contamination by the lower orders. These hunting aficionados preserved the market for well-made firearms and organized powerful lobbying efforts to reinvigorate the militia through government action.

Hunting has always drawn mixed reviews in America. From the earliest Colonial settlements, frontier families had relied on the Indians and on professional white hunters for wild game, and the Colonial assemblies regulated all forms of hunting, as had Parliament.[60] As in England, most hunters were actually trappers, finding traps more efficient and less expensive than the time-consuming process of tracking animals with guns. Most Americans in the seventeenth and eighteenth centuries got almost all their meat from domesticated animals, and it was rather unusual to use a musket to slaughter a cow or pig. From the start, hunting was an inessential luxury, associated either with the elite gentleman with too much time on his hands, or with the poorest fringes of civilization, if not outright savagery.[61]

In the first decades of the nineteenth century, hunting was held up to ever increasing ridicule as a waste of time, money, and resources, and mocked as the play of insufficiently grown-up boys. In the popular press, hunting had become both exotic and foolish. Hunters themselves were often portrayed as tedious bores looking for any opportunity to tell the same tired story of the glorious hunt. An 1828 hunting story ends: "A friend of mine has one, and only one, good story, respecting a gun, which he contrives to introduce upon all occasions." Whenever he hears any loud noise, he pretends that it sounded like a gun and then leaps into the story, "'By the by, speaking of guns.' . . . and the company is condemned to smell powder for twenty minutes to come!"[62]

A typical motif in these less serious hunting stories, as in one published in the *Knickerbocker* in 1844, was the careful building of a sense of danger in the hunt, only to have the peril appear as a couple of stray dogs. An 1825 article in the *Atheneum* described the incredible number of animals killed by various aristocratic hunters, the thousands of deer, ducks, and rabbits, and expressed amazement at the pride that these aristocrats took in totting up such statistics: "A magnificent list of animal slaughter carefully and systematically recorded as achievements." Another article warned that citizens of Philadelphia interested in a walk in the country should "go a considerable distance from the city, to avoid the showers of shot" sent skyward by a few overenthusiastic bird hunters.[63] The *New England Farmer* called for legislation to protect the robin "from the bloody fangs of the fowler"—a group they later labeled "wanton insensible persons." They questioned the value of hunting itself: "Perhaps no *amusement* (if it deserves the name) is so lame in defence as this." The birds ate insects that destroyed crops, and were therefore far more useful than hunters. The journal concluded by calling for legislation against "leaving loaded guns standing about the house."[64]

At the very end of the 1820s two separate strands of interest in hunting, both influenced by the English example, came together to form a gun-centered subculture. Members of the southern elite had long demonstrated their wealth through ostentatious hunting parties. These hunts were rarely isolated forays into the wilderness, but usually large parties of gentlemen accompanied by groups of slaves to carry their provisions, beat the bushes for game, and do all the messy cleaning. The southern gentleman found his beau ideal in the English country aristocrat. That role model supplied the essential link to the second group interested in hunting, an urban middle class seemingly desperate for status. Starting in the 1820s, these city gentlemen organized themselves into hunting clubs, purchased luxurious hunting lodges in "wilderness" areas like the Catskill Mountains, and did their best to replicate the imagined life of the English squire.[65]

These two groups of hunters—plantation owners and city merchants—would have surely gone their separate ways but for the unifying effect of two popular journals. Largely through the efforts of John Stuart Skinner's *American Turf Register and Sporting Magazine,* which began publication in 1829, and William T. Porter's *Spirit of the Times,* first published in 1831, hunting became an appropriate enterprise for aspiring gentlemen. In the first issue of the first hunting magazine in the United States, Skinner wrote that hunting as a sport was just beginning to attract the attention of American men. He, Porter, and a few particularly popular authors such as William Elliott and Henry William Herbert accomplished a great deal over the next twenty years in evangelizing for their faith in this manly activity.[66]

The determinant code word for hunting was "gentleman." It is extremely difficult to find an article published in either *American Turf Register* or *Spirit of the Times,* or a gun advertisement in any newspaper for that matter, that did not use the word "gentleman" in describing a hunter. Amateur hunters seeking legitimacy looked to the British aristocracy, modeling their notions of sportsmanship, hunting styles, clothing, appropriate game, and even patterns of speech after the British elite. The very portraits of hunters that the magazines published mimic the style of those available in British sporting journals. Porter, Skinner, and their loyal supporters sought to rescue hunting from public disdain and to translate it into "the very corinthian columns of the community," the mark of the true gentleman and of a real man. The magazines pushed for the acceptance of the idea, first expressed in *Spirit of the Times* in 1837, that "our rifles and our liberties are synonymous." Owning and using a firearm therefore became "a moral decision." And since guns had always been expensive, their use was in some ways self-limiting, their price serving as a barrier against the poor.[67]

These authors found the ultimate legitimization of their passion for hunting in England. While the mainstream press mocked the body counts racked up by English lords out hunting with their retainers, the hunting press praised their skill and sought to emulate their standards. Most intriguing in this regard was the popularity of fox hunting, that "most delightful of all field sports." Every issue of American Turf Register had at least one article on "this most manly and healthy sport," complete with a little woodcut of a gentleman fox hunter. Fox hunting clubs were organized throughout the country, including Chicago, but they were particularly popular in the South. As late as 1834, the Turf Register reported on fox hunting within sight of the Capitol at Washington. This elevation of fox hunting is particularly intriguing as the gentleman hunts the fox without a weapon.[68]

These American gentlemen hunters were very practical, and honest— using almost no euphemisms. They, at least, understood that competent shooters are not born; they are trained and they practice regularly. The stories published by Porter and Skinner had their romantic qualities, but never moved too far from realism. There are tales of good shooting, but they are perfectly reasonable, such as praise for a pair shooting from horseback, who each hit a pheasant, one of which was sitting on the ground at thirty-five yards, the other perched in a nearby tree. The author thought it extraordinary that the latter shot came from a pistol.[69] Contemporary works of fiction gave the impression that the professional hunter never missed. Based on the first-person accounts published in popular magazines in the 1830s and 1840s, hunters missed more often than they found their targets—which matches the travelers' accounts. The nonfiction accounts did not pretend; the narrators and their friends were often poor shots, having fun and making mistakes, relying on dogs and drivers to assist them, occasionally being too frightened or startled to shoot, and looking forward to luxurious meals at day's end. Having fired a shot and missed, William Elliott wrote, "I dash down my now useless gun," and then killed the deer with a knife. Such were his "spirit-stirring incidents" of the hunt. There were many such failed hunts, and worse, as when every member of a hunting party missed the target except one, who killed one of the dogs. Or in a western hunt in which no one seemed able to hit a deer they were chasing, so they "knocked him on the head with the tomahawk" when the dogs had cornered it. After another hunter carefully aimed at a deer, took a few steps closer, and fell off his scaffold ten feet up a tree, breaking his leg, he lamely said, "it is true that the deer were not killed this time, but you see clearly they might have been."[70]

But the westerners were at a disadvantage, not being able to practice as often as the urban hunter, who had readier access to guns and powder. The author of one story mocked a country host who was first astonished and then angry when his guest, a city dandy, proved himself a far better shot. There is no mystery here, as shooting skill was the product of "long and constant practice." A shooter needed "firmness of nerve, keenness of sight, and that glorious natural attribute distinguished by the name of presence of mind." Nevertheless, "the lovers of the captivating amusement of the gun" should recognize the futility of these natural attributes without practice. It "needs only resolution and perseverance, in any person capable of presenting his piece, to become, in due time, a good shot, at any object." Referring to the English guide *Scott's Field Sports* the editor of *American Turf Register* reminded the reader that he must become almost mechanical in his shooting; "all accuracy of aim is out of the question," until the "gunner, in pulling the trigger, should feel no more emotion . . . than in taking a pinch of snuff." The shooter should start with targets, move on to small birds (though not the swallow, which is "highly useful for the destruction of insects; and besides, too difficult for the aim of a beginner"), and then graduate to the deer. There is an almost universal willingness to blame the equipment—the gun, powder, and shot—for missed shots, but the real cause is always a "lack of skill" caused by not practicing. Young hunters particularly were warned to heed this advice, as they "often forget they have a gun," so enamored were they of the sight of wild game. This article mentioned one hunter who was so surprised by a deer that he grabbed his gun by the muzzle and used it as a club to drive the deer off. Thus the "great secret" for successful hunting was "the attainment of philosophical calmness."[71]

But there were real problems with the equipment. One of William Elliott's friends, an experienced hunter, complained that "I had *wounded* the six last deer I'd fired at, so I thought I'd *kill* one to-day." Elliott tried to explain these errors away: "once, your powder was too weak; and next, your shot were too small; and next, your aim was somewhat wild," one nicked an ear and the next a tail. "You are bound to set up an infirmary across the river, for the dismembered deer you have dispatched there!"

Elliott assured him he just needed yet more practice; "let it grow into a habit." The friend went forth renewed in his dedication and missed his next two shots.[72] William Elliott, like most of these authors, knew a hunter could hope to shoot a deer or bear only when it was standing completely still; the rest was luck. But Elliott appreciated that many of his friends hated being told that. When he told "a man who was priding himself on having made a magnificent shot, that it was nothing but luck," the shooter responded, "To have met the bears was my good luck, I grant you; but to have disposed of them, thus artistically, excuse me!" His "wounded self-love" led him to boast of his shooting skill.[73]

The hunting magazines attempted to tell their readers everything they needed to know, acknowledging a real dearth of knowledge on firearms and their use up until that time. As a consequence, their advice was not always very good, as when "Leatherstocking" wrote that the best way to load a rifle was to "take the gun between your knees—the butt on the ground and the barrel towards your face." Conflicting information was also available on how much powder to use. Most recommended a light charge, for the safety of the shooter, but one writer quoted an "old hunter" as recommending a heavy charge, since "I like to make the blood and bones fly, when I shoot." Writers offered a wide, and often wildly inaccurate, amount of information on animal behavior, some with an eye to killing them more efficiently, occasionally with the notion that it might be best to preserve enough for future slaughter. Those who shot out of season were just "*pretending* to be gentlemen." Another writer condemned the "bird murderers" who shot "indiscriminately" whatever bird they saw without concern for the future, recommending that New Jersey's and Virginia's limited deer-hunting seasons be adopted for all game.

This tension between the need to preserve game and the competitive spirit to kill more is evident in a story that first praised a Cincinnati hunter who killed 1,226 partridges in one year, and then issued a call for a limit on their destruction. Some writers remained sanguine about the inexhaustible sources of American game. As one reader wrote to the *Turf Register,* "It is not, perhaps, generally known that Long Island is one of the finest sporting countries in the world. . . . I have hunted for twenty years, and [there] are now full as many [deer], if not more, than there used to be. . . . The only game which has decreased is the grouse, which has become almost entirely extinct." William Elliott, one of the premier proponents of hunting, worried about this attitude, warning that "in another generation, this manly pastime will no longer be within our reach."

Elliott insisted that he was no softy: "I am not one of those who regret the destruction of the forests, when the subsistence of man is the purpose. . . . It is the wanton, the uncalled-for destruction of forests and of game, that I reprehend." His view contrasted with another hunter, who described how "I fired indiscriminately at every bird which rose within proper distance."[74]

Doubts by the sporting writers matched a slight hesitancy and healthy skepticism about hunting, which continued into the 1830s. A few articles in the hunting magazines worried that shooting animals might lower the quality of life in the cities. One author wrote of "the rail-shooting gentry" of Philadelphia, that "their work of murder and destruction among these poor little birds" just outside the city could make the days less musical. There is also evidence in these early years of a gentle mocking of hunters, especially of the pretensions of city gentlemen to be great hunters. Even the pages of the *American Turf Register* featured clumsy hunters dropping their powder horns into the water, being knocked overboard by the gun's recoil, buying game on their way home, which they would claim to have shot, accidentally shooting one another, and excuse-making ("the sun was right in my eyes . . . but my gun was dirty, and the powder bad"). Humorous hunting stories appeared often in the first years of the *Turf Register* and *Spirit of the Times,* such as one about two brothers who always shared their one gun—"they . . . use it alternately"—making every preparation for a day's hunt, only to reach the field of action and discover that "They had forgotten the gun."[75]

Likewise, a suspicion of outrageous hunting stories peppered these journals. Questioning some descriptions of exceptional shooting, one author pointed out that the measurement of distances was hardly a science: "I have been sporting with many who were professed shots, . . . but found them all woefully deficient in estimating distances, even when they stepped them off." A shooting match among the best shots in Baltimore ended without the death of a single pigeon, but these failures were made up for by excellent food and drink. And the gun was not always the correct weapon. Dogs were generally preferred for dealing with varmints; the humans should be armed with sticks to avoid accidentally shooting a dog. William Tappan Thompson, a southern humorist, wrote in an 1845 edition of *Spirit of the Times* of going hunting with Samuel Sikes, a "backwoodsman" and thus, by definition, an incompetent hunter. Sikes "pretended to cultivate a small spot of ground," but devoted so much time to "the pursuit of game, that his agricultural interests suffered." Though Thompson did not carry a gun, Sikes did, and blasted away at everything without effect until he killed his favorite mule. He then lost his gun, became lost himself, and it started raining.[76]

But then these magazines, and most of the sporting writers of the 1820s and 1830s, did not see themselves as primarily dedicated to hunting over other activities. Their goal was the encouragement of all outdoor male activities, with horse racing and fishing taking the lead. The *Turf Register* and *Spirit of the Times* received occasional letters complaining about the paucity of hunting stories. "I always read about the shooting first," grumbled one subscriber to the *Turf Register, "when there is any to be read of.* . . . You must, Mr. Editor, be hard run for matter, . . . and I suppose that somewhat accounts for your Magazine being so completely trampled over by such droves of horses, to the almost entire exclusion of the manly sports of the field." The editor responded that his magazine was a "pioneer," that "the field appeared to be unoccupied," and he hoped to give his readers what they wanted.[77] Later that year another reader wrote, "It is with great pleasure that I perceive attempts made, in your Sporting Magazine, to revive and encourage the manly practice of rifle shooting." This reader called for the establishment of shooting clubs, mentioning that he had attended shooting matches in several eastern states in which contestants fired at animals tied to stakes—chickens at fifty yards. "Though I never saw a great shot among them," and sometimes everyone missed, "yet the practice gave them some skill and greatly promoted social feelings." The problem was that few Americans "arrive at a very great degree of perfection in rifle shooting," which could be a problem as "there is nothing an invading foe so much dreads as an American rifleman."[78]

This initial skepticism and sense of humor gave way by the middle 1830s to a seriousness fed by the glory of the hunt and the sense that hunters were part of a movement to strengthen the American male. And after being a gentleman, the most important value to these sports writers was manliness. As the 1830s proceeded, the word "manly" became ever more intimately linked with the use of a gun. A reader complimented the *Turf Register* on their firearms coverage. "I am much pleased to find . . . that the subject of rifle shooting is beginning to assume a station among the sports of the day. The exercise is manly and healthful; . . . no amusement can be more exciting or interesting." Governor Alexander McNutt of Mississippi, who wrote several hunting stories under the name "The Turkey Runner," stated in 1845 that the "gentleman devoted to the chase" excelled at all the "manly virtues."[79] By the end of the decade it would have been very difficult to find a single sports writer who did not perceive the use of a gun as a sure sign of masculinity.

Seeking legitimization, the hunting magazines constantly searched for great men who enjoyed hunting. Unfortunately for their democratic and nationalist sympathies, these men were too often monarchs. Thus an article in the *Turf Register,* "Destruction of Game by Crowned Heads," praised Charles III of Spain for killing "539 wolves, and 323 foxes!" Far more satisfying was the discovery that founding father George Mason enjoyed hunting "in support of our constant doctrine, that the sports of the field, while they invigorate the body, exhilarate and prepare the mind for its greatest exertion."[80]

What is intriguing, though, is that in their first decade, one subject on which these magazines offered absolutely no help was the selection of a gun. "It is presupposed," the *American Turf Register* said, "that the sports-man has provided himself with the kind of gun most convenient to his taste." Guns were so distinctive, one from another, that there was no way that anyone could provide advice; the gun "must, of course, be fitted to the shooter, who should have his measure for them as carefully entered on a gunmaker's books, as that for a suit of clothes on those of his tailor."[81]

Along with the hunting magazines, and as a further indication of the spread of gun use, the 1820s witnessed the first civilian American instruction manuals on the use of guns. These works appreciated that most Americans did not know how to use a gun. The first of these to gain much circulation was the *American Shooter's Manual* written by "A Gentleman of Philadelphia," Lee Kester, in 1827. Kester was probably the first American writer to express concern that American shooters paid no attention to safety. There was a general failure on the part of most American shooters to follow the most basic safety standards, and many tended to go hunting with their muskets already cocked, as though to save time. Kester offered pages of advice on how to use a gun safely, acknowledging that "these cautionary rules to the imprudent . . . may appear womanish," but were absolutely necessary.[82] Other writers followed Kester's lead. John Stuart Skinner stated the obvious: "A gun is a dangerous instrument, therefore care is indispensible." Henry William Herbert warned against leaving a gun loaded, as "scarcely a week passes, but we see that some unhanged idiot has had, as it is glibly termed, the misfortune to blow out the brains of his sweetheart, wife, or child." Elliott warned that his readers "only take care, as we stand so close, that we do not shoot each other!"[83]

The surest route to gun safety was gun care, keeping the gun clean so as to avoid dangerous misfires. The shooter "should never sleep after a day's shooting, without cleaning his gun completely; and he had better do it himself, than trust to servants." And servants bore most of the blame for anything that went wrong on a hunt. After one hunter found his gun inoperative he said, "So much for trusting careless servants and not cleaning one's own gun." The narrators of the hunting tales constantly examined their firearms, fearful of misfire. An army captain in one story prepared for the hunt by examining "the lock of his rifle with . . . affection."[84] Rust was a special concern of these hunters, yet they did not really understand it. Some authors recommended gloves "as the warmth of the skin is apt to produce rust," while another felt that the gun should never be stored clean since "the smoke of the powder in the barrel is the best preventive against rust." Lee Kester warned that gun barrels corroded quickly, therefore the need to oil the barrel immediately after each use. The real gun enthusiast should have been able to take apart the lock and keep it cleaned that way, leading the *American Turf Register* to publish an article on that subject complete with a glossary of terms so that the gun user would know the proper name of each part. Kester's recommendation was simpler: the gun should be taken to a gunsmith to have the interior sanded as "Barrels cannot be too smooth inside."[85]

The advocates of hunting moved slowly but certainly toward the advocacy of general gun use in the 1830s. They understood that they did so in the face of some opposition. Henry Herbert, writing in 1852, thought public hostility to hunting so pervasive that "the rifle will ere long be as rare in the western, as it now is in the eastern states." A Baltimore man writing in *Spirit of the Times* in 1850 was certain that "a majority of our citizens . . . think it a crime and wrong to shoot a gun." But he felt certain that if they only tried hunting, "they would find that there is more good to be derived from it than they imagine," as "excursions of this sort bring out the character of [a] man; they tend to warm his heart and soul."[86] Most men were not conversant with this way of thinking, but signs of the spread of a new gun-centered subculture could be discovered in the sudden popularity of pistols, the creation of urban pistol galleries, and the increased number of hunting clubs in the 1840s. Most hunting clubs, like that at Doguc's Neck, Virginia, provided "all necessary equipments" to their members and guests for hunting, and had strict rules aimed at "the increase and preservation of the Game," as well as maintaining social order: "No hired person, servant, negro, or other dependant, shall be allowed, on any pretext whatever, to keep a gun." Most of these clubs also devoted as much energy to fishing as hunting, though not all proved successful. The Cincinnati Hunting Club, organized in 1831 with twenty-five members, had fourteen hunters, including nonmembers, at their first annual "Grand Hunt" in November, and just twelve at their 1833 hunt. In that latter year they held their first shooting contest, firing at pigeons from twenty paces; only three of the eleven contestants hit a bird.[87]

Most, though not all, of these clubs were relatively elite institutions centered in the East. The West Coast was exceptional in this regard. The first shooting club in California was the Sacramento Swiss Rifle Club, which held its first shooting match on July 4, 1853. The Sacramento *Union* reported after this event that "the Swiss are in the front ranks in all pertaining to the use of the weapon [rifle]." For the next several years the club held annual Fourth of July shooting matches before large crowds, firing at targets at an impressive 180 yards (80 yards being the norm for rifle contests, 20 for muskets). Between 1855 and 1860 five ethnically based rifle clubs started in San Francisco: the Turner Schuetzen, the San Francisco Shooting Club, the Deutsche Rifle Club, the Swiss Rifle Club, and the Schuetzen Verein. Swiss and German immigrants seemed to have a greater familiarity with firearms than did the native Americans, at least in the West.[88]

Despite increasing interest in firearms in the United States in the 1830s, white American hunters continued to defer to the English, who served as their model of good hunters, good shooters, and even good poachers. Henry Herbert wrote that "whatever faults, whatever weaknesses, follies, deficiencies or vices, may be justly laid to the charge of the English gentry and nobility, want of manliness . . . is not of them," as a consequence of their devotion to hunting.[89] That deference extended even to the selection of firearms. When advising their readers "On the Choice of a Gun," the *Turf Register* simply reprinted an article from "an early volume of the English Sporting Magazine," with the note: "if improvements have since been made, in what do they consist?" This last comment was telling. Not even the premier hunting magazine in America had a clear understanding of the technology of firearms, and certainly not of the newest developments. One expert wrote in 1846 that "there is scarcely anything so little understood as a gun" and called for the establishment of a single "Government Standard for Guns." Such a standard was particularly important for rifles, which "cannot be depended upon." The *Turf Register* continued to advise its readers that "the barrel should be of a tolerably large bore, and very smooth, with a handsome outside," while the "mounting may be according to fancy." To test the gun, the reader should shoot at a barn door. Every guide to guns published from 1820 to 1850 maintained the superiority of English guns, some even commenting that American gunmakers did not understand "the proper proportion" of a well-made gun. "How any man of sense should risk his life forty times a day with such a weapon," Johnson J. Hooper wrote of cheap American guns, "I cannot comprehend." Lee Kester focused his attention on European guns, noting with pride that "in this country we receive guns from all the manufactories in Europe." He thought the French guns "very handsome ... but they are too light for the shooting in this country," while he found Dutch and German guns poorly made. Kester did think some American guns well made, but there is a "prevailing prejudice against our own manufactures" and his opinion was that English guns were vastly superior. "The English are, without doubt, the neatest and best gunmakers in the world," he wrote. However, Americans made better percussion caps and the best gunpowder. In 1850 Charley Chase called the rifle "our national weapon," and then stated that "the best rifles are made in England."[90]

Henry William Herbert, the single most popular hunting writer in America, under the pseudonym Frank Forester, maintained the superiority of English guns throughout his career. His *Complete Manual for Young Sportsmen,* which was the most successful guide to gun use in America in the 1850s, directed the serious shooter to order a European gun, though none "can compare with the best English" firearm. One must order a gun only from "a house of established character and reputation." This was necessary because fraudulent versions of good English guns were regularly foisted upon the American public. As for American guns, such "exceedingly cheap guns ... are to be found in ... every gunsmith's shop." These cheap guns were bound to burst; they will "at some time or another, apart from any carelessness of the shooter, fail in some part of its mechanism; and then, woe to the holder." Such "mere rubbish" was to be avoided; "every person who has the taste and means to follow field-sports at all" must be willing to spend $300 in order to get a quality English gun (roughly ten times the cost of a cheap American gun). There was no mystery why guns made in London were the best, for "London concentrates the largest number of the wealthiest men and the best sportsmen . . . probably in the world—men who will have nothing but what is the best, and will have the best, whatever it may cost." But if one had to buy an American gun, Herbert insisted on spending at least $100 and having it made in one of the eastern cities "by American gunmakers of standing reputation. It will be understood, that the locks and barrels are all English made and English bored." It would be an English gun assembled in New York.[91]

The sporting writers displayed surprising ignorance of just how guns worked. Into the 1850s enthusiasts debated the relative value of a long or short barrel. The long-barrel advocates mistakenly believed that a larger bore made the shot steadier, while Skinner himself thought that long barrels could shoot farther. Likewise, hunters debated what size shot a *"real sportsman"* should use, and how much powder, and even how to aim the gun. One writer in this debate noted that "it is a difficult matter to find two pieces, though the same length and calibre, which require precisely the same charge." Kester found the barrel "a mystery . . . which has never been explained. For it is within the knowledge of every sportsman, that two barrels may be made by the same man, of the same metal, caliber," etc., and "will shoot differently.—In fact, it is very rare that the barrels of a double gun shoot alike." Some critics hated the rifle and predicted its imminent demise as a hunting weapon: "In a few years it [the rifle] will be entirely laid aside, and we shall not have a gunsmith amongst us who understands the cutting of a rifle." The new percussion guns, which used a percussion cap rather than a flint to ignite the gunpowder, defeated the understanding of many sportswriters in the 1830s. When one letter writer praised the "double barrel percussion gun, made by Constable, of Philadelphia," as far superior to any flintlock, the editor responded with tales of shooters injured when the percussion cap flew off. Others spoke out against those "infatuated with the detonating, or percussion, system." One author suspected a conspiracy by gunmakers promoting percussions because they "are sooner shook to pieces and worn out." He suspected that they even "employ people, who will write any thing for so much a sheet, to overrate them to the credulous." In contrast, Lee Kester admired the percussion cap, but stated that "the gun is capable of little or no important improvement." Nor did it need any, "as every useful purpose appears to be completely answered by the common lock." And Henry Herbert rejected entirely the revolver as "unpardonably clumsy, hideous, and unsportsmanlike."[92]

North and South came together in this love of the hunt.[93] The pages of the sporting magazines and books introduced northern readers to the many opportunities for hunting in the still-wild areas of the South, while southern readers were assured of a warm welcome in the more civilized but still well-stocked hills of New York and Pennsylvania. The only noticeable difference between the two settings was the presence of slaves in the South in the place of northern servants—though even that was covered over by calling the slaves "servants." No southern slave owner need ever worry that some questioning of their "peculiar institution" would find its way into conversations of the sporting life, other than the occasional reference to the fact that the best hunting dogs were those used to "hunt the maroons or runaway slaves."[94]

There were a few minor divisions among sportsmen, such as those who condemned hunting on Sunday. There were even a few who thought the gun too easy. General C. R. Floyd of Georgia preferred to hunt with the Polish lance, and for a few years after 1829 there was a fad for Robin Hood bow-and-arrow clubs.[95] Otherwise, the hunting journals emphasized the naturalness of hunting binding together all true men. "Men are naturally created hunters," John Stuart Skinner explained, "as is evinced by their having little other employment in the barbarous ages of the world, [and] that every man, whatever may be his creed, philosophy or pursuit, feels a strong glow of pleasurable excitement upon hearing a pack of hounds." Killing one's first deer took on transcendent significance for these sporting writers: "To say that the heart of my young friend was not large enough to contain all his joy, would not convey any idea of the ecstasy he was in" upon shooting his first deer. After he had calmed down a bit he "declared he would go immediately home and tell his mother."[96]

Hunting—in these years before social Darwinism provided a coherent theoretical justification for male violence—was seen to make men stronger, preparing them through its "conflict" and "combat" for the real world. "So far as physical education is concerned," wrote the philosopher of hunting, William Elliott, "it stands preeminent. Its manliness none will deny." The hunter learns "punctuality" and "observation through the study of nature and habits of the quarry," as well as "the sagacity, that anticipates its projects of escape—and the promptitude that defeats them!—the rapid glance, the steady aim, the quick perception, the ready execution." Hunting was more than a sport; it was "preparatory school for war." Ironic, then, that Elliott spoke with revulsion of many of his prey, such as "the undoubted instinct of a cruel nature" evidenced in the wildcat. He and his fellow hunters "looked with abhorrence on the savage animal" that had just killed a rooster before their eyes, "and we wondered still more, that in the providence of God, he had seen fit to create an animal with an instinct so murderous." That very abhorrence leads to "the consolatory conclusion—that the instincts of a man naturally differ from those of a wild-cat."[97]

Elliott grappled, though not self-consciously, with the delicate line between the savage and civilizing influences of hunting. He horrified that a wildcat would kill a rooster for pleasure, but saw no contradiction in his own desire to drop birds from the sky for his entertainment. That contradiction was evocative of what would become an intellectual problem in the latter part of the nineteenth century: whether civilization enhanced or crushed the nature of man. Elliott anticipated this debate in his belief that city life made men soft. The answer to many sportswriters seemed obvious: small doses of savage nature imparted valuable lessons and skills. And the gun, the product of human intellect, came to symbolize that safe reach into man's primal past. "Field sports are both innocent and manly," Elliott wrote. "Its tendency is actually promotive of good morals. . . . [Of] all the associates who have acted with me in field sports, and were interested enough to excel in them, not one has been touched with the vice of gaming!" Most important, one did not hunt alone, but as part of a group, so that hunting promoted "social intercourse, and the interchange of friendly offices between neighbors."[98]

This last point decisively separated American hunting from either the more "barbaric" form of the Indians or the too-effete practices of the aristocrats. Hunting was a democratic (as understood among white males in the age of Jackson) social event, to be enjoyed in the retelling "through the medium of the sparkling glass," in Elliott's words. Alexander Hunter of Virginia said that "It is a matter of indifference to me whether or not my companions are good shots, as but a fraction of the time spent on the trip is spent in actual shooting." Hunting parties were always to consist of four men, so that if things got boring, they could have a good hand of whist instead. "It need scarcely be mentioned that the liquor flask is a very necessary appendage" to hunting, Elliott wrote, "but on no account should cold water be drank alone."[99]

There is much in mid-nineteenth century hunting literature that the modern reader would recognize. Though they took a little time to emerge, the themes of male bonding and the deep romantic affection for a favorite gun stand out. In the 1830s the first loving descriptions of every detail of a firearm appeared in print. No longer was it sufficient simply to say "He held a musket in his arms." From this date the dedicated author of hunting articles had to have the precise name and maker of the piece noted, with sensual descriptions of the well-oiled stock and the long, gleaming barrel, as well as the delicate intricacies of the lock. The gun was no longer held; it was now "cradled," "caressed," "hugged," and ultimately "grasped with firmness" in order to fulfill its "deadly purpose." A hunter now wrote of his rifle, without embarrassment, "she's a beauty— tall and slim, with a sight that would ravish you. Next to Miss — —, I love her better than any thing living." One writer went even further, proclaiming "give me my dog and gun, a clear October morning, and place me on the 'Blue Ridge,' and I will envy the life of no poor demented creature, who has been silly enough to prefer a *wife* to his *gun!*" Real men hunted, while "the effeminate young man may die at home, or languish in a dead calm for the want of some external impulse to give circulation to the blood."[100]

On the other hand, the sportswriters sought to separate the participants in their luxurious sport from the hoi polloi. Lee Kester worried that "Living in a country destitute of game laws, and almost without any legal restrictions, ... every man, whose leisure, or circumstances, will permit, may become a shooter. But of the multitude who shoot, few indeed, will be found entitled to the appellation of sportsman; they are very generally game killers, and nothing more."[101] Thus there were constant references to servants almost as necessities of the proper hunt. Close attention was paid to the quality of the dogs, horses, food, and spirits appropriate for a fruitful hunt. Country lodges free from female fripperies brought the hunters together over manly—which is to say gigantic—meals. The decadence of this elite romanticism was savored by connoisseurs, those with the education and intelligence to appreciate the deeper meanings of this close contact with nature.[102] This mixture of nature, sociability, and killing comes together perfectly in one of the many hunting songs popular at the time:

> The cordial takes its merry round,
> The laugh and joke prevail,
> The huntsman blows a jovial sound,
> The dogs snuff up the gale;

The upland hills they sweep along,
   O'er fields, through breaks they fly,
The game is roused; too true the song,
   This day a stag must die.[103]

The gentleman hunter found it necessary to distance himself from the coarse, violent sports of the lower classes. Though Skinner endorsed hunting of all kinds, he held boxing "in the deepest abhorrence," and refused to publish any news of boxing matches. He did not feel the same qualms about printing a letter from "A Lover of Sport" in Nashville who described treeing a raccoon and then sending a servant up the tree to whack away at the poor animal with a stick until it fell to the ground amid a pack of dogs. Skinner was a little doubtful about a "gander pulling" in Mobile, in which a gander was tied to the top of a post with his neck greased while contestants rode by and tried to grab the gander's neck and yank his head off. The editor wonders "if Mrs. Trollope was present" at a gander pulling, implying that it would feed her disdain for the Americans.[104]

While gentlemen hunters rarely criticized their fellows, they often used the image of the western hunter for humorous effect, focusing particular attention on the frontiersman's outrageous clothes and dialect. But no animosity appeared toward even the more primitive western hunter in the pages of any of these sporting works. It was the "pothunter" they despised. Gentlemen hunters resented the competition from these poor people and described them as too lazy to work as they filled their cooking pots with animals captured in an unsporting fashion in traps, often without regard to the ownership of that trap, or by beating the animal to death. The latter aspect made the pothunter especially unattractive to the gentleman hunter, who did not care that the poor could not afford a gun and ammunition—or, in the case of blacks, were not allowed to own a gun. When pothunters used guns, according to Johnson J. Hooper, they did not know what they were doing, overloading their guns with powder and blasting away indiscriminately, and were thus dangerous to themselves and others. As late as 1858, the *Spirit of the Times* heaped derision on those who hunted out of necessity, calling for legislation against "the rascally pot hunter."[105]

Even that gentlest of gentlemen hunters, William Elliott, rejected the pothunter as practicing "poaching" rather than "legitimate hunting." Their "fire hunting," going about at night with torches in an effort to startle animals, was particularly obnoxious, as well as dangerous. Elliott recounted stories of pothunters shooting horses and slaves they thought were deer. He complained that "the modern improvements in gunnery," making it easier for just anyone to hunt, were leading to a serious depletion of all game east of the Mississippi. These pothunters were turning professional, making a living by hunting for the new hotels springing up around the United States. "It is too much to expect this class of men to refrain from 'fire hunting,'" he said, "though forbidden by law. . . . In a few years, the game is destroyed, or driven off" and then no one would be able to hunt without traveling to the far West. The gentleman hunter would never behave in this fashion: "the sport, in their hands, is not apt to be pursued so recklessly, or carried to the extent of extermination." Elliott spoke from personal experience in complaining against these pothunters, these "*amateurs*" "who took a malicious pleasure in destroying the game which a proprietor had presumed to keep for himself," and railed against the ridiculous sense of entitlement "held by the great body of the people" of "a right to hunt wild animals." Elliott sounded precisely like the English gentlemen he emulated in proclaiming that only the owners of the soil should have the right to hunt. But Elliott was hopeful. Once the game was gone, "the mass of people shall have no interest in hunting their neighbors' grounds," and then may gentlemen "without offence, or imputation of aristocracy, preserve the game from extermination—and perpetuate, in so doing, the healthful, generous, and noble diversion of hunting." Elliott left the question open, though: If hunting is so good for men, why limit it to the great landowners?[106]

The hunting subculture got off to a slow and isolated start, most certainly because of the class biases inherent in its message. Mainstream magazines and newspapers occasionally republished a hunting story, but otherwise Skinner and the rest spoke to a small audience confined largely to the East Coast, and faced a degree of opposition. *Niles' Weekly Register* spoke out on several occasions in the late 1830s against hunting as wanton slaughter for pleasure and linked the spread of hunting to the greater availability of guns and ammunition.[107]

But all that changed in the 1840s, as the *Turf Register* and *Spirit of the Times* enjoyed substantial national success, inspiring several competitors, while other magazines began to print hunting stories for their readers. Members of the urban middle class, eager to acquire the aura of the English gentleman, flocked to the sport. The *Turf Register* boasted in 1833 that "Field Sports [are] Becoming Popular The spirit for field sports we may suppose to be spreading, by the fact that *buttons,* emblematic of the various sports, are now made at several manufactories." Hunting became a safe, middle-class group activity, which could even include the ladies— though only on special occasions. Participants in such hunts enjoyed using literary names for one another, such as Hawkeye and Nimrod, and did not seem to mind too much if no one killed any animals. It was, after all, a sport.[108]

At no time in the mid-nineteenth century did hunting become completely accepted. Mockery continued. By the 1840s most critics found hunting simply a waste of money: "An amusing affair, termed a 'Buffalo Hunt,' came off at Hoboken last week—the Buffaloes however, objected to the sport, and declined being hunted, so taking the first opportunity, they bolted, and many of them are still enjoying their freedom among the New Jersey marshes. . . . [But] for the melancholy accident whereby one man lost his life, there was nothing to regret—those who went to see it, were made fools of, and those who got it up made money." Some opponents were a bit harsher in their critique, seeing hunting as a throwback to primitive ages. In 1854 an author regretted that hunting persisted despite "the introduction of rail-roads and recent changes in the habits of society."[109] Nonetheless, there is evidence that by 1850 carrying a gun had become a firm part of male identity for a significant number of Americans.

Hunting received an additional boost from the romance associated with the westward migration of the United States across the Great Plains. While the sporting magazines continued their focus on hunting as a gentleman's sport, with most of its descriptions placed in the East, the popular press began an association of hunting with the West, especially with shooting buffalo. By the late 1850s the hunting magazines had learned to exploit this connection, and featured stories of grand western excursions in search of game.

Most of the literature on the westward migration shared the practical approach of the sporting magazines. During the antebellum period guidebooks written for migrants headed west generally included a "good gun" on the list of items to bring. But for some reason the subject did not take up any more room than those three words. Few guidebooks had anything else to add, while several did not provide even this unhelpful entry. An anonymous guide for migration to Texas published in 1840 contained three pages on the necessities, with emphasis on "substantial wagons" but no "ardent spirits," yet made no reference to a gun. A typical longer entry can be found in an 1844 series of letters published in the New York *Herald*. The author, Peter H. Burnett, wrote that guns "are useful, and some of them necessary on the road, and sell well here" in Oregon. A gun that cost $20 in New York would fetch $50 in Oregon. This value remained high particularly because of the absence of gunsmiths in the West prior to the 1850s. Similarly, Ole Rynning advised his Norwegian readers to bring "good rifles with percussion locks," as such good guns were far too expensive in America and could be sold there for a solid profit. Guns thus had an economic value, but if thought requisite for self-protection, it remained an unstated assumption.[110]

The other obvious reason for bringing a gun was to shoot game along the trail west. Yet most of the guidebooks and travelers' accounts do not mention hunting, or warn against wasting one's time hunting. The guidebooks focused on what most concerned the vast majority of migrants: farming and jobs. William Darby's popular *Emigrant's Guide* did not even mention hunting as a way to supplement one's diet. The West offered employment not only for farmers, but for all trades, and Darby listed a wide variety of artisans, from masons and carpenters to tailors and shoemakers, yet somehow skipped gunsmiths. Or as William Oliver pointed out in 1843, it is "unnecessary to say much about hunting, . . . [as] it ought not to influence the intending emigrant. The hunter is always poor, and in some measure despised by his industrious neighbours."[111]

Migrants moving across the Great Plains in the 1840s wrote in astonishment of the massive herds of buffalo, and of how easy it was to shoot one. Indians were known to walk right up to a bison and take careful aim with their bow, dispatching the animal with a single, carefully aimed arrow. Even the clumsiest musket could serve in such circumstances, though several shots might be necessary. But the guidebooks warned that all those animals gave a false security. Peter Burnett advised those following him West: "When you reach the country of buffalo, never stop your wagons to hunt, as you will eat up more provisions than you will save. . . . Buffalo hunting is very hard upon horses, and . . . prudent care should be taken" of them. Lansford Hastings's *Emigrants' Guide to Oregon and California,* the book carried but not read closely by the Donner party, also addressed this issue. Hastings knew that most people thought "meat can be very readily obtained" by hunting on the overland trail, "but this is an error, which, unless cautiously guarded against, will be very apt to prove fatal." To depend on hunting for food "in that wild and remote region . . . would, in nine cases out of ten, result in immediate or ultimate starvation." Hunting took a great deal of time and energy, slowing down an expedition, "and unless you pass over the mountains early in the fall, you are very liable to be detained, by impassable mountains of snow, until the next spring, or, perhaps, forever." Yet many men devoted that time to hunting, not wanting to pass up the opportunity to shoot buffalo. As John Mack Faragher wrote, "Men had this opportunity for play, and play it was. The amount of usable food produced by these masculine sorties was dismally low." Lacking the equipment to render the dead buffalo into usable food, migrants shot the animals for sport and then left them to rot on the plains.[112]

The letters and memoirs of many western explorers and mountain men attest to the limitations of hunting as a source of food. Jedediah Smith discovered during his western travels in the mid-1820s that, while hunting was far too time-consuming and unreliable, eating his own horses proved far more convenient: "The balance of the horses I was compelled to eat as they gave out." Zenas Leonard's 1833 expedition also ended up eating their horses, after they determined that hunting was hard work and led to either feast or famine. John C. Fremont's expedition in 1843 ate their horses, and more: "We had tonight an extraordinary dinner—pea soup, mule, and dog." Kit Carson, who was also known to eat a horse on occasion, wrote in his memoirs that those who spent much time in the West quickly figured out that trapping worked, while hunting made work. The winter created a false confidence, as the snow revealed the tracks of foxes and rabbits and deer; yet somehow the animals themselves always seemed invisible. Trapping, which did not require tracking, was thus far superior. In the winter of 1844 a young man named Moses Schallenberger survived fine in a small cabin in the Sierra Nevada by trapping animals. Two years later the Donner party used Schallenberger's cabin but not his methods, wasting valuable time and energy attempting to hunt food. Their one successful hunting foray came when William Eddy, who did not own a gun, borrowed a rifle and tracked down a bear. Another such effort ended with William Pike killing himself with his own pepperbox pistol—or so they said. After eating their horses, they ate one another. As John Muir dryly noted, "They were not good mountaineers. The whole winter could have been spent delightfully in so beautiful a spot."[113]

But such practical concerns could not overcome the need to demonstrate masculinity, and by the 1840s hunting was widely seen as a sure indication of male prowess: "We started [off] to bring in some buffalo meat and thus prove our skill as hunters from the Hoosier State." This particular Hoosier and his friend, "a crack shot," chased buffalo for a few hours, until the frustrated crack shot dismounted, walked up to a buffalo, and shot him in the head. He had his kill. For the migrants, as for the Indians among whom they passed, killing the first or the largest buffalo imparted instant status. Where the migrants differed from the Plains Indians was in also admiring those who could kill the most buffalo. Such a need to kill as many buffalo as possible—a policy that eventually led to the animal's near extinction—indicates to many scholars some sort of mental disorder, what John Mack Faragher called "weak ego development."[114]

In the later 1840s and 1850s, this desire to slaughter bison inspired men to purchase firearms before heading west. The women were not always as impressed. "Our men are all well-armed," wrote Lucy R. Cooke. "William carries a brace of pistols and a bowie knife. Aint that blood-curdling? I hope he won't hurt himself!" The women were equally cynical about the men's hunting prowess: "The young men of our party . . . went out this morning for the purpose of hunting buffalo. They soon discovered a herd of a hundred and fifty, rushed into their midst, fired their guns without effect and finally succeeded in capturing a cow." Another young woman sympathized with the animals: "Two antelopes were coming toward the camp and two of the fellows took guns and chased them, but did not get any and I was very glad, for the poor things were at home and we were the intruders."[115]

Fortunately, this desire to use their new guns against the animals of the plains generally did not extend to people, though one particularly sensible woman thought "the gentlemen were somewhat disappointed that they had not *even seen an Indian*." The Indians themselves, who still relied overwhelmingly on bows, mostly ignored the white migrants, except for stealing the occasional horse. When migrants were attacked—as in 1853, when a group of Oglala killed a family of four in retaliation for an unprovoked attack upon them by some soldiers—they did not rely on themselves for their defense, but called on the U.S. Army for protection. The men on the overland trail did behave aggressively toward one another. John Mack Faragher reported that "nearly every diary recorded at least one . . . fistfight." But these were generally always one-punch affairs, with one combatant hitting the ground and the other retreating victoriously. The violence usually stopped there, even in the stressful conditions of the overland migration. But then, again contrary to the popular image of the West, migrants traveled in family groups, and the women not only disapproved of aggressive behavior, but also usually put a quick stop to it.[116]

Men crafted an image of the heroic and dangerous westward journey, and hoped to place themselves at the center of these grand tales. Washington Irving perfectly expressed this vision in his popular biography of the overrated Captain Benjamin Bonneville: "With his horse and his rifle, he is independent of the World, and spurns all its restraints." One guidebook explained that "your wives and daughters . . . can do but little for you here—herding stock, . . . breaking bush, swimming rivers, attacking grizzly bears or savage Indians, is all out of their line of business." The image of battling grizzlies and Indians while the adoring family watched in wonder apparently appealed to many men. But the migration west could be disappointing, because it was in reality rather boring, and several guidebooks pointed out that the dangers were wildly exaggerated. Buying the emerging symbol of masculinity, the rifle, and hunting along the trail made up for the absence of other adventures. Still, men generally understood that this trail hunting was an interlude between the more pedestrian pursuits of farming and shopkeeping, what they were leaving and that toward which they traveled.[117]

Writers of hunting stories played a significant role in elevating the gun to the central icon of the American frontier. After Cooper, one of the most important was probably William Darby, a racist Indian-hater and author of a popular guidebook. In the 1830s he brought before the public "the white hunter-warrior." In a score of stories Darby described this hero visiting death upon the Indians. Mostly, though, the heroes talked—with poor grammar. Darby's own biography reflects the careful avoidance of reality necessary to construct the heroic frontier image. Though militia from his hometown took part in the 1782 massacre of the Moravian Indians, Darby made the militia commander one of his heroes, and the Moravians essentially deserving of their fate. His stories focus on Indian massacres of white women and children, and cast the frontiersman as an avenging hero armed with a deadly rifle.[118]

In stories like "The Hunter's Tale" of 1831, Darby placed the gun at the center of his story, while establishing the basic motif for generations of western heroes. The narrator, Kingsley Hale, looks back on events in 1775 as he tells his grandchildren, "we sit on a spot" the first white settlers "dared not visit without their terrible weapon, the rifle; nor did their rifle always save them from a foe who seemed to issue from the earth. But if the motion of the white hunter-warrior was slow, his march was steady and he sustained his post or fell; the white wave never flowed backwards towards its native ocean." The hero of this tale, Lewis Wetzel, had the miraculous ability to reload while running. Where most people in the 1770s needed three minutes to load a rifle, Wetzel could do so in fifteen seconds. And, another anticipation of future American heroes, he never missed: "The piece was pointed, and the unerring ball sped through the heart of the animal." His protégé, Conrad Mayer, was also a sure shot, but untrained in war.[119]

Like Cooper's Judge Templeton and Leatherstocking, Wetzel and Mayer first meet when they shoot a deer at the same time. The ensuing fight is a contest of brute strength, with Wetzel subduing the younger man. Wetzel sits on his opponent, grabs Mayer's knife, and throws it aside. They then become best friends. Though Darby returns to the rifle as the key weapon in the whites' triumph over the savage Indians, he never describes the gun, which remains a generic weapon. Wetzel warns Mayer not to rely too much on his gun; his advice in warfare is "do not fire unless sure of your mark. When you do fire, instantly retreat and reload."[120]

Darby evoked the traditional fighting stories, but with deadlier violence. Frederick Mayer (father of Conrad) avoids the shots of three Indians by falling to the ground. With their guns empty, the Indians are now reduced to hand-to-hand combat. Mayer shoots one, and uses his rifle as a club on another: "But the stock of the piece flew to shivers against a joist as the owner was grappled and thrown on the floor." Mayer kills another Indian by using the "iron bar" of the barrel before he himself is killed and his helpless family massacred.[121] The younger Mayer learns his lessons from Wetzel, avoiding an Indian bullet by falling to the ground, and then using his hatchet to kill his foe before he can reload. And again, when attacking a man armed with a rifle, Mayer wins though using only a hatchet because his opponent misses. The hatchet does not miss: "The ball passed harmless, but the hatchet lodged in the brain."[122] Despite the apparent limitations of the rifle, Darby's stories were among the very first to portray gunfire as a regular feature, while highlighting the deadly accuracy of the frontier hero—only the villains are poor shots. Darby may also have been the first writer to suggest that, on the frontier, "we were all hunters."[123]

Like many western authors, Darby was caught in the ambiguity of attempting to promote a rugged and heroic version of frontier life, while regretting its savagery. Darby insisted that the frontier was not more violent: "These calumnies do very little harm to the objects; but are extremely mischievous to those who travel the interior of the United States under their influence." Nonetheless, Darby also worried that frontier settlers degenerated into barbarians living on, "as they term it, [the] verge of civilized life." As one moved away from the East Coast, "the scale of civilization lowers, until upon the Ohio and Mississippi the savage state commences." Because he overdid the violence, Darby, unlike James Fenimore Cooper, could not reconcile his competing images of the frontier.[124]

Darby missed one leitmotif that would become a standard in frontier stories later in the 1830s, the shooting match. In 1836 the Boston-based *American Magazine of Useful and Entertaining Knowledge* published an account of an Arkansas contest. The author described some twenty "brown hunters; equipped in leather, with their broad knives at their sides, rifles in hand," competing for an ox. Shooting at a wooden target from forty yards, each contestant was allowed eleven shots. The author was surprised that the contest moved so slowly, not realizing until then how long it took to reload a rifle. This account has the ring of truth, in that there are no immoderate examples of marksmanship, and the distance of forty yards is perfectly reasonable. Nonetheless, the author is effusive in his praise of the frontiersmen: "You have made a show of Davy Crockett; but there are thousands of men in the West who are better marksmen, better bear hunters, and every whit as smart as Davy himself."[125]

Eastern writers were creating a mythology about the frontiersmen, often by distorting or fabricating a historic past. Even the *Army and Navy Chronicle,* which should have cared about the differences in firearms, made the soldiers at Bennington into frontier marksmen armed with rifles, rather than the muskets and axes they actually carried. In "The Rifleman's Song at Bennington," the poet placed these heroes in the trees, which they certainly never climbed:

Full soon ye'll know the ringing
Of the rifle from the tree!

The rifle, the sharp rifle!
In OUR hands it is no trifle![126]

By the late 1840s the frontiersman had become a completely romanticized figure, but one who was largely extinct. It may seem curious that this vision of a vanished frontiersman emerged at the very moment that America's westward expansion accelerated, but the writers of the 1840s got around this contradiction by maintaining that the modern settler was different. Darby's hunter warrior, like Cooper's more famous Natty Bumppo, was in the past; the lone frontiersman had served his purpose and was replaced by well-behaved American families moving west to plant civilization. The rifle had cleared the way; the ax followed. As the *Western Miscellany* summarized the situation in 1849, the "profession" of hunting gave way to "the axe of industry." In 1847 *De Bow's Review* praised the western hunters who "cleared the way for us, their fortunate successors, and laid the foundations of that greatness, to which . . . we are rapidly marching. They, however, were going the way of the animals they have exterminated—were disappearing in the direction of the setting sun, expending their remaining energies and final services, in lighting the way and guiding the footsteps of the emigrant and the settler." The hunter-warrior would always be in the past; that remains the attraction of the Western—the civilizing settlers do not have to live with these lone heroes who, like the movie figure Shane, move on. As the article in *De Bow's* concluded, the frontiersman's experiences were "stranger and more romantic than fiction."[127]

Of course it is difficult to determine what is fiction and what a strange and romantic reality. Many westerners understood the silliness of the image of the eagle-eyed frontiersman being created by the eastern press. Western writers from Johnson Jones Hooper to Mark Twain mocked such exaggerated claims of marksmanship. Nonfiction accounts also became ever more self-conscious of the gap between reality and imagery in the 1840s. A settler described how he aimed at a chicken and pulled the trigger of his rifle, but "she spluttered, an' spootered, and sizzled till the chicken got tired waitin' an' went over in the field to hunt June bugs. I had both eyes shet, fur the sparks wuz jest a b'ilin' out'n the tech hole, an' I dasn't take 'er down from my shoulder, 'cause I knowed she'd go off *some* time that day." It did go off, just as an old sheep wandered by, "'n' got the whole load right behin' the shoulder, an' keeled over deader'n a shad."[128]

Magazines published in the West tended to carry much more realistic accounts of the use of firearms. In a story of Daniel Boone's rescue of the women captives from Indians in 1779, which appeared in an 1833 edition of the *Western Monthly Magazine,* Boone fires once and finds his mark, while McMillan's shot is deflected by a tree and he grapples with his opponent and kills him with a knife. Two years later the same magazine described a shooting match as essentially frivolous. Just two individuals, "a noble pair of odd ones—the pride of Tennessee and the last resort of Freedom," fired away at the target while the rest "reposed with quite a Turkish air of nothing to do." There was no fancy shooting, just two men trying to hit a target with shots from their beat-up old rifles. The author noted that the gap between this real shooting match and the imagined one was the product of believing old stories that expanded with time, and asked, "If a Tennessee rifle has a charmed power, is not the talisman to be sought in the memory that clings round" tales of the frontier?[129]

John Audubon observed that many westerners, especially in the Southwest, were a bit sensitive about their poor shooting, given their emerging reputation for being great shots. One must ask, " 'Pray, friend, what have you killed?' for to say, 'What have you shot at?' might imply the possibility of his having missed, and so might hurt his feelings." Audubon thought none of the five frontiersmen with whom he went hunting very good shots; they relied more on their dogs than their guns to bring down their prey. But he kept that opinion to his journal, until he got back east.[130]

That great observer of early America, Alexis de Tocqueville, mentioned guns once. In explaining why democratic armies—"this small uncivilized nation," as he called it—are dangerous, he wrote that the army "has arms in its possession and alone knows how to use them; for, indeed, the pacific temper of the community increases the danger to which a democratic people is exposed from the military turbulent spirit of the army." In "an unwarlike nation" like the United States, "the excessive love of the whole community for quiet continually puts the constitution at the mercy of the soldiery." Tocqueville offered the Whig vision of America: a country that wanted quiet to pursue business, and found peace in its equality. Only their army could bring violence: "Democratic nations are naturally prone to peace from their interests and their propensities, they are constantly drawn to war and revolutions by their armies." The great transformation would come in the 1840s with the Mexican War, when the

United States had to decide between the pacific pursuit of business and aggressive expansion. Expansion won.[131]

Violence Becomes American

In 1834 John Murrell attempted to steal two slaves in Mississippi. Caught in the act, he was sentenced to prison, where he died from tuberculosis ten years later. A minor criminal of no discernible intelligence, Murrell was not known to have ever committed a violent act and would certainly have been completely forgotten today but for the imagination of Virgil A. Stewart, whose testimony put him in prison. In 1835 Stewart wrote a small pamphlet full of the most unbelievable stories portraying Murrell as a mass murderer and criminal genius who led a ruthless gang called the "Mystic Clan of the Confederacy," which planned to lead a giant slave rebellion and slaughter all the whites. People outside of the Southwest, always willing to believe the worst of that benighted region, fell for these tales of the "Great Western Land Pirate," as Stewart labeled Murrell. A few people in Madison County, Mississippi, also panicked, and killed two whites suspected of opposing slavery, and an unknown number of slaves. John F. H. Claiborne called the Murrell biography "one of the most extraordinary and lamentable hallucinations of our times." Yet it helped to form the image of the Southwest as a violent and lawless region up to our own time. That it was completely unconnected to reality, highly improbable, and internally contradictory mattered not in the least.[132]

During the twenty years before the Civil War, Americans began constructing an image of themselves as a violent people and to act on that self-perception. A core tension existed in the United States between violence and civilization, between a tough self-image and the desire to attain European social standards. Since the early eighteenth century, the English ideal placed emphasis on the gentleman mastering his passions. There is substantial evidence that during the first three decades of the nineteenth century America continued the eighteenth-century cultural standard of controlling emotions and violence. But the 1840s and 1850s marked a shift toward ever-accelerating passion and violence.

These differing paths for America, between a basically Victorian and European conception of society and a perceived authenticity of violent Americanism, played themselves out politically and sectionally. The

Whigs saw themselves as the party of "sober moderation," the party of order in a society becoming more rather than less violent with age. They feared what they called "the bowie-knife style of civilization," their perception of the Democrats' cultural manner. They certainly had before them enough negative examples. In April 1832 Sam Houston clubbed Ohio representative William Stansberry over a political disagreement; President Jackson praised Houston and remitted his $500 fine from a Washington, D.C., court. John Q. Adams's son was assaulted by a Democrat in the Capitol building; Alabama Representative Albert Rust beat Horace Greeley; Representative Preston Brooks caned Senator Charles Sumner on the floor of the Senate. And then there was Alexander Stephens's problem with taller men (which included most men). Stephens challenged four men to duels in order to prove his manliness; his first three opponents rejected the offer; the fourth seemed to accept it with alacrity. Stephens hit Judge Francis Cone with his cane as the first step in a challenge to a duel; Cone responded by pulling out a knife and lunging at Stephens, who defended himself with an umbrella. Cone knocked the umbrella aside and stabbed Stephens repeatedly, even getting atop Stephens as he lay bleeding. Amazingly Stephens survived, and Cone pled guilty and was fined $1,000, a large sum for the time.[133]

Whigs held the common conviction that civilization should produce a decline in the level of violence. Whig leader Henry Clay had put the "spirit of commercial enterprise" as the one great American "passion as unconquerable as any with which nature has endowed us." He held that "All legislation, all government, all society, is formed upon the principle of mutual concession, politeness, comity, courtesy." There was disturbing evidence that the opposite was happening in America. Could it be that the world's great democracy was collapsing into barbarity and anarchy? If so, most people in the northern part of the country knew just where to look: the southern part of the United States. In this context, stories of the Murrell gang confirmed the worst suspicions of northerners.[134]

The image of the Southwest as violent went back to the beginning of the century. Friends warned Winthrop Sargent, the first U.S. governor of the territory, that the people living there were little more than "wild beasts," "the fugitives from justice & all the lawless characters . . . have taken refuge in that country." Yet he found very little violence. One of the first judges in the area, Ephraim Kirby of Washington County, hated his neighbors, describing them in 1804 as "illiterate, wild and savage, of depraved morals, . . . litigious, disunited, and knowing each other, universally distrustful of each other." But here "litigious" is the key word, for they settled their disputes in court, keeping Kirby far too busy for his own liking. And Kirby had to admit that the people showed little inclination toward actual violence; they certainly were not interested in the militia, which he thought a bad joke. The attorney Francis Martin seconded this judgment of the litigious nature of the people in 1811: "They keep me tightly at work here. . . . There is not a day in the year that the court does not sit somewhere in the territory."[135]

Criminal gangs existed, but they tended to focus on stealing movable goods and livestock, and did not last very long. The most famous of these gangs, the Kempers of southern Mississippi, was typical. They mostly raided across the border into Spanish west Florida or stole from their rivals, the Horton gang. The one gang known for the use of force, the Masons, apparently never murdered anyone. Samuel Mason acquired his few guns from the militia force that came in pursuit of him. Mason's gang operated for longer than any other known criminal group, two years. He was finally killed by two of his followers, who put a tomahawk in his head in order to claim the reward. Mason's death in 1803 marked the end of gang operations in the territory, terminating a period of ten years when the Mississippi government struggled to assert its authority.[136]

Nonetheless, shortly thereafter a single notorious robbery set the image for decades to come. In 1805 a robber stopped a mail carrier named Swaney and his companion as they rode along the Natchez Trace. When the unnamed companion went for his pistol, the robber shot him dead. Swaney fled before the robber could reload, which demonstrated for many future robbers the need for a second gun.[137]

Agents of the law often proved more dangerous to the public peace than did the common thief. Mississippi had particular problems in this regard. In 1815 Judge George Poindexter, who had a history of drunken fights, shot and killed a Natchez merchant in a duel. The rumor circulated that the judge turned and fired on the second of ten paces. The following year former governor Robert Williams attacked the land register, Nicholas Gray, with a knife. But Williams forgot to take the knife from its sheath, just bruising Gray. On the whole, though, the territory adhered to the letter of the law, even allowing two horse thieves to claim the ancient "benefit of clergy," proving that they could read and therefore getting off with being branded on their thumbs. Slaves could also escape worse punishment through benefit of clergy until 1814. Robert V. Haynes, a leading historian of frontier Mississippi, found very few murders and a level of violence equal to contemporary New York City and Philadelphia, and absolutely no evidence of any lynchings of whites in the territory prior to 1835.[138]

Vigilantes are often located primarily in the West and identified with cowboys or rednecks.[139] In reality, vigilante groups appeared throughout the country in the antebellum years, and generally with middle-class and elite support. Vigilantism always supported white supremacy, often worked as a tool of party politics, occasionally as a class weapon against workers, and rarely against criminals.[140] Vigilantes were no more likely to have guns than the local militia. They tended to beat or exile their victims, rather than hang them in the fashion preferred by vigilantes after the Civil War. One group in Alabama, called the Slicks, kept undesirables, including slaves and free blacks, in line. These vigilantes, like others in Arkansas and Illinois in the late 1840s, met resistance, but with fists, a club, or an ax. If the miscreants subject to the regulators' fury had guns, surely they would have used them for self-defense, but there are no such recorded instances prior to 1840. Eventually members of the community in both Alabama and Illinois organized another vigilante group to put a halt to the activities of this first vigilante group.[141]

The first lynching by a vigilante group to capture the attention of the American public came in 1835. In that year a group of citizens in Vicksburg, Mississippi, tired of the failure of their courts to deal with professional gamblers, took the law into their own hands and hanged five gamblers, running several others out of town. The gamblers were thieves, not murderers; it was the lynch mob that brought violence to Vicksburg, as the local newspapers charged.[142]

Vigilantism was a fraud, a claim to preserve public virtue while pursuing self-interest or hierarchy; the slave patrol was its perfect exemplar. And vigilantes, especially in the South, became ever more violent in the years leading up to the secession crisis. Their premier target tended to be those who opposed or in any way questioned the structure of slavery. In Louisiana in 1859 a group led by Alexander Mouton, a former governor, senator, and speaker of the U.S. House of Representatives, killed six people and beat forty-one others in an effort to stop the trade between slaves and whites. Alexandre Barde wrote an odd little poem on these events:

> Women rent their gloves applauding with their beautiful
> White hands, and a bursting fanfare welcomed the hunters. . . .

Kill! kill! Shoot! shoot!
Fire for the beautiful black eyes watching you!

Vigilantism was terrorism. It generally sought to make a few very public examples in order to control those on their list of the disapproved. Vigilantes tended to beat and hang; they rarely shot. David Grimsted offers a perfect summation of vigilantism in the years just before the Civil War: "It was a rule of lies whose self-righteous perpetrators commonly committed acts much less just and more brutal than any their victims dreamed of."[143]

Vigilantism is an apt indicator of the way in which white society mostly reserved its violence for nonwhites. Murder rates support this assertion. Based purely on statistics, the least violent state in the country in the thirty years prior to the Civil War was South Carolina, which averaged just 120 acts of legally charged violence a year; fewer than five of these acts were murders. In contrast, Massachusetts in those years, only 10 percent larger in population, averaged 331 violent acts per year, nine of which were murders. But of course it was the nature of that population that made the difference; just over half of South Carolina's population was enslaved. Acts of violence against them do not even appear in the records, and there is very good reason to believe that there was quite a bit of violence against slaves. There is also some evidence to indicate that violence against slaves reduced violence among whites. The larger point is that the presence of a growing number of men owning and interested in firearms, as represented by the hunting subculture, did not, of necessity, produce greater levels of violence. But matching the spread of gun ownership with institutionalized racism did have a powerful impact on American society.[144]

Murder statistics provide another measurement of the gun's noncentrality in American life prior to the Civil War, for the gun was not then the weapon of choice. It is difficult to build up a compelling statistical base on this issue, since murder was so rare in the antebellum period. For instance, during Vermont's frontier period, from 1760 to 1790, there were five reported murders (excluding those deaths in the American Revolution), and three of those were politically motivated.[145] In 1799 Mississippi Territory had its most violent year, with two men charged with murder and eight with assault—and this in an area with twenty-eight licensed taverns. The next peak came in the four years from 1802 through 1805, which witnessed six murders. The average for this rugged frontier territory is indicated by the two years of 1817 and 1818, during which one man was murdered and eleven assaulted. Also one slave who fired a gun was fined $4 and put in the stocks. In 1830 the sole prosecuted murder came when a man beat his wife to death. And many alleged antebellum murders never actually occurred, but were the product of literary imagination, as with Stewart's report of the Murrell gang's homicidal spree. Many other cases were like one in Noble County, Indiana, in which the supposed victim showed up after a vigilante mob had hanged his "murderer."[146]

A study of 735 prominent nineteenth-century murders indicates that the gun was the preferred weapon in just 18.1 percent of the murders committed prior to 1846; for the years from 1846 to 1860, that figure nearly doubled, to 34.9 percent; over the next thirty years, it climbed to 59 percent. Prior to the Mexican War, the knife was the weapon of choice. By the 1880s, guns were being used almost five times as often as knives.[147] Close-quarter murders (including "by hand," stabbing, and ax murders) account for 73.2 percent of the murders in the first forty-five years of the century, 49 percent in the immediate antebellum years, and 29.5 percent in the later period. After the Civil War, beating and stabbing gave way in popularity to the gun. Samuel Colt's own brother, John C. Colt, preferred an ax to one of his brother's revolvers when he murdered a rival in 1841. Samuel Colt did take advantage of the publicity surrounding the trial to give a shooting display in the courtroom, convincingly demonstrating the superiority of his revolver to his brother's ax as a murder weapon, though failing to aid John Colt in any comprehensible fashion.[148]

It is not difficult to understand this preference for bladed weapons in homicide. First, most murders then, as now, were acts of passion. Since guns were not in every home, the impassioned potential murderer had plenty of time to cool down while attempting to locate a firearm. And if there was a cleaned gun and ammunition at hand, it took too long to load a musket for a satisfying quick kill. Second, guns remained unusual enough through the 1840s that their use in a homicide carried the assumption of premeditation. Many murderers received reduced sentences and even pardons by arguing that they committed their crimes in the heat of passion, reaching for the first weapon at hand. The use of a tool or a kitchen knife conveyed that lack of planning, but the use of a gun convinced juries and governors that the murder must have been planned.[149] Third, guns prior to Colt's revolver lacked the reliability of bladed weapons. And as pistols prior to Colt's were single-shot, a misfire often terminated the effort at homicide, as was evidenced in a pair of famous attempted assassinations. In 1835 Richard Lawrence fired at Andrew Jackson with a pair of pocket pistols from within five feet. Both pistols misfired, perhaps because the powder was damp. In 1850 political opponents of the courageous Kentucky abolitionist Cassius Clay plotted his murder. Twenty men set upon Clay, one seizing his favorite weapon, a bowie knife. Clay was severely beaten and stabbed, and then a pistol placed against his head, but the gun misfired three times. Incredibly, Clay seized his knife by the blade and tore it away, killing the man with the pistol. A knife plunged into the chest was certain to kill; a musket or pistol was anyone's guess. This uncertainty of the firearm made it the favored weapon in duels.[150]

Duels, it must be recalled, were fought primarily to preserve honor, not to kill or injure. There were occasional psychopaths, like Vice President Aaron Burr and President Andrew Jackson, who saw dueling as a way to murder opponents, but most men who fought duels sought a dramatic gesture rather than a corpse—especially as the latter might be themselves. Dueling pistols, unless rifled, were notoriously inaccurate. No one could tell which way a shot from one of these early pistols might go, especially once each party had marched off ten paces, placing themselves roughly fifty feet apart. Often the participants deliberately fired into the air as an appropriate indication of their gentlemanly desire to avoid bloodshed and heal any personal disagreement. Often they were just terrible shots.

The famous duel between John Randolph of Virginia and Henry Clay of Kentucky in 1826 is worthwhile in this regard. Clay, then secretary of state, appears to have misunderstood something Randolph said in the Senate about foreign policy. All their friends tried to talk them out of the duel, and it was unclear that either party had any idea why they were proceeding with the affair. Randolph informed Thomas Hart Benton that he hoped only to "disable" Clay. Clay, the hero of the West, told his second that he "was not accustomed to the use of the pistol," and feared that he "might not be able to fire within the time" allotted to aim, so Randolph allowed him extra time. Randolph's pistol went off before he had raised it to fire; his second shot hit a stump rather than Clay. Clay missed twice, knocking up the gravel some distance from his opponent. Randolph fired into the air, and then offered his hand to Clay. The two men shook hands, and "social relations were formally and courteously restored."[151]

Duels appear to have become more frequent in the 1830s, but they did not become much deadlier. Fairly typical was a duel in Vicksburg in 1839 in which two newspaper editors each fired twice, without visible effect. The two men met later that afternoon and tried again before a crowd of one thousand people. This time one of the men hit the other in the thigh.[152] There was a certain fashionable aura among southern gentlemen to speak of dueling as a social grace. Texas senator Louis T. Wigfall held that dueling "engendered courtesy of speech and demeanor—had a most restraining tendency on the errant fancy, and was a preservative of the domestic relations without an equal." A dueling society was a polite society. In the 1830s dueling grounds became popular places to visit, the number of people killed at a site such as the Bladensburg grounds outside of Washington, D.C., growing with the telling. At "The Oaks" in New Orleans, one could even take lessons in dueling. Charleston had a society for those who had emerged victorious from duels (though the society came to an end with the death of their president in a duel). Despite such indicators of support—Governor John L. Wilson of South Carolina published a tract on the proper methods of dueling in 1838—dueling did not claim many lives. Far more typical was Representative Preston Brooks's caning of Senator Charles Sumner in 1856. This was the southern white male's preferred mode of violence, beating an unarmed opponent. After all, it was how they treated their slaves.[153]

Antebellum literature also shied away from firearms. The fight story was remarkably popular, but involved fists and knives rather than guns. Robert Bolling's epic poem of the 1760s, *Neanthe,* is credited with containing the first such story, a battle between Euphenor and Dolon on Virginia's Eastern Shore, ending with Dolon being kicked to death. Similarly, the Reverend Charles Woodmason's "Burlesque Sermon" of the 1760s describes a backcountry fight complete with gouging and nose-biting, but no gun appears. Little changed in the popular almanacs of Davy Crockett and any other of the stories of the frontier published in the first half of the nineteenth century. Fights recur in American literature; fists fly, knives are wielded, hair is pulled, and noses bitten, yet firearms remain strangely silent.[154]

The emerging middle-class culture of the mid-nineteenth century despised the ugliness and dirtiness of violence, shrinking from the very idea of personal confrontation. Violence became associated with workers and the poor in general. There is strong evidence that workers equated manhood with an ability to assert oneself violently, yet with absolutely no reference to firearms. Fists made the man.[155]

Adding deaths resulting from mob actions to the homicides listed above further clarifies the rare usage of firearms by private citizens. There were a few instances of mobs shooting prominent individuals, most notably Joseph Smith and Elijah Lovejoy. But antebellum crowds seldom displayed guns, and the authorities rarely responded with firearms. Rioting in antebellum America remained relatively mild compared with the upheavals in Europe at the same time. State violence has always been more extreme in the United States, from the slaughter of the Indians to the bombing of Vietnam. Slavery alone does not fit the pattern, for here was state-supported private violence. But when antebellum Americans took to the streets, they tended to throw rocks rather than fire bullets, and soldiers rarely fired on crowds, which was the single most dramatic difference from the European experience. It was possible for an official like Colonel J. P. Miller of Montpelier, Vermont, to stop an anti-abolitionist mob in 1835 by warning one of its leaders: "if you do not stop this outrage now, I'll knock you down." In the face of such a threat, the crowd dispersed. Without the comparative perspective, as Peter Way wrote, "the reader is left with the stereotype of the preternaturally violent American."[156]

Many contemporaries appreciated this comparative advantage. In 1833 the *Western Monthly Magazine* expressed gratitude that the American West was not as bloody and violent as Europe, where "banditti" robbed travelers at every turn. These criminals had more honor than Napoleon or Wellington, "who shed oceans of blood in the prosecution of ambitious schemes for personal or national aggrandizement." In Europe "even the poor cottager sleeps in continual terror of the knife and the firebrand," and the American reader "cannot but rise from the perusal" of a study of modern Europe "with renewed love for our republican institutions."[157]

Fairly typical was the 1837 flour riot in New York City. A crowd angry over the high price of flour broke into the storehouse of Eli Hart & Co. A company of militia was called out and the crowd dispersed. Anticipating trouble, the city government kept the militia in readiness, stationed in a flour warehouse and treated to dinner by the flour merchants. But nothing came of these fears, and the militia was dismissed with a loaf of bread for their troubles.[158]

Significantly, the one large-scale, gun-related crowd action of the first half of the nineteenth century ended up as a farce. Pennsylvania's "Buckshot War" of 1838 began with a disputed election in which the Whigs, allied with the Anti-Masons, carried a key district. A group of armed Democrats, led by a trio of federal officeholders, including a deputy marshal, descended on the capitol in Harrisburg with the intention of intimidating the legislature into nullifying the election results. The Democratic press was filled with militarist language proclaiming "civil government is at an end," and calling for bloodshed if necessary. The Whigs charged that the crowd was recruited from "grog shops," supplied with arms, and paid a per diem. The crowd burst into the legislative chambers, the Whigs left, and the governor declared a state of insurrection, calling for federal troops. The secretary of war demurred, but the federal arsenal in Philadelphia did supply arms to the militia, which moved into Harrisburg to restore order. The Democratic mob left and the "war" was at an end, the backlash aiding the Whigs. There were no deaths, and the only casualty came when some Democrats beat a witness.[159]

Deadly violence, and even sometimes the threat of real violence, induced crowds to back down and political leaders to halt party warfare in an effort to reach peaceful reforms. Democrats and Whigs, shocked by the *potential* violence of the Buckshot War, compromised on a new constitution. In Rhode Island, Dorr's Rebellion of 1840 ended when Governor Samuel Ward King armed six hundred volunteers intent on restoring order with guns from the Providence arsenal. Dorr's own brother and father had joined the force defending the arsenal, and Dorr's militia simply dissolved. The deadly St. Louis riots of 1854, which witnessed a run on the gun stores and left ten shot, beaten, and stabbed to death, induced party leaders to work together in establishing a professional police force.[160]

In April 1834 New York was rocked by an election riot. Some five hundred Whigs rushed to the armory, convinced that Democrats from the 6th ward were marching on it to arm themselves. They occupied the building and were then surrounded by a Democratic crowd armed with clubs and bricks—obviously neither side ordinarily owned guns. Mayor Gideon Lee arrived, backed by a unit of volunteer militia. Lee pleaded with the Whigs to avoid bloodshed and just go home, promising that they would be protected from the Democratic crowd and that no charges would be brought. The Whigs laid down their arms and left, and the crowd outside dispersed. Thus ended the 1834 riot without fatalities. Riots could produce deaths, of course. Philadelphia's fall election riot that year was the deadliest prior to the 1850s, ending with two deaths: one young man knifed and another man beaten to death with a cane.[161]

The expectation of nonviolent crowds was so great that states even held the militia responsible for any violations of decorum. Missouri had revived its militia in the early 1840s, but when the militia committed acts of violence repressing a riot in St. Louis in 1844, the legislature terminated the entire system. When they revised the laws of Missouri in 1845, the assembly did not even mention the militia.[162]

In the public mind, at least, firearms were still associated largely with the military—and with good cause. The military was the premier source of violence in the United States, called upon to battle and suppress uprisings from slaves and political radicals. Throughout the antebellum years, the War Department remained not only the predominant purchaser of firearms, but also the premier manufacturer of guns. This association of the U.S. Army with defensive violence held even, or perhaps especially, on the frontier. During the Civil War, Minnesota's representative Ignatius Donnelly spoke of the frontier's nationalism. He insisted that westerners were not deferential to state authority: "We who come . . . from the far West have not that deep and ingrained veneration for State power which is to be found among the inhabitants of some of our older States." Yet a moment later he admitted that "We look to the nation for protection." Not to themselves, but to the nation; not their own guns, but the army's.[163]

By 1840 the U.S. government was well supplied with firearms. A War Department census found just over 568,690 serviceable muskets, 29,706 rifles, and 7,654 pistols. Almost all of these weapons were stored in twenty-three armories, arsenals, and depots. The War Department did locate one very large problem in the shortage of gunsmiths—they had none—to care for these weapons, and of tools for those armorers even if they could hire any. Just fourteen of those twenty-three repositories had an anvil, a bare necessity for any smith, and only two of them had emery wheels, required for the fine detail work on locks.[164]

The War Department also found its forts grossly under-armed. The nation's fifty-eight forts had just over two thousand firearms, one-fifth of which were completely unserviceable, an average of twenty-nine serviceable firearms per fort. Particularly troublesome were the service's rifles, which broke much more often than muskets; only 12 percent of the muskets required repair, compared with one-third of the rifles. But it hardly mattered, since none of the forts had an armorer on staff, only seven had any sort of hammer, and only three had files. All but the simplest form of gun repair therefore bordered on the impossible; a broken gun had to be sent to one of the nation's armories.[165]

Though the United States in 1846 can hardly be called well prepared for its next war effort, the country did, for the first time, have a large stockpile of guns. It entered the Mexican War with a small army, but one that was supplemented quickly by volunteers armed out of that reserve of firearms. Also unlike previous wars, these volunteers did not come from the militia, but joined up as individuals or as part of specially recruited companies. In the War of 1812 the militia had constituted 88 percent of the total force committed; in the Mexican War the militia composed just 12 percent of the total strength of the U.S. military. That decline in reliance on the militia may go a long way toward explaining the often brilliant performance of the U.S. forces in the latter war.[166]

In 1845 Indiana's Adjutant General David Reynolds surveyed his state's militia and was most dissatisfied. Public interest appeared to him at an all-time low, but he offered a prediction: "War, with its thrilling incidents, could . . . revive military discipline." In Indiana's case, that was exactly the result of the Mexican War. Though the governor was unable to respond to President James K. Polk's call for troops because the state lacked an organized militia, thousands of volunteers enlisted, enough to fill fifty-six companies within three weeks.[167]

President Polk hoped to rely on the state militia for the war, but was sorely disappointed.[168] As with Indiana, most states did not have an organized militia in 1846. Yet there was evidence of enthusiasm for the war. Even before the declaration of war, General Edmund Gaines, acting without authority, called for volunteers from Missouri, Louisiana, Mississippi, and Alabama; 12,600 men mustered in New Orleans. Though most of these men lacked firearms, and Gaines had few to give them, he sent eight thousand of them on to General Zachary Taylor. But the militarism of these men melted under the Mexican sun, and so all but a single company decided that their enlistment was unconstitutional—which it was—and took the first opportunity to return to New Orleans.[169]

Once war was declared, Congress authorized the president to call for fifty thousand volunteers. The volunteers were to provide their own uniforms, and the federal government would provide the guns. The response varied dramatically. Several state governments ignored the war: Delaware sent no organized companies of volunteers; only one company of eighty-four men from Vermont volunteered to serve; no Florida troops ever saw combat in Mexico, though four companies of specially assembled militia did arrive after the battles had ended to conduct police duties. In

Massachusetts the war with Mexico almost destroyed the one truly active militia system in the country, as militia participation dropped dramatically. Many elite volunteer companies disbanded in opposition to the war, which many Americans saw as a giant landgrab intended to extend the area of slavery, and membership overall fell from 10,000 to 4,588 men. In addition, a number of officers expressed their distaste for this war of aggression; Captain Erastus Leuck wrote Adjutant General Henry K. Oliver that "the war with Mexico . . . has rendered human butchery rather unpopular and the war is considered here but little better than butchery for the purpose of Robbery." Other volunteer companies lacked this political motivation but also sat out the war. New York's 7th Regiment, an elite volunteer unit, held several parades, but otherwise confined their duties to serving as New York City's front line of defense against attack from the Mexicans. The company's records contain not a single reference to any of its members seeing service in the war.[170]

Opposition to the war undermined militia service in several states. Wisconsin's constitutional convention coincided with the declaration of war, and led to a bitter debate over the propriety of maintaining a state militia. One critic charged that the militia existed just so "some quasi great men on a small scale may wear epaulettes and side arms." Another wrote, "We are . . . likely to be cursed with the farce of militia trainings and musters to gratify the vanity of would-be great men, and to dub with high military titles, some of the aspiring, to the great annoyance of and expense of the people." The promilitia faction won by a vote of 66–21; but the legislature refused to order musters and only volunteers joined the war effort. Just two years later, in 1848, Wisconsin had another constitutional convention, and, by a vote of 35–26, placed serious limitations on the militia in the new constitution. Many people agreed with Ulysses S. Grant's later assertion that the Mexican War was "the most unjust war ever waged by a stronger against a weaker nation." Opposition to the war and its militarism was clearly widespread.[171]

In contrast, the governor of Illinois called for thirty companies of volunteers, and seventy-five showed up. In Tennessee, thirty thousand men volunteered for three thousand positions; they drew lots for the honor of going to Mexico. During the Mexican War 58 percent of the 104,556 U.S. combat troops were volunteers, 30 percent regulars, and just 12 percent regular militia. Some of these troops were privately armed, though by rich benefactors. Robert F. Stockton not only raised a private army of three thousand men in Texas for service against Mexico, he also supplied their guns, a precedent followed ten years later in Kansas. The first great free-market war was on.[172]

Not that the regular army was terribly pleased by this turn of events. The commanders of the U.S. war effort, Zachary Taylor and Winfield Scott, had few kind words for their volunteer hordes, though they had no choice but to accept them. General Scott thought the volunteers undisciplined barbarians, and said that the United States had "committed atrocities to make Heaven weep and every American of Christian morals blush for his country. Murder, robbery and rape of mothers and daughters in the presence of tied-up males of the families have been common all along the Rio Grande." Lieutenant George C. Meade called the volunteers serving in the Mexican War "a set of Goths and Vandals without discipline." Even some of the officers of the volunteer companies had their doubts. Captain Luther Giddings of Ohio described his troops' firing ability as limited to making lots of noise, "a capital one for a funeral escort."[173]

Fortunately for the Americans, they did not rely on shooting skill to win the Mexican War. For the first time American troops went into combat well armed, though still with flintlock muskets.[174] Thanks to the increased output of the Springfield and Harpers Ferry armories, the U.S. government armed not only their regular soldiers, but also the several thousand short-term volunteers. One unit at least, the Mounted Rifles, carried the most modern percussion rifles and, in the place of swords, Colt revolvers. But this unit was the exception, as Taylor, Scott, and the other American commanders did not expect their troops to fire their muskets often; it was still the bayonet at the end on which they relied. The officers of the army had all been trained in the classic infantry tactics of the Napoleonic Wars, with an emphasis on tightly packed formations, a single volley of concentrated musket fire, and the bayonet charge, with artillery in support. His general orders before the Battle of Palo Alto state that General Taylor "wishes to enjoin upon the battalions of Infantry that their main dependence must be in the bayonet."[175] The Mexican War convinced the vast majority of American officers and military experts of the value of the bayonet over all other weapons; the majority of battles in the war were decided in hand-to-hand combat, the type of fighting in which the bayonet was most effective. As John S. D. Eisenhower wrote of the Battle of Churubusco, "the bayonet was the final, decisive weapon." While the rifle was just beginning to lose its reputation as far too difficult a gun for military use, most officers still saw it as a special-use weapon, useful for scrimmaging and keeping the enemy off-balance by picking off individuals at long range, but only specially trained marksmen could be relied upon to use the rifle properly.[176]

Little attention was paid to the quick victory of Colonel Alexander Doniphan's mounted riflemen over the Mexicans outside El Paso. The Battle of Brazito on Christmas Day, 1846, lasted about half an hour before the Mexicans retreated. In that time, the Americans killed or wounded one hundred of their enemy. The Mexicans never came close enough to inflict casualties, though their cannon wounded seven Americans. Doniphan's victory was unusual in many ways, and later, at the Battle of Sacramento, his troops used their rifles as clubs rather than guns to bash their way through the Mexican redoubts. But it is still surprising that few contemporaries appreciated the implications of the startling victory at Brazito and its demonstration of the long-range accuracy of rifles.[177]

The American commanders erred in not realizing the advantages of percussion rifles, even if they still took longer to load than muskets. They were probably also wrong in their estimation of what won the war. The U.S. forces were outnumbered at every major battle, and often faced determined opposition from brave Mexican soldiers armed and trained, for the most part, in the same fashion. American guns certainly made little difference. As Ulysses S. Grant famously described musket fire during the Mexican War, "a man might fire at you all day without your finding it out."[178] The Mexican army had fewer bayonets than the Americans, but made up for that shortage by the energetic use of mounted lancers, who managed to halt U.S. forces on several occasions. And it must be said that the Americans were far more fortunate in their officer corps than were the Mexicans. Nonetheless, though the U.S. officers did not expect it at the start of the war, their artillery proved remarkably effective, and most military historians now credit this branch of the service as the decisive factor in the war.[179]

The U.S. Army may have been well supplied with guns, but the public still was not, based on those volunteers appearing for service.[180] Men anxious to move right to the front generally showed up for service, as with every American war up to 1846, either unarmed or carrying ancient firearms labeled "useless" by their commanders. The creation of the Bear Flag Republic in California is a fair example of the continuing shortage of privately held firearms. Only a few of the forty men who surprised the small Mexican garrison at Sonoma carried guns, but then the commander, Manuel Vallejo, invited them in and offered drinks, not expecting any conflict. The rebels took the drinks, eighteen prisoners, and 250 stands of arms, "with the arms the . . . main object of the expedition." With that one act they suddenly had a well-armed force, courtesy of the Mexican government. What followed was a bit farcical, as John C. Fremont took over the "revolutionary" force and Monterey surrendered without firing a shot. The pro-U.S. forces in Los Angeles faced stiffer resistance in the form of a masterful display of horsemanship by the Mexican garrison. The Americans fired their muskets but could not hit any of the Mexican moving targets, while the Mexicans killed four men with their single cannon. The Americans finally left, leaving Los Angeles in Mexican hands.[181]

In December General Stephen Kearny arrived with three hundred dragoons. He had one problem: though all his troops carried guns, they were flintlocks. The dragoons' gunpowder became soaked during a sudden rainstorm the night before they met the Mexican lancers under Andreas Pico at the Battle of San Pascual. Unable to fire their guns, the Americans were reduced to fighting with the butts of their weapons; in a matter of a few minutes the Mexicans, using only their lances, killed eighteen Americans, wounded another thirteen, including Kearny, and captured one of the two American cannon. Kearny's forces dragged their way to San Diego and claimed a victory. Southern California would fall to the Americans, but not as the result of any significant military endeavor.[182]

The victory of the United States in the Mexican War changed the nation's politics and culture in many ways. A vast new area of the country was opened to occupation by white Americans, and thousands of settlers made the decision to head west into California and Oregon Territories, with Samuel Colt making every effort to persuade them that they needed one of his new revolvers for the overland journey. For the first time in American history, people who had no obvious reason to possess a gun acquired them, even to the point that a pistol, the new Colts being favored, became essentially a tourist accoutrement in the West. European tourists particularly loved to dress in the "Wild West" costumes, complete with multiple firearms. The Sir St. George Gore hunting expedition of 1854 to 1857 spent $500,000 and covered seven thousand miles. Gore carried seventy rifles and thirty other firearms, and bagged thousands of animals—on a single day he claimed one thousand buffalo, much to the disgust of Jim Bridger, the famous mountain man, who was appalled by such purposeless slaughter.[183]

Firearms became much more common in the West after the Mexican War, but they still did not dominate frontier life. A fine example of the ability of settlers to establish security in their settlements can be found in the gold camps of California. In myth, these gold fields were home to ruthless individualists who mined with one hand while holding their neighbors at bay with a .45 in the other. Yet the reality was rather different. In an area covering some ten thousand square miles and inhabited by a hundred thousand men and very few women, and rich in resources worth stealing, from tools to gold, there was not only very little crime, but generally no locks on the doors. Bayard Taylor, a traveler in this area at the height of the gold rush, was stunned to report that "there was as much security of life and property as in any part of the Union." The Butterfield stage line operated for three years between Missouri and California just before the Civil War, was never stopped by thieves, and was halted by hostile Indians only once. Of course there was crime in these regions, and nothing approaching a liberal judge in sight. Those found guilty of a serious crime were usually hanged without appeal. A miner who took part in the 1849 Gold Rush thought "the marvel of marvels is, that mob-law and failure of justice were so infrequent, that society was so well and swiftly organized."[184] As a scale of reference, the famous San Francisco vigilante movement started after a merchant was assaulted by a robber. George R. Stewart wrote that "modern citizens . . . must feel some humiliation to think that our ancestors could get so excited about what we would consider a very mild crime."[185]

Racism determined the presence and nature of American violence more than any other factor. The most obvious example was the entire institution of slavery, of which violence was a routine component, seen by its adherents as an absolute necessity. Slaves, who could not defend themselves, made an easy target for violence. But a similar racism swept west with conquest, provoking acts of violence completely unrelated to slavery, leaving the Plains Indians, Mexicans, and Chinese to pay the heaviest price for national expansion. A leading California politician boasted in 1856, "I can maintain a better stomach at the killing of a Mexican than at the crushing of a body louse."[186]

In Trinity County, California, in 1854 two competing groups of Chinese immigrants from Canton and Hong Kong agreed to meet in open battle. For three weeks they prepared, and then on the day of the confrontation, the two sides hurled insults at one another. The white audience grew bored and started to push the two sides toward one another in hopes of creating a real battle. A drunken Swedish miner opened fire on the crowd, and was immediately shot by another white. A chaotic battle ensued in which ten Chinese and twelve whites were killed. Two years later another silly brawl erupted into deadly violence. In Toulumne County a Chinese company spent an estimated $40,000 buying muskets and bayonets in preparation for a showdown with a competing immigrant group, which spent about $20,000 for weapons. But both sides used the guns as clubs and the bayonets as large sticks, aiming to hurt rather than kill. Again, white spectators joined the fight, killed two Chinese, and then everyone fled. In this context, the sarcastic comments of Henry Ward Beecher on missionary efforts among the Chinese are comprehensible: "We have clubbed them, stoned them, burned their houses and murdered some of them; yet they refuse to be converted. I do not know any way, except to blow them up with nitroglycerin, if we are ever to get them to Heaven."[187]

California aside, the presence of more guns did not instantly transform American society. Some Americans were just a bit afraid of guns. One indication of this shift was the termination of the *feu de joie*. A discharge of blank cartridges at the end of a parade, the *feu de joie* was the hallmark of uniformed companies prior to the Mexican War. But more spectators came to complain that the noise and the unreliability of the amateur soldiers, who "occasionally fire off a ramrod," acted to "the terror of spectators." With enthusiasm for military displays waning after the war, the *feu de joie* died off, and was last performed in New York City by the 7th Regiment on July 4, 1850.[188] Most communities and cities in the United States remained quiet, peaceful places. John Mack Faragher described a bitter political fight in 1860 in which Democrats and Republicans exchanged charges of being liars and damned liars. For such an outburst the local justice fined the participants. Antebellum tough guys still confined themselves to talk and the occasional fisticuffs.[189]

As always in American history, there were many different currents of thought and belief in the country, some directly contradictory. But in a nation that was coming to prize middle-class respectability and religious morality to an ever greater degree, those with an interest in firearms remained a small minority. Their numbers had grown in response to the cult of the gentleman hunter and the success of American forces in the Mexican War, but the attitude of most Americans toward firearms continued to be, at best, ambiguous.

In the years after the Mexican War violence became noticeably more common in the United States. Some of this violence was exaggerated, especially by the press, which leaped upon any tale of bloodshed. After the 1852 election riot in St. Louis in which one person died, Ned Buntline telegraphed his New York paper that he alone had shot and killed several rioters.[190] Travelers observed this increased level of violence in the 1850s, but not in the West. It was the South that captured their attention. For the first time authors repeatedly referred to a region of the United States as noticeably armed. An English visitor advised that it was "absolutely necessary to carry arms in the South"; another was shocked to read in a paper in Louisville, Kentucky, of a man entering a hotel and "deliberately shooting at another in the dining-saloon when full of people, missing his aim, and the ball lodging in the back of a stranger's chair." Bad shooting aside, the whip and the bowie knife remained the symbol of southern violence; the first for the slaves, the second for use among white men. Henry Murray, traveling in the South in 1854, read of a debtor who "seized a bowie knife in each hand, and rushed among" his creditors until someone took the liberty of "burying a cleaver in his skull." But that was not all; Murray also heard of a man who, in the midst of an argument, decapitated his opponent with "one blow" of a bowie knife, and of a third who stabbed an acquaintance for stepping on his toe. Murray did not witness any of these events, but he did feel them typical of the South's "heartless apathy."[191]

What set the South apart from the rest of the country, obviously, was slavery. David Grimsted has brilliantly demonstrated a compelling link between the perceived need of southern slave owners to defend their racist system and the growing use of violence as a means of resolving political disputes. In their vicious assault on slaves suspected of questioning their bondage and upon abolitionists who rejected the entire system, southern whites broke with the traditional forms of crowd actions, which almost always confined themselves to intimidation and property damage. Southern defenders of slavery even demanded that the North treat its abolitionists similarly. Violence in defense of slavery, Grimsted argued, drove frustrated northerners to the ever greater use of force in the defense of freedom. The evidence in support of this thesis appears overwhelming, and one component of that development is the newfound willingness of crowds to use guns against their opponents.[192]

Several scholars found that southern violence accelerated from 1835. In that year the abolitionists launched a major pamphlet campaign, and a slave-insurrection hysteria swept the South. The southern leadership

responded by nullifying the First Amendment; southern crowds reinforced this closure of public discussion of slavery with the greatest possible brutality. Alexander Stephens summarized the view of the southern
leadership perfectly: "I have no objection to the liberty of speech, when
the liberty of the cudgel is left free to combat it."[193] The vast majority of
those who died as a result of mob violence were African Americans.
These southern mobs did not shoot down their opponents; they beat them
and burned them and tore them to shreds with a savagery unknown in
other parts of the country, and did so—another distinction from the rest
of the country—all with the complete support of the authorities. Northern crowds from the Colonial period forward targeted property; southern crowds killed people with a sadism that defies easy explanation.
Northern and western crowds did not skin their victims alive, set wild
animals upon their bound prey, or play kickball with the head of someone
they had just torn asunder. Nor could northern crowds expect to be led in
these activities by their local sheriffs, militia commanders, and governors,
as was the case with southern mobs. Racism warped every aspect of southern society, twisting the law and civilization into the most grotesque
shape imaginable, and all of it rationalized as a Christian duty to the
victims.[194]

At the slightest rumor of a slave insurrection—and most of these slave
uprisings were figments of the whites' imagination—local whites frantically requested guns from the state government. The North Carolina
slave-insurrection scare of Christmas 1830 led the governor to issue arms
to several communities. Despite efforts to beat confessions out of slaves,
there was no evidence of a planned uprising. Nine months later there was
another scare, this one leading to the murder of about thirty slaves. Again,
no evidence of rebellion was produced, though the slaves certainly had
sufficient justification to rebel. And if whites found a black with a gun,
they went berserk. When a free black in Livingston, Mississippi, was discovered with a gun in 1835, his claim that he used it only to hunt squirrels
was ignored and he was hanged on the spot.[195]

It is vital to emphasize that at no point did the United States have anything like a unified culture, even in the South. The southern planter elite
found it necessary to foreclose basic freedoms for their fellow whites in
the late 1830s precisely because of people like Cassius Clay, the Grimké
sisters, and other southern whites who insisted on questioning racial slavery. Additionally many southern whites who supported slavery objected
strenuously to the incredible savagery of white mobs and the increased

daily violence of southern life. In South Carolina hundreds of common people signed a total of thirty-seven petitions in the late 1830s calling on the legislature, in David Grimsted's words, to place "restrictions on the carrying of deadly weapons in order to curb a system of social bullying and intimidation." An 1838 petition from Abbeville supported a ban on carrying all private arms, including the "murderous Bowie knife, Dirks, Pistols, Sword-Canes, etc. Your petitioners look upon this practice as a violation of civilization, barbarous in its origin, derogatory to our free institutions, shackling the liberty of opinion, and at war with the laws of God and civilized man."[196]

Crowds continued to employ traditional forms of physical force from 1835 to 1861, though guns appeared with greater frequency, especially in self-defense. In Cincinnati in 1841, blacks and Irish clashed and a few gunshots were reported, though no one was hit by a bullet. City officials rejected the request for protection from African Americans, who then acquired firearms and responded to the next white mob attack by opening fire. The blacks also seized a cannon that the whites had dragged up the street. Several people were injured, though no one was killed until, interestingly, the blacks agreed to disarm, and the two crowds then resorted to beatings that killed one black and one white. Two years later William Birney led a group of fourteen armed abolitionists against a small mob supporting a Louisiana slave owner attempting to seize a girl he claimed as his property. The only injuries came from thrown bricks. But guns appeared in the Philadelphia riot of 1844. An observer reported that "These are strange things for Philadelphia. We have never had anything like it before, but now that firearms have been once used and become familiar to the minds of the mob, we may expect to see them employed on all occasions, and our riots in the future will assume a more dangerous character."[197] Cities appeared more dangerous places than ever before and, starting in 1846, guns appeared as "house protectors" in advertisements.[198]

In the increasing tension of the 1850s, modes of violence shifted dramatically. The most violent of all antebellum political riots came in Louisville in 1854, with twenty-two people beaten and shot to death. Baltimore's riots between Know-Nothings and Democrats the following year involved bowie knives and slingshots—but no guns—leaving four dead. When another riot later that year left a policeman dead, Virginia's Governor Henry Wise offered his state's militia to the Maryland governor to put down opponents of the Democrats. In New Orleans in 1855 nativists and the foreign-born exchanged dozens of shots, killing two

people. When the Know-Nothings took control of the New Orleans government, Democrats began purchasing arms for future battles. While
urban crowds began bringing guns into the streets, especially in the slave
states, southern mobs continued to use extremely vicious methods against
their perceived enemies.[199]

But Kansas stood out like a warning beacon of what lay ahead for a
nation that was slowly arming itself. "Bleeding Kansas," as it is so often
called, fell far short of the bloodbath that name implies. Between 1855 and
1858 fifty-two people were murdered in the territory. Twice as many
people would be killed in three days in New York City in the draft riots of
1863. The proslavery faction proved more prone to commit murder,
thirty-six compared to the fourteen killed by the free-state faction (two
proslavery men died accidentally while committing acts of violence).
Even though guns were pouring into Kansas from supporters of both
sides, old-fashioned beatings and hackings accounted for a great many of
these deaths. John Brown's small company of followers, the Potawatomie
Rifle Company, did not actually use rifles to kill five men in retaliation for
the burning of Lawrence; they hacked them to death with swords. Others
employed more modern methods: in 1858 the Kansas state militia led by
Charles Hamilton of Georgia captured and shot ten free-staters, five of
whom survived by pretending to be dead. By either method, the supporters of slavery determined to bring Kansas into the Union as a slave state.
Benjamin Stringfellow encouraged the citizens of Missouri to "mark
every scoundrel . . . that is the least tainted with free-soilism or abolition-
ism, and exterminate him. . . . I advise you, one and all, to enter every
election district in Kansas . . . and vote at the point of the bowie-knife and
the revolver."[200]

Those who rushed to Kansas showed a dangerous willingness to use
firearms for a political cause, replacing the ballot with the bullet for the
first time in American history. That more guns were not brought into use
was the product of ignorance rather than intent, as volunteers on both
sides had little working knowledge of firearms. Two free-staters were
taken captive because "not one of the four guns" in their possession "could
be fired for want of caps." The Republican James Montgomery therefore
advised that in the future volunteers be trained in keeping their guns "in
condition for use."[201] There was not, however, any shortage of firearms.
Members of the Connecticut Kansas Colony wrote in 1856, "Before leaving Connecticut, and without any agency of our own, we were presented
with fifty Rifles, which we gladly accepted, to be used *only* in extreme

emergencies." Henry Ward Beecher stated succinctly that a Sharps rifle carried "more moral power . . . so far as the slave-holders were concerned than [are] in a hundred Bibles." For the next decade the Sharps rifle would be known as Beecher's Bibles.[202]

Bleeding Kansas was but part of an acceleration of political violence throughout the rest of the country. By 1857 militia units had fired on one another and upon crowds of civilians. In that year, for the first time ever, U.S. troops shot members of a peaceful crowd—in this case, a crowd of people voting in Washington, D.C. In June 1857 President James Buchanan, worried that the Know-Nothings would win the city election, provided Mayor William Magruder, a Democrat, with a personal guard of just over one hundred marines. For reasons that still remain unclear, the marines fired upon a group of voters, killing ten and wounding twenty-five.[203]

As some scholars have recently noted, the 1840s mark a fundamental turning point in American history, when the nation's entire culture seemed to swing in entirely new directions. It appeared that Americans sought anew for their identity, with many finding surety in an ugly racism and aggressive expansionism, and others seeking redemption through social reform. The militia began a slow rebirth as a voluntary organization, often constituted along ethnic lines, and occasionally doing battle with one another. In the aftermath of a number of slave rebellions, southern whites turned with greater fervor to armed repression and an uncompromising and violent defense of their "way of life" (read slavery). And the spread of the United States across the continent, culminating in the Mexican War, placed heavy demands on the gunmakers and the U.S. Army. These two impulses, hunting and militarism, fed the enthusiasm of many Americans for guns, and for the enhancement of American arms production.

Chapter Ten

The Arming of the
American People

The good people of this world are very far from
satisfied with each other & my arms are the best
peacemakers.

—Samuel Colt, 1852[1]

The Technological
Transformation

Gentlemen hunters were terrible for
business, at least for American gun-
makers. They did a fine job supporting dealers in good food, fine spirits,
the DuPont gunpowder company, and English gunmakers, but they may
have actually hurt the development of the American gun industry
through their constant castigation of firearms made in the United States.
War, on the other hand, was great for business. The U.S. Army acquired
almost all its firearms from the national armories and thus, unlike in previous wars, offered little profit to private gunmakers. But thousands of
volunteers either supplied themselves or were supplied by wealthy benefactors and officers with muskets from domestic sources. And in the
aftermath of the Mexican War, new opportunities opened up for the promotion of gun sales to migrants heading west. Nonetheless, American
gun manufactories remained small-scale through the 1850s, only the Colt
Firearms Company coming anywhere near the level of production at
either of the national armories.

The gentlemen hunters were not alone in demanding European firearms, for American Indians did so as well. The American Fur Company

insisted on European guns for their Indian trade, informing James Henry of the Boulton Gun Works of Nazareth, Pennsylvania, in 1836 that "We have already sent our requisitions to England for probably all we shall require. . . . We cannot hold out any encouragement for North West guns. Our people will not take any but the English." American-made guns broke more often and were too heavy and bulky. Despite their greater accuracy, American rifles were disliked by the western Indians because the rifling required the use of a ramrod on each loading, a nearly impossible task on horseback.[2] Even the U.S. Army found that the Indians with whom they traded demanded English guns, which were nearly a foot shorter and half the weight of the average American musket. Trying to break free of the English monopoly, the U.S. government ordered the production of carbines at the national armories "not as a martial weapon . . . but as a light-weight, half-ounce caliber smooth bore . . . made for the Indian Department." On the orders of Secretary of War Henry Dearborn in 1807, Springfield had produced twelve hundred of these carbines by the end of 1810. The army admitted that these short carbines were not very good in field action and far from accurate, but easy to use on horseback. By the 1840s some American gunmakers, led by Jacob Hawkins of St. Louis, had learned enough from the Indians to shorten the barrel of their rifles to just under three feet, making it easier to use on horseback without losing accuracy.[3]

Though guns were the preferred weapon among Indians, as consumers they were far from connoisseurs. They received guns from any source they could and then devoted their energy to obtaining shot and powder. One U.S. Army officer described how the Indians "were armed with guns of the most nondescript character, old Tower [of London] muskets, and smooth-bores of every antique pattern." The Indians used bullets that "were purposely made so much smaller than the bore of the gun as to run down when dropped into the muzzle," thus avoiding the need to use a ramrod but seriously diminishing the bullet's velocity and force. "When going into a fight, the Indian filled his mouth with bullets. After firing he reloaded in full career, by turning up the powder-horn, pouring into his gun an unknown quantity of powder and then spitting a bullet into the muzzle." Such a method allowed them to fire three or four shots on the run, whereupon the war club or ax came into play. It was this alacrity in firing, rather than any degree of marksmanship, that earned the Indians a reputation for mastery of firearms. The obvious pride and often totemic quality of guns among Indians secured that identification. The vast majority of whites did not share that fascination at least until the 1850s.[4]

The antebellum years were an age of missed opportunities in gun production. As early as 1819, John H. Hall began making workable breech-loading rifles for the Ordnance Department. His rifle performed brilliantly in its army board tests, yet no one seemed to realize what a significant breakthrough had occurred, and production remained low. Several private companies attempted to make the Hall rifle, but only Simeon North succeeded, selling twelve hundred to the government in the late 1820s. Though Harpers Ferry continued to manufacture a small number of the rifles under Hall's personal direction, demand remained low. Hall could not even interest the military in his clever invention, the army displaying an astounding lack of interest in the latest developments in gun technology. It was not until 1836 that an army board finally got around to comparing the relative advantages of various kinds of firearms.[5]

The report of that 1836 army board is a masterpiece of inaccuracy and myopia. A board of officers compared the arms made by Hall, Samuel Colt, John W. Cochran, Baron Hackett, S. Fisher, D. Leavitt, and the armory musket. The rate of firing ranged from 1.2 times a minute for the muzzle-loading musket to five times a minute for the breechloaders of Hall and Hackett. The problem with all the early breechloaders, as well as Colt's revolver, was the escape of gas from the breech. The most noticeable effect was an unpleasant smell, but the escaping gas also reduced the shot's velocity while fouling the breech and barrel, often to the point that the gun no longer functioned properly. The board therefore rejected the breechloaders and repeaters as unsafe, more liable to breakage, and more difficult to repair. The best of the lot, Hall's rifle, was dismissed with the comment, "an arm which is complicated in its mechanism and arrangement deranges and perplexes the soldier." It is little wonder that four years later, Hall, who lost money in his effort to produce a breechloader, gave up on his rifle.[6]

The one objection against these new firearms that would be repeated continually for the next thirty years was the assurance of military men that a rapid-fire gun would lead troops to waste ammunition: "It is the opinion of the board that a larger proportion of fire from rapidly repeating guns would be thrown away than from those that receive but one charge at a time." Rapid fire diminished the steadiness and deliberation that encouraged good, effective shooting in volleys. The board was also unimpressed with percussion caps, noting that "the difficulty of placing an object so small as the cap, during the excitement of action, in excessively cold weather, and in dark nights, has prevented this improvement in fire-arms" from use in the military. They were also dangerous, liable to explode. The board thought that these gunmakers, Hall included, allowed their "desire to reach perfection in construction of the arms," to overlook "the convenience, physical power, and safety of those who are to use them." In other words, it was all a fad.[7]

The U.S. military found it hard to accept that there was ample room for improvement in firearms. The basic flintlock still used by the U.S. Army in the Mexican War differed little from the Brown Bess of the early eighteenth century. Little wonder then that the bayonet, not the musket, was perceived and used as the decisive military weapon. Contemporaries sensed that the vast majority of musket shots did not hit their targets, and a few studies confirmed this impression. Studies of battles in the century spanning the Seven Years' War to the Crimean War indicate that, at best, 5 percent of all projectiles fired actually inflicted casualties. At the siege of Gibraltar in 1781 two hundred shots were fired per man hit. In the Battle of Vitoria in 1813, the British fired more than 3.5 million rounds, killing and wounding eight thousand of their enemy, a rate of 460 rounds per casualty. In the Battle of Churubusco during the Mexican War, the Mexicans had a ratio of 800 shots fired per man hit, compared to the American ratio of 125 shots per Mexican casualty. All sides in the Crimean War fired nearly one thousand shots per casualty. The one thing the U.S. Army did not want was for its soldiers to aim their guns; even the rifles made at the national armories had fixed sights, meaning that the individual could not elevate the sight to adjust for distance. Volley fire inflicted an effective psychological shock, but it was the ensuing bayonet charge that persuaded the other side to flee the field. Napoleon noted that the value of morale outweighed material in a battle by a factor of three to one. The point therefore was to demoralize the enemy as quickly as possible. American military forces adhered to this logic into the Civil War, ignoring some of the most important technological changes in the history of firearms.[8]

In 1822 Joshua Shaw patented the percussion cap, which he had been working on for over eight years. As noted, the Ordnance Board rejected the cap's utility in 1836, and experts argued over its value well into the 1850s. In 1844 the national adjutant general's office issued instructions on how to use the new muskets with percussion caps, noting that many militia were adopting the percussion system, though the adjutant general did not recommend their use. Even after most gentlemen hunters had finally accepted Shaw's invention, the U.S. Army continued to issue outdated weapons; four-fifths of the troops in the Mexican War were armed with flintlock muskets, and the national armories did not halt production of the flintlock until 1848. Secretary of War Joel Poinsett rejected all these improvements in 1840 with the flat statement that "every attempt to increase the rapidity of fire will fail, . . . after involving the government in great expense."[9]

Simeon North, probably the greatest gunmaker of the 1820s, developed a multiple-shot musket in 1825, followed in 1828 by a similar development by Reuben Ellis, but the gun did not find a market, and production ceased after a few years. In the 1830s the Reverend John Somerville created several safety features to prevent the accidental discharge of firearms, including the slide stop or catch—what is now called a safety. Again, this innovation evoked little enthusiasm from gunmakers. Many other developments in the 1830s sought to prevent explosions and other accidents in guns. In 1842 came the percussion lock, which could have completely transformed gun use in America; but experts in and out of the military rejected it as too dangerous.[10]

The more established gunmakers and the national armories also demonstrated a hesitancy to adopt the new technologies. They had their formula and intended to stick to it. Until 1842 the official U.S. military smooth-bore remained the French Charleville Model 1763 adopted during the Revolution. The armories and arms manufacturers displayed a deep-seated fear of change for perfectly sound reasons. Contract arms made for the government had to equal those made at national armories, and pattern arms rather than blueprints were used. Obviously, then, any change to the pattern might lose a valuable contract and would prove expensive to the private gunmakers and the armories, as both would have to retool. In 1817, well before any of the truly significant changes in gun production became available, Roswell Lee, the superintendent of the Springfield armory, wrote the Ordnance Department rejecting all proposals for change: "After experiencing the inconveniences and noticing the immense expense of frequently changing the model of muskets in this establishment, I have come to the conclusion that it is better to adhere to an uniform pattern than to be frequently changing, although the model may not be the most perfect." Most gunmakers resisted the modernization of firearms.[11]

The new technical improvements did find an interested audience among gun enthusiasts, many of whom perceived sure signs of human progress in better guns. An 1837 article in the *American Magazine of Useful and Entertaining Knowledge* praised an invention by John W. Cochran as likely to transform human society for the better. His invention was a repeating rifle. The magazine admitted that, "If the consequences of such improvements" in firearms was "to make wars more destructive, or to induce nations to engage in them with less reluctance, we would wish for no improvements. But the tendency of all improvements of this nature, is to make nations more cautious in commencing a war and also in carrying it on." They gave as an example the invention of gunpowder, which demonstrates that "Wars in modern times, though complicated with horrors at the thought of which humanity shudders, are far less destructive and carried on with far less ferocity than formerly, when less effective weapons were in use." That improvements in gun technology all enhance the defensive qualities of weaponry rather than the offensive "affords the lovers of peace good grounds to congratulate each other in the prospect that war may eventually become useless and unpopular." Unfortunately Cochran would have to seek financial support for his inventions abroad, the article noted, as Americans had shown no inclination to "reward those inventive powers" of gun innovators.[12]

By the 1850s this argument that gunpowder diminished "the frequency, duration, and destructiveness of wars" had become an article of faith among all forward-looking men. In 1852 the *Hartford Daily Times* praised Samuel Colt's revolver as just the latest example of how "men of science can do no greater service to humanity than by adding to the efficiency of warlike implements, so that the people and nations may find stronger inducements than naked moral suasion to lead them towards peace." This belief demonstrates an amazing tenacity.[13]

The Mexican War made the career of the most innovative gunmaker of the nineteenth century. Samuel Colt, like most New Englanders, opposed the war as an imperialist enterprise. But when the Texan captain Sam Walker arrived at Colt's Boston hotel room with a commission from General Zachary Taylor to buy one thousand Colt revolvers, Colt's sympathies shifted on the spot. Colt failed to tell Walker that his Patent Arms Manufacturing Company of Paterson, New Jersey, had gone bankrupt in 1843 and that he no longer had a factory where he could make the revolvers, but he intended to fulfill the contract. He did so by paying Eli Whitney Jr. and Thomas Warner to make the parts for him, and then Colt assembled the pistols himself. The war ended too soon for this enterprise to grow much beyond the initial order of one thousand revolvers, and Colt made little money from the effort. That hardly mattered to Samuel Colt, for whom the war was his greatest publicity coup. From 1847 on Colt traveled the world telling anyone who would listen how his revolvers, though few in number, had led the United States to victory over superior Mexican forces—he had woodcuts of battle scenes made to prove it. It was astounding how many people believed him.[14]

In 1848 Samuel Colt opened a new gun factory in his hometown of Hartford. Few pistols had been made in the United States prior to the opening of the Hartford factory, pistols having found little market beyond the officers in the army and navy.[15] Colt initially appealed to the gentlemen hunters with his elegant revolvers, but his ambitions demanded a broader market. Colt had hit on the perfect weapon for a gun culture: his revolvers were relatively inexpensive; fired several rounds quickly, negating the need for skill; were perfect for urban life, being easy to conceal; had no function other than "self-defense," being useful neither in hunting nor militia service; and, in short, were clearly intended for personal use in violent situations. Colt also did all he could to link his revolver with an image of the heroic frontier and to find a market for his guns among the migrants heading west. He populated the Great Plains with "hordes of aborigines" who launched massive suicide attacks upon innocent travelers on the overland trail and soldiers, attempting to "overwhelm small bodies of American soldiers by rushing down on them in . . . superior numbers." Against these savages the "enterprising pioneer" stood alone, only "his personal ability" with a gun standing between his family and death. It was a masterfully crafted mythology that has enraptured generations of moviemakers and historians. Many scholars, turning to the image of the Colt revolver, have argued that the frontier pushed the technological development of firearms. In a thesis repeated by many scholars, Walter Prescott Webb argued that the revolver was a natural outgrowth of westward expansion from woodlands to grasslands and the need in the latter for mounted combat. Yet Colt invented his revolver at sea and developed it in New Jersey and Connecticut, making the connection to the frontier tenuous at best.[16]

Colt also took advantage of the 1847 decision of the Texas Rangers to replace their flintlock pistols with Colt revolvers. From that date forward his advertisements in eastern newspapers made every possible reference to the brave Rangers and their preference for Colt revolvers. An 1850 flier quoted a Texas Ranger: "We state, and with entire assurance of the fact, that your six-shooter is the arm which has rendered the name of Texas Ranger a check and terror to bands of our frontier Indians." Such an assertion led Carl P. Russell to state that "only the Colt is strongly in evidence as the arm which marked the turning point in Indian warfare in the Far West by giving the white man superiority." But while Colt used the frontier image at every turn, his sales were concentrated in the East.[17]

Colt spent a great deal of energy attempting to rope in the biggest customer of all, the U.S. military. As he once told a committee of Parliament, "government patronage . . . is an advertisement, if nothing else." But the military continually rebuffed Colt firearms because they failed their performance tests in 1836, 1837, 1840, and 1850. In the latter test, the Ordnance Board considered and rejected Colt's revolver as much too complicated for military use. Ordnance Chief George Talcott wrote that "Colt's pistols may be used to advantage in the hands of skillful or careful men," but the pistol is "calculated and suitable for personal defense alone," and will find little military application. A revolver "cannot be advantageously used by the mass of our private soldiers for want of the necessary discretion, coolness, and skill."[18]

Unable to discover a large demand for such weaponry, Samuel Colt tried to create one through the cleverest advertising yet seen in America. Colt made available to the average American for the first time one of the premier status symbols of the elite, the beautifully crafted firearm. In a stroke of genius, Colt was the first entrepreneur to apply Waterman Ormsby's grammagraph to a mass-produced item. Ormsby had figured out a way to engrave the same design repeatedly on steel using a roll-die. The grammagraph worked perfectly on Colt's revolvers, transferring onto the gun such heroic scenes as a man protecting his wife and child against a pack of savage Indians, armed only with a Colt revolver. These scenes, mostly the product of Gustave Young's imagination (one features centaurs armed with Colt revolvers), were engraved on the distinctive blue-black metal of Colt's firearms, the product of "bluing," the chemical cooling of steel, which protects against rust. Replacing cast iron with steel, which was declining in price in the 1850s, reduced at one stroke the need for constant gun care. Colt filled eastern newspapers with advertisements identifying his revolver with the romance of the West, commissioning artist George Catlin to craft beautiful portraits of himself hunting buffalo with a Colt revolver. His most ingenious move was to include instructions, carefully printed on the cleaning rag that came with every Colt firearm; he realized that most Americans did not actually know how to use a gun. Colt discovered that the public would pay more than the government for the nearly half of his total production that failed to meet military standards.[19]

But Colt's best customers were governments—not, however, his own. The majority of his sales in the 1850s were to foreign governments, often enemies in the midst of war. Colt's demonstration and display at the Great Exhibition (the Crystal Palace) in London in 1851 made his reputation. He delivered a talk before London's Institution of Civil Engineers on the use of machines in gunmaking and was the first American elected to membership in that body, which also awarded him their Telford Medal. Understanding that he was his company's best salesman, Colt returned to Europe in 1852 to visit the nations gearing up for a conflict over the Crimea. He sold five thousand pistols to the Russian government by telling them that the Turks were buying his pistols. He then went to Constantinople and told the sultan the same thing. Turkey ordered five thousand pistols as well. Colt lectured the British government that they would drive the Russians from Sebastopol if they only supplied all of Lord Raglan's troops with Colt revolvers. At the same time he promised the Russians that a properly armed Russian force would sweep the Allies from the Crimea. Colt understood that the end of the Crimean War would bring a business slump, so he was hoping to encourage further business in other ways. Even as he was closing a deal with the Austrian government, Colt was presenting engraved revolvers to the revolutionary leaders Kossuth and Garibaldi. Colt instructed his agents to help the pair in any way they could, including augmenting their public meetings with hired crowds. These efforts paid off, as the frightened Austrian government purchased more Colt guns. His best customers, though, were Britain and, curiously, Mexico.[20]

Colt's other great technological contribution to gunmaking was his remarkably successful application of machine production to what remained essentially an artisanal craft. His drilling, jigging, and stocking machines were state-of-the-art, and attracted the attention of the U.S. government, other gun manufacturers, and the British Parliament. The jigging machine, which allowed the worker to attach a number of different cutting tools, freed Colt from the long-term dependence of all American gunmakers on English locks. For the first time, an American gunmaker manufactured gun locks equal to anything in Great Britain, and in great numbers. Colt's guns did not become truly interchangeable until the Civil War, but he did attain levels of gun production unsurpassed in American history. By 1860 Colt had the largest gun factory in the United States, employing 369 workers and making as many guns as every private manufacturer in the country in 1840. So many people wanted to visit his factories that he issued tickets. Prominent writers, including Charles Dickens, wrote articles on his factories and machine-made guns—for which Colt rewarded them amply. And briefly, from 1853 until 1857, Colt had done the unthinkable: operated a gun manufactory in England.[21]

Interchangeable production had first been attained through the cooperation of George Bomford of Harpers Ferry and Simeon North at his nearby gun factory in 1834. But it took Cyrus Buckland's gauges to make the Springfield firearms truly interchangeable in 1850. Colt tried, but could not replicate this process. Parts for his pistols were machine made and immediately filed and fitted by artisans. Each part was stamped with matching serial numbers so that they could be reassembled. The parts were machine made, but the Colt revolver, like all other guns in America, remained handmade.[22]

During the 1850s the production of revolvers skyrocketed, increasing from a few hundred a year to tens of thousands, largely thanks to Colt and the fact that Congress refused to renew his patent in 1857. Other companies, such as Remington, Starr, and Whitney, immediately rushed revolvers into production. Another new firm, Smith & Wesson, entered the revolver business after Colt lost his patent. The Smith & Wesson revolver was the first American gun to use the new metal cartridges, an entirely self-contained bullet similar to those in use today. That Smith & Wesson used it first was the product of Samuel Colt's one great error, for it was one of his workers, Rolin White, who invented the metallic cartridge. But Colt failed to realize its value and allowed White to shop it around.[23]

The 1850s witnessed a slower increase in the production of rifles, but a notable shift nonetheless. In the mid-1840s the rifle was more difficult to make and to use. Most gunmakers found rifling the barrel far too difficult, which raised the price beyond what most people were willing to spend. Similarly, loading a rifle was time-consuming and required a degree of skill. In addition, rifles became clogged with powder residue more quickly than muskets, with most experts recommending that the barrel be cleaned after every four shots. Neither private citizens nor the military showed much interest in the rifle.[24]

The leading book on the subject, Newton Bosworth's *Treatise on the Rifle*, published in 1846, found it necessary to defend the rifle as a useful weapon. Bosworth declared that "the rifle is the hero of my work," while a "perfect rifle"—which is attained when the shooter "treats his rifle as a friend"—was correctly seen as more than a weapon; it was "a philosophical instrument." Bosworth bemoaned the absence of technical change in the previous century and called upon the federal government to support and reward those seeking innovation.[25]

Bosworth accurately identified the basic problem with the rifle as the bullet. The bullet had to fit tightly into the barrel, and therefore had to be rammed home, taking more time and creating a potential danger if it became stuck when the powder exploded. Bosworth's hoped-for technological breakthrough came just three years after he published his book, but in France rather than the United States. In 1849 Captain Claude-Étienne Minié patented a conical bullet with a hollow base and a diameter smaller than the barrel's, which allowed it to be dropped into the rifle; when fired, the base expanded to a perfect fit with the rifling. With Minié's breakthrough it was possible to fire a rifle rapidly without concern of a dangerous clogging of the barrel. The Minié bullet spelled the end of the smooth bore.[26]

Ordnance Board tests on the new rifle bullets conducted in 1854 and 1855 demonstrated their worth, but Secretary of War Jefferson Davis urged "great caution" before manufacturing a new gun to take advantage of the conical bullet. A rifled musket, Model 1855, was planned, but production was delayed until further tests could be conducted the following year. Comparing smooth-bore muskets and rifles, with professional soldiers shooting at a ten-foot-square target at different distances and in different forms (volleys, by files, individual), revealed the superiority of the rifle, though the advantage was still not that impressive. At two hundred yards, twenty-four of the fifty soldiers shooting the rifles could hit the hundred-square-foot target, and only three hit within the two-foot-by-six-foot bull's-eye. These were individual shots; the volley shooting found that only eighteen of the soldiers could hit the giant target.[27] These findings matched contemporary European tests. French soldiers using fixed gun rests could hit a five-foot-by-nine-foot target 60 percent of the time at eighty-two yards. German marksmen, using cutouts of cavalry at one hundred yards, hit 53 percent of the time, 30 percent at two hundred yards; ordinary soldiers had rates of 40 percent and 18 percent. These tests also indicated that the musket ball lost considerable force in traveling beyond fifty yards. Nothing had changed the physics of guns: balls from smooth-bored guns had irregular flights because they tumbled, while rifling impelled a spin that prevented the ball from tumbling. These tests persuaded the War Department to order an end to the production of smooth-bore muskets in 1856 and the immediate alteration of its entire stock of six hundred thousand firearms to percussion locks and the rifling of all smooth-bore muskets. They also ordered the armories to begin manufacturing the Model 1855 rifled musket—just in time so far as the future of the Union was concerned.[28]

The technology may have improved considerably by 1850, but the manufacturing of firearms remained locked in the eighteenth century. Hindrances of several kind persisted. Ordnance officers and gun experts agreed that the iron used in the construction of guns in the United States was often of the poorest quality, with the English getting the best. Those hoping for an improvement in American armaments felt that the government should take over iron production as a matter of national defense, yet the national armories were having no better luck acquiring high-grade iron, and steel was just too expensive for use in firearms. The far larger problem remained the lack of skilled workers. With guns still made by hand, the task required trained workers, and by the late 1840s the national armories were in stiff competition with the expanding gunmaking firms of New England for the limited number of skilled workers.[29]

Workers had good reason for seeking a job at the Springfield armory. The government armories pioneered the modern labor system, shifting from piecework to a wage scale and a ten-hour day, while those working for private armsmakers continued to labor for twelve hours, six days a week. From 1817 the armories even had a relief system for those temporarily incapacitated. The Springfield armory consistently had more applicants than positions; until 1833 workers held their positions as fungible rights that could be sold or inherited. Except for the last detail, Colt replicated many of the welfare practices of Springfield, adding a few innovations of his own, in order to attract the best workers.[30]

Until the Mexican War, then, guns were tools, luxury items, or broken relics; they were either mass-produced for the military or handmade for specific customers rather than for general sale. Dictionaries even defined a musket as a tool of war, "a fire-arm borne on the shoulder, and used in war." The notion of private gun ownership remained confined to a specific class, with firearms widely perceived as expensive and complicated mechanisms of limited applicability. A truism, repeated "by the best gunmakers," ran that no two guns were alike, not even the double barrels of a single shotgun.[31] Guns remained the product of individual craftsmanship throughout the first half of the nineteenth century, handmade by highly skilled artisans. Hand cranks, foot treadles, treadmills, and water wheels supplied the power for such crude machinery as the pole lathe and rifling bench, and most locks were still imported from Europe into the 1840s. Axes and scythes made up the greater part of any smith's business, and demand for firearms practically vanished when the country was not at war.[32]

The termination of the War Department's contract system in the late 1830s led a number of once-prominent gunmakers—including Simeon North, Asa Waters, and Lemuel Pomeroy—to go out of business. The end of government subsidies and purchases meant there was simply not enough demand for guns to keep these manufacturers in business. After the Mexican War the government did come slowly to support those experimenting with new technology, the so-called patent manufacturers of weapons like the Colt revolver and Sharps rifle. These innovators also benefited from a half-century of government-supported technological development at the national armories. Major James Wolfe Ripley, superintendent of the Springfield armory for much of the 1850s, resented this service, charging that the patent companies "owe many of their modifications and much of their successful working to the ingenuity and skill of the mechanics in government employ, for which the inventor obtains all the compensation and lays claim to all the credit."[33]

The 1850s saw a notable growth in gun production throughout the United States. A number of once-small gunshops expanded considerably, especially in Connecticut and Pennsylvania. Henry Leman was one of a dozen gunmakers in Lancaster, Pennsylvania, in the 1830s. During the 1840s his business slowly expanded on the basis of his government contracts for Indian trade guns. By 1850 he was calling his firm the Conestoga Rifle Works, employed thirty men, and claimed a capital investment of $18,000. The 1850 census listed his annual output at twenty-five hundred rifles. By the 1860 census Leman employed sixty workers in a plant valued at $30,000 that used steam power to produce five thousand guns a year. The 1860 census found 239 gunmakers in America, employing a total of 2,056 workers, or 8.6 workers per site. The nine largest private firms, all in Connecticut, employed 969 workers, or an average of 108 workers. Absent these nine firms and the two national armories, and the average gunmaking plant employed four people.[34]

New England dominated arms manufacturing in the United States. As gunmaking factories grew, the need for ever greater numbers of skilled workers and large amounts of capital helped to concentrate production in the Connecticut River Valley. In 1860 New England accounted for 55.2 percent of all the arms workers in the United States, 82.1 percent of the capital invested in armsmaking, and nearly 85 percent of all the guns made in America.[35] Much of the remaining value of guns produced nationally was concentrated at Harpers Ferry. Elsewhere in the country gunmaking remained a matter of small-scale operations. Out in California, at the height of its wildest frontier years, there were only two gunsmiths: James McDowell, who arrived in 1845 at Sutter's Mill, and Henry Huber, who set up shop in San Francisco in 1847. Neither man made guns, limiting service to repairs. Newspaper advertisements indicate that as the number of gunshops increased in the 1850s, they sold guns made in Europe or the eastern United States, not local productions.[36]

In the early 1850s, with tens of thousands of privately made firearms available for the first time, cities all over the country witnessed the opening of gunshops that sold solely guns and their accessories. The level of specialization reached a point by the end of the decade that competing shops became agents for Remington or Colt. But only Massachusetts and New York made any effort to modernize their armaments, despite the fact that all the states were weighed down by ancient musketry. In 1853 Massachusetts's Adjutant General Ebenezer Stone reported that the state arsenal still had 800 entirely useless muskets from 1814, another 6,000 flintlock muskets that could be converted to the percussion system, perhaps, and 2,174 serviceable percussion muskets. But the state legislature did not share his sense of urgency, and decided to wait for the federal government to replace their archaic arms.[37]

The federal government attempted to promote this increased arms production by maintaining a stiff import duty of 30 percent on foreign-made guns until the start of the Civil War.[38] That their efforts paid off is evident by comparing two meticulous calculations of American manufacturing capacity undertaken by the secretary of the treasury's office in 1833 and 1858. In 1833 there were so few gun factories in the country that each could be easily listed by name. The report included Harpers Ferry and Springfield, which made 24,000 muskets that year. The states reported eleven gunmakers capitalized at $207,550 and employing 161 workers paid between $1 and $1.50 per day. These eleven factories made 21,000 muskets and rifles per year, plus an additional seven hundred gun barrels, all valued at $644,100. Rhode Island, Vermont, Delaware, and Maine specifically reported that they had no gunsmiths. American gunmaking, and record keeping, had changed remarkably by 1858. There were now 317 gunmaking facilities in the country, capitalized at $577,509, using $269,673 worth of raw materials and employing 1,547 workers at an annual pay of $518,292. Unfortunately, this account does not list the total number of arms made, but the total value of their production is given as $1,073,014, a 66 percent increase from 1833. With the average price of a gun running around $25, this figure indicates a total production of 42,920 guns; the two national armories added another 21,000 guns to the total. Obviously the government was taking greater care in counting all those involved in gunmaking in 1858 than ever before, and the 1833 count did not bother with gunsmiths who employed no additional workers. Nonetheless, the comparison of the two counts does give a valid indication of the increase in arms production in the late 1840s and 1850s.[39]

The first hindrance to arming America was swept away in the 1840s as American arms manufacturers reached new heights of productivity. Industry created the supply and encouraged the demand for firearms. Production took off in the 1850s with the organization of a series of large gun manufacturers: Colt, Sharps, Remington, Robbins and Lawrence, Smith & Wesson, and Winchester. But the government's participation was vital in this as in many other early industries: the federal government provided capital, patent protection, technological expertise, and the largest market for guns.[40]

The probate records from the late 1850s reinforce this portrait of increased gun use in America. Culminating a rapid rise through the 1840s and 1850s, guns appeared in just over 40 percent of all studied southern probate inventories by the end of the decade. Guns had become a regular feature of southern life by 1859, and were on their way to becoming so in the West as well, where nearly a third of all probate inventories contained firearms. Though the percentage of northern inventories containing guns actually dropped from the late 1840s to the late 1850s as a result of the phenomenal population growth of northern cities, the absolute number of guns in these records is notable. Also highly significant is the near disappearance of commentary on the condition of these firearms. By 1859 an old gun was unusual in the inventories, and one can almost read the surprise of the executors as they write "*very* old gun" or "*rusted* gun of some sort," underlining their distinction from the more common modern guns.[41]

The new technology attracted a great deal of attention and admiration in the 1850s, and the popular press ran a number of articles on the industrial production of guns. Some of these writers, however, wanted to assure their readers that they had nothing to fear from this mass production. Thus an 1852 article in *Harper's Magazine* on the Springfield Armory waxed enthusiastic about these new miracles of production, complete with gorgeous woodcuts and admiring commentary on the near perfection of these new weapons; and yet concluded with the affirmation that only a small number of "these terrible instruments of carnage and destruction . . . are destined ever to be used." Those actually distributed "are never called to any other service than to figure in peaceful drilling and parades," while the greater portion are "stored in the nations arsenals, where they lie, and are to lie, as we hope, forever, undisturbed."[42]

The new sudden growth of interest in firearms in the 1840s encouraged a few brilliant entrepreneurs to seek their fortunes in gunmaking. Samuel Colt exemplified and, in the public mind, led this new arms race; in 1860 his company made 27,374 pistols (the only gun Colt made at that time), compared to Remington's 1,000 and Starr's 200 that year.[43] By the late 1850s, foreign observers praised American gunmakers for their technological innovations. But more significantly, gunmakers convinced an ever-wider audience that they needed guns in order to be real Americans. By the middle of the decade, the subculture of firearms enthusiasts had become mainstream, with middle-class men joining prestigious militia units and hunting clubs, and with pistols becoming a popular murder weapon. Though the majority of adult white males remained ignorant of firearms and their use, a large minority of Americans found confidence in their guns and longed to demonstrate their proficiency. They would get their opportunity.

The Volunteer Militia Movement

While it is difficult to speak of cultures confined by state borders, a spectrum of attitudes toward firearms is evident in the nature of the support extended to the militia in the 1830s and 1840s. Officials of every state mouthed the platitudes of a militia as the bulwark of liberty even while decrying their lack of preparation. Yet with only a few exceptions, the state governments did not back up that ideal with action or money. Probably the least militaristic state was Delaware, which essentially eliminated its militia in 1811—excellent timing that. At the other extreme, the most consistent and effective supporter of its militia and the best-armed state in the union was Massachusetts. South Carolina and Kentucky reflect the paradoxes of American attitudes. South Carolina certainly was the most bellicose in its militarism, yet the elite remained terrified of the consequence of uncontrolled access to firearms, and its parsimonious legislature was unwilling to spend the funds necessary to support its militia effectively. As a frontier state, Kentucky was caught between its perceived need for a defensive military force and its relative poverty; in addition, the majority of its settlers had an overwhelming desire to appear civilized, as did the state's dominant politician, Henry Clay, exemplar of Whig propriety.

The southern and frontier states particularly suffered from a shortage of firearms for their militia. While a lower percentage of the adult white males may have owned guns in the Northeast, most domestic gun production was located in that region and more merchants with access to European sources were concentrated there. As William C. Davis wrote, "The Southwesterners never developed a true martial spirit. Only the social elite who paraded in gaudy uniforms in the cities' private militia companies ever developed any real love of regimented service, and even that was more for show than anything else." A southern joke making the rounds in the 1840s asked, "How would a Southerner defeat a well-armed Yankee?" The answer: "Buy his gun from him."[44]

Despite hunting enthusiasts and victory against Mexico, the official state militias remained dormant. There had been a slight rush of enthusiasm during the war itself, but even in the western states that surge of interest quickly died. Between 1846 and 1860, more than half the states used outdated militia figures to claim firearms from the federal government. Federal law required each state to submit an annual return listing the number of its active militia. In exchange, the federal government would supply firearms to the state for use by its military. Yet just eleven of the thirty-four eligible states and territories bothered to submit more than five returns during these fifteen years; only Massachusetts and New York came anywhere near the legal standard of a yearly return, issuing eleven and ten returns, respectively. All the states continued to rely on the federal government for their firearms, and yet the minimal effort of most of these states in claiming those guns kept the federal government from spending the $200,000 per year on firearms and accoutrements for state use mandated by the 1808 Militia Act in all but four of these years.[45]

State after state shut down its militia in the 1840s. Even the frontier militias collapsed in these years: Arkansas, Iowa, Wisconsin, and Texas struggled for some time, but all gave up eventually. Regardless of fears of slave uprisings, North Carolina pulled the plug in 1850. For many communities the withdrawal of state support for the militia terminated a number of traditions, from drunken musters to parades. *Record of the Times,* a newspaper in the Wyoming Valley of Pennsylvania, reported in 1855 on the complete absence of militia in the region, adding that "It will be a sad thing, to be without soldiers on the fourth of July."[46]

Those state governments that continued to express any interest in the militia did so in the face of a persistent public apathy and outright hostility aroused by opposition to the Mexican War. Though New York's executive branch continued its support for the militia, the legislature abolished militia parades in 1852. Massachusetts, which most observers agreed had the best militia in the country, found that the number of officially enrolled members of the militia grew slowly in the 1840s, while those showing up for the musters, the "active militia," kept shrinking. In 1840, when the *Quincy Patriot* already worried that the militia "have been on the retrograde march," there were 83,602 enrolled militia, 7,255 (8.7 percent) of whom appeared for muster; in 1850 the figures were 110,050 enrolled and 4,791 active (4.4 percent). When the adjutant general ordered in 1858 that all companies with fewer than thirty-two privates should disband, one-third of the state's active companies ceased to exist.[47]

In some states it seemed that the militia continued to function solely as a source of titles—a charge leveled against New York's 1857 militia law for allowing any man who had served in the militia for twenty years to become automatically a colonel. When the Indiana legislature hoped to attract more interest in the militia in 1855 by creating lots of officers, the adjutant general sadly admitted that, while "We have sowed commissions broadcast through the state," it was all to no purpose: "Our desires fell off from an entire reorganization to simply a new enumeration, yet even in these modest efforts we have signally failed, and we have to abide by the enumeration of 1833." Even Virginia, the most militarily active of the southern states, effectively terminated its militia in 1853, after watching the militia shrink every year since the end of the Mexican War. By 1856 the state could field 105 cavalry and a seventy-five-man artillery company; no one wanted to serve in the infantry.[48]

Though the majority of Americans showed not the least bit of interest in guns or their possible uses, in the afterglow of the Mexican War militarism did spread in an unexpected place. Just as hunting had gained popularity during the previous decade among the middle and upper classes, so a fascination with the military and their weapons found favor with many of the same people. By the mid-1850s a military subculture was firmly in place, "a broad military brotherhood," as one historian labeled it, seeing itself separate and with interests distinct from "civilians." In the 1850s the traditional structure of the universal militia that had collapsed in 1815 was replaced by a series of volunteer companies supported by the state. Public disinterest had undermined the federal government's arms-giveaway program; as militia companies disintegrated in the 1830s, Washington found few takers for its free guns. The government needed a constituency for its arms program and found it in middle-class militarists. From 1840 on, presidential speeches continued to praise the concept of the militia, but encouraged volunteer companies as the only way of maintaining that institution. These companies, most common in the cities, usually organized along ethnic or class lines and no longer represented the larger community.[49]

But just as they sought to separate hunting from its plebeian American roots, so urban militia companies rejected the traditional republican ideal of universal citizen service and embraced the notion of elite volunteer companies, fostering the emerging gun subculture. Volunteers purchased colorful uniforms and shining new swords; they acquired their guns from the government. In some states the volunteer companies led efforts to revise state support for the militia, so long as it was the volunteer militia that received the benefits. Though small in number, the volunteer militia included some of the most respectable citizens in the state. In New York the elite 7th Regiment took advantage of the temporary enthusiasm generated by the Mexican War to pressure the legislature into passing a new militia act in 1847 that recognized the legitimacy of the uniformed militia and gave them priority in the distribution of firearms.[50] Its membership intended the volunteer militia to be exclusive, not large. Under the standard militia, regiments tended to have between seven hundred and one thousand members. In 1848 New York's 7th Regiment, one of the most successful in the country, mustered 328 men; several companies lost half their membership to gold fever the following year, as young men went out to California to try their luck. The regiment grew to a peak of 519 active members in 1853. Curiously, the single largest company was the regimental band, which had sixty-nine members.[51]

The volunteer movement got off the ground in Massachusetts. The state legislature finally got tired of trying to make its tradition-bound but nearly invisible militia system work, so in 1840 it created a volunteer militia. A new "active militia" of no more than ten thousand soldiers would form the core of this reorganized structure, with all other adult males theoretically enrolled in the inactive "enrolled militia."[52] The state also acknowledged its other key problem of arming these soldiers by no longer requiring each soldier to supply his own musket; the new volunteer militia companies were to apply to the adjutant general's office for arms, which they were required to maintain. The volunteers were thus not only better armed than the old militia, but they kept their arms in good repair—a striking innovation. Volunteer companies attracted those who valued guns and enjoyed the military style, and the state rewarded them with all the arms they needed. Within four years the state had issued more than ten thousand of its seventeen thousand muskets to the active militia.[53]

While these uniform companies focused their energies on firearms more than most Americans, there is little evidence that they were ever very good with them. They certainly kept them well polished, but after the Mexican War interest in target practice waned. With New York's 7th Regiment, "the annual target-excursions of military organizations . . . rapidly decline[d] in popular favor. After the year 1848 such excursions by the companies of the Seventh Regiment were rare, and soon ceased entirely." The 7th Regiment had abandoned target practice for much the same reason as had most of their predecessors: they found that practicing even twice a year did "not make them expert marksmen." By the 1850s "the citizen soldier, however well instructed in the manual of arms, rarely had an opportunity to load or fire a musket." Not even during the crisis of 1861 did the 7th Regiment make any plans for shooting at targets. Until 1872, when target shooting began at Creedmoor, New York, "there were frequent instances of militiamen performing faithfully a full term of seven years' service without discharging a gun."[54]

Just as in the past, uniforms remained the single most important issue for militia companies. The decision to stop target shooting passed without dissent, but the argument over a new uniform led to a schism in New York's 13th Regiment in 1858. Hartford's Putnam Phalanx, which was founded in 1858 and included Sam Colt among its members, wore Revolution-era uniforms in honor of General Israel Putnam. The militia may well have been "the palladium of liberty," but revelry was its true purpose and chief activity. As Edward McCrady reported to the South Carolina legislature in 1859, "the success of a Volunteer Corps depends upon its perfection as a social club."[55]

The United States had moved far from the militia heritage. These companies included a small minority of the community, were usually organized along ethnic and class lines, and demonstrated a new and disturbing willingness to use their guns against their fellow citizens. The inherent danger of having a few better-armed volunteer militia units emerged quickly. The competition among volunteer companies could get tense. In 1848 New York's 1st Division held its first parade. In marching through the streets of New York City, the 2nd Regiment tried to pass the 7th, which led to a battle between the two. But fortunately the two regiments used their muskets only to shove one another. The 7th bullied their way to the lead, thereby earning a reputation for a "belligerent spirit." The parade did hint, however, at some future problems of supplying even well-to-do young men with firearms.[56]

Far more troubling were events in Philadelphia in 1844. What started as a rather traditional riot, with shoving, intimidation, and rock throwing, devolved into a battle between nativist, Irish, and state militia that ended with twelve deaths and at least forty-three wounded. The 1849 Astor Place Riot demonstrated clearly the widening class barriers between the volunteers and the broader citizenry that once constituted the militia. It began as a protest against an English actor and the pretensions of the city's elite. When the police could not restrain the huge crowd in Astor Place, they sent for the militia. Just over two hundred members of the 7th Regiment forced their way to the front of the theater, and turned to face the largest crowd yet assembled in the city's history, perhaps as many as twenty thousand people. The crowd began throwing rocks at the militia; the mayor refused to give General Hall the order to fire and then vanished, leaving Sheriff Westervelt in charge, who did give the order. The 7th Regiment fired their *loaded* muskets above the heads of the crowd, seemingly forgetting that the shots had to come down someplace, such as on innocent onlookers behind the crowd. When the crowd continued to throw rocks, Hall ordered a second volley and the crowd fled in terror. The militia's fire killed twenty-two people and seriously injured another fifty; fifty-three militiamen were injured and thirty-one of their muskets broken by thrown rocks. One minor but telling effect of the Astor Place Riot was that the 7th Regiment immediately required its sergeants to carry muskets rather than swords. For the first time, American militia showed itself willing to open fire on unarmed fellow citizens.[57]

But those citizens did not remain completely unarmed for long. Starting in the 1850s, the crowd demonstrated a newfound willingness to fire back. In 1853 the Cincinnati police attacked an anti-Catholic demonstration consisting mostly of Germans, beating one member of the crowd to death. Someone in the crowd fired a gun, and a police officer fell dead. In 1857, during an election riot in Chicago, a German crowd exchanged shots with the police, leaving one of the Germans dead. In each instance the community responded quickly to try to put an end to the violence, which they saw as having reached extreme levels.[58] The volunteer militia companies used the increased number of riots in the 1850s to justify their requests for government support. Essentially the uniform companies presented themselves as the only force standing between the state and chaos. Leaders of the volunteer movement reinvented the militia tradition, scrapping appeals to the heroism of Bunker Hill in favor of the terror of urban mobs.[59]

Some states hesitated to grant a group of volunteers the power to fire upon their fellow citizens. New York required that volunteer companies keep their guns in armories or drill rooms rather than at home in order to avoid any unauthorized firings. The state had the right to determine where individuals kept their guns, and in 1834 the New York legislature thought that volunteer militia should call upon their arms only for musters and public emergencies. In return, the state granted a lifetime exemption from jury duty and paid for an armorer to care for each regiment's weapons, freeing the volunteers from a task few enjoyed, or performed.[60]

Despite the advantage of having others care for the guns, it appears that most volunteers felt that guns, even though provided by the state, should be distributed to the individual for safekeeping. What started as a gift became a right. Some justified this logic on the simple grounds that armories made easy targets for insurgents, a position that proved especially persuasive in the South. Other enthusiasts offered more ideological justifications. The practice of keeping state arms in armories, editorialized the *Citizen Soldier,* "is dangerous to civil liberty." If this practice became general, citizens "would have no longer any guarantee of their rights. . . . [For] suppose . . . the rulers become corrupt, and wish to perpetuate their power, or establish an aristocracy. They have only, the state arms being within their control, to recall them, under some plausible pre-text or other, and the people are left defenseless." Acknowledging that the majority of people did not own guns and holding that the state should arm the people for their own defense against the state, the *Citizen Soldier* also admitted its fear of the foreign-born as a threat to order. Volunteer militia should be given state arms "neither for anarchy or revolution . . . but as a preventative for both." Uniform companies needed state arms to battle "popular insurrection."[61]

Only on this last point did the *Citizen Soldier*'s position find much res-onance. Most members of the volunteer militia movement upheld an older ideal of the state as the ultimate symbol of the people's will. And since the government expressed that will, no one could legitimately resist its authority. An 1836 act of the New York legislature clarified the duties of the volunteer militia as aiding the authorities "to quell riots, suppress insurrection, to protect the property, or preserve the tranquillity" of the state. The nature of that tranquillity was well revealed in 1840, when workers on the new Croton waterworks struck for higher wages. Twice the city called upon the volunteer 27th Regiment to protect the scabs, and on both occasions the crowd dispersed immediately, the strike collapsing before this show of force.[62]

The volunteer companies even found that firing on crowds earned the support of the propertied class. The *Boston Evening Transcript* extended its support for the city's uniformed companies, observing that "there is an excellent, and unanimous feeling also, prevailing in the city, which goes directly to the suppression of all mobs." Would-be members of such a mob "may rest assured, it ever be necessary to call citizen soldiers into action, *ball* cartridges will be discharged *first,* and *blanks* afterwards."[63]

To their supporters, the volunteer militia upheld civic order. As New York City's Common Council resolved in their message of thanks to the 27th Regiment after the 1834 election riot, civic disorders "proved the necessity to the city of a well-disciplined militia in time of peace." General Morton concurred; riots showed "the necessity . . . of a well-regulated militia, prepared at all times to support the magistracy in sustaining law and order in the community."[64] Back in 1829 Governor Gideon Tomlin-son, requesting state funds for arming the militia, had told the Connecti-cut assembly: "No danger exists, that arms placed in the hands of the whole body of the enrolled citizens, will be used for the suicidal purpose of subverting their own happiness by overthrowing the governments they have established." Roughly the same message was repeated by each of

Tomlinson's successors, as they struggled to keep the militia alive by offering state arms for service. The state government perceived little choice as, in the words of Governor Henry W. Edwards, only the militia could be "called upon to aid the civil power in the preservation of the public peace in time of great local excitement." In 1846 Governor Isaac Toucey told the legislature that only the militia protected "the security of person and property, the supremacy of law and order." But the vast majority of citizens would not serve. Given popular reluctance, the state had no choice but to turn to volunteers, who would gladly serve if given guns by the state.[65]

Some Americans angrily rejected the use of troops for law enforcement. An editorial in the *United States Magazine* in 1849 proclaimed that "the bayonet and cartridge are not elements of the administration of American laws." But with only six American cities having uniformed police forces by 1860, the volunteer militia served in the place of police in the fast-growing cities. It was not until 1857 that Baltimore became the first city to authorize its police to use firearms, but only "in emergencies." New Orleans's sheriff, in refusing to allow his officers to carry guns, offered a different vision in 1861: "nothing would ever put an end to the murders, manslaughters, and deadly assaults, till it was made penal to carry arms."[66]

The 1857 New York City police riots reflect the centrality of the volunteer companies to civic order, as well as revealing the increased use of guns. Until that year, the police had carried truncheons and found them sufficient. A study of complaints against the New York police between 1845 and 1854 reveals not a single shooting incident. But 1855 and 1856 witnessed a sudden rise in homicides in the city, with guns as the primary weapon. The *New York Times* and the New York police commissioners urged gun control legislation. In the midst of this debate, the state attempted to modernize the city's police by creating the Metropolitan Police force. Mayor Fernando Wood resisted this move and kept his Municipal Police on the streets. After a number of brawls between the two police forces, the Metropolitans laid siege to city hall. The 7th Regiment was marching to the pier to take a steamer for Boston when General William Hall ordered them into action to arrest Mayor Wood. When Wood saw the bayonets, he and his Municipal Police surrendered, the battle ended, and the Metropolitans took over law enforcement.

But in the midst of this strange scene of militia and two police forces battling for law and order, a gang war broke out between the Bowery

B'hoys and the Dead Rabbits. For the first time some police captains gave their officers permission to carry revolvers. It came as a nasty shock to the city when it discovered on July 14, as a result of an officer shooting an innocent bystander during a German riot in the 17th Ward, that some of their police were carrying concealed weapons. Several police captains condemned the use of firearms by their men, and Chief George W. Matsell "made it a standing rule to look upon every man as a coward and unfit to be put a second time on duty, where he had descended to the use of a pistol." The Metropolitan Police commissioners hoped to contain the use of firearms by creating a special armed riot squad, but public opposition to this idea continued into the 1870s. As a consequence, individual police continued to carry pistols, though without official sanction; they would appear in great numbers in 1863.[67]

Volunteer militia happily stepped into the role of the police in serving the security interests of the state. Members of the uniform companies often expressed contempt for common citizens who failed to support adequately the volunteer militia. A prime complaint was the failure of officials to collect the commutation fees from those who did not serve in the militia, the source of most funding for the volunteer companies. In New York no effort was made in the 1850s to collect this fifty-cent fee despite direct instructions to that effect from the New York Supreme Court and a federal court of appeals. This failure represented a great deal of money lost to the volunteers. The state's 3rd Brigade of regular militia officially had a total strength of 18,253 in 1853, but John S. Cocks, inspector for that brigade, reported that only 1,049 men (5.7 percent) appeared for the annual muster. In theory Cocks should have been able to raise $8,602 from those not attending. The reality was that the officials responsible for collecting the fees did not want to risk losing reelection. Cocks noted that this was the first inspection in years for the 3rd Brigade, and that it collapsed because of the tardiness even of those who did show up, leaving Cocks with barely enough time to line up the brigade and gather their names. Only one company was prepared to go further, and they proved unable to "execute the loading and firing" of their guns.[68]

But even worse than the regular militia, in the eyes of most volunteers, was the increased number of volunteer companies drawn from the immigrant population. The German immigrants played a particularly significant role in this regard. Great numbers of Germans came over after the failed revolutions of 1848 and organized themselves into shooting clubs and private militia companies. They also began hosting *schutzenfest,* formal shooting matches with prizes. Many scholars identify the *schutzenfest* as the first organized public shooting contests in the United States, with a match planned by Remington workers in Ilion, New York, in 1853 as the first non-German match. H. W. S. Cleveland, one of the leading gun experts of the period, wrote in 1862 that he had traveled widely on the frontier and that the "best target-shooting we have ever seen was in New England."[69]

In a few cities immigrant companies came to dominate the volunteer movement. For a brief period in 1853, four thousand of New York City's six thousand volunteer militiamen were foreign-born. Serving in a volunteer company gave immigrants the opportunity to become American while associating with cultural peers. It also gave them guns. It was the image of armed immigrants that so terrified the native-born elite. General Thomas Guyer warned Connecticut's Adjutant General E. W. N. Starr in 1852 that, "if we don't have some better legislation on military laws than we have had, the time is not far distant when we shall have little els[e] than adopted Citizens to quell riots mobs &c (generally created by the same)." The *Hartford Courant* was astounded that the state was paying to arm "bands of foreigners in our streets, . . . prepared at any moment to interfere decisively in behalf of their country-men." Several commentators referred to a confrontation on the night of January 22, 1844, between a nativist and German company, each of which wanted to use the drill room above New York's Centre Market. When the Germans began loading their muskets, the nativist company retreated; the peril seemed clear to many state officials.[70]

Nativist volunteer militia companies took advantage of these fears to get the various state governments to meet most of their expenses. The Connecticut volunteer companies adroitly manipulated the legislature not only into paying the volunteers $1.50 for every day they served, but also into supplying their arms and ammunition, paying armory rent, and granting lifetime exemptions from the poll tax. The complete lack of public interest in most things military and a blatant appeal to the legislature's fear of social disorder made it easy for the uniform companies to obtain funding and guns from state governments. The volunteers became an agency of the state under the government's directing authority—no longer representative of the people or community under local control.[71]

Most volunteer companies were self-consciously Yankee or Anglo-Saxon. But the fact that these Irish and German companies had an equal right to claim arms from the state proved sufficient to send most legislatures into paroxysms of alarm. Recent immigrants, who were perceived as inherently violent, particularly frightened the state governments. Connecticut Adjutant General Joseph D. Williams referred to them as "an ignorant and excitable population, many of whom do not comprehend the nature, or estimate the value of our institutions. . . . [S]uch a class of the community are apt to be easily stimulated by the acts of demagogues, or by their own ill regulated passions." And yet, at least in the state of Connecticut, the only large-scale violent incidents in the years from 1840 to 1860 were a pair of nativist attacks on Catholic churches.[72]

Despite the absence of any evidence of an immigrant threat to social order, the Know-Nothing candidate William T. Minor won election as governor of Connecticut in 1855 with the promise to disarm all foreign-born militia. Stating that "military organizations, composed entirely of those born on foreign soil, should not exist by the sanction of the law," Minor immediately disbanded six companies of volunteer militia, repossessing their firearms. Minor's successor was Know-Nothing Alexander H. Holley, who also kept the foreign-born out of the state militia. When one group of Germans applied to form a company in 1857 and earned the warm endorsement of the regiment's American-born colonel, the governor dismissed the petition out of hand. Holley's adjutant general supported the governor with the observation, "With a large increase among us of ignorant and excitable populations, it is not too much to say that we should at all times be prepared promptly to meet and to suppress the deeds of violence to which a class of the community are apt to be easily stimulated." As an example he offered the Astor Place Riot, in which New York's volunteer militia fired on an unarmed crowd.[73]

Connecticut was not alone in its fear of the foreign-born. As early as 1838 a group of twenty-one men withdrew from New York's 9th Regiment "on account of the predominance of the foreign element in that organization," and joined a nativist regiment. Throughout the country, volunteer "Yankee" companies formed in response to the presence of foreign-born companies such as New York's 71st Regiment, also known as the American Rifles, which was disarmed by the governor in 1852. Over the next three years other units had their guns taken from them, such as the 250 members of the Long Island Irish Volunteers. Know-Nothing governors, and even a few Whigs and Republicans, denied petitions from immigrants to form companies. Massachusetts governor Henry Gardner did not concern himself with legal complications when he declared his intention to "disband all military companies composed of persons of foreign birth." In the 1850s nativist companies could always rely on the state governments to supply firearms, while any company that accepted the foreign born was frozen out of this government largesse.[74]

Also ignored by the state governments were the few African American companies, which most legislatures perceived as illegal. The Militia Act of 1792 had specified that the militia would include only white males, and most states had restrictions on gun ownership by blacks, slave or free. Starting in the 1820s urban blacks attempted to circumvent this prohibition on their participation in the militia, and thus the limitation of their rights as citizens, by organizing volunteer companies. Their petitions to gain recognition were generally rejected.[75]

It is in this context that the sudden turn by the militarist journals to an examination of "street fighting" in the 1850s makes sense. One problem of special concern was how to determine friend from foe during an "insurrection of certain classes." The *Eclaireur* (which means mounted scout), edited by New York's Adjutant General J. Watts De Peyster, made these fears obvious. Insurrections from "the turbulent or fanatic neighborhoods" threatened to overwhelm "order, life and property, with the volcanic fury of Red Republicanism." The newspaper claimed that the United States, unlike the European governments, was at a real disadvantage in its ability to confront these new urban challenges because it lacked adequately armed troops. The volunteer militia companies must be prepared to respond immediately to this threat: "Instant and decided measures always compel submission. Temporizing, negotiating, and compromising, waste the force, moral and physical, of authority." De Peyster bluntly advised that troops must be ready to fire on civilians, even the unarmed in the process of fleeing. The mob "trust that troops, unless under the grossest provocation and injury, will show further forbearance, whereas mercy cannot be expected from a bullet." "The suppression of every dangerous riot in the city of New York has hitherto been awfully bungled," the *Eclaireur* declared; if the Astor Place rioters had been led by a capable leader, they could have taken over the city. To avoid such a danger, De Peyster called for a new arsenal in New York, one in an open area with a clear field of fire in case of attacks from the populace. He also promoted firing by ranks, called "street-firing."[76]

This obsession for order extended beyond fear of the foreign born. In the South, volunteer militia companies continued to act in conjunction with the older slave patrols to maintain racial order. William Sumner of Massachusetts pointed out to North Carolina's adjutant general, Beverly

Daniel, that "the slaveholding States require an organized and disciplined militia force more than us." While many southerners agreed, not even the fear of slave rebellion could motivate some states, including Florida and Texas, to offer anything more than verbal support to the militia. However, volunteer companies used the threat of slave uprisings to extort guns from their state governments, as when the Marengo Blues of Alabama asked the governor for guns by stating that "our principle object in raising the company was to enable us to get arms to guard against the extensive slave population in this vicinity."[77]

In the North especially, volunteer companies stood for middle-class propriety. The *Eclaireur* devoted extensive coverage to the June 1855 liquor riot in Portland, Maine. To the Yankee militiamen, this riot demonstrated yet again immigrant disorder, as the foreign-born battled against Maine's effort to prohibit alcohol. The *Eclaireur* expressed concern, however, not with the fact that the militia opened fire and killed one person, but with the news that one of the company commanders rejected Mayor Dow's command to fire on the unarmed crowd. Equally disturbing was the information that another company had no ammunition, a third had no cartridges, and a fourth no bayonets. The police, who were still unarmed, and the regular militia could not hope to confront "ruffians" who "only fear the bullet." A single well-armed volunteer unit had saved Portland from some unknown disaster.[78]

In the literature of the volunteer movement, northern and southern, the ideal militiaman looked like the ideal hunter: he should be a gentleman. Though they occasionally battled street toughs, the militia used the gentleman's weapon, a gun, to do so, and avoided descending to those indicators of lower-class violence, fists and knives. The militia journals held up the citizen soldier as the archetype of virile masculinity, in a fashion similar to the hunting magazines. But just as being a real man did not require one to be uncomfortable while hunting, so nothing in the male bonding of militia service necessitated such discomforts as getting wet; after all, most volunteer militia companies kept their headquarters in taverns for a reason. In the New York *Herald* A. Oakley Hall satirized General William Hall's postponement of his volunteer brigade's annual parade because of rain. "Latest from the Seat of War," Hall began his "City Intelligence" column. "We regret to state that one of the most disastrous and sudden retreats recorded in the annals of our citizen-soldiery took place yesterday." At an early hour there appeared the "splendid brigade of General Hall, numbering upwards of six hundred able-bodied men, armed and equipped as the law directs, and including that world-renowned corps, the Twenty-Seventh Regiment." They came "supplied with blank cartridges, blankets, cheese and crackers, and many of them fortified by a strong dose of Gough's Tonic Mixture." But then "the heavens suddenly assumed a threatening aspect, and General Hall, who had just pulled on one of his boots, happening to look out of the window, and perceiving the alarming prospect, with that humane consideration for the safety of his troops, and cool appreciation for the duties devolving upon him in such a trying emergency," canceled the parade, "cheating the hostile elements, and sinking to the very depths of agonized disappointment forty-three chivalric urchins and seventeen Irish chambermaids in the immediate vicinity of Tompkins Square." Not to be so easily intimidated by mockery, General Hall again canceled the parade because of rain. A few companies did not want to appear so soft, and paraded anyway, to the delight of those chivalric urchins and Irish chambermaids.[79]

The volunteer companies were bastions of nativism, middle-class propriety, and masculinity. They uniformly rejected the universal militia ideal and feared the consequences of allowing just anyone to form themselves into militia companies. Most units allowed just a few members to blackball any applicant, a useful device for keeping out the foreign born and unrespectable. Their paranoia could drive the volunteer militarists to see threats everywhere. On one occasion the *Eclaireur* reported that some women were thinking of forming a militia company; the journal humorlessly mistook a traditional burlesque muster, still called "fantasticks," for the real thing. Bad enough that "Negro military companies have shocked the sense of the community," now this! "Are we aping the barbarian customs of the negro kingdom of Dahomey, whose miserable savage sovereign maintains his regiments of unsexed women? . . . Twenty well dressed young women marched through the street, two abreast, in military order. . . . They giggled like so many girls just let loose from school." The *Eclaireur* simply could not tolerate these women mocking the masculinity they saw inherent in militia service.[80]

The serious civilian militarists did not handle lampoons well. One children's book from this period wrote that young men used to go to militia musters "because the law made them do so." They all "thought it very foolish, and so they did not try to behave well at all, but made all the sport out of it they could, and the people, and especially the boys, used to look on and laugh." Now people enrolled in the militia and trained only because they wanted to. "They all dress alike, and dress very nicely, and they have bright guns and swords. . . . But I think it is rather foolish business any way. It costs a great deal of time and money, and it does not amount to much." Despite such mockery, which continued through 1860, the volunteers found a great deal of public support, especially in the aftermath of a riot.[81] The Boston Lancers, a new volunteer company, were called into service before their uniforms arrived to suppress a riot. Four days after scattering the crowd, the Lancers paraded before some ten thousand spectators, and Governor Edward Everett presented them with a banner reading "Liberty, the Union, and the Laws." The newspapers proclaimed them "a favorite with the citizens."[82]

The volunteer militias remained the favorites of most state governments. No state, North or South or on the frontier, enforced its militia laws by maintaining a regular militia. Several states followed the example of New Hampshire's legislature, which allowed only volunteer companies to drill, stating that they would call on these companies first in a crisis. Apparently the state governments found the volunteer militia companies a good deal, as every state supplied guns to these units, no matter how wealthy their membership. In 1854 Connecticut armed the 2,462 men enrolled in its "Yankee" volunteer companies. In 1855, after New Jersey's Adjutant General Cadwallader declared the militia "comparatively useless to the state," the legislature agreed to fund volunteer companies; by 1857 there were 147 private companies in New Jersey. The last state to make this transition was Pennsylvania. In 1858 its legislature voted to arm and fund the private companies in the state. Doing so led to a sudden sharp increase in membership to 17,500, second only to New York in the total membership of volunteer companies—and still only 5 percent of the 350,000 men eligible for militia duty.[83]

Southern governments also used tax dollars to fund volunteer companies. As the South Carolina legislative committee on the militia summarized this reasoning, the state must "regard these organized, fully equipped, well armed and drilled bodies of men, as her first means of defense." The volunteers were not only better armed than the official militia, but they kept their arms in good repair—almost unheard of among the militia companies of this state. The volunteers expected the state to supply their arms; they just promised to take better care of them.[84]

The uniform companies occasionally came into conflict with the legislatures. In August 1857 the New Haven Grays became angry with Connecticut's new militia law, which lowered the amount of money awarded for participating in the annual parades and musters. To indicate their disapproval, the Grays returned their muskets to the state and appointed a committee to acquire guns for the company. This gesture is doubly interesting not simply for demonstrating that the members of one of the nation's elite units did not own their own guns, but also because it worked. The legislature agreed to retain the old fees and persuaded the Grays to take back their muskets.[85]

Not everyone interested in the health of the militia favored the volunteer militia movement. Adjutant General W. H. Richardson of Virginia wrote in 1856 that the state had been forced to rely on volunteer militia by the legislature's decision to end the regular militia three years earlier. But Richardson thought the volunteer units "an expensive nuisance" that had "drawn four times as many arms as they have men, and soon go down [are disbanded]—the Arms are thrown away or lost and cannot be recovered." Several adjutants general worried over the fact that volunteer companies formed and broke up at an astonishing rate, though most states kept these units on their organizational charts well after they ceased to exist. In Massachusetts in the 1840s, seventy-eight volunteer companies disbanded, mostly during or right after the Mexican War, and another twenty-nine organized. Others worried over the way many volunteer companies organized as adjuncts to the political parties. As early as 1840, Worcester, Massachusetts, had a Whig company, the Worcester Guards, and a Democratic company, the Light Infantry. The amount of material and other support they received followed the success of their parties. In Florida competing Whig and Democratic militias threatened to fire on one another during a particularly heated election. Events in Kansas brought home to many Americans the danger of allowing rival militias.[86]

Interest in militarism seemed on the wane in the mid-1850s, and opposition to volunteer companies increased. At the 1855 encampment in Kingston, New York, a woman and her infant child were shot accidentally during the drill, even though the guns were supposed to contain blank cartridges. The child died and a public uproar ensued, many critics charging that this event demonstrated the danger of allowing just anyone to carry a loaded weapon. In the following few years, membership in the state's uniform companies declined. Even the 7th Regiment felt the heat of the newspaper attacks, the regiment's board of officers ordering in 1856 and again in 1858 that members of the regiment should not respond to these denunciations, which served only to extend the debate. During these same years the board found it difficult to replace its officers as several retired. For five years the regiment did not have a major, several men refusing election before a lieutenant agreed to an instant promotion to that rank.[87]

However, starting in 1858 a few northern states, responding to the growing militarism of the South, made active efforts to revive or at least train their militia, and actually discovered some public support. Massachusetts insisted that its militia meet for three days a year in order to learn how to use a gun, while the Wisconsin legislature ordered a four-day muster as an "annual school of practice." Both these states and New York attempted to discover how many men were actually eligible for the militia. As a consequence, Wisconsin, in which not a single company had issued a report in 1857, saw its militia count increase from its previous report of 50,781 enrolled militia to 95,806. In 1859 the entire active militia of the state of Massachusetts met for the first time ever. New York reached a peak in 1860 when 26 percent of its enrolled militia (82,078 men enrolled, while 70,667 eligible men refused to even register) appeared for muster.[88]

More typical was the experience of Alabama's governor in 1857. John Winston proposed the termination of the state's militia, as "The want of a proper military spirit, and the absence of any general organization throughout the State are lamentable facts." Ending the facade of a militia would simply be accepting reality. With a notion that conflict with the North might be approaching, the legislature agreed to reform the system. First, though, they needed to figure out what that system should look like. Lacking militia returns, the legislative committee on the militia turned to the adjutant general. But no one, including the governor, knew who held that position, or if anyone did. At the end of January 1858 the committee announced that they had found the state's adjutant general. His name was Thomas E. McIver, but they could not locate him. They could say that, contrary to law, McIver kept his office in Camden, Alabama, but, like Major Major of *Catch-22,* he was never seen there. The legislature determined that they would have to create a militia system all over again. Florida and Maryland had almost precisely the same experience.[89] In Dickson Bruce's formulation, the South had the "trappings of a martial spirit, ... a stylized militarism." There was little behind the titles and epaulettes.[90]

It is easy to imagine that the volunteer militia movement might have maintained its elitist path for years to come. But 1859 witnessed a surprising revival. The exciting performances of the excellently trained and colorfully dressed units of Elmer Ellsworth's Chicago Zouaves and Lew

Wallace's Montgomery Guards inspired a sudden outpouring of the martial spirit in the Midwest and Northeast. Even jaded New Yorkers who
initially thought the reputation of the Zouaves a product of midwestern
provincialism, flocked to the demonstration of military skill. Individual
units, like New York's 7th Regiment, saw their membership double in the
excited response to these performances. Most northern state legislatures,
responding to the sense of dread at the approaching 1860 election as well
as to the energy generated by the Zouaves, renewed their support for the
uniform companies. The Massachusetts legislature launched a massive
revitalization program, quickly rebuilding their volunteer system, providing all the arms and equipment needed. As a consequence, these companies were the first to arrive in Washington, D.C., to defend the capital
in April 1861.[91]

The militia revival was not universal nor always that impressive. In
Vermont, where the National Guard still likes to call itself the Green
Mountain Boys, only nine militia companies with 450 men responded to
the governor's 1858 invitation to a general muster. Lacking anyone who
knew drill, Governor Ryland Fletcher invited the adjutant general of
Massachusetts, Ebenezer Stone, to command the muster. The enthusiasm
for uniform companies spread, though, and by August 1860 the number
attending the muster doubled to nine hundred men in seventeen companies. The secession crisis added five new companies, representing phenomenal growth in terms of percentages, but unimpressive in overall
numbers.[92]

The Zouaves motivated Northerners; John Brown's raid on Harpers
Ferry inspired the creation of scores of volunteer companies in the South.
Immediately after the attack, which had sought to capture the rich store
of armaments at Harpers Ferry for use in a slave rebellion, James J. Pettigrew of South Carolina wrote that "unfortunately the Militia and Patrol
system are dying out everywhere. The want of the commonest military
knowledge, on the part of the militia of Virginia was truly lamentable,
even farcical, and it looks as if a thousand organized men led with skill,
could have marched from one end of the state to the other." Brown's
attack inspired Pettigrew to promote the reorganization of his state's militia, though he was ignored as South Carolina continued to rely upon elite
volunteer units. Such volunteer companies sprang up throughout the
South in 1860; even in remote St. Augustine three companies quickly
organized and began competing for scarce firearms. The Mississippi
assembly responded to John Brown's raid by appropriating $150,000 to

purchase firearms. Most significant was the sudden decision by the Virginia legislature to appropriate $320,000 to refurbish the Virginia Manufactory of Arms, abandoned since 1822, with the goal of making five thousand rifle muskets a year.[93]

The fracture lines were visible throughout American society, with the volunteer militia companies increasing the stress rather than maintaining order. Uniform companies effectively started the greatest carnage in American history: the Civil War. Through the winter of 1860—61, existing volunteer companies around the South seized federal property; from Harpers Ferry in Virginia to Fort Moultrie in South Carolina to the United States Arsenal at Apalachicola in Florida, they grabbed all the federal armaments they could. It was a wise move; the South lacked a single gun manufacturer other than Harpers Ferry, which federal troops burned and Confederate troops destroyed. In Texas, volunteer companies forced the regular United States Army forces under General D. E. Twiggs to abandon the state and all United States military property. When war came in April 1861 South Carolina turned first to the volunteers, not calling out the militia until May 27.[94] Both sides in this conflict now faced the same internal crisis: they needed guns, many more guns. Their efforts would finally succeed in arming the American people.

The Civil War

The technological transformation of the 1850s fed a growing militarization of American society. Especially in the South, politicians called for military preparedness and the arming of every good citizen. Ironically, though, it was the North that attained this latter goal after the Southern states seceded from the Union. President Lincoln pulled out all the stops in supporting the maximization of Northern arms production. By the war's end, more than a million firearms a year were manufactured in the North and nearly every adult male in the country had been trained in the use of guns. The 1850s witnessed the expansion of gun production in the United States—or rather, in the northeastern part of the United States. The Southern states did not share in this growth in gunmaking, except insofar as they purchased guns made in the North.

The Southern faith in a quick victory over the Yankees persuaded most of the leadership that the absence of productive capacity would not be an issue. Most white Southerners simply overlooked recent history—

the dormant militia, the gentleman hunters' derision of pothunters, the Southern reliance on federal arms, the tradition of New Englanders as militarists—and constructed a vision of themselves as perfect soldiers. Writing in *De Bow's Review,* the house journal of secessionism, George Fitzhugh, the leading defender of slavery, reminded his readers that "A master race"—in this case Southern whites—"improves upon itself, and practices as severe a drill as it subjects its inferiors to." Transforming theory into reality, Fitzhugh claimed that "gentlemen of the South are better horsemen, better marksmen, have more physical strength and activity, and can endure more fatigue than their slaves." As if that were not enough to remove any worries about a quick Southern victory, Fitzhugh added that the plantation owners "have the lofty sentiments and high morals of a master race, that would render them unconquerable. Their time is occupied in governing their slaves and managing their farms— they are slaves themselves to their duties, and have no taste for that prurient love of licentious liberty which has depraved and demoralized free society." No one ever claimed that Fitzhugh was a keen observer of the world around him.[95]

Such insistence on Southern martial skills—and there were many, oft repeated by historians—flew in the face of the scramble by the Southern states to acquire firearms. As Nathaniel F. Cabell of Virginia wrote in 1860, "we must arm & discipline our people, nor must the Military Spirit ever again be allowed to become dormant." That need indicates that the South was indeed less than its self-image.[96] Even after a year of war, the *Richmond Whig* insisted that Southern "familiarity . . . with arms and horses gives them advantages for aggression. . . . Ten thousand Southerners, before the Yankees learnt to load a gun, might have marched to Boston without resistance." The paper failed to explain why they had not done so after Bull Run, but then this myth was being constructed for a purpose, to convince themselves and the rest of the world that Southerners were a militaristic people who could not be defeated. Thus Confederate president Jefferson Davis, who certainly knew better based on his many frustrations while secretary of war, told the sympathetic English reporter, William Howard Russell, that "the fact is, we are a military people. . . . We are not less military because we have had no great standing armies." He must have been gratified when Russell repeated these statements to his London audience.[97]

The biggest problem facing all the Southern states was the lack of firearms. With secession came the customary American scramble for weapons. The Confederacy had the volunteers, but not the guns. Over the previous twenty years only South Carolina had made any effort at arming its militia. Virginia immediately halted the shipment of the forty-two thousand old flintlocks in its arsenals being sold to a New York contractor in order to pay for the rebuilding of the Virginia Manufactory of Arms, now called the Richmond Armory. These guns, some dating from the Revolution, the majority between forty and sixty years old, were converted to percussion for use by the new Confederate Army. Jefferson Davis also sent the naval officer Raphael Semmes north to purchase guns; and he actually succeeded in purchasing and shipping many before the war started. In spite of these efforts, several Confederate commanders asked governors to stop sending them unarmed soldiers.[98]

Virginia began issuing weapons to its militia companies in early January 1861, before it seceded. The guns were not all that they could have been. Captain William Seth reported that "On Saturday we had a Target-Shooting and about one gun in five would fire without snapping Three or Four times, from all indications in a vary short time we will have to be in the field and I will not go with guns that are *very little better than clubs.*"[99]

This experience was replicated in units everywhere in the country at the start of the Civil War. In spite of the enthusiasm for arms generated by hunters and volunteer militia, regardless of improved technology and the increase in the total number of arms in the 1850s, the same problems of caring for these weapons remained. And as states began issuing guns they had stored since the Mexican War, they discovered that they served little purpose beyond the one suggested by Captain Seth, as clubs. Indiana was fairly typical. Back in 1831 the legislature passed a law requiring the state's quartermaster to keep receipts on all guns issued by the state. The first such receipt was written in 1844, by which time at least twenty-four hundred guns had been issued. With the coming of the Civil War, the adjutant general reported that he had no idea where most of the state's guns had gone, being "scattered through-out different parts of the State, in some places stacked up in a house, in other places lying in shops, broken and rusted," most in such poor condition that they were not worth bringing in for repair in any case. Massachusetts converted the 11,240 flintlocks in its armory to the percussion system in 1852. When it came time to use these improved guns, it was found that they broke constantly and misfired more often than had the old flintlocks. The adjutant general charged that the Springfield Armory had just sought to make a profit on these alterations.[100]

New York's 7th Regiment had better luck. In 1854 the regiment ignored the warnings about the danger of percussion locks and sent all of their flintlock muskets to the state arsenal in Albany for conversion, at state expense, to the new percussion system. The members of the regiment were sufficiently impressed with the improvements to welcome an exchange with the U.S. government in November 1858, arranged by Senator William Seward. In return for their thousand muskets, the regiment received an equal number of the new Springfield rifled muskets. These new weapons loaded at the rate of a musket, but fired with nearly the accuracy of a rifle. These were the arms that the 7th carried to the defense of Washington in 1861, stopping along the way to buy ammunition in Philadelphia. The day before the 7th passed through Baltimore, the "imperfectly armed and equipped" 6th Massachusetts had to fight its way through the city. The 7th reached Washington on April 25 without incident, except for a private who shot himself in the leg and the accidental discharge of a musket, which set others to firing, thinking they were under attack.[101]

April 1861 found the North a little better prepared for war than the South in terms of firepower. The government owned some 576,800 firearms, though Secretary of War John B. Floyd had transferred 105,000 of these guns south. Only 35,000 of these guns, the .58 caliber rifles and rifled muskets, could meet anyone's standard of excellence (Floyd failed to move any of these guns south); half of the rest had been made between 1822 and 1842, and bordered on useless. In addition, pistols, especially revolvers, were still relatively unusual in America, and the government had distributed every revolver it could purchase on the domestic market by June 1861. Further depleting Union stores was the Confederate capture of Harpers Ferry and every one of the thirteen thousand Model 1855 rifles made to that date. On the positive side, those Harpers Ferry guns accounted for two-thirds of the rifles in the South at the start of the war.[102]

The U.S. Army was less impressive at the start of 1861. It consisted of sixteen thousand troops scattered all over the country, mostly out west, and with a great number resigning to serve the Confederacy. Lincoln therefore called upon the militia, North and South, to put down this domestic insurrection, as the Constitution and the Militia Act of 1792 specified. The results were discouraging, constituting the greatest single failure of the militia system. Communities throughout the country, like Sangamon, Illinois, were rudely reminded that they did not have a militia, and had not for the previous fifteen years. Several governors, most bluntly Governor William Burton of Delaware, informed Lincoln that their militia did not actually exist.[103]

While the Southern volunteer militia was initiating the war, the Northern militia was grotesquely unprepared to fight any sort of war. Not that the Northern states did not try. Northern leadership responded to Lincoln's call with enthusiasm. Most state governments followed the lead of Connecticut's governor, who immediately began buying powder and firearms on the international market. Wisconsin appropriated $100,000 while Indiana sent Robert Dale Owen to England, where he bought forty thousand Enfield rifles for the state in 1862 for $753,000. Even after the heightened gun enthusiasm of the 1850s, which had focused primarily on private arms, the state militias were in no condition to go to war. Not only were these states competing with one another for limited supplies, but they were also coming into competition with the Confederacy, which desperately needed guns for its insurrection.[104]

After Massachusetts, New York had the best-armed militia. In January 1861 Frederick Townshend, New York's adjutant general, reported that the state should be able to field 18,846 officers and men with "8,000 serviceable weapons (muskets and rifles) in the hands of the troops, and this comprises all that the State possesses." Townshend noted that the militia budget had just been reduced by one-third "to the pittance of $10,000. . . . Certainly in view of the present questionable status of the Union, parsimony like this appears to have been singularly malopportune." He intelligently recommended the immediate purchase of fifty thousand rifled muskets, adding that "I am aware of the difficulty of procuring these arms at present, owing to the recent heavy orders for the South, which have perhaps drained the market of fire arms." An agent, he suggested, should be dispatched to England and France to purchase guns.[105]

The volunteer companies went to war first. Massachusetts conducted a quick inventory of its resources in January 1861. Several of the volunteer companies owned excellent armaments; these were the units rushed to Washington in April. But the state's military officials expressed surprise at how ill-equipped were some of the volunteer companies. Colonel Edwin F. Jones reported to General Benjamin Butler that four of his eight companies did not have enough weapons, while the other four were armed with ancient muskets that could be more dangerous to them than the foe. New Hampshire had 750 men enrolled in their uniform militia, while Vermont formed its eight best volunteer companies into the 1st Regiment and sent them on to Washington, after borrowing the requisite guns from Massachusetts. The 1,993 men enrolled in Wisconsin's fifty-two private companies formed the state's first regiment. Michigan could field twenty-eight volunteer militia companies, but only after Governor Austin Blair secured a loan from a Detroit businessman to arm them. The volunteer companies provided not simply the first troops, North and South, but also much of the officer corps of the two armies.[106]

The regular militia, even in states that had been working to reactivate their militia over the previous year, remained fairly pathetic. Major G. F. Van Beck, inspector for New York's 8th Brigade, reported at the end of 1860 that 247 of the 835 (30 percent) enrolled men had appeared for muster. But they did not show up with much in the way of firearms, as most men still did not own guns. A few companies were fairly well armed: "Company C has only 22 muskets; wants 20 more." Others carried arms supplied by the state in the past; company F and H "have forty old muskets which were furnished to them temporarily. They are unfit for the service, . . . they need now 46." Most of the privately owned guns "are not in order and cannot be made good short of the State Arsenal; ought to be exchanged." And as for equipment, "The belts and cartridge boxes date, no doubt, of the last century." Van Beck would not even inspect Company D, so pathetic were they. And all but the last company were rated as enormously improved from just the previous year. Every regiment had similarly missed reports; some units were well armed while others, such as the 12th Regiment, had ninety-two muskets for 378 men (24.3 percent). A few inspectors also noted that units were sharing arms for the inspections, passing them from one to another as needed. The worst units were the "rural companies," whose arms were described as "utterly useless," "entirely unfit for service," "of an inferior quality and generally unserviceable and useless, as well as dangerous to those handling them when powder is used," or, as one inspector put it, "arms could not be poorer or more unfit for any service." The review of the 76th Regiment must have been quite something: its inspector wrote, "There has been so much said in the public prints about this parade, that I shall forbear commenting on it, lest I should make it worse if it were possible."

The best-armed units were all in New York City. The new 71st Regiment had arms "in perfect condition," inspector Major Charles H. Smith stated, though their drill was "clumsily performed." The inspector did note that the captain of one company had rented muskets for his use at the inspection, and he had to call attention "to the worthless condition of the greater part of muskets in the hands of the" 2nd Regiment; these guns "would be utterly useless and even dangerous to their possessors in service, and there is not a full supply even of these arms." And then there was Staten Island's 73d Regiment. They were "in a deplorable condition as regards arms, uniform, equipments, drill," and everything else Major Smith valued. "No attempt was made . . . to perform the manoeuvres." Most discouraging was Brooklyn's 28th Rifle Regiment, which had just received new rifles from the state that were already rusting from a lack of proper care. In contrast, the 35th Regiment included former members of the Chicago Zouaves: "Their muskets glittered with brightness, and the ringing of rammers . . . and distinct click of the locks, at inspection, made music." Euphoria for the lucky inspector.[107]

North and South, volunteers rushed to do battle. North and South, state governments discovered that most of these new soldiers—except those in volunteer companies—owned no arms and that the state arsenals were empty. In Ohio thirty thousand volunteers sprang forth to fill the state's quota of thirteen thousand troops. But George McClellan reported that the state arsenal contained only a few boxes of rusty muskets, leaving the state no choice but to send its first two regiments to Washington without guns. An Indiana inventory in 1861 found 3,436 firearms "of sixteen different kinds, but of uniform inferiority" in state arsenals, while fifteen militia companies reported that their members owned 692 muskets—505 of which were "worthless and incapable of repair"—26 Sharps rifles, and 95 pistols. Illinois could boast eight hundred men holding serviceable arms available in the state militia. The governor of Iowa reported a total of "1,500 old muskets, [and] about 200 rifles and rifled muskets" in his state. In 1860 Maryland's adjutant general reported that the state's three arsenals held 780 muskets and 19 rifles that were "tolerable good," plus an additional 700 that desperately needed repair, 44 condemned rifles, and 687 condemned and entirely worthless muskets. Florida possessed 259 antiquated muskets, 433 rifles, 348 old and rusty pistols, and 252 rifled muskets, all stored inadequately in the capitol itself. Mississippi found that the state arsenal contained 110 rifles and 234 muskets in fair order. Like other Southern states, Mississippi responded by calling for contributions of arms, and many wealthy planters exchanged personal arms caches for field commands. Northern states turned to the federal government for their weapons.[108]

In these first few months of the war there was a great popular faith that militarism would revive the United States from its capitalist stupor, in much the same way that militaristic enthusiasm swept Europe in July and August 1914 (and with much the same result). Many commentators held that the country had been focused on selfish pursuits for too long, and that this confrontation would lift people to a higher moral plain. Horace Greeley expressed this sense well: "Let no one feel that our present troubles are deplorable, in view of the majestic development of Nationality and Patriotism which they have occasioned. But yesterday we were esteemed a sordid, grasping money-loving people, too greedy to gain to cherish generous and lofty aspirations. Today vindicates us from that reproach and demonstrates that beneath the scum and slag of forty years of peace, and in spite of the insidious approaches of corruption, the fires of patriotic devotion are still burning."[109] The nation would rise above materialism through violence. Here was not just a moral, but a militant democracy.

This fervor grabbed many, and maybe even most, former pacifists, from Frederick Douglass to Julia Ward Howe. It was the latter who wrote those famous words proclaiming "the coming of the Lord" at the beginning of the Civil War. Howe saw Union soldiers acting in God's name, letting "loose the fateful lightning of His terrible swift sword." The faith of tens of thousands of religious people moved irrevocably to the gun as the path of not just their nation's salvation, but their personal salvation as well. They somehow failed to realize that it was capitalist materialism, as expressed in the massive manufacturing capacity of the North, that made their victory possible. Nor did they fully appreciate the ways in which secession unleashed more than the dogs of war. Almost from the start, the entire country, on all points of the compass, seemed to give way to violent urges long contained. In Texas, lynch parties were hanging blacks and white who opposed secession. One member of a mob wrote a friend, "Judge Lynch has had the honor to preside only in ten cases of whites (northern Lincolnites) and about sixty-five negroes, all of whom were hung or burnt, as to the degree of their implication in the rebellion."[110]

Lincoln's call for volunteers met with energetic outpourings in the North; the border states proved a different matter. Maryland's Governor

Thomas Hicks told Lincoln that he would furnish troops only for the defense of Washington. Governor Beriah Magoffin declared, "Kentucky will furnish no troops for the wicked purpose of subduing her sister Southern states." But the most hostile response came from Claiborne F. Jackson of Missouri, who ranted that Lincoln's request was "illegal, unconstitutional, and revolutionary; in its objects inhuman and diabolical."[111]

Volunteer militia companies throughout the South seized all the federal arsenals within their states' borders. These seizures came without a fight in every state but one, Jackson's Missouri. Lacking popular support to take Missouri out of the Union, Governor Jackson created a situation that guaranteed chaos, as competing volunteer militia battled for federal arms and control of the state. Francis P. Blair created the Home Guards to keep Missouri in the Union, receiving guns from the federal arsenal in St. Louis courtesy of General Nathaniel Lyon, commander of the nearby Jefferson Barracks, who ordered the arsenal's commander "to arm the loyal citizens to protect the public property and execute the laws." Militia favoring secession immediately seized the state's other arsenal, at Liberty, and its one thousand muskets, sending half these arms for use by the five-hundred-strong force under General Daniel M. Frost, commander of the state militia. But the St. Louis arsenal's stockpile of over fifty thousand guns was the real prize, and whichever side seized the arsenal would instantly be the only well-armed force in the region.[112]

On the day of Lincoln's inauguration, March 4, 1861, the competing forces met outside the secessionist headquarters, the Berthold mansion. Though many guns were in evidence, neither side used them as anything other than clubs in the brawl that ensued. The leader of the secessionists, Basil Duke, held a knife to the throat of one Unionist leader, David Dickey, but there were no serious injuries as the Unionists retreated. These Americans, at least, hesitated to make the leap to serious violence, and General Frost hoped to capture the arsenal peacefully, as had militia leaders in the Southern states. But when the Missouri convention refused to secede, Frost decided to take the St. Louis arsenal by force, if necessary. There followed a period of careful maneuvering and escalating violence.[113]

Back in Washington, General Winfield Scott saw the threat and ordered seven hundred federal troops to protect the St. Louis arsenal. The War Department also approved the transfer of seven thousand muskets from the arsenal to the Blair's Home Guards. Lincoln appointed Lyon commander of the arsenal, and the general set about fortifying it and placing artillery on the heights commanding the area. Frost reviewed his troops and discovered that the five hundred arms from the Liberty arsenal formed the bulk of his armaments; most secessionists lacked personal firearms. He therefore requested, through Governor Jackson, guns from the Confederate government. The Confederates complied and ordered eight hundred muskets and ammunition sent from the recently captured federal arsenal in New Orleans.

With the firing on Fort Sumter, Lyon understood that battle with the secessionists was imminent. He received news that the Confederate arms had arrived at the Confederate militia's Camp Jackson (named for the governor). As a surety that they would not get more guns, Lyon removed the arms from the St. Louis arsenal across the river to Alton, Illinois. Lyon wanted to attack Camp Jackson at once and seize the guns before the secessionists had an opportunity to train in their use, but the Unionist Committee of Public Safety insisted that he follow due process and send the U.S. marshal to demand the return of federal property. This he did, though backing the marshal with a force of Home Guards and a battalion of U.S. regulars. Lyon was astounded when, on May 10, the secessionist militia surrendered to the Home Guard without resistance, handed over their arms, and marched back through the city under guard. A hostile crowd lined the route of the march, and the Home Guard opened fire on the crowd, many of whom returned fire. The charm of nonviolence was broken, as twenty-eight people were killed or wounded. From that moment forward, the contending parties did not hesitate to use force. There were two other clashes over the next twenty-four hours, including one in front of the arsenal that led to the killing of eight civilians. In all three instances it was the untrained Home Guard, and not the regulars, who opened fire. City officials appealed to General Harney to send in more regulars to restore order, U.S. troops with artillery arriving within a few days. Thus began a long and bloody civil war in Missouri, but the state stayed in the Union and the federal arms stayed in Unionist hands.[114]

Since the states lacked arms, the federal government moved to arm its volunteers. Even in the hills of Kentucky, Unionists had very few guns at their disposal. A naval officer, William Nelson, took personal responsibility for arming those loyal to the country, succeeding over the next several months in channeling ten thousand guns to Union volunteers. Other states lacking the romantic association with the rifle were equally underarmed, and arms procurement quickly devolved to political infighting. Representatives and senators worked the levers of power in an attempt to get the best possible guns for volunteers from their states. The most favored were, of course, the few British Enfields in government arsenals. But these were quickly apportioned, and then the battle came down to the .58 calibers. Lost in the struggle for prestige were the very real needs of the troops. Nearly every Union officer complained, in the words of John C. Fremont, "We have plenty of men, but absolutely no arms." Within two months the Union had exhausted their supply of rifles and rifled muskets and began issuing the older smooth-bore muskets. By August 1861 these weapons had also been handed out and the government purchased every gun it could find on the domestic market, thirty thousand firearms of every imaginable kind by November 1862. The United States government had no choice but to turn to Europe for arms.[115]

American agents were rather overwhelmed by the number and variety of arms available in Europe. Colonel George L. Schuyler, the War Department's first agent, was staggered to learn that Enfield (the descendant of the old gunmakers' guild) produced fifteen thousand rifled muskets a month, which exceeded the total production of the Springfield Armory in the entire year of 1860 by more than 20 percent. But American agents, representing several states as well as the U.S. government, kept tripping over one another as well as Confederate buying agents, helping to drive up the prices of European guns. Congress aided these endeavors by lifting all import duties on firearms for the first time in American history. In the first year of war, Schuyler purchased 137,000 guns for the Union armies from England, Austria, France, and Germany, while the U.S. counsel in Belgium, H. S. Sanford, purchased 56,000 muskets there, and the trading house of Herman Boker acquired an additional 100,000 European firearms. Many of these arms, especially the Belgian, were criticized for their inferiority to English guns, but they still constituted a much needed boost to the nation's armaments. In July 1862 Marcellus Hartley, a member of a gun-importing firm in New York City, replaced Schuyler as the U.S. representative with specific instructions to buy only the best guns. Hartley therefore concentrated on British arms, buying more than 100,000 Enfields, plus an additional 100,000 of the best Continental firearms. By the end of the war the United States had purchased 1,165,000 European firearms; 436,000 of these arms came from Enfield, making it the second most common gun in the Union Army after the Springfield.[116]

Far more significant in the long term was the government's encouragement of domestic manufacturers. In the first year of the war the government issued contracts to just about anyone. Some of these enterprises went bust fast. For instance, a P. S. Justice, who had no experience making guns but had imported some Enfields for sale to the government, con-tracted to make four thousand stands of arms. Justice did not make these guns, but in the traditional American way, assembled them. The barrels were crooked Springfield rejects, the locks were ineptly attached con-demned castoffs, the sights came from Enfield but were put on incor-rectly, the stocks were green wood and rusted the barrels with their moisture, and the hammers tended to break off when fired. In his defense, Justice pointed out that his guns passed inspection, which was true. Government inspectors were rather lax in their standards, as several other such errors indicated. As Carl L. Davis said, "Poor arms were con-sidered better than no arms at all." Worse were a number of contracts that were never fulfilled, as the would-be gunmakers discovered it a far more difficult task than they had initially assumed and as skilled workers were already fully employed at established shops.[117]

The government had better luck with established manufacturers, for the most part. The oldest of these firms, the Eli Whitney works, had a long history of failed federal contracts. At the beginning of the war it undertook to make 55,000 Springfield-style rifled muskets; the company delivered only 15,000 by 1865. James Mulholland contracted for 50,000 of these muskets, and delivered 5,500. The U.S. government contracted for the manufacture of 1,525,000 of its Springfield rifled muskets from pri-vate firms; Alfred Jenks and Son made 98,000, Colt 75,000 (plus 40,000 under subcontracts), Remington 40,000, and twenty other firms produced their share. Production delays and institutional resistance did hinder some companies. The Colt company would have made many more guns had its factory not burned down in February, 1864. The Sharps Rifle Company made only fifty-eight hundred carbines and one hundred rifles in 1861, hindered by a shortage of skilled workers and the hostility of many in the army, including Chief of Ordnance James Wolfe Ripley, to breech-loading rifles. Though it never met government demand, the Sharps company expanded enormously as a result of the war, supplying the army with ninety thousand breechloaders. The war saved some com-panies, like Winchester, which was about to declare bankruptcy in 1861, but came too late for Robbins & Lawrence, which closed shop in fall 1859. The government encouraged every gunmaker it could locate, regularly promising to buy whatever could be produced, even if the war ended sud-denly. Colt's initial contract with the government was a telegram from

Chief of Ordnance Ripley: "Deliver weekly until further orders as many of your pistols . . . as you can make." New England prospered.[118]

Once the truth sank in after Bull Run that a single victory would not win the war, the Confederate government began frantic efforts to acquire sufficient arms and ammunition to sustain its army. Coastal units actually had to abandon the defenses they had just built because troops were largely unarmed. As Kenneth McCreedy has observed, "the notion that citizen soldiers would rush to their country's defense suitably armed and equipped by their own resources most certainly did not match the reality of the mad scramble for weapons and supplies among the state and national governments" in 1861. The state governments pursued every possible lead in their efforts to acquire firearms in a fashion that would have been recognized by the governors of Revolutionary America.[119]

The Confederacy's ordnance chief, Josiah Gorgas, counted all the guns at his disposal but kept the total, 159,010, a secret from everyone but those who absolutely had to know. Most of these guns were captured federal arms. By June 30, 1861, Gorgas reported the entire Confederate reserve of arms as 2,992 muskets, 978 rifles, 58 carbines, 456 Colt revolvers, 164 other pistols, 156 sabers, and 9 musicians' swords. It was evident that there was no way that the Confederates could fight an extended war. The first task was the rushed completion of the Richmond Armory. The Virginia legislature had originally intended to purchase the machinery from Northern manufacturers, but not even Samuel Colt would sell to the South once the war began. However, one of the first acts of the war had been a raid by Southern troops on Harpers Ferry. Before burning the buildings, the raiders carried off most of the machinery to Richmond, where it sat in a tobacco warehouse until October, when the armory building was finished. The first rifled musket was completed in January 1862, and for the next three years the Richmond Armory was the South's only major gunmaking plant.[120]

The Confederacy faced a wide variety of problems in manufacturing arms. First and foremost, as Gorgas informed President Davis, very few people in the South knew how to make firearms. Then they lacked the resources and even the places in which to build guns. Gorgas identified two alternatives: capturing guns on the battlefield, which was inexpensive but dependent on continuing victories, and buying them overseas and then running the federal blockade. Lee took care of the first option, while the government called upon a Yankee professor, Caleb Huse, to act as their agent in Europe. Huse arrived in Montgomery and met immediately with President Davis and Colonel Gorgas. It quickly became apparent to Huse that the Confederacy had no plans for acquiring arms for their war and very little money. Davis sent Huse to Europe with orders to purchase twelve thousand stands of arms, which Davis thought would be sufficient. Huse spent the next four years arranging the purchase and shipment of guns to the Confederacy, usually in direct competition with U.S. agents. He also established the procedure that allowed the Confederates to pay for these armaments with cotton. The Confederacy could not have kept its forces armed but for Huse. By August 1862 Huse had sent 63,510 guns to the South, equal to 40 percent of total Confederate armaments a year earlier. Another 113,504 got through the blockade over the next year. In the end, Huse supplied two-thirds—330,000 stands of arms—of the Confederacy's total firearms. It must be recalled that the Confederate states mobilized some 750,000 men during the war, which means that they never had enough guns.[121]

Many of these European arms did not get past the Union blockade and thus helped to arm the North. The Confederates therefore experimented with a number of alternate routes. One of the more successful ones ran European guns through Mexico. For much of the war the Confederates kept open a route up the Rio Grande from Bagdad, Mexico, across the border to Matamoros, and then through the desert from Brownsville to Houston. The King Ranch was the center of operations for these gun runners, and Richard King, who owned two steamboats that ran the cotton downriver to Bagdad, made a fortune in this trade. King took cotton selling for four cents a pound in Texas and sold it in Mexico for fifty cents; an Enfield costing $21 in England went for $60 in Matamoros, with an appropriate markup for King in the transfer to the Confederacy. Given the Union blockade, this "Cotton Road," as it was called, proved vital to Confederate troops in the West.[122]

The Confederate government enjoyed two successes in their efforts to make guns in the South: the armories at Richmond and Fayetteville, North Carolina. The former could produce one thousand firearms a month, the latter five hundred at most. In four years they could thus make up for the seventy thousand guns the South lost at Vicksburg and Gettysburg in a few days in July 1863. But in fact, they never made that many. Total arms production in the South from all sources during the war was just twenty thousand guns. The government's promotion of private production was an abysmal failure. The various plants encouraged by the government fought over scarce skilled workers, machines, and resources.

The Confederate Ordnance Office had to become involved at the highest levels when Virginia's Ordnance Department offered higher wages to a single worker as an inducement for him to leave the Richmond Armory. On another occasion production dropped by one-third when a worker, John Jones, was killed during a Union raid on Richmond in March 1864. Jones was the only trained barrel straightener at the armory.[123]

Indicative of the problems facing the Confederacy in its struggle to make firearms was the Spiller & Burr Revolver Company. In 1861 Edward Spiller and Joseph Burr hired James H. Burton, a former master armorer at Harpers Ferry and director of the Enfield rifle plant in England, to establish a pistol factory in Georgia. After a frustrating period dealing with the poor managerial skills of his bosses, Burton recommended that the Confederate government buy Spiller & Burr and merge it with the new Macon Armory—all under Burton's control, of course. Gorgas endorsed Burton's position and gave the company every support for the remainder of the war, including the authority to confiscate public and private materials and slave labor for use in the plant. Lacking capital, skilled workers, access to raw materials, machinery, and preexisting industrial sites, Burton had to reinvent the wheel in order to attain even the most modest production levels. Machinery rarely performed as intended; Burton had to make due with a "rifling machine [that] would not rifle a good barrel." Worse, he had to deal with the labyrinth of Confederate politics. Guns made for the Confederate Army were often seized for use by state forces while workers were lost to service on the front lines. Burton spent weeks exchanging long letters with General Joe Johnston in an effort to keep a single skilled laborer. It took a year for Spiller & Burr to turn out their first twelve pistols. Necessity forced the company to take a number of shortcuts, which led to a series of production disasters. Every single center pin made in May 1864 was condemned, and four-fifths of their guns failed the inspection tests. For a period, Spiller could not get a single pistol to pass the test. In fact the company workforce actually drilled with Austrian rifles rather than the products of their own labor. By the end of the war, Spiller & Burr had succeeded in making a total of 1,875 pistols, the Macon Armory producing 1,500. By contrast, Colt alone made 400,000 pistols for the U.S. government during the war.[124]

The Confederacy acted much like the Union, its central government arming all draftees and volunteers—but only if they were under Confederate Army command. The government also felt justified in confiscating any privately owned firearms its agents could locate. And they most definitely needed a standing army. In his inaugural address, Jefferson Davis specified that no reliance could be put on the militia: "there should be a well-instructed and disciplined army." The militia's core task continued as it had always been, even when Yankee troops were in the area: staffing the slave patrol.[125]

The Confederacy also discovered, as did the Union, that it had to train a great number of its soldiers in the use of firearms. On both sides of the sectional divide, young men enlisting, or drafted after 1862, did not know how to use guns. Instructors had to show these men how to load, fire, clean, and care for their firearms, just as Washington's officers had eighty years earlier. And even many officers were basically unfamiliar with guns. No less an authority than the Massachusetts master of ordnance did not realize that paper cartridges had to be torn open before loading. Two Union officers, William Conant Church and George Wood Wingate, would make the correction of this ignorance of firearms a lifelong crusade.[126]

Despite the best efforts of Huse, Gorgas, and Robert E. Lee to make, purchase, or capture as many guns as possible, the Confederacy simply could not compete with the North. By 1862 Confederate commanders were forced to hold unarmed recruits in reserve until enough soldiers had died to supply the necessary arms for their replacements. By July 1863 Florida had exactly eighteen muskets; the rest had all been allocated to troops, and the adjutant general doubted that any were left in private hands.[127] In contrast, the North mobilized 2.2 million men for war; their industry produced nearly three million guns.[128]

The heightened demand for firearms generated by the arms race between North and South also inspired technological innovation. Nearly five hundred firearms-related patents were filed between 1860 and 1871. One of the most important of these developments was metallic ammunition, which aided the development of breech-loading, repeating, and magazine rifles. By 1865 the government had tested sixty different breech-loading designs and purchased guns made according to the specifications of twenty-seven of these designs. Of course such diversity created a maze of supply problems, especially with ammunition, but also with repairs. One of the most telling indicators of the novelty of gunmaking in these years is the fact that many gunmakers did not have names for the different parts of their guns, especially the new breechloaders, and those who did often used names peculiar to themselves. As a consequence, the Ordnance Department faced the unique problem of not knowing what to call a part they wanted to order.[129]

Curiously, the Union Army did not recognize the advantages of breech-loading rifles until the very end of the war, and then only the cavalry employed breech-loading carbines, with great effectiveness. When commanders requested breechloaders, they were either rebuffed or advised against their use. Benjamin Butler was so frustrated with the runaround he received that he bought Sharps rifles directly from the company and billed the War Department. This resistance to the breechloaders extended even to the rifle invented by Union general Ambrose Burnside and made by the Burnside Rifle Company of Rhode Island. At the start of the war Burnside had difficulty acquiring his own rifle for use by his troops. Opponents of the breechloader worried that soldiers would waste ammunition and stay behind cover if they had guns that could fire rapidly and accurately at a safe distance. Common soldiers did not see a problem there, and appreciated early on the superiority of the breech-loading rifle to the rifled musket, but it was only in the last two years of the war that a great number of Union commanders came to this conclusion. At that point, the Ordnance Department finally took the hint, ordering every one of the new rifles they could. By 1865 the Union had purchased 430,000 breechloaders, and Alexander B. Dyer, the chief of ordnance at that time, concluded that "The experience of the war has shown that the breech-loading arms are greatly superior to muzzleloaders for infantry as well as for cavalry."[130]

The repeating rifle stood forth as the most powerful development in firearms during the war. Again, there was much initial resistance to the repeater, and Chief of Ordnance Ripley refused even to meet with Christopher Spencer to discuss his invention, even after the ordnance board fired a Spencer rifle 120 times in six minutes without a single misfire. It took the personal intervention of President Lincoln to get the Ordnance Department to start buying repeaters. It was not until Ripley's replacement, George D. Ramsay, examined the test results carefully in 1864 that the government seriously promoted the manufacture of repeating rifles. The repeaters were made by four companies: Colt, Ball, Spencer, and Henry. The Ball rifle entered production late in the war, while Colt sold just seven thousand revolving rifles to the Union Army, mostly in the first year of war, as troops hated the proximity of the explosion to their faces. The Henry was widely admired for its magazine of sixteen rounds and its ease of loading. Though the Spencer's magazine held only seven rounds, soldiers favored it for its durability and reliability. It also found favor with the Ordnance Department as a result of Spencer's ability to mass-produce its guns, whereas Oliver Winchester's fifty-three workers produced an average of only 200 Henry rifles a month, reaching a peak of 260 in 1865. The government would have purchased many more Henry repeaters, but ended up buying just 1,730. In contrast, the Spencer company, whose plant was in a Boston piano factory, delivered 75,000 repeaters before the war ended. Given that Christopher Spencer did not have a plant when the war started, this accomplishment was all the more impressive.[131]

Arms production took off in the Civil War, never to settle back down. Gunmakers had increased productive capacities to the limits of demand. With Harpers Ferry out of the picture, the Springfield Armory bore the burden of making the army's small arms. The armory did a remarkable job: in 1860 the two national armories made twenty thousand guns total; at its peak in 1864, Springfield alone produced one thousand guns *a day,* for a total annual output of 247,664 finished stands of arms. By war's end, Springfield had produced 802,000 rifled muskets. Private manufacturers did even better, as the Civil War created a secure market for Colt and the other Northern gunmakers. The United States purchased four million firearms during the war, one-fourth of them from Europe. Of special long-term significance was the spur these levels of arms production gave to the manufacture of what had previously been a specialty weapon, the pistol. Colt Firearms made 130,000 .44-caliber army and navy revolvers and 260,000 other pistols during the war, distributing them widely among Union, and even some Confederate, troops. Remington made 1,000 guns a year in 1861; by the end of the war it had delivered 133,000 revolvers to the government. The Starr Arms Company, which made two hundred pistols in 1860, sold fifty thousand revolvers to the Ordnance Department by 1865. Smith & Wesson and many other companies, though they did not make as many revolvers, added tens of thousands to the total. The result was an increased familiarity not just with firearms, but with easily transportable and concealable revolvers.[132]

Not only did the Northern manufacturers make more guns, they made better guns. By the end of the Civil War, American-made guns were sturdier, more accurate, and much easier to use than they had ever been. It no longer took twenty steps to prepare a weapon for firing; Colt no longer needed to print long instructions on the use of a gun. American guns no longer misfired an average of one time in four, nor did the barrel have to be cleaned after every fourth shot: with the new metallic bullets an individual could fire off thousands of rounds without mishap, and dozens of shots without having to clean the weapon. And with the new small revolvers, it was at last possible for a young child to learn the use of a gun, though the advantages of doing so were questionable.

The U.S. government concentrated all its efforts on arming the front-line troops, not even thinking that local militia might ever figure into the conflict. On the few instances when Confederates raided deep into Northern territory, they found the local militia relying on personal fire-arms, which generally meant very little. The militia's finest hour in the war came in Ohio in July 1863. General John Hunt Morgan led his twenty-four hundred Confederate cavalry on a slashing raid through Indiana and Ohio for two weeks, pursued the whole way by Burnside's Union troops. Morgan hoped to lose his shadow by crossing the Ohio River into West Virginia, but towns along Morgan's route mobilized their ill-equipped militia units in an effort to slow him down. The New Lisbon militia was typical. On July 25, the town gathered together its assortment of weapons: "Squirrel rifles, muskets of various and sundry bores, shot-guns, horse pistols, swords, and axes." The axes proved key, as militia throughout that part of the state chopped down trees to block Morgan's raiders, requiring the Confederates to halt their march repeatedly to chop their way through while Burnside's forces tightened the noose. On the 26th, the New Lisbon militia under Judge Cornelius Curry stood guard behind a barricade when one of their scouts came riding up the road screaming "Morgan is a-coming, run for your lives!" The militia did just that. But Morgan's forces were coming under a white flag attempting to surrender, hoping to gain passage out of the state by surrendering to the militia rather than the U.S. Army. Judge Curry had to be convinced that the white flag the Confederates were carrying meant that they desired a truce before he would return to the barricade to speak with the Confeder-ate officers. By the time the negotiations got under way, Union general James M. Shackelford arrived and Morgan became a permanent guest of the U.S. government.[133]

Of course, the Civil War was really about mass murder, and for that task nothing yet surpassed the rifle. It was not a question of rifles in the hands of expert marksmen. Marksmen existed, most famously in Colonel Hiram Berdan's New York company of sharpshooters (the name origi-nates with their gun, the Sharps Model 1859 breech-loading open-sight rifle). The best shot in this company of expert shots—expert because they practiced regularly—was the company chaplain, the Reverend Lorenzo Barber of Troy, a calm, quiet minister who could outshoot anyone else in Berdan's regiment.[134] This handful of East Coast eagle eyes did not win the Civil War for the Union; massed rifle fire did.

Commanders on both sides of the Civil War had learned their tactics in the Mexican War or from those who had fought in that war. Not that the Mexican War had introduced any major innovations to combat—the reliance on close-ordered ranks of professional soldiers moving forward, firing a single concentrated volley, and then charging with fixed bayonets was standard since Culloden. Napoleon had added a few twists to this standard model—the quick movement and concentration of forces and mobile artillery—which Generals Scott and Taylor followed in Mexico, but otherwise Butcher Cumberland would have recognized the tactics of his successor, Robert E. Lee.

The charge is a romantic vision of heroism, which, as many scholars have noted, seemed an illness among Confederate troops. Grady McWhiney and Perry D. Jamieson perfectly summarized this approach to warfare in the title of their book, *Attack and Die*.[135] But charging is an especially attractive option for those with limited munitions; a bayonet does not need to be reloaded. At the Battle of Murfreesboro, half of the men in one Confederate regiment charged entrenched Union forces armed with sticks and clubs, while another regiment's rifles were wet from the rain, though their bayonets still worked fine.[136]

The standard manual for infantry tactics after the Mexican War, written by Winfield Scott, failed to appreciate the advantages of rifles. Officers in the first years of the Civil War continued to use rifles for skirmishing, sniping, and protecting flanks. Troops were still expected to march forward into enemy fire with their elbows touching. Such an approach may appear ludicrous now, but it rested on the knowledge that musket fire was remarkably inaccurate, so that the marching troops should concentrate their fire in that one massed volley, and it did not really matter where they were when they received the enemy's volley in return. But none of this applied once breech-loading rifles were involved, for such a weapon could be reloaded five and six times before the enemy had a chance to charge, and fired with deadly accuracy. What is most astounding about American military thought in the years just before the Civil War is that the change in weaponry had no impact on tactical theory. In his memoirs, written during the war, Scott sought, with emphasis, to "dismiss this subject for ever:— *It is extremely perilous to change systems of tactics in an army in the midst of a war, and highly inconvenient at the beginning of one.*"[137]

Not even the one branch of the service for which the breech-loading rifles were perfect, the cavalry, benefited from the new technology until later in the war. There was just something about being on top of a horse that seemed to mandate the use of the saber. All the manuals agreed with General Henry Halleck that "the saber is the best weapon" for cavalry, though he did think lances would work very nicely in the charge. Halleck thought the rifle was also "useless for the great body of infantry." The cavalry simply ignored the lesson of Balaklava in the Crimean War.[138]

Oddly, one of the few works from this period to realize that rifles had changed warfare was an artillery manual by John Gibbon, who became a general during the war. Gibbon acknowledged the value of the bayonet charge, but "the fact is now incontestable that the efficiency of a body of infantry resides essentially in its accuracy of fire," as should be "apparent from the recent improvements in fire-arms." Still, Gibbon agreed with most of those writing on the subject that soldiers armed with the new rifles would fire too often and at too great a distance, resulting in a waste of ammunition; he just worried about the rifle's greater range and accuracy.[139]

While scholars debate the reasons for this adherence to outdated battle tactics, few can mistake their impact in the tens of thousands killed. More than likely it was a simple case of sticking with what one knew worked. General William S. Rosecrans sounded like General Zachary Taylor when he told his troops before the Battle of Murfreesboro to "Close steadily in upon the enemy, and, when you get within charging distance, rush on him with the bayonet." It was easy to give the order, harder to count the resulting dead. The man some rate the greatest general of the war, Thomas J. "Stonewall" Jackson, wanted some of his troops armed with pikes, a request approved by General Lee and ignored by Josiah Gorgas. Jackson's attitude toward battle cost twenty thousand Confederate casualties. A Confederate Army newspaper stated in 1862 that "The greatest minds in the South are coming to the conclusion, that our liberties are to be won by the bayonet," as "no Federal regiment can withstand a bold and fearless bayonet charge." One of those great minds, Robert E. Lee, ordered George Pickett to lead the most famous and glorious of these charges at the Battle of Gettysburg; 62 percent of those who followed him across that field into the artillery and rifle fire, about sixty-five hundred men, did not make it back. Though they made constant calls for the use of the bayonet, officers seemed not to notice that their troops rarely had the chance to use it as they were mowed down by rifle fire.[140]

Military officers in the mid-nineteenth century predicted that improved technology would actually lead to a decline in the ability of their troops to hit the enemy. These critics correctly predicted that the faster firing rate of the breechloader would induce forces to shoot at one another from a greater distance, leading them to waste ammunition at an astounding rate. Britain's adjutant general in the mid-nineteenth century, Sir Thomas Troubridge, opposed issuing faster-firing rifles to the infantry for this waste of ammunition and probable undermining of military discipline.[141] As a consequence of this fear of change, it took Union commanders several years to appreciate that the breech-loading rifle, and even more the repeating rifle, had completely transformed warfare. Rapid-fire rifles were almost unbeatable on defense, a point made well at Fredericksburg and against Pickett's troops at Gettysburg. With an effective range three times that of the smooth-bore musket, opposing forces could be decimated before they came close enough to utilize the bayonet charge so loved by mid-nineteenth-century military theory. Attacking rifles required a complete change in tactics, the abandonment of close-order formations and of the cavalry charge. This was a lesson that only a few brilliant officers and guerrilla forces understood until World War II. William T. Sherman was the master of maneuvering into a position where the Confederates would attack his rifle-carrying troops, with a resultant enormous loss of life for the Confederates. Several other Union generals came to appreciate that the rifle had shifted warfare to the defensive: Emory Upton, James H. Wilson, William B. Hazen, O. O. Howard, and, rather late in the war, U. S. Grant. The famous Confederate cavalry commander John S. Mosby thought the only use for a saber "was to hold a piece of meat over a fire for frying. I dragged one through the first year of the war, but when I became a commander, I discarded it" and relied instead on guns. Somehow most of his fellow Southern officers never learned this lesson. The result for the South was 258,000 deaths (164,000 by disease), or one-third of those who served, plus another 37 percent wounded. The North suffered 360,000 dead (250,000 from disease), or one-sixth of its soldiers, plus an additional 17.5 percent wounded.[142]

There can be little doubt that the number and quality of Union firearms determined the outcome of the war. The Confederacy had promoted gunmaking the same way the United States had over the previous seventy years. Jefferson Davis's government attempted to persuade individual gunmakers to produce more than four guns a month (the average per skilled gunsmith in 1860), subsidized a few gun entrepreneurs who promised to deliver any number of guns, and attempted to find, hire, and train more artisans to work in the government arsenals repairing firearms. It seemed to have worked in the past, but against the massive productive capacity of the North, such procedures were as grotesquely out-of-date as the peculiar institutions they were meant to defend.

The Union had shifted gears entirely. Lincoln's government needed tens of thousands of guns, as did the Confederates. But Washington no longer wasted its time on gunsmiths and artisans; the goal had become the mass production of firearms. The Northern gunmakers were delighted to accommodate this objective. The United States had discovered industrial gunmaking.

After the U.S. Navy tightened its blockade in 1863, the Confederate forces remained armed only because they had captured thousands of Union guns and because they suffered so many casualties that they could spread these weapons among their remaining troops. But the Union attained an entirely different scale of warfare and arms production. The North could afford to lose the guns—the government just ordered more. This process pleased the Northern industrialists, who increased production to unheard-of levels, hiring ever more workers, attracting more immigrants from Europe to work in their factories—plus many who were drafted into the army to replace Union casualties. It was a very efficient system, and it kept the North awash in guns. After its opening months, the Civil War was America's first conflict in which commanders did not need to spend much of their time attempting to find guns for their troops. And once the Union military leaders perceived the advantages of the breech-loading and repeating rifles, Lee might as well have armed his desperate survivors with pikes. The Confederacy never stood a chance against the combined force of Colt, Remington, Spencer, and the Springfield Armory.

In the first seventy years of their nation's history, Americans struggled with the meaning of violence in a "civilized" society. The Civil War clarified this relationship, as some people thought violence had attained a great moral good. The Civil War introduced thousands of American men to guns, showed them how to use firearms, and made them willing to use them to kill others.[143] Guns also proved extremely effective for suicide, and their use for that end became common during the Civil War years. At the war's end, Edmund Ruffin put a musket in his mouth and pulled the trigger. Many people found this an unusual way of doing it—"scattering his brains and snowy white hair against the ceiling"—but others recognized a trend.[144]

The Civil War dramatically accelerated the slow cultural shift instigated by the increase in arms production in the 1840s. By 1865 it would seem that most Americans believed that the ability to use a gun made one a better man as well as a patriot more able to defend the nation's liberties—they certainly showed a willingness to act on that assumption. Technological innovation coupled with government support had powerfully altered the national character and sensibilities within a single generation. The Civil War established these attitudes permanently by demonstrating the need for one American to be able to kill another. In 1865 the army allowed Union soldiers to take their firearms home with them. General Grant allowed Confederates to keep their side arms. Incredibly, there was no general disarming of Confederates after the war. The government had finally succeeded in arming America.[145]

Epilogue

Blessed are the peacemakers:
for they shall be called the children of God.

—Matthew 5:9

In 1861 the home of Hartford's Reverend T. C. Brownell was burglarized. The next day Samuel Colt wrote the minister a letter, releasing a copy to the press: "I take the liberty of sending you a copy of my latest work on 'Moral Reform,' trusting that, in the event of further depredations being attempted, the perpetrators may experience a feeling effect of the moral influence of my work." Enclosed was a Colt revolver.[1]

Samuel Colt referred to his guns as "peacemakers." In 1872, after Colt's death, his company brought out the first of their revolvers to fire self-contained metallic cartridges and called it "The Peacemaker." Samuel Colt's vision triumphed; by the year the Peacemaker appeared, guns were everywhere in America. The *Wichita Eagle* reported in May 1874 that "Pistols are as thick as blackberries." By that time a gun seemed to most men a requisite for their very identity: "I would as soon go out into the street without my pants as without my Colt," wrote a man in El Paso. Some settlers in Idaho were so fond of the Winchester repeating rifle that they named their town in its honor.[2]

The Civil War transformed the gun from a tool into a perceived necessity. The war preserved the Union, unifying the nation around a single icon: the gun. The gun had solved the problems of slavery and disunion; it would now be put to uses that the framers of the Constitution never conceived. As Gordon Wood wrote of a different war, "it was the Revolution, and only the Revolution, that made them one people."[3] Similarly, the Civil War reinforced the need for violence in crafting a national identity. For thousands of Confederates, firearms came to represent their struggle against Northern aggression, that "noble cause." Their government had struggled hard to acquire these guns, or else they had been taken from a dead comrade or dead Yankee. The articles of surrender required Confederate soldiers to turn in their guns, and thousands did, but Union commanders made little effort at enforcement, and thousands of Confederate soldiers took their guns home with them. Many of these firearms reappeared during Reconstruction to again do battle for white supremacy. In the North, too, guns took on symbolic power, representing for veterans of the Grand Army of the Republic the preservation of the Union. No one could mistake the significance of guns in winning the war for freedom in the United States.

In 1862 gun expert H. W. S. Cleveland noticed that "Rifle-clubs are organizing in our country-towns, and target-practice" is becoming popular. Cleveland was pleased that one positive effect of the war was the way it increased interest in firearms: "The chief obstacle to the immediate and extensive practical operation of this interest lies in the difficulty of procuring serviceable guns." With the average price of a good gun at that time being $50, requiring saving from several months' wages, there was little chance that most American men would buy their own gun, but Cleveland had hopes that increased production would lower prices. Until that golden day he called upon the state legislatures to provide all "able-bodied men" with guns, and to organize "public shooting matches" as an encouragement to practice. "The interest which is beginning to be awakened in target-practice is the germ of a great movement," Cleveland predicted, accurately.[4]

The 1860 census calculated that all the gunmakers in the country, private and public, produced fifty thousand firearms, the highest level yet attained in the United States. In the four years of war, Union gunmakers produced nearly three million firearms. In 1865 the U.S. government found itself in possession of more than 2.5 million muskets made obsolete by the development of the repeating rifle. To save money, Congress did not interfere with demobilized troops—Union or Confederate—taking their weapons home. The government also dumped its remaining muskets on the open market, drastically lowering prices for not only used guns, but all firearms. This action coincided with a crisis of overproduction, as the northern gunmakers sought to keep the same levels of output while struggling to sell their arms to a public already armed by the government. The war had introduced the majority of American males to the use of firearms; peace brought those weapons into their homes.[5]

The end of the war created a crisis for the American arms industry. Several companies that had prospered during the war collapsed as a consequence of the surplus of firearms on the market. Most notably, the Spencer Firearms Company went bankrupt in 1869, despite the fact that it made one of the best rifles in America. But Spencer did not lower its prices nor craft compelling advertising. With gun prices spiraling downward, Spencer appeared a dinosaur in a dynamic new market.[6] Remington had its multimillion-dollar government contract canceled three days after the surrender at Appomattox, and, like many manufacturers, bought its own guns back from the government for half what they sold them for in hopes of reselling them to the general public. The public wanted only the latest armaments, and yet even Winchester, the maker of that most modern of weapons, the repeater, came close to bankruptcy in 1873 as the market was simply saturated with firearms.[7]

Those companies that survived the 1873 depression prospered. The fear of John Anderson and the other British experts in the 1850s—that American machinery showed such promise that Americans might soon be exporting firearms to England—came true in the years after the Civil War.[8] Turks armed with Winchester repeaters fought Russians carrying Colts; Chinese forces using Remington-Lee rifles defeated the French at Langson; the British used American Gatling guns to expand their empire in Africa; and while the Franco-Prussian War saved Remington, American gun manufacturers learned that outdated armaments could always be dumped overseas. Much of the world used Winchester cartridges, that company producing one million rounds a day by 1875. By the 1870s the United States had become the major exporter of small arms, a position it would hold from that decade forth. But this production became more concentrated. The 1860 census listed 239 firms producing small arms in the United States; the 1900 census named just 26 firms.[9]

The production of firearms is not in itself sufficient to create a gun culture; otherwise Britain would have developed such a culture sooner than did the United States. There needed to be a conviction, supported by the government, that the individual ownership of guns served some larger social purpose; for instance, that they preserved the nation's freedom or the safety of the family. The advertising campaigns of all the gun manufacturers played up these two themes, with the added incentive of low prices. Coupled with the expansion of advertising that built on Samuel Colt's antebellum equation of firearms possession and manly security, high levels of production led to the wide distribution of guns, both geographically and socially.

The cost of firearms continued to fall after the Civil War, finally reaching a level at which anyone could afford the so-called "suicide special" of the 1890s. Guns were now the standard for murders and suicide—both rates attaining new highs. These inexpensive pistols, produced in mass quantities, could be bought for the price of a day's labor. Such pistols were given away as prizes and incentives, allowing anyone to carry a concealed weapon. In 1879 one religious magazine offered a pistol with every new subscription. Apparently the offer was very popular, eliciting only four complaints and many subscriptions from clergymen.[10]

A few events during the war anticipated the change that had come over America, none more dramatically than the New York City Draft Riot. Angry workers, mostly Irish, began the riots on July 13, 1863, by destroying the building that housed conscription headquarters. Over the next three days the rioters turned their anger on the homes of the wealthy and, most violently, upon individual blacks. For the first time, American police fired revolvers at a crowd, but that was not sufficient to curtail the crowd's violence. As the crowds crossed into black neighborhoods and burned the Colored Orphan Asylum to the ground, city officials frantically called upon the militia to restore order. To the shock of many in the militia and the press, members of the mob pulled pistols from pockets and shot at the troops, the first time that a crowd had opened fire first. It took the arrival of forces straight from the battlefield at Gettysburg, including the Irish Brigade of New York City, to end the riots on July 17, as federal forces returned fire on the rampaging crowd. No one can determine the total number of casualties, as so many bodies were destroyed by fire or thrown into the river; but at least 120 people were killed and several hundred wounded, making this the bloodiest riot in American history to that date.[11]

The Civil War itself led to brutality at a whole new, mass level. Individual acts of cruelty and murder had certainly occurred before the war, most particularly in the wars against the Indians. But few events in U.S. history matched such events as the slaughter of fifty Germans who attempted to flee Texas in 1862 in hopes of avoiding the war. Unwilling to allow them not to fight, the Texas militia hunted them down, killed thirty outright, and then lined up the survivors and killed them all. Later that same year Texas secessionists hanged another hundred Texans suspected of Unionist sympathies. In January 1863, in what is known as the Shelton Laurel Massacre, a North Carolina regiment gunned down thirteen men who had avoided service in the Confederate Army. New York's police commissioners called the Civil War "a school of violence and crime," as pithy a summary as any.[12]

Only the official murder ended in April 1865; an unofficial explosion of homicide followed the war. The murder rate reached such levels in the 1870s that many experts felt the nation was in the midst of a serious crisis. One influential book, H. V. Redfield's *Homicide, North and South,* argued for stricter concealed-weapons laws in order to reduce the number of murders. Communities from Dodge City to New York City attempted to control the use of firearms, while states around the country passed legislation against the carrying of concealed firearms. Eastern cities were becoming particularly dangerous places, as dozens of murders a year convinced citizens that their lives were in daily danger. It was not simply that the number of murders increased; the very nature of the crime shifted dramatically. The rare prewar murders had been seen in the public imagination as outbursts of madness or acts of demons. After the war, murder took on an air of calculation or anonymity. The gun itself changed the workings of murder. The face-to-face fury of strangling or the ax attack gave way to the bullet in the back of the head. Prior to the war, the emerging middle class viewed with disdain the ugliness of personal confrontation and violence, though workers tended to find some defining manliness in the ability to fight well. The resort to violence in antebellum America rarely involved the use of firearms. That attitude changed considerably after the war, especially in the cities, with revolvers now small enough to fit in a coat pocket.[13]

Civil War service inspired a number of criminal careers. Half of Quantrill's 296 raiders pursued criminal careers after the war. The most famous of these included the James, Dalton, and Younger families, Ike Flannery, Dick Burns, and Thomas Little. Their opponents, the Jay-hawkers, counted Wild Bill Hickok, Buffalo Bill Cody, and Theodore Bartles among their number. What set these groups apart from criminal predecessors was their close attachment to and constant use of firearms. They actually had sufficient ammunition to practice regularly, and many of them became excellent shots as a consequence. And all showed a willingness to shoot to kill.[14] The homicide rate in the West reached historic highs in the twenty years after Appomattox, though without attaining the levels of the great eastern cities or the South—with one exception. In the towns of Abilene, Ellsworth, Wichita, and Dodge City, Kansas, and in Caldwell, Oklahoma, forty-five people died from gunshots between 1870 and 1885.[15] The exception was Texas. The State Constitutional Convention of 1868 received a report that 1,035 murders had occurred in the three years since the end of the war, more than half being white-on-white.[16]

Much western violence is mythology. The most violent year in the history of Deadwood, South Dakota, was 1876. Four people, including Wild Bill Hickok, were murdered. Tombstone's most violent year, 1881, witnessed the slaughter at the O.K. Corral, in which the Earps and Doc Holliday gunned down three men. The town reacted strenuously against these murders, draping a banner on the caskets, "Murdered in the Streets of Tombstone." A Citizens' Safety Committee threatened to hang the Earps if they were responsible for any more violence. It is no wonder a British visitor who came to Virginia City in 1876 hoping to see western violence was grievously disappointed. No one was shot, and the city was guilty of "the most perfect order and decorum." Individuals could be just as disappointing. Billy the Kid is generally credited with killing twenty-two men. While he was a psychopath, it appears that he actually killed only three men. Similarly, Bat Masterson used to be credited with killing some twenty men, whereas three again seems accurate. Masterson was so hounded on this point in later life that he bought an old .45 Colt in a gun-shop in New York, carved twenty-two notches in it, and sold it for a sizable profit. Masterson never claimed that he used this gun to kill anyone: "I simply said that I hadn't counted Mexicans and Indians, and he went away tickled to death."[17]

The great Oklahoma land rush of 1889 was famous for bringing together fifteen thousand men from around the world and armed to the teeth, each fighting desperately for the best claim. Yet "not a single killing, gunshot wound, or fist fight took place." Disputes were settled by the flip of a coin. Few of these settlers knew one another; yet within thirty-six hours of establishing Guthrie, the mob of tough guys had elected a mayor and city council, and adopted a city charter and head tax. Within a few weeks Baptists, Methodists, and Presbyterians were holding services in tents and planning the construction of churches. Even contemporary critics of western culture, such as A. S. Mercer, admitted that the western United States in the last half of the nineteenth century was less violent and lawless than most other places in the world, a view supported by most serious historians of the subject.[18] The law could certainly be brutal; federal judge Isaac Parker of Fort Smith, Arkansas, tried 13,500 cases between 1875 and 1896; 9,500 people were convicted or pled guilty and

172 of these were hanged.[19] But the real western violence came from industry, not guns. In any given year in the last forty years of the nineteenth century, more industrial accidents occurred than murders during this entire period.[20]

Even if the number of western murders does not match those killed in the popular imagination, a substantial increase had occurred from the antebellum period. It was not only the numbers that had changed, but attitudes, too. In 1871 a group of ranchers trailed and murdered a group of thirty Digger Indians in the Sacramento Valley: "Kingsley could not bear to kill them [the Indian children] with his 56-calibre Spencer rifle. 'It tore them up so bad.' So he did it with his 38-calibre Smith and Wesson revolver."[21]

Guns were used in ways that had never been anticipated prior to the Civil War, and violence reached levels that would have staggered antebellum society. In 1866 Louisiana Republicans, supposedly backed by the federal government, convened a constitutional convention at the Mechanics Institute in New Orleans with the intention of writing a democratic constitution extending civil rights to blacks. As the meeting came to order, angry whites led by police officers attacked the building, firing at the crowd through the windows, and shooting down others as they attempted to flee. Thirty-eight people were killed and 150 wounded. Nothing like that had ever happened before in America. In 1877 as strikes swept the country, private detective agencies like the Pinkertons shot workers, and the workers returned fire, battling militia and even federal troops. In Chicago strikers paraded the streets crying, "We want arms," breaking into gun stores along the way. The *Chicago Tribune* estimated that one-tenth of all adults in the city carried a concealed pistol at this time: "Every man who could beg, buy, or borrow a revolver carried it." In Pittsburgh workers supported by armed police laid siege to the Pennsylvania militia in a railyard roundhouse and sent burning trains into their midst in an effort to burn them out. The militia escaped but fled the city. It took six thousand troops to restore order; at least forty-five people were killed. The United States had never witnessed anything like it.[22]

The most prestigious gun manufacturers continued to appeal to the English standard of consumption throughout the century. For instance, Colt advertised its Model 1888 Hammerless Double Shotgun as "made of the best materials and workmanship, and is in all respects equal to the most costly and best English sporting guns." Remington also compared its guns to the superior English models, but in one instance aimed higher, labeling their guns "Fit for the Gods." But most gunmakers played on the fear of a heavily armed society. Colt's one-word ad, "Protection," with a picture of a revolver, summed it up. In the 1870s there was a "tramp" scare, the conviction that thousands of tramps were wandering the country with murder on their minds. The Western Gun Works of Chicago issued a "Tramps' Terror" pistol for only $3. This gun was "for Police, Bankers, and Household use," and was "specially adapted for the Pocket." Their advertisement warned that "Tramps, Burglars and Thieves infest all parts of the Country." But the solution was obvious: "Everyone should go Armed."[23]

The fear becomes the danger, as Americans acted on the imagined terrors around them and armed themselves for private protection. Accidental shootings became common, and family arguments too often ended with gunshots. In *Innocents Abroad,* Mark Twain described how many of his fellow "pilgrims" had read romantic guidebooks that put "melodramatic nonsense" into their heads: "All at once, when one is jogging along stupidly in the sun . . . here they come, at a stormy gallop . . . and as they whiz by out comes a little potato gun of a revolver, there is a startling little pop, and a small pellet goes singing through the air." Twain's fellow travelers were firing at imaginary perils, but it was Twain who was endangered: "I do not mind Bedouins—I am not afraid of them; because neither Bedouins nor ordinary Arabs have shown any disposition to harm us—but I *do* feel afraid of my own comrades." He was certain that "Some of us will be shot before we finish this pilgrimage." Hearing stories of the dread all around them, they "keep themselves in a constant state of quixotic heroism. They have their hands on their pistols all the time, and every now and then, when you least expect it, they snatch them out and take aim at Bedouins who do not exist."[24]

There was wide acceptance by the 1870s of the saying "God created men; Colonel Colt made them equal." The belief was widely held that two men with guns were two equals. However, the reality of gun use during Reconstruction demonstrated the gun's ability to undermine equality in America. With freedom, many blacks took to carrying pistols as a symbol of their newly gained authority. A Senate investigating committee was told that the South "is the greatest place on the face of the earth for pistols. No man is comfortable down there unless he has got his pistols." Whitelaw Reid reported that one could not brush against a white southerner "without being bruised by his concealed revolver." Observer after observer reported fights with fists, knives, and guns as daily occurrences in the South. Even Union officers were shocked by the level of violence in the South after the war. "Our tragedies are crimes," wrote John William De Forest, "their tragedies are gentilities which the public voice does not condemn and for which the law rarely exacts a penalty."[25] Some governments hoped to contain this violence through legislation; Kansas passed a law forbidding former Confederates from owning firearms, while Congress passed the Army Appropriation Act in March 1867, terminating the entire southern militia because it was limited to whites. In contrast, black militia units were disarmed in Baltimore after the war.[26] These efforts were wasted, as even southern whites noticed a remarkable and troubling shift toward greater violence after the war.[27]

Defeated Confederates stockpiled guns in preparation for a "war of the races." This preparation actually increased with time, despite the absence of any evidence that free blacks were about to launch their long-delayed day of retribution. The result was that every year for a decade after the war ended, former Confederates murdered hundreds of people who dared to resist the restoration of racist governments. These whites even organized themselves into an illegal militia, the Ku Klux Klan. The Klan was a well-armed continuation of the slave patrol, and like the antebellum slave patrols, the Klan focused on terrorizing blacks and preventing their self-defense by seizing any guns found in their possession. As one visitor to the South after the war observed, the whites now intended to "govern . . . by the pistol and the rifle."[28]

In response, many freed blacks organized themselves into protective militia companies to protect their access to the rights of citizenship. The freedmen in turn clearly enjoyed bearing the symbol of white power. Though responsible for negating integrated militia, whites were deeply resentful of black-dominated militia companies; the idea of an armed black violated their understanding of the universe—guns were for whites, and that was all there was to it. The editor of the *Charleston Mercury* wrote that if blacks were allowed to bear arms they would become "swaggering buck niggers" and would of course attack white women (it was a pity that the concept of projection had not yet been developed). White racists were not about to wait for the black militia to become familiar with their firearms, but launched preemptive strikes.[29]

One of these battlegrounds was South Carolina. In 1871 the federal government supplied ten thousand obsolete Springfield muskets to South Carolina for use by the black militia. The state paid Remington $90,000 to convert them to breechloaders and bought an additional thousand Winchesters; but these eleven thousand guns were hardly sufficient for the ninety thousand enrolled members of the nearly all-black militia. "Still," as Lou Falkner Williams wrote, "eleven thousand armed former slaves must have seemed enormously threatening to a white population long established in the belief that one black with a squirrel gun represented a serious danger of insurrection." The result of that fear was thirty-eight murders in South Carolina in the few months between the 1870 election and April 1871, a murder rate that dwarfed anything in the antebellum years. Though the victims were all either blacks or their white supporters, Governor Robert K. Scott caved in to white pressure in 1871 and ordered the disarming of the black militia.[30]

President U. S. Grant attempted to control this homicidal epidemic in the South by issuing an executive order in October 1871 requiring "all persons composing the unlawful combinations and conspiracies" in the South to turn over their weapons to U.S. marshals. He also suspended habeas corpus, which was unprecedented in peacetime, and launched a number of federal trials of Klan members. But executive orders and trials were no longer sufficient against a well-armed and broad-based conspiracy. The South Carolina racists responded to these trials by going public. Their effort to seize control of the state government was no longer a secret conspiracy—it was out in the open. With the goal of terrifying blacks into not voting in the 1874 election, the Democrats organized rifle clubs as fronts for the Klan, with the slogan "force without violence." These "social clubs" demonstrated their real purpose in the 1876 election when at least 125 blacks were murdered, as rifle club members poured into black-dominated areas and broke up political rallies. As one member recorded, the rifle clubs "determined to kill all the negroes they could find with arms." Put bluntly, these clubs were seizing the guns of other citizens without due process, a clear violation of the Constitution.[31]

South Carolina was not alone in this exercise of terror against blacks. In Vicksburg, Mississippi, in December 1874, armed whites drove black Sheriff Peter Crosby from office. Crosby returned to town on the morning of December 7 with more than one hundred armed supporters. The blacks hesitated to use violence; the whites under the command of former Confederate officer Horace H. Miller did not waver. Witnesses reported that "not one-half" of the blacks were "armed with any weapon but a pistol, and many wholly unarmed and none of them armed with weapons of effectiveness." One of the whites stated, "There wasn't any danger for we were firing with long-range guns at long range, and they with shot guns or short-range guns." The whites held a number of military rifles, which they fired on the blacks after the latter had turned to leave. "It was no battle," the Congressional committee of inquiry concluded, "it was a simple massacre, unutterably disgraceful to all engaged in it." The purpose was clearly stated: "to strike a wholesome terror into colored people." At least twelve blacks and one white were killed. The white southern press played up this new "Battle of Vicksburg" as a great military success.[32]

In 1875 the gun industry put out a little book titled *The Pistol as a Weapon of Defense in Its Home and on the Road*. This work praised the pistol as an equalizer that "renders mere physical strength of no account, and enables the weak and delicate to successfully resist the attacks of the strong and brutal." The book optimistically did not consider the possibility that the gun could be used for attack as well as defense, and baldly stated that "There can be no objections to it [a pistol] on moral or prudential grounds."[33] Inexpensive and readily available guns changed many social equations, as the Ku Klux Klan demonstrated in their terror campaigns in the South, most notoriously in Louisiana's Colfax Massacre of 1873.

In Colfax Parish, Louisiana, 150 freedmen gathered together at the county courthouse to defend themselves against a threatened attack by whites angry at local Republican electoral successes. The black farmers carried shotguns, muskets, and twelve Enfields. On Easter Sunday, 1873, a force of roughly 150 whites, armed with rifles and a cannon, began firing on the blacks from several hundred yards, well beyond the range of the blacks' guns. The blacks retreated into a stable, which the whites set on fire. When the blacks threw down their arms and rushed out with their hands in the air, the whites shot them down; several freedmen preferred to burn to death. The whites found themselves with between forty and fifty prisoners; they lined them up and shot them dead. Two days later two federal officials arrived and found the dead bodies still on the ground. They counted at least 105 dead blacks and three whites, a figure that does not include those who died in the fire, nor the twenty or so who were killed along the riverbank, nor those who crawled into the woods and died of their wounds.[34]

When local authorities would not bring murder charges against the whites, the federal government brought ninety-eight people to trial for violating the 1870 Force Act. Among other arguments, the government insisted that the white mob, in seeking to disarm black citizens, violated the Second Amendment right to possess firearms. In the centennial year of 1876, the U.S. Supreme Court ruled in *U.S. v. Cruikshank* that the right "of bearing arms for a lawful purpose is not a right granted by the Constitution nor is it in any manner dependent upon that instrument for its existence. . . . This is one of the amendments that has no other effect than to restrict the power of the national government." The Fourteenth Amendment, the court explained, "prohibits a State from depriving any person of life, liberty, or property, without due process of law; but this adds nothing to the rights of one citizen as against another." Since private persons had acted to deprive individuals of their rights, there was nothing the federal government could do—it remained a question of state authority. The irony of the Cruikshank decision is that it reaffirmed the framers' conception of the Second Amendment while insuring that it would be ignored. Private citizens were empowered to use deadly force to attain political ends without fear of prosecution, so long as the state government agreed with their objectives. Since the goal was white supremacy, the Supreme Court handed white racists all the legitimization they needed to institute a reign of terror that would last nearly a hundred years.[35]

And yet, despite all this horrific violence, the gun also became a plaything. Railroads organized special trips that allowed passengers to shoot buffalo from the train—at least while supplies lasted. It has been estimated that there were one hundred million bison in 1500, and perhaps fifty million in 1800; in 1887 the U.S. government counted 1,091. In the single year of 1872, 1.5 million buffalo were killed. Even then, nothing could stop the fascination of killing bison for many people. In 1885 Pat T. Tucker described one such kill: "At the first crack of the rifle I dropped the leader of the herd, a magnificent creature that had done well to preserve this last remnant of a once countless herd." From 1865 on, Fourth of July celebrations were routinely punctuated by gunfire, as people shot into the air, constantly forgetting Newton's discovery. The Hartford *Daily Times,* in reporting without comment the "hundreds of explosions of pistols" around the city, mentioned one "4th of July celebration mishap" that "accidentally shot" Harriet Beecher Stowe's daughter when one of those bullets came back to earth.[36]

After the Civil War, the major gun manufacturers attempted to maintain public enthusiasm for firearms by sending teams of marksmen to give public displays of shooting skills. Captain A. H. Bogardus was one such champion, becoming nationally famous for his demonstrations, such as shooting fifty-five hundred glass balls with a shotgun in seven hours. In

1888 Dr. W. F. Carver fired his Winchester every day for a week, hitting 60,000 wooden balls thrown in the air, missing only 670. Most famous of course was Annie Oakley, who toured with her husband, Frank Butler, as representatives of Remington. Winchester competed with their own husband-and-wife team, Adolph and Elizabeth "Plinkey" Topperwein. Adolph Topperwein spent ten days shooting at targets, missing only nine times out of 72,500 shots fired. Three facts stand out in such displays: the widespread public interest in them; the astounding amount of ammunition wasted in such displays; and the equal billing given to women, probably the first time a sport had allowed them such equality. The .22 was developed in the 1880s specifically to encourage such casual marksmanship among the public, and was even referred to as "the youth rifle" within the industry.[37]

And of course guns filled the literature of the period. There were the Western dime novels of Edward S. Ellis, Ned Buntline (Edward Z. C. Judson), Prentiss Ingraham, and dozens of imitators who glorified and exaggerated the violent lives of heroes, imaginary and real. More than five hundred of these dime novels were written about a western scout named Buffalo Bill Cody. He became a myth in his own lifetime, and he returned the favor by traveling the world with his Wild West Show, reinforcing the popular image of the frontier before appreciative crowds. Guns found their way also into the more refined literature of the period, and established a permanent place in the nation's humor. Mark Twain especially enjoyed mocking those who thought the gun elevated them to heroic status, while occasionally reminding his readers of the real cost of gun violence. And it was in these years that artists and politicians crafted the mythical image of the heroic Minuteman, winning American independence with his ever-ready musket. In 1875 Daniel Chester French gave this imagined past form with his statue *The Minuteman,* the classic embodiment of the well-regulated and well-armed militia.[38]

Guns had become everyday items, their presence in American life no longer questioned. To take a single example, in 1911 the Remington Company brought out a "Boy Scout Special," which included a bayonet. The Boy Scouts came under fire as a militarist group and were defended on precisely those grounds. New York's adjutant general hoped the Boy Scouts would reverse the decline of martial spirit in the United States brought on by "female school-teachers, . . . Suffragettes," and, of course, socialists. Using a gun seemed the best and most appropriate way to battle these insidious forces. Some people disagreed, but they were the minority.

When the National Council of the Boy Scouts of America voted in 1916 to award a Marksmanship Merit Badge, many active supporters, including members of their board, left the group. But the marksmanship badge is still available.[39]

Having finally succeeded in arming its citizens, the government generally maintained a benign neutrality in the further promotion of the gun culture, with one exception: subsidies to the National Rifle Association (NRA). The very existence of the National Rifle Association is a testament to the absence of a widespread gun culture in the antebellum period. Many former Union officers recalled their soldiers' lack of familiarity with firearms and hoped to avoid that situation in the future. The NRA's founders, the Union veterans William Conant Church and George Wood Wingate, sought to maintain a familiarity with firearms in times of peace. Doing so required teaching a new generation of American men to shoot. Church and Wingate understood that accuracy was irrelevant with the traditional muzzle-loading musket, while the new mass-produced breech-loading rifles offered the opportunity to develop sharpshooting skills. But American men had to own guns and use them regularly to develop these skills. With support from the State of New York—monetary backing that would later be taken over by the federal government—the NRA opened its first target-shooting range at Creedmore in 1872. The NRA enjoyed its greatest success in the East, and followed up Creedmore with the first great indoor shooting range, a hundred-yard-long tunnel built at 260 Broadway in New York City. The NRA's influence, along with its emphasis on individual gun ownership, spread west from Long Island.[40]

By the mid-1870s guns were everywhere in American life. From living rooms to theaters, literature to art, popular songs to patriotic parades, the gun defined American character. This cultural identification became so complete that by the centennial celebrations of 1876 it was impossible to conceive that America had ever been any other way. Guns filled the newspapers that year: Buffalo Bill Cody shot Yellow Hand; Jack McCall shot Wild Bill Hickok in the back; Frank Eclestadt, a dispatch rider with the army, fought off twelve Indians with a pair of revolvers, killing two; and in Hamburg, South Carolina, a white militia attempting to disarm a black militia shot and killed five blacks. One of the more indicative incidents that year of the presence of firearms in American life came in Northfield, Minnesota, on September 7, when the James gang swept into town to rob the bank. After shooting a teller, they found themselves under fire from the good people of Northfield. These were not sheriffs drawing their guns, merely people who lived in town running home for their rifles, many of which had last seen service in the Civil War. Every member of the eight-man gang was shot, two of them dead. Nothing like this had ever happened before.[41]

What had changed by 1876 from just twenty years earlier was the supply of guns and ammunition, which had increased astronomically. After the war, when the U.S. Army was armed with the best new breechloaders, their rate of accuracy did not improve over Mexican War standards, as they tended to shoot from a greater distance. General George Crook's troops fired off twenty-five thousand rounds during their 1876 campaign against the Cheyenne and Sioux, hitting 252 of their enemy, or a ratio of 99:1. All those experts had been right: rapid-fire rifles did lead troops to waste ammunition.[42]

Too much confidence could be placed in the new guns, as George Armstrong Custer discovered on June 25, 1876. Custer knew that as white men armed with repeating rifles, his troops had nothing to fear from a bunch of savages. Custer must have been ignorant of the Greek concept of hubris as he marched his 225 men into the midst of the largest concentration of Indian warriors ever assembled, 1,500 men under the brilliant leadership of Crazy Horse. It is impossible to know how many and what kind of guns the Sioux and their allies used at Little Bighorn. At the Fetterman Massacre in 1866, the Indians had killed eighty-one U.S. soldiers, only four of them with bullets. Some scholars have estimated that half the Sioux carried firearms by 1876, and guns were widely available by that date. But the firearms the Indians acquired never matched the quality of the Springfield Model 1873 .45-70s carried by Custer's troops. When Crazy Horse surrendered, his remaining 250 warriors had forty-six breechloaders, thirty-five muzzle-loading muskets, and thirty-three revolvers, enough guns for 45 percent of his warriors. Sitting Bull's gun was a forty-year-old Hawken rifle. The Battle of Little Bighorn proved to be the last victory of America's first gun culture. Just beyond the horizon, a more massive gun culture waited to squash the Indians once and for all. By the time Crazy Horse surrendered with his exhausted band of followers in May 1877, America's gun culture had attained complete victory. The Peacemakers triumphed.[43]

Appendix

Table One

Percentage of Probate Inventories Listing Firearms

	1765–90	1808–11	1819–21	1830–32	1849–50	1858–59
Frontier	14.2	15.8	16.9	20.4	27.8	31.6
Northern coast:						
urban	16.1	16.6	17.3	20.8	27.3	25
rural	14.9	13.1	13.8	14.3	18.7	19.2
South	18.3	17.6	20.2	21.6	33.3	40.3
NATIONAL AVERAGE	14.7	16.1	17.0	20.7	27.6	32.5

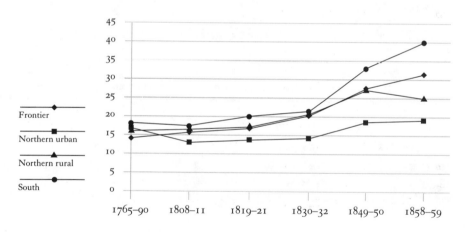

NOTES: No differentiation is made between functioning and dysfunctional firearms in these figures.

SOURCES: Forty counties have been divided into four regional groups. Frontier counties moved into other categories with each new time period. Several of the counties examined changed their name over time; for easier identification, the modern names are used. Counties included: Bennington, Rutland, Windham, and Windsor, Vermont; Luzerne, Northampton, Philadelphia, Washington, and Westmoreland, Pennsylvania; Litchfield and New Haven, Connecticut; Essex, Hampshire, Plymouth, Suffolk, and Worcester, Massachusetts; Burlington, New Jersey; Kent, Delaware; Anne Arundel and Queen Anne, Maryland; Fairfax, Spotsylvania, Chesterfield, Charlotte, Halifax, Mecklenburg, Brunswick, and Southampton, Virginia; Orange and Halifax, North Carolina; Charleston, South Carolina; Baldwin, Chatham, and Glynn, Georgia; Jefferson and Knox, Indiana; Adams and Washington, Ohio; San Francisco and Los Angeles, California.

Table Two

Census of American Militia Members and Firearms, 1803–30

	1803	1810	1820	1830
Militia members	524,086	677,681	837,498	1,128,594
Muskets	183,070	203,517	315,459	251,019
Rifles	39,648	55,632	84,816	108,036
Other	13,113	49,105	0	0
TOTAL ARMS	235,831	308,254	400,275	359,055

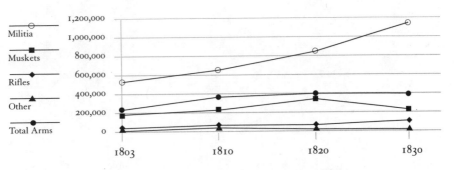

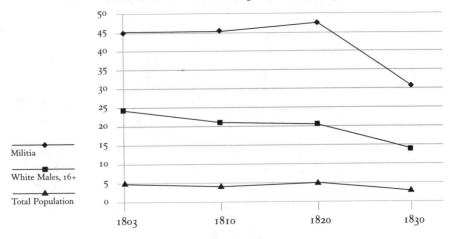

Total Firearms as a Percentage of Selected Populations, 1803–30

NOTES: "Other" includes pistols, fowling pieces, blunderbusses, and other curiosities. From 1820 on, such pieces were included with muskets.

SOURCES: *American State Papers: Documents, Legislative and Executive, of the Congress of the United States*, class V: *Military Affairs*, 7 vols. (Washington, DC, 1832–61), 1: 162, 169–72, 258–62; 2: 319–23, 361–64; 4: 683–85; *Census for 1820* (Washington, DC, 1821); *Fifth Census; or Enumeration of the Inhabitants of the United States, 1830* (Washington, DC, 1832).

Table Three

Private Gun Ownership in Massachusetts

	NUMBER OF PRIVATELY OWNED MUSKETS OR RIFLES	POPULATION	PERCENT OF POPULATION WITH GUNS	
			TOTAL POPULATION	WHITE MALES 16 OR OLDER
1789	27,619	475,327	5.81	23.0
1795	34,000	524,946	6.48	25.6
1808	50,000	675,509	7.4	28.7
1812	49,000	482,289	10.16	27.8
1815	50,000	497,664	10.05	29.8
1824	32,128	557,978	5.76	19.4
1839	21,760	724,931	3.0	9.5

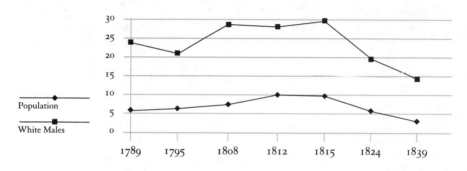

NOTES: Population estimates are based on per-year increase during the decade. The adjutant general tended to round up the number of muskets in that state.

SOURCES: Adjutant General, *Annual Return of the Militia for Massachusetts, and Quartermaster General's Letter Book* 6: 9, Commonwealth of Massachusetts Military Division, Military Records (National Guard Armory, Natick, MA).

Table Four

Federal Arms Delivered to the States, 1808–18

	ENTITLED	RECEIVED	DUE	EXTRA
Connecticut	1,571	2,000		429
Delaware	639	1,650		1,011
District of Columbia	192	2,200		2,008
Georgia	2,358	3,000		642
Illinois	*	657	657	
Indiana	430	0	430	
Kentucky	4,266	1,500	2,766	
Louisiana	*	3,250		3,250
Maryland	2,762	4,000		1,238
Massachusetts	5,935	3,100	2,835	
Michigan	*	0		
Mississippi	454	0	454	
Missouri	241	0	241	
New Hampshire	2,136	1,400	736	
New Jersey	3,171	3,156	16	
New York	8,153	16,012		7,859
North Carolina	3,708	2,180	1,528	
Ohio	3,155	3,000	155	
Pennsylvania	8,529	4,258	4,271	
Rhode Island	708	2,000		1,292
South Carolina	2,763	2,000	763	
Tennessee	2,504	1,500	1,004	
Vermont	1,738	2,500		762
Virginia	7,195	3,244	3,949	
TOTAL	63,265	61,950	19,194	19,148

*No militia return. Where a state received more than its due, that amount was subtracted from the next year's quota.

NOTES: The federal government supplied 6,195 guns per year.

SOURCE: *American State Papers: Military Affairs* 1: 678, 4: 683–85.

Table Five

Federal Arms Delivered to the States, 1836

	LAST RETURN	NUMBER OF MILITIA	NUMBER OF ARMS DELIVERED
Alabama	1829	14,892	167
Arizona	1825	2,028	23
Connecticut	1836	23,826	268
Delaware	1827	9,229	104
District of Columbia	1832	1,249	14
Florida	1831	827	9
Georgia	1834	48,461	545
Illinois	1831	27,386	309
Indiana	1833	53,913	606
Kentucky	1836	71,483	805
Louisiana	1830	14,808	166
Maine	1836	42,468	478
Maryland	1836	46,854	528
Massachusetts	1836	44,911	505
Michigan	1831	5,476	62
Mississippi	1830	13,724	154
Missouri	1835	6,170	70
New Hampshire	1836	27,473	310
New Jersey	1829	39,171	442
New York	1836	184,728	2,078
North Carolina	1835	64,415	724
Ohio	1836	146,428	1,647
Pennsylvania	1834	202,281	2,275
Rhode Island	1832	1,377	15
South Carolina	1833	51,112	576
Tennessee	1830	60,982	687
Vermont	1824	25,581	287
Virginia	1836	101,838	1,146
Wisconsin	none		
TOTALS		1,333,091	15,000

SOURCE: *American State Papers: Military Affairs* 7: 739–40.

Table Six

Nineteenth-Century Murder Methods

	BY HAND	STABBING	AX	GUN	POISON	OTHER	TOTAL
1801–15	17	9	8	10	3	1	48
1816–30	30	19	11	13	6	2	81
1831–45	45	25	14	21	7	2	114
1846–60	37	32	11	52	14	3	149
1861–75	43	33	14	76	7	4	177
1876–90	27	19	2	98	11	9	166
TOTALS	199	137	60	270	48	21	735

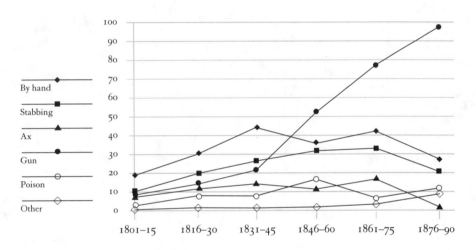

NOTES: "By hand" is defined as beating, drowning, and strangling; "other" includes abortion, cannon, bomb, and chloroform.

Grouped in fifteen-year periods to allow for annual volatility because of small numbers involved.

The executions of rebellious slaves have not been included in these statistics, though they certainly were unjustifiable homicides. A few notable beating deaths of slaves have been included as they reached the newspapers, though the law did not always consider them murder. Also excluded from this data are all war-related murders and deaths and deaths in the New York City Draft Riot of July 1863.

SOURCES: 501 cases drawn from Thomas M. McDade, *The Annals of Murder: A Bibliography of Books and Pamphlets on American Murders from Colonial Times to 1900* (Norman, OK, 1961); an additional 184 cases drawn from the following newspapers: *Baltimore Weekly Magazine*; *Niles' Weekly Register* (Baltimore); *Boston Gazette*; *Southern Patriot* (Charleston, SC); *Western Monthly Magazine* (Cincinnati); *Western Miscellany* (Dayton, OH); *Connecticut Courant* (Hartford); *Southern Recorder* (Milledgeville, GA); *New York World*; *New York Tribune*; *Graham's American Monthly Magazine* (Philadelphia); *Pennsylvania Packet* (Philadelphia); *Southern Literary Messenger* (Richmond, VA); *Vermont Journal* (Windsor).

Table Seven

Contractors Under the 1808 Militia Act

This list includes most of the major private gunmakers in the
United States in the years from 1808 to 1820.

CONTRACTORS	STATE	NUMBER CONTRACTED	NUMBER DELIVERED
W & I Henry	PA	10,000	4,246
Goetz & Westphall	PA	2,500	1,019
John Miles	NJ	9,200	2,407
Winner & Nipes	PA	9,000	3,900
Waters & Whitmore	MA	5,000	3,000
Ethan Stillman	CT	2,500	825
Dan Gilbert	MA	5,000	875
French, Blake, & Kinsley	MA	4,000	2,175
I & C Barstow	NH	2,500	1,625
Wheeler & Morrison	VA	2,500	125
Oli Bidwell	CT	4,000	750
O & E Evans	PA	4,000	1,960
Steph Jenks	RI	4,000	2,300
R & C Leonard	MA	5,000	2,125
A & P Bartlett	MA	2,500	1,500
Rufus Perkins	MA	4,500	200
I & N Brooke	PA	4,000	1,257
W & H Shannon	PA	4,000	1,101
Sweet & Jenks	RI	3,000	250
TOTALS		87,200	31,640 (36.3%)

DELIVERY LEVELS

1809: 2,371
1810: 9,129
1811: 12,074
1812: 7,816
1813: 3,087

TOTAL: 34,477

NOTE: The difference of 2,837 guns appears to have been older muskets refurbished by a number of different gunmakers.

SOURCE: *American State Papers: Military Affairs* 1: 255–58, 302–7, 327–29, 335–38, 624–26, 677–80, 848–60.

Table Eight

Average Yearly Arms Production at the Springfield and Harpers Ferry Armories, 1795–1870

	HARPERS FERRY	SPRINGFIELD
1795–1800	na	2,102
1801–10	3,107	5,099
1811–20	7,318	10,473
1821–30	11,855	14,770
1831–40	10,264	13,047
1841–50	8,551	12,603
1851–60	8,081	12,586
1861–70		90,992

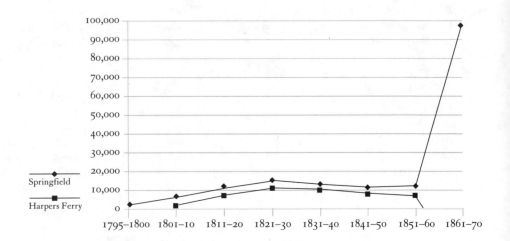

SOURCES: Merritt Roe Smith, *Harpers Ferry Armory and the New Technology: The Challenge of Change* (Ithaca, NY, 1977), 342–47; Felicia J. Deyrup, *Arms Makers of the Connecticut Valley* (Northampton, MA, 1948), 233. The statistics include all firearms made at these armories (muskets, rifles, pistols, carbines, and pattern arms). Confederate troops destroyed most of the armory at Harpers Ferry in June 1861.

Table Nine

Arms Manufactured in the United States, 1823

STATE	NUMBER	MARKET VALUE GOODS PRODUCED	CAPITAL	WORKERS	VALUE OF RAW MATERIALS	WAGES
Massachusetts	1	$28,000	$30,000	35	$5,000	$4,000
Connecticut	3	83,000	155,000	132	14,700	44,000
New York	6	8,650	17,000	17	2,935	2,580
Pennsylvania	4	8,800	7,300	14	1,860	2,250
Virginia	4	2,175	490	8	805	130
Tennessee	27	20,074	4,877	60	3,417	660
Ohio	7	10,150	18,908	19	2,233	1,044
Missouri	1	1,500	n/a	2	350	100
North Carolina	2	1,000	n/a	2	300	n/a
Georgia	6	4,211	375	17	472	180
Alabama	2	700	100	2	50	5
Illinois	1	n/a	n/a	2	200	n/a
Louisiana	1	2,400	750	1	250	n/a
TOTALS	65	170,660	223,000	311	32,572	54,949

NOTES: The national armories are not included in these figures. "Workers" does not include apprentices.

SOURCE: *Digest of Accounts of Manufacturing Establishments in United States, and of Their Manufactures* (Washington, DC, 1823).

Table 10

Arms Manufacturers in the United States, 1833

Massachusetts

1. Greenfield, Martin Smith, gun factory, capitalized at $3,800, 6 workers paid $1.25/day each, produces 600 guns per year at $12 each = $7,200.

2. Sherburn, gunsmith, capitalized at $800, 3 workers paid $1 per day each, produces 100 rifles per year at $15 each = $1,500, 100 muskets = $700, other work = $2,700.

3. Millbury, Asa Waters (in business since 1816), capitalized at $47,500, 40 workers paid $14,875, 2,000 muskets = $24,500, iron = $5,400, total production of $29,900.

4. Millbury, Luke Harrington (1831), capitalized at $4,600, 4 workers paid $1,375, 1,100 muskets at $5 each = $5,500, 100 rifles = $1,000, total production of $6,500.

5. Sutton, capitalized at $3,200, 2 workers paid $620, 600 rifle barrels, $1,800 (using Russian iron), 100 gun barrels, $300 = $2,100.

6. Shrewsbury, gunsmiths, capitalized at $9,500, 16 workers paid $4,340, (using English locks) 10,000 rifles, 2,000 muskets. No total value listed.

New Hampshire

1. Keene, capitalized at $1,150, use English iron, 3 workers, total production of $1,600.

2. Hinsdale, gunsmith, capitalized at $1,150, 3 workers, total production of $1,600.

Connecticut

1. Middletown, 3 gun factories, capitalized at $137,000 (iron from Salisbury, CT), 90 workers paid $1.50 per day each, 12-hour days, 5,000 muskets = $60,000, sold entirely within U.S.

SOURCE: Secretary of the Treasury McLane, *Documents Relative to the Manufactures in the United States* (Washington, DC, 1833), vols. 3–7 of Thomas C. Cochran, ed., *The New American State Papers: Manufactures,* 9 vols. (Wilmington, DE, 1972), 3: 318–19; 4: 19–20, 181–82, 201–02, 205–06, 251–52; 5: 35–36, 119–20, 359–61.

Notes

A complete bibliography is located at the
author's web site at Emory University:
www.emory.edu/HISTORY/ATLAS/faculty.

Introduction
In Search of Guns

1. *Time,* 6 April 1998, 28–37; *Newsweek,* 6 April 1998, 20–26. This notion of teaching very young children to shoot is a standard component of the gun culture, with special guns made for those under ten years old. See, for instance, "Shooting Fun for the Whole Family," which appeared in *Guns & Ammo* after the events at Columbine High School, and features the training of a four-year-old boy in gun use. *Guns & Ammo,* July 1999, A–N.

2. In 1990 there were 36,866 deaths involving firearms in the United States. The high point for American murders so far was 1991, with 24,703. In 1993 there were 22,540 murders and 1,932,270 violent crimes reported; in 1994 there were 1,924,188 violent crimes. U.S. Department of Justice, *Uniform Crime Reports for the United States 1993* (Washington, DC, 1994), 20–24; *The World Almanac, 1994* (Mahwah, NJ, 1994), 963–64, 967; *Statistics Canada, 1995* (Ottawa, ONT, 1995); Osha Gray Davidson, *Under Fire: The NRA and the Battle for Gun Control* (New York, 1993), 117; *Creative Loafing,* 25 May 1996; *Herald Tribune,* 13 August 1993.

3. Dave Grossman, *On Killing: The Psychological Cost of Learning to Kill in War and Society* (Boston, 1995); *Atlanta Constitution,* 18 June 1992, 1.

4. Daniel J. Boorstin, *The Americans: The Colonial Experience* (New York, 1958), 353. See also, for instance, Richard Maxwell Brown, *Strain of Violence: Historical Studies of American Violence and Vigilantism* (New York, 1975); Robert Elman, *Fired in Anger* (Garden City, NY, 1968); John Hope Franklin, *The Militant South, 1800–1861* (Cambridge, 1956), 20–25.

5. Richard Slotkin, *Regeneration Through Violence: The Mythology of the American Frontier, 1600–1860* (Middletown, CT, 1973).

6. Richard Maxwell Brown, *Strain of Violence;* Richard Slotkin, *Regeneration Through Violence;* Arnold Madison, *Vigilantism in America* (New York, 1973);

Richard E. Nisbett and Dov Cohen, *Culture of Honor: The Psychology of Violence in the South* (Boulder, CO, 1996).

7. See, for example, *Guns & Ammo,* April 1999, 44–49; July 1999, 38–44, 104.

8. *Guns & Ammo,* May 1998, 28, 30–34, 66–69, 74–75; December 1998, 54–55. Many gun owners see a direct connection between Christianity and guns. In Parkville, Maryland, there is a shop called Christian Soldiers, which caters to this market. *Los Angeles Times,* 25 August 1998, E2.

9. *Guns & Ammo,* October 1995, 19; May 1998, 9; November 1998, 42; February 1999, 5.

10. *Guns & Ammo,* November 1998, 34; April 1999, 34; *Baltimore Sun,* 30 April 1999, 27.

11. *Guns & Ammo,* November 1998, 14–15.

12. Davidson, *Under Fire,* 44; *Guns & Ammo,* November 1998, 64–78.

13. John Collins of Holand & Holand, New York City; *Wall Street Journal,* 24 March 1997, 1; *San Francisco Chronicle,* 2 May 1999, 11; *Guns & Ammo,* May 1998, 65; August 1998, 11, 44–51; December 1998, 33, 101, 108–09; January 1999, 31, 46, 109; March 1999, 12.

14. D'Angelo, "Sh*t, Damn, Motherf*cker," *Brown Sugar* CD; Samuel Charters, *The Poetry of the Blues* (New York, 1963), 45–46. My thanks to Meta Jones for these citations.

15. *New York Times,* 31 August 1997, 5; Omnibus Consolidated Appropriations Bill, HR 3610, Pub. L #104–208; Wash. Rev. Code 9.41.129; Arthur L. Kellermann, "Obstacles to Firearm and Violence Research," *Health Affairs* (winter 1993): 142–53; Kellermann, "Comment: Gunsmoke—Changing Public Attitudes toward Smoking and Firearms," *American Journal of Public Health* 87 (1997): 910–13.

16. Quoted, Hollon, *Frontier Violence: Another Look* (New York), 107.

17. William C. Davis, *A Way Through the Wilderness: The Natchez Trace and the Civilization of the Southern Frontier* (New York, 1995), 88. See also http://www.nra.org/wi/voice198.html.

18. Wesley Frank Craven, *The Colonies in Transition, 1660–1713* (New York, 1968), 30–31.

19. Harold L. Peterson, "The Military Equipment of the Plymouth and Bay Colonies, 1620–1690," *The New England Quarterly* 20 (1947): 197.

20. James B. Whisker, *The Gunsmith's Trade* (Lewiston, NY, 1992), 71, 91.

21. James B. Whisker, *The American Colonial Militia,* 5 vols. (Lewiston, NY, 1997), 1: 87, 171. This book was funded by The Second Amendment Foundation.

22. Jenkins, "Old Reliable," *The American Rifleman,* December 1931; Harold F. Williamson, *Winchester, the Gun that Won the West* (Washington, DC, 1952), 5.

23. Lee Kennett and James LaVerne Anderson, *The Gun in America: The Origins of a National Dilemma* (Westport, CT, 1975), 108; Warren Moore, *Weapons of the American Revolution* (New York, 1967), vi.

24. John M. Dederer, *War in America to 1775: Before Yankee Doodle* (New York, 1990), 116, 251.

25. Milton, *Paradise Lost,* book 5, lines 859–61.

26. *Guns & Ammo,* January 1999, 114.

27. John K. Mahon, "Anglo-American Methods of Indian Warfare, 1676–1794," *Mississippi Valley Historical Review* 45 (1958): 254. The scholarship of many military historians will be employed at many places in this book. In general see Mahon, *History of the Militia and the National Guard* (New York, 1983); Fred Anderson, *A People's Army: Massachusetts Soldiers and Society in the Seven Years' War* (Chapel Hill,

NC, 1984); Don Higginbotham, *War and Society in Revolutionary America: The Wider Dimensions of Conflict* (Columbia, SC, 1988); Harold E. Selesky, *War and Society in Colonial Connecticut* (New Haven, CT, 1990); Russell F. Weigley, *History of the United States Army* (New York, 1967).

28. A. Conan Doyle, *Memoirs of Sherlock Holmes* (Garden City, NY, 1990), 23.

29. Eric Hobsbawm and Terence Ranger, eds., *The Invention of Tradition* (Cambridge, 1993). And thanks to Jack Rakove for a helpful discussion on this point.

30. Information courtesy of Josh Sugarmann of the Violence Policy Center, Washington, DC.

31. *New York Times Magazine,* 5 November 1995, 20.

32. R. G. Collingwood, *The Idea of History* (Oxford, 1993), 390; Gordon Wood, "America in the 1790s," *Atlantic Magazine,* December 1993, 134. See also Perry Miller, *The Responsibility of Mind in a Civilization of Machines,* ed. John Crowell and Stanford Searl (Amherst, MA, 1979). For the contrary view, see David Harlan, *The Degradation of American History* (Chicago, 1997).

33. Hegel, *Lectures on the Philosphy of History,* quoted in Theodore S. Hamerow, *Reflections on History and Historians* (Madison, WI, 1987), 229.

Chapter One
The European Gun Heritage

1. Lynn White Jr., *Medieval Technology and Social Change* (Oxford, 1962), 93–95; J. R. Partington, *A History of Greek Fire and Gunpowder* (Cambridge, 1960), 91–129; J. R. Hale, "Gunpowder and the Renaissance: An Essay in the History of Ideas," in Charles H. Carter, ed., *From the Renaissance to the Counter-Reformation: Essays in Honor of Garrett Mattingly* (New York, 1965), 115–18.

2. Greek fire was invented by a Syrian named Kallinikos in the late seventh century. W. Y. Carman, *A History of Firearms: From Earliest Times to 1914* (London, 1955), 1–9; Partington, *History of Greek Fire,* 10–22, 28–32.

3. William H. McNeill, *The Pursuit of Power: Technology, Armed Force, and Society Since A.D. 1000* (Chicago, 1982), 81; L. Carrington Goodrich and Feng Chia-sheng, "The Early Development of Firearms in China," *Isis* 36 (1946): 14–23; O. F. G. Hogg, *Artillery: Its Origins, Heyday and Decline* (London, 1970), 29–49, 66–75; Carman, *History of Firearms,* 15–21; Henry Wilkinson, *Engines of War: Or, Historical and Experimental Observations on Ancient and Modern Warlike Machines and Implements* (London, 1841), 45–69.

4. White, *Medieval Technology,* 95–101, 164–65; Carlo M. Cipolla, *Guns, Sails and Empires: Technological Innovation and the Early Phases of European Expansion 1400–1700* (New York, 1965), 21–71; Carman, *History of Firearms,* 22–49, 131–41, 149–55, 189–91; Partington, *History of Greek Fire,* 160–77.

5. Sir Ralph Payne-Gallwey, *The Crossbow: Medieval and Modern, Military and Sporting* (London, 1903), 3–10, 43–53, 237–42; McNeill, *Pursuit of Power,* 38, 68. The success of the Catalan Company in the early fourteenth century was particularly notable.

6. McNeill, *Pursuit of Power,* 83; Payne-Gallwey, *The Crossbow,* 279–319; Thomas Esper, "The Replacement of the Longbow by Firearms in the English Army," *Technology and Culture* 6 (1965): 382–93.

7. Partington, *History of Greek Fire,* 144–58, 314–29; Carman, *History of Firearms,* 157–62; Wilkinson, *Engines of War,* 132–83; D. Cotterman, "Harnessing the

Powder Demon," in T. Bridges, ed., *Black Powder Gun Digest* (Northfield, MA, 1972); Jenny West, *Gunpowder, Government and War in the Mid-Eighteenth Century* (Woodbridge, UK, 1991), 7–22. The limitations of corning were recognized in the nineteenth century; Andrew Une, *A Dictionary of Arts, Manufactures and Mines* (London, 1846), 620–29.

8. In contrast, the Chinese and the Muslim countries abandoned experimentation after developing large cannon. Partington, *History of Greek Fire,* 186–288.

9. McNeill, *Pursuit of Power,* 83n; Payne-Gallwey, *The Crossbow,* 39; Martin Davidson and Adam Levy, *Decisive Weapons: The Technology that Transformed Warfare* (London, 1996), 52–54. J. R. Hale supports McNeill in seeing the gun take "over from the sword as a virility symbol." "Gunpowder and the Renaissance," 133.

10. Michel de Montaigne, "Of War Horses," Donald M. Frame, trans., *The Complete Essays of Montaigne* (Stanford, CA, 1958), 211. See also Chevalier Bail, *Essais historiques et critiques sur l'organisation des armies* (Paris, 1817), 42–44.

11. Miguel de Cervantes [Saavedra], *The History of the Valorous and Witty Knight-Errant Don Quixote of the Mancha,* trans. Thomas Shelton (New York, 1906), 206–07, book 4, chapter 11.

12. John Hale, "War and Public Opinion in the Fifteenth and Sixteenth Centuries," *Past & Present* 22 (1962): 28; Erasmus, *Complaint of Peace,* ed. W. J. Hirten (New York, 1946), 32; Milton, *Paradise Lost,* book 6; Blaize de Montluc, *The Commentaries of Messire Blaize de Montluc, Mareschal of France,* trans. Charles Cotton (London, 1674), 9, 118; Sir Charles Oman, *A History of the Art of War in the Middle Ages,* 2d ed., 2 vols. (New York, 1924), 2: 308–09; John U. Nef, *War and Human Progress: An Essay on the Rise of Industrial Civilization* (Cambridge, MA, 1950), 42–45.

13. Malcolm Vale, *War and Chivalry: Warfare and Aristocratic Culture in England, France and Burgundy at the End of the Middle Ages* (Athens, GA, 1981), 129–46; Hale, "Gunpowder and the Renaissance," 117–26. The contemporary Chinese shared this perspective. As Wang An-Shih said, "The educated men of the land regard the carrying of arms as a disgrace." McNeill, *Pursuit of Power,* 40.

14. Machiavelli is referring to the battles of Zagonara in 1424, in which three men fell off their horses and were smothered in the mud, and the long encounter at Molinella in 1427, which ended in the loss of some horses. Niccolo Machiavelli, *The Prince,* trans. James B. Atkinson (Indianapolis, IN, 1976), 231; Niccolo Machiavelli, *History of Florence: From the Earliest Times to the Death of Lorenzo the Magnificent* (New York, 1901), 180.

15. Cervantes, *Don Quixote,* 206.

16. As J. R. Hale has written, "Gunpowder, in short, revolutionized the conduct but not the outcome of wars." Hale, "Gunpowder and the Renaissance," 115.

17. Shakespeare, *Henry VI,* part 1; Jim Bradbury, *The Medieval Archer* (Bury St. Edmunds, UK, 1985), 160–64; Oman, *Art of War in the Middle Ages,* 301–12; Hale, "Gunpowder and the Renaissance," 123–25; Brian J. Given, *A Most Pernicious Thing: Gun Trading and Native Warfare in the Early Contact Period* (Ottawa, ONT, 1994), 15.

18. Davidson and Levy, *Decisive Weapons,* 38–59; Charles Oman, "Columns and Line in the Peninsular War," *Proceedings of the British Academy* 4 (1909–1910): 322–23; Carman, *History of Firearms,* 89–120; John M. Dederer, *War in America to 1775: Before Yankee Doodle* (New York, 1990), 88–91. With thanks to John Juricek for this insight.

19. 1503, 19 Henry VII, chapter 4; 1541, 33 Henry VIII, chapter 6; Margaret

Rule, *The Mary Rose: The Excavation and Raising of Henry VIII's Flagship* (London, 1982), 26–27, 172.

20. J. F. Hayward, *The Art of the Gunmaker,* 2 vols. (New York, 1962), 1: 106–20.

21. Lindsay Boynton, *The Elizabethan Militia, 1558–1638* (Toronto, 1967), 57–62; Hogg, *Artillery,* 49–56.

22. On this debate see Maurice J. D. Cockle, *A Bibliography of Military Books up to 1642* (London, 1900), 7–56; Esper, "Replacement of the Longbow," 382–93; C. G. Cruikshank, *Elizabeth's Army,* 2d ed. (Oxford, 1966), 102–29; Henry J. Webb, *Elizabethan Military Science: The Books and the Practice* (Madison, WI, 1965), 86–107; Sir Charles Oman, *A History of the Art of War in the Sixteenth Century* (London, 1937), 379–85. Those favoring archery included Roger Ascham, *Toxophilus: The Schoole, or Partitions of Shooting* (London, 1589); Sir John Smythe, *Certain Discourses . . . Concerning the Formes and Effects of Divers Sorts of Weapons* (London, 1590) [no page numbers, pagination set by counting the dedication as the first page]; R. S., *A Briefe Treatise to Proove the Necessitie and Excellence of the Use of Archerie* (London, 1596). Among those supporting the new armaments were Sir Roger Williams, *A Briefe Discourse on Warre* (London, 1590); Humphrey Barwick, *A Briefe Discourse Concerning the Force and Effect of All Manuall Weapons of Fire* (London, 1594) [every two pages numbered as one]. Little has been written on similar arguments among military experts on the continent. Payne-Gallwey, *The Crossbow,* 38–39.

23. Oman, "Columns and Line," 322; Esper, "Replacement of the Longbow," 382–83; Carman, *History of Firearms,* 98–100; Cruikshank, *Elizabeth's Army,* 102–03, 107; Ewart Oakeshott, *The Archaeology of Weapons: Arms and Armour From Prehistory to the Age of Chivalry* (Woodbridge, UK, 1994), 297; Rule, *Mary Rose,* 182; Given, *A Most Pernicious Thing,* 93–110.

24. Smythe, *Certain Discourses*; Barwick, *A Briefe Discourse*; White, *Medieval Technology,* 36–38; Bradbury, *Medieval Archer,* 17–38.

25. Smythe, *Certain Discourses,* 68–69, 72–79, 90–91, 124; Barwick, *A Briefe Discourse,* 4, 24; Robert Barret, *The Theorike and Practise of Moderne Warres* (London, 1598), 32–34; Payne-Gallwey, *The Crossbow,* 39; Given, *A Most Pernicious Thing,* 105–07. On Barwick, see Webb, *Elizabethan Military Science,* 49–50. Trained archers in the sixteenth century were timed at a rate of twelve arrows a minute. Rule, *Mary Rose,* 182.

26. Smythe was also first cousin to Edward VI. On Smythe, see Webb, *Elizabethan Military Science,* 38–42.

27. Smythe, *Certain Discourses,* 70–71, 82–83; Webb, *Elizabethan Military Science,* 11–19.

28. Smythe, *Certain Discourses,* 14, 37, 59–66, 102–03.

29. Given, *A Most Pernicious Thing,* 16–18; Turner Kirland, "Loading and Shooting Black Powder Guns," in T. Bridges, ed., *Black Powder Gun Digest.* The wheelock, though superior to the matchlock, was reserved for the rich, as it was four times the price and required expert repair. The English made notoriously inferior wheelocks. Harold L. Peterson, *Arms and Armor in Colonial America, 1526–1783* (New York, 1956), 17–25.

30. Thomas Venn, *Military and Maritime Discipline* (London, 1672), 7–14; John S. Cooper, *For Commonwealth and Crown: English Gunmakers of the Seventeenth Century* (Gillingham, UK, 1993), 101–02.

31. See especially Thomas Styward, *The Pathwaie to Martiall Discipline* (London, 1588); Francois de La Noue, *The Politike and Militarie Discourses of the Lord De*

La Nowe (London, 1587); Niccolo Tartaglia, *Three Books of Colloquies Concerning the Art of Shooting in Great and Small Peeces of Artillerie* (London, 1588); Don Bernardino de Mendoza, *Theorizue and Practise of Warre* (London, 1597). However, no English writer completely accepted Continental methods, all insisting on the special needs and styles of the English. Webb, *Elizabethan Military Science,* 47–49.

32. Smythe, *Certain Discourses,* 4–6. Though associated by the English with France, this new military organization had originated in Spain in 1534. Called the *tercio,* in these infantry units of three thousand men, one-half were equipped with pikes, one-fourth with javelins and short swords, and one-sixth with arquebuses and later muskets. J. H. Elliott, *Imperial Spain, 1469–1716* (New York, 1964), 123–25. Gustavus Adolphus of Sweden perfected the method of pikemen protecting musketeers while they reloaded, which became the standard in the seventeenth century.

33. Cruikshank, *Elizabeth's Army,* 130–42.

34. Esper, "Replacement of the Longbow," 384–85; John Bruce, ed., *Correspondence of Robert Dudley, Earl of Leycester, During His Government of the Low Countries* (London, 1844), 244–45; Cruikshank, *Elizabeth's Army,* 109–13.

35. Smythe, *Certain Discourses,* 3–5.

36. Ibid., 22–23.

37. Barwick, *A Briefe Discourse,* passim, quote 16; Oakeshott, *Archaeology of Weapons,* 282–300; Rule, *Mary Rose,* 173; Robert Hardy, *Longbow: A Social and Military History* (New York, 1976), 135.

38. Rule, *Mary Rose,* 183; Davidson and Levy, *Decisive Weapons,* 28–29; Barwick, *A Briefe Discourse,* 11–12.

39. Barwick, *A Briefe Discourse,* preface, 8–9, 20, 23, 27.

40. Webb, *Elizabethan Military Science,* 95–96; Barwick, *A Briefe Discourse,* 7; Barret, *Theorike and Practise,* 27; Cruikshank, *Elizabeth's Army,* 169.

41. Esper, "Replacement of the Longbow," 393; Oakeshott, *Archaeology of Weapons,* 297; Edwin Tunis, *Weapons* (Cleveland, 1954), 61–64; Gervase Markham, *The Souldiers Accidence* (London, 1648).

42. Esper, "Replacement of the Longbow," 392; Calendar of Close Roles, Edward III, 1364–68, 12 June 1365. There is one curiosity about archery: almost every author notes that the longbow required "years of training," and most of the English archers at Agincourt were between twelve and twenty. Davidson and Levy, *Decisive Weapons,* 34; Bradbury, *Medieval Archer,* 160–64.

43. Davidson and Levy, *Decisive Weapons,* 29–30; John Keegan, *The Face of Battle* (London, 1976), 79–116; Bradbury, *Medieval Archer,* 116–38; Oakeshott, *Archaeology of Weapons,* 297.

44. Esper, "Replacement of the Longbow," 392–93; Acts of the Privy Council, 21: 174–75 (June 6, 1591); William Blackstone, *Commentaries on the Laws of England,* 4 vols. (Chicago, IL, 1979), 4: 175; P. B. Munsche, *Gentlemen and Poachers: The English Game Laws, 1671–1831* (Cambridge, 1981), 8–32.

45. Quoted in Roger B. Manning, *Hunters and Poachers: A Cultural and Social History of Unlawful Hunting in England, 1485–1640* (Oxford, 1993), 65.

46. Boynton, *Elizabethan Militia,* 21–26, 61–62, 111–19; T. A. Critchley, *The Conquest of Violence: Order and Liberty in Britain* (London, 1970), 46–54.

47. Cruikshank, *Elizabeth's Army,* 110–13; Boynton, *Elizabethan Militia,* 257–97; J. R. Western, *The English Militia in the Eighteenth Century: The Story of a Political Issue, 1660–1802* (London, 1965), 3–29; Norman Longmate, *Island Fortress: The Defence of Great Britain, 1603–1945* (London, 1993), 6–21.

48. Smythe, *Certain Discourses,* 25–26, 35–37; Hogg, *Artillery,* 56–85.

49. Anthony North and Ian V. Hogg, *The Book of Guns and Gunsmiths* (London, 1977), 50.

50. The exact number of gunsmiths at this time is subject for some debate. Based on the petition, the number seems to be fifty-six, though several estimates run lower. Walter M. Stern, "Gunmaking in Seventeenth-Century London," *Journal of the Arms and Armour Society* 1 (1954): 55–60, 70–75; Cooper, *For Commonwealth and Crown,* 171, 175–80; Hayward, *Art of the Gunmaker* 1: 201; Howard L. Blackmore, *A Dictionary of London Gunmakers, 1350–1850* (Oxford, 1986), 14–15; W. Keith Neal and D. H. L. Back, *Great British Gunmakers, 1540–1740* (Norwich, 1984), 11–13.

51. A later master, William Fell Jr., was prosecuted in 1660 for counterfeiting the company's proof mark. Cooper, *For Commonwealth and Crown,* 11–16, 106–08, 188; Stern, "Gunmaking in Seventeenth-Century London," 55–56, 61, 79, 83–85; Blackmore, *Dictionary of London Gunmakers,* 65. The records of the Gunmakers' Company are in the Muniment Room of the Guildhall Library in London; ordnance records for the seventeenth century are WO 46–51, Public Records Office, Kew, UK.

52. Cooper, *For Commonwealth and Crown,* 173.

53. Ibid., 175.

54. Much of this Civil War–era production was in fact the selling of old muskets as new. Many of these antiquated weapons proved extremely dangerous to their possessors. Stern, "Gunmaking in Seventeenth-Century London," 61–70; G. I. Mungeam, "Contracts for the Supply of Equipment to the 'New Model' Army in 1645," *Journal of the Arms and Armour Society* 6 (1968): 53–115; Cooper, *For Commonwealth and Crown,* 18, 24–28, 109, 169–70; Blackmore, *Dictionary of London Gunmakers,* 15–18.

55. Cooper, *For Commonwealth and Crown,* 59–64; Mungeam, "Contracts," 53; Blackmore, *Dictionary of London Gunmakers,* 20–23, 147, 210–19.

56. Cooper, *For Commonwealth and Crown,* 170–72.

57. Stern, "Gunmaking in Seventeenth-Century London," 82–83; Cooper, *For Commonwealth and Crown,* 35, 40, 78.

58. Stern, "Gunmaking in Seventeenth-Century London," 69–70; Cooper, *For Commonwealth and Crown,* 114–61, 207; Mungeam, "Contracts," 53–55; Howard L. Blackmore, *British Military Firearms, 1650–1850* (New York, 1961), 24–27; Blackmore, *Dictionary of London Gunmakers,* 197–98.

59. Cooper, *For Commonwealth and Crown,* 68–69; Stern, "Gunmaking in Seventeenth-Century London," 65–68.

60. Cooper, *For Commonwealth and Crown,* 72 73, 207; Stern, "Gunmaking in Seventeenth-Century London," 62–63.

61. Cooper, *For Commonwealth and Crown,* 78, 85; Neal and Back, *Great British Gunmakers,* 88–96, 126–30; Stern, "Gunmaking in Seventeenth-Century London," 83.

62. Stern, "Gunmaking in Seventeenth-Century London," 69, 78–79; Blackmore, *Dictionary of London Gunmakers,* 17–22; Hayward, *Art of the Gunmaker* 1: 203, 213–17, 2: 61–62, 76–87; Cooper, *For Commonwealth and Crown,* 91; Blackmore, *Dictionary of London Gunmakers,* 18–20; Neal and Back, *Great British Gunmakers,* 97–116.

63. Joyce Lee Malcolm, *To Keep and Bear Arms: The Origins of an Anglo-American Right* (Cambridge, MA, 1994), 21, 84 85; Ian Gilmour, *Riot, Risings and Revolution: Governance and Violence in Eighteenth-Century Britain* (London, 1992), 135–206; Alan Macfarlane, *The Justice and the Mare's Ale. Law and Disorder in Seventeenth-Century*

England (Oxford, 1981), 189–96; E. P. Thompson, *Whigs and Hunters: The Origins of the Black Act* (New York, 1975), 81–115.

64. David Underdown, *Revel, Riot, and Rebellion: Popular Politics and Culture in England, 1603–1660* (Oxford, 1985), 34–35; J. A. Sharpe, *Crime in Early Modern England, 1550–1750* (London, 1984), 94–120; V. H. T. Skipp, *Crisis and Development: An Ecological Case Study of the Forest of Arden, 1570–1674* (New York, 1978), 39–42, 78–89, 106–07.

65. Underdown, *Revel, Riot, and Rebellion,* 96; E. P. Thompson, *Customs in Common* (London, 1991), 467–538.

66. Underdown, *Revel, Riot, and Rebellion,* 128; Thomas Birch, ed., *The Court and Times of Charles the First,* 2 vols. (London, 1848), 1: 364–65; E. P. Thompson, "Patrician Society, Plebian Culture," *Journal of Social History* 7 (1974): 387; Thompson, *Customs in Common,* 185–258.

67. Underdown, *Revel, Riot, and Rebellion,* 69; Thompson, *Customs in Common,* 16–96.

68. It is important to note that all British rights were seen as restricted rights, adjusted to social condition. J. G. A. Pocock, *The Ancient Constitution and the Feudal Law: A Study of English Historical Thought in the Seventeenth Century* (Cambridge, 1957).

69. Underdown, *Revel, Riot, and Rebellion,* 108–19; Buchanan Sharp, *In Contempt of All Authority: Rural Artisans and Riot in the West of England, 1586–1660* (Berkeley, CA, 1980), 36–42, 86–96; D. G. C. Allan, "The Rising in the West, 1628–1631," *Economic History Review,* 2d series, 5 (1952): 76–85; Eric Kerridge, "The Revolts in Wiltshire against Charles I," *The Wiltshire Archaeological & Natural Magazine* 57 (1958–60): 64–75.

70. Underdown, *Revel, Riot, and Rebellion,* 109. See also Allan, "Rising in the West," 78–82.

71. Underdown, *Revel, Riot, and Rebellion,* 161, 185, 235; Joyce Lee Malcolm, *Caesar's Due: Loyalty and King Charles, 1642–1646* (Atlantic Highlands, NJ, 1983), 45–50.

72. Underdown, *Revel, Riot, and Rebellion,* 186; "Letters from a Subaltern Officer," *Archaeologia* 35 (1853): 321–22.

73. Sharp, 117–23, 228; Allan, "Rising in the West," 78–80.

74. Underdown, *Revel, Riot, and Rebellion,* 115; Thompson, *Whigs and Hunters,* 68–70.

75. Underdown, *Revel, Riot, and Rebellion,* 131–32; Thompson, *Whigs and Hunters,* 67–73, 165–66, 190–92; Thompson, *Customs in Common,* 97–184; Brian Manning, *The English People and the English Revolution, 1640–1649* (London, 1976), 46–70. This notion that the state holds a monopoly on violence goes back to the Roman republic. Citizens were allowed to develop military skills so that the state "may appropriate to [its] own use the great and more important part of our courage, our talents, and our wisdom." Cicero, *De Re Publica* 1: 4.8. Cato warned his son, recently discharged and wanting to rejoin his unit, "be careful not to go into battle; for the man who is not legally a soldier has no right to be fighting the foe." Cicero, *De Officiis* 1: 11. Grotius and Emmerich de Vattel endorsed these classic ideals. Dederer, *War in America to 1775,* 162–65.

76. David Underdown, "The Chalk and the Cheese: Contrasts Among the English Clubmen," *Past and Present* 85 (1979): 30–32; J. S. Morrill, *The Revolt of the Provinces: Conservatives and Radicals in the English Civil War, 1630–1650* (London, 1976), 99–103.

77. Underdown, *Revel, Riot, and Rebellion,* 161; Sharp, *In Contempt of All Authority,* 95, 224–25; Allan, "Rising in the West," 81–83.

78. Sharp, *In Contempt of All Authority,* 94.

79. Underdown, *Revel, Riot, and Rebellion,* 166.

80. Ibid., 168.

81. Sharp, *In Contempt of All Authority,* 225–26; Allan, "Rising in the West," 81.

82. Sharp, *In Contempt of All Authority,* 220–56; Underdown, *Revel, Riot, and Rebellion,* 221.

83. Underdown, *Revel, Riot, and Rebellion,* 252.

84. Ibid., 125.

85. Cruikshank, *Elizabeth's Army,* 113; Underdown, *Revel, Riot, and Rebellion,* 142; C. H. Firth, *Cromwell's Army: A History of the English Soldier During the Civil Wars, the Commonwealth and the Protectorate* (London, 1905), 13, 379–80. Almost every illustration of troops from the English Civil War picture soldiers with blades and pole weapons rather than firearms. There is a good collection of such illustrations in Underdown, *Revel, Riot and Rebellion*.

86. John Brewer, *The Sinews of Power: War, Money and the English State, 1688–1783* (London, 1989), 7; Lawrence Stone, *The Crisis of the Aristocracy, 1558–1641* (Oxford, 1965), 266.

Chapter Two

The Role of Guns in the Conquest of North America

1. Also known as a "hackbut" and an "arquebus." Claude Blair, ed., *Pollard's History of Firearms* (New York, 1983), 55, 92–93.

2. H. P. Biggar, ed., *The Works of Samuel de Champlain,* 6 vols. (Toronto, 1922–36), 2: 94–107; Ian K. Steele, *Warpaths: Invasions of North America* (New York, 1994), 65; Bruce G. Trigger, *The Children of Aataentsic: A History of the Huron People to 1660,* 2 vols. (Montreal, 1976), 1: 246–54. Champlain's report that he downed three men with a single shot is highly unlikely. Modern tests with a short-barrel blunderbuss such as Champlain used cannot replicate such a shot, the spread of the pellets being a mere four inches. The use of multiple shot in a musket decreases the lethality of a musket, as the shot cannot "form an effective gas-seal." Brian J. Given, *A Most Pernicious Thing: Gun Trading and Native Warfare in the Early Contact Period* (Ottawa, ONT, 1994), 77.

3. Weber quoted in John M. Dederer, *War in America to 1775: Before Yankee Doodle* (New York, 1990), 89. See also Geoffrey Parker, "The 'Military Revolution,' 1560–1660—a Myth?" *Journal of Modern History* 48 (1976): 208–10.

4. George Abbott, *A Brief Description of the Whole World* (London, 1600), 11; James Axtell, *After Columbus: Essays in the Ethnohistory of Colonial North America* (New York, 1988), 125–43; Neal Salisbury, *Manitou and Providence: Indians, Europeans, and the Making of New England, 1500–1643* (New York, 1982), 7–12; Daniel K. Richter, *The Ordeal of the Longhouse: The Peoples of the Iroquois League in the Era of European Colonization* (Chapel Hill, NC, 1992), 2–5, 54–56.

5. The first large order for flintlocks came in 1666 from the Maryland General Assembly, which ordered 140 cutlasses and fifty flintlocks from England for distribution to the county militia, under the care of local officials. Flintlocks were available earlier, but the enormous demands of the competing factions in the English Civil War absorbed the entire production of firearms in Great Britain in the 1640s, as

did Cromwell's New Model Army in the 1650s. *Archives of Maryland,* 72 vols. (Baltimore, MD, 1883–1972), 2: 19–20.

6. Blair, ed., *Pollard's History of Firearms,* 62–105, 161–87; "Fowling-piece," in G. G. and J. Robinson, *The Sportsman's Dictionary; Or, The Gentleman's Companion* (London, 1800); Given, *A Most Pernicious Thing,* 106–07.

7. Given, *A Most Pernicious Thing,* 6–18, 24–25, 30–31, 108–09; Ned H. Roberts, *The Muzzle-Loading Cap Lock Rifle* (Harrisburg, PA, 1958), 84–85, 98–113, 203–04; Robert Held, *The Age of Firearms* (New York, 1957), 70–97; Thomas Johnson, *Shooter's Guide* (London, 1816); George C. Nonte Jr., *Black Powder Guide* (South Hackensack, NJ, 1976); C. Kenneth Ramage, *Black Powder Handbook* (Middlefield, CT, 1975); Basil P. Hughes, *Firepower: Weapons Effectiveness on the Battlefield, 1630–1850* (New York, 1974); W. W. Greener, *The Gun and Its Development* (New York, 1967); Frederick Wilkinson, *British and American Flintlocks* (Feltham, UK, 1971).

8. Blair, ed., *Pollard's History of Firearms,* 84–85, 139–43, 183–85; Given, *A Most Pernicious Thing,* 89–91.

9. Given, *A Most Pernicious Thing,* 98–99.

10. Thomas Church, *The History of King Philip's War,* ed. Henry Martyn Dexter (Boston, 1865), 122–23.

11. Dave Grossman has suggested that most soldiers attempted to avoid killing their enemy in battle. Dave Grossman, *On Killing: The Psychological Cost of Learning to Kill in War and Society* (Boston, 1995), 17–28.

12. Rene Laudonniere, *A Notable Historie Containing Foure Voyages . . . ,* trans. Richard Hakluyt (London, 1587), 29–30.

13. Daniel Usner, *Indians, Settlers and Slaves in a Frontier Exchange Economy: The Lower Mississippi Valley Before 1783* (Chapel Hill, NC, 1992), 18; John Worth, "Prelude to Abandonment: The Interior Provinces of Early 17th-century Georgia," *Early Georgia* 21, (1993): 45.

14. William H. McNeill, *Plagues and Peoples* (New York, 1977); Alfred W. Crosby, *Ecological Imperialism: The Biological Expansion of Europe, 900–1900* (Cambridge, 1986).

15. Edmund S. Morgan, *American Freedom, American Slavery: The Ordeal of Colonial Virginia* (New York, 1975), 71–91.

16. A point well developed by George Raudzens, in "Why Did Amerindian Defences Fail? Parallels in the European Invasions of Hispaniola, Virginia and Beyond," *War in History* 3 (1996): 331–52. Those early Spanish expeditions have a feudal quality in terms of armament. The officers were outfitted in full armor, the common cavalry in three-quarter armor from knee to neck, and the infantry wore light armor, even in the heat of the Southwest. The Spanish troops had a wide variety of weapons, with lances, swords, and daggers preferred by the cavalry, and crossbows, pikes, swords, shields, and poleaxes among the infantry, with a few wheellock carbines, muskets, and pistols—no two alike.

17. Francis Jennings, *The Invasion of America: Indians, Colonialism, and the Cant of Conquest* (Chapel Hill, NC, 1975), 165–70; J. Frederick Fausz, "Fighting Fire with Firearms: The Anglo-Powhatan Arms Race in Early Virginia," *American Indian Culture and Research Journal* 3, no. 4 (1979): 34–35; Richter, *Ordeal of the Longhouse,* 17–18, 35–38, 54, 103 04; Robert Beverley, *The History and Present State of Virginia,* ed. Louis B. Wright (Chapel Hill, NC, 1947, orig. London, 1705), 192; James W. Covington, "Relations between the Eastern Timucuan Indians and the French and

Spanish, 1564–1567," in Charles M. Hudson, ed., *Four Centuries of Southern Indians* (Athens, GA, 1975), 11–27.

18. Gentleman of Elvas, *The Discovery and Conquest of Terra Florida, by Don Ferdinando de Soto,* trans. Richard Hakluyt (London, 1851, orig. 1609), 28; James W. Covington, "Relations," 20, 23. Indian bows were not longbows. The longbow had a range, or cast, of three hundred yards; the Indian bows had a range of 100 to 150 yards at most. Given, *A Most Pernicious Thing,* 106; Charles Chenevix French, *A History of Marksmanship* (Chicago, 1954), 24, 31–33, 71 , 113.

19. Carl O. Sauer, *Sixteenth Century North America: The Land and the People as Seen by the Europeans* (Berkeley, CA, 1971), 25–31; Paul E. Hoffman, *A New Andalucia and a Way to the Orient: The American Southeast During the Sixteenth Century* (Baton Rouge, LA, 1990), 3–33.

20. Álvar N. Cabeza de Vaca, *Adventures in the Unknown Interior of America,* trans. Cyclone Covey (New York, 1961), 31–52; David B. Quinn, ed., *New American World: A Documentary History of North America to 1612,* 5 vols. (New York, 1979), 2: 3–14; Sauer, *Sixteenth Century North America,* 36–46; Hoffman, *A New Andalucia,* 84–101. The claim that the Indian arrows pierced Spanish armor is probably an exaggeration. More likely, arrows, which came in thick flights, entered at the joints in the armor. However, some chroniclers compared the Indian bows to English longbows, reporting that they took just as much strength to launch their arrows. Charles M. Hudson, *The Southeastern Indians* (Knoxville, TN, 1976), 245.

21. Quinn, ed., *New American World* 2: 158–83, 187–88; Steele, *Warpaths,* 13–19; Sauer, *Sixteenth Century North America,* 157–80; Hoffman, *A New Andalucia,* 87–98. The Spanish also made good use of war dogs as offensive weapons. Michael G. Lemish, *War Dogs: Canines in Combat* (Washington, DC, 1996).

22. Steele, *Warpaths,* 17; M. L. Brown, *Firearms in Colonial America: The Impact on History and Technology, 1492–1792* (Washington, DC, 1980), 43–44.

23. Quinn, ed., *New American World* 2: 382–463; Sauer, *Sixteenth Century North America,* 214–18; Eugene Lyon, *The Enterprise of Florida: Pedro Menendez de Aviles and the Spanish Conquest of 1565–1568* (Gainesville, FL, 1976), 19–70; Paul E. Hoffman, *The Spanish Crown and the Defense of the Caribbean, 1565–1585: Precedent, Patrimonialism, and Royal Parsimony* (Baton Rouge, LA, 1980), 138–46, 218–30; Paul Quattlebaum, *The Land Called Chicora: The Carolinas Under Spanish Rule with French Intrusions, 1520–1670* (Gainesville, FL, 1956), 57–77. There are two different versions of the Moyano de Morales story. Either the Spanish were so confident that they went to sleep, letting the matches go out, or (according to the cacique Escamacu) the guns frightened the women and children, and the Spanish put them out. Hoffman, *A New Andalucia,* 270; Quattlebaum, *Land Called Chicora,* 73.

24. Steele, *Warpaths,* 34.

25. John H. Hann, *Apalachee: The Land Between the Rivers* (Gainesville, FL, 1988), 14–20.

26. D. J. R. Walker, *Columbus and the Golden World of the Island Arawaks: The Story of the First Americans and their Caribbean Environment* (Lewes, UK, 1992), 282–84. On this general point see Raudzens, "Why Did Amerindian Defences Fail?"; Cronon, *Changes in the Land*; Crosby, *Ecological Imperialism.*

27. By the early seventeenth century, when Onate conquered New Mexico, most cavalry and infantry contented themselves with half-suits of armor and helmets, though the weaponry remained roughly the same with the addition of harquebus. Even by the end of the seventeenth century, when armor had largely vanished from

European battlefields, the Spanish continued to wear it in the Southwest—though thick leather reinforced with metal had become the norm among infantry when Spanish troops reconquered New Mexico in the 1690s. Frank Raymond Secoy, *Changing Military Patterns of the Great Plains Indians* (Lincoln, NE, 1992), 6–20; F. S. Curtis Jr., "Spanish Arms and Armor in the Southwest," *New Mexico Historical Review* 2 (1927): 107–33.

28. J. Manuel Espinosa, *Crusaders of the Rio Grande: The Story of Don Diego de Vargas and the Reconquest and Refounding of New Mexico* (Salisbury, NC, 1977), 62–63, 156–61, 197–98; David J. Weber, *The Spanish Frontier in North America* (New Haven, CT, 1992), 217–19. Indians rushed to adopt the Spanish style of leather armor, just as they had the horse. Those tribes that did so triumphed over their non-armored opponents. As one observer described the Indians at the siege of Santa Fe in 1694, they were "equipped for war in Spanish fashion, even to leather jackets, leather horse armor, and shields." These accoutrements rather than firearms marked the Spanish soldier. Secoy, *Changing Military Patterns,* 18–19; Espinosa, *Crusaders of the Rio Grande,* 151, 267–72.

29. Marcel Trudel, *The Beginnings of New France, 1524–1663,* trans. Patricia Claxton (Toronto, 1973), 34–53, 93–106; Trigger, *Children of Aataentsic* 1: 177–208, 463–67; Reuben G. Thwaites, ed., *The Jesuit Relations and Allied Documents,* 73 vols. (Cleveland, 1896–1901), 10: 52–53. This desire to fight to attain access to European metal goods persisted into the eighteenth century. See John Lawson, *A New Voyage to Carolina* (London, 1709), 33; Joseph Jablow, *The Cheyenne in Plains Indian Trade Relations, 1795–1840* (Lincoln, NE, 1994), 7–25.

30. W. J. Eccles, *France in America* (New York, 1972), 21; Trigger, *Children of Aataentsic* 1: 258; Biggar, ed., *Works of Champlain* 2: 124–34. This technique of dropping to the ground at the moment of firing became rather common among Indians throughout the Americas. Trigger, *Children of Aataentsic* 2: 754–55; Thwaites, ed., *Jesuit Relations* 32: 178–83; Gentleman of Elvas, *Discovery and Conquest of Terra Florida,* 27–28.

31. Biggar, ed., *Works of Champlain* 3: 65–80, 6: 51–74; Trudel, *Beginnings of New France,* 172–78; Eccles, *France in America,* 21, 27–28; Trigger, *Children of Aataentsic* 1: 312–14, 2: 456–59; S. James Gooding, *The Canadian Gunsmiths, 1608 to 1900* (West Hill, ONT, 1962), 21.

32. Biggar, ed., *Works of Champlain* 5: 3.

33. Thwaites, ed., *Jesuit Relations* 25: 26–27.

34. Trigger, *Children of Aataentsic* 1: 273, 2: 546–51, 629–33, 699–724, 754–55; Trudel, *Beginnings of New France,* 217–19; Elizabeth Tooker, "The Iroquois Defeat of the Huron: A Review of the Causes," *Pennsylvania Archeologist* 33 (1963): 115–23. The exact number of Huron who converted is not known, but French sources indicate that by 1648 they had given 120 Christian Huron each an inferior trade gun. Thwaites, ed., *Jesuit Relations* 32: 178–79.

35. David Beers Quinn, ed., *The Roanoke Voyages, 1584–1590,* 2 vols. (London, 1955), 1: 371. Francis Higginson expressed this same self-confidence thirty years later: "We neither feare them nor trust them, for fourtie of our Musketeeres will drive five hundred of them out of the Field." Higginson, *New England's Plantation* (London, 1630).

36. Philip L. Barbour, ed., *The Jamestown Voyages Under the First Charter, 1606–1609,* 2 vols. (Cambridge, 1969), 1: 52.

37. John Smith, *Travels and Works of Captain John Smith, President of Virginia,*

and Admiral of New England, 1580–1631, ed. Edward Arber, 2 vols. (Edinburgh, 1910), 2: 458, 578; Fausz, "Fighting Fire with Firearms," 38.

38. Walker, *Columbus and the Golden World,* 286–312.

39. Barbour, ed., *Jamestown Voyages* 1: 95–98, 110; J. Frederick Fausz, "An 'Abundance of Blood Shed on Both Sides': England's First Indian War, 1609–1614," *Virginia Magazine of History and Biography* 98 (1990): 13; Smith, *Travels and Works* 1: 7–8.

40. Barbour, ed., *Jamestown Voyages* 1: 94–95; William Strachey, *The Historie of Travell into Virginia Britania (1612),* ed. Louis B. Wright and Virginia Freund (London, 1953), 108–10.

41. For similar developments among other tribes, see Covington, "Relations," 23–24.

42. Smith, *Travels and Works* 1: xxxvi, 8–13; Barbour, ed., *Jamestown Voyages* 1: 52–54. This desire to not let the Indians see inferior shooting skills was rather common. As Brian J. Given wrote, "One might speculate that they were trying to convince themselves, as well as the Indians, that their superior technology gave them the upper hand." Given, *A Most Pernicious Thing,* 49.

43. Quinn, ed., *New American World* 5: 317; Smith, *Travels and Works* 2: 456, 474; George Percy, " 'A Trewe Relacyon,' Virginia from 1609 to 1612," *Tyler's Quarterly Historical and Genealogical Magazine* 3 (1922): 267; Fausz, "An 'Abundance of Blood,' " 15–21.

44. Fausz, "An 'Abundance of Blood,' " 22–23; Smith, *Travels and Works* 2: 486; Anon., "Good Newes from Virginia, 1623," *William and Mary Quarterly* 3rd ser., 5 (1948): 357.

45. George Percy, " 'A Trewe Relacyon,' " 273–76; Strachey, *Historie of Travell into Virginia,* 64–67; Smith, *Travels and Works* 2: 61–62; Fausz, "An 'Abundance of Blood,' " 24–35; Leroy V. Eid, " 'National' War Among Indians of Northeastern North America," *Canadian Review of American Studies* 16 (1985): 125–54.

46. Beverley, *History and Present State of Virginia,* 36–37; Fausz, "An 'Abundance of Blood,' " 26–27; Percy, " 'A Trewe Relacyon,' " 266–70; Strachey, *Historie of Travell into Virginia,* xxiv, 67–69, 90–93, 105–07.

47. Smith, *Travels and Works* 2: 500–04, 682; Lyon G. Tyler, ed., *Narratives of Early Virginia, 1606–1625* (New York, 1907), 211–12, 422–23; Helen Rountree, *Pocahontas's People: The Powhatan Indians of Virginia Through Four Centuries* (Norman, OK, 1990), 48–65; Fausz, "An 'Abundance of Blood,' " 32–34.

48. William L. Shea, *The Virginia Militia in the Seventeenth Century* (Baton Rouge, LA, 1983), 16–17; Steele, *Warpaths,* 42, 61; Susan M. Kingsbury, ed., *The Records of the Virginia Company of London,* 4 vols. (Washington, DC, 1906–1935), 4: 279–81.

49. Percy, " 'A Trewe Relacyon,' " 270–71, 274–75, 277.

50. Ibid., 279–80; Fausz, "An 'Abundance of Blood,' " 37–39.

51. Percy, " 'A Trewe Relacyon,' " 270–74; Strachey, *Historie of Travell into Virginia,* 65–66. Many scholars argue that the methods used against the Irish were transported for use against the Indians. Dederer, *War in America to 1775,* 129–35; James Muldoon, "Indian as Irishman," *Essex Institute Historical Quarterly* 111 (1975): 267–89; Nicholas Canny, "The Ideology of English Colonization: From Ireland to America," *William and Mary Quarterly* 3rd ser., 30 (1973): 575–98. It seems equally likely that the settlers developed their tactics in response to the local situation in America, or that this brutality was not limited to the English treatment of the Irish.

Henry VIII's suppression of the northern uprisings, in which he ordered executions in every town and village regardless of guilt, certainly matches the worst behavior of Europeans in America. And it was a French commander speaking of French Protestants who said, "Kill them all. God will know which are His." Quoted in Roland H. Bainton, *Christian Attitudes toward War and Peace: A Historical Survey and Critical Reevaluation* (London, 1961), 115.

52. Percy, "'A Trewe Relacyon,'" 276; Kingsbury, ed., *Records of the Virginia Company* 2: 100.

53. Percy, "'A Trewe Relacyon,'" 275–77; Beverley, *History and Present State of Virginia,* 37; Fausz, "An 'Abundance of Blood,'" 55–56; Morgan, *American Freedom, American Slavery,* 79–81. The best that Percy could say for for Virginia in 1612 was that "If we Trewly Consider the diversity of miseries mutenies and famishmentts wch have Attended upon discoveries and plantacyons in theis our moderne Tymes we shall nott fynde our plantacyon in Virginia to have Suffered Aloane." Percy, "'A Trewe Relacyon,'" 260.

54. Cronon, *Changes in the Land,* 39–41; Salisbury, *Manitou and Providence,* 30–49; Richard R. White, *The Middle Ground: Indians, Empires, and Republics in the Great Lakes Region, 1650–1815* (Cambridge, 1991), 1–49; Shea, *Virginia Militia,* 19–21. Feed fights have a long European tradition. The Roman historian Flavius Vegetius wrote that "the main and principal point in war is to secure plenty of provisions and to destroy the enemy by famine." Quoted in Dederer, *War in America to 1775,* 103.

55. Beverley, *History and Present State of Virginia,* 44–45; Harold L. Peterson, *Arms and Armor in Colonial America, 1526–1783* (New York, 1956), 321.

56. H. R. McIlwaine, ed., *Minutes of the Council and General Court of Colonial Virginia, 1622–32, 1670–76* (Richmond, VA, 1924), 28; Quinn, ed., *New American World* 5: 311–12; Tyler, ed., *Narratives of Early Virginia,* 270; Fausz, "Fighting Fire with Firearms," 40–41; Morgan, *American Freedom, American Slavery,* 97–98; Smith, *Travels and Works* 2: 563–64, 601–02.

57. Smith, *Travels and Works* 2: 572–78; Joseph Mead, "The Indian Massacre of 1622: Some Correspondence of the Reverend Joseph Mead," *Virginia Magazine of History and Biography* 71 (1963): 409; Beverley, *History and Present State of Virginia,* 51; Morgan, *American Freedom, American Slavery,* 98–101.

58. Anon., "Good Newes from Virginia, 1623," 353. This ballad mentions three villages being torched by the English.

59. Smith, *Travels and Works* 2: 597–606; Kingsbury, ed., *Records of the Virginia Company* 4: 58–62; Rountree, *Pocahontas's People,* 54–58, 70–77; Steele, *Warpaths,* 46–47.

60. Smith, *Travels and Works* 2: 600–01; Anon., "Good Newes from Virginia, 1623," 354.

61. Kingsbury, ed., *Records of the Virginia Company* 4: 61.

62. Ibid. 4: 61, 147.

63. Fausz, "Fighting Fire with Firearms," 43.

64. Tyler, ed., *Narratives of Early Virginia,* 425; Kingsbury, ed., *Records of the Virginia Company* 2: 96, 99–100, 135, 3: 447, 676, 4: 475, 507–08, 540–41, 545, 566.

65. Beverley, *History and Present State of Virginia,* 54; Shea, *Virginia Militia,* 27–38; Fausz, "Fighting Fire with Firearms," 43–44; Axtell, *After Columbus,* 215–19.

66. The Crown also sent over several barrels of powder in 1624 and again in 1626. McIlwaine, ed., *Minutes of the Council,* 62, 106, 151; Kingsbury, ed., *Records of the Virginia Company* 3: 676, 4: 93–94, 229–30, 234–37, 476, 528, 568–69; Tyler, ed.,

Narratives of Early Virginia, 423–24; W. L. Grant and James Munro, eds., *Acts of the Privy Council of England, Colonial Series, 1613–1680,* 6 vols. (Hereford, UK, 1908–12), 1: 54, 65–66, 80, 92–95, 97, 108, 131.

67. William W. Hening, ed., *The Statutes at Large, Being a Collection of All the Laws of Virginia,* 13 vols. (Richmond, 1809–23), 1: 255–56.

68. Beverley, *History and Present State of Virginia,* 61–62; Anon., "Good Newes from Virginia, 1623," 355–57; Steele, *Warpaths,* 48–49. "Nor did they fear the Indians, but kept them at a greater Distance than formerly: And they for their Parts, seeing the English so sensibly increase in Number, were glad to keep their Distance, and be peaceable." Beverley, *History and Present State of Virginia,* 57.

69. William Bradford, *Of Plymouth Plantation, 1620–1647,* ed. Samuel Eliot Morison (New York, 1952), 81–84; Salisbury, *Manitou and Providence,* 106–08.

70. English settlers continued to use armor until at least 1650. Bradford, *Of Plymouth Plantation,* 50–51, 64; [Bradford], "A Relation, or Journal, of the Beginning and Proceedings of the English Plantation settled at Plymouth," in Edward Arber, ed., *The Story of the Pilgrim Fathers, 1606–1623 A.D.; as told by Themselves, their Friends, and their Enemies* (London, 1897), 411–12, 449, 457–60; Nathaniel B. Shurtleff, ed., *Records of the Governor and Company of the Massachusetts Bay in New England,* 5 vols. (Boston, 1853–61), 1: 25–26; H. L. Peterson, "The Military Equipment of the Plymouth and Bay Colonies, 1620–1690," *New England Quarterly* 20 (1947): 197–208; "Acts, Orders and Resolutions of the General Assembly of Virginia: At Sessions of March 1643–1646," *Virginia Magazine of History and Biography* 23 (1915): 231.

71. [Bradford], "A Relation," 411–15, 431–34; Salisbury, *Manitou and Providence,* 110–14; Bradford, *Of Plymouth Plantation,* 69–70.

72. Bradford, *Of Plymouth Plantation,* 204, 207–08.

73. Ibid., 247–48.

74. Shurtleff, ed., *Records of Massachusetts Bay* 1: 26–37, 392, 2: 42; Arber, ed., *Story of the Pilgrim Fathers,* 411–15, 457; John Winthrop, *Winthrop Papers,* 6 vols. (Boston, 1929–92), 1: 305. On the militarist nature of Colonial Massachusetts see Darrett B. Rutman, "A Militant New World: 1607–1640" (Ph.D. diss., University of Virginia, 1959). On the lack of militia organization in early Plymouth, see Douglas E. Leach, "The Military System of Plymouth Colony," *New England Quarterly* 24 (1951): 342–50.

75. Shurtleff, ed., *Records of Massachusetts Bay* 1: 125, 4 part 2: 331; J. Hammond Trumbull et al., eds., *The Public Records of the Colony of Connecticut,* 15 vols. (Hartford, CT, 1850–90), 1: 239–44.

76. William H. Whitmore, ed., *The Colonial Laws of Massachusetts* (Boston, 1890), 107–15, 204, 226–28, 231–32, 265–66; Shurtleff, ed., *Records of Massachusetts Bay* 1: 85, 102, 124, 210, 2: 43, 5: 212; Leach, "Military System of Plymouth Colony," 350–51; George M. Bodge, *Soldiers in King Philip's War* (Boston, 1906), 456. See also John D. Cushing, ed., *The Earliest Laws of the New Haven and Connecticut Colonies, 1639–1673* (Wilmington, DE, 1977), 43–46, 123–25.

77. J. Franklin Jameson, ed., *Johnson's Wonder-Working Providence, 1628–1651* (New York, 1910), 148–50.

78. Bradford, *Of Plymouth Plantation,* 295–96; John Underhill, *News from America* (London, 1638) in *Collections of the Massachusetts Historical Society,* 3rd ser., 6 (1837): 27.

79. Jameson, ed., *Johnson's Wonder-Working Providence,* 170.

80. There is certainly much disagreement on this point. There were incidents in both Europe and North America of civilian populations put to the sword prior to

1500, yet neither made such conduct an integral aspect of its approach to war until the seventeenth century. Jennings, *Invasion of America,* 3–14, 146–70; Axtell, *After Columbus,* 182–221; Salisbury, *Manitou and Providence,* 41–47, 70–71, 229; Richter, *Ordeal of the Longhouse,* 32–41; White, *Middle Ground,* 2–6; 117–19; Adam J. Hirsch, "The Collision of Military Cultures in Seventeenth-Century New England," *Journal of American History* 74 (1988): 1187–1212; Lawrence H. Keeley, *War Before Civilization* (New York, 1996). Many contemporaries certainly saw Indians as less violent than Europeans. John Mason, in 1637, disdained the Pequot's "feeble Manner" of war, which "did hardly deserve the name of fighting." Quoted in Jill Lepore, *The Name of War: King Philip's War and the Origins of American Identity* (New York, 1998), 118. Roger Williams, in 1643, thought Indian wars were "farre less bloudy and devouring than the cruell Warres of Europe." Quoted in Hirsch, "Collision of Military Cultures," 1191.

81. Steele, *Warpaths,* 93.

82. George Willison, *Saints and Strangers* (New York, 1945), 392. Earlier, the Calvinist John Robinson wrote Governor Bradford in a different vein on December 19, 1623: "Oh, how happy a thing had it been, if you had converted some before you had killed any!" Bradford, *Of Plymouth Plantation,* 374–75.

83. Shurtleff, ed., *Records of Massachusetts Bay* 1: 25–26.

84. Shurtleff, ed., *Records of Massachusetts Bay* 4 part 2: 562, 5: 22, 343, 378, 602. Whenever the colony acquired new firearms, it ordered them to be "equally devided amongst the severall planations" to be kept in "readynes as a towne stocke." Shurtleff, ed., *Records of Massachusetts Bay* 1:125.

85. J. Franklin Jameson, ed., *Narratives of New Netherlands, 1609–1664* (New York, 1909), 84–85; Allen W. Trelease, *Indian Affairs in Colonial New York: The Seventeenth Century* (Ithaca, NY, 1960), 46–47.

86. Trelease, *Indian Affairs,* 48–49, 63–64; Richter, *Ordeal of the Longhouse,* 55–57, 79–85; Francis Jennings, *The Ambiguous Iroquois Empire: The Covenant Chain of Indian Tribes with English Colonies from Its Beginnings to the Lancaster Treaty of 1744* (New York, 1984), 51, 71–81. The French traded four hatchets and fifty knives for every gun. White, *Middle Ground,* 136.

87. Arnold J. F. Van Laer, trans., *Council Minutes, 1639–1649,* vol. 4 of *New York Historical Manuscripts* (Baltimore, MD, 1974), 426, 520–25. The various Europeans regularly blamed one another for violating their own laws and trading guns with the Indians. Given, *A Most Pernicious Thing,* 58–59; Trigger, *Children of Aataentsic* 2: 630–31; Trelease, *Indian Affairs,* 51–54; Patrick M. Malone, *The Skulking Way of War: Technology and Tactics Among the New England Indians* (Lanham, MD,1991), 42–51.

88. There is some disagreement among the sources as to the exact number of firearms in Mohawk hands by 1645, but the total seems between three hundred and four hundred. Thwaites, ed., *Jesuit Relations* 24: 270–71, 294–95, 45: 204–05; Jennings, *Invasion of America,* 24–29. The Mohawk seem to have been the only tribe prior to 1660 that preferred to use firearms. Given, *A Most Pernicious Thing,* 65; George E. Hyde, *Indians of the Woodlands from Prehistoric Times to 1725* (Norman, OK, 1962), 120–27, 133; Trigger, *Children of Aataentsic* 1: 191, 2: 736.

89. The River Indians were a mixed group of Weckquaesgeek and Tappan. Evan Haefili, "Kieft's War and the Cultures of Violence in Colonial America," in Michael A. Bellesiles, ed., *Lethal Imagination: Violence and Brutality in American History* (New York, 1999), 26–29; Jennings, *Ambiguous Iroquois Empire,* 52–57; Trelease, *Indian Affairs,* 69–73.

90. Van Laer, trans., *Council Minutes, 1639–1649,* 128–29; Haefili, "Kieft's War," 31–34; Trelease, *Indian Affairs,* 76–80.

91. Haefili, "Kieft's War," 34–35; Thwaites, ed., *Jesuit Relations* 21: 32–39, 22: 250–51, 24: 232–37, 270–71, 288 95, 32: 18–21, 44: 102–05, 192–93; E. B. O'Callaghan and B. Fernow, eds., *Documents Relative to the Colonial History of the State of New York,* 15 vols. (Albany, NY, 1856–87), 14: 15, 83; Raoul Naroll, "The Causes of the Fourth Iroquois War," *Ethnohistory* 16: 51–81; Trigger, *Children of Aataentsic* 2: 632–33, 700–06; Salisbury, *Manitou and Providence,* 76–84; Richter, *Ordeal of the Longhouse,* 61–65.

92. Charles M. Andrews, *The Colonial Period of American History,* 4 vols. (New Haven, CT, 1937), 3: 53–63, 102–11, 149–52.

93. O'Callaghan and Fernow, eds., *Documents* 3: 260–62; Richter, *Ordeal of the Longhouse,* 133–61; Jennings, *Ambiguous Iroquois Empire,* 148–67.

94. John S. Cooper, *For Commonwealth and Crown: English Gunmakers of the Seventeenth Century* (Gillingham, UK, 1993); J. F. Hayward, *The Art of the Gunmaker,* 2 vols. (New York, 1962), 1: 130–246; Carlo M. Cipolla, *Guns, Sails and Empires: Technological Innovation and the Early Phases of European Expansion 1400–1700* (New York, 1965), 35–97; Howard L. Blackmore, *British Military Firearms, 1650–1850* (New York, 1961), 28–44.

95. Board of Trade, Plantations, CO323/4, PRO.

96. Strachey, *Historie of Travell into Virginia,* 105, 110; Peterson, "Military Equipment," 202; Thwaites, ed., *Jesuit Relations* 5: 220–25, 10: 52–53, 42: 178–81; Trigger, *Children of Aataentsic* 1: 339, 430–31, 2: 629, 634, 638–39. Of course that confidence imparted by guns could work the other way: Colonial militia were known to use being low on powder as an excuse to go home. Percy, "'A Trewe Relacyon,'" 263–64.

97. Smith, *Travels and Works* 1: 141–42, 2: 458–59.

98. Thomas Venn, *Military and Maritime Discipline* (London, 1672), 7–14; L. E. Nolan, *Calvary: Its History and Tactics* (London, 1854), 82–84; Cooper, *For Commonwealth and Crown,* 101–03.

99. Chester Raymond Young, ed., *Westward into Kentucky: The Narrative of Daniel Trabue* (Lexington, KY, 1981), 45–46.

100. James Adair, *The History of the American Indians* (London, 1775), 407–16; John Heckewelder, *History, Manners, and Customs of the Indian Nations* (Philadelphia, 1876), 100–06, 187–91; John Phillip Reid, *A Better Kind of Hatchet: Law, Trade, and Diplomacy in the Cherokee Nation during the Early Years of European Contact* (University Park, PA, 1976), 1–12; Haehli, "Kieft's War," 17–26; Stephen E. Ambrose, *Crazy Horse and Custer: The Parallel Lives of Two American Warriors* (New York, 1975), 12–14, 55–64; Anthony McGinnis, *Counting Coup and Cutting Horses: Intertribal Warfare on the Northern Plains, 1738–1889* (Evergreen, CO, 1990), 129–48.

101. Richter, *Ordeal of the Longhouse,* 64; Steele, *Warpaths,* 16.

102. Morgan, *American Freedom, American Slavery,* 136–37.

103. Malone, *Skulking Way of War,* 56–60; Given, *A Most Pernicious Thing,* 13–32.

104. White, *Middle Ground,* 136, 180–82.

105. Raudzens, "Why Did Amerindian Defences Fail?" 348; see also Raudzens, "So Why Were the Aztecs Conquered, and What Were the Wider Implications? Testing Military Superiority as a Cause of Europe's Pre-Industrial Colonial Conquests," *War in History* 2 (1995): 87–104.

106. Percy, "'A Trewe Relacyon,'" 277.

107. Rountree, *Pocahontas's People,* 75; Mead, "Indian Massacre of 1622," 409; Kingsbury, ed., *Records of the Virginia Company* 3: 555–56; Smith, *Travels and Works* 2: 399.

Chapter Three
Guns in the Daily Life of Colonial America

1. Isabel M. Calder, ed., *Colonial Captivities, Marches, and Journeys* (New York, 1935), 54.

2. Robert Beverley, *The History and Present State of Virginia,* ed. Louis B. Wright (Chapel Hill, NC, 1947; orig. London, 1705), 269, 271.

3. Ibid., 272.

4. Ibid., 253, 268–69.

5. Douglas E. Leach, *Arms for Empire: A Military History of the British Colonies in North America, 1607–1763* (New York, 1973), xi–xii. The official wars during this period include: the English Civil War (1642–49); the Anglo-Dutch War (1664–67); the Glorious Revolution (1688–89); the War of the League of Augsburg (1689–97), also known as King William's War; the War of the Spanish Succession (1702–13), also known as Queen Anne's War; the War of Jenkins' Ear (1739–42); the War of the Austrian Succession (1740–48), which included King George's War, 1744–48; and the French and Indian War (1755–63), also known as the Seven Years' War.

6. Pennsylvania's government did pay companies of rangers a few times in the eighteenth century, and allowed Benjamin Franklin to organize a private militia company in 1747. Francis Jennings, *Empire of Fortune: Crowns, Colonies, and Tribes in the Seven Years War in America* (New York, 1988), 86–87, 255–56. Connecticut did not experience a military threat from the end of Philip's War in 1676 until the American Revolution a century later. Harold E. Selesky, *War and Society in Colonial Connecticut* (New Haven, CT, 1990), 32.

7. Frederick Stokes Aldridge, "Organization and Administration of the Militia System of Colonial Virginia" (Ph.D. diss., American University, 1964), 77; "Causes of the Discontent in Virginia, 1676," *Virginia Magazine* 2 (1895): 168.

8. J. A. Sharpe, *Crime and the Law in English Satirical Prints, 1600–1832* (Cambridge, 1986), 12.

9. Nathaniel B. Shurtleff, ed., *Records of the Governor and Company of the Massachusetts Bay in New England,* 5 vols. (Boston, 1853–54), 1: 211–12; William H. Browne et al., eds., *Archives of Maryland,* 72 vols., (1883–1972), 3: 345–46, 5: 32–33, 52: 448–74. South Carolina law required that freed indentured servants receive a firelock musket. Masters generally used the paucity of firearms as a reasonable excuse to not supply these guns. Theodore Jabbs, "The South Carolina Colonial Militia, 1663–1733" (Ph.D. diss., University of North Carolina, 1973), 137–38.

10. William Strachey, comp., *For the Colony in Virginea Britannia: Laws Divine, Morall and Martiall, etc.,* ed. David H. Flaherty (Charlottesville, VA, 1969), 9–25; *The Colonial Laws of New York from the Year 1664 to the Revolution,* 5 vols. (Albany, NY, 1894), 1: 49–50; Lyon G. Tyler, ed. *Narratives of Early Virginia, 1606–1625* (New York, 1907), 273; William W. Hening, ed., *The Statutes at Large, Being a Collection of All the Laws of Virginia,* 13 vols. (Richmond, VA, 1809–23), 2: 304, 405; Harold L. Peterson, *Arms and Armor in Colonial America, 1526–1783* (Harrisburg, PA, 1956), 321–22; Walter Clark, ed., *The State Records of North Carolina,* 30 vols.

(Goldsboro, NC, 1886–1909), 22: 311–14; Browne et al., eds., *Archives of Maryland* 3: 103, 46: 398–99, 58: 122–24, 340–42, 390, 395, 59: 146–47; Herbert L. Osgood, ed., *Minutes of the Common Council of the City of New York, 1675–1776,* 8 vols. (New York, 1905), 6:54; J. Hammond Trumbull et al., eds., *The Public Records of the Colony of Connecticut,* 15 vols. (Hartford, CT, 1850–90), 1: 134, 6: 363, 406, 8: 386, 9: 473, 580, 14: 343, 392; William Brigham, ed., *The Compact with the Charter and Laws of the Colony of New Plymouth* (Boston, 1836), 84; Charles J. Hoadly, ed., *Records of the Colony and Plantation of New Haven, from 1638 to 1649* (Hartford, CT, 1857), 131–32; Hoadly, ed., *Records of the Colony or Jurisdiction of New Haven, from May 1653, to the Union* (Hartford, CT, 1858), 500; Jabbs, "The South Carolina Colonial Militia," 62; William J. Rivers, *A Sketch of the History of South Carolina to the Close of the Proprietory Government* (Charleston, SC, 1856), 348; Shurtleff, ed., *Records of Massachusetts Bay* 1: 25–26, 84, 125, 2: 72–73, 134–35, 222; Alexander S. Salley Jr., ed., *Journal of the Grand Council of South Carolina,* 2 vols. (Columbia, SC, 1907), 1: 10–12; Thomas Cooper and David J. McCord, eds., *Statutes at Large of South Carolina,* 14 vols. (Columbia, SC, 1836–73), 7: 397, 417–19; John Russell Bartlett, ed., *Records of the Colony of Rhode Island and Providence Plantations, in New England,* 10 vols. (Providence, RI, 1856–65), 1: 79–80, 94, 223–34; William J. Novak, *"Salus Populi:* The Roots of Regulation in America, 1787–1873" (Ph.D. diss., Brandeis University, 1992), 188–89.

11. Edmund S. Morgan, *American Freedom, American Slavery: The Ordeal of Colonial Virginia* (New York, 1975), 239–40; Bruce C. Baird Jr., "The Social Origins of Dueling in Virginia," in Michael A. Bellesiles, ed., *Lethal Imagination: Violence and Brutality in American History* (New York, 1999), 207, 210–11, 230–31; J. A. Leo Lemay, "Southern Colonial Grotesque: Robert Bolling's Neanthe," *Mississippi Quarterly* 35 (1982): 116, 142n.

12. Fred Anderson, *A People's Army: Massachusetts Soldiers and Society in the Seven Years' War* (Chapel Hill, NC, 1984), 75–76; Carole Shammas, *The Pre-Industrial Consumer in England and America* (New York, 1990), 206–08; Alan Macfarlane, *The Justice and the Mare's Ale: Law and Disorder in Seventeenth-Century England* (Oxford, 1981), 191–92; Michael A. Bellesiles, "The Origins of American Gun Culture, 1760–1865," *Journal of American History* 83 (1996): 425–55; Kathleen M. Brown, *Good Wives, Nasty Wenches, and Anxious Patriarchs: Gender, Race, and Power in Colonial Virginia* (Chapel Hill, NC, 1996), 177–79; William L. Shea, *The Virginia Militia in the Seventeenth Century* (Baton Rouge, LA, 1983), 53–54, 92–94; James Titus, *The Old Dominion at War: Society, Politics, and Warfare in Late Colonial Virginia* (Columbia, SC, 1991), 42–44, 66, 106–08; John C. Fitzpatrick, ed., *The Writings of George Washington from the Original Manuscript Sources, 1795–1799,* 39 vols. (Washington, DC, 1931–44), 1: 31–32, 128–29, 170, 187–89, 200–04, 391, 405, 494–96, 499–501; Robert A. Brock, ed., *The Official Records of Robert Dinwiddie, Lieutenant-Governor of the Colony of Virginia, 1751–58,* 2 vols. (Richmond, VA, 1883), 1: 41, 82, 94–95, 121, 125.

13. Hening, *Statutes at Large* 1: 127, 198, 401–02, 2: 335; Susan M. Kingsbury, ed., *The Records of the Virginia Company of London,* 4 vols. (Washington, DC, 1906–35), 4: 422; John C. Miller, *The First Frontier* (New York, 1966), 55; Trumbull et al., eds., *Public Records of Connecticut* 1: 239, 2: 25, 44–46, 52, 244, 270, 361, 3: 63, 432, 4: 37, 178, 349, 485, 6: 363, 406, 8: 386, 10: 460; Salley, ed., *Journal of the Grand Council* 1: 59; Aldridge, "Organization and Administration," 37–38; Hoadly, ed., *Records of the Colony and Plantation,* 205. Maryland had an odd version of a law in 1642 prohibiting the excess firing of guns: "Noe man to discharge 3 Gunns within the Space

of 1/4 hour nor concurr to the dischargeing [of] Soe many." Browne et al., eds., *Archives of Maryland* 3: 103.

14. Trumbull et al., eds., *Public Records of Connecticut* 2: 375.

15. Hening, *Statutes at Large* 2: 344, 348; H. R. McIlwaine, ed., *Minutes of the Council and General Court of Colonial Virginia, 1622–1632, 1670–1676* (Richmond, VA, 1924), 489; Aldridge, "Organization and Administration," 73, 207–08.

16. Michael A. Bellesiles, "Gun Laws in Early America: The Regulation of Firearms Ownership, 1607–1794," *Law and History Review* 16 (1998): 567–89. This census was generally called "taking the assize of arms" and was the annual responsibility of the captain or clerk of each militia company. Shurtleff, ed., *Records of Massachusetts Bay* 2: 118; Trumbull et al., eds., *Public Records of Connecticut* 1: 542; Bartlett, ed., *Records of Rhode Island* 1: 77, 80, 2: 196–97; Hoadly, ed., *Records of the Colony and Plantation,* 96–97, 131–32, 201–02; Hoadly, ed., *Records of the Colony or Jurisdiction,* 602; Brigham, ed., *Compact with . . . the Laws of . . . New Plymouth,* 145; Nathaniel B. Shurtleff and David Pulsifer, eds., *Records of the Colony of New Plymouth in New England,* 12 vols. (Boston, 1855–61), 3: 50, 11: 181.

17. Hening, *Statutes at Large* 1: 219, 255–56, 441, 518, 525, 2: 215, 336–37, 403, 3: 343; Trumbull et al., eds., *Public Records of Connecticut* 1: 1, 52, 74, 79, 138–39, 145–46, 163, 240, 294, 351, 2: 119, 271; Tyler, ed., *Narratives of Early Virginia,* 270; Browne et al., eds., *Archives of Maryland* 1: 36, 291–92, 3: 103, 126, 144, 146–47, 160, 260; Shurtleff and Pulsifer, eds., *Records of New Plymouth* 3: 192, 9: 181, 10: 13–14; Salley, ed., *Journal of the Grand Council* 1: 33; Hoadly, ed., *Records of the Colony and Plantation,* 60, 206; Hoadly, ed., *Records of the Colony or Jurisdiction,* 594; Patrick M. Malone, *The Skulking Way of War: Technology and Tactics Among the New England Indians* (Lanham, MD, 1991), 43–51; Shea, *Virginia Militia,* 57–58; Morgan, *American Slavery, American Freedom,* 250–58. Even Rhode Island, which favored free trade policies in much else, had laws forbidding the sale or trade of firearms to the Indians. Bartlett, ed., *Records of Rhode Island* 1: 123, 139, 155, 226, 320–21, 346, 2: 193–94.

18. Clayton Colman Hall, ed., *Narratives of Early Maryland, 1633–1684* (New York, 1910), 107–08; Hening, *Statutes at Large* 1: 255, 3: 335, 4: 118, 5: 16, 6: 93–106.

19. Hening, *Statutes at Large* 1: 226, 2: 481, 3: 459, 4: 119, 131, 5: 17, 6: 109–10, 9: 268; *William and Mary Quarterly* 2d ser., 4 (1924): 147; T. H. Breen and Stephen Innes, *"Myne Owne Ground": Race and Freedom on Virginia's Eastern Shore, 1640–1676* (New York, 1980), 26; Shea, *Virginia Militia,* 114–17.

20. Peter H. Wood, *Black Majority: Negroes in Colonial South Carolina from 1670 through the Stono Rebellion* (New York, 1974), 324–25; Jabbs, "The South Carolina Colonial Militia," 33–34.

21. Gooch to Commissioners for Trade, 29 June 1729, 11 August 1742, CO 5/1322, CO 5/1325, Public Records Office, Kew, UK (hereafter PRO); H. R. McIlwaine et al., eds., *Executive Journals of the Council of Colonial Virginia, 1680–1754,* 6 vols. (Richmond, VA, 1925–66), 4: 471; Hening, *Statutes at Large* 5: 19; Aldridge, "Organization and Administration," 114–21.

22. Shurtleff and Pulsifer, eds., *Records of New Plymouth* 5: 173; Trumbull et al., eds., *Public Records of Connecticut* 4: 18, 5: 86–87, 6: 381–82, 8: 379; McIlwaine et al., eds., *Executive Journals of the Council* 2: 360.

23. Trumbull et al., eds., *Public Records of Connecticut* 1: 3, 15, 543. In November 1675 the Massachusetts General Court ordered that every town should provide each militia member with six flints, since the assize of arms revealed that many had none and the majority just one. Shurtleff, ed., *Records of Massachusetts Bay* 5: 63.

24. E.g., 1639 and 1643, a twenty-shilling fine per town. Trumbull et al., eds., *Public Records of Connecticut* 1: 30, 91, 1741, 8: 386. For a similar sequence of events in Rhode Island, see Bartlett, ed., *Records of Rhode Island* 1: 104–05, 113, 121–22, 153–54, 221–22, 402–03, 2: 117, 282–83, 409–10, 4: 424–25, 428, 566.

25. Hening, *Statutes at Large* 3: 13–14, 338–39, 4: 200–01, 5: 90, 6: 116, 533, 537–38; Trumbull et al., eds., *Public Records of Connecticut* 1: 74, 134, 542–43, 2: 390, 3: 430; Hoadly, ed., *Records of the Colony and Plantation*, 25–26, 96–97, 131, 201, 500; *Collections of the Connecticut Historical Society*, 31 vols. (Hartford, CT, 1860–1967), 13: 83–85, 15: 191.

26. Trumbull et al., eds., *Public Records of Connecticut* 1: 239, 2: 25, 44–46, 52, 244, 270, 361, 3: 63, 432, 4: 37, 178, 349, 485, 6: 363, 406, 8: 386, 10: 460, *Collections of the Connecticut Historical Society* 1: 268–69, 276–77, 291–94; Hoadly, ed., *Records of the Colony and Plantation*, 214; Hoadly, ed., *Records of the Colony or Jurisdiction*, 174.

27. Trumbull et al., eds., *Public Records of Connecticut* 1: 282, 350, 2: 19–20, 181, 347; McIlwaine, *Minutes of the Council*, 484–85; Salley, ed., *Journal of the Grand Council* 1: 11, 39–40, 62; Aldridge, "Organization and Administration," 85.

28. Trumbull et al., eds., *Public Records of Connecticut* 6: 436, 8: 382–83, 10: 461, 559, 612. Other colonies also complained of the militia not showing up for musters. Alexander S. Salley Jr., ed., *Journals of the Commons House of Assembly*, 21 vols., orig. 1697 (Columbia, SC, 1907–46), 5; Emmons Clark, *History of the Seventh Regiment of New York, 1806–1889*, 2 vols. (New York, 1890), 1: 5, 15–16.

29. 1695, 7 William and Mary, chapter 5 (Ireland); 1739, 13 George II, chapter 6 (Ireland); 1715, I George I, stat. 2, chapter 54; 1746, 19 George II, chapter 39; C. H. Firth and R. S. Rait, eds., *Acts and Ordinances of the Interregnum, 1642–1660* (London, 1911), 2: 1317–19; William Blackstone, *Commentaries on the Laws of England*, 4 vols. (Chicago, 1979), 2: 412; William Nelson, *The Office and Authority of a Justice of the Peace* (London, 1729).

30. Trumbull et al., eds., *Public Records of Connecticut* 2: 217, 3: 431, 4: 177, 485, 6: 363, 406, 9: 111, 10: 479. See also Brigham, ed., *Compact with the Laws of New Plymouth*, 114–15; Shurtleff and Pulsifer, eds., *Records of New Plymouth* 3: 138; Salley, ed., *Journals of the Commons House*, 16; Cooper and McCord, eds., *Statutes at Large* 2: 15–18; Shurtleff, ed., *Records of Massachusetts Bay* 1: 84, 414 (arms "to be provided by the several towns for their inhabitants"); E. B. O'Callaghan and B. Fernow, eds., *Documents Relative to the Colonial History of the State of New York*, 15 vols. (Albany, NY, 1856–87), 1: 156, 166; Bartlett, ed., *Records of Rhode Island* 1: 221. At the end of any campaign, the militia was "to lodge ye Armes in some convenient and safe place." *Collections of the Connecticut Historical Society* 13: 306–07.

31. Hening, *Statutes at Large* 7: 26–27, 125–26, 9: 292, 10: 218, 11: 493, 12: 12–13, 24; Trumbull et al., eds., *Public Records of Connecticut* 1: 282, 350, 2: 19–20, 181, 347, 8: 380, 9: 341–44, 473, 580.

32. Hening, *Statutes at Large* 4: 202–03. South Carolina required the patrols to search slave dwellings once a month for firearms and other weapons. Cooper and McCord, eds., *Statutes at Large* 7: 343–47.

33. According to Valerio Kinter, *A Traveller's History of Italy* (New York, 1997), during the eleven years of Pope Climent XIII's reign, 1758 to 1769, the Papal states recorded thirteen thousand murders, at a time when their population was three million. In Venice between 1741 and 1762 there were seventy-three thousand executions and life sentences in the galleys. Venice imposed summary justice with a traveling court of a judge, lawyer, priest, policemen, and hangman. Criminals were hanged on the spot after they were found guilty.

34. Sally Smith Booth, *Seeds of Anger: Revolts in America, 1607–1771* (New York, 1977), ix. One gets the feeling that Booth did not read her own introduction, for nearly every conflict she described ended "through peaceful, not violent means" (39).

35. Peter Young and Wilfred Emberton, *The Cavalier Army: Its Organization and Everyday Life* (London, 1974), 31–38; Quentine Bone, *Henrietta Maria: Queen of the Cavaliers* (Urbana, IL, 1972), 143–44.

36. Board of Trade, Plantations, CO 323/4, PRO; Wallace B. Gusler and James D. Lavin, *Decorated Firearms, 1540–1870* (Williamsburg, VA, 1977).

37. Dave Grossman, *On Killing: The Psychological Cost of Learning to Kill in War and Society* (Boston, 1995); Konrad Lorenz, *On Aggression* (New York, 1963).

38. J. A. Sharpe, *Crime in Early Modern England, 1550–1750* (London, 1984), 143–67; Clive Emsley, *Crime and Society in England, 1750–1900* (London, 1996), 21–85; J. M. Beattie, *Crime and the Courts in England, 1660–1800* (Princeton, NJ, 1986), 74–198; D. Rumbelow, *I Spy Blue: The Police and Crime in the City of London from Elizabeth I to Victoria* (London, 1971). For a completely different perspective, see Joyce Lee Malcolm, *To Keep and Bear Arms: The Origins of an Anglo-American Right* (Cambridge, MA, 1994), 79–91.

39. Donna J. Spindel and Stuart W. Thomas Jr., "Crime and Society in North Carolina, 1663–1740," in Eric H. Monkkonen, ed., *Crime and Justice in American History: The Colonies and Early Republic,* 2 vols. (Westport, CT, 1991), 2: 699–720; Arthur P. Scott, *Criminal Law in Colonial Virginia* (Chicago, 1930), 314–19, Byrd quoted 321; Hugh F. Rankin, *Criminal Trial Proceedings in the General Court of Colonial Virginia* (Williamsburg, VA, 1965), 204–15; Hoadly, ed., *Records of the Colony and Plantation* 1: 22; Cornelia Hughes Dayton, *Women Before the Bar: Gender, Law, and Society in Connecticut, 1639–1789* (Chapel Hill, NC, 1995), 8n, 144; Shurtleff and Pulsifer, eds., *Records of New Plymouth* 7: 6, 35, 56, 58, 116. Carl Bridenbaugh insisted that the "crimes of violence" were on the rise throughout American cities in the 1730s. He offered no statistics, only one amazing event, in which a "Troop of young Ladies" set upon a man walking across the Boston Neck and "strip't down his Breaches and whip't him most unmercifully." A compelling story, though hardly compelling evidence. Carl Bridenbaugh, *Cities in the Wilderness: The First Century of Urban Life in America, 1625–1742* (New York, 1955), 382, quoting the New York *Journal,* 8 November 1736.

40. William Bradford, *Of Plymouth Plantation, 1620–1647,* ed. Samuel Eliot Morison (New York, 1952), 210; Shurtleff, ed., *Records of Massachusetts Bay* 1: 48; Charles F. Adams, *Three Episodes of Massachusetts History,* 2 vols. (Boston, 1893), 194–208; Charles M. Andrews, *The Colonial Period of American History,* 4 vols. (New Haven, CT, 1937), 1: 332–34, 362–63.

41. J. Mills Thornton III, "The Thrusting Out of Governor Harvey: A Seventeenth Century Rebellion," *Virginia Magazine of History and Biography* 76 (1968): 11–26; Sir John Harvey, "The Mutiny in Virginia, 1635," *Pennsylvania Magazine of History and Biography* 1 (1893): 416–30; Thomas J. Wertenbaker, *Virginia under the Stuarts, 1607–1688* (Princeton, NJ, 1914), 60–84; Richard L. Morton, *Colonial Virginia,* 2 vols. (Chapel Hill, NC, 1960), 1: 82, 137–46. Oddly, Thornton, who labeled this "America's first rebellion against royal authority," and considered it a "triumph" (12), failed to mention Harvey's return to power. Harvey was removed from office by the Privy Council in 1639.

42. Hall, ed., *Narratives of Early Maryland,* 73, 107–08, 150–54, 158–59.

43. Shea, *Virginia Militia,* 73–77; Morgan, *American Slavery, American Freedom,*

147–48, 400–04; Wertenbaker, *Virginia under the Stuarts,* 99–101; Morton, *Colonial Virginia* 1: 171–73.

44. Andrews, *Colonial Period* 2: 319; B. Bernard Browne, "The Battle of the Severn: Its Antecedents and Consequences, 1651–1655," *Maryland Historical Magazine* 14 (1919): 154–71; Matthew Page Andrews, *History of Maryland: Province and State* (Hatboro, PA, 1965), 117–29; Hall, ed., *Narratives of Early Maryland,* 235–44, 256–67.

45. Alexander C. Flick, ed., *History of the State of New York,* 10 vols. (New York, 1933–37), 1: 310–13, 315–17, 2: 56–57, 75–80; O'Callaghan and Fernow, eds., *Documents* 1: 550–55, 14: 213, 231–32, 237–40, 544–48, 551–59; Allen W. Trelease, *Indian Affairs in Colonial New York: The Seventeenth Century* (Ithaca, NY, 1960), 107–08.

46. Flick, ed., *History of New York* 2: 92–95.

47. Shea, *Virginia Militia,* 89–94.

48. Shea, *Virginia Militia,* 75, 92–93; Morgan, *American Slavery, American Freedom,* 244–48. South Carolina found itself in a similar position at the beginning of an Indian war in 1671. The council voted that "it is thought unsafe" to keep all its twelve barrels of powder—barely enough for a month's campaigning—in one central location, so sent several barrels for safekeeping to two militia officers. Salley, ed., *Journal of the Grand Council* 1: 9–10.

49. Charles M. Andrews, ed., *Narratives of the Insurrections, 1675–1690* (New York, 1943), 105.

50. Beverley, *History and Present State of Virginia,* 77; Andrews, ed., *Narratives of the Insurrections,* 16–19, 105–07; W. L. Grant and James Munro, eds., *Acts of the Privy Council of England, Colonial Series, 1613–1680,* 6 vols. (Hereford, UK, 1908–12), 1: 593; Morgan, *American Slavery, American Freedom,* 250–59; Shea, *Virginia Militia,* 97–99.

51. Beverley, *History and Present State of Virginia,* 78; Andrews, ed., *Narratives of the Insurrections,* 20–22, 108–12, 123–24; Morgan, *American Slavery, American Freedom,* 259–62; Shea, *Virginia Militia,* 100–04.

52. Andrews, ed., *Narratives of the Insurrections,* 22–27, 121–28; Morgan, *American Slavery, American Freedom,* 262–69; Shea, *Virginia Militia,* 104–11.

53. Andrews, ed., *Narratives of the Insurrections,* 27–39, 66–71, 128–40; Morgan, *American Slavery, American Freedom,* 269–70; Shea, *Virginia Militia,* 111–18.

54. Andrews, ed., *Narratives of the Insurrections,* 39–40; Beverley, *History and Present State of Virginia,* 85–86; Morgan, *American Slavery, American Freedom,* 271–79; Wertenbaker, *Virginia under the Stuarts,* 196–201, 207–11; Morton, *Colonial Virginia* 1: 278–80, 288–90.

55. CO 5/1355: 68–75, 5/1371: 48, PRO; "Virginia in 1682," *Virginia Magazine of History and Biography* 28 (1920): 227–28; Shea, *Virginia Militia,* 118–20.

56. "Virginia in 1682," 117–27, 229–33; Beverley, *History and Present State of Virginia,* 92; Morgan, *American Slavery, American Freedom,* 286–88; Shea, *Virginia Militia,* 125–26.

57. Shea, *Virginia Militia,* 120–21; W. Noel Sainsbury et al., eds., *Records in the British Public Record Office Relating to South Carolina, 1663–1782,* 36 vols. (Columbia, SC, and Atlanta, GA, 1928–47), 5: 109–11.

58. David S. Lovejoy, *The Glorious Revolution in America* (New York, 1972), 122–59, 235–50.

59. E. B. O'Callaghan, ed., *Documentary History of the State of New-York,* 4 vols. (Albany, NY, 1849–51), 2: 3–4, 14–15; Andrews, ed., *Narratives of the Insurrections,* 362–63; Lovejoy, *Glorious Revolution,* 106 14, 251–57.

60. Andrews, ed., *Narratives of the Insurrections,* 364; O'Callaghan, ed., *Documentary History* 2: 6, 68, 185.

61. Flick, ed., *History of New York* 2: 109–16; O'Callaghan, ed., *Documentary History* 2: 40, 106–08, 113–14, 120–32; Andrews, ed., *Narratives of the Insurrections,* 338; Lovejoy, *Glorious Revolution,* 313–14.

62. O'Callaghan, ed., *Documentary History* 2: 263, 268–69; Lovejoy, *Glorious Revolution,* 312–24, 330–31.

63. O'Callaghan, ed., *Documentary History* 2: 309–10; Lovejoy, *Glorious Revolution,* 322–23.

64. O'Callaghan, ed., *Documentary History* 2: 320–30, 340–46, 358–64; Andrews, ed., *Narratives of the Insurrections,* 368–70, 390–93; Lovejoy, *Glorious Revolution,* 337–40. For a more sympathetic treatment of Leisler's Rebellion, see Gary B. Nash, *The Urban Crucible: Social Change, Political Consciousness, and the Origins of the American Revolution* (Cambridge, MA, 1979), 44–49, 88–93.

65. Andrews, *Colonial Period* 2: 343–44; Aubrey C. Land, *Colonial Maryland: A History* (Millwood, NY, 1981), 79.

66. Browne et al., eds., *Archives of Maryland* 5: 312–34; Andrews, *The Colonial Period* 2: 347–51; Lovejoy, *Glorious Revolution,* 84–87; Land, *Colonial Maryland,* 79–80, 83–84.

67. Browne et al., eds., *Archives of Maryland* 8: 56–57, 65–67; Lovejoy, *Glorious Revolution,* 257–60; Lois G. Carr and David W. Jordan, *Maryland's Revolution of Government, 1689–1692* (Ithaca, NY, 1974), 17, 41, 46–48.

68. Browne et al., eds., *Archives of Maryland* 8: 100–12; Lovejoy, *Glorious Revolution,* 265–66; Andrews, ed., *Narratives of the Insurrections,* 311–13; Land, *Colonial Maryland,* 86–93; Carr and Jordan, *Maryland's Revolution,* 53–61.

69. Browne et al., eds., *Archives of Maryland* 8: 134–38, 147–56, 181–204, 211–28, 263–70; Carr and Jordan, *Maryland's Revolution,* 74–83, 158–63, 201–16; Lovejoy, *Glorious Revolution,* 267–68, 302–07, 364–67.

70. Hugh F. Rankin, *Upheaval in Albemarle: The Story of Culpeper's Rebellion, 1675–1689* (Raleigh, NC), 16–17, 27–30, 36–39.

71. Ibid., 40–48, 62–63.

72. Gove was the only one tried. Convicted and sentenced to death, he was pardoned by the Privy Council and set free. Jere R. Daniell, *Colonial New Hampshire: A History* (Millwood, NY, 1981), 90–95.

73. Jeremy Belknap, *The History of New-Hampshire,* 2 vols. (Dover, NH, 1831), 1: 98–100.

74. Gary B. Nash, *Urban Crucible,* 43. There have been a number of studies of crowd action in Colonial America, most focusing on the Revolutionary period. Those studying the years prior to the Stamp Act crisis in 1765 have found surprisingly few incidences, compared with contemporary Europe, only a handful involving violence. In addition to those crowd actions mentioned here, there were three nonviolent mobs in Boston, in 1689, 1710, and 1736, protesting economic issues; some election crowds in Philadelphia in 1727–29 and 1742; a bloodless anti-impressment riot in Boston in 1747, to which the militia refused to respond; a small nonviolent protest against the overevaluation of pennies in New York in 1753; a minor anti-impressment demonstration in New York in 1758, and another in 1759 concerning a food shortage; an anti-inoculation riot in Marblehead in 1730; and two attacks on houses of prostitution in Boston, in 1734 and 1737. Nash, *Urban Crucible,* 38–44, 76–80, 132–33, 152–54, 222–23, 228–31, 266; Bridenbaugh, *Cities in the Wilderness,*

70–71, 383–84, 388–89; Christine L. Heyrman, *Commerce and Culture: The Maritime Communities of Colonial Massachusetts, 1690–1750* (New York, 1984), 304–13. Bridenbaugh, who has a much looser definition of riot, located several more: officials attacked in the streets of Boston, 1701 and 1741, and New York, 1705; the governor's coach damaged in Boston, 1725; "vile Miscreants" tore up the mayor's plants and sailors stole a city pump in Philadelphia, 1729 and 1741; a "rabble" drinking confiscated claret in front of the customs officers in Newport, 1719; and a crowd of women who threw chamber pots at returning soldiers in 1707. Bridenbaugh, *Cities in the Wilderness,* 223–24, 382–83. Only one of these riots may have involved a gun. Nash identified a Boston riot in 1713 in which the lieutenant governor was shot; Bridenbaugh says he was wounded. Nash, *Urban Crucible,* 77; Bridenbaugh, *Cities in the Wilderness,* 196. Their source, Samuel Sewall's diary, says only that a riot "Wounded the Lt. Govr. and Mr. Newton's Son." There is no reference to a gun or gunshot. *Collections of the Massachusetts History Society,* 5th ser., 6: 384. I can locate no contemporary account of what must have been a very dramatic event that surely would have evoked a royal response. On Colonial and Revolutionary traditions of crowd action, see Pauline Maier, *From Resistance to Revolution: Colonial Radicals and the Development of American Opposition to Britain, 1756–1776* (New York, 1972); Dirk Hoerder, *Crowd Action in Revolutionary Massachusetts, 1765–1780* (New York, 1977); Edward Countryman, *A People in Revolution: The American Revolution and Political Society in New York, 1760–1790* (Baltimore, MD, 1981); Michael A. Bellesiles, *Revolutionary Outlaws: Ethan Allen and the Struggle for Independence on the Early American Frontier* (Charlotesville, VA, 1993); Alan Taylor, *Liberty Men and Great Proprietors: The Revolutionary Settlement on the Maine Frontier, 1760–1820* (Chapel Hill, NC, 1990).

75. Booth, *Seeds of Anger,* 150.

76. Michael A. Bellesiles, "Guns Don't Kill, Movies Kill: The Media's Promotion of Frontier Violence," in *Western Historical Quarterly* (fall 2000).

77. Salley, ed., *Journals of the Commons House,* 110; Wood, *Black Majority,* 53, 260–62.

78. Sally E. Hadden, "Colonial and Revolutionary Era Slave Patrols," in Michael A. Bellesiles, ed., *Lethal Imagination,* 69–85.

79. There was a hysterical terror of a slave uprising in New York in 1741 that led to the official torture and execution of thirty-five people. Nash, *Urban Crucible,* 108–11; Kenneth Scott, "The Slave Insurrection in New York in 1712," *New-York Historical Society Quarterly* 45 (1961): 43–74; Farenc M. Szasz, "The New York Slave Revolt of 1741: A Re-Examination," *New York History* 48 (1967): 215–30; Herbert Aptheker, *American Negro Slave Revolts* (New York, 1983), 168–73, 192–96.

80. Wood, *Black Majority,* 308–23.

81. Ibid., 321–23; Aptheker, *American Negro Slave Revolts,* 187–91.

82. Browne et al., eds., *Archives of Maryland* 28: 188–90; Aptheker, *American Negro Slave Revolts,* 191–92.

83. Albert Henry Smyth, ed., *The Writings of Benjamin Franklin,* 10 vols. (New York, 1905–07), 4: 289–314.

84. For example, "Instructions from the Church of Natick to William and Anthony," *Collections of the Massachusetts Historical Society,* 1st ser., 6: 201–03; Charles H. Lincoln, ed., *Narratives of the Indian Wars: 1675–1699* (New York, 1913), 5, 8 17; Shurtleff and Pulsifer, eds., *Records of New Plymouth* 10: 439 40; Edward Wharton, *New-England's Present Suffering under Their Cruel Neighboring Indians* (London, 1675), 4–6; William Hubbard, *The Happiness of a People* (Boston, 1676), 46.

Colonial Americans seem to have lacked a coherent justification for war. Jill Lepore, *The Name of War: King Philip's War and the Origins of American Identity* (New York, 1998), 97–121.

85. Daniell, *Colonial New Hampshire,* 91–92; Andrews, ed., *Narratives of the Insurrections,* 21–25; Morgan, *American Slavery, American Freedom,* 253–57; *Collections of the Connecticut Historical Society* 13: 247–48, 257–58.

86. Rankin, *Upheaval in Albemarle,* 12–13, 20–22; Alexander S. Salley Jr., ed., *Narratives of Early North Carolina, 1650–1708* (New York, 1911), 328–29.

87. Lovejoy, *Glorious Revolution,* 218; Andrews, ed., *Narratives of the Insurrections,* 196–97; Andros to Blathwayt, 4 April and 4 October 1688, William Blathwayt Papers, John O. Rockefeller Jr. Library Colonial Williamsburg Foundation, Williamsburg, VA.

88. Board of Trade, Plantations, CO 323/4, PRO; Beverley, *History and Present State of Virginia,* 269; Grant and Munro, eds., *Acts of the Privy Council* 1: 422–23; Morgan, *American Slavery, American Freedom,* 252. Another problem was that all the gunpowder came from Europe as well. Gunpowder was thus expensive, difficult to transport, and just simply dangerous to handle or store. And it was essentially useless if shaken into a dust form or if it got wet. There were drying areas in European powder mills, but that was considered the single most dangerous part of the mill, and none existed in America. Jenny West, *Gunpowder, Government and War in the Mid-Eighteenth Century* (Woodbridge, Suffolk, UK, 1991), 7–22.

89. Malcolm, *To Keep and Bear Arms,* 20–21.

90. Military historians who have looked at militia records: Shea, *Virginia Militia,* 87–96, 127–34; Selesky, *War and Society,* 3, 13–14; Titus, *Old Dominion at War,* 1–23; Don Higginbotham, "The Military Institutions of Colonial America: The Rhetoric and the Reality," in Don Higginbotham, *War and Society in Revolutionary America: The Wider Dimensions of Conflict* (Columbia, SC, 1988), 19–41.

91. Shurtleff and Pulsifer, eds., *Records of New Plymouth* 1: 22.

92. Browne et al., eds., *Archives of Maryland* 1: 77–78, 84, 347, 406–08, 410–13, 2: 475–76, 3: 107–08, 130–34, 344–51, 411, 502, 5: 21, 7: 53–63, 8: 223 (quote), 15: 47–49, 97–99, 124–27, 142–44, 20: 186, 313, 315, 317. Some other colonies were even more lax in maintaining militia musters, their legislatures struggling for decades to keep their militia alive in the face of public indifference. In 1677, for instance, the Rhode Island legislature informed the Crown that the Colonial militia was defunct and the colony "at this time is in effect wholly destitute of the military forces for the preservation of itself." Bartlett, ed., *Records of Rhode Island* 2: 567–58. See also ibid. 1: 153–55, 218, 381, 2: 51–52, 114–18, 190, 211–12, 215–19, 3: 15, 4: 149, 155, 173, 211; Aaron Leaming and Jacob Spicer, eds., *The Grants, Concessions, and Original Constitutions of the Province of New-Jersey* (Philadelphia, 1758), 17–19, 85, 94, 135, 277, 331, 348, 424; *Colonial Laws of New York* 1: 49–55, 161–62, 219–20, 231–36, 454–55, 500–07, 546–48, 611–12, 675, 706–07, 745, 778–79, 781–82, 868, 885–88, 917, 1001; Cooper and McCord, eds., *Statutes at Large* 1: 22–40, 48–49, 135, 148, 2: 9–12, 15, 20–21, 25, 44–50, 254–55, 623–24, 691, 3: 23, 108–11, 183, 255–57, 272, 301, 362, 395–98, 465–66, 568–73, 577, 595–96, 4: 104–06, 113–28, 144–48, 7: 1–12, 22–27, 33, 49–56, 346–49, 417–19, 9: 617–24, 638–57, 664–65, 682–88; Hoadly, ed., *Records of the Colony and Plantation* 1: 131–32, 202–205; Hoadly, ed., *Records of the Colony or Jurisdiction,* 173–75, 603–04.

93. John Winthrop, *Winthrop's Journal "History of New England," 1630–1649,* ed. J. K Hosmer, 2 vols. (New York, 1908), 1: 91–92, 2: 42.

94. Fifteen thousand men were eligible for service in the militia in 1690.

Chincheley to Privy Council, 16 July 1672, Winder Transcripts, Virginia State Library, 1: 277; Effingham to the Lords for Trade, 28 May 1689, CO 5/1358: 1, PRO; Effingham to the Lords for Trade, 12 May 1691, *Calendar of State Papers, Colonial Series, America and the West Indies, 1689–1692,* 434–35; Henry Chicheley to Thomas Chicheley, 16 July 1673, CO 1/30, PRO; Shea, *Virginia Militia,* 130; Morgan, *American Slavery, American Freedom,* 252, 395–410; Aldridge, "Organization and Administration," 66, 211.

95. Richard B. Davis, ed., *William Fitzhugh and His Chesapeake World, 1676–1701* (Chapel Hill, NC, 1963), 238. Fitzhugh's will and probate carefully record every bequest, right down to which son gets which waistcoat and his favorite chocolate pot, as well as every detail of his personal possessions; but there is no reference to a gun. See ibid., 38–39, 373–85.

96. Nicholson to Lords of Trade, 20 August, 4 November 1690, 26 January 1691, 26 February, 16 July 1692, 2 December 1701, CO 5/1305, 1306, 1358, 1360, PRO; Abstract of Militia Lists, October 1701, CO 5/1312, PRO; Query to Commissioners for Trade, March 1702, and to Lords of Trade, 17 March 1702, CO 5/1312, CO 5/1360, PRO; Gov. Edward Nott to Lords of Trade, 1705, CO 5/1315: 26–29, PRO; McIlwaine, et al., eds., *Executive Journals of the Council* 1: 111–14, 117–21, 132–34, 141–42, 2: 333–34; William P. Palmer et al., eds., *Calendar of Virginia State Papers and Other Manuscripts,* 11 vols. (Richmond, VA, 1875–93), 1: 80–81; Morgan, *American Slavery, American Freedom,* 351–54; Aldridge, "Organization and Administration," 92–104; Richard L. Morton, *Struggle Against Tyranny* (Williamsburg, VA, 1957), 50. Nicholson's successor as governor, Edmund Andros, shared the view that the militia was "very Indifferently Armed," and "unsuiteably (and not well) Armed" but concentrated on coastal defenses. Andros to Commissioners for Trade, 22 July 1693, CO 5/1308, PRO; Shea, *Virginia Militia,* 131–34.

97. William Byrd, *The Secret Diary of William Byrd of Westover, 1709–1712,* eds. Louis B. Wright and Marion Tinling (Richmond, VA, 1941), 389–96.

98. Ibid., 234, 399, 403, 405, 414–17, 424.

99. Jack Verney, *The Good Regiment: The Carignan-Salieres Regiment in Canada, 1665–1688* (Montreal, 1991), 37–40.

100. Ibid., 45–53; W. J. Eccles, *Canada under Louis XIV, 1663–1701* (London, 1964), 39–41. For a different reading of these events, see Trelease, *Indian Affairs,* 242–43.

101. Henry True, Memorandum and Account Book, 1696–1719, New York Public Library Mss. Room; *Collections of the Connecticut Historical Society* 13: 83–85, 269–76, 15: 133–36, 191.

102. Robert E. Wall, "Louisbourg, 1745," *New England Quarterly* 37 (1964). 64–83; Louis Effingham De Forest, ed., *Louisbourg Journals, 1745* (New York, 1932), 5–6 (quote), 10–28, 174–76; G. A. Rawlyk, *Yankees at Louisbourg* (Orono, ME, 1967), 98–117.

103. Thomas Proctor to Samuel Waldo, 26 May 1744, Samuel Waldo Papers, John Marshall Diary, Massachusetts Historical Society, Boston, MA.

104. South Carolina *Gazette* for 8 November 1735, 6 March 1736 (in reverse order); H. Telfer Mook, "Training Day in New England," *New England Quarterly* 11 (1938): 681; John W. Shy, *Toward Lexington: The Role of the British Army in the Coming of the American Revolution* (Princeton, NJ, 1965), 6; Ronald L. Boucher, "The Colonial Militia as a Social Institution: Salem, Massachusetts, 1764–1775," *Military Affairs* 37 (1973): 125–30; Morison Sharp, "Leadership and Democracy in the Early New England System of Defense," *American Historical Review* 50 (1945): 252; Louis

Morton, "The Origins of American Military Policy," *Military Affairs* 22 (1958): 75–82; Walter Millis, *Arms and Men: A Study in American Military History* (New York, 1956), 22–23.

105. Calder, ed., *Colonial Captivities*, 36, 56; Henry True, Memorandum and Account Book, 1696–1719, New York Public Library Mss. Room; O'Callaghan, and Fernow, eds., *Documents* 14: 597–609; Samuel Sewall, *Diary of Samuel Sewall, 1674–1729*, vols. 5 and 6 of *Collections of the Massachusetts Historical Society* 5th ser. (Boston, 1878–88), 5: 350.

106. On the mythology of hunting, see Matt Cartmill, *A View to a Death in the Morning: Hunting and Nature Through History* (Cambridge, MA, 1993).

107. Percy Wells Bidwell and John I. Falconer, *History of Agriculture in the Northern United States, 1620–1860* (Washington, DC, 1925); Bettye H. Pruitt, "Self-Sufficiency and the Agricultural Economy of Eighteenth-Century Massachusetts," *William and Mary Quarterly* 41 (1984): 333–64.

108. John Lawson, *A New Voyage to Carolina* (London, 1709), 14–42; Lawrence J. Burpee, ed., "Journal of Matthew Cocking, From York Factory to the Blackfeet Country, 1772–73," *Proceedings and Transactions of the Royal Society of Canada* 3rd ser., 2: 89–119; Kathryn E. Holland Braund, *Deerskins & Duffels: The Creek Indian Trade with Anglo-America, 1685–1815* (Lincoln, NE, 1993), 66. For other legal limitations on hunting, see, for example, *The Colonial Laws of New York from the Year 1664 to the Revolution*, 5 vols. (Albany, NY, 1894), 1: 585–86, 618–20, 888, 2: 323–24; Stephen Aron, *How the West Was Lost: The Transformation of Kentucky from Daniel Boone to Henry Clay* (Baltimore, MD, 1996), 15–17.

109. Lawson, *A New Voyage to Carolina*, 86, 88.

110. See, for instance, the account books of William Heywood, Stephen Peabody, Thomas Vail, Elijah Washburn, American Antiquarian Society (Worcester, MA); Jonas Fay, Isaac Greene, Nathan Stone, Samuel Thrall, Vermont Historical Society (Montpelier, VT); the Brownson family, David Mallory, Arlington Library (Arlington, VT); Stephen Fay, Bennington Historical Museum (Bennington, VT); Stephen Fay, Ambros Hubbert, Bennington, VT, Probate Records; Asa Sanger, Keene Public Library (Keene, NH); Harold B. Gill Jr., *The Gunsmith in Colonial Virginia* (Williamsburg, VA, 1974), 63–68.

111. Indians also relied heavily on traps for hunting. Very little research has been done on hunting in Colonial America. The topic is better developed in the nineteenth century. Michael A. Bellesiles, "The Autobiography of Levi Allen," *Vermont History* 60 (1992), 85–87; Beverley, *History and Present State of Virginia*, 309–10; Thomas E. Norton, *The Fur Trade in Colonial New York, 1686–1776* (Madison, WI, 1974), 60–120; Colin G. Calloway, *The Western Abenakis of Vermont, 1600–1800: War, Migration, and the Survival of an Indian People* (Norman, OK, 1990), 132–42; Colin G. Calloway, ed., *Dawnland Encounters: Indians and Europeans in Northern New England* (Hanover, NH, 1991), 193–211; Paul C. Phillips, *The Fur Trade*, 2 vols. (Norman, OK, 1961), 1: 377–403; Burpee, ed., "Journal of Matthew Cocking," 106–07; Braund, *Deerskins & Duffels*, 66–73.

112. John Phillip Reid, *A Better Kind of Hatchet: Law, Trade, and Diplomacy in the Cherokee Nation during the Early Years of European Contact* (University Park, PA, 1976), 34–36; Braund, *Deerskins & Duffels*, 61–66; Daniel K. Richter, *The Ordeal of the Longhouse: The Peoples of the Iroquois League in the Era of European Colonization* (Chapel Hill, NC, 1992), 90–91; Trelease, *Indian Affairs*, 215–25. Rhode Island employed Indians as hunters; Bartlett, ed., *Records of Rhode Island* 1: 125–26. Maryland

attempted in 1650 to outlaw the practice of employing Indians as hunters for white settlers. Nothing came of this effort. Browne et al., eds., *Archives of Maryland* 3: 260.

113. Bellesiles, *Revolutionary Outlaws,* 27; Jackson T. Main, *The Social Structure of Revolutionary America* (Princeton, NJ, 1965), 18–27, 50–54, 104–13; Walter Nugent, *Structures of American Social History* (Bloomington, IN, 1981), 39–53.

114. Main, *Social Structure,* 34–44, 67, 75–83, 112–13, 132–35; Shammas, *Pre-Industrial Consumer,* 121–88.

115. Main estimates the average annual income of a skilled artisan at £25 to £30. Main, *Social Structure,* 68–114; Shammas, *Pre-Industrial Consumer,* 123–33. On the paucity of currency in British North America, see John J. McCusker, *Money and Exchange in Europe and America, 1600–1775: A Handbook* (Chapel Hill, NC, 1978), 125–31; John J. McCusker and Russell R. Menard, *The Economy of British America, 1607–1789* (Chapel Hill, NC, 1985), 337–41.

116. Gill, *The Gunsmith in Colonial Virginia,* 22–32, 63–68; James Whisker, *The Gunsmith's Trade* (Lewiston, NY, 1992), 144–63.

117. S. James Gooding, *The Canadian Gunsmiths, 1608 to 1900* (West Hill, ONT, 1962), 31–32. The first gun known to be made in Canada was in the early nineteenth century, though some forty smiths and armorers, mostly employed by the Hudson's Bay Company, repaired and maintained firearms in the eighteenth century. Ibid., 34, 59–185.

118. James Blair, president of the Virginia council, wrote in 1768 that "We do not make a saw, auger, gimlett, file, or nails, nor steel; and most tools in the Country are imported from Britain." Quoted in Gill, *The Gunsmith in Colonial Virginia,* 45. The few surviving gunsmith account books from the eighteenth century, such as those of James Anderson of Williamsburg, which covers the years 1778 to 1799 (Research Department, Colonial Williamsburg), indicate that they repaired but did not make guns. And Colonial assemblies regularly paid smiths to repair arms, but almost never purchased guns from these smiths.

119. Gill, *The Gunsmith in Colonial Virginia,* 21–32; Whisker, *The Gunsmith's Trade,* 47–66. The Jager rifle, an ornamental German gun with a short barrel and large bore, came to Pennsylvania in the early eighteenth century. Those few gunsmiths making rifles in America reduced the caliber to conserve powder and lead, and lengthened the barrel. Felix Reichman, "The Pennsylvania Rifle: A Social Interpretation of Changing Military Techniques," *Pennsylvania Magazine of History and Biography* 69 (1945): 8–9.

120. Salley, ed., *Journal of the Grand Council* 1: 7–8, 39–40, 46, 51–52, 62; Jabbs, "The South Carolina Colonial Militia," 96–97. There is a smith named John Dandy who appears in the Maryland records of the 1640s. In 1644 he may have made or assembled the first gun in the American colonies—the parts were surely imported. On at least one occasion Dandy stocked a gun, and in 1647 he claimed to have made a gun lock eight years earlier, though that must have been in England, if true, since he arrived in Maryland in 1642. Dandy was charged with murdering an Indian boy in 1644, but was found innocent. In 1650 he beat an indentured servant to death and was hanged. Browne et al., eds., *Archives of Maryland* 4: 122, 247, 254–55, 284, 10: 283.

121. Reichman, "The Pennsylvania Rifle," 9–10; James B. Whisker, *Arms Makers of Colonial America* (Selinsgrove, PA, 1992), 102–04, 129–30; M. L. Brown, *Firearms in Colonial America: The Impact on History and Technology, 1492–1792* (Washington, DC, 1980), 256–59, 264.

122. Gill, *The Gunsmith in Colonial Virginia,* 6–7, 27–29, 69–108. On David and William Geddy's ability to rifle barrels, see the *Virginia Gazette,* 8 August 1751.

123. Rita S. Gottesman, comp., *The Arts and Crafts in New York, 1726–1776,* vol. 69 of *Collections of the New York Historical Society* (New York, 1938), 82, 165; quoting *New York Gazette,* 18 September 1769, 7 November 1774 (in reverse order). On other artisans repairing guns, see also ibid., 197, 201, for a brass founder (*Rivington's New York Gazetteer,* 18 May 1775) and a cutler (*New York Gazette,* 6 April 1767). As Rita S. Gottesman writes in the introduction, "The early New York artisan had apparently not yet won the confidence of his community, for most articles offered for sale in New York were imported. Even repairs were made abroad" (xiii).

124. Ibid., 304; Gottesman, *Arts and Crafts in New York* quoting *New York Gazette* 1 August 1748.

125. George F. Dow, comp., *The Arts and Crafts in New England, 1704–1775* (Topsfield, MA, 1927), 264–65.

126. At the very least one can safely say that gunsmiths saw no advantage in advertising their services. Alfred C. Prime, comp., *The Arts and Crafts in Philadelphia, Maryland, and South Carolina, 1721–1785* (Philadelphia, 1929). During the Revolution, fifty artisans from trades as diverse as clockmaker to tinsmith cleaned and repaired firearms for Pennsylvania; not one of them was a gunsmith. Whisker, *The Gunsmith's Trade,* 88; Roy Chandler et al., *Arms Makers of Eastern Pennsylvania* (Bedford, PA, 1984).

127. H. R. McIlwaine, ed., *Legislative Journals of the Council of Colonial Virginia, 1680–1774,* 3 vols. (Richmond, VA, 1918), 2: 695; Whisker, *The Gunsmith's Trade,* 68–73.

128. Hening, ed., *Statutes at Large* 1: 208, 2: 85, 294, 3: 363; McIlwaine, ed., *Executive Journals of the Council* 1: 215. Other colonies also expropriated the labor of gunsmiths, often in similar wording. In 1661, for instance, the Maryland council ordered "That all Smiths which have tooles be forced to fixe armes for the Soldiers." Four years later Connecticut's assembly proclaimed that no smith could do any other work until all the militia's arms were properly repaired. Browne et al., eds., *Archives of Maryland* 3: 531, 4: 46, 19: 586; Trumbull et al., eds., *Public Records of Connecticut* 2: 19–20.

129. Gill, *The Gunsmith in Colonial Virginia,* 17–18, 33–44. Though many different artisans were involved in gun repair and maintenance, it is unclear how often they conducted such work. For instance, Jonathan Haight, a rural New York blacksmith, kept an account book between 1771 and 1789. His fifty-two hundred transactions involving 350 customers included only one minor gun repair. American Antiquarian Society, Worcester, MA.

130. McIlwaine, ed., *Executive Journals of the Council* 1: 215; The Council to the Board of Trade, CO 5/1309: 223–24, CO 5/1358: 29–33, 41–45, PRO. See also CO 323/4, PRO.

131. Gill, *The Gunsmith in Colonial Virginia,* 21–31. There are a few instances of gunsmiths coming to America as indentured servants and finding themselves with little opportunity to use their skills, eventually turning to other lines of employment. See for instance John Austin and John Spencer of Maryland and Henry Hawkins of Pennsylvania; *American Weekly Mercury,* 28 November 1728; *Maryland Gazette,* 31 July 1755; Whisker, *The Gunsmith's Trade,* 96.

132. One critic explained the paucity of firearms in probate inventories by stating that "it is well known that the inventory of an estate is what is left after family members pick over the items." Maybe that is the way people behave in his family, but

it was and remains highly illegal to ransack an estate before a court-appointed executor can conduct an inventory. Anyone who works with the probate court records from this early, perhaps more honest, period knows that exact reference was made to every item, no matter how trivial, that had been passed on to a friend or family member before the death of the testator. The courts are packed with suits between family members arguing over who gets the sheets, plow, and the family Bible. Mike Brown, "Constitution Framers Backed the Right to Bear Arms," St. Louis *Post-Dispatch,* 5 December 1998.

133. This data is drawn from Horatio Rogers et al., eds., *The Early Records of the Town of Providence,* 21 vols. (Providence, RI, 1892–1915), vols. 6, 7, and 16.

134. Leach, *Arms for Empire,* 12. Incredibly, Leach demonstrated this assertion with a *fictional* account of a militia muster (24–38).

Chapter Four
Creation of the First American Gun Culture

1. William Hubbard, *The History of the Indian Wars in New England,* ed. Samuel G. Drake (Roxbury, MA, 1865, orig. 1677), 144.

2. An Act to Prevent Outrages against the Indians, 4 May 1681, J. C. Brown Library; J. Hammond Trumbull et al., eds., *The Public Records of the Colony of Connecticut,* 15 vols. (Hartford, CT, 1850–90), 2: 359–60; Jill Lepore, *The Name of War: King Philip's War and the Origins of American Identity* (New York, 1998), 182–83; Harold E. Selesky, *War and Society in Colonial Connecticut* (New Haven, CT, 1990), 19.

3. Christine L. Heyrman, *Commerce and Culture: The Maritime Communities of Colonial Massachusetts, 1690–1750* (New York, 1984), 225–26.

4. Social scientists call this desire to eliminate groups of people identified as parasites or cancers "prophylactics," the Nazis being the leading historical example of this disease. Mary Poovey, *Making a Social Body* (Chicago, 1995), 90–94; Robert Nye, *Crime, Madness and Politics: The Medical Concept of National Decline* (Princeton, NJ, 1984); Claude Lefort, "The Image of the Body in Totalitarianism," in Lefort, *The Political Forms of Modern Society,* ed. John Thompson (Cambridge, 1986). These scholars locate prophylactics in the twentieth century, yet it is evidently not confined to that century.

5. Benjamin Trumbell, *History of the Indian Wars* (Boston, 1846), 87.

6. Theodore Jabbs, "The South Carolina Colonial Militia, 1663–1733" (Ph.D. diss., University of North Carolina, 1973), 71–72, 116; Alexander Salley Jr., ed., *Journal of the Grand Council of South Carolina,* 2 vols. (Columbia, SC, 1907), 1: 62–63; W. Noel Sainsbury et al., eds., *Records in the British Public Record Office Relating to South Carolina, 1663–1782,* 36 vols. (Columbia, SC, and Atlanta, GA, 1928–47), 5: 204. The first settlers at Cape Fear had few arms after the proprietors' shipment capsized. When these settlers came into conflict with the local Indians they simply abandoned their settlement as undefendable in 1667. Alexander S. Salley Jr., ed., *Narratives of Early North Carolina, 1650–1708* (New York, 1911), 84; William L. Saunders, ed., *The Colonial Records of North Carolina,* 30 vols. (Raleigh, NC, 1886–1914), 1: 153–55, 159–60.

7. Robert Ferguson, *The Present State of Carolina with Advice to the Settlers* (London, 1682), 21; Langdon Cheves, ed., *The Shaftesbury Papers and Other Records Relating to Carolina,* vol. 5 of *Collections of the South Carolina Historical Society*

(Charleston, SC, 1897): 31, 49–50, 147–52; Saunders, ed., *The Colonial Records of North Carolina* 1: 77; Thomas Cooper and David J. McCord, eds., *The Statutes at Large of South Carolina,* 14 vols. (Columbia, SC, 1836–73), 2: 20–21, 82–84, 307; Sainsbury et al., eds., *Records in the British Public Record Office* 2: 223; Jabbs, "The South Carolina Colonial Militia," 49–50, 62–64, 163–64, 193. For similar efforts see Charles J. Hoadly, ed., *Records of the Colony and Plantation of New Haven, from 1638 to 1649* (Hartford, CT, 1857), 500; John Russell Bartlett, ed., *Records of the Colony of Rhode Island and Providence Plantations, in New England,* 10 vols. (Providence, RI, 1856–65), 2: 487–88, 504–05.

8. Alexander S. Salley Jr., ed. *Journals of the Commons House of Assembly,* 21 vols. (Columbia, SC, 1907–46), [1697]: 5, 16–17, [1701] 14–15, [1702] 67–69, 72–73; Jabbs, "South Carolina Colonial Militia," 204–05, 228–40, 267–68; Cooper and McCord, eds. *Statutes at Large* 2: 96, 182–85, 227–28. Sailors were particularly valued because of their greater experience with firearms. In 1703 the assembly granted any militia officer the power to impress seamen during times of crises. Cooper and McCord, *Statutes at Large* 9: 617–24.

9. Salley, ed. *Journals of the Commons House* [1702]: 69, 84, [1707]: 91, [1707–08]: 21–22; Cooper and McCord, eds., *Statutes at Large* 3: 272; Sainsbury et al., eds., *Records in the British Public Record Office* 5: 35–36. Contradicting, or ignoring, this declining interest in the militia, Thomas Nairne wrote in 1710 that "It is not here as in England, where an ordinary mechanic thinks himself too good to be a soldier. Every one among us is versed in arms, from the governour to the meanest servant, and all are so far from thinking it below them, that most People take Delight in military Affairs." Nairne went on to praise the militia as "superiour in making a true shot." As Theodore Jabbs wrote, "Ironically, Nairne was among the first to die during the Yamasee War, a conflict that made a mockery of much of his earlier praise of the militia." Jabbs, "South Carolina Colonial Militia," 275–76; Thomas Nairne, "A Letter from a Swiss Gentleman to His Friend in Bern," *North Carolina University Magazine* 4 (September 1855): 297.

10. Saunders, ed., *Colonial Records of North Carolina* 2: 254.

11. The South Carolina government even accused Virginia of selling arms to the hostile Indians. Saunders, ed., *Colonial Records of North Carolina* 2: 242–43, 246–47; Sainsbury et al., eds., *Records in the British Public Record Office* 6: 132, 264–67; Verner W. Crane, *The Southern Frontier, 1670–1732* (Ann Arbor, 1929), 176–77.

12. South Carolina's agents did eventually acquire 160 muskets from Virginia and 500 in New England. The other colonies all made South Carolina pay dearly for this aid, and Massachusetts demanded cash up front. Saunders, ed., *Colonial Records of North Carolina* 2: 188; Cooper and McCord, eds., *Statutes at Large* 2: 623–25; Sainsbury et al., eds., *Records in the British Public Record Office* 6: 104–07, 134; Saunders, ed., *Colonial Records of North Carolina* 2: 225, 255; David H. Corkran, *The Creek Frontier, 1540–1783: Conflict and Survival, 1740–62* (Norman, OK, 1962), 56–81; W. S. Robinson, *The Southern Colonial Frontier, 1607–1763* (Albuquerque, NM, 1979), 110–18, 185–86; Jabbs, "South Carolina Colonial Militia," 98, 136–37; Salley, ed., *Journal of the Grand Council* 1: 8–9; Salley, ed., *Narratives of Early North Carolina,* 182, 284–87, 329; Crane, *Southern Frontier,* 19–24; Edward McCrady, *History of South Carolina under the Proprietary Government, 1670–1719* (New York, 1897), 478; Steven J. Oatis, "A Colonial Complex: South Carolina's Changing Frontiers in the Era of the Yamasee War, 1680–1730" (Ph.D. diss., Emory University, 1999), 242–63.

13. Sainsbury et al., eds., *Records in the British Public Record Office* 6: 100, 7: 254–55, 8: 170–74, 12: 120–23; Jabbs, "South Carolina Colonial Militia," 322–29,

356–59. The new royal governor was ordered to "arm, muster, command and employ" the militia. Toward that end the government sent three hundred muskets and seventy-two cannon as a gift in August 1731. The problem then became where to store these weapons, as the Charleston armory was too small. The governor requested several times that the assembly turn its attention to this matter, but until 1736, the weapons rusted outside. Sainsbury et al., eds., *Records in the British Public Record Office* 8: 51–52, 124–25, 11: 188–89, 14: 292–93, 15: 39.

14. Louis B. Wright and Marion Tinling, eds., *The Secret Diary of William Byrd of Westover, 1709–1712* (Richmond, VA, 1941), 466; R. A. Brock, ed., *The Official Letters of Alexander Spotswood, Lieutenant-Governor of the Colony of Virginia, 1710–1722,* 2 vols. (Richmond, VA, 1882–85), 1: 132, 2: 1–7, 34, 41–43, 210–12; Ian K. Steele, *Warpaths: Invasions of North America* (New York, 1994), 161–62; Selesky, *War and Society,* 66.

15. James Fitzroy Scott, the Duke of Monmouth, *An Abridgment of the English Military Discipline* (Boston, 1690), 10–11, 28–32. See also Anon., *The Exercise for the Militia of the Province of the Massachusetts-Bay* (Boston, 1758), 12–15.

16. Selesky, *War and Society,* 14. In 1666 the Connecticut legislature ordered that one-fifth of the militiamen should bear pikes. Trumbull, ed., *Public Records of Connecticut* 2: 46.

17. Urian Oakes, *The Soveraign Efficacy of Divine Providence* (Boston, 1682), 26; Lepore, *The Name of War,* 113; Thomas S. Abler, "Scalping, Torture, Cannibalism and Rape: An Ethnohistorical Analysis of Conflicting Cultural Values in War," *Anthropologica* 34 (1992): 6–15; John E. Ferhling, *A Wilderness of Miseries: War and Warriors in Early America* (Westport, CT, 1980), 34–36.

18. William L. Shea, *The Virginia Militia in the Seventeenth Century* (Baton Rouge, LA, 1983), 79–80.

19. Charles M. Andrews, ed., *Narratives of the Insurrections, 1675–1690* (New York, 1943), 18–19, 47–48, 105–07; Lyon G. Tyler, ed., "Colonel John Washington," *William and Mary Quarterly,* 1st ser. (1893–94), 2: 38–43; Edmund S. Morgan, *American Slavery, American Freedom: The Ordeal of Colonial Virginia* (New York, 1975), 251–52; Shea, *Virginia Militia,* 97–99.

20. Lepore, *The Name of War,* xv–xxi, makes a strong case for the use of Philip, but I prefer Metacom.

21. Douglas E. Leach writes of these "savages" that, after turning in their guns, Philip "and his retinue stalked back to Mount Hope weaponless, like little boys deprived of their slingshots at school." Douglas E. Leach, *Flintlock and Tomahawk: New England in King Philip's War* (New York, 1958), 26–27. Such comments highlight the unreliability of some historians of the Indian wars.

22. Nathaniel B. Shurtleff and David Pulsifer, eds., *Records of the Colony of New Plymouth in New England,* 12 vols. (Boston, 1855–61), 5: 63–64, 73–80, 97–98, 176–77, 183–86, 200, 10: 364; Charles H. Lincoln, ed., *Narratives of the Indian Wars, 1675–1699* (New York, 1913), 7–13, 24–29; Thomas Church, *The History of Philip's War,* ed. Samuel G. Drake (Exeter, NH, 1829, orig. 1712), 19–34; William Hubbard, *History of the Indian Wars,* ed. Samuel G. Drake (Roxbury, MA 1865; orig. 1677), 53–67; Francis Jennings, *The Invasion of America: Indians, Colonialism, and the Cant of Conquest* (Chapel Hill, NC, 1975), 293–97; Philip Ranlet, "Another Look at the Causes of King Philip's War," *New England Quarterly* 61 (1988): 90–100.

23. Nathaniel B. Shurtleff, ed., *Records of the Governor and Company of the Massachusetts Bay in New England,* 5 vols. (Boston, 1853–61), 5: 47; John Dutton, *Letters Written from New England, A.D. 1681,* ed. W. H. Whitmore (Boston, 1867), 140;

William Harris, *A Rhode Islander Reports on King Philip's War: The Second William Harris Letter of August, 1676,* ed. Douglas Edward Leach (Providence, RI, 1963), 35–36; George M. Bodge, *Soldiers in King Philip's War* (Boston, 1906), 45–46; Jack S. Radebaugh, "The Militia of Colonial Massachusetts," *Military Affairs* 43 (1954): 1–18; *Massachusetts Historical Society Collections* 43 (1909–10): 491.

24. *Collections of the Massachusetts Historical Society* 7: 352–53.

25. The troops found fifty muskets among the Narragansett. Lincoln, ed., *Narratives of the Indian Wars,* 31, 38–39, 57–64; Hubbard, *History of the Indian Wars,* 79–94; Church, *History of Philip's War,* 50–63; Harris, *A Rhode Islander Reports,* 37–39; Bodge, *Soldiers in King Philip's War,* 185–94; Steele, *Warpaths,* 102–07; Jennings, *Invasion of America,* 302–12. Leach (*Flintlock and Tomahawk,* 145–47) doubted that there were any neutral Indians, and even refers to "The Problem of the 'Friendly Indians.'" Apparently their "savage instincts" led them to acts of "deliberate treachery" against the whites.

26. Lincoln, ed., *Narratives of the Indian Wars,* 118–22; Hubbard, *History of the Indian Wars,* 165–67.

27. Lincoln, ed., *Narratives of the Indian Wars,* 81–85; Hubbard, *History of the Indian Wars,* 131–32, 201–15; Harris, *A Rhode Islander Reports,* 41–45; Increase Mather, *A Brief History of the War with the Indians in New-England* (London, 1676), 206; Bodge, *Soldiers in King Philip's War,* 347–49; Lepore, *The Name of War,* 71–96.

28. Church, *History of Philip's War,* 39–47.

29. Trumbull, *History of the Indian Wars,* 78–80, 90, 96. On other fights in which the Indians had few or no guns, see ibid., 67, 72, 84–85, 91–93. Rhode Island made an effort to diversify its weapons use in 1647. With its supplies of arms and ammunition dangerously low, the legislature passed an archery law ordering all adult males to own a bow and arrows and requiring every father to give his son a bow at age seven. Everyone was to practice regularly "to the end also that we may come to out shoot these natives in their owne bow." Nothing much came of this effort. Bartlett, *Records of Rhode Island* 1: 186–87.

30. Trumbull, *History of the Indian Wars,* 67–69, 90; Church, *History of Philip's War,* 42–43.

31. Lincoln, ed., *Narratives of the Indian Wars,* 95–96; Hubbard, *History of the Indian Wars,* 230–37; Bodge, *Soldiers in King Philip's War,* 241–47; Jennings, *Invasion of America,* 317–19.

32. Shurtleff, ed., *Records of Massachusetts Bay* 5: 47–49; Trumbull et al., eds. *Public Records of Connecticut* 2: 383–84; Church, *History of Philip's War,* 125–27, 149–49; Hubbard, *History of the Indian Wars,* 88–96, 265–68; Harris, *A Rhode Islander Reports,* 18, 64–67; Jennings, *Invasion of America,* 313–26; Selesky, *War and Society,* 20–21.

33. Harris, *A Rhode Islander Reports,* 22; Lepore, *The Name of War,* 175–76.

34. Shurtleff, ed., *Records of Massachusetts Bay* 5: 242; Michael J. Puglisi, *Puritans Beseiged: The Legacies of King Philip's War in the Massachusetts Bay Colony* (Lanham, MD, 1991), 156–59.

35. On the war's consequences, see Puglisi, *Puritans Beseiged,* 58–76; Stephen Saunders Webb, *1676: The End of American Independence* (New York, 1984), 227–44. Webb holds that the economy of New England did not recover from Philip's War until 1775 (243).

36. Thomas E. Burke Jr., *Mohawk Frontier: The Dutch Community of Schenectady, New York, 1661–1710* (Ithaca, NY, 1991), 104–08; W. J. Eccles, *Canada under Louis XIV, 1663–1701* (London, 1964), 172–73, 176; E. B. O'Callaghan and Fernow,

eds., *Documents Relative to the Colonial History of the State of New York,* 15 vols. (Albany, NY, 1856–87), 3: 693–704, 715–18, 735–36.

37. O'Callaghan and Fernow, eds., *Documents* 3: 390–94, 708–10, 715–19, 751–54, 4: 193–96; Richard S. Dunn, *Puritans and Yankees: The Winthrop Dynasty of New England, 1630–1717* (Princeton, NJ, 1962), 289–94; David S. Lovejoy, *The Glorious Revolution in America* (New York, 1972), 323–24; Alexander C. Flick, ed., *History of the State of New York,* 10 vols. (New York, 1933–37), 2: 207–13.

38. Eccles, *Canada under Louis XIV,* 186–87.

39. Robert Caverly, *Heroism of Hannah Duston* (Boston, 1874), 14–29, 389–408; Laurel Thatcher Ulrich, *Good Wives: Image and Reality in the Lives of Women in Northern New England, 1650–1750* (New York, 1982), 167–72, 234–35.

40. W. Noel Sainsbury et al., eds., *Calendar of State Papers, Colonial Series, America and the West Indies,* 44 vols. (London, 1860–1969), 15: 165; Salley, ed., *Journal of the Grand Council* 1: 39.

41. John Williams, *The Redeemed Captive,* ed. Edward W. Clark (Amherst, MA, 1976), 44–45; George Sheldon, *A History of Deerfield, Massachusetts,* 2 vols. (Deerfield, MA, 1895–96), 302; Richard I. Melvoin, *New England Outpost: War and Society in Colonial Deerfield* (New York, 1989), 211–53.

42. Shea, *Virginia Militia,* 122; Selesky, *War and Society,* 26–27, 48–49, 58–63; O'Callaghan and Fernow, eds., *Documents* 5: 261; Trumbull et al., eds., *Public Records of Connecticut* 5: 164–65, 181, 291–92, 353, 15: 586–88; Brock, ed., *The Official Letters of Alexander Spotswood* 1: 142–43, 145, 2: 115–16. They failed to specify, however, that the soldiers could keep these muskets. Those who wanted to found it necessary to reenlist. Some of those who turned in their muskets were still petitioning for their return in 1737.

43. Douglas E. Leach, *Arms for Empire: A Military History of the British Colonies in North America, 1607–1763* (New York, 1973), 9; Lindsay Boynton, *The Elizabethan Militia, 1558–1638* (Toronto, 1967), chapters 7–8; J. R. Western, *The English Militia in the Eighteenth Century: The Story of a Political Issue, 1660–1802* (London, 1965), chapter 1.

44. "A Ranger's Report of Travels with General Oglethorpe, 1739–1742," in Newton D. Mereness, ed., *Travels in the American Colonies* (New York, 1916), 223–27; John Juricek, ed., *Georgia Treaties, 1733–1763* (Washington, DC, 1990), 30; Leach, *Arms for Empire,* 220–23. General James Oglethorpe initially intended that his settlers "might be taught the use of the Musket" on the ship over; but these plans did not produce a reliable defensive force. James Oglethorpe, *Some Account of the Design of the Trustees for Establishing Colonys in America,* eds. Rodney M. Baine and Phinizy Spalding (Athens, GA, 1990), 31.

45. H. R. McIlwaine and J. P. Kennedy, eds., *Journals of the House of Burgesses of Virginia, 1619–1776,* 13 vols. (Richmond, VA, 1905–15), 5: 13, 91; Beverly Fleet, ed., *Virginia Colonial Abstracts,* 34 vols. (Baltimore, MD, 1961), 2: 15; Carl P. Russell, *Guns on the Early Frontiers* (Berkeley, CA, 1957), 10–14.

46. William H. Browne et al., eds., *Archives of Maryland,* 72 vols. (Baltimore, MD, 1883–1972), 3: 146–48. In 1675 the Connecticut assembly attempted to define "how they may be able to distinguish the friendly Indians from others." The criterion would be that friendlies "doe not approach any of our plantations . . . but at set times and places." Later the assembly took hostages from friendly Indians, just to be sure. Trumbull et al., eds., *Public Records of Connecticut* 2: 272, 378.

47. Verner S. Crane, *Southern Frontier,* 17–21; John T. Juricek, "The Westo Indians," *Ethnohistory* 11 (1964): 134–73; W. L. McDowell, ed., *Journals of the*

Commissioners of the Indian Trade, September 20, 1710–August 29, 1718 (Columbia, SC, 1955), 5, 70–75, 123, 152–53, 295–96; Saunders, ed., *Colonial Records of North Carolina* 1: 811, 893–94; Russell, *Guns on the Early Frontiers,* 23–24, 41–49; Thomas Hatley, *The Dividing Paths: Cherokees and South Carolinians Through the Era of Revolution* (New York, 1993), 32–41. The Spanish encountered similar difficulties in Florida; John H. Hann, *Apalachee: The Land Between the Rivers* (Gainesville, FL, 1988), 8–11.

48. Crane, *Southern Frontier,* 12–21.

49. Lord Proprietors to the Governor and Council, 7 March 1681; Sainsbury et al., eds., *Calendar of State Papers* 11: 16–17.

50. Jabbs, "The South Carolina Colonial Militia," 135–36; Sainsbury et al., eds., *Records in the British Public Record Office* 1: 115–18; Cooper and McCord, eds., *Statutes at Large* 2: 64–68, 309–16.

51. T. M. Hamilton, *Early Indian Trade Guns: 1625–1775,* Contributions of the Museum of the Great Plains (Lawton, OK, 1968), 1, 7; Russell, *Guns on the Early Frontiers,* 13–23, 104–30; Charles E. Hanson Jr., "The Indian Trade Fusil," *Gun Digest* (Chicago, 1959), 128; James B. Whisker, *The Gunsmith's Trade* (Lewiston, NY), 67. Some historians have argued that the Eastern Woodland Indians adapted firearms in great number almost the moment they first saw them. As George T. Hunt has written, "The European trade instantly divided the tribes into highly competitive groups, and the competition for trade was, or soon became, a struggle for survival." Yet Hunt gives no indication how many firearms were acquired, nor where they came from. George T. Hunt, *The Wars of the Iroquois: A Study in Intertribal Trade Relations* (Madison, WI, 1972), 19. Brian J. Given offers fairly compelling evidence that "as late as 1676 the gun was by no means the Indian's primary weapon." His study of the early Indian trade demonstrates that very few guns actually found their way into Indian hands prior to the last quarter of the seventeenth century, and that the gun was just one of many weapons used by the Indians through the mid-nineteenth century. Brian J. Given, *A Most Pernicious Thing: Gun Trading and Native Warfare in Early Contact Period* (Ottawa, 1994), see esp. 57–92. See also Neal Salisbury, *Manitou and Providence: Indians, Europeans, and the Making of New England, 1500–1643* (New York, 1982), 158, 185.

52. Louis-Armand Baron de Lahontan, *New Voyages to North-America,* 2 vols., ed. Reuben G. Thwaite (Chicago, 1905, orig. 1703), 93.

53. John Winthrop, *Winthrop's Journal "History of New England," 1630–1649,* 2 vols., ed. J. K. Hosmer (New York, 1908), 2: 157–58.

54. Some historians have perceived the Indians holding a technological advantage. Without benefit of citation, Douglas E. Leach wrote that Philip's followers were "equipped with modern firearms." In contrast, the whites had a "miscellaneous" collection of old firearms; the "most common type of firearm" was the "cumbersome" matchlock, which required a rest for firing. Oddly, he later noted that the whites all carried flintlocks, and, again lacking a source, that the white settler "Owning his own gun, he was naturally familiar with its use." Benjamin Church offered a more accurate portrayal: meeting with a group of Indians during the war, he observed them "armed with guns, spears, hatchets, &c." Also, the settlers were desperate for firearms, confiscating all guns for public use and purchasing more from England. Leach, *Flintlock and Tomahawk,* 12–13, 51, 106; Church, *History of Philip's War,* ed. Drake, 79; Shurtleff, ed., *Records of Massachusetts Bay* 5: 47–49. In the film *Winchester 73* the actor James Stewart mouths a similar argument to explain the defeat at Little Bighorn in 1876: the Sioux all had repeaters while Custer's forces had

single-shot muskets. This was a complete fabrication. Custer's forces "had the best available equipment and supplies (they were armed with the 1873 Model Springfield .45s-70s)," precisely the weapon the film claims as an Indian monopoly. Stephen E. Ambrose, *Crazy Horse and Custer: The Parallel Lives of Two American Warriors* (New York, 1975), 385.

55. Steele, *Warpaths,* 101–9. Patrick M. Malone, *The Skulking Way of War: Technology and Tactics Among the New England Indians* (Latham, MD, 1991), 60–66, maintains that the New England Indians attained a superior command of guns in this period. But George Raudzens is surely correct in his criticism that "his arguments about the aimed fire capabilities of smooth-bore flintlock muskets are probably too speculative. Most experts agree that aimed musket fire was highly erratic." George Raudzens, "Why Did Amerindian Defences Fail? Parallels in the European Invasions of Hispaniola, Virginia and Beyond," *War in History* 3 (1996): 351n.

56. The evidence on this point is rather mixed. For instance, in 1652 a group of eighty Iroquois surprised some French and Huron standing in the shallows inspecting their fish lines. The Iroquois opened fire, and missed. "They fired, on both sides, several volleys without effect," before the French and Huron made the tree line and the Iroquois left. Reuben G. Thwaites, ed., *The Jesuit Relations and Allied Documents,* 73 vols. (Cleveland, 1896–1901), 37: 106–07.

57. John Lawson, *A New Voyage to Carolina* (London, 1709), 27, 32, 45, 50.

58. Johann Ewald, *Diary of the American War: A Hessian Journal,* ed. and trans. Joseph P. Tustin (New Haven, CT, 1979), 145. There is an excellent drawing of a Stockbridge Indian armed with these weapons on 148.

59. W. Vernon Kinietz, *The Indians of the Western Great Lakes, 1615–1760* (Ann Arbor, MI, 1940), 254–55, 322, 363, 369, 407–08. Calvin Martin offered an exceedingly weird explanation of this dependency as the outgrowth of a psychological need on the part of the Indians to wage war on animals. Calvin Martin, *Keepers of the Game: Indian-Animal Relationships and the Fur Trade* (Berkeley, CA, 1978). Francis Jennings has summarized the nature of this dependency perfectly: "Indian dependency was the outcome of rational decisions by rational persons caught up in an objective situation that limited choice. The Indians simply could not foresee the implications of their initiative for the trade in guns. By the time its effects in dependency became clear, the Indians had lost their power of choice." Francis Jennings, *The Ambiguous Iroquois Empire: The Covenant Chain of Indian Tribes with English Colonies from Its Beginnings to the Lancaster Treaty of 1744* (New York, 1984), 81. See also Shepard Krech, ed., *Indians, Animals and the Fur Trade: A Critique of "Keepers of the Game"* (Athens, GA, 1981); Richard R. White, *The Middle Ground: Indians, Empires, and Republics in the Great Lakes Region, 1650–1815* (Cambridge, 1991), 94–99, 482–86.

60. John Phillip Reid, *A Better Kind of Hatchet: Law, Trade, and Diplomacy in the Cherokee Nation during the Early Years of European Contact* (University Park, PA, 1976), 37.

61. Howard L. Blackmore, *A Dictionary of London Gunmakers, 1350–1850* (Oxford, 1986), 21; Reid, *A Better Kind of Hatchet,* 38.

62. Mary Rowlandson reports a gun used along with spears and bows in a war ritual in 1675. There is a vague earlier reference to such symbolic use in a 1666 document from New York. By the mid-eighteenth century guns are involved in many Indian rituals, from marriage to torture, among some tribes. Lincoln, ed., *Narratives of the Indian Wars,* 152–53; E. B. O'Callaghan, ed., *Documentary History of the State of New-York,* 4 vols. (Albany, NY, 1849–51), 1: 6; Reid, *A Better Kind of Hatchet,* 38;

Kinietz, *The Indians of the Western Great Lakes,* 205, 208–09, 218, 281, 360–62, 393–94.

63. Reid, *A Better Kind of Hatchet,* 193.

64. "Coloniel Chicken's Journal to the Cherokees, 1725," in Mereness, ed., *Travels in the American Colonies,* 112–13, 127. The quotation is taken from two different speeches delivered July 28 and August 21, 1725.

65. "Captain Fitch's Journal to the Creeks, 1725," in Mereness, ed., *Travels in the American Colonies,* 181. Fitch delivered his address on July 20, 1725.

66. Bruce G. Trigger, *The Children of Aataentsic: A History of the Huron People to 1660,* 2 vols. (Montreal, 1976), 2: 794–95; Thwaites, *Jesuit Relations,* 37: 108–11, 44: 150–53, 69: 100–03; Daniel K. Richter, *The Ordeal of the Longhouse: The Peoples of the Iroquois League in the Era of European Colonization* (Chapel Hill, SC, 1992), 220–21; Peter Force, ed., *American Archives* (Washington, DC, 1837–53), 5th ser., 2: 91. Some authors have proposed that Indians routinely repaired their firearms, an absurd statement that demonstrates unfamiliarity with both gunsmithing and guns. As James B. Whisker has written, it was not just that only gunsmiths or armorers could repair firearms, but that "The delicate and sometimes unreliable arms had to be repaired at or near the place where they were used." He added that "there is precious little evidence that . . . any Indians could really do any gunsmithing work." Whisker, *The Gunsmith's Trade,* 67, 87.

67. John Lawson noted this method of repair in 1701 in South Carolina. He wrote that Indians would shoot "about 100 Loads of Ammunition, before they bring the Gun to shoot according to their mind." This seems unlikely, as one hundred loads with bullets would not only take the whole day, requiring constant cleaning, and dangerously overheat the gun often, but would also be extremely expensive. Lawson noted that they stocked guns well, though their only tools were knives, a point made also by James Adair, a merchant with the Chickasaw. Lawson, *A New Voyage to Carolina,* 27, 172; James Adair, *The History of the American Indians* (London, 1775), 457. See also M. L. Brown, *Firearms in Colonial America: The Impact on History and Technology, 1492–1792* (Washington, DC, 1980), 157; Malone, *Skulking Way of War,* 69–72; Hamilton, *Early Indian Trade Guns,* 103–07; Given, *A Most Pernicious Thing,* 90–92.

68. Frank Raymond Secoy, *Changing Military Patterns of the Great Plains Indians* (Lincoln, NE, 1992), 33–38; *Collections of the State Historical Society of Wisconsin* 18 (1908): 87–88; J. B. Tyrrell, ed., *David Thompson's Narrative of His Explorations in Western America, 1784–1812* (Toronto, 1916), 225–28; Richter, *Ordeal of the Longhouse,* 54–55; Jennings, *Ambiguous Iroquois Empire,* 80. As the Quebecois Marc Lescarbot poetically described a battle between the Abenaki and Micmac: "There are more laid low on the [Abenaki] side: because their arrows / With heads of bone, do not make as mortal a wound / As those used by the neighbours of the French / Which have steel tips at the end of their wooden shafts." Thomas Goetz, trans., "The Defeat of the Armouchiquois Savages," in William Cowan, ed., *Papers of the Sixth Algonquian Conference, 1974* (Ottawa, ONT, 1975), 172.

69. Secoy, *Changing Military Patterns,* 1–5; Hubert E. Bolton, *Athanase de Mezieres and the Louisiana-Texas Frontier, 1768–1780,* 2 vols. (Cleveland, 1914), 1: 88–97, 277–82; David J. Weber, *The Spanish Frontier in North America* (New Haven, CT, 1992), 143, 177–79, 227.

70. Secoy, *Changing Military Patterns,* 46–47; Lawrence J. Burpee, ed., "Journal of Matthew Cocking, From York Factory to the Blackfeet Country, 1772–73," *Proceedings and Transactions of the Royal Society of Canada* (1908), 3rd ser., 2: 109–11.

71. Tyrrell, ed., *David Thompson's Narrative*, 330–32.

72. Ibid., 335–40, 367–71; Elliott Coues, ed., *New Light on the Early History of the Greater Northwest: The Manuscript Journals of Alexander Henry . . . and David Thompson*, 2 vols. (New York, 1897), 2: 722–25; Secoy, *Changing Military Patterns*, 36–41, 52–54; Joseph Jablow, *The Cheyenne in Plains Indian Trade Relations, 1795–1840* (Lincoln, NE, 1994), 6, 35–39.

73. There are several reports even in the nineteenth century of western Indians pointing out the superiority of bows to traders attempting to sell them on guns. They were, however, most impressed with cannon. In 1843 the trader Roderick Finlayson used one at Fort Victoria to destroy an empty house, convincing the Songhee to negotiate rather than fight. Three years later Finlayson failed to impress the Songhee with muskets, and they explained to him the greater value of bows. Robin Fisher, *Contact and Conflict: Indian-European Relations in British Columbia, 1774–1890* (Vancouver, BC, 1977), 16–17, 39–40; Roderick Finlayson, *Biography of Roderick Finlayson* (Victoria, BC, 1913), 17; Given, *A Most Pernicious Thing*, 49–53.

74. Coues, ed., *New Light* 2: 513; Walter P. Webb, *The Great Plains* (New York, 1931), 168–69. Flintlocks could be used from horseback; it was the reloading process that made them so disadvantageous in a hunt. Secoy, *Changing Military Patterns*, 96–103.

75. The Cherokee waited several weeks before launching a surprise attack on the Waco village, having acquired some ammunition for their guns in the interim. When held off by arrows, the Cherokee burned the village, killing fifty Waco. Frank H. Watt, "The Waco Indian Village and Its People," *The Central Texas Archeologist* 9 (1969): 217; J. W. Wilbarger, *Indian Depredations in Texas* (Austin, TX, 1889), 174–79.

76. Jablow, *The Cheyenne*, 18.

77. Coues, ed., *New Light* 2: 513; Secoy, *Changing Military Patterns*, 44–47; Burpee, ed., "Journal of Matthew Cocking," 104, 109–11.

78. Tyrrell, ed., *David Thompson's Narrative*, 461–63; Secoy, *Changing Military Patterns*, 51–52.

79. The government of New Netherlands brought charges against their two armorers for stealing the guns in their care and selling them to the Indians. O'Callaghan and Fernow, eds., *Documents* 1: 312, 428.

80. Even a few of these guns could exert a powerful impact on French relations with the Indians. In 1683 Oliver Morel presented just two guns to the Iroquois. As Richard White wrote, "The guns had little material impact on the outcome of the Iroquois wars, but as gifts, they helped hold the alliance together during a crisis and placed hundreds of warriors in the field." White, *Middle Ground*, 104; *Collections of the Illinois Historical Library*, 38 vols. (Springfield, IL, 1903–78), 23: 60–67.

81. White, *Middle Ground*, 113–19, 174–77; Kathryn E. Holland Braund, *Deerskins & Duffels: The Creek Indian Trade with Anglo-America, 1685–1815* (Lincoln, NE, 1993), 36–37; Richter, *Ordeal of the Longhouse*, 94–95, 247–48. Contemporaries perceived that the gun trade with the Indians was born of imperial rivalries. The same politics led them to exaggerate this trade and constantly accuse their enemies of mercilessly supplying the Indians with great numbers of firearms. Increase Mather, *A Relation of the Troubles Which Have Happened in New England by Reason of the Indians There, from the Year 1614 to the Year 1675* (Boston, 1677), 67–68; Lahontan, *New Voyages to North-America* 1: 92–95; Salisbury, *Manitou and Providence*, 156–58, 162.

82. Weber, *The Spanish Frontier*, 168–71; Secoy, *Changing Military Patterns*, 80–82; Alfred B. Thomas, trans. and ed., *After Coronado: Spanish Exploration Northeast of*

New Mexico, 1696–1727 (Normon, OK, 1935), 19–21, 31–37, 74–75, 154–62, 171–74, 245–46; Hubert E. Bolton, *Athanase de Mezieres and the Louisiana-Texas Frontier,* 1: 42–61. In 1759 a group of Spanish soldiers and allied Indians attacked a Taovaya village only "to find a large body of Indians entrenched behind a strong stockade with breastworks, flying a French flag, and skillfully using French weapons and tactics." The Spanish suffered a humiliating defeat. Hubert E. Bolton, *Texas in the Middle 18th Century: Studies in Spanish Colonial History and Administration* (Berkeley, CA, 1915), 90.

83. Secoy, *Changing Military Patterns,* 84–85; H. Bailey Carroll and J. Villasana Haggard, eds., *Three New Mexico Chronicles* (Albuquerque, NM, 1942), 200–03; Frank Russell, "Pima Annals," *American Anthropologist* 5 (1903): 78.

84. Weber, *The Spanish Frontier,* 227–30.

85. Selesky, *War and Society,* 3. For praise of these well-trained Colonial militia units, see Leach, *Arms for Empire,* 8–38.

86. Selesky, *War and Society,* 10–11; Malone, *Skulking Way of War,* 78–90.

87. Thwaites, ed., *Jesuit Relations* 21: 36–37; White, *Middle Ground,* 128–45; S. James Gooding, "Gunmakers to the Hudson's Bay Co.," *The Canadian Journal of Arms Collecting* (February 1973): 19; O'Callaghan and Fernow, eds., *Documents* 3: 806–08, 836–44, 4: 20–24, 41–44; Russell, *Guns on the Early Frontiers,* 14. James Whisker provides a probate inventory of one Indian trader. It contained five guns and twenty-three "new axes," a fairly clear indication of the level and nature of the Indian gun trade. Whisker, *The Gunsmith's Trade,* 127; O'Callaghan and Fernow, eds., *Documents* 14: 42–44.

88. Thwaites, *Jesuit Relations* 60: 160–61; S. James Gooding, *The Canadian Gunsmiths, 1608 to 1900* (West Hill, ONT, 1962), 27.

89. Lahontan, *New Voyages to North-America* 2: 497–502; Thwaites, *Jesuit Relations* 48: 76–79, 52: 70–77, 152–53; O'Callaghan and Fernow, eds., *Documents* 3: 25–52, 9: 280–82; Richter, *Ordeal of the Longhouse,* 98–99, 228–29; Secoy, *Changing Military Patterns,* 68–69.

90. Secoy, *Changing Military Patterns,* 26.

91. Ibid., 31; Thomas, trans. and ed., *After Coronado,* 38–39, 114–16, 170–71, 193–95.

92. John C. Ewers, introduction to Secoy, *Changing Military Patterns,* xii.

93. Secoy, *Changing Military Patterns,* 51–61, 66–69, 81–85.

94. John C. Ewers, "The Indian Trade of the Upper Missouri Before Lewis and Clark: An Interpretation," *Bulletin of the Missouri Historical Society* 10 (1954): 429–46; Lawson, *A New Voyage to Carolina,* 211.

95. Steven J. Oatis, "A Colonial Complex," chapter 1.

96. John Heckewelder, *History, Manners, and Customs of the Indian Nations* (Philadelphia, 1876), 216; Marian W. Smith, "The War Complex of the Plains Indians," *Proceedings of the American Philosophical Society* 78 (1937): 425–61.

97. Tyrrell, ed., *David Thompson's Narrative,* 229; Lawrence J. Burpee, ed., *Journals and Letters of Pierre Gautier de Varennes de la Verendrye and His Sons* (Toronto, 1927), 134–39, 427–32; Jablow, *The Cheyenne,* 52–55; Secoy, *Changing Military Patterns,* 54–55, 59–60, 72–74; George E. Hyde, *Red Cloud's Folk: A History of the Oglala Sioux Indians* (Norman, OK, 1937), 9–52, 85–98.

98. Secoy, *Changing Military Patterns,* 74–75.

99. Tyrrell, ed., *David Thompson's Narrative,* 423–25, 551–52. Thompson reported that three accomplished white hunters were with the Flathead. Between them they fired 131 shots, killing two and wounding three Piegan (425).

100. Coues, ed., *New Light* 2: 540–41, 719–22, 733–36; Tyrrell, ed., *David Thompson's Narrative,* 239–41; *Collections of the State Historical Society of Wisconsin* 19 (1910): 240.

101. Coues, ed., *New Light* 2: 736–37; Secoy, *Changing Military Patterns,* 57; Jablow, *The Cheyenne,* 16–17.

102. Jablow, *The Cheyenne,* 45, 75; Rupert N. Richardson, *The Comanche Barrier to South Plains Settlement* (Glendale, CA, 1933), 87–88, 190–91, 296.

103. Coues, ed., *New Light* 2: 523; Secoy, *Changing Military Patterns,* 60, 69–73; Jablow, *The Cheyenne,* 21–22.

104. Secoy, *Changing Military Patterns,* 69; Burpee, ed., *Journals and Letters of de Varennes,* 136.

105. Secoy, *Changing Military Patterns,* 60–61.

106. Ibid., 62–63, 68; Oscar Lewis, *The Effects of White Contact upon Blackfoot Culture: With Special Reference to the Role of the Fur Trade* (New York, 1942), 51–59.

107. Secoy, *Changing Military Patterns,* 64; J. W. Schultz, *My Life as an Indian* (New York, 1907), 197–99. See also Secoy, *Changing Military Patterns,* 76–77; Thomas H. Leforge, *Memoirs of a White Crow Indian,* ed. Thomas B. Marquis (Lincoln, NE, 1974), 91–95; Ambrose, *Crazy Horse and Custer,* 58–60, 308–9.

108. Reid, *A Better Kind of Hatchet,* 195; William L. McDowell, Jr., ed., *Documents Relating to Indian Affairs May 21, 1750–August 7, 1754* (Columbia, SC, 1958), 158.

109. David H. Corkran, *The Cherokee Frontier: Conflict and Survival, 1740–62* (Norman, OK, 1962), 174.

110. Secoy, *Changing Military Patterns,* 46–64; Burpee, ed., "Journal of Matthew Cocking," 113–14.

111. Reid, *A Better Kind of Hatchet,* 196.

112. Chester Raymond Young, ed., *Westward into Kentucky: The Narrative of Daniel Trabue* (Lexington, KY, 1981), 38, 59; Marco Sioli, "Huguenot Traditions in the Mountains of Kentucky: Daniel Trabue's Memories," *Journal of American History* 84 (1998): 1325.

113. William Brigham, ed., *The Compact with the Charter and Laws of the Colony of New Plymouth* (Boston, 1836), 201, 211–15; Shurtleff and Pulsifer, eds., *Records of New Plymouth* 6: 109, 214–15, 223–24; Douglas E. Leach, "The Military System of Plymouth Colony," *New England Quarterly* 24 (1951): 362–63.

114. Selesky, *War and Society,* 66, 68, 73–74, 82–84; *Connecticut Historical Society Collections* 5: 192–93, 230–43, 251, 304, 11: 351, 13: 60–61, 15: 448; Trumbull et al., eds., *Public Records of Connecticut* 9: 95–97; Lahontan, *New Voyages to North-America* 21 496 97.

115. *Connecticut Historical Society Collections* 13: 203, 231–34, 237–39, 242, 247, 258–59, 269–73, 276, 278–79, 283, 330, 350, 15: 114–60; Trumbull et al., eds., *Public Records of Connecticut* 9: 210–14, 231–32; Selesky, *War and Society,* 90–91.

Chapter Five

Brown Bess in the Wilderness

1. Quoted in Hew Strachan, *European Armies and the Conduct of War* (London, 1983), 24.

2. John Brewer, *The Sinews of Power: War, Money and the English State, 1688–1783* (London, 1989), 8; Geoffrey Parker, "The 'Military Revolution,' 1560–1660: A Myth?" *Journal of Modern History* 48 (1976): 195–214.

3. Brewer, *Sinews of Power,* 3–24.

4. England did fight two long wars in this half century: the War of the Spanish Succession, 1702–13, and the Wars of Jenkins' Ear and the Austrian Succession, 1739–48. In each of these wars the army's personnel increased dramatically, to ninety-two thousand in the first, and sixty-two thousand in the second. In each instance the standing army shrank to around thirty-five thousand troops once the war ended. Brewer, *Sinews of Power,* 30–32.

5. Norman Longmate, *Island Fortress: The Defence of the Great Britain 1603–1945* (London, 1993), 153–57, 164–66; Jeremy Black, *Culloden and the '45* (New York, 1990), 66–133; W. A. Speck, *The Butcher: The Duke of Cumberland and the Suppression of the '45* (Oxford, 1981), 27–102.

6. John Prebble, *Culloden* (London, 1961), 185–202, 324–32; Speck, *The Butcher,* 164–203; Black, *Culloden,* 188–201.

7. Howard L. Blackmore, *A Dictionary of London Gunmakers, 1350–1850* (Oxford, 1986), 221; Howard L. Blackmore, *British Military Firearms, 1650–1850* (New York, 1961), 17–42.

8. J. A. Houlding, *Fit for Service: The Training of the British Army, 1715–1795* (Oxford, 1981), 138–39, 279–80; De Witt Bailey, *British Military Longarms, 1715–1815* (Harrisburg, PA, 1971), 13–18; Richard Lambert, *A New System of Military Discipline Founded upon Principle* (Philadelphia, 1776), 18–25; Edward Ely Curtis, *The Organization of the British Army in the American Revolution* (New Haven, CT, 1926), 16–21.

9. Humphrey Bland, *A Treatise of Military Discipline,* 4th ed. (London, 1740), 135, see also 65–83, 132–34.

10. Basil P. Hughes, *Firepower: Weapons Effectiveness on the Battlefield, 1630–1850* (New York, 1974), 26, 64.

11. Houlding, *Fit for Service,* 262–63; J. R. Western, *The English Militia in the Eighteenth Century: The Story of a Political Issue, 1660–1802* (London, 1965), 414; Theodore Ropp, *War in the Modern World* (Durham, NC, 1959), 32–34.

12. William Muller, *The Elements of the Science of War* (London, 1811); Hughes, *Firepower,* 10, 26–30, 59, 64, 164–65; Curtis, *Organization of the British Army,* 20.

13. Martin Davidson and Adam Levy, *Decisive Weapons: The Technology that Transformed Warfare* (London, 1996), 52–59; Ropp, *War in the Modern World,* 30–31; Houlding, *Fit for Service,* 160–63, 282–84; Black, *Culloden,* 155–62, 170–71; Prebble, *Culloden,* 100–06; Jay Luvaas, ed. and trans., *Frederick the Great on the Art of War* (New York, 1966), 70, 142–46. There is some disagreement whether the bayonet or the artillery deserved most credit for the victory at Culloden. Yet if Stuart had ordered an immediate charge, as Murray suggested, the English artillery would have had little impact, while the bayonet would have exerted the same impact.

14. Luvaas, ed. and trans., *Frederick the Great,* 171; Prebble, *Culloden,* 83–148; Ropp, *War in the Modern World,* 82, 145–47, 150; Hughes, *Firepower,* 11–13, 165; Christopher Duffy, *The Military Experience in the Age of Reason* (London, 1987), 204–06; Paddy Griffith, *Battle Tactics of the Western Front: The British Army's Art of Attack, 1916–18* (New Haven, CT, 1994), 20–44.

15. Strachan, *European Armies,* 23–24; Duffy, *Military Experience,* 212. Humphrey Bland stated that "the Point then to be aimed at is, that of receiving the Enemy's Fire first." Bland, *A Treatise of Military Discipline,* 134.

16. Luvaas, ed. and trans., *Frederick the Great,* 146; Strachan, *European Armies,* 16–22; Duffy, *Military Experience,* 212–14.

17. Richard E. Beringer et al., *Why the South Lost the Civil War* (Athens, GA, 1986), 48–49.

18. Francis Jennings, *Empire of Fortune: Crowns, Colonies, and Tribes in the Seven Year War in America* (New York, 1988), 3–7; Speck, *The Butcher*, 187–203; Prebble, *Culloden*, 231–38, 252; Black, *Culloden*, 199–201.

19. The most concise formulation of the Commonwealth view is John Trenchard, *A Short History of Standing Armies* (London, 1698). See also Western, *The English Militia in the Eighteenth Century*, 89–92; Bernard Bailyn, *The Ideological Origins of the American Revolution* (Cambridge, MA, 1967), 34–54; Caroline Robbins, *The Eighteenth-Century Commonwealthmen: Studies in the Transmission, Development and Circumstances of English Liberal Thought from the Restoration of Charles II until the War with the Thirteen Colonies* (Cambridge, MA, 1959), 3–21, 98–125.

20. J. R. Western has ably summarized this debate and the dormancy of the militia in *The English Militia in the Eighteenth Century*, 30–33, 41–74, 89–103, quote 53. Western writes of the English militia that "Never did an institution better deserve to be called a relic of the bad old days. Its passing was a step towards taking the gun out of politics and bringing civilisation and humanity into our political life" (74). See also Longmate, *Island Fortress*, 37–41, 86–98; Max Beloff, *Public Order and Popular Disturbances, 1660–1714* (London, 1938).

21. Anon., "A Short Discourse on the Present State of the Colonies with Respect to the Interest of Great Britain," William L. Saunders, ed., *The Colonial Records of North Carolina*, 30 vols. (Raleigh, NC, 1886–1914), 2: 632–33.

22. Western, *The English Militia in the Eighteenth Century*, 94–111, quote 102. Many of the Whig leaders stated in Parliament that such militarism contradicted the spirit of industry required in a modern nation. War was fit only for subsistence farmers or those without an alternative means of employment. See the speeches of William Lyttelton, who found the universal militia "an utopean scheme," and Lord Hardwicke in T. C. Hansard, comp., *The Parliamentary History of England, From the Earliest Period to the Year 1803*, 36 vols. (London, 1806–20), 14: 1093–98, 15: 724–40.

23. Brewer, *Sinews of Power*, 40; John M. Dederer, *War in America to 1775: Before Yankee Doodle* (New York, 1990), 198–204. Western found only a few instances in the entire eighteenth century in which men of property willingly served in the militia; these instances were confined to the years 1757–59 and 1796. Western, *The English Militia in the Eighteenth Century*, 255–57.

24. Bailyn, *The Ideological Origins*, 55–93; Robbins, *Eighteenth-Century Commonwealthmen*, 335–77, 384–86; Joyce Lee Malcolm, *To Keep and Bear Arms: The Origins of an Anglo-American Right* (Cambridge, MA, 1994), 124–25, 138–43.

25. Western, *The English Militia in the Eighteenth Century*, 127–54.

26. Houlding, *Fit for Service*, 139–41; Western, *The English Militia in the Eighteenth Century*, 342–43. In the 1770s Richard Lambert, Earl of Cavan, found that as many as half the weapons in some companies of the British army were dysfunctional because of poor workmanship. Lambert, *A New System of Military Discipline*, 22–24.

27. R. A. Brock, ed., *The Official Letters of Alexander Spotswood, Lieutenant-Governor of the Colony of Virginia, 1710–1722*, 2 vols. (Richmond, VA, 1882–1885), 1: 166–67; *Calendar of State Papers, Colonial Series, America and the West Indies, 1689–1692*, 136–37, 550; Earl of Dartmouth to Lords of Trade, 22 April 1712, CO 5/1316, PRO; William W. Hening, ed., *The Statutes at Large, Being a Collection of all the Laws of Virginia*, 13 vols. (Richmond, VA, 1809–23), 4: 120, 5: 16, 21; Frederick Stokes Aldridge, "Organization and Administration of the Militia System of Colonial Virginia" (Ph.D. diss., American University, 1964), 130–31.

28. New York *Gazette*, 16 March 1747.

29. Worcester County Militia Returns, May 1744, Massachusetts Collection, Box

4, folder 4, American Antiquarian Society; William Pencak, "Warfare and Political Change in Mid-Eighteenth-Century Massachusetts," *Journal of Imperial and Commonwealth History* 8 (1980): 51–73.

30. Paine to Osborne, 6 September 1756, Worcester muster return, September 1756, Act of the Massachusetts House 15 January 1757, Chandler to Committee of War 29 March 1757, Chandler to Osborne, 20 July 1757, Massachusetts Collection, Box 4, folder 4, American Antiquarian Society.

31. W. Noel Sainsbury et al., eds., *Calendar of State Papers, Colonial Series, America and the West Indies,* 44 vols. (London, 1860–1969), 41: 169–75; Bull quoted John W. Shy, "A New Look at Colonial Militia," *William and Mary Quarterly,* 3rd ser., 20 (1963): 181; W. Noel Sainsbury et al., eds. *Records in the British Public Record Office Relating to South Carolina, 1663–1782,* 36 vols. (Columbia, SC, and Atlanta, GA, 1928–47), 23: 23–25, 213, 26: 330–31, 27: 192–93, 201, 262–63; Alexander S. Salley Jr., ed., *Journal of the Commons House of Assembly,* 21 vols. (Columbia, SC, 1907–46) for 31 May and 6 June 1747; David W. Cole, "The Organization and Administration of the South Carolina Militia System, 1670–1783" (Ph.D. diss., University of South Carolina, 1953), 76–77.

32. Washington to Loudoun, 10 January 1757, John C. Fitzpatrick, ed., *The Writings of George Washington from the Original Manuscript Sources, 1745–1799,* 39 vols. (Washington, DC, 1931–44), 1: 18–19; Marion Tinling, ed., *The Correspondence of the Three William Byrds of Westover, Virginia, 1684–1776,* 2 vols. (Charlottesville, VA, 1977), 2: 616, 724–25, 729–30, 747–48.

33. Bouquet to Loudoun, 25 August, 16 October 1757, Sylvester K. Stevens and Donald H. Hunt, eds., *The Papers of Col. Henry Bouquet,* 20 vols. (Harrisburg, PA, 1940–43), 9: 64–69, 107–14; Lawrence Henry Gipson, *The Great War for the Empire: The Victorious Years, 1758–1760* (New York, 1949), 32–33.

34. Jennings, *Empire of Fortune,* 86; William T. Parsons, "The Bloody Election of 1742," *Pennsylvania History* 36 (1969): 290–306.

35. "Observations in Several Voyages and Travels in America," *William and Mary College Quarterly* 16 (1907): 5–6.

36. The oddest and least informed of such formulations has been offered by Daniel Boorstin. Calling the American colonies "a nation of minute men," Boorstin not only insisted that "nearly everyone" owned a gun, but also that "there was an impressive uniformity in the way colonists organized (or failed to organize) their defense." Yet not only did the militia change over time and from colony to colony, but also, as Boorstin noted, these universally armed colonists were somehow never prepared for war. Boorstin offered no supportive evidence for these apparently contradictory conclusions. Daniel J. Boorstin, *The Americans: The Colonial Experience* (New York, 1958), 353–57.

37. "Capt. William Lee, of Northumberland County," *Virginia Magazine of History and Biography* 38 (1930): 80–81; Brock, ed., *The Official Letters of Alexander Spotswood* 2: 41–42; Aldridge, "Organization and Administration," 95.

38. Quoted in Richard Slotkin, *Regeneration Through Violence: The Mythology of the American Frontier, 1600–1860* (Middletown, CT, 1973), 232; from William Smith, *Historical Account of Bouquet's Expedition against the Ohio Indians* (1868), 19.

39. R. Ernest and Trevor N. Dupuy, *The Encyclopedia of Military History From 3500 B.C. to the Present,* 2d ed. (New York, 1986), 619–21; Michael Calvert, *A Dictionary of Battles, 1715–1815* (London, 1978), 45.

40. Benjamin Franklin, *The Autobiography of Benjamin Franklin,* ed. Leonard Labaree et al. (New Haven, CT, 1964), 224.

41. Lawrence L. Gipson, *The Great War for the Empire: The Years of Defeat, 1754–1757* (vol. 6 of *The British Empire Before the American Revolution* [New York, 1946]), 93; Jennings, *Empire of Fortune,* 157n. Daniel J. Beattie followed the lead of the British officers in blaming the common troopers, in this case for ignoring "the orders of some of their officers to use cold steel in the European manner." But Beattie offered no supportive citation, and the evidence indicates a different causality. Daniel J. Beattie, "The Adaptation of the British Army to Wilderness Warfare, 1755–1763," in Maarten Ultee, ed., *Adapting to Conditions: War and Society in the Eighteenth Century* (University, AL, 1986), 59.

42. Jennings, *Empire of Fortune,* 158; Gipson, *The Years of Defeat,* 92–98; Ian K. Steele, *Warpaths: Invasions of North America* (New York, 1994), 188–89.

43. Franklin, *Autobiography,* 226; Gipson, *The Years of Defeat,* 127–29, 133–34; Jennings, *Empire of Fortune,* 321–22.

44. Jennings, *Empire of Fortune,* 208; John W. Shy, *Toward Lexington: The Role of the British Army in the Coming of the American Revolution* (Princeton, NJ, 1965), 129.

45. John Hawks, *Orderly Book and Journal of Major John Hawks on the Ticonderoga-Crown Point Campaign, Under General Jeffrey Amherst, 1759–1760* (New York, 1911), 15; Stanley McCrory Pargellis, *Lord Loudoun in North America* (New Haven, CT, 1933), 98, 300–1; Charles H. Lincoln, ed., *Correspondence of William Shirley, Governor of Massachusetts and Military Commander in America, 1731–1760,* 2 vols. (New York, 1912), 2: 456–59; Harold E. Selesky, *War and Society in Colonial Connecticut* (New Haven, CT, 1990), 108.

46. Shy, *Toward Lexington,* 129; Pargellis, *Lord Loudoun,* 98, 299–305; Robert Rogers, *Journals of Major Robert Rogers,* ed. Franklin B. Hough (Albany, NY, 1883), 14–15, 97–98; Stanley Pargellis, ed., *Military Affairs in North America, 1748–1765: Selected Documents from the Cumberland Papers in Windsor Castle* (Hamden, CT, 1969), 251, 255–56, 269, 279, 337–39; Norreys Jephson O'Conor, *A Servant of the Crown in England and North America, 1756–1761* (New York, 1938), 92–96; Beattie, "Adaptation of the British Army," 76–78.

47. Jennings, *Empire of Fortune,* 289–91; Pargellis, ed., *Military Affairs,* 200–01; William G. Godfrey, *Pursuit of Profit and Preferment in Colonial North America: John Bradstreet's Quest* (Waterloo, ONT, 1982), 77–81. Bradstreet's casualties may have surpassed those of the French, but the battle remains a victory since the Americans were able to supply Oswego.

48. Jennings, *Empire of Fortune,* 187–99, 209–17.

49. Ibid., 232.

50. Samuel Hazard, ed., *Minutes of the Provincial Council of Pennsylvania,* 10 vols. (Harrisburg, PA, 1852), 6: 652–53, 662–65, 678–81, quote 679; Leonard Labaree et al., eds., *The Papers of Benjamin Franklin,* 20 vols. (New Haven, CT, 1959–76), 6: 165, 170–71, 229 n3; Jennings, *Empire of Fortune,* 166–67, 255–56.

51. *Pennsylvania Journal,* 4 and 11 March 1756; Labaree et al., eds., *Papers of Franklin* 6: 410–11. The King disallowed this militia almost immediately, terminating Franklin's military career.

52. Steele, *Warpaths,* 198.

53. Pargellis, ed., *Military Affairs,* 218–21; Pargellis, *Lord Loudoun,* 148–62; Gipson, *The Years of Defeat,* 197–203.

54. Selesky, *War and Society,* 110, 135–36; Pargellis, *Lord Loudoun,* 228–52; *Collections of the Connecticut Historical Society,* 31 vols. (Hartford, CT, 1860–1967), 9: 197–265, 17: 348–49; Gipson, *The Victorious Years,* 148–49. At the same time that

the New York militia was deserting in droves, the New Hampshire force of five hundred militia at Fort No. 4 were doing the same, every last one abandoning their post between September and November 1757. Ibid., 165.

55. Selesky, *War and Society,* 185.

56. Bland, *A Treatise of Military Discipline,* 133; Houlding, *Fit for Service,* 358–63. Volley fire required twenty-four separate steps, not one of which was "aim." Lambert, *A New System of Military Discipline,* 67–115. Platoon firing and alternate firing did not appear in the manuals until 1764, though James Wolfe seems to have trained his troop in both in 1755. *New Manual, and Platoon Exercise: with an Explanation* (Dublin, 1764); Houlding, *Fit for Service,* 318–21.

57. Field Officers to Shirley, September 1755, Schuyler to Shirley, 20 September 1755, Lincoln, ed., *Correspondence of William Shirley* 2: 276–78.

58. Shirley to Fox, 12 April 1756, Lincoln, ed., *Correspondence of William Shirley* 2: 427–28; see also 298–99, 401–2.

59. Pargellis, ed., *Military Affairs,* 486; Jennings, *Empire of Fortune,* 417–19.

60. Quoted, Beattie, "Adaptation of the British Army," 73; Pargellis, *Lord Loudoun,* 299–300; Peter R. Russell, "Redcoats in the Wilderness: British Officers and Irregular Warfare in Europe and America, 1740–1760," *William and Mary Quarterly* 34 (1978): 629–52. Single combat generally produced lower casualty rates than was the case in European battles. But disease was the big killer, claiming eight times as many lives in the Seven Years' War than did combat. Sylvia R. Frey, *The British Soldier in America: A Social History of Military Life in the Revolutionary Period* (Austin, TX, 1981), 28.

61. Steele, *Warpaths,* 211; Henri R. Casgrain, ed., *Voyage au Canada dans le Nord de L'Amerique Septentrional fait depuis L'an 1751 a 1761 par J.C.B.* (Quebec, 1887), 62–66, 93–107, 117–20, translated as "A French Soldier on the Ohio Frontier," in Michael A. Bellesiles, trans. and ed., *BiblioBase* (Boston, 1998).

62. J. Hammond Trumbull et al., eds., *The Public Records of the Colony of Connecticut,* 15 vols. (Hartford, CT, 1850–90), 10: 460–94; militia records, Massachusetts Collection and Local Records, American Antiquarian Society.

63. Hening, ed., *Statutes at Large* 6: 118, 521–25; see also 2: 349, 5: 90; Washington to Robert Dinwiddie, 27 June 1757, Fitzpatrick, ed., *Writings of Washington* 2: 78–79; see also "Memorandums Concerning the Militia," ibid. 1: 344–53.

64. Selesky, *War and Society,* 152–53; Trumbull et al., eds., *Public Records of Connecticut* 11: 122–24.

65. Owen Aubrey Sherrard, *Lord Chatham: Pitt and the Seven Years' War* (London, 1955), 170–73, 281–85; Gertrude Selwyn Kimball, ed., *Correspondence of William Pitt, When Secretary of State, with Colonial Governors and Military and Naval Commissioners in America,* 2 vols. (New York, 1906), 1: xxix–xxxviii; Selesky, *War and Society,* 137–40. British military spending increased from £660,000 on the army and £220,000 on the navy between 1749 and 1755 to £5,489,000 on the army and £966,000 on the navy from 1756 to 1763. Julian Gwyn, "British Government Spending and the North American Colonies, 1740–1775," *Journal of Imperial and Commonwealth History* 8 (1980): 77.

66. Selesky, *War and Society,* 144.

67. Pitt to the Governors, 30 December 1757, Kimball, ed., *Correspondence of William Pitt* 1: 136–40. After the war disputes arose over these reimbursements, with several colonies insisting that they contributed more than the other colonies. Jack P. Greene, "The Seven Years' War and the American Revolution: The Causal Relationship Reconsidered," *Journal of Imperial and Commonwealth History* 8 (1980): 98;

Pencak, "Warfare and Political Change," 65–68. Lawrence Henry Gipson compiled a painstaking examination of the government's reimbursement of the American colonies: *The Triumphant Empire: Thunder-Clouds Gather in the West, 1763–1766* (New York, 1961), 38–110.

68. *Collections of the Connecticut Historical Society* 1: 331; Pitt to the Governors, 30 December 1757, Kimball, ed., *Correspondence of William Pitt* 1: 139, 142; Pargellis, *Lord Loudoun,* 228–52.

69. De Lancey to Pitt, 1 June 1758, Kimball, ed., *Correspondence of William Pitt* 1: 264; De Lancey to Abercromby, 17 and 22 May 1758; Abercromby to De Lancey, 1 June 1758, WO 34: 29, PRO; M. John Cardwell, "Mismanagement: The 1758 British Expedition Against Carillon," *The Bulletin of the Fort Ticonderoga Museum* 15 (1992): 262–63.

70. Pitt to Abercromby, 30 December 1757, Abercromby to Pitt, 22 May 1758, Kimball, ed., *Correspondence of William Pitt* 1: 143–48, 248–56.

71. Abercromby to Colonial Governors, 5 March 1758, WO 34: 25, PRO.

72. Pownall to Abercromby, 25 March, 3 April, 7 May, and 12 June 1758, Fitch to Abercromby, 17 and 30 March, 4 May 1758, WO 34: 25, 28, PRO.

73. Abercromby to Reading, 3 April and 3 May 1758, Reading to Abercromby, 13 April 1758, WO 34: 32, PRO; Abercromby to Pitt, 22 and 27 May 1758 in Kimball, ed., *Correspondence of William Pitt* 1: 248–50, 261–62.

74. Abercromby to Pitt, 28 April 1758, in Kimball, ed., *Correspondence of William Pitt* 1: 225–30; Trumbull et al., eds., *Public Records of Connecticut* 11: 121–27.

75. Pownall to Abercromby, 22 April, 1 and 14 May, 1 and 12 June 1758, Hancock to Abercromby, 19 May 1758, WO 34: 25, 62, PRO.

76. Cardwell, "Mismanagement," 263–64; Pownall to Abercromby, 19 May, 1 June 1758, WO 34: 25, PRO.

77. Abercromby to Pitt, 22 May 1758, Kimball, ed., *Correspondence of William Pitt* 1: 250; Cardwell, "Mismanagement," 289.

78. Archeleus Fuller, "Journal of Col. Archeleus Fuller of Middleton, Mass., in the Expedition Against Ticonderoga in 1758," *Essex Institute Historical Collections* 46 (1910): 209–11; Daniel Shute, "A Journal of the Rev. Daniel Shutte, D.D., Chaplain in the Expedition to Canada in 1758," *Essex Institute Historical Collections* 12 (1874): 135–37; "The Journal of Captain Samuel Cobb, May 21, 1758–October 29, 1758," *The Bulletin of the Fort Ticonderoga Museum* 14 (1981): 15, 18. For similar efforts to arm troops while on the march, see "Selections from the Military Correspondence of Colonel Henry Bouquet, 1757–1764," ed. Helen Jordan, *Pennsylvania Magazine of History and Biography* 33 (1909): 104. If these militia were all rushing forth with their muskets, why was it always necessary to arm them?

79. Cardwell, "Mismanagement," 268; Fred Anderson, *A People's Army: Massachusetts Soldiers and Society in the Seven Years' War* (Chapel Hill, NC, 1984), 74–77. See, for example, the four different incidents leaving three dead and two seriously wounded and the almost killed milking girl in F. M. Ray, ed., "The Journal of Dr. Caleb Rea written During the Expedition against Ticonderoga in 1758," *Essex Institute Historical Collections* 18 (1881): 96–99; the two killings in Moses Dorr, "A Journal of an Expedition Against Canaday," *New York History* 16 (1935): 453–54; the two incidents that left one dead and one wounded in Lemuel Lyon, "Military Journal for 1758," in Abraham Tomlinson, comp., *The Military Journals of Two Private Soldiers, 1758–1775* (Poughkeepsie, NY, 1855), 17–18; the killing and wounding in Fuller, "Journal of Col. Archeleus Fuller," 212; man shot in the stomach in "Journal of Captain Samuel Cobb," 18.

80. "Amos Richardson's Journal, 1758," *The Bulletin of the Fort Ticonderoga Museum* 12 (1968): 274.

81. Abercromby to Pitt, 12 July 1758, Kimball, ed., *Correspondence of William Pitt* 1: 297–302; Pargellis, *Lord Loudoun,* 353–55; *Collections of the Connecticut Historical Society* 17: 350–53; O'Conor, *A Servant of the Crown,* 99–115; Selesky, *War and Society,* 113–14.

82. Steele, *Warpaths,* 210–11; Jennings, *Empire of Fortune,* 185, 366–67.

83. Jennings, *Empire of Fortune,* 374–75; Hazard, ed., *Minutes of the Provincial Council* 8: 78–84, 112; Stevens and Hunt, eds., *Papers of Col. Bouquet* 2: 23–28; Alfred P. James, ed., *Writings of General John Forbes Relating to His Service in North America* (Menasha, WI, 1938), 92, 109–12; Gipson, *The Victorious Years,* 247–86.

84. Prebble, *Culloden,* 101; Gipson, *The Victorious Years,* 371–427.

85. Lyttleton to Loudoun, 20 October 1757, in Gipson, *The Victorious Years,* 33. As Gipson wrote of the South Carolina militia, "the [white] men of the province were too prosperous to want to bother with military service even to ensure the safety of their families and possessions," and always turned to British Regulars for protection (32).

86. David H. Corkran, *The Cherokee Frontier: Conflict and Survival, 1740–62* (Norman, OK, 1962), 187–215.

87. Corkran, *The Cherokee Frontier,* 216–22; Lawrence Henry Gipson, *The Triumphant Empire: New Responsibilities within the Enlarged Empire, 1763–1766* (New York, 1956), 68–70, 76–80.

88. Corkran, *The Cherokee Frontier,* 236–72; Gipson, *New Responsibilities,* 80–87.

89. Richard R. White, *The Middle Ground: Indians, Empires, and Republics in the Great Lakes Region, 1650–1815* (Cambridge, 1991), 279–85; Gregory E. Dowd, *A Spirited Resistance: The North American Indian Struggle for Unity, 1745–1815* (Baltimore, MD, 1992), 27–37.

90. White, *Middle Ground,* 256–60.

91. Howard H. Peckham, *Pontiac and the Indian Uprising* (Princeton, NJ, 1947), 201–13; Gipson, *New Responsibilities,* 105–13; White, *Middle Ground,* 288–89.

92. Jennings, *Empire of Fortune,* 423.

93. Western, *The English Militia in the Eighteenth Century,* 104–26, 245–64.

94. Sherrard, *Lord Chatham,* 94–97, 109, 172–75, 226–27, 276 (quote); *Gentleman's Magazine* 26 (1756): 457–60, 509–10; Jennings, *Empire of Fortune,* 185. The riots, based on an "aversion of the people to being armed," served, in J. R. Western's words, as "a warning against any rapid move towards universal military training." Western, *The English Militia in the Eighteenth Century,* 291, 302, see also 127–54, 253–54, 290–302.

95. Lewis Namier, *England in the Age of the American Revolution,* 2nd ed. (London, 1963), 118 n6.

96. Western, *The English Militia in the Eighteenth Century,* 174; Sherrard, *Lord Chatham,* 360–62.

97. Brewer, *Sinews of Power,* 33; Western, *The English Militia in the Eighteenth Century,* 193–204.

98. Brewer, *Sinews of Power,* 52–53; Houlding, *Fit for Service,* 67–73, 82–84; Tony Hayter, *The Army and the Crowd in Mid-Georgian England* (Totowa, NJ, 1978), 155–58, 176.

99. Abercromby to Loudoun, 25 February 1758, Loudoun Papers No. 5668, Huntington Library, San Marino, CA; Washington to Governor Dinwiddie,

9 March 1754, Fitzpatrick, ed., *Writings of Washington* 1: 31–32; *Collections of the Connecticut Historical Society* 18: 109–10.

100. Selesky, *War and Society,* 224–25; *Connecticut Gazette,* 8 May 1762.

101. See for instance, Edmund S. Morgan, *American Slavery, American Freedom: The Ordeal of Colonial Virginia* (New York, 1975), 240. Rhys Isaac was a little more cautious, linking manliness to aggressive behavior, especially fighting, and noting that only gentlemen could afford the equipment required by the militia. Rhys Isaac, *The Transformation of Virginia, 1740–1790* (Chapel Hill, NC, 1982), 256, see also 95–99, 255–69.

102. Brewer, *Sinews of Power,* 59.

103. *The Exercise for the Militia of the Province of Massachusetts-Bay* (Boston, 1758), 3; Bailyn, *The Ideological Origins,* 83–84; Shy, *Toward Lexington,* 376–81.

104. Quotes from *Essex Gazette* 1770, Ronald L. Boucher, "The Colonial Militia as a Social Institution: Salem, Massachusetts, 1764–1775," *Military Affairs* 37 (1973): 125–26.

105. Jennings, *Empire of Fortune,* 449.

106. Gwyn, "British Government Spending," 74–84; Pargellis, *Lord Loudoun,* 352–53; Brewer, *Sinews of Power,* 30; Blackmore, *British Military Firearms,* 32.

Chapter Six

A People Numerous and Unarmed

1. Peter Force, ed., *American Archives* (Washington, DC, 1837–53), ser. 4, 1: 486–501; Allen French, *The Day of Concord and Lexington: The Nineteenth of April, 1775* (Boston, 1925), 95–99.

2. French, *The Day of Concord,* 105–19; Henry De Berniere, *General Gage's Instructions of 22d February 1775 . . . With a Curious Narrative of Occurences During Their Mission* (Boston, 1779), 17; [John Barker], "A British Officer in Boston in 1775," ed. R. H. Dana Jr., *Atlantic Monthly* 39 (1877): 398–99; depositions of eyewitnesses, Richard Frothingam Jr., *History of the Siege of Boston, and of the Battles of Lexington, Concord, and Bunker Hill* (Boston, 1849), 365–72; Christopher Ward, *The War of the Revolution,* ed. John Richard Alden, 2 vols. (New York, 1952), 1: 32–39.

3. Gage believed that more than ninety barrels of powder were stored at Concord. In fact that was the size of the entire Massachusetts reserve, which was stored in several towns. French, *The Day of Concord,* 58–59; De Berniere, *General Gage's Instructions,* 15–16; Percy to General Harvey, 1 November 1774, and to Grey Cooper, 13 December 1774, Charles Knowles Bolton, ed., *Letters of Hugh Earl Percy from Boston and New York, 1774–1776* (Boston, 1902), 41–43, 46–47; Clarence Edwin Carter, ed., *The Correspondence of General Thomas Gage with the Secretaries of State, 1763–1775,* 2 vols. (New Haven, CT, 1931–33), 1: 396–97; 2: 198–200.

4. Force, ed., *American Archives,* ser. 4, 2: 359–63; French, *The Day of Concord,* 177–96; De Berniere, *General Gage's Instructions,* 17–18.

5. French, *The Day of Concord,* 197–202; [Barker], "A British Officer in Boston," 398–99; Ward, *The War of the Revolution* 1: 40–51.

6. [Barker], "A British Officer in Boston," 400; French, *The Day of Concord,* 215–25, quote 224; De Berniere, *General Gage's Instructions,* 18.

7. French, *The Day of Concord,* 12, 22–30, 254–58, quote 27; William Lincoln, ed., *The Journals of Each Provincial Congress of Massachusetts in 1774 and 1775, and of*

the Committee of Safety (Boston, 1838), 131–33; Frank Warren Coburn, *The Battle of April 19, 1775* (Port Washington, NY, 1970), 156–59, 165–79.

8. De Berniere, *General Gage's Instructions,* 18–20; Percy to Gage, and to General Harvey, 20 April 1775, Bolton, ed., *Letters of Hugh Earl Percy,* 49–53; French, *The Day of Concord,* 237–50.

9. Richard Maxwell Brown, *The South Carolina Regulators* (Cambridge, MA, 1963), 83–95, quote 94.

10. William S. Powell et al., eds., *The Regulators in North Carolina: A Documentary History, 1759–1776* (Raleigh, NC, 1971), 309–24, 457–97, 522–27, 578–93; Paul D. Nelson, *William Tryon and the Course of Empire: A Life in British Imperial Service* (Chapel Hill, NC, 1990), 70–89.

11. Merrill Jensen, *The Founding of a Nation: A History of the American Revolution, 1763–1776* (New York, 1968), 145–53, 339–54, 408–14; Robert Middlekauff, *The Glorious Cause: The American Revolution, 1763–1789* (New York, 1982), 192–208.

12. Pauline Maier, *From Resistance to Revolution: Colonial Radicals and the Development of American Opposition to Britain, 1756–1776* (New York, 1972).

13. Margaret Marion Spector, *The American Department of the British Government, 1768–1782* (New York, 1940), 74–95; Elizabeth Miles Nuxoll, "Congress and the Munitions Merchants: The Secret Committee of Trade during the American Revolution, 1775–1777" (Ph.D. diss., City University of New York, 1979), 3–4.

14. Pickering, "A Military Citizen," in Pickering, *Life of Timothy Pickering,* 1, 17, 26–27.

15. Winthrop Sargent, ed., "Letters of John Andrews, Esq., of Boston," *Proceedings of the Massachusetts Historical Society, 1864–1865,* 1st ser., 8 (1866): 321, 371–72.

16. James Curtish Ballagh, ed., *The Letters of Richard Henry Lee,* 2 vols. (New York, 1911), 1: 130–31; W. Noel Sainsbury, comp., *Records in the British Public Record Office Relating to South Carolina, 1663–1782,* 36 vols. (Columbia, SC, and Atlanta, GA, 1928–47), 34: 188–91.

17. Madison to Bradford, 19 June 1775, Council Minutes, 10 November and 23 December 1778, William T. Hutchinson et al., eds., *The Papers of James Madison,* 17 vols. (Chicago, 1962–91), 1: 153, 259, 278–79.

18. Lt. Col. William Coats to the Pennsylvania Council, 6 May 1779, Samuel Hazard et al., eds., *Pennsylvania Archives* (Philadelphia, 1852–1935), ser. 1, 4: 376; Charles Royster, *A Revolutionary People at War: The Continental Army and American Character, 1775–1783* (Chapel Hill, NC, 1979), 25–53; William P. Palmer et al., eds., *Calendar of Virginia State Papers and Other Manuscripts,* 11 vols. (Richmond, VA, 1875–93), 1: 385, 418–21.

19. Timothy Pickering Jr., *An Easy Plan of Discipline for a Militia* (Salem, MA, 1775), 11; Royster, *A Revolutionary People at War,* 228.

20. See, for instance, Greene to Adams, 2 June 1776, Richard K. Showman et al., eds., *Papers of General Nathanael Greene,* 10 vols. (Chapel Hill, NC, 1976–96), 1: 222–27; Royster, *A Revolutionary People,* 11–13, 35–43. As Don Higginbotham has pointed out, there was a general perception in New England that the inhabitants of none of the other colonies knew anything about war. Don Higginbotham, *George Washington and the American Military Tradition* (Athens, GA, 1985), 2–3.

21. William H. Browne et al., eds., *Archives of Maryland,* 72 vols. (Baltimore, MD, 1883–1972), 29: 363–64.

22. H. R. McIlwaine, ed., *Journals of the House of Burgesses of Virginia, 1619–1776,* 13 vols. (Richmond, VA, 1905–15), 13: 223–24; Force, ed., *American Archives,* ser. 4, 2: 1206–08.

23. Jensen, *Founding of a Nation,* 546–50.

24. Don Higginbotham, "The American Militia: A Traditional Institution with Revolutionary Responsibilities," in Higginbotham, ed., *Reconsiderations on the Revolutionary War: Selected Essays* (Westport, CT, 1978), 83–103; Lawrence Delbert Cress, *Citizens in Arms: The Army and the Militia in American Society to the War of 1812* (Chapel Hill, NC, 1982), 41–50.

25. Walter Clark, ed., *The State Records of North Carolina,* 30 vols. (Goldsboro, NC, 1886–1909), 23: 585, 597, 787–88, 941; Benjamin B. Winborne, *The Colonial and State Political History of Hertford County, N.C.* (Murfreesboro, NC, 1906), 36–37.

26. William E. Hemphill, ed., *Extracts from the Journals of the Provincial Congresses of South Carolina, 1775–1776* (Columbia, SC, 1960), 29, 44, 55, 103–04, 117–18, 135–39, 142–47, 152, 178, 188, 195–99, 251.

27. Lincoln, ed., *The Journals of Each Provincial Congress,* 30–34; Allen French, *The Day of Concord,* 21.

28. Westboro town meeting, 21 February 1775, Sudbury records, 22 July 1775, Box 1, U.S. Revolutionary Collection, American Antiquarian Society; Lincoln, ed., *The Journals of Each Provincial Congress,* 63, 103, 507–10; French, *The Day of Concord,* 24–25.

29. Lincoln, ed., *The Journals of Each Provincial Congress,* 756. Gage also acquired 634 pistols, 972 bayonets, and thirty-eight blunderbusses. French, *The Day of Concord,* 56.

30. J. Hammond Trumbull et al., eds., *The Public Records of the Colony of Connecticut,* 15 vols. (Hartford, CT, 1850–90), 14: 327–28.

31. "Pot-valor" means alcohol induced. Frothingam, *History of the Siege of Boston,* 36; De Berniere, *General Gage's Instructions,* 9–10.

32. Harold E. Selesky, *War and Society in Colonial Connecticut* (New Haven, CT, 1990), 228–29; Trumbull et al., eds., *Public Records of Connecticut* 14: 499; *Collections of the Connecticut Historical Society,* 31 vols. (Hartford, CT, 1860–1967), 20: 220–21; *Collections of the Massachusetts Historical Society,* 5th ser., 9: 493.

33. Trumbull et al., eds., *Public Records of Connecticut* 14: 417–19; Palmer et al., eds., *Calendar of Virginia State Papers* 1: 268–69, 387, 605. Several states shared guns during crises, attempting to forward them to areas where British troops were expected. See, for example, Palmer et al., eds., *Calendar of Virginia State Papers* 1: 350.

34. Westboro town meeting, 21 February 1775, Charlestown, NH, equipment list, 1775, U.S. Revolutionary Collection, Box 1, American Antiquarian Society.

35. "Armes & Accutrements of Col. Learneds Regt.," 1775, U.S. Revolutionary Collection, Box 1, American Antiquarian Society.

36. Percy to Northumberland, 19 June 1775, and to General Harvey, 28 July 1775, Bolton, ed., *Letters of Hugh Earl Percy,* 56–58; depositions of eyewitnesses, Frothingam, *History of the Siege of Boston,* 372–401; Middlekauff, *The Glorious Cause,* 281–92.

37. Jefferson to Giovanni Fabbroni, 8 June 1778, Julian P. Boyd et al., eds., *The Papers of Thomas Jefferson,* 27 vols. to date (Princteon, NJ, 1950–97), 2: 195, 198n.

38. Burgoyne to Lord Germain, 20 August 1775, Germain Papers, Clements Library, quoted in John N. Shy, *A People Numerous and Armed: Reflections on the Military Struggle for American Independence* (New York, 1976), 103, see also 42–43; Gage to Barrington, 26 June 1775, Carter, ed., *Correspondence of General Gage* 2: 686.

39. Invoice of goods, 20 July 1767, John C. Fitzpatrick, ed., *The Writings of George Washington from the Original Manuscript Sources, 1745–1799,* 39 vols.

(Washington, DC, 1931–44), 2: 464; Harold B. Gill Jr., *The Gunsmith in Colonial Virginia* (Williamsburg, VA, 1974), 13.

40. Gill, *The Gunsmith in Colonial Virginia,* 69–108; Berkeley R. Lewis, *Small Arms and Ammunition in the United States Service,* vol. 129 of Smithsonian Miscellaneous Collections (Washington, DC, 1956), 40–41; Paine to Schuyler, 2 April 1776, in Paul H. Smith, ed., *Letters of Delegates to Congress, 1774–1789,* 24 vols. (Washington, DC, 1976–96), 3: 477.

41. M. L. Brown, *Firearms in Colonial America: The Impact on History and Technology, 1492–1792* (Washington, DC, 1980), 318; Richard Henry Lee to William Henry, 28 September 1777, *Pennsylvania Magazine of History and Biography* 11 (1887): 502; James B. Whisker, *Arms Makers of Colonial America* (Selingsgrove, PA, 1992), 103.

42. Michael A. Bellesiles, *Revolutionary Outlaws: Ethan Allen and the Struggle for Independence on the Early American Frontier* (Charlottesville, VA, 1993), 112–20; Allen French, *The Taking of Ticonderoga in 1775: The British Story* (Cambridge, MA, 1928), 45–55.

43. Allen quoted in Bellesiles, *Revolutionary Outlaws,* 121; Washington C. Ford et al., eds., *Journals of the Continental Congress, 1774–1789,* 34 vols. (Washington, DC, 1904–37), 2: 24–25, 52, 56, 68–70, 75.

44. New York's government hesitated in this, as in most matters, the longest. Local patriots waited until September 6, 1775, to steal the 522 muskets in the city hall in New York. Force, ed., *American Archives,* ser. 4, 3: 882.

45. *Virginia Military Records* (Baltimore, MD, 1983), 449–642; Committee of Safety Ledger, 1775–76, Virginia State Library; Account of Army Stores, June to August 1775, Box 1, U.S. Revolutionary Collection; Col. Doolitle's Orderly Book, 1775, Orderly Books collection, American Antiquarian Society; Lincoln, ed., *The Journals of Each Provincial Congress,* 536–37, 575, 584–87, 590–95; *Pennsylvania Archives,* ser. 1, 4: 190; W. W. Abbot et al., eds., *The Papers of Washington, Revolutionary War Series,* 8 vols. to date (Charlottesville, VA, 1985–98), 4: 326; Hemphill, ed., *Extracts from the Journals of South Carolina,* 109, 121–22; "Miscellaneous Papers of the General Committee, Secret Committee and Provincial Congress, 1775," *South Carolina Historical and Genealogical Magazine* 8 (1907): 132–50, 9 (1908): 9–11, 67–72; Arthur Bowler, *Logistics and the Failure of the British Army in America, 1775–1783* (Princeton, NJ, 1975), 150; Middlekauff, *The Glorious Cause,* 527. The ordnance records are full of these remarkable small-scale exchanges. To take just a single page from June 1781, Ebenezer Cowell bills the U.S. government $280 for cleaning and repairing sixty muskets, while James Black is paid $20 "for one musket sold . . . for the use of the United States." James E. Hicks, *Notes on United States Ordnance,* 2 vols. (Mount Vernon, NY, 1940), 2: 11.

46. Connecticut Committee of Safety, May 1777, Charles J. Hoadly et al., eds., *The Public Records of the State of Connecticut,* 11 vols. (Hartford, CT, 1894–1967), 1: 246 (Connecticut ended this immunity from service in 1781; ibid. 3: 341); *Pennsylvania Archives,* ser. 1, 4: 202, 238, 1659, 5: 726, ser. 2, 13: 299, ser. 5, 1: 1570; Force, ed., *American Archives,* ser. 4, 1: 1002, 1340, 2: 490, 1349; ibid. ser. 5, 1: 760; Browne et al., eds., *Archives of Maryland* 21: 68–69. James P. Whisker, *Arms Makers of Pennsylvania* (Selingsgrove, PA, 1990), 14; Palmer et al., eds., *Calendar of Virginia State Papers* 1: 359, 605. Harold B. Gill Jr. has made the most careful study of the gunsmith trade in early America. Between 1740 and 1769 there were seven gunsmiths and seventeen artisans capable of some gunsmithing skills in Virginia. Between 1770 and 1799 Gill found forty-seven gunsmiths plus another eighty-three artisans working on guns

(with seventeen possible gun workers), mostly during the years of the Revolutionary War. Gill, *The Gunsmith in Colonial Virginia,* 69–108.

47. Carson to President Joseph Reed, 24 May 1779, *Pennsylvania Archives,* ser. 1, 4: 437; report of Rez Beall, 29 May 1776, Force, ed., *American Archives,* ser. 4, 2: 613; Browne et al., eds., *Archives of Maryland* 11: 155, 16: 377; James B. Whisker, *The Gunsmith's Trade* (Lewiston, NY, 1992), 83; Daniel D. Hartzler, *Arms Makers of Maryland* (York, PA, 1977), 210–11.

48. Lochry to President Wharton, 13 May 1778, to President Reed, 20 July 1779, Lewis Gronow to President Wharton, 13 May 1778, Joseph Erwin to President Reed, 20 July 1779, Hazard et al., eds. *Pennsylvania Archives,* ser. 1, 6: 495–96, 503, 514, 7: 563–64; Committee of Safety, 29 January 1777, Boyd Crumrine, *History of Washington County, Virginia* (Philadelphia, 1882), 186; Whisker, *The Gunsmith's Trade,* 169; Frederic P. Wells, *History of Newbury, Vermont* (St. Johnsbury, VT, 1902), 72–73. The nine volumes of the first series of the *Pennsylvania Archives* are packed with similar reports.

49. Mathias Ogden, *Journal of Major Mathias Ogden* (Morristown, NJ, 1928), 13; Kenneth L. Roberts, ed., *March to Quebec: Journals of the Members of Arnold's Expedition* (New York, 1938), 264–66; Abbot et al., eds., *Papers of Washington, Revolutionary War Series* 4: 326–27, 329.

50. Proceedings of a Council of General Officers, 23 September 1777, Showman et al., eds., *Papers of General Nathanael Greene* 2: 164.

51. Charles Rumsey to the Council of Safety, 26 September 1776, Browne et al., eds., *Archives of Maryland* 12: 302; "Extracts from the Letter-Books of Lieutenant Enos Reeves," *Pennsylvania Magazine of History and Biography* 21 (1897): 387.

52. Pennsylvania Committee of Safety, 4 July 1775; Rodney Hilton Brown, *American Polearms, 1626–1865: The Lance, Halberd, Spontoon, Pike and Naval Boarding Weapons* (New Milford, CT, 1967), 51–52; Robert W. Bingham, "The American Military Pike of '76," in *A Miscellany of Arms and Armor* (New York, 1927), 39–40.

53. Ford et al., eds., *Journals of the Continental Congress* 4: 215, 224; Lincoln, ed., *The Journals of Each Provincial Congress,* 392; Washington, General Orders of 23 July 1775, Abbot et al., eds., *Papers of Washington, Revolutionary War Series* 1: 158; Fitzpatrick, ed., *The Writings of George Washington,* 4: 362, 10: 190–91; James A. Huston, *Logistics of Liberty: American Services of Supply in the Revolutionary War and After* (Newark, DE, 1991), 113; Friedrich W. L. G. A. Baron von Steuben, *Regulations for the Order and Discipline of the Troops of the United States* (Philadelphia, 1779), 5; Showman et al., eds., *Papers of General Nathanael Greene* 1: 151–52, 198–99, 213. Rodney Hilton Brown wrote that "The Revolutionary War saw a revival in the use of polearms, and especially pikes, due to the colonists' scarcity of weapons." *American Polearms,* 51.

54. Fitzpatrick, ed., *The Writings of George Washington* 3: 338, 4: 362, 364 (quote), 5: 51, 99, 105, 10: 314, 17: 18; Abbot et al., eds., *Papers of Washington, Revolutionary War Series* 4: 325, 458, 5: 673, 6: 18; Robert W. Gibbes, ed., *Documentary History of the American Revolution: Consisting of Letters and Papers Relating to the Contest for Liberty, Chiefly in South Carolina,* 3 vols. (New York, 1853–57), 2: 45–46; Browne et al., eds., *Archives of Maryland* 12: 307, 493; H. R. McIlwaine et al., eds., *Journals of the Council of State of Virginia,* 4 vols. (Richmond, VA, 1931–67), 1: 45; *Pennylsvania Archives* 7: 190; Palmer et al., eds., *Calendar of Virginia State Papers* 1: 407; Wylma A. Wates, ed., *Stub Entries to the Indents Issued in Payment of Claims against South Carolina* (Columbia, SC, 1957), No. 59, book D: 143; "American Pole Arms or Shafter Weapons," *The Bulletin of the Fort Ticonderoga Museum* 5 (1939): 74–76.

55. Washington to Hancock, 9 February 1776 (twice), Abbot et al., eds., *Papers of Washington, Revolutionary War Series* 3: 275, 278, see also 4: 452, 458–59.

56. Washington to Philip Van Renssalaer, 17 May 1776, Abbot et al., eds., *Papers of Washington, Revolutionary War Series* 4: 329; Charles K. Bolton, *The Private Soldier Under Washington* (New York, 1902), 113–14.

57. Paine to Schuyler, 2 April 1776, in Smith, ed., *Letters of Delegates to Congress,* 3: 477; Ford et al., eds., *Journals of the Continental Congress* 1: 102–06, 2: 85–86, 218–19, 465, 3: 453, 4: 170–71; Orlando W. Stephenson, "The Supply of Gunpowder in 1776," *American Historical Review* 30 (1925): 271–80; E. Wayne Carp offers the best study of these congressional efforts to supply the Continental army in *To Starve the Army at Pleasure: Continental Army Administration and American Political Culture, 1775–1783* (Chapel Hill, NC, 1984).

58. Carp, *To Starve the Army at Pleasure,* 177, see also 21–23; Ford et al., eds., *Journals of the Continental Congress* 13: 353–56, 545–46, 812–13, 4: 103, 128, 169, 215, 221–23, 312, 354, 363. The efforts of the states to supply their own firearms was, in the words of a special committee of the Virginia assembly, "entirely deranged." Palmer et al., eds., *Calendar of Virginia State Papers* 1: 586–87, see also 2: 106–07.

59. Whisker, *Gunsmith's Trade,* 232–37, 242–43; Lewis, *Small Arms,* 22–27. Orlando Stephenson provides the following estimates of gunpowder held by American forces at the beginning of the Revolution:

in private hands or by seizure:	80,000 pounds
made from American saltpeter:	115,000 pounds
made from imported saltpeter:	698,245 pounds
imported:	1,454,210 pounds

Excluding the first category, whose provenance is unknown, 64 percent of the remaining 2,267,455 pounds was imported from Europe, 31 percent was made with imported saltpeter, and only 5 percent was made from American saltpeter. "The Supply of Gunpowder in 1776," 271–81.

60. Ford et al., eds., *Journals of the Continental Congress* 2: 85, 219, 3: 246–48, 4: 170–71; David L. Salay, "The Production of Gunpowder in Pennsylvania during the American Revolution," *Pennsylvania Magazine of History and Biography* 99 (1975): 422–42; Donald Reynolds, "Ammunition Supply in Revolutionary Virginia," *Virginia Magazine of History and Biography* 73 (1965): 56–77; Norman B. Wilkinson, *Explosives in History* (Chicago, 1966), 10–14; James E. Hicks, *U.S. Military Firearms, 1776–1956* (Alhambra, CA, 1962), 11; Huston, *Logistics of Liberty,* 81–82, 118–20.

61. Brown, *Firearms in Colonial America,* 130.

62. Brown, *Firearms in Colonial America,* 309.

63. Arcadi Gluckman, *United States Muskets, Rifles, and Carbines* (Buffalo, NY, 1948), 43–48, quote 44; *Pennsylvania Gazette,* 26 June 1776; *Pennsylvania Archives,* ser. 1, 4: 12, 239, 294–96, 376, 711, 748; Arthur Merwyn Carey, *American Firearms Makers: When, Where, and What They Made from the Colonial Period to the End of the Nineteenth Century* (New York, 1953), 28, 90, 104–09; Robert E. Gardner, *Small Arms Makers: A Directory of Fabricators of Firearms, Edged Weapons, Crossbows and Polearms* (New York, 1962), 50, 140–43, 149, 153, 194; Alexander C. Flick, *The American Revolution in New York: Its Political, Social and Economic Significance* (Albany, NY, 1926), 187–93; Brown, *Firearms in Colonial America,* 314; Harold L. Peterson, *Arms and Armor in Colonial America, 1526–1783* (New York, 1956), 185.

64. Lincoln, ed., *The Journals of Each Provincial Congress,* quotations 291, 330, 592, see also 474, 476, 498–99, 540, 542, 548–53, 562, 565, 590, 595; Edward C. Janes

and Roscoe S. Scott, *Westfield Massachusetts 1669–1969: The First Three Hundred Years* (Westfield, MA, 1968), 115–16, 348. After the war, Falley ran a small gun factory that did out work for the Springfield Armory until the War of 1812; the exact termination date is unknown.

65. Lewis to Washington, 6 March 1776, W. W. Abbot et al., eds., *The Papers of George Washington, Revolutionary War Series* 3: 419; Hunter to Jefferson, January 1781, Boyd et al., eds., *Papers of Thomas Jefferson* 4: 448–49; Davies to the governor, 11 September 1781, War Office Orders, 15 August to 1 November 1781: 56, and Executive War Office Letter Book, 1 August 1782 to 12 July 1786: 30–31, Virginia State Library; Virginia *Gazette,* 22 June and 15 November 1776; Palmer et al., eds., *Calendar of Virginia State Papers* 1: 268–69, 372–73, 386, 418–19, 430, 454–56, 606, 2: 336, 339, 411, 502; William W. Hening, ed., *The Statutes at Large; Being a Collection of All the Laws of Virginia,* 13 vols. (New York, 1823), 9: 303–06; Donald E. Reynolds, "Ammunition Supply in Revolutionary Virginia," 56–77; Gardner, *Small Arms Makers,* 37–38, 91, 98–99, 126, 157, 170, 200, 209. More often quoted is Ebenezer Hazard's comment after his visit to the gun works in May 1777 that there were "about 60 persons" working there and they made "about 20 Muskets, complete with Bayonets," every week. Yet those numbers do not match Lewis's figures, and the director seems a better source. Fred Shelley, ed., "The Journal of Ebenezer Hazard in Virginia, 1777," *Virginia Magazine of History and Biography* 62 (1954): 404.

66. Force, ed., *American Archives,* ser. 4, 2: 1227, 1296, 1321, 1335, 3: 303 (quote), 885, 5: 253. Trumbull et al., eds., *Public Records of Connecticut* 15: 18–19, 317–18; John Russell Bartlett, ed., *Records of the Colony of Rhode Island and Providence Plantations in New England,* 10 vols. (Providence, RI, 1856–65), 7: 271; J. Hoadly et al., eds., *The Public Records of the State of Connecticut* 3: 325; Whisker, *The Gunsmith's Trade,* 99, 166.

67. McIlwaine et al., eds., *Journals of the Council* 1: 177–78; Force, ed., *American Archives,* ser. 4, 1: 1256, 3: 1232, 1496, 4: 71, 305, 6: 1721, ser. 5, 1: 50, 2: 70, 79; Hazard et al., eds., *Pennsylvania Archives,* ser. 1, 10: 250–52. There were also examples of war profiteering, of gun contractors hoarding firearms until states became desperate enough to pay exorbitant rates. Hazard et al., eds., *Pennsylvania Archives,* ser. 1, 4: 731; Gardner, *Small Arms Makers,* 181.

68. Jefferson to George Muter, 14 February 1781, Boyd et al., eds., *Papers of Thomas Jefferson* 4: 609; Force, ed., *American Archives,* ser. 4, 1: 1334, 3: 131, 5: 470, 6: 1393; Browne et al., eds., *Archives of Maryland* 12: 412, 16: 219, 21: 68–69, 141.

69. McIlwaine et al., eds., *Journals of the Council* 3: 297; Browne et al., eds., *Archives of Maryland* 11: 75, 81; Gill, *The Gunsmith in Colonial Virginia,* 41–48; Peterson, *Arms and Armor,* 209–08, Carey, *American Firearms Makers,* 109. An average rate of production was twenty muskets per month by an experienced gunsmith with a full staff of ten workers, and with the state supplying the parts. On other small-scale efforts at gun production during the Revolution, see Ford et al., eds., *Journals of the Continental Congress* 4: 128, 169; Gardner, *Small Arms Makers,* 20, 67, 91, 141–42, 157, 211, 217; Carey, *American Firearms Makers,* 11, 40, 133, 138; Brown, *Firearms in Colonial America,* 315; Browne et al., eds., *Archives of Maryland* 16: 377–78; Hemphill, ed., *Extracts from the Journals of South Carolina,* 209–10.

70. Ford et al., eds., *Journals of the Continental Congress* 4: 220–21; Nuxoll, "Congress and the Munitions Merchants," 27–37.

71. Washington to Greene, 18 March 1777, Greene to Washington, 25 March 1777, Showman et al., eds., *The Papers of General Nathanael Greene* 2: 44, 48; Coy Hilton James, *Silas Deane, Patriot or Traitor?* (East Lansing, MI, 1975), 9–10, 18–20;

George C. Neumann, *The History of Weapons of the American Revolution* (New York, 1967), 22; ordnance stores in Boston, January 1777, Box 2, U.S. Revolutionary Collection, American Antiquarian Society; Helen Augur, *The Secret War of Independence* (New York, 1955), 13–20, 51–91; Samuel Flagg Bemis, *The Diplomacy of the American Revolution* (New York, 1935), 24–37, 48–54; Nuxoll, "Congress and the Munitions Merchants," 112–72, 343–421. Every volume of Jared Sparks, ed., *The Diplomatic Correspondence of the American Revolution,* 12 vols. (Boston, 1829–30), is packed with material on efforts to acquire firearms, as are the first two volumes of Henri Doniol, ed., *Histoire de la participation de la France a l'etablissement des Etats-Unis D'Amerique,* 6 vols. (Paris, 1886–92). Private gunrunning and the capture of British munitions at sea supplied only a small portion of American needs; Nuxoll, "Congress and the Munitions Merchants," 10–12, 17–18; Robert G. Albion and Jennie B. Pope, *Sea Lanes in Wartime: The American Experience, 1775–1945* (Hamden, CT, 1968), 45–48, 63–65; Bowler, *Logistics and the Failure of the British Army,* 149–50; Augur, *The Secret War,* 60–62. Not just Congress bought arms abroad during the Revolution. Every state sent agents first to the Caribbean—which proved a weak market—and then to France and the Netherlands to purchase firearms for their militia. *Pennsylvania Archives,* ser. 1, 4: 125–26, 386, 417; Force, ed., *American Archives,* ser. 4, 1: 1077; Palmer et al., eds., *Calendar of Virginia State Papers* 1: 500, 587–88; Flick, *The American Revolution in New York,* 186–93; Albion and Pope, *Sea Lanes in Wartime,* 54–57; Nuxoll, "Congress and the Munitions Merchants," 12–14; Ernest E. Rogers, *The Connecticut Naval Office at New London During the War of the American Revolution* (New London, CT, 1933), 11, 24–26, 262–70.

72. Force, ed., *American Archives,* ser. 4, 2: 341, 841; John Shy, *A People Numerous and Armed,* 147–55, 160–62.

73. James T. Mitchell and Henry Flanders, eds., *The Statutes at Large of Pennsylvania from 1682 to 1801,* 8 vols. (Harrisburg, PA, 1886–1902), chapter 731, sect. 10; Enos Reeves, "Extracts from the Letter-Books of Lieutenant Enos Reeves," *Pennsylvania Magazine of History and Biography* 21 (1897): 387; Arthur J. Alexander, "Pennsylvania's Revolutionary Militia," *Pennsylvania Magazine of History and Biography* 69 (1945): 23; *Pennsylvania Archives,* ser. 1, 4: 578–79, 7: 401, 679–80; Shy, *A People Numerous and Armed,* 155. Every state allowed members of the militia to pay for substitutes, and they did so to an astounding degree. Volumes 6–8 of *Pennsylvania Archives,* ser. 5, are full of muster lists noting substitutes. In one typical company twenty-four of the thirty-two privates were substitutes (8: 75–77).

74. Lee to Patrick Henry, 15 September 1776, William Wirt Henry, ed., *Patrick Henry: Life, Correspondence and Speeches,* 3 vols. (New York, 1891), 3: 10–11; Higginbotham, *George Washington,* 12.

75. Washington to Hancock, 10 July 1775, Abbot et al., eds., *Papers of Washington, Revolutionary War Series* 3: 327, see also 379–80, 486–87.

76. Washington to the New England Governments, 5 December 1775, Abbot et al., eds., *Papers of Washington, Revolutionary War Series* 2: 492, see also ibid. 3: 156, 185, 278, 5: 682–85, 6: 200, 388, 7: 262–63.

77. Washington to Hancock, 2 September 1776, Abbot et al., eds., *Papers of Washington, Revolutionary War Series* 6: 199.

78. Washington, "Circular to the States," 18 October 1780, Fitzpatrick, ed., *Writings of George Washington* 20: 209.

79. Reed to Col. William Henry, 23 September 1794, *Pennsylvania Archives,* ser. 1, 4: 711; Samuel Haws, "A Journal for 1775," in Abraham Tomlinson, comp., *The*

Military Journals of Two Private Soldiers, 1758–1775 (Poughkeepsie, NY, 1855), 54; Bolton, *The Private Soldier,* 112–13; "Diary of Rev. Benjamin Boardman," *Proceedings of the Massachusetts Historical Society,* 2nd ser., 7: 404; "Orderly Books and Journals Kept by Connecticut Men While Taking Part in the American Revolution, 1775–78," *Collections of the Connecticut Historical Society* 7: 123, 226, 268.

80. Greene to John Hancock, 21 December 1776, Showman et al., eds., *Papers of General Nathanael Greene* 1: 374; ibid. 334–35, 365–69; E. Milton Wheeler, "Development and Organization of the North Carolina Militia," *North Carolina Historical Review* 41(1964): 318–19, 323; Clark, ed., *The State Records of North Carolina* 14: 860; *Pennsylvania Archives,* ser. 1, 4: 747–49; Henry, ed., *Patrick Henry* 1: 483–89; Ford et al., eds., *Journals of the Continental Congress* 2: 336; Louis Clinton Hatch, *The Administration of the American Revolutionary Army* (New York, 1904), 71–77, 84; Force, ed., *American Archives,* 5th ser., 2: 1067; Morgan quoted in Royster, *A Revolutionary People at War,* 322. Captain Windsor Brown accepted an offer to be commissary of military stores for Virginia as he "wishes never to command militia again." Brown to Colonel G. Muter, 13 February 1781, Palmer et al., eds., *Calendar of Virginia State Papers* 1: 511.

81. Greene to Governor Nicholas Cooke of Rhode Island, 17 September and 4 December 1776, to Jacob Greene, 28 September 1776, Showman et al., eds., *Papers of General Nathanael Greene* 1: 300, 303, 362.

82. Middlekauff, *The Glorious Cause,* 456–57; Otho Holland Williams, "A Narrative of the Campaign of 1780," in William Johnson, ed., *Sketches of the Life and Correspondence of Nathanael Greene,* 2 vols. (Charleston, SC, 1822), 1: 485–510, quotes 496–97.

83. Elliott to Jefferson, 7 November 1780, Steuben to Jefferson, 6 January 1781, Palmer et al., eds., *Calendar of Virginia State Papers* 1: 385, 418; Greene to Washington, 3 December 1777, to William Green, 7 March 1778, Showman et al., eds., *The Papers of General Nathanael Greene* 2: 234, 302, see also ibid. 234, 268–72, 316, 384; Washington to General Horatio Gates, 6 March 1779, Fitzpatrick, ed., *The Writings of George Washington* 14: 199; Palmer et al., eds., *Calendar of Virginia State Papers* 1: 440, 556–57, 605.

84. William W. Harris, *The Battle of Groton Heights* (New London, CT, 1882), 90–102; Willard Sterne Randall, *Benedict Arnold: Patriot and Traitor* (New York, 1990), 586–88; Broadus Mitchell, *The Price of Independence: A Realistic View of the American Revolution* (New York, 1974), 275–83.

85. Don Higginbotham, *Daniel Morgan, Revolutionary Rifleman* (Chapel Hill, NC, 1961), 125–42; Banastre Tarleton, *A History of the Campaigns of 1780 and 1781 in the Southern Provinces of North America* (London, 1787), 210–26.

86. John Peter Gabriel Muhlenberg, "Orderly Book of Gen. John Peter Gabriel Muhlenberg," *Pennsylvania Magazine of History and Biography* 34 (1910): 471–72, 35 (1911): 77; Worthington C. Ford, ed., *General Orders Issued by Major-General Israel Putnam* (Brooklyn, NY, 1893), 39.

87. Lt. John Brooks to Inspector General, December 1781, Return of the New Wine Hospital, December 1781, oversized box, U.S. Revolutionary Collection, American Antiquarian Society. Even high-ranking officers often pursued a single musket, as when General Muhlenburg wrote Virginia's Committee of War in 1780 in an effort to recover a confiscated musket. Palmer et al., eds., *Calendar of Virginia State Papers* 1: 373.

88. Greene's Orders, 12 November 1775, Greene to Samuel Ward, 31 December

1775, Showman et al., eds., *Papers of General Nathanael Greene* 1: 151, 173; Fitzpatrick, ed., *Writings of George Washington* 4: 102–03, 152–53. See also Palmer et al., eds., *Calendar of Virginia State Papers* 2: 607.

89. Showman et al., eds., *Papers of General Nathanael Greene* 1: 161, 197, 230, 325.

90. Peter Force, *American Archives,* ser. 5, 3: 1058–59.

91. General Sullivan to New Hampshire Committee of Safety, 5 August 1775, *Pennsylvania Magazine of History and Biography* 14 (1890): 119; "Orderly Book Fourth Pennsylvania Battalion, Col. Anthony Wayne, 1776," *Pennsylvania Magazine of History and Biography* 30 (1906): 212; Daniel Grout's Orderly Book, 1779, Orderly Books Collection; Charlestown, NH, equipment list, 1775, U.S. Revolutionary Collection, Box 1, returns for General Heath's Army, 1782, oversized box, U.S. Revolutionary Collection, American Antiquarian Society; Brown, *Firearms in Colonial America,* 330; Letter Books of Lt. Enos Reeves, 1782, *Pennsylvania Magazine of History and Biography* 21 (1897): 387.

92. Greene's Orders, 29 May 1776, Showman et al., eds., *Papers of General Nathanael Greene* 1: 220.

93. Neumann, *Weapons of the American Revolution,* 22; Bowler, *Logistics and the Failure of the British Army,* 239–64. England's difficulties were exasperated by incompetence. The accounts of the navy and army were not rendered or examined between 1767 and 1783, an amount of £171 million. Carp, *To Starve the Army at Pleasure,* 132; Victor L. Johnson, "Internal Financial Reform or External Taxation: Britain's Fiscal Choice, 1763," *Proceedings of the American Philosophical Society* 98 (1954): 31–37.

94. Bowler, *Logistics and the Failure of the British Army,* 150–53.

95. Reports of the Inspector General, May 1779, Box 3, U.S. Revolutionary Collection, American Antiquarian Society; Greene to Samuel Ward, 4 January 1776, Showman et al., eds., *Papers of General Nathanael Greene* 1: 178–79.

96. "Return of Arms Wanting to Compleat the Pennsylvania Line," 13 June 1779, Box 3, "Remarks on the Connecticut Line," n.d. [probably 1779], Return on Col. Hazen's Regiment, 27 April 1780, oversized box, U.S. Revolutionary Collection, American Antiquarian Society. See also the many other returns in this box from 1779 to 1780.

97. Orderly Book of the Pennsylvania Regiment of Foot, 1777, *Pennsylvania Magazine of History and Biography* 22 (1898): 205–06. See any other orderly book, for instance, ibid., 200, 205, 208–09, 303–06, 317; "Orderly Book Fourth Pennsylvania Battalion, Col. Anthony Wayne, 1776," *Pennsylvania Magazine of History and Biography* 29 (1905): 476, 30 (1906): 99, 215; "Extracts from the Orderly-Book Lieutenant William Torrey," *Pennsylvania Magazine of History and Biography* 29 (1905): 117–19; "Orderly Book of Captain Sharp Delany," *Pennsylvania Magazine of History and Biography* 32 (1908): 307; John Peter Gabriel Muhlenberg, "Orderly Book of Gen. John Peter Gabriel Muhlenberg," *Pennsylvania Magazine of History and Biography* 33 (1909): 257–78, 454–74; Ford, ed., *General Orders Issued by General Putnam,* 27.

98. Muhlenberg, "Orderly Book," 177.

99. Muhlenberg, "Orderly Book," 180; John W. Jordan, ed., "Orderly-Book of the Pennsylvania State Regiment of Foot, May 10 to August 16, 1777," *Pennsylvania Magazine of History and Biography* 22 (1898): 208; Ford, ed., *General Orders Issued by General Putnam,* 36, 46, 52, 54; "Orderly Book Fourth Pennsylvania Battalion, Col. Anthony Wayne, 1776," *Pennsylvania Magazine of History and Biography* 30 (1906): 207; Showman et al., eds., *The Papers of General Nathanael Greene* 1: 146, 277, 280; Abbot et al., eds., *Papers of Washington, Revolutionary War Series* 4: 445.

100. General Orders, 3 March 1776, Fitzpatrick, ed., *Writings of George Washington,* 4: 364; Ford, ed., *General Orders Issued by General Putnam,* 19.

101. Return of Arms for the 2nd Massachusetts Brigade of Foot, 12 January 1782, Return of Arms for the 3rd Massachusetts Regiment, 22 December 1781, Return of Arms for the 5th Massachusetts Regiment, January 1782, Box 3, U.S. Revolutionary Collection, American Antiquarian Society. One can follow the progress of the 2nd Massachusetts Brigade of Foot through its weekly reports. Its absolute low point was July 1780, when the regiment reported that 84 percent of its soldiers fit for duty did not have a gun. Returns of 3rd Mass Brigade of Foot, Folio vol. 1, U.S. Revolutionary Collection, American Antiquarian Society.

102. General Orders, 24 July 1776, Fitzpatrick ed., *Writings of George Washington* 5: 336.

103. "Orders by Maj.-Gen. Daniel Jones," *Collections of the New-York Historical Society* 16 (1883): 606–19, 621–23; Benjamin F. Stevens, *General Sir William Howe's Orderly Book at Charleston, Boston and Halifax, 17 June 1775 to 26 May 1776* (London, 1890), 201–4; Allen French, ed., *Diary of Frederick Mackenzie,* 2 vols. (Cambridge, 1930), 1: 4, 144; Peter Paret, "Colonial Experience and European Military Reform at the End of the Eighteenth Century," *Bulletin of the Institute of Historical Research* 37 (1964): 52–53; Sylvia R. Frey, *The British Soldier in America: A Social History of Military Life in the Revolutionary Period* (Austin, TX, 1981), 101–02. The failure of the British army to realize the technological advantages of the Ferguson rifle is one of the greatest military errors of all time. See David Patten, "Ferguson and His Rifle," *History Today* 28 (1978): 446–54; Peterson, *Arms and Armor in Colonial America,* 218–21.

104. Adams to Adams, 17 June 1775, *Familiar Letters of John Adams and His Wife Abigail Adams During the Revolution,* ed. Charles F. Adams (Boston, 1875), 65; Higginbotham, *Daniel Morgan,* 57, 64–77; Fitzpatrick, ed., *Writings of George Washington* 8: 246. After the Saratoga campaign, Washington effectively dismantled Morgan's unit, sending companies of riflemen off to serve as support for other commands. Higginbotham, *Daniel Morgan,* 92; Fitzpatrick, ed., *Writings of George Washington* 11: 440, 12: 190, 251–52, 13: 110, 439.

105. Report of the Board of War, 20 and 21 March 1776, Ford et al., eds., *Journals of the Continental Congress* 4: 215, 224; Fitzpatrick, ed., *Writings of George Washington* 8: 236–37, 272; Peterson, *Arms and Armor in Colonial America,* 200, 292–93; Charles J. Stille, *Major General Anthony Wayne* (Philadelphia, 1893), 118; *American State Papers* 1: 53; *Pennsylvania Archives,* ser. 1, 4: 679.

106. Felix Reichman, "The Pennsylvania Rifle: A Social Interpretation of Changing Military Techniques," *Pennsylvania Magazine of History and Biography* 69 (1915): 5; Peter Paret, *Yorck and the Era of Prussian Military Reform, 1807–1815* (Princeton, NJ, 1966), 15–16.

107. Steuben, *Regulations,* 32, 64; on maintenance of firearms, see 88–89, 117–21; on compliance, see Showman et al., eds., *The Papers of General Nathanael Greene* 1: 150, 200–02, 208, 286–87. Compare with the British manual Richard Lambert, Earl of Cavan, *A New System of Military Discipline Founded upon Principle* (Philadelphia, 1776), 67–112.

108. French, ed., *Diary of Frederick Mackenzie,* 1: 45; Percy to Northumberland, 1 September 1776, Bolton, ed., *Letters of Hugh Earl Percy,* 68; Edward Ely Curtis, *The Organization of the British Army in the American Revolution* (New Haven, CT, 1926), 20–21.

109. Burgoyne, general orders, 20 June 1777, J. M. Hadden, *A Journal Kept in*

Canada upon Burgoyne's Campaign (New York, 1884), 74; Franklin and Mary Wick-wire, *Cornwallis: The American Adventure* (Boston, 1970), 63–65, 298–300; Middle-kauff, *The Glorious Cause*, 461–62, 480–87; Bolton, ed., *Letters of Hugh Earl Percy*, 67–75; Showman et al., eds., *Papers of General Nathanael Greene* 2: 169. On British doubts of the reliability of firearms, see Lambert, *A New System of Military Discipline*, 23–25; H. C. B. Rogers, *Weapons of the British Soldier* (London, 1960), 90–93, 110–15.

110. Roger Lamb, *An Original and Authentic Journal of Occurrences during the Late American War* (Dublin, 1809), 344–48, quote 344; Tarleton, *A History of the Campaigns of 1780 and 1781*, 222–31. See also the descriptions of the Battle of Guilford Court House, where the Highlanders' bayonets routed the American militia; Wick-wires, *Cornwallis*, 274–310.

111. Washington's order to Wayne before Stony Point stated that the soldiers "are to advance . . . with fixed bayonets and muskets unloaded." Charles J. Stille, *Major General Anthony Wayne*, 118.

112. Muhlenberg, "Orderly Book," 33 (1909): 455, 464; Worthington C. Ford, ed., *General Orders Issued by Major-General Israel Putnam*, 34, 69.

113. General Orders, 3 March 1776, Fitzpatrick, ed., *Writings of George Washington* 4: 364; Showman et al., eds., *The Papers of General Nathanael Greene* 2: 181, 455.

114. Instructions to General John Sullivan, 31 May 1779, Fitzpatrick, ed., *The Writings of George Washington* 15: 189, 191; Colin G. Calloway, *The American Revolution in Indian Country: Crisis and Diversity in Native American Communities* (Cambridge, 1995), 26–51, quote 49. On March 6, 1779, Washington wrote General Horatio Gates that the point of Sullivan's campaign was to "carry the war into the Heart of the six nations; . . . destroy their next Years crops, and do them every other mischief of which time and circumstances permit." Fitzpatrick, ed., *The Writings of George Washington* 14: 199.

115. Calloway, *The American Revolution in Indian Country*, 47, 50; Hazard et al., eds., *Pennsylvania Archives*, ser. 1, 9: 523–25.

116. Carp, *To Starve the Army at Pleasure*, 216; Return of Arms for the Massachusetts Line, October 1783, Box 4; Returns for General Heath's Army, 1782, oversized box, U.S. Revolutionary Collection, American Antiquarian Society.

117. Royster, *A Revolutionary People*, 351. See also ibid., 331–68; Higginbotham, *George Washington*, 96–105.

Chapter Seven

Government Promotion of Gun Production

1. Jefferson to John Adams, 28 October 1813, in "Jefferson and Adams on Aristocracy," Michael A. Bellesiles, ed., *BiblioBase* (Boston, 1998), 9.

2. Knox to Congress, 3 January 1784, Knox Papers, New England Genealogical Society.

3. William Guthman, *March to Massacre: A History of the First Seven Years of the United States Army, 1784–1791* (New York, 1975), 91.

4. Knox to Congress, 1784, Worthington C. Ford et al., eds., *Journals of the Continental Congress, 1774–1789*, 34 vols. (Washington, DC, 1904–37), 13: 123.

5. Doughty to Knox, 9 October 1784, Knox Papers.

6. Lawrence Delbert Cress, *Citizens in Arms: The Army and the Militia in American Society to the War of 1812* (Chapel Hill, NC, 1982), 75–93.

7. Washington to Hamilton, 2 May 1783, John C. Fitzpatrick, ed., *The Writings of George Washington from the Original Manuscript Sources, 1745–1799,* 39 vols. (Washington, DC, 1931–44), 26: 388–89.

8. Hamilton, "Report on a Military Peace Establishment," 18 June 1783, Harold C. Syrett and Jacob E. Cooke, eds., *The Papers of Alexander Hamilton,* 26 vols. (New York, 1961–79), 3: 382, 392–95.

9. Kenneth R. Bowling and Helen E. Veit, eds., *The Diary of William Maclay and Other Notes on Senate Debates* (Baltimore, 1988), 246.

10. On the grievances of the Shaysites, see William Whiting, "Some brief Remarks on the Present State of Publick Affairs" (1786) and "Some Remarks on the Conduct of the Inhabitants of the Commonwealth of Massachusetts in Interrupting the Sitting of the Judicial Courts in Several Counties of that State" (1787) in Stephen T. Riley, "Dr. William Whiting and Shays' Rebellion," *Proceedings of the American Antiquarian Society* 66 (1956): 131–35, 140–66. On conditions in Massachusetts in the 1780s see Robert J. Taylor, *Western Massachusetts in the Revolution* (Providence, RI, 1954), chapter 6; David P. Szatmary, *Shays' Rebellion: The Making of an Agrarian Insurrection* (Amherst, MA, 1980), chapter 2.

11. Shays to General Lincoln, 30 January 1787, in John Lockwood et al., *Western Massachusetts: A History, 1636–1925,* 4 vols. (New York, 1926), 1: 172–73.

12. *Acts and Laws of Massachusetts, 1786* (Boston, 1786), 494–95, 497, 502–03, 510; Massachusetts Senate to Governor Bowdoin, 4 February 1787, Massachusetts Archives, State House (Boston); "Address to the People" from the General Court, *Hampshire Gazette,* 3 December 1786; William Shepard to Bowdoin, 26 January 1787, and Lincoln to Bowdoin, 28 January 1787, Joseph P. Warren, "Documents Relating to Shays' Rebellion," *American Historical Review* 2 (1897): 694–96; Szatmary, *Shays' Rebellion,* 70–105. Since the lower house of the general court had not declared a rebellion, General Lincoln violated civil law in his encounters with the Regulators, failing to read the riot act and give the crowd one hour to disperse, as required by law. Lincoln understood this legal technicality, but rejected it. The general court finally declared a state of "horrid and unnatural Rebellion" on 5 February 1787, *after* the attack at Petersham. Benjamin Lincoln to Washington, 22 February 1787, Washington Papers, Presidential Papers Microfilm Collection, Library of Congress, Washington, DC; Lincoln to General John Paterson, 31 January, 1 and 6 February 1787, Paterson to Lincoln, 5 February 1787, Thomas Egleston, *The Life of John Paterson, Major-General in the Revolutionary Army* (New York, 1898), 360–66; Francis Bowen, "Life of Benjamin Lincoln," in Jared Sparks, ed., *The Library of American Biography,* 25 vols. (Boston, 1847), 23: 393–95, 402.

13. Washington to Madison, 5 November 1786, Fitzpatrick, ed., *Writings of Washington* 29: 50–52. On the impact of Shays's Rebellion on the militia's reputation, see Cress, *Citizens in Arms,* 95–98.

14. Lockwood et al., *Western Massachusetts,* 183. George Washington wrote Benjamin Lincoln Jr. on February 24, 1787, that the insurgents "had by their repeated outrages forfeited all right to Citizenship." Fitzpatrick, ed., *Writings of Washington* 29: 168.

15. Washington to David Humphreys, 22 October, to Henry Lee, 31 October, Fitzpatrick, ed., *Writings of Washington* 29: 26–28, 33–35; Knox to Congress, 18 October 1786, Ford et al., eds. *Journals of the Continental Congress* 31: 887; Knox to

Washington, 23 October 1786, Henry Knox Papers, Massachusetts Historical Society (Boston).

16. Max Farrand, ed., *The Records of the Federal Convention of 1787,* 4 vols. (New Haven, CT, 1937), 1: 19–20, 25, 293, 2: 47.

17. Ibid. 2: 220–22, 330–31. The debate over the federal regulation of the militia may be followed through the records. See esp. 2: 47–49, 133–37, 144–48, 159, 168, 174, 182, 316–18, 323–33, 352–56, 368, 380–90, 459, 466–67, 602, 656, 662.

18. Madison to Jefferson, 24 October 1787, William T. Hutchinson et al., eds., *The Papers of James Madison,* 17 vols. (Chicago, 1962–91), 10: 212–14; Jack N. Rakove, *Declaring Rights: A Brief History with Documents* (Boston, 1998), 147–66. In general see H. Jefferson Powell, "Rules for Originalists," *Virginia Law Review* 73 (1987): 673–84; Jack N. Rakove, ed., *Interpreting the Constitution: The Debate over Original Intent* (New York, 1990); Rakove, *Original Meanings: Politics and Ideas in the Making of the Constitution* (New York, 1997).

19. Farrand, ed., *Records of the Federal Convention* 2: 207–09, quote 207.

20. Ibid. 2: 386–87.

21. Don Higginbotham, "The Federalized Militia Debate: A Neglected Aspect of Second Amendment Scholarship," *William and Mary Quarterly,* 3rd ser., 55: 39–58, 44; Farrand, ed., *Records of the Federal Convention* 2: 182, 323, 330–33, 352–56, 380–90.

22. Robert E. Shalhope, "To Keep and Bear Arms in the Early Republic," *Constitutional Commentary* 16 (1999): 269–82.

23. Don Higginbotham, "The Second Amendment in Historical Context," *Constitutional Commentary,* 16 (1999): 263–68.

24. The precise concept of eminent domain was not known under English common law; until the 1770s the taking of property by the sovereign required a special act of Parliament. William Blackstone, *Commentaries on the Laws of England,* 4 vols. (Chicago, 1979), 1: 138–39, 222, 290–96, 4: 154–59; Forrest McDonald, *Novus Ordo Seclorum: The Intellectual Origins of the Constitution* (Lawrence, KS, 1985), 9–24.

25. See, for instance, J. Hammond Turnbull, et al., eds., *The Public Records of the Colony of Connecticut,* 15 vols. (Hartford, CT, 1850–90), 1: 351, 2: 217, 8: 380, 9: 341–44, 473, 580; William H. Browne et al., eds., *Archives of Maryland,* 72 vols. (Baltimore, 1883–1972), 29: 10–11, 47, 98, 153–55, 237–39, 376–78, 30: 20–21, 38–39, 461–63, 42: 87–90; Thomas Cooper and David J. McCord, eds., *The Statutes at Large of South Carolina,* 14 vols. (Columbia, SC, 1836–73), 2: 15; Walter Clark, ed., *The State Records of North Carolina,* 30 vols. (Goldsboro, NC, 1886–1909), 10: 158; Robert M. Calhoon, *The Loyalists in Revolutionary America, 1760–1781* (New York, 1965), 281–311, 397–414, 439–78; Alexander C. Flick, *Loyalism in New York During the American Revolution* (New York, 1901), 58–94; Robert S. Lambert, *South Carolina Loyalists in the American Revolution* (Columbia, SC, 1987), 33–58.

26. Anon., *Militia Laws of the United States and Massachusetts* (Boston, 1836), 1–2.

27. Rakove, *Declaring Rights,* 86–87; James T. Mitchell and Henry Flanders, eds., *The Statutes at Large of Pennsylvania* (Philadelphia, 1903), 9: 110–14, 346–48; Saul Cornell, "Commonplace or Anachronism: The Standard Model, the Second Amendment, and the Problem of History in Contemporary Constitutional Theory," *Constitutional Commentary* 16 (1999): 221–46.

28. Higginbotham, "The Federalized Militia Debate, 39–58, quote, 40.

29. Higginbotham, "The Federalized Militia Debate," 41; Samuel E. Morison, ed., *Sources and Documents Illustrating the American Revolution,* 2d ed. (Oxford, 1929), 151.

30. Henry, 5 June 1788, Merrill Jensen et al. eds., *The Documentary History of the Ratification of the Constitution,* 18 vols. (Madison, WI, 1976–95), 9: 954–59, quote 957; Cress, *Citizens in Arms,* 98–102; Lyle D. Brundage, "The Organization, Administrations, and Training of the United States Ordinary and Volunteer Militia, 1792–1861" (Ph.D. diss., University of Michigan, 1958), 41. For additional Anti-Federalist views on the militia, see Jensen et al. eds., *The Documentary History of the Ratification* 1: 482, 539–40, 2: 37–38, 60, 184–85, 290–92, 318–19, 3: 20–22, 30–31, 408–12, 4: 58. As Higginbotham points out, it is odd that the Anti-Federalists did not quote Blackstone on the militia as "not compellable to march out of their counties, unless in case of invasion or actual rebellion." Higginbotham, "The Federalized Militia Debate," 47n; Blackstone, *Commentaries* 1: 399.

31. Farrand, ed., *Records of the Federal Convention* 3: 272. For Martin's response, see 286–95; Landowner #10, Jensen et al., eds., *Documentary History of Ratification* 16: 267.

32. Higginbotham, "The Federalized Militia Debate," 49; Jensen et al., eds., *Documentary History of Ratification* 9: 1014, 1074, 1102, 10: 1288–96, 1311–12, 1324–25, 1486, 1531; a point also made in Federalist Papers #29 and 46.

33. Higginbotham, "The Federalized Militia Debate," 50; Cress, *Citizens in Arms,* 102–09.

34. Jensen et al., eds., *Documentary History of Ratification* 2: 318–19.

35. Ibid., 2: 420; Alexander Hamilton, James Madison, and John Jay, *The Federalist, or the New Constitution* (Norwalk, CT, 1979), 161. See also ibid., 151–56 (#24), 180–86 (#29), 313–20 (46); Jensen et al., eds., *Documentary History of Ratification* 1: 435–36, 3: 321–22, 401–02, 457, 508, 532, 4: 125, 265–67, 419.

36. Higginbotham, "The Federalized Militia Debate," 48; Helen E. Veit et al., eds., *Creating the Bill of Rights: The Documentary Record from the First Federal Congress* (Baltimore, MD, 1991), 12, 30, 38–39n, 182–85, 267.

37. William C. diGiacomantonio et al., eds., *Documentary History of the First Federal Congress, Volume XIV: Debates in the House of Representatives Third Session, December 1790–March 1791* (Baltimore, MD, 1996), 173; Higginbotham, "The Federalized Militia Debate," 48; Stuart Leibiger, "James Madison and Amendments to the Constitution, 1787–1789: 'Parchment Barriers,'" *Journal of Southern History* 59 (1993): 441–68.

38. Rakove, ed., *Declaring Rights,* 176–77.

39. Veit et al., eds., *Creating the Bill of Rights,* 182–84, 198–99; see also 4, 30, 37–41, 48, 247–48, 293. Roger Sherman's version of the Bill of Rights, which played a key role in the congressional debates, addresses only the militia, with no reference to a right to bear arms. Ibid., 266–68.

40. 1 Stat. 264 (2 May 1792); *Militia Laws,* 16; Michael A. Bellesiles, "Gun Laws in Early America: The Regulation of Firearms Ownership, 1607–1794," *Law and History Review* 16 (1998): 567–89.

41. Joel Barlow, *Advice to the Priveleged Orders of Europe* (London, 1792; reprint Ithaca, 1956), 45–46; John Taylor, *An Inquiry into the Principles and Policy of the Government of the United States* (Fredericksburg, VA, 1814), quoted in Cress, *Citizens in Arms,* 158; Walter Millis, *Arms and Men: A Study in American Military History* (New York, 1956), 38–39; Michael A. Bellesiles, "Suicide Pact: New Readings of the Second Amendment," *Constitutional Commentary* 16 (1999): 247–62.

42. R. Ernest and Trevor N. Dupuy, *The Encyclopedia of Military History from 3500 B.C. to the Present,* 2d ed. (New York, 1986), 725; Russell F. Weigley, *History of the United States Army* (New York, 1967), 82–94.

43. United States Congress, *American State Papers: Documents, Legislative and Executive, of the Congress of the United States,* class 2: *Indian Affairs,* 2 vols. (Washington, DC, 1832–34), 1: 92–93.

44. Ebenezer Denny, *Military Journal of Major Ebenezer Denny* (Philadelphia, 1860), 344.

45. Israel Chapin to Secretary of War Henry Knox, 29 April 1794, O'Reilly Papers 10: 19, New-York Historical Society.

46. Charles S. Sargent, ed., "Winthrop Sargent's Diary While with General Arthur St. Clair's Expedition Against the Indians," *Ohio Archeological and Historical Publications* 33 (1924): 258–65, quote 262; Arthur St. Clair, *A Narrative of the Manner in Which the Campaign against the Indians, in the Year 1791, Was Conducted* (Philadelphia, 1812), 199; Guthman, *March to Massacre,* 220–44.

47. Guthman, *March to Massacre,* 93; St. Clair, *A Narrative,* 11–13, 26–27, quote 26; Weigley, *History of the United States Army,* 90–92; Cress, *Citizens in Arms,* 170.

48. Gayle Thornbrough, *Outpost on the Wabash* (Indianapolis, 1957), 125, 155.

49. Brundage, "Organization, Administrations, and Training," 28; *Pennsylvania Magazine of History and Biography* 45 (1921): 370.

50. Lee to James Wood, 16 September 1794, Edward Carrington to Wood, 16 September 1794, Account against the United States for Arms, 19 September 1794, Thomas Mathews to Wood, 6 and 12 October 1794, William P. Palmer et al., eds., *Calendar of Virginia State Papers,* 11 vols. (Richmond, VA, 1875–93), 7: 316–19, 341–43; Martin K. Gordon, "The Militia of the District of Columbia, 1790–1815" (Ph.D. diss., George Washington University, 1975), 29–30, 33, 53–54; Cress, *Citizens in Arms,* 121–27; Thomas P. Slaughter, *The Whiskey Rebellion: Frontier Epilogue to the American Revolution* (New York, 1986), 192–204.

51. Slaughter, *The Whiskey Rebellion,* 205–06.

52. Frank A. Cassell, "Samuel Smith: Merchant Politician, 1792–1812" (Ph.D. diss., Northwestern University, 1968), 44–45; *Columbian Chronicle,* 23 January 1795; Gordon, "The Militia of the District of Columbia," 32; Richard H. Kohn, "The Washington Administration's Decision to Crush the Whiskey Rebellion," *Journal of American History* 59 (1972): 567–84; Weigley, *History of the United States Army,* 100–03; Slaughter, *The Whiskey Rebellion,* 206–21; Saul Cornell, "Aristocracy Assailed: The Ideology of Backcountry Anti-Federalism," *Journal of American History* 66 (1990): 1148–72.

53. Cress, *Citizens in Arms,* 128; Cornell, "Commonplace or Anachronism," 231–37, 242–46.

54. William Findley, *History of the Insurrection in the Four Western Counties of Pennsylvania* (Philadelphia, 1796), 165–68; Washington's Sixth Annual Message to Congress, 19 November 1794, Fitzpatrick, *Writings of Washington* 34: 3–6, 34–35; General Smith to the Maryland Troops, 15 November 1794, Samuel Hazard et al., eds., *Pennsylvania Archives* (Philadelphia, 1852–1935), 2nd ser., 4: 253–54; *Debates and Proceedings in the Congress* 4: 1067–71, 1214–20. Thomas Slaughter had noted "an attempt at the time, and largely successful for the last 190 years, to hide [the] reluctance of citizens to serve" in the militia putting down the Rebellion (*The Whiskey Rebellion,* 275).

55. West Point Waste Books, 1784–92, USMA Library West Point; Guthman, *March to Massacre,* 93.

56. DiGiacomantonio et al., eds., *Documentary History of the First Federal Congress, Volume XIV,* 56, 84, 93–94; see also 48–76, 102–32, 161–67.

57. 1 Stat. 381 (5 June 1794); *Debates and Proceedings in the Congress* 3: 343–48,

762–90; Richard H. Kohn, *Eagle and Sword: The Beginnings of the Military Establishment in America* (New York, 1975), 120–23, 145–48; Cress, *Citizens in Arms*, 130–34.

58. Friedrich W. L. G. A. Baron von Steuben, *A Letter on the Subject of an Established Militia* (New York, 1784), 7–8; Washington to Hamilton, 2 May 1783, Fitzpatrick, ed., *Writings of Washington* 26: 388–89; Henry Knox, *A Plan for the General Arrangement of the Militia of the United States* (Philadelphia, 1786); Cress, *Citizens in Arms*, 84–85, 90–92. Secretary of War James McHenry would use this artisan metaphor in 1800, arguing that a universal militia required universal training, which was as senseless as training everyone in all the essential crafts. Professionals, McHenry argued, existed for a reason. McHenry to the Speaker of the House, 5 January 1800, United States Congress, *American State Papers: Documents, Legislative and Executive, of the Congress of the United States,* class V: *Military Affairs,* 7 vols. (Washington, DC, 1832–61), 1: 133–35.

59. *American State Papers: Military Affairs* 1: 6–13; Knox to the Speaker of the House, 18 January 1790, *Debates and Proceedings in the Congress* 2: 2087–107. Knox's original plan was very complicated, but Washington simplified it for presentation to Congress in 1791. Weigley, *History of the United States Army,* 89–90; Cress, *Citizens in Arms,* 116–19.

60. Jensen et al., eds., *The Documentary History of the Ratification* 2: 509.

61. See George Mason's speech to the Virginia Convention, ibid. 10: 312; "Federal Farmer" [perhaps Melancton Smith], "An Old Whig" [perhaps Smilie], Herbert J. Storing, ed., *The Complete Anti-Federalist,* 7 vols. (Chicago, IL, 1981), 2: 224–27, 341–42, 3: 49; Edmund S. Morgan, *Inventing the People: The Rise of Popular Sovereignty in England and America* (New York, 1988), 173.

62. Bowling and Veit, eds., *The Diary of William Maclay,* 245; Weigley, *History of the United States Army,* 89–94; *Debates and Proceedings in the Congress* 2: 1804–26; Theodore J. Crackel, *Mr. Jefferson's Army: Political and Social Reform of the Military Establishment, 1801–1908* (New York, 1987), 162–64; Cress, *Citizens in Arms,* 119–21.

63. Otis in the House of Representatives, *Debates and Proceedings in the Congress* 10: 304–6; *American State Papers: Military Affairs* 1: 133–35, 142–44; Cress, *Citizens in Arms,* 136–49; Crackel, *Mr. Jefferson's Army,* 17–35.

64. James Roger Sharp, *American Politics in the Early Republic: The New Nation in Crisis* (New Haven, CT, 1993), 203; Adrienne Koch and Henry Ammon, "The Virginia and Kentucky Resolutions," *William and Mary Quarterly* 5 (1948): 163–65; Richard R. Beeman, *The Old Dominion and the New Nation, 1788–1801* (Lexington, KY, 1972), 202.

65. Sharp, *American Politics in the Early Republic,* 222, Lisle A. Rose, *Prologue to Democracy: The Federalists in the South, 1789–1800* (Lexington, 1968), 219–23.

66. Sharp, *American Politics in the Early Republic,* 252; quoting the *General Advertiser,* 11 December 1800.

67. Gordon, "The Militia of the District of Columbia," 38, 40; Stone to James McHenry, 29 May and 7 August 1797, Council to the Governor, 13 April 1797, John Henry to John Adams, 18 April 1798, Council Letterbooks; *The Times and District of Columbia Advertiser,* 15 November 1798. Secretary of War James McHenry wrote the chair of the House Committee on Defense that "Even in times of the greatest danger, we cannot give to our militia that degree of discipline . . . upon which a nation may safely hazard its fate." McHenry to Harrison G. Otis, 31 January 1800, *American State Papers: Military Affairs* 1: 142.

68. Gordon, "The Militia of the District of Columbia," 36–37.

69. Ibid., 58–59; *The Times and Alexandria Advertiser,* 18, 21, and 31 May 1798; Roger West to James Wood, 6 June 1798, Statement of Public Arms, 22 June 1799, Palmer et al., eds., *Calendar of Virginia State Papers* 8: 487–88, 9: 31–32.

70. Levi Lincoln Jr. et al., to the General Court, January 1804, Senate and House approval 23 and 28 January 1804, Records of the Worcester Light Infantry Company, 1804–61, Records of the Worcester County Regiment of Cavalry, 1786–90, Worcester Collection, American Antiquarian Society; George D. Moller, *Massachusetts Military Shoulder Arms, 1784–1877* (Lincoln, RI, 1988), 13–15.

71. Thomas Carpenter, comp., *The Two Trials of John Fries on an Indictment of Treason* (Philadelphia, 1800), 21, 75; Francis Wharton, ed., *State Trials of the United States* (Philadelphia, 1849), 545 (in general see 458–648); Sharp, *American Politics in the Early Republic,* 209–10; Peter Levine, "The Fries Rebellion: Social Violence and the Politics of the New Nation," *Pennsylvania History* 40 (1973): 241–58.

72. Hamilton to McHenry, 18 March 1799, Syrett and Cooke, eds., *Papers of Hamilton* 22: 552–53; Levine, "Fries Rebellion," 244–46, 249–50.

73. Sharp, *American Politics in the Early Republic,* 268; quoting Bleckley to A. Gallatin, 15 February 1801, Gallatin Papers, New-York Historical Society.

74. Sharp, *American Politics in the Early Republic,* 269.

75. Ibid., 270; Randolph to Monroe, 14 February 1801, Monroe Papers, Library of Congress (Washington, DC).

76. Sharp, *American Politics in the Early Republic,* 269; McKean to Jefferson, 19 March 1801 [a rewrite of a February letter], McKean papers, Historical Society of Pennsylvania.

77. Sharp, *American Politics in the Early Republic,* 209–10; Levine, "Fries Rebellion," 267–68; quoting *Washington Federalist,* 12 February 1801.

78. Gordon, "The Militia of the District of Columbia," 84.

79. James Richardson, comp., *A Compilation of the Messages and Papers of the Presidents,* 20 vols. (New York, 1897–1917), 1: 57.

80. Hamilton, "Final Version of the Report of Manufactures," 5 December 1791, Syrett and Cooke, eds., *The Papers of Alexander Hamilton* 10: 230, 291.

81. The remaining gunsmiths in New York were John Martin, "Gun and White Smith," who also made printer's type; David Provost of Long Island, who died in 1781; Hendrick Van Dewater, who died in 1785; James and John Youle, also a cutler, who worked at the fly market from 1787 to 1792. *New-York Journal,* 16 March 1775; *New York Packet,* 25 April 1782, 20 April 1787; *New York Daily Advertiser,* 24 April 1788, 12 May 1796; Rita S. Gottesman, comp., *The Arts and Crafts in New York, 1777–1799,* vol. 81 of *Collections of the New-York Historical Society* (New York, 1954), 222–24, 238–40, 304.

82. Gottesman, comp., *The Arts and Crafts in New York, 1777–1799,* 239; see also 67–68, 74, 132–34, 219–23.

83. Alfred C. Prime, comp., *The Arts and Crafts in Philadelphia, Maryland, and South Carolina, 1786–1800* (Philadelphia, 1932); *Pittsburgh Gazette,* 1 August 1789. It is remarkably difficult to determine how many gunmakers there were at any time in early America. Those who compile lists tend to include scores of artisans who cleaned and repaired guns without regard to the amount of time they were involved in those trades or the number of guns involved. McGunnigle appears on several of these lists. The lists also tend to be biased toward the mid-nineteenth century. A great number of apocryphal stories are repeated along the way. It is vital in this context to recall the distinctions among smith, gunsmith, and gunmaker. As James B.

Whisker, one of the most careful scholars of the subject, notes, "Gunsmiths remained scarce on the frontier, but in the cities the supply of these craftsmen outnumber the positions available." James B. Whisker, *The Gunsmith's Trade* (Lewiston, NY, 1992), 89. For such compilations, see Holman J. Swinney, *New York State Gunsmiths* (Cooperstown, NY, 1951); Robert E. Gardner, *Small Arms Makers: A Directory of Fabricators of Firearms, Edged Weapons, Crossbows and Polearms* (New York, 1962); Albert Lindert, *Gunsmiths of Indiana* (Homewood, IL, 1968); Donald Hutslar, *Gunsmiths of Ohio* (York, PA, 1973); Daniel D. Hartzler, *Arms Makers of Maryland* (York, PA, 1977); Curtis Johnson, *Illinois Gunsmiths* (York, PA, 1982); Frank Sellers, *American Gunsmiths* (Highland, NJ, 1983); James B. Whisker, *Arms Makers of Pennsylvania* (Selingsgrove, PA, 1990).

84. Hamilton, "Final Version of the Report of Manufactures," 5 December 1791, Syrett and Cooke, eds., *The Papers of Alexander Hamilton* 10: 317.

85. *Militia Laws,* 8–10, 13; *U.S. Statutes* 1: 271–74 (reenacted 2 February 1813, 2: 797); *Debates and Proceedings in the Congress* 3: 1392–95; Kohn, *Eagle and Sword,* 128–35. See also acts on the calling out of the militia, *U.S. Statutes* 1: 264 (2 May 1792), 424 (28 February 1795—repealed 1861), 2: 241 (3 March 1803), 383–84 (18 April 1806), 478–79 (30 March 1808), 705–07 (10 April 1812—reenacted 1814).

86. James E. Hicks, *Notes on United States Ordnance,* 2 vols. (Mount Vernon, NY, 1940), 1: 14; *Report of the Committee of Commerce and Manufactures, To Whom Were Referred the Petitions of the Manufacturers of Gun-Powder . . .* (Washington, DC, 1802).

87. Knox to the Senate, 16 December 1793, Washington to Congress, 21 January 1790, *American State Papers: Military Affairs* 1: 7–8, 44; Brundage, "Organization, Administrations, and Training," 53.

88. Pickney to the House, 30 November 1792, Moultrie to the House, 14 December 1792, Michael E. Stevens, ed., *Journals of the House of Representatives, 1792–1794* (Columbia, SC, 1988), 38–39, 182.

89. Ibid., 233, 285, 421–22, 440, 499–500.

90. Gordon, "Militia of the District of Columbia," 21–22; John K. Mahon, *The American Militia: Decade of Decision, 1789–1800* (Gainesville, FL, 1960), 14.

91. *American State Papers: Military Affairs* 1: 69–70.

92. Ibid. 1: 44; Raphael P. Thian, *Legislative History of the General Staff of the Army of the United States, 1775–1901* (Washington, DC, 1901), 569–72; Merritt Roe Smith, *Harpers Ferry Armory and the New Technology: The Challenge of Change* (Ithaca, NY, 1977).

93. Hicks, *Notes on United States Ordnance* 1: 14–18; Simeon N. D. North and Ralph H. North, *Simeon North, First Official Pistol Maker of the United States* (Concord, NH, 1913), 18–19; Moller, *Massachusetts Military Shoulder Arms,* 26–27; James A. Huston, *Logistics of Liberty: American Services of Supply in the Revolutionary War and After* (Newark, DE, 1991), 312–14. The United States purchased 6,040 muskets and 271 cannon from three British firms, receiving delivery in 1800, eight years after the initial congressional act to acquire muskets for the approaching emergency.

94. Secretary of War to the Senate, 12 December 1798, *American State Papers: Military Affairs* 1: 110; Felicia J. Deyrup *Arms Makers of the Connecticut Valley* (Northampton, MA, 1948), 37.

95. Merritt Roe Smith, "Eli Whitney and the American System of Manufacturing," in *Technology in America: A History of Individuals and Ideas,* ed. Carroll W. Pursell Jr. (Cambridge, MA, 1981), 46–47; Jeannette Mirsky and Allen Nevins, *The World of Eli Whitney* (New York, 1952), 128–37.

96. Mirsky and Nevins, *The World of Eli Whitney,* 137–46; Deyrup, *Arms Makers of the Connecticut Valley,* 21, 233; Thian, *Legislative History of the General Staff,* 573; Hicks, *Notes on United States Ordnance* 1: 20–22.

97. Deyrup, *Arms Makers of the Connecticut Valley,* 87–95.

98. Jefferson to Monroe, January 1801, quoted David A. Hounshell, *From the American System to Mass Production, 1800–1932: The Development of Manufacturing Technology in the United States* (Baltimore, MD, 1984), 31.

99. As Merritt Roe Smith points out, the equipment list for Whitney's Mill Rock armory indicates little movement toward mechanization. Smith, "Eli Whitney," 47–49.

100. Thaddeus M. Harris, comp., *The Minor Encyclopedia, or Cabinet of General Knowledge,* 4 vols. (Boston, 1803), 3: 118.

101. Robert S. Woodbury shattered that myth in 1960, and yet it continues to appear in many recent histories, such as M. L. Brown, *Firearms in Colonial America: The Impact on History and Technology, 1492–1792* (Washington, DC, 1980), 383–85; Huston, *Logistics of Liberty,* 300–05; *Webster's Biographical Dictionary*; Robert S. Woodbury, "The Legend of Eli Whitney and Interchangeable Parts," *Technology and Culture* 1 (1960): 235–53; Edwin A. Battison, "Eli Whitney and the Milling Machine," *Smithsonian Journal of History* 1 (1966): 9–34; Smith, *Harpers Ferry Armory,* chapters 7–8; Smith, "Eli Whitney," 49–65; Hounshell, *From the American System to Mass Production,* 28–32.

102. Smith, "Eli Whitney," 60. Smith writes of the 1842 muskets that it "was the first regular-issue weapon ever to be mass-produced with interchangeable parts and, as such, constitutes a milestone in the history of technology" (57).

103. Mirsky and Nevins, *The World of Eli Whitney,* 205–10; Smith, "Eli Whitney," 53.

104. Wadsworth to the Secretary of the Treasury, 24 December 1800, Eli Whitney Papers, Yale University Library (New Haven, CT); Mirsky and Nevins, *The World of Eli Whitney,* 210–12.

105. Deyrup, *Arms Makers of the Connecticut Valley,* 46; Stephen Vincent Benet, *A Collection of Annual Reports . . . Ordnance Department, 1812–1889,* 4 vols. (Washington, DC, 1890), 1: 26.

106. Hicks, *Notes on United States Ordnance* 1: 23–24, North and North, *Simeon North,* 40–47, 95–99.

107. *New York Evening Post,* 22 October 1804; Rita S. Gottesman, comp., *The Arts and Crafts in New York, 1800–1804,* vol. 82 of *Collections of the New-York Historical Society* (New York, 1965), 104–06, 154, 218–22, 237–39, 245, 401. The other gunsmiths were Joseph Finch, Robert McCormick, William McKee, and Thomas Smith.

108. Giles Cromwell, *The Virginia Manufactory of Arms* (Charlottesville, VA, 1975), 2–57.

109. The Lancaster gunmakers were Henry Dehulf, Jacon Dickert, Peter Gonter, John Graeff, Christopher Gumpp, Jacob and John Haeffer, Atram Henry, Benjamin Hutz, and Abraham Pieper. *Memorial of Sundry Gun Manufacturers of the Borough of Lancaster in the State of Pennsylvania* (Washington, DC, 1803).

110. Ibid., 3–5. On the Lancaster contracts, see Hicks, *Notes on United States Ordnance* 2: 88–103.

111. For instance, twelve Massachusetts gunmakers failed to fulfill their government contracts: Silas Allen of Shrewsbury; Asher Bartlett, Henry Osborne, and

Caswell & Dodge of Springfield; Thomas French, Adam Kinsley, and Rudolph & Charles S. Leonard of Canton; Rufus Perkins of Bridgewater; Alvin Pratt, Elijah and Asa Waters, and Luke Wood of Sutton; Lemuel Pomeroy of Pittsfield. Hicks, *Notes on United States Ordnance* 1: 42–43.

112. Mirsky and Nevins, *The World of Eli Whitney,* 212–16.

113. Smith, "Eli Whitney," 50–51.

114. Mirsky and Nevins, *The World of Eli Whitney,* 217–19.

115. Hicks, *Notes on United States Ordnance* 1: 25–26.

116. Deyrup, *Arms Makers of the Connecticut Valley,* 35–67.

117. Ibid., 37, 233; Smith, *Harpers Ferry,* 69.

118. *American State Papers: Military Affairs* 2: 429.

119. *U.S. Statutes* 2: 490; *Militia Laws,* 16–17.

120. Richardson, comp., *Compilation of the Messages of the Presidents* 1: 323; Crackel, *Mr. Jefferson's Army,* 36–53. Lawrence Delbert Cress makes a very good point that Jefferson, as "governor of Virginia during the Revolution . . . had learned well the inadequacies of militia soldiers during wartime. . . . Certainly Benedict Arnold had found Virginia's militia no deterrent to his campaign through the Piedmont early in 1781—a situation that had led Jefferson to ask the Virginia assembly to consider raising regular troops for the state's protection." *Citizens in Arms,* 151–52. Jefferson's rhetorical support for the militia is all the odder as a consequence.

121. 8–10 February 1803, *The Debates and Proceedings in the Congress of the United States,* 42 vols. (Washington, DC, 1834–56), 12: 489–507; see also ibid. 18: 1472–86, 1512–22, 1620–39, 1860–83, 1901–2064, 2850–52, 19: 946–69, 1192–1229, 20: 557–70, 21: 1471–79, 1497–1531, 1566–1604; Richardson, comp., *Messages and Papers of the Presidents* 1: 443, 454–55, 476, 486–87; Weigley, *History of the United States Army,* 104–05; Gordon, "The Militia of the District of Columbia," 97–98; Cress, *Citizens in Arms,* 150–71; Crackel, *Mr. Jefferson's Army,* 74–97.

122. Hugh Hastings, ed., *Public Papers of Daniel D. Tompkins,* 3 vols. (New York, 1898), 2: 11–12, 67–69; Brundage, "Organization, Administrations, and Training," 141–42.

123. *American State Papers: Military Affairs* 1: 162, 198–99, 215–17. Three years later a congressional committee estimated that there were 250,000 guns in America. Ibid. 1: 198.

124. Ibid. 1: 190.

125. *Debates and Proceedings in the Congress* 27: 1002–05, 1019–45, 2175–97.

126. *American State Papers: Military Affairs* 1: 255, 327–29, 337. Congress had made a similar offer in 1798, but was ignored. *U.S. Statutes* 1: 576.

127. Tench Coxe apparently rejected only one experienced gunsmith, because his shop was too small. Hicks, *Notes on United States Ordnance* 2: 24.

128. *American State Papers: Military Affairs* 1: 328, 335–37; Hicks, *Notes on United States Ordnance* 1: 32–35, 2: 20–25, 29, 35–36, 115–28; Benet, *A Collection of Annual Reports . . . Ordnance Department* 1: 113, 177; Deyrup, *Arms Makers of the Connecticut Valley,* 41–42. For individual contracts and delivery levels, see appendices.

129. United States Congress, *American State Papers: Documents, Legislative and Executive, of the Congress of the United States,* class III: *Finance,* 5 vols. (Washington, DC, 1832–59), 2: 687, 696.

130. Tallmadge to Huntington, 18 December 1809, Huntington to Tallmadge, 5 January 1810, *American State Papers: Military Affairs* 1: 263–66, quotes 264–65.

131. Maximillian Godefroy, *Military Reflections, on Four Modes of Defence, for the*

United States (Baltimore, MD, 1807), 22; Joseph Priestley, *Lectures on History, and General Policy* (Philadelphia, 1803); John Taylor, *An Inquiry; Annals of Congress,* 12th Congress, 2nd Session (House), 630.

132. David Humphreys, *Considerations on the Means of Improving the Militia for the Public Defence* (Hartford, CT, 1803), 16.

133. *American State Papers* 1: 266–27. See also *Annals of Congress,* 12th Congress, 2nd Session (House), 923–28.

134. Mirsky and Nevins, *The World of Eli Whitney,* 231–37; Hicks, *Notes on United States Ordnance* 2: 68–69; *American State Papers: Military Affairs* 1: 255; Moller, *Massachusetts Military Shoulder Arms,* 38, 57; Cromwell, *The Virginia Manufactory of Arms,* 72–75.

135. Whitney to Lee, 19 March 1818, SAR; Irvine to Perkins, 4 August 1814, Hicks, *Notes on United States Ordnance* 2: 67; Irvine to Whitney, 16 October 1813, Whitney Papers, Yale University Library; Huston, *Logistics of Liberty,* 307–08.

136. Whitney to Irvine, 11 and 25 November 1813, Whitney Papers, Yale University Library; Huston, *Logistics of Liberty,* 308–11.

137. Irvine to Whitney, 17 November 1813, Whitney Papers, Yale University Library; Mirsky and Nevins, *The World of Eli Whitney,* 244–53.

138. Huston, *Logistics of Liberty,* 311–12; Mirsky and Nevins, *The World of Eli Whitney,* 254–65.

139. Smith, "Eli Whitney," 59–61; North and North, *Simeon North,* 78–133.

140. Hicks, *Notes on United States Ordnance* 1: 45; North and North, *Simeon North,* 136–37.

141. Douglas R. Egerton, *Gabriel's Rebellion: The Virginia Slave Conspiracies of 1800 and 1802* (Chapel Hill, NC, 1993), 50–68.

142. Ibid., 58.

143. Ibid., 55 quotation from the trial papers.

144. Ibid., 55–56, 64–65.

145. Ibid., 72, 75–79; see the payroll accounts in Gabriel's Insurrection: Military Papers, Virginia State Library. The state spent a total of $5,431.90 on militia expenses in putting down Gabriel's plot. That included pay, rations, rum, extra guards for the county jails, and even extra candles. It does not, of course, include the much larger expense of compensating masters for executed slaves. Personal communication from Douglas Egerton.

146. Egerton, *Gabriel's Rebellion,* 76; William Wilkinson to James Monroe, 1 October 1800, Executive Papers, Negro Insurrection, Virginia State Library; *Norfolk Herald,* 2 October 1800, *Virginia Argus* (Richmond), 10 October 1800.

147. Egerton, *Gabriel's Rebellion,* 77; Callender to Jefferson, 13 or 18 September 1800, Jefferson Papers, Library of Congress; John Randolph to Joseph Nicholson, 26 September 1800, Nicholson Papers, Library of Congress.

148. Thomas Newton to Monroe, 29 December 1800, John Bracken to Monroe, 20 September 1800, Executive Papers, Negro Insurrection, Virginia State Library; Egerton, *Gabriel's Rebellion,* 75, 77.

149. Egerton, *Gabriel's Rebellion,* 133–34; Monroe to Richard Adams, 26 July 1802, Letterbook, Executive Papers, Virginia State Library.

150. Egerton, *Gabriel's Rebellion,* 173; Howard to William Preston, 25 October 1800, Preston Family Papers, Library of Congress.

151. Little to the Governor, 26 June 1793, Palmer et al., eds., *Calendar of Virginia State Papers* 6: 411; *Centinel of Liberty* 22 January and 6 August 1799; Gordon, "The Militia of the District of Columbia," 41–42, 50–51.

152. Emmons Clark, *History of the Seventh Regiment of New York, 1806–1889,* 2 vols. (New York, 1890), 1: 38–43, 47–49, 53.

153. Governor Mitchell to the Assembly, 4 August 1807, Public Archives Commission of Delaware, *Delaware Archives, Military Records,* 5 vols. (Wilmington, DE, 1911–19), 4: 155–56, 271–76, 307–09. Every volume of these records contains material on the unarmed condition of Delaware's citizens.

154. Claiborne to Madison, 23 January and 3 March 1802, Dunbar Rowland, ed., *Official Letter Books of W. C. C. Claiborne, 1801–1816,* 6 vols. (Jackson, MS, 1917), 1: 39, 54; *American State Papers: Military Affairs,* 1: 162. See also Rowland, ed., *Official Letter Books of W. C. C. Claiborne,* 1: 113, 152, 155, 182–83, 202, 237–38.

155. Claiborne to Col. Freeman, 25 October 1806, and speeches to the Assembly, 13 January 1807, 14 January 1809, and 29 January 1811, Rowland, ed., *Official Letter Books of W. C. C. Claiborne* 4: 32, 92, 297, 5: 124; see also 4: 73, 111, 302, 5: 189, 194–95, 216, 259–60, 6: 165–67, 174–75, 225–26.

156. 7th Congress, 2nd Session, "A Bill more effectually to provide for the Organization of the Militia of the District of Columbia" (1803); *Alexandria Gazette,* 24 December 1803; Gordon, "The Militia of the District of Columbia," 200–05. In 1813 Washington, DC, passed a similar ordinance, with exemption for military exercises. *Acts of the Corporation of Washington Passed by the Tenth Council* (Washington, DC, 1813), 41.

157. Gordon, "The Militia of the District of Columbia," 230–31; *National Intelligencer* (Washington, DC), 17, 19, 21, and 28 June, 8 and 15 July 1805; *Alexandria Gazette* 2, 3, 5, and 6 July 1805.

158. *National Intelligencer,* 7, 9, and 16 July 1806, 1, 3, 8, and 10 July 1807; *Alexandria Gazette,* 21 May 1807; Gordon, "The Militia of the District of Columbia," 238–40, 243, 247–48.

159. Brent to Jefferson, 23 July 1807, Jefferson to Smith, 30 July 1807, Jefferson Papers, Library of Congress; *National Intelligencer,* 17, 22, and 29 July, 14, 21, and 26 August, 2, 11, and 18 September 1807; *Alexandria Gazette,* 11 July 1807; Gordon, "The Militia of the District of Columbia," 249–50, 254.

160. *National Intelligencer,* 15, 20, 22, and 24 July, 7, 10, and 26 August 1807. With the passing of the 1808 war scare, the government retrieved many of its weapons, including those of Washington's 2d Legion just days before their muster. Ibid., 20 July, 17 August, 12 September, 19 and 21 October 1808; Gordon, "The Militia of the District of Columbia," 251–52, 266.

161. Gordon, "The Militia of the District of Columbia," 284; *National Intelligencer* 18 June, 21 September, 1, 17, and 29 October, 15 November, 18 and 25 December 1810; *Alexandria Gazette,* 8 August, 1 September, 26 October, 16 and 23 November 1810.

162. Harrison, "Militia Discipline," *National Intelligencer,* 21 September 1810 (continued in the 1 October issue).

163. *American State Papers: Military Affairs* 1: 303–04. The government also owned 4,655 pairs of pistols, 3,666 rampart arms, and 6,911 rifles.

164. Ibid. 1: 318.

165. Thomas C. Cochran, ed., *The New American State Papers: Manufactures,* 9 vols. (Wilmington, DE, 1972), 1: 157.

166. John R. Elting, *Amateurs, To Arms!: A Military History of the War of 1812* (New York, 1995), 2; Ernest and Dupuy, *Encyclopedia of Military History,* 756, 765; Crackel, *Mr. Jefferson's Army,* 98–125; C. Edward Skeen, *Citizen Soldiers in the War of 1812* (Lexington, KY, 1999), 1–3, 39–61.

167. *American State Papers: Military Affairs* 1: 491–92.

168. T. H. Palmer, ed., *The Historical Register of the United States,* 4 vols. (Washington, DC, 1814–16), 1: 59; *American State Papers: Military Affairs* 1: 323; Rowland, ed., *Official Letter Books of W. C. C. Claiborne* 6: 179–80, 218–19. Congress was also wrong about American self-sufficiency in gunpowder. The United States imported at least 472,475 pounds of gunpowder ("at least," as this total is the amount upon which duties were paid; more may have entered the country illegally). *American State Papers: Finance* 3: 55.

169. "Pennsylvania Militia," *Niles' Weekly Register,* 12 December 1812, 240; *American State Papers: Military Affairs* 1: 338; Lenoir quoted, Skeen, *Citizen Soldiers,* 52; *Annals of Congress,* 12th Cong., 1st Session (Senate), 283. See also *Niles' Weekly Register,* 27 June 1812, 274; 26 September 1812, 50; 24 October 1812, 115–16; 12 December 1812, 209–11; Skeen, *Citizen Soldiers,* 72–77.

170. Cress, *Citizens in Arms,* 152.

171. *American State Papers: Military Affairs* 1: 337; Gordon, "The Militia of the District of Columbia," 301–03; *Alexandria Gazette,* 17 and 19 June 1812; *National Intelligencer,* 14 and 19 May, 2, 13, and 20 June 1812; John Brannan, ed., *Official Letters of the Military and Naval Officers of the United States* (Washington, DC, 1823), 103, 109; Rowland, ed., *Official Letter Books of W. C. C. Claiborne* 6: 231–32. The War Department also loaned 250 muskets to Rhode Island, 650 to Delaware, and 3,500 to Ohio. *American State Papers: Military Affairs* 1: 329.

172. Edward D. Ingraham, *A Sketch of the Events Which Preceded the Capture of Washington* (Philadelphia, 1849), 44–45; Elting, *Amateurs, To Arms!* 198–243.

173. *American State Papers: Military Affairs* 1: 554, 563–64.

174. James Madison, militia report, 21 March 1810, ibid. 1: 258–62. See also the appendix on pages 445–54 of this volume.

175. Moller, *Massachusetts Military Shoulder Arms,* xi, 39–40, 49–50, 55; Report of 16 June 1813, Papers on the Defense of Boston and other places, 295, Massachusetts State Archives; *Annual Report of the Massachusetts Adjutant General for 1835* (Boston, 1836), 4–8; *Quartermaster General Letter Book* 1: 2, Account of Powder, Arms, Accoutrements, Standards & Music Delivered, Military Records, Massachusetts Military Division, National Guard Armory, Natick, MA.

176. Davis to Governor Caleb Strong, 6 October 1812, Moller, *Massachusetts Military Shoulder Arms,* 39; Return of Ordnance Stores, 1789–1824, Papers on the Defense of Boston and Other Places, Military Records, Massachusetts Military Division, National Guard Armory, Natick, MA.

177. "Records and Orderly Book of the Boston Rifle Corps, 1814," *Regiments and Armories of Massachusetts,* 2 vols. (c. 1900), 113–23, American Antiquarian Society.

178. Claiborne to Louisiana Senators, 10 June 1813, and to General Flournoy, 17 June 1813, Rowland, ed., *Official Letter Books of W. C. C. Claiborne* 6: 220–21, 226. The government supplied twenty-one hundred more muskets, bringing the total given to Louisiana to thirty-six hundred, but Secretary of War Armstrong insisted that no more would be forthcoming as "The State of the public arsenals will not justify so great a supply of arms to any one State." Nonetheless, Claiborne insisted that they needed sabers for their cavalry, which "is best adapted to the Climate of Louisiana." These guns took a long time to arrive, finally all reaching New Orleans after the war was over. Until then, Claiborne complained about his "unarmed, & undisciplined Militia." Ibid. 6: 231–32, 242–46, 268–70.

179. Van Renesselaer to Dearborn, to Tompkins, and to Fenwick, 1 and 15 September 1812, Solomon Van Renesselaer, *A Narrative of the Affair at Queenstown: In the*

War of 1812 (New York, 1836), Appendix: 37, 49, 53; Charles W. Elliot, *Winfield Scott: The Soldier and the Man* (New York, 1937), 69.

180. Elting, *Amateurs, To Arms!* 47; McClure to Armstrong, 25 December 1813, *American State Papers: Military Affairs* 1: 487; Elliot, *Winfield Scott,* 67. For more diasterous militia campaigns, see *Niles' Weekly Register,* 28 November and 26 December 1812, 204–05, 264–65; 22 May and 19 June 1813, 190, 261; 15 October 1814, 70; Robert B. McAfee, *History of the Late War in the Western Country* (Lexington, KY, 1816), 49–52, 72–75, 147–51. The most balanced account of the militia's performance during the War of 1812 can be found in Skeen, *Citizen Soldiers,* 77–125.

181. Brannan, ed., *Official Letters of the Military and Naval Officers,* 71–72, 77–78.

182. "Selections from the Gano Papers," *Quarterly Publication of the Historical and Philosophical Society of Ohio* 18 (1923): 5–36; Return J. Meigs Papers, Box 2, Folder 3, Ohio Historical Society; Weigley, *History of the United States Army,* 117–26, 131–32; Johnathan D. Hills, "Made Packhorses: A Study of the Differing Attitudes of the Ohio and New York Militias Towards the Regular Army in the War of 1812," Paper delivered at the British Association for American Studies Conference, Glasgow, 1999; Elting, *Amateurs, To Arms!* 61–64, 79–80, 136–55, 162–74, 269–81.

183. Cress, *Citizens in Arms,* 172–73; *American State Papers: Military Affairs* 1: 514–17; Skeen, *Citizen Soldiers,* 1–3.

184. Elting, *Amateurs, To Arms!* 48–49.

185. Jackson to Monroe, 9 January 1815, Palmer, ed., *The Historical Register of the United States* 4: 291; Elting, *Amateurs, To Arms!* 297–99.

186. Jackson to Monroe, 9 January 1815, Palmer, ed., *Historical Register of the United States* 4: 291.

187. John William Ward, *Andrew Jackson: Symbol for an Age* (New York, 1955), 17; Jackson to Monroe, 3 January 1815, A. Lacarriere Latour, *Historical Memoir of the War in West Florida and Louisiana in 1814–1815* (Philadelphia, 1816), 142; Claiborne to Monroe 25 October 1814 and 4 January 1815, Rowland, ed., *Official Letter Books of W. C. C. Claiborne* 6: 290, 330.

188. Elting, *Amateurs, To Arms!* 304–08; Ward, *Andrew Jackson,* 17–22.

189. *Kentucky Palladium,* 30 January 1815; Ward, *Andrew Jackson,* 21–22; Latour, *Historical Memoir,* clxxxii–v, 147–48. For other contemporary accounts, all reporting on the centrality of artillery in winning the Battle of New Orleans, see the *Liberty Hall* (Cincinnati), 4 February 1815; *National Intelligencer,* 7 and 27 February 1815; *Albany Argus,* 10 February 1815; *The Enquirer* (Richmond, VA), 22 February 1815; "A Contemporary Account of the Battle of New Orleans by a Soldier in the Ranks," *Louisiana Historical Quarterly* 9 (1926): 11–15.

190. On this mythology, see especially Ward, *Andrew Jackson,* 13–17, 22–45.

191. Ward, *Andrew Jackson,* 26; Alexander Walker, *The Life of Andrew Jackson, To Which is Added an Authentic Narrative* (New York, 1858), 158–59.

Chapter Eight

From Indifference to Disdain

1. Joseph Story, *Commentaries on the Constitution of the United States,* 2 vols. (Boston, 1851, orig. 1833), 2: 620–21.

2. Report of the House Committee on the Militia, 27 February 1827, House Report #92, 19th Congress, 2nd Session, 8; Leonard D. White, *The Jeffersonians: A Study in Administrative History, 1801–1829* (New York, 1951), 528–45.

3. There is not, to my knowledge, a study of these gun censuses based on the manuscript material in the National Archive. However, every volume of the *American State Papers: Documents, Legislative and Executive, of the Congress of the United States,* class V: *Military Affairs,* 7 vols. (Washington, DC, 1832–61) contains correspondence on gun censuses, not a single note of which is hostile to the intention of these enumerations.

4. These questions are particularly well considered from a critical perspective in J. A. Sharpe, *Crime in Early Modern England, 1550–1750* (London, 1984), 41–72; David Henige, *Numbers from Nowhere: The American Indian Contact Population Debate* (Norman, OK, 1998), 3–16.

5. See appendix. By comparison, the current figures, based on FBI estimates, would be enough firearms for 102.5 percent of the total population, 334.9 percent of the adult white male population, and 49,765.8 percent of the militia (the current National Guard, which has 512,400 members, or 0.2 percent of the population). Under Article 1, section 8 of the Constitution, only congressionally regulated militia can be the legal militia of the United States. Since the Dick Act of 1903, the National Guard, and only the National Guard, has held that status. Frederick Bernays Wiener, "The Militia Clause of the Constitution," *Harvard Law Review* 54 (December 1960): 181–219; *American State Papers: Military Affairs* 1: 162, 169–72, 258–62, 2: 319–23, 361–64, 4: 683–85; *Census for 1820* (Washington, DC, 1821); *Fifth Census; or Enumeration of the Inhabitants of the United States, 1830* (Washington, DC, 1832). In 1803 Tennessee, Delaware, and Maryland did not respond to Secretary of War Henry Dearborn's request for information. Population figures were based on the 1800 census, producing an understatement in percentages since the population had grown in the intervening three years. On the other hand, Dearborn's study would not have indicated those instances in which an individual owned several firearms, nor the arms of those avoiding the militia officers who conducted this survey (though there is no evidence of anyone doing so). The 1810 returns from Michigan, Louisiana, and Illinois Territories were incomplete and are therefore not included. By 1820 statistics were becoming significantly less reliable. The adjutant general noted that Delaware last made a return in 1814, Maryland in 1811, South Carolina in 1815, and Mississippi in 1812; Arkansas never returned, Alabama's return left out sixteen regiments, and the District of Columbia vanished. Most surveys were actually conducted in 1821. The 1820 census was used for population figures, leading to a slight understatement in percentages.

6. The Northeast is defined as the New England states plus New York, New Jersey, and Pennsylvania; the Southeast as Maryland, Delaware, the District of Columbia, Virginia, the Carolinas, and Georgia; the western states and territories in these years included Ohio, Indiana, Illinois, Michigan, Kentucky, Tennessee, Alabama, Mississippi, Louisiana, and Missouri. These national audits depended on the willingness and ability of the states to count accurately the number of firearms within their borders. With several states ignoring the whole procedure, the results cannot be considered entirely reliable.

7. See appendix. In 1813 the U.S. government shipments totaled 2,300 muskets to Massachusetts, another 2,835 in 1817 in two shipments, 2,091 in 1819, and 4,431 in 1824; the 1,260 rifles came in five shipments between 1829 and 1842. George D. Moller, *Massachusetts Military Shoulder Arms, 1784–1877* (Lincoln, RI, 1988), 47, 49, 51, 70; *Annual Report of the Massachusetts Adjutant General, 1835* (Boston, 1836), 4, 8; *Annual Report of the Massachusetts Adjutant General, 1841* (Boston, 1842), 2; *Annual Report of the Massachusetts Adjutant General, 1842* (Boston, 1843), 4.

8. "Pennsylvania Militia," *Niles' Weekly Register,* 12 December 1812, 240; "Militia System," *Army and Navy Chronicle* 6 (1838): 168; Census of Troops in Charleston, 1825, Capt. John Mathis to Governor Manning, 27 November 1826, Williams-Chestnut-Manning Families Papers, Caroliniana Collection, University of South Carolina, Columbia; Adjutant General to Governor Pierce M. Butler, 27 November 1837, Military Affairs Committee File, Legislative Group, South Carolina Department of Archives and History, Columbia.

9. *Annual Report of the Massachusetts Adjutant General, 1840,* 30, *Annual Report of the Massachusetts Adjutant General, 1849,* 32, *Quartermaster General's Letter Book* 3, 76, Commonwealth of Massachusetts Military Division, Military Records, National Guard Armory, Natick. See also Adjutant General to Governor Pierce M. Butler, 27 November 1837, Military Affairs Committee File, Legislative Group, South Carolina Department of Archives and History, Columbia; Frederick Townsend, "Annual Report of the Adjutant General of the State of New York, Transmitted to the Legislature March 20, 1857," Assembly Document #15 (Albany, 1857), 9; Doc. 36, *Documents Accompanying the Journal of the Senate of the State of Michigan, at the Annual Session of 1841,* 2 vols. (Detroit, 1841), 2: 83–86; *Annual Report of the Adjutant General of the State of Michigan for the Year of 1856* (Lansing, MI, 1857), 3–5, 21; *Annual Report of the Adjutant and Quarter Master General of the State of Michigan for the Year 1858* (Lansing, MI, 1859), 15–16.

10. G. W. Gooch to Commanding Officer, 3rd Regt., Orange, 20 September 1817, and to Regimental Commanders, 7 March 1818, sect. 58, Barbour Family Papers (Virginia Historical Society, Richmond), 919, 923. In 1807 the Pennsylvania legislature required each militia captain to appoint one person to care for arms supplied by the state. *An Act for the Regulation of the Militia of the Commonwealth of Pennsylvania* (Lancaster, PA, 1807), 31–32, 56, 59.

11. George Bomford to Lewis Cass, 19 January 1832, *American State Papers: Military Affairs* 4: 829.

12. Winfield Scott, *Infantry Tactics; or Rules for the Exercise and Manoeuvres of the Infantry of the U.S. Army,* 2 vols. (Washington, DC, 1825), 2: 209, 211–12. Reprinted every few years until 1862.

13. Lyle D. Brundage, "The Organization, Administrations, and Training of the United States Ordinary and Volunteer Militia, 1792–1861" (Ph.D. diss., University of Michigan, 1958), 160–62, 165; Doc. 36, *Documents Accompanying the Journal of the Senate of the State of Michigan, at the Annual Session of 1841,* 2 vols. (Detroit 1841), 2: 83–86; *Annual Report of the Adjutant General of the State of Michigan for the Year of 1856* (Lansing, MI, 1857), 3–5, 21; *Annual Report of the Adjutant General of Michigan for the Year 1858,* 15–16.

14. *American State Papers: Military Affairs* 1: 675; Report of the Committee on Militia, 22 January 1819 (Doc. 108), *House of Representatives Executive Documents* in *United States Congressional Serial Set* (microfiche, Library of Congress), 22: 3–7; *House of Representatives Journal,* 1st Sess., 15th Congress, 4: 128; Joseph J. Holmes, "The Decline of the Pennsylvania Militia, 1815–1870," *The Western Pennsylvania Historical Magazine* 57 (1974): 207; William P. Clarke, *Official History of the Militia and National Guard of the State of Pennsylvania,* 2 vols. (Philadelphia, 1909–12), 2: 30–31.

15. *Army and Navy Chronicle* 6 (1838): 263–64; U.S. Congress, Senate, "Report of the Secretary of War," 30 November 1839, *Senate Journal, Congressional Serial Set* 354, 26 Congress, 1st Session, 1839, 44. See also *American State Papers: Military Affairs* 1: 318; Thomas H. McKee, comp., *Reports of the Committee on the Militia, House of Representatives* (Washington, DC, 1887), Report 584, 26th Congress, 1st session. Calls

for reform came from the states as well. See, for instance, H. A. S. Dearborn, "Annual Report of the Adjutant General for 1839," Commonwealth of Massachusetts Military Division, Military Records.

16. Alice Hanson Jones, *American Colonial Wealth: Documents and Methods,* 3 vols. (New York, 1977), I: 13–24, III: 1847–59; Gloria L. Main, "Probate Records as a Source for Early American History," *William and Mary Quarterly* 32 (1975): 89–99; Daniel S. Smith, "Underregistration and Bias in Probate Records: An Analysis of Data from Eighteenth-Century Hingham, Massachusetts," *William and Mary Quarterly* 32 (1975): 100–10; Lois Green Carr and Lorena S. Walsh, "Inventories and the Analysis of Wealth and Consumption Patterns in St. Mary's County, Maryland, 1658–1777," *Historical Methods* 13 (1980): 81–104; Peter Benes, ed., *Early American Probate Inventories* (Boston, 1989); Carole Shammas, *The Pre-Industrial Consumer in England and America* (Oxford, 1990), 18–46, 95–112.

17. No differentiation is made between functioning and dysfunctional firearms in these figures. See appendix. Forty counties have been divided into four regional groups. Frontier counties moved into other categories with each new time period. Several of the counties examined changed their name over time; for easier identification, the modern names are used. Counties included: Bennington, Rutland, Windham, and Windsor, Vermont; Luzerne, Northampton, Philadelphia, Washington, and Westmoreland, Pennsylvania; Litchfield and New Haven, Connecticut; Essex, Hampshire, Plymouth, Suffolk, and Worcester, Massachusetts; Burlington, New Jersey; Kent, Delaware; Anne Arundel and Queen Anne, Maryland; Fairfax, Spotsylvania, Chesterfield, Charlotte, Halifax, Mecklenburg, Brunswick, and Southampton, Virginia; Orange and Halifax, North Carolina; Charleston, South Carolina; Baldwin, Chatham, and Glynn, Georgia; Jefferson and Knox, Indiana; Adams and Washington, Ohio; San Francisco and Los Angeles, California.

18. James E. Hicks, *Notes on United States Ordnance,* 2 vols. (Mount Vernon, NY, 1940), vol. 1.

19. Giles Cromwell, *The Virginia Manufactory of Arms* (Charlottesville, VA, 1975), 148–52; *American State Papers: Military Affairs* 1: 773; Hicks, *Notes on United States Ordnance* 1: 49.

20. Hicks, *Notes on United States Ordnance* 2: 73–85; Jeannette Mirsky and Allen Nevins, *The World of Eli Whitney* (New York, 1952), 274–76; Felicia J. Deyrup, *Arms Makers of the Connecticut Valley* (Northampton, MA, 1948), 56–65.

21. United States Government, *Digest of Accounts of Manufacturing Establishments in United States, and of Their Manufactures* (Washington, DC, 1823); see appendix.

22. *Niagara Journal,* 1 July 1817, 4, 6 March 1819, 3; *Buffalo Emporium,* 14 May 1825, 3; Robert W. Bingham, *Early Buffalo Gunsmiths* (Buffalo, NY, 1934), 13–18. See, for instance, the account books of Emerson Bixby, Barre, Massachusetts, blacksmith, 1824–55; Jonathan Haight, rural New York, blacksmith, 1771–89; Elihu Burritt, Worcester, Massachusetts, blacksmith, 1839; Janes & Shumway, West Sutton, Massachusetts, blacksmiths, 1833–35—all at the American Antiquarian Society.

23. See, for instance, James B. Whisker, *Arms Makers of Colonial America* (Selingsgrove, PA, 1992), 17–19; Moller, *Massachusetts Military Arms,* 35–56; Solomon Van Renesselaer, *A Narrative of the Affair at Queenstown: In the War of 1812* (New York, 1836), appendix: 36–53; George C. Bittle, "In the Defense of Florida: The Organized Florida Militia from 1821 to 1920" (Ph.D. diss., Florida State University, 1965), 213–14.

24. James Richardson, comp., *A Compilation of the Messages and Papers of the Presidents,* 20 vols. (New York, 1897–1917), 1: 468, 553; John M. Dederer, *War in America to 1775: Before Yankee Doodle* (New York, 1990), 214. Contemporaries made this same observation. "A Militia-Man" appealed "to the experience of other nations as well as our own" to demonstrate the uselessness of the militia. And "if a particular instance is required, we will point to the ruins of our capitol." *National Intelligencer,* 3 March 1815. For more comments on the lessons of the militia's performance in the War of 1812 see ibid., 24 and 28 February and 1 April 1815.

25. Quoted Michael S. Fitzgerald, "Rejecting Calhoun's Expansible Army Plan: The Army Reduction Act of 1821," *War in History* 3 (1996): 161; Russell F. Weigley, *History of the United States Army* (New York, 1967), 133–43; C. Edward Skeen, *Citizen Soldiers in the War of 1812* (Lexington, KY, 1999), 175–84. Jackson's clear abuse of authority in using that standing army to invade Florida, and the successful acquisition of Florida through negotiation in 1821, convinced Congress to cut back the army to the prewar maximum of sixty-two hundred men with the Army Reduction Act of March 2, 1821. Over the next fifteen years, Congress generally supported the slow growth and greater professionalization of the army. Fitzgerald, "Rejecting Calhoun's Expansible Army Plan," 163–177; Weigley, *History of the United States Army,* 144–72.

26. Calhoun to the House of Representatives, 27 February 1815, 2 January 1816, to Speaker, 11 December 1818 and 12 December 1820, Robert L. Merriwether and W. Edwin Hemphill, eds., *The Papers of John C. Calhoun,* 5 vols. (Columbia, SC, 1959–71), 1: 277–78, 287–90, 3: 374–78, 5: 480–90; Lawrence Delbert Cress, *Citizens in Arms: The Army and the Militia in American Society to the War of 1812* (Chapel Hill, NC, 1982), 173–77.

27. House Committee report on Militia Reform, 17 January 1817, and Calhoun's military reduction plans, 12 December 1820 and 7 November 1822, *American State Papers: Military Affairs* 1: 633–35, 2: 189–94, 450–51; Richardson, comp., *Compilation of the Messages of the Presidents* 2: 7–8, 15–16, 45–46, 61–62, 78; Carleton B. Smith, "Congressional Attitudes towards Military Preparedness during the Monroe Administration," *Military Affairs* 40 (1976): 22–26.

28. Quoted Henry Lee, *The Militia of the United States. What It Has Been. What It Should Be* (Boston, 1864), 57.

29. See reports of Calhoun, 1821, Crawford, 1822 and 1823, select committee, 1822, *American State Paper: Military Affairs* 2: 314, 329, 389, 527.

30. Ibid. 2: 315–18, 332, 391–92, 527–28; White, *The Jeffersonians,* 536–39, quote 539.

31. One aspect of militia service rarely mentioned then or now is that it was exceedingly boring. A careful recapitulation of the duties of the New York City militia on active duty during the War of 1812 indicates that they spent the war digging and drilling. Emmons Clark, the 7th Regiment's official historian, felt that this dullness explained the loss of enthusiasm for military activities after the war's end. Emmons Clark, *History of the Seventh Regiment of New York, 1806–1889,* 2 vols. (New York, 1890), 1: 60–85.

32. *Mercantile Advertiser,* 29 August 1814; Alexis de Tocqueville, *Democracy in America,* 2 vols., trans. Henry Reeve and Francis Bowen (New York, 1963), 1: 191–98. Volunteer companies had problems getting members to turn out for musters as well. The elite 7th Regiment of New York had 66.6 percent of its members appear for their 1823 muster, 64.5 percent the following year, and 58.3 percent in 1826. Clark, *History of the Seventh Regiment* 1: 99, 111, 144.

33. Stewart L. Gates, "Disorder and Social Organization: The Militia in Connecticut Public Life, 1660–1860" (Ph.D. diss., University of Connecticut, 1975), 159–65; Records of the Military Department: Militia, Connecticut State Library, Hartford. An added twist, but one difficult to prove, to these volunteer companies was that they were occasionally used to avoid militia service. Those who joined volunteer military companies did not have to report for the annual musters of the town companies. Some volunteer companies were formed solely to avoid service, and sometimes picked up extra money by selling memberships to those seeking a legal avoidance of militia duty. Kenneth O. McCreedy, "Palladium of Liberty: The American Militia System, 1815–1861" (Ph.D. diss., University of California, Berkeley, 1991), 40–46.

34. Clark, *History of the Seventh Regiment* 1: 136–37, 149–51.

35. Ibid. 1: 102, 133, 286. On the tavern as headquarters, see ibid. 1: 108–28, 147–48, 169–72, 205, 212–13, 253. On the uniform debate, see ibid. 1: 96–107, 125, 128, 131–33, 169–70, 175–76, 200–01, 225, 229–35, 240–41, 245, 259–60, 271–72, 285–87, 295–96, 354, 363–64, 367–68, 387–88, 403. Members usually purchased their guns at Moore's on Broadway. These guns were fowling pieces "small, with small flint-lock, light stocks, the stocks varying in style, some being very crooked and some almost straight, and generally very badly balanced and quite unsuited for purposes of uniform military drill." Ibid. 1: 176.

36. *Militia Laws of the United States and Massachusetts* (Boston, 1836), viii–ix, 33–37; Jerome B. Lucke, *History of the New Haven Grays* (New Haven, CT, 1876), 29–30; D. A. Winslow, "The Old Vermont June Training," *The Vermonter* 6 (1901): 250; J. Trasker Plumer, "The Old Times Muster," *Manchester Historical Association Collections* 3 (1902–03): 176; Regimental Orders, 22 June 1816, 75th Regiment, New York State Infantry, 1815–20, New-York Historical Society; John L. Sibley, *History of the Town of Union* (Boston, 1851), 350–86; E. G. Austin, "Memorandum of the Boston Light Infantry from its Foundation in 1798 to 1838," collections of the Massachusetts Historical Society, Boston; Dutcher, "June Training in Vermont," *Vermont Historical Gazetteer* 2 (1871): 347–51.

37. Charles K. Gardner, *Compend of the United States System of Infantry Exercise and Maneuvers* (New York, 1819), 247; Oxford, Massachusetts, Militia Muster Records, Local Records (American Antiquarian Society); Regimental Orders, 75th Regiment, New York State Infantry, 1815–20, 22 June 1816, New-York Historical Society, New York; Minutes of the Charleston Washington Light Infantry, 21 April 1841, Caroliniana Collection, University of South Carolina; *American State Papers,* class V: *Military Affairs* 1: 20–21, 26, 2: 314–19, 329–37, 389–95, 527–29; Gayle Thornbrough, *Outpost on the Wabash* (Indianapolis, IN, 1957), 125, 155; Arthur St. Clair, *A Narrative of the Manner in Which the Campaign against the Indians, in the Year 1791, Was Conducted* (Philadelphia, 1812), 199; William Guthman, *March to Massacre: A History of the First Seven Years of the United States Army, 1784–1791* (New York, 1975), 93, 105–06; Ebenezer Denny, *Military Journal of Major Ebenezer Denny* (Philadelphia, 1860), 344. Members of the New Haven Grays fired four shots once a year. Lucke, *New Haven Grays,* 15–17, 26, 29–31, 44, 47, 107.

38. Emmons Clark, *History of the Second Company, Seventh Regiment, New York State Militia* (New York, 1864), 62. Only about half the members attended these target practices, and far fewer actually participated. Clark, *History of the Seventh Regiment* 1: 176.

39. *Commercial Advertiser,* 8 August 1825; Clark, *History of the Seventh Regiment*

1: 120–21, 143. The Worcester County Regiment of Cavalry, organized in 1786, held its first target shooting in 1837. Record of the Worcester County Regiment of Cavalry, 1786–90, Worcester, MA, Collection, American Antiquarian Society.

40. William Zierdt, "Narrative History of the 109th Field Artillery," *Wyoming Historical and Genealogical Society* 22 (1938): 67; Lucke, *History of the New Haven Grays,* 30–31, 50–51. By 1833, with the target back at one hundred feet, one-third of the company was hitting the target, ibid., 79–80. H. Telfer Mook noted that militiamen "were not marksmen, for they could not be. For two reasons, the poorness of their guns and the lack of practice." Mook, "Training Day in New England," *New England Quarterly* 11 (1938): 696. Likewise, Allen French wrote that "the opportunity for practice was lacking for sheer absence of powder." French, *The Day of Concord and Lexington: The Nineteenth of April, 1775* (Boston, 1925), 255–56.

41. Edmund S. Morgan, *American Freedom, American Slavery: The Ordeal of Colonial Virginia* (New York, 1975), 239–40, 377–79; Bertram Wyatt-Brown, *Southern Honor: Ethics and Behavior in the Old South* (New York, 1982), 357–60; John Hope Franklin, *The Militant South, 1800–1861* (Cambridge, MA, 1956), 14–62.

42. Fred Anderson, *A People's Army: Massachusetts Soldiers and Society in the Seven Years' War* (Chapel Hill, NC, 1984), 75–76; Anthony Marro, "Vermont's Local Militia Units, 1815–1860," *Vermont History* 40 (Winter 1972): 28, 31; *American Turf Register and Sporting Magazine* 1 (1829–30): 338–39, 359; *Western Monthly Magazine* 3 (1835): 65–66; *Brother Jonathan* 6 (1843): 43.

43. Records of the Uxbridge Grenadier Company, 1818–1831, Uxbridge, MA, Local Records, American Antiquarian Society.

44. Barbour to President Adams, 28 November 1826, *American State Papers, Military Affairs* 3: 331; Martin K. Gordon, "The Militia of the District of Columbia, 1790–1815" (Ph.D. diss., George Washington University, 1975), 121; Thomas Cooper and David J. McCord, eds., *The Statutes at Large of South Carolina,* 14 vols. (Columbia, SC, 1836–73), 8: 2650. On the popularity and masculine image of fire companies, see Amy S. Greenberg, *Cause for Alarm: The Volunteer Fire Department in the Nineteenth-Century City* (Princeton, NJ, 1998), 12–79. The exemption of federal workers upheld in *Ex parte William S. Smith* (2 Cranch 693 [1826]), in which the circuit court ruled that clerks in the executive and judicial branches were federal officers as defined in section two of the Militia Act of 1792 and therefore not subject to militia duty.

45. The adjutant general of Delaware wrote in 1820 that removing militia fines terminated the militia. "The consequences naturally flowing from that law have been a total neglect of every appearance of military duty; for, in removing the obligation to muster, on the part of the private, every incentive having a tendency to urge the officer to the performance of his duty ceases to exist." He doubted that the militia would revive "until Congress shall interpose their strong arm in support of the militia . . . and by their fostering care preserve from annihilation those pillars of our national safety." W. Kennedy to General Daniel Parker, 22 December 1820, *American State Papers, Military Affairs* 2: 320. Maryland was the next state to follow suit.

46. McCreedy, "Palladium of Liberty," 185–87; J. Thomas Scharf, *History of Delaware, 1609–1888,* 2 vols. (Philadelphia, 1888), 1: 816–17; Emory Upton, *The Military Policy of the United States* (Washington, DC, 1912), 228. For similar patterns in other states, see McCreedy, "Palladium of Liberty," 187; Everett Stackpole, *History of New Hampshire* (New York, 1916), 93, 159; Marro, "Vermont's Local Militia," 29–39; Military Reports and Recommendations, 1830–1831, and Militia Reports and

Recommendations, 1834 (microfilm, reel 64), Commonwealth of Massachusetts Military Division, Military Records; An Act supplemental to an act to organize the Militia, 15 January 1831, and An Act supplemental to the several acts to organize the Militia, 14 January 1833, *Laws of a Public and General Nature of the State of Missouri, 1824–1836,* 2 vols. (Jefferson City, MO, 1842), 2: 237–39, 320–22.

47. Sumner, Adjutant General's Report of 1834, 39; C. M. and Alexander Hyde, eds., *Lee: The Centennial Celebration* (Springfield, MA, 1878), 166; A. C. Niven to General Burt, 11 July 1843, Clemons Papers, Box 2, Cornell University; J. P. Bradley to Adjutant General H. K. Oliver, 24 November 1846, Militia Reports and Recommendations, 1846, Military Records, Reel 64, Massachusetts Adjutant General's Office. In general, see the excellent studies by Steven C. Bullock, *Revolutionary Brotherhood: Freemasonry and the Transformation of the American Social Order, 1730–1840* (Chapel Hill, NC, 1996); Greenberg, *Cause for Alarm;* Mark Pitcavage, "An Equitable Burden: The Decline of the State Militias" (Ph.D. diss., Ohio State University, 1995).

48. Edward B. Bourne, *The History of Wells and Kennebunk* (Portland, 1875), 698; Maud Burr Morris, "William A. Bradley, Eleventh Mayor of the Corporation of Washington," *Records of the Columbia Historical Society* 25 (1923): 130–33; Pennsylvania House of Representatives, *Report of the Committee on the Militia System* (Harrisburg, PA, 1833), 3–4; Frederic P. Wells, *History of Newbury, Vermont,* (St. Johnsbury, VT, 1902), 289–90; Marro, "Vermont's Local Militia," 32; *Principles of the Non-Resistance Society* (Boston, 1839); New England Non-Resistance Society, *National Organizations* (Boston, 1839); William Little, *The History of Weare, New Hampshire, 1735–1888* (Lowell, 1888), 383; William H. Kilby, ed., *Eastport and Passamaquoddy: A Collection of Historical and Biographical Sketches* (Eastport, ME, 1888), 472; Valerie H. Ziegler, *The Advocates of Peace in Antebellum America* (Bloomington, IN, 1992), 18–47. As the legislature of New York put it in an 1832 petition to Congress arguing that the country no longer needed a universal militia: "The sources of danger are diminished, and are more remote. . . . Our population is comparatively dense and powerful." *American State Papers, Military Affairs* 5: 240.

49. Quoted in Mook, "Training Day in New England," 694. See also Report of Samuel Power, Adjutant General of Pennsylvania, *Hazard's Register of Pennsylvania* 7 (1831): 189; Edward R. Foreman, ed., *Centennial History of Rochester, New York,* 2 vols. (Rochester, NY, 1932), 1: 177; Lena London, "The Militia Fine, 1830–1860," *Military Affairs* 15 (1951): 133–44.

50. *Brother Jonathan* 6 (1843): 186; T. L. Hagood to William C. Bouck, 15 December 1843, Box 3, William C. Bouck Papers, Department of Archives and Manuscripts, Cornell University, Ithaca, NY; London, "The Militia Fine," 142; *Ten Dialogues on the Effects of Ardent Spirits* (n.p., c. 1826), 6–7. A favorite phrase for the militia seems to have been "a promiscuous assemblage"; e.g., Adjutant General A. C. Nevin, "Report of the Adjutant General for 1843," New York Senate Doc. 5, 4 January 1844, American Antiquarian Society.

51. Everett Dick, *The Dixie Frontier* (New York, 1948), 268–69; Charles Edward Banks, *History of York, Maine,* 2 vols. (Boston, 1935), 2: 218; Raymond W. Albright, *Two Centuries of Reading, Pennsylvania, 1748–1948* (Reading, PA, 1948), 153; *Eclaireur* 2 (March/April 1855): 116; Poinsett, "Report of the Secretary of War," 30 November 1839, *Senate Journal* in *U.S. Serial Set* 354: 44. For more examples, see Warren Brown, *History of the Town of Hampton Falls, New Hampshire* (Manchester, NH, 1900), 261; David Duncan Wallace, *The History of South Carolina,* 4 vols. (New York, 1934), 3: 148; Henry Bushnell, *The History of Granville, Licking County, Ohio*

(Columbus, OH, 1889), 162; Ernest C. Hynds, *Antebellum Athens and Clarke County* (Athens, GA, 1974), 39; John B. Armstrong, "General Simon Goodell Griffin's Account of Nelson and the New Hampshire Militia," *Historical New Hampshire* 21 (1966): 43; Wingfield, *Franklin County, Virginia,* 20; Maud Carter Clement, *The History of Pittsylvania County, Virginia* (Lynchburg, VA, 1929), 215; David Turpie, "The Pioneer Militia," *Indiana History Bulletin* 38 (1961): 48.

52. A. T. Andreas, *History of Cook County, Illinois* (Chicago, 1884), 206–07; *Report of the Adjutant General and Acting Quartermaster General Accompanying the Annual Returns of the Militia of Massachusetts,* Senate Doc. 27 (1834), 91, Commonwealth of Massachusetts Military Division, Military Records; Joseph J. Holmes, "The Decline of the Pennsylvania Militia, 1815–1870," *The Western Pennsylvania Historical Magazine* 57 (1974): 208; Beverly Daniel, *Report of the Adjutant General of North Carolina for the Year 1827,* Legislative Doc. #9, Raleigh, NC, 1828, 4. See also Charles W. Burpee and Charles F. Chapin, "Military Life Since the Revolution," in Joseph Anderson, ed., *The Town and City of Waterbury, Connecticut,* 3 vols. (New Haven, CT, 1896), 3: 1186; Randall Parrish, *Historic Illinois: The Romance of the Earlier Days* (Chicago, 1905), 368; Oxford, Massachusetts, Militia Muster Records, Local Records; *American State Papers, Military Affairs* 2: 320; *Statute Laws of Connecticut, 1835,* 410–11; *The Public Statute Laws of the State of Connecticut . . . 1838* (Hartford, CT, 1838), 35; *Public Acts, Passed by the General Assembly of the State of Connecticut in the Years 1839, 1840, 1841, 1842, and 1843* (Hartford, CT, 1845), 157–58; State of Connecticut, *Public Acts, 1846* (New Haven, CT, 1846), 29; Gates, "Disorder and Social Organization," 147–49; Sibley, *History of the Town of Union,* 350–86; Howard F. Dyson, ed., *History of Schuyler County* (Chicago, IL, 1908), 725; Morris, "William A. Bradley," 130–33; Frederic Kidder, *History of New Ipswich* (Boston, 1852), 247.

53. David Crockett, *A Narrative of the Life of David Crockett of the State of Tennessee* (Lincoln, NE, 1987), 72–75. Vermont passed an antiburlesque law in 1834, Maine in 1838, Rhode Island in 1840, and Louisiana in 1850. David Turpie, "The Pioneer Militia," *Indiana History Bulletin* 38 (1961): 48; Richard W. Musgrove, *History of the Town of Bristol, Grafton County, New Hampshire,* 2 vols. (Bristol, NH, 1904), 1: 187; French, *The Day of Concord,* 17; Cooper and McCord, eds., *The Statutes at Large* 8: 2650, 11: 2856; Skeen, *Citizen Soldiers,* 182. For more burlesques, see Marro, "Vermont's Local Militia Units," 36; Gates, "Disorder and Social Organization," 142, 147; Charles W. Burpee, *The Military History of Waterbury* (New Haven, CT, 1891), 31; Elizabeth J. Varney, "Panorama of Rochester," *Rochester Historical Society* 8 (1929): 222; *Statute Laws of Connecticut, 1835* (Hartford, CT, 1835), 410–11; McCreedy, "Palladium of Liberty," 129–44; Alexander Davidson and Bernard Stuve, *A Complete History of Illinois from 1673 to 1873* (Springfield, IL, 1874), 362; Holmes, "The Decline of the Pennsylvania Militia," 209.

54. William H. Sumner, "An Inquiry into the Importance of the Militia to a Free Commonwealth," *North American Review* 19 (1824): 279–80; *Niles' National Register* 58 (22 August, 1840): 397–99; London, "The Militia Fine, 1830–1860," 140–41. See also John R. Commons et al., eds., *A Documentary History of American Industrial Society,* 11 vols. (Cleveland, OH, 1910–11), 1: 29, 119, 161; ibid. 5: 114, 119–20, 157, 160–61; "A Poor Man's Son," *Remarks on the Militia System* (New York, 1831).

55. A theme Ray repeated, Messages to the General Assembly, 4 December 1827, 8 December 1829, 6 December 1831, Dorothy Riker and Gayle Thornbrough, eds., *Messages and Papers Relating to the Administration of James Brown Ray, Governor of Indiana, 1825–31* (Indianapolis, IN, 1954), 290–92, 464–67 (quote), 684–85, Message

to the General Assembly 3 December 1834, Riker and Thornbrough, eds., *Messages and Papers Relating to the Administration of Noah Noble, Governor of Indiana, 1831–1837* (Indianapolis, IN, 1958), 340, see also 57–58, 64; Dorothy Riker, ed., *Messages and Papers Relating to the Administration of David Wallace, Governor of Indiana, 1837–1840* (Indianapolis, IN, 1963), 185–87; *A History of the National Guard of Indiana* (Indianapolis, IN, 1901), 69–78. See similar complaints from New Hampshire's governor Samuel Dinsmoor, and the adjutants general of Connecticut and New York. Stackpole, *History of New Hampshire,* 93, 150, 159; Joseph D. William, *Annual Report of the Adjutant General of the State of Connecticut for the Year 1856* (Hartford, CT, 1857), 3; A. C. Niven, "Report of the Adjutant General [of NY] for 1843," Senate Doc. #5, 4 January 1844, 4; McCreedy, "Palladium of Liberty," 187–89.

56. *American State Papers, Military Affairs* 3: 690; Marro, "Vermont's Local Militia Units," 35; *The Citizen Soldier,* 12 February 1841. In 1825 Governor James B. Ray felt that Indiana had never received its fair share of federal arms because of poor militia returns. He decided to remedy this shortfall by expanding the official returns from 20,322 to 40,000. The federal government ignored his creative math. Ray to Secretary of War James Barbour, 20 November 1826, Message to General Assembly, 8 December 1826, Dorothy Riker and Gayle Thornbrough, eds., *Messages and Papers Relating to the Administration of James Brown Ray* (Indianapolis, 1954), 152, 189; Ray to Secretary of War James Barbour, 28 November 1826, *House of Representatives Documents,* 19th Congress, 2: 205, 335.

57. Petition of South Carolina, 11 January 1830, and Committee Reports, *American State Papers: Military Affairs* 4: 219–20, 769–800; An Act further to alter . . . the Militia laws, Cooper and McCord, eds., *The Statutes at Large* 8: 2560. On May 29, 1813, Governor Alston informed General Pickney that "the military equipments of the State are too inconsiderable to be relied on." *American State Papers: Military Affairs* 4: 224, see also 226–31.

58. On militia legislation, see Cooper and McCord, eds., *The Statutes at Large* 8: 1916 (1815), 2220 (1819), 2318 (1823), 2341 (1824), 2560 (1832), 2612 (1833), 2650 (1835), 11: 2815 (1840), 2856 (1841), 2997 (1846). On opposition to militia, see Memorial to the Legislature, . . . from Officers of the 12th Regt., 1840, Petition from the Citizens of Lexington District, n.d., Military Affairs Committee Files, Legislative Group, South Carolina Department of Archives and History, Columbia, SC.

59. Quoted, McCreedy, "Palladium of Liberty," 341.

60. An Act supplemental to an act . . . to organize . . . the Militia, 15 January 1831, *Laws of a Public and General Nature . . . of the State of Missouri, 1824–1836,* 2 vols. (Jefferson City, MO, 1842), 2: 237–39.

61. Henry W. Edwards, *Message from His Excellency Henry W. Edwards, . . . May 1835* (Hartford, CT, 1835), 9–10; John S. Peters, *The Annual Message of His Excellency John S. Peters* (New Haven, CT, 1832), 10–11; *Report of the Joint Standing Committee on the Militia* (Hartford, CT, 1835), 3; *Statute Laws of Connecticut, 1835* (Hartford, CT, 1835), 5–7; *The Public Statute Laws of the State of Connecticut . . . 1836 [and] 1837* (Hartford, CT, 1837), 57; State of Connecticut, *Public Acts, 1845* (Hartford, CT, 1845), 37; State of Connecticut, *Public Acts, 1846* (New Haven, CT, 1846), 55–58; State of Connecticut, *Public Acts, 1847* (Hartford, CT, 1847), 39–41, 49, 52, 57; Chauncey F. Cleveland, *Message from His Excellency Chauncey F. Cleveland, . . . May Session, 1843* (Hartford, CT, 1843), 10; *Public Acts, Passed by the General Assembly of the State of Connecticut in the Years 1839, 1840, 1841, 1842, and 1843* (Hartford, CT, 1845), 157; Gates, "Disorder and Social Organization," 144–46, 151, 186–89, 194–204 (fireworks on 204).

62. *Militia Laws,* iii, viii–x; Avery to Sumner, 23 June 1834, Military Reports and Recommendations, 1830–31, Militia Reports and Recommendations, 1834, Military Records, Reel 64, Massachusetts Adjutant General's Office.

63. Adjutant General Veverense to Connecticut's Adjutant General E. W. N. Starr, 21 July 1850, Records of the Military Department: Militia, Box 101, Connecticut State Library, Hartford; *Niles' National Register* 70 (6 June 1846): 213; Joseph J. Holmes, "The Decline of the Pennsylvania Militia," 210–11; Marro, "Vermont's Local Militia Units," 36; Paul Tincher Smith, "Militia of the United States from 1846 to 1860," *Indiana Magazine of History* 15 (1919): 44–47; Johnson "The Militia Fine," 142; Federal Writers Project, *Military History of Kentucky* (Frankfort, KY, 1939), 145–46.

64. *Pensacola Gazette,* 22 September 1826; Rodman to Barbour, 11 July 1826, Duval to Barbour, 29 August 1826, Clarence E. Carter, ed., *The Territorial Papers of the United States,* 26 vols. (Washington, DC, 1934–62), 23: 604–05, 635–36; Bittle, "In the Defense of Florida," 20–31.

65. Clarence E. Carter, ed., *Territorial Papers of the United States,* 26 vols. (Washington, DC, 1934–62), 22: 721–22, 744, 23: 629, 684–85, 713, 24: 284; *Niles' Weekly Register,* 13 January 1827, 312, 369; John P. Duval, comp., *Compilation of the Public Acts of the Legislative Council of the Territory of Florida* (Tallahassee, FL, 1839), 394–95; *American State Papers: Military Affairs* 2: 152, 249, 502; Bittle, "In the Defense of Florida," 32–44. In the 1840s the legislature changed its tack, increasing the percentage that local officers earned from militia fines to 50 percent. But no one dared enforce these fines. Ibid., 169, 177.

66. Bittle, "In the Defense of Florida," 27–28.

67. *Houston v. Moore* 5 Wheat. 1–37 (US 1820); *Martin v. Mott* 12 Wheat. 19–39 (US 1827).

68. *American State Papers: Military Affairs* 2: 671–72; White, *The Jeffersonians,* 532–33; *Army and Navy Chronicle* 6 (1838): 205–07. William Henry Harrison's committee on the militia said much the same thing in its report of 9 January 1818. The committee did not "approve of putting public arms into the hands of the militia, when not necessary. That mode would expose the arms to be lost and destroyed." Instead, the government should establish arsenals, "from which the militia of every part of the United States could draw arms when necessary." *American State Papers: Military Affairs* 1: 675. In 1836 the Connecticut legislature ordered the distribution of arms to the militia, requiring that they "shall be used for no other purposes, excepting in cases of insurrection, rebellion and invasion, and shall be kept in some suitable and convenient place in such town, and in good order for immediate use." *The Public Statute Laws of the State of Connecticut . . . 1836 [and] 1837* (Hartford, CT, 1837), 54–57; Lucke, *History of the New Haven Grays,* 25.

69. *Army and Navy Chronicle* 6 (1838): 205–07. Congress authorized the construction of ten new arsenals between 1813 and 1819: in 1813 and 1814 at Rome, New York; West Troy (the Watervliet), New York; and Pittsburgh, 1814; five in 1816 at Richmond, Virginia; Pikesville, Maryland; Washington, D.C.; Watertown, Pennsylvania; and Philadelphia; one in 1817 at Augusta, Georgia; and one at Baton Rouge 1819. Congress again considered a third armory in the West, but nothing came of it. James A. Huston, *Logistics of Liberty: American Services of Supply in the Revolutionary War and After* (Newark, DE, 1991), 313; *American State Papers: Military Affairs* 1: 773.

70. Report of Henry Storms to Gov. William H. Seward, 29 March 1842, Box 1, William C. Bouck Papers, Department of Archives and Manuscripts, Cornell University.

71. Guignard to J. L. Wilson, 23 November 1824, Williams-Chestnut-Manning Family Papers, South Caroliana Library, University of South Carolina; William C. Kibbe, *Annual Report of the Adjutant General for the Year 1861* (Sacramento, CA, 1861), 171.

72. *American State Papers: Military Affairs* 4: 302.

73. Report of the House Committee on Militia, 4 February 1829, ibid. 4: 87. The committee was inspired by the recommendations of General Edmund P. Gaines, 2 December 1826, ibid. 4: 134–40.

74. Barbour to Adams, 28 November 1826, ibid. 3: 331.

75. Barbour's circular letter to the states, 11 July 1826, ibid. 3: 394. The responses can be found in ibid. 3: 395–488; and "Report of the Board of Officers Relative to the Militia," 28 November 1826, *House of Representatives Executive Documents* 2: 269–506.

76. Harwood to Gov. Joseph Kent, 1 August 1826, Harvie to Barbour, 7 August 1826, Coles to Barbour, 8 September 1826, Murphy to Barbour, 29 August 1826, Cadwalader to Barbour, 14 August 1826, *American State Papers: Military Affairs* 3: 395, 400, 416, 429, 431.

77. Watmough to Cadwalader, 31 July 1826, Williams to Cadwalader, 16 August 1826, "Amicus Patriae" [of Kentucky] to Barbour, 7 October 1826, ibid. 3: 432, 435, 455.

78. Peyton to Barbour, 5 August 1826, ibid. 3: 396. According to the sources here, volunteers constituted 5 percent in North Carolina, 10 percent of the militia in Georgia, 5 percent in Mississippi, 9 percent in Louisiana, 8.3 percent in Illinois, 10 percent Indiana, 25 percent in Maine, 20 percent in Pennsylvania, 7.7 percent in New York, and between 25 percent and 33 percent in Massachusetts, ibid. 3: 404, 413–14, 416–17, 426, 430, 453, 468. General John M. McCalla of Kentucky made a telling observation when he noted that about one-third of his state's militia was in the volunteer corps, but then they had so few total that it was one-third of a small number. Ibid. 3: 418.

79. Cocke to Col. Bernard Peyton, 7 August 1826, Kibbe to Oliver Wolcott, 31 October 1826, Johnson to Barbour, 10 October 1826, Wallace to Barbour, 8 August 1826, ibid. 3: 397, 410, 415–16, 421.

80. Daniel to Barbour, 9 August 1826, Sewall to Barbour, 17 August 1826, Appleton to W. H. Sumner, 10 October 1826, ibid. 3: 404–03, 422, 428, 477.

81. Browne to Cadwalader, 14 August 1826, Sill to Barbour, 16 August 1826, ibid. 3: 445–46, 453.

82. McCalla to Barbour, 18 September 1826, ibid. 3: 418.

83. "Amicus Patriae" [of Kentucky] to Barbour, 7 October 1826, ibid. 3: 457–58.

84. Wolcott to Barbour, 30 November 1826, Huntington to Barbour, 30 November 1826, *American State Papers: Military Affairs* 3: 407–9.

85. Elmer to Barbour, 14 August 1826, Swift to Barbour, 6 September 1826, ibid. 3: 437–38, 452.

86. O'Fallon to Barbour, 1 October 1826, ibid. 3: 418–19.

87. O'Neall to Richard J. Manning, 3 November 1826, Ray to Barbour, 20 November 1826, Anon. to Barbour, 1826, ibid. 3: 404–5, 417, 467.

88. Pickering to W. H. Sumner, 10 September 1826, Rufus Amory to Barbour, 8 October 1826, ibid. 3: 471, 475.

89. John H. Hall to Barbour, 28 October 1826, ibid. 3: 448–49.

90. Barbour to Congress and Report of the Board of Officers, 28 November 1826, Report of the House Committee on the Militia, 27 February 1827, ibid. 3:

330–92, 597–602; John K. Mahon, "A Board of Officers Considers the Condition of the Militia in 1826," *Military Affairs* 15 (1951): 85–94.

91. Report of the Secretary of War, 30 November 1839, *Senate Journals* in *Congressional Serial Set* 354: 44–45; *Army and Navy Chronicle* 6 (1838): 263–64; *American State Papers: Military Affairs* 4: 806–07, 935, 5: 6, 238–41, 518, quotes 238, 241.

92. *New York Herald,* 25 September 1840.

93. Triplett and Keim, "Militia," 6 June 1840, in Thomas H. McKee, comp., *Reports of the Committee on the Militia, House of Representatives* (Washington, DC, 1887), 584.

94. *American State Papers: Military Affairs* 2: 671, 4: 266–69, 300–01.

95. There were a few journals published in the late 1830s and early 1840s supportive of the militia. Most of these vanished after a few issues. As Anthony Marro described one of these, *The Citizen Soldier,* it was "a short-lived pro-militia newspaper" that "ceased publication for want of subscribers" in 1841. Marro, "Vermont's Local Militia Units," 36. See also the *Army and Navy Chronicle.*

96. Petition of the officers of the Massachusetts militia, 23 February 1831, Convention of Militia Officers of Pennsylvania, 6 February 1832, *American State Papers, Military Affairs* 4: 701–05, 856–65; Resolutions of the Legislature of New York, 10 April 1833 (Doc. 14), *Senate Documents* in *Congressional Serial Set* 283: 414; Memorial of the Officers of the 7th Brigade, 17 February 1834, *House of Representatives Journals* in *Congressional Serial Set* 253: 338.

97. Henry I. Tragle, ed., *The Southampton Slave Revolt of 1831: A Compilation of Source Material* (Amherst, MA, 1971), 43, 255; Marvin E. Gettleman, *The Dorr Rebellion: A Study in American Radicalism: 1833–1849* (New York, 1973), 107–38.

98. Philip St. George Cooke, *Scenes and Adventures in the Army* (Philadelphia, 1857), 223; Williams to Lewis Cass, 27 May 1832, and to Stevens T. Mason, 31 May 1832, C. M. Burton, ed., "The Black Hawk War: Papers of Gen. John R. Williams," *Collections and Researches Made by the Michigan Pioneer and Historical Society* 31 (1901): 388–90, 397–98; Brundage, "Organization, Administrations, and Training," 135, 144; John Hauberg, "The Black Hawk War, 1831–1832," *Transactions of the Illinois Historical Society* 39 (1932): 90–134.

99. Call to Cass, 3 April 1832, Duval to Cass, May 1832, Hernandez to the Secretary of War, 27 November 1835, Carter, ed., *Territorial Papers* 24: 686–87, 706–07, 25: 198–99.

100. *Jacksonville Courier,* 10 and 24 December 1835; Weigley, *History of the United States Army,* 160–61; Bittle, "In the Defense of Florida," 58–61; Frank Laumer, *Massacre!* (Gainesville, FL, 1968), 135–56. It is not completely clear where the Indians got their guns, though some contemporaries reported that the Seminoles carried small-bore Spanish guns acquired from Cuba. Many observers commented on what terrible shots were the Seminole, who apparently had little experience with firearms. John K. Mahon, *History of the Second Seminole War, 1835–1842* (Gainesville, FL, 1967), 120–21.

101. Myer M. Cohen, *Notices of Florida and the Campaigns* (Charleston, SC, 1836), 88–89; *Jacksonville Courier,* 10 December 1835, 11 February 1836; *Pensacola Gazette,* 23 January 1836; *Florida Herald* (St. Augustine), 14 March 1839; "Reminiscences of the Life of James Ormond of Atlanta, GA," Yonge Library, Gainesville; *Niles' Weekly Register,* 2 July 1836, 309–10; Bittle, "In the Defense of Florida," 62–64, 87–94, 125–26; Mahon, *History of the Second Seminole War,* 110–13, 135–42, 268–70. On militia arriving without arms, *American State Papers: Military Affairs* 7: 108–10, 115–16, 180–83, 202–05, 224–25, 231, 254, 326–29, 337.

102. *American State Papers: Military Affairs* 7: 171–72, 184–85, 326. Major Edmund Kirby, paymaster of the army, reported that he "mustered into the service of the United States forty-five companies of the Georgia troops. . . . They were generally entirely destitute of arms and accoutrements. The few arms they had were generally unfit for service." Ibid. 7: 169.

103. Carter, ed., *Territorial Papers* 25: 299, 303. U.S. Congress, *Senate Document 278*, 26th Congress, 1st Session, 126, 179; *Key West Inquirer,* 3 February 1836; Bittle, "In the Defense of Florida," 124, 152–57, 180–82.

104. *Florida Herald* (St. Augustine), 25 August 1837. That same year the Wisconsin house and senate requested three thousand stands of arms from the federal government in order to arm its militia for an upcoming Indian war. *American State Papers, Military Affairs* 6: 1003.

105. General Orders, 5 March 1836; Capt. E. Harding to General Scott, 14 June 1836, Scott to Jesup, 10 June 1836, *American State Papers, Military Affairs* 7: 204, 248, 321, 326. Scott's evaluation of the situation was supported by Major Kirby, ibid. 7: 326. Georgia's Governor William Schley admitted to an official army court of inquiry looking into the failure of this campaign, that his troops were under-armed and expected to be armed by the federal authorities. The court's opinion in favor of General Scott stated that Scott "took the earliest measures to provide arms, munitions, and provisions for his [volunteer] forces, who were found almost wholly destitute." Ibid. 7: 176, 179; in general see 7: 365–465.

106. Bittle, "In the Defense of Florida," 166–67.

107. Ibid., 178–79, 194–204; U.S. Congress, *House Executive Document 2,* 32nd Congress, 1st Session, 452; *Florida House Journal, 1854,* appendix: 42–43; *Florida House Journal, 1852,* appendix: 122–23.

108. *Report of U.S. Army Ordnance Office,* 28 October 1851, *Congressional Serial Set* 611, Department of War (Washington, DC, 1851), 452. The seven uninterested states were New Jersey, Delaware, Maryland, Georgia, Mississippi, Tennessee, and Indiana. On the difficulties of adjutants general attempting to reach accurate returns, or any returns at all, see Richard Harwood, *Report of the Adjutant General to the Executive of Maryland* (Annapolis, MD, 1833), 3; John E. Schwarz, *Annual Report of the Adjutant General and Quarter Master General [of Michigan] for the Year 1849* (Lansing, MI, 1850), 12.

109. "Report of Commissioners and the Adjutant General to codify and amend [the Militia Laws], April 1, 1853," Senate Doc. 66, New-York Historical Society.

110. See for example, *Annual Report of the Adjutant General of Michigan for the Year 1858,* 15–16; G. W. Gooch to Commanding Officer, 3rd Regt., Orange, 20 September 1817, Gooch to Regimental Commanders, 7 March 1818, Barbour Family Papers, Sect. 58: 919, 923, Virginia Historical Society; Gordon, "The Militia of the District of Columbia," 301–03; Ebenezer Stone, *Annual Report of the Adjutant General of the Commonwealth of Massachusetts for the Year Ending Dec. 31, 1852* (Boston, 1853), 31; *Florida Senate Journal* (Tallahassee, FL, 1859), appendix: 7–8; Frederick Townsend, *Annual Report of the Adjutant General of the State of New York* (Albany, NY, 1857), 9; "Report of Committee on Volunteer Companies," 18 September 1856, "Petition of Volunteer Companies of St. Philip's and St. Michael's" [1849], Military Affairs Committee Files, Legislative Group, South Carolina Department of Archives and History, Columbia, SC; George Bomford to Lewis Cass, 19 January 1832, *American State Papers: Military Affairs* 4: 829.

111. Don Higginbotham, *War and Society in Revolutionary America: The Wider Dimensions of Conflict* (Columbia, SC, 1988), 106–31; Donald R. Hickey, *The War of*

1812: A Forgotten Conflict (Chicago, 1989), 33–34, 221–23; McCreedy, "Palladium of Liberty"; Pitcavage, "An Equitable Burden"; Harry L. Coles, *The War of 1812* (Chicago, 1965), 265; Upton, *Military Policy,* 91–106.

112. Jacob Abbott, *Marco Paul's Adventures in Pursuit of Knowledge* (Boston, 1843), 104–05.

113. Ibid., 108, 110–12.

114. Ibid., 114–16.

115. Henry C. Wright, *A Kiss for a Blow: or, a Collection of Stories for Children* (Boston, 1842), 119–21, see also 114–18.

116. Sylvester Judd, *A Moral Review of the Revolutionary War, or Some of the Evils of the Event Considered* (Hallowell, ME, 1842). See also *The Non-Resistant,* 2 March 1839, 25 May and 8 and 29 June 1842; *Advocate of Peace,* August and September 1842; Henry David Thoreau, "On Civil Disobedience," in *The Writings of Henry David Thoreau,* 10 vols. (Boston, 1893), 10: 131–70; Ziegler, *The Advocates of Peace,* 48–115; London, "The Militia Fine," 135–36.

117. Joseph Alden, *The Old Revolutionary Soldier* (New York, 1849), 95, 116, 129, 133. See David Grossman, *On Killing: The Psychological Cost of Learning to Kill in War and Society* (Boston, 1995).

118. Alden, *The Old Revolutionary Soldier,* 55–58, 86–88, 95, 119–20, 123.

119. Ibid., 60, 62, 67–68. See also Increase N. Tarbox, *Winnie and Walter's Evening Talks with Their Father About Old Times* (Boston, 1861); Anon., *Evils of the Revolutionary War* (Boston, 1846); *Parley's Magazine* 3 (1835): 17, 81; Wright, *A Kiss for a Blow,* 112–14; *Western Monthly Magazine* 2 (1834): 268.

120. Johnson Jones Hooper, "Adventures of Captain Simon Suggs," 15; Augustus Baldwin Longstreet, "The Militia Company Drill," 1, Michael A. Bellesiles, ed., *BiblioBase* (Boston, 1998), 15; from *Adventures of Captain Simon Suggs, Late of the Tallapoosa Volunteers* (n.p., 1845), 65–103; Augustus Baldwin Longstreet, *Georgia Scenes, Characters, Incidents, &c., in the First Half Century of the Republic* (New York, 1840), 145–51.

121. The magazine printed an incorrect figure of 163 companies not mustering. *The Non-Resistant,* 16 February 1839; Charles W. Hall, *Regiments and Armories of Massachusetts,* 2 vols. (Boston, 1899), 1: 120. See also *The Non-Resistant,* 21 September, 16 November, and 21 December 1839, and 2 (1840): 11, 18, 49 (they began sequential numbering with vol. 2).

122. *Herald of Freedom,* quoted in *The Non-Resistant,* 21 December 1839; *Journal of Commerce,* 16 November 1839; *Christian Watchman,* 21 December 1839.

123. *Principles of the Non-Resistance Society* (Boston, 1839), 5–6, 8. See also *National Organizations* (Boston, 1839), 5, 32, which states that the people of the United States "stand before heaven and earth as an organized and practised band of oppressors, robbers, pirates, and murderers." This group was a little more violent in declaring that "the arm of violence must be broken."

124. Ohio legislature to Congress, 7 April 1834, *American State Papers, Military Affairs* 5: 307; Resolution of Representative Davy Crockett, 25 February 1830, *Gale's and Seaton's Debates in Congress* (Washington, DC, 1830), 583; J. Thomas Fleming, *West Point: The Men and the Times of the United States Military Academy* (New York, 1969), 110–13.

125. Henry J. Bogue, "The Hunter—A Fragment," *The Ladies' Garland* 5 (October 1841): 101; B. Blanque, "Border Bullets; Or, Reports from the Rifle of an Old Frontier Man," *Holden's Dollar Magazine* 2 (November 1848): 667; Wahopekah, "Deer Hunting by Lamp Light," *The Ariel* 5 (3 March 1832): 363.

126. Laura McCall, "Armed and 'More or Less Dangerous': Women and Violence in American Frontier Literature, 1820–1860," in Michael A. Bellesiles, ed., *Lethal Imagination: Violence and Brutality in American History* (New York, 1999), 171–83. This theme will be developed further in the following chapter.

127. *Army and Navy Chronicle*. Collections of printing type from this period reinforce this point. For instance, Elihu White, *Specimen of Printing Types, and Ornaments, From the Letter-Foundry of E. White* (New York, 1829) contains portrait of soldiers, all without guns and carrying swords in plates 9, 12, 25, 137, 159, 228, 237. Plate 25 contains a whole troop, none with guns, all with swords. See also plates 48, 49, 51, 119, 137, 203, and 235. When guns are pictured, as in plates 33, 34, and 58, they are pictured simply as long sticks, with no attention to the detail of the gun. It is also notable that in these three prints, guns are held by soldiers at attention, whereas those with swords are mostly in motion. The only other print (out of 250) with a gun is the one exception: plate 97 is a military scene with artillery in the foreground and a group of marching soldiers with rifles in background. See also J. Howe & Co., *Specimen of Printing Types, and Ornaments, From the Letter-Foundry of J. Howe, & Co.* (Philadelphia, 1830), plates 265, 269, 300, 302, 313, 324, 417, 418, 428; Boston Type Foundry, *Specimen of Modern Printing Types and Stereotype Cuts* (Boston, 1826), plates 34, 37, 53, 58, 60, 63–69, 84, 126, 130, 161–63, 264, 271, 283, 333, 335, 344; Isaiah Thomas, *A Specimen of Isaiah Thomas's Printing Types* (Worcester, MA, 1787); Russell and Cutler, *A Specimen of Printing-Types, and Ornaments, Attached to the Office of Russell & Cutler* (Boston, 1806); Thomas Day, *The Forsaken Infant; or Entertaining History of Little Jack* (Philadelphia, 1813); illustrations facing 32, 36, 39; *Parley's Magazine* 3 (1835): 341; *Western Miscellany* 1 (1849): 213, 330; *The Ariel* 3 (1829): 49, 121. See also Robert W. Johannsen, *To the Halls of the Montezumas: The Mexican War in the American Imagination* (New York, 1985), 40–41.

Chapter Nine

Creation of a Gun Subculture

1. *American Turf Register and Sporting Magazine* 2 (1830): 180.

2. Frederick Jackson Turner, "The Significance of the Frontier in American History" (1893), in Michael A. Bellesiles, ed., *BiblioBase* (Boston, 1999), 3, 13.

3. Many of these quotations are from memoirs published much later in the nineteenth century. Three such books often used are William C. Smith, *Indiana Miscellany* (Cincinnati, OH, 1867); Sandford C. Cox, *Recollections of the Early Settlement of the Wabash Valley* (Freeport, NY, 1970); Charles H. Haswell, *Reminiscences of New York by an Octogenarian* (New York, 1896), all of which offer exciting portraits of violent societies in which everyone went around armed.

4. This technique of using travel accounts to get at the exceptional qualities of American life was developed by Arthur M. Schlesinger in "What Then Is the American, This New Man?" *American Historical Review* 48 (1943): 225–44. Ray Allen Billington, *America's Frontier Heritage* (New York, 1966) used a similar approach to answer the question "The Frontier: Cradle of Barbarism or Civilization?" He comes down on the latter side (p. 69).

5. The travel accounts examined were Franklin G. Adams, *The Homestead Guide* (Waterville, KA, 1873); Agnes Stewart, "The Journey to Oregon—A Pioneer Girl's Diary," ed. Claire Warner Churchill, *Oregon Histocial Quarterly* 29 (1928): 77–98; Christopher C. Andrews, *Minessota and Dacotah: In Letters Descriptive of a*

Tour Through the North-west, in the Autumn of 1856 (Washington, DC, 1857); Thomas Ashe, *Travels in America, Performed in 1806 for the Purpose of Exploring the Rivers Alleghany, Monongahela, Ohio, and Mississippi,* 3 vols. (London, 1808); Caleb Atwater, *Remarks Made on a Tour to Prairie du Chien: Thence to Washington City, in 1829.* (Columbus, OH, 1831); John J. Audubon, *Delineations of American Scenery and Character* (New York, 1926, orig. 1839); William A. Baillie-Grohman, *Camps in the Rockies* (New York, 1882); Francis Baily, *Journal of a Tour in the Unsettled Parts of North America in 1796 and 1797* (London, 1856); Robert Baird, *View of the Valley of the Mississippi, or the Emigrant's and Traveller's Guide to the West,* 2d ed. (Philadelphia, 1834); Karl Bernhard, *Travels Through North America During the Years 1825 and 1826,* 2 vols. (Philadelphia, 1828); William N. Blane, *An Excursion through the United States and Canada, during the Years 1822–3* (London, 1824); John D. Borthwick, *Three Years in California, 1851–1854* (Edinburgh, 1857); Samuel Bowles, *Across the Continent: A Summer's Journey to the Rocky Mountains, the Mormons, and the Pacific States, with Speaker Colfax* (Springfield, MA, 1866); John Bradbury, *Travels in the Interior of America in the years 1809, 1810, and 1811,* in Reuben Gold Thwaites, ed., *Early Western Travels, 1748–1846,* 32 vols. (Cleveland, OH, 1904–1907, orig. 1819), vol. 4; Joe Cowell, *Thirty Years Passed among the Players in England and America: Interspersed with Anecdotes and Reminiscences of a Variety of Persons* (New York, 1844); Fortescue Cuming, *Sketches of a Tour to the Western Country through the States of Ohio and Kentucky,* ed. Reuben Gold Thwaites (Cleveland, OH, 1904, orig. 1810); Charles G. B. Daubney, *Journal of a Tour Through the United States* (Oxford, 1843); Charles Dickens, *American Notes for General Circulation,* 2 vols. (London 1842); Theodore C. Blegen, trans. and ed., *Frontier Parsonage: The Letters of Olaus Frederik Duus, Norwegian Pastor in Wisconsin, 1855–1858* (Northfield, MN, 1947); George W. Featherstonhaugh, *Excursion through the Slave States, from Washington on the Potomac, to the Frontier of Mexico* (New York, 1844), and *A Canoe Voyage up the Minnay Sotor,* 2 vols. (London, 1847); James B. Finley, *Autobiography of Rev. James B. Finley: or, Pioneer Life in the West* (Cincinnati, OH, 1853); James Flint, *Letters from America* (Edinburgh, 1822); Timothy Flint, *Recollections of the Last Ten Years, Passed in Occasional Residences and Journeyings in the Valley of the Mississippi* (Boston, 1826); Friedrich Gerstacker, *Wild Sports in the Far West: The Narrative of a German Wanderer beyond the Mississippi, 1837–1843* (Durham, NC, 1968); Thomas H. Gladstone, *The Englishman in Kansas; or, Squatter Life and Border Warfare* (Lincoln, NE, 1971, orig. 1857); Marie Fontenay de Grandfort, *The New World,* trans. E. C. Wharton (New Orleans, LA, 1855); D. Griffiths Jr., *Two Years' Residence in the New Settlements of the Ohio, North America* (London, 1835); Baynard R. Hall, *The New Purchase: or, Seven and a Half Years in the Far West,* 2 vols. (New York, 1843); James Hall, *Sketches of History, Life, and Manners, in the West,* 2 vols. (Philadelphia, 1835); Thomas Hamilton, *Men and Manners in America,* 2 vols. (London, 1833); Adam Hodgson, *Remarks During a Journey through North America in the Years 1819, 1820, and 1821: In a Series of Letters* (New York, 1823); Abner D. Jones, *Illinois and the West* (Boston, 1838); Paul J. Lindholdt, ed., *John Josselyn, Colonial Traveler: A Critical Edition of Two Voyages to New-England* (Hanover, NH, 1988); William Kingsford, *Impressions of the West and South* (Toronto, 1858); Caroline Kirkland, *A New Home—Who'll Follow?* (New York, 1839); Franklin D. Scott, ed., *Baron Klinkowstron's America, 1818–1820* (Evanston, IL, 1952); Charles Joseph Latrobe, *The Rambler in North America,* 2 vols. (London, 1836); Lambert Lilly, *The History of the Western States* (Boston, 1833); Charles Lyell, *A Second Visit to the United States of North America,* 2 vols. (New York, 1849); Caroline Dale Snedeker, ed., *Diaries of Donald MacDonald, 1824–1826,* vol. 14 of *Indiana*

Historical Society Publications (Indianapolis, IN, 1942); Alexander Mackay, *The Western World or, Travels in the United States in 1846–47,* 2 vols. (Philadelphia, 1849); Frederick Marryat, *A Diary in America: With Remarks on its Institutions,* ed. Sydney Jackson (New York, 1962, orig. 1839); Harriet Martineau, *Society in America,* 3 vols. (London, 1837); Charles McKnight, *Our Western Border: Its Life, Combats, Adventures, Forays, Massacres, Captivities, Scouts, Red Chiefs, Pioneer Women, One Hundred Years Ago* (New York, 1970, orig. 1875); Newton D. Mereness, ed., *Travels in the American Colonies* (New York, 1916); Francois A. Michaux, *Travels to the Westward of the Allegheny Mountains* (London, 1805); Thomas M. Marshall, ed., "Journal of Henry B. Miller," *Missouri Historical Society Collections* 6 (1931): 213–87; Masao Miyoshi, *As We Saw Them: The First Japanese Embassy to the United States (1860)* (Berkeley, CA, 1979); Charles A. Murray, *Travels in North America during the Years 1834, 1835, & 1836,* 2 vols. (London, 1839); Henry Anthony Murray, *Lands of the Slave and the Free: or, Cuba, The United States, and Canada* (London, 1857); Thomas Nuttall, *Journal of Travels into the Arkansas Territory, During the Year 1819* (Philadelphia, 1821); William Oliver, *Eight Months in Illinois; with Information to Emigrants* (Newcastle-Upon-Tyne, UK, 1843); Frederick Law Olmsted, *A Journey in the Seaboard Slave States in the Years 1853–1854, with Remarks on their Economy,* 2 vols. (New York, 1904, orig. 1856); Frederick Law Olmsted, *A Journey Through Texas: or, A Saddle-trip on the South-western Frontier* (New York, 1857); Joel Palmer, *Journal of Travels over the Rocky Mountains, to the Mouth of the Columbia River* (Cincinnati, OH, 1847); John Palmer, *Journal of Travels in the United States of America* (London, 1818); Amos A. Parker, *Trip to the West and Texas* (Concord, NH, 1835); John M. Peck, *A New Guide for Emigrants to the West* (Boston, 1836); Tyrone Power, *Impressions of America During the Years 1833, 1834, and 1835,* 2 vols. (London, 1836); Gunnar J. Malmin, trans. and ed., *America in the Forties: The Letters of Ole Munch Raeder* (Minneapolis, MN, 1929, orig. 1848); John S. Robb, *Streaks of Squatter life, and Far-West Scenes,* ed. John Francis McDermott (Gainesville, FL, 1962, orig. 1847); Anne Newport Royall, *Letters from Alabama, 1817–1822,* ed. Lucille Griffith (University, AL, 1969); Theodore C. Blegen, trans. and ed., *Ole Rynning's True Account of America* (Minneapolis, MN, 1926, orig. 1838); Christian Schultz Jr., *Travels on an Inland Voyage Through the States of New-York, Pennsylvania, Virginia, Ohio, Kentucky and Tennessee, and Through the Territories Of Indiana, Louisiana, Mississippi, and New-Orleans,* 2 vols. (New York, 1810); Sidney Smith, *The Settler's New Home: Or, Whether to Go, and Whither?,* 2 vols. (London, 1850); Eliza R. Steele, *A Summer Journey in the West* (New York, 1841); James Stirling, *Letters from the Slave States* (London, 1857); James Stuart, *Three Years in North America,* 2 vols. (Edinburgh, 1833); Bayard Taylor, *Eldorado, or, Adventures in the Path of Empire: Comprising a Voyage to California, via Panama,* 2 vols. (New York, 1850); Theodore C. Blegen, trans. and ed., *Peter Testman's Account of His Experiences in North America* (Northfield, MN, 1929, orig. 1839); David Thomas, *Travels through the Western Country in the Summer of 1816* (Auburn, NY, 1819); Alexis de Tocqueville, *Democracy in America,* trans. Henry Reeve and Francis Bowen, ed. Phillips Bradley, 2 vols. (New York, 1963); Frances Trollope, *Domestic Manners of the Americans* (London, 1832); Adlard Welby, *A Visit to North America and the English Settlements in Illinois,* in vol. 12 of Thwaites, ed., *Early Western Travels*; Isaac Weld, *Travels Through the States of North America, and the Provinces of Upper and Lower Canada, During the years 1795, 1796, and 1797,* 2 vols. (London, 1800); John Woods, *Two Years' Residence in the Settlement on the English Prairie in the Illinois Country* (London, 1822). The accounts of several Western explorers are not included.

6. Murray, *Travels in North America* 1: 213–14, 2: 152–54, 299. It should be noted in this context that most generalizations about the United States, then and now, define Americans as white males. Thus Billington, writing in the 1960s, could comment with ease about how Americans treated their wives—the wives themselves not being Americans. Billington, *America's Frontier Heritage,* chapter 3.

7. In general, see "Advertisements for Runaway Slaves," in Bellesiles, ed., *BiblioBase;* Featherstonhaugh, *Excursion through the Slave States;* Kingsford, *Impressions of the West and South;* Murray, *Lands of the Slave and the Free,* 360–69; Olmsted, *A Journey in the Seaboard Slave States* 1: 32–43, 60–62, 128–31, 142–48, 2: 269–75; Stirling, *Letters from the Slave States.*

8. Trollope, *Domestic Manners;* Marryat, *A Diary in America;* Hamilton, *Men and Manners in America.*

9. Marryat, *A Diary in America,* 328.

10. Hamilton, *Men and Manners* 1: 232, 2: 386–88; Schultz, *Travels on an Inland Voyage* 2: 134–46, quote, 146; Latrobe, *The Rambler* 1: 300; Featherstonhaugh, *Excursion through the Slave States* 2: 238–45. See also Snedecker, ed., *Diaries of Donald Mac-Donald,* 341–43; Steele, *A Summer Journey,* 227–29; McDermott, ed., *Before Mark Twain,* 83–85.

11. Martineau, *Society in America* 1: 162–64, quote, 164; Marryat, *A Diary in America,* 59; Malmin, trans. and ed., *America in the Forties,* 171–74.

12. Billington, *America's Frontier Heritage,* 256; Baillie-Grohman, *Camps in the Rockies,* 27; Blane, *An Excursion,* 147; Jones, *Illinois and the West,* 25–26.

13. Murray, *Travels in North America* 1: 212–13; *Acts Passed at the Called Session of the General Assembly of the State of Alabama* (Tuscaloosa, AL, 1837), 11–7; *Acts Passed at the First Session of the Twenty-Second General Assembly of the State of Tennessee* (Nashville, TN, 1838), 200–01. On picking teeth and fingernails with bowie knives impressing foreign visitors, see also John Francis McDermott, ed., *Before Mark Twain: A Sample of Old, Old Times on the Mississippi* (Carbondale, IL, 1968), 65.

14. Moore quoted Billington, *America's Frontier Heritage,* 164; Latrobe, *The Rambler* 1: 298; Tocqueville, *Democracy in America* 1: 51. See also Hamilton, *Men and Manners* 1: 131.

15. Lindholdt, *John Josselyn,* 20–21, 90, 99, 125–26.

16. Murray, *Travels in North America* 1: 128–29 (quotes), 325–28, 335–39, 366–70, 2: 120–30. William Oliver shared this judgment of the American rifle and shooting ability. Oliver, *Eight Months in Illinois,* 84–87. On professional hunters, see Stephen Aron, *How the West Was Lost: The Transformation of Kentucky from Daniel Boone to Henry Clay* (Baltimore, MD, 1996), 21–27.

17. Oliver, *Eight Months in Illinois,* 83–84.

18. Cuming, *Sketches of a Tour to the Western Country,* 133–34; "The Backwoods of America," originally published in the *London Sporting Review,* reprinted in P. Hawker, *Instructions to Young Sportsmen in all that Relates to Guns and Shooting* (Philadelphia, 1846), 295–97.

19. Murray, *Travels in North America* 2: 129–30.

20. Gerstacker, *Wild Sports in the Far West,* v (quote), xvii–xix, 41 (quote), 174 (quote), 175–77, 184–87, 200–08, 227.

21. Gerstacker, *Wild Sports in the Far West,* 75–76, 86–88, 179–84, 269–70, 292, 298, 308, 326, quotes 86, 178–83, 269–70, 290, 303–04. On one occasion Gerstacker leapt on a wounded stag, dropped his knife, and bit the animal's neck while his dog bit its legs, and finished it off with a large rock. Ibid., 303–04. For more on dogs, see *Turf Register* 2 (1830): 170–77, 179–80; 2 (1831): 221–25, 232–35, 273–80, 289; 4 (1832):

187–90; 4 (1833): 303–04, 401–02; William Elliott, *Carolina Sports by Land and Water* (New York, 1859), 160–63, 165–66, 171–73, 189, 215. The very title of Johnson Jones Hooper's last book speaks to this close association: *Dog and Gun: A Few Loose Chapters on Shooting, Among Which will be Found Some Anecdotes and Incidents* (Tuscaloosa, AL, 1992, orig. 1856). Hooper writes that "the shooting of game birds" in the company of dogs "has been, time out of mind, the *gentleman's* amusement" (7).

22. Gerstacker, *Wild Sports in the Far West,* 40, 179 (quote), 235, 249 (quote), 259.

23. Ibid., 329–36 (quotes, 329, 335).

24. Ibid., 191–92, 337. Gerstacker notes that hunting with others has the added advantage that when one misses, the other still has a shot (291–92).

25. Ibid., 241 (quote), 312, 327–29. On axes, see Carl P. Russell, *Firearms, Traps, & Tools of the Mountain Men* (New York, 1967), 232–311.

26. Writing in 1889 about hunting in the Western Reserve in 1818, Milton Pierce recalled that "Rifles were scarce in those days and those who owned them could readily rent them for 12.5 cents a day without ammunition." *American Field,* 28 December 1889, 617.

27. Gerstacker, *Wild Sports in the Far West,* 208, 268, 271. See also *American Turf Register and Sporting Magazine* 1 (1830): 388–89; 2 (1830–1831): 68, 281; *Spirit of the Times* 24 (1854): 244; Ashe, *Travels in America* 1: 26.

28. Gerstacker, *Wild Sports in the Far West,* 266–67.

29. Ibid., 314–23. Kit Carson had a roughly similar experience in 1834. Having just shot a deer, he turned around to face two bears. Since he did not have time to reload, he dropped his gun and climbed a tree, where he spent the night. Milo Milton Quaife, ed., *Kit Carson's Autobiography* (Chicago, 1935), 38–39.

30. Gerstacker, *Wild Sports in the Far West,* 96–97, 151, 171–72 (quote), 263, 340–48. On the deadly mosquitoes, see also McDermott, ed., *Before Mark Twain,* 61; Steele, *A Summer Journey,* 199–200.

31. Gerstacker, *Wild Sports in the Far West,* 348. Gerstacker went hunting one last time near New Orleans, but from "anxiety . . . I trembled in every limb, and could not steady the rifle," missing the buck (p. 304).

32. Ibid., 351.

33. Ralph L. Rusk, *The Literature of the Middle Western Frontier* (New York, 1925), 1: 75n; Elliott J. Gorn, " 'Gouge and Bite, Pull Hair and Scratch': The Social Significance of Fighting in the Southern Backcountry," *The American Historical Review* 90 (1985): 18–43.

34. Hall, *The New Purchase* 2: 158–59; Smith, *The Settler's New Home,* 96–97; Featherstonhaugh, *A Canoe Voyage up the Minnay Sotor* 1: 152; Cuming, *Sketches of a Tour to the Western Country,* 137; William Darby, *The Emigrant's Guide to the Western and Southwestern States and Territories* (New York, 1818), 206. As Zadock Cramer noted in his footnote to this passage, somehow these accounts never seem to be about anyone, they tend to be about everyone on the frontier; they never witness, they always hear these tales. Darley, *Emigrants' Guide,* 138n.

35. Adams, *The Homestead Guide,* 113; Flint, *Recollections,* 189.

36. Michael A. Lofaro, ed., *Davy Crockett: The Man, the Legend, the Legacy, 1786–1986* (Knoxville, TN, 1985).

37. Billington, *America's Frontier Heritage,* 143, 145. Billington does a fine job demolishing the mythology of individualism with example after example (see also pp. 139–57); Garry Wills, *Reagan's America: Innocents at Home* (Garden City, NY, 1987). Miners almost never acted alone, just bare survival in western mountains required group effort; digging a claim was certainly not a one-person operation, a

point made abundantly clear in the case studies by scholars like W. Turrentine Jackson, *Treasure Hill: Portrait of a Silver Mining Camp* (Tucson, AZ, 1963).

38. John Phillip Reid, *Law for the Elephant: Property and Social Behavior on the Overland Trail* (San Marino, CA, 1980), and *Policing the Elephant: Crime, Punishment, and Social Behavior on the Overland Trail* (San Marino, CA, 1997). See also John Mack Faragher, *Women and Men on the Overland Trail* (New Haven, CT, 1979); Noah Smithwick, *Texas Frontiersmen: The Evolution of a State* (Austin, TX, 1910); Everett Dick, *The Sod House Frontier* (New York, 1937); Dick, *The Dixie Frontier* (New York, 1948).

39. R. Carlyle Buley, *The Old Northwest: Pioneer Period, 1815–1840,* 2 vols. (Indianapolis, 1950), 1: 367–69; Borthwick, *Three Years in California,* 369; McKnight, *Our Western Border,* 185. See also Thomas, *Travels through the Western Country,* 124. Tocqueville also emphasized this quality of association as unique to America. Tocqueville, *Democracy in America* 1: 190–98, 2: 106–20.

40. Quoted, Dixon Wecter, "Instruments of Culture on the Frontier," *Yale Review* 36 (1947): 246; Bowles, *Across the Continent,* 327–28; R. L. Hartt, "The Ohioans," *Atlantic Monthly* 84 (November 1899): 682; Malmin, trans. and ed., *America in the Forties,* 148–52.

41. Elise D. Isely, *Sunbonnet Days* (Caldwell, ID, 1935), 180; Tocqueville, *Democracy in America* 1: 317. Billington claimed that "Morality, education, and learning bulked larger in the consciences of the 'better sort' in the West than among their counterparts in the East." *America's Frontier Heritage,* 75. See also Louis B. Wright, "The Westward Advance of the Atlantic Frontier," *Huntington Library Quarterly* 11 (1946): 261–75; Howard M. Jones, *America and French Culture* (Chapel Hill, NC, 1927), 50–51; Earl Pomeroy, "Toward a Reorientation of Western History: Continuity and Environment," *Mississippi Valley Historical Review* 41 (1955): 582–83, 591–93.

42. Walter A. Agard, "Classics on the Midwest Frontier," in Ealker D. Wyman and Clifton B. Kroeber, eds., *The Frontier in Perspective* (Madison, WI, 1957), 165–83; Frank Klassen, "Persistence and Change in Eighteenth-Century Colonial Education," *History of Education Quarterly* 2 (1962): 83–99; *Western Review* 3 (1820): 145; Finley, *Autobiography,* 113–14; Flint, *Recollections,* 48; Griffiths, *Two Years' Residence in the New Settlements,* 83–84; *Niles' Weekly Register* 11 (8 February 1817), 392; Hodgson, *Remarks During a Journey,* 269; William W. Ferrier, *Ninety Years of Education in California, 1846–1936* (New York, 1927), 36–40; Dick, *The Sod House Frontier,* 315; Edward A. Miller, "The History of Educational Legislation in Ohio from 1803 to 1850," *Ohio Archaeological and Historical Society Publications* 27 (1918): 1–27; Merle Curti, *The Making of an American Community: A Case Study of Democracy in a Frontier County* (Stanford, CA, 1959), 384–85.

43. Benjamin Thomas, *Lincoln's New Salem* (Springfield, IL, 1934), 29–36. See also Curti, *Making of an American Community;* John Mack Faragher, *Sugar Creek: Life on the Illinois Prairie* (New Haven, CT, 1986).

44. Thomas, *Lincoln's New Salem,* 29–36; Billington, *America's Frontier Heritage,* 82; Curti, *Making of an American Community;* John Mack Faragher, *Sugar Creek*; Edward P. Anderson, "Intellectual Life of Pittsburgh, 1786–1836," *Western Pennsylvania Historical Magazine* 14 (1931): 101–05; Joseph S. Schick, *The Early Theater in Eastern Iowa* (Chicago, 1939), 161–65; Howard H. Peckham, "Books and Reading on the Ohio River Frontier," *Mississippi Valley Historical Review* 44 (1958): 652; Louis B. Wright, *Culture on the Moving Frontier* (Bloomington, IN, 1955), 71–75; Richard C. Wade, *The Urban Frontier: The Rise of Western Cities, 1790–1830* (Cambridge, MA, 1959), 140; Madeleine B. Stern, *Imprints on History: Book Publishers and American*

Frontiers (Bloomington, IN, 1956), 137–38. Classics were particularly popular throughout America, though more than half of all the books published in the western part of the country before 1815 were almanacs, gazetteers, and religious works. That same appreciation for classics can be seen in the theater. James M. Miller, *The Genesis of Western Culture: The Upper Ohio Valley, 1800–1825* (Columbus, OH, 1938), 147–51; Peckham, "Books and Reading on the Ohio River Frontier," 657–60; Rusk, *Literature of the Middle Western Frontier* 2: 1–38, 352–57; Anderson, *Intellectual Life of Pittsburgh,* 225–31; Wade, *Urban Frontier,* 143–46; Buley, *The Old Northwest* 2: 573–76; Esther C. Dunn, *Shakespeare in America* (New York, 1939), 175–204.

45. Sarah Cutler, "The Coonskin Library," *Ohio Archaeological and Historical Quarterly* 26 (1917): 58–77; Flora H. Apponyi, *Libraries in California* (San Francisco, 1878), 3–15; Eleanora A. Baer, "Books, Newspapers, and Libraries in Pioneer St. Louis, 1808–1842," *Missouri Historical Review* 56 (1962): 358–60; Wade, *Urban Frontier,* 254–56; W. T. Norton, "Early Libraries in Illinois," *Journal of the Illinois Historical Society* 6 (1913): 246–51; John F. McDermott, "Private Libraries in Frontier St. Louis," *Papers of the Bibliographical Society of America* 51 (1957): 19–37; Edward E. Dale, "The Frontier Literary Society," *Nebraska History* 31 (1950): 167–82.

46. Michaux, *Travels to the Westward,* 160–61; Jones, *Illinois and the West,* 102–03. See also Bernhard, *Travels Through North America* 2: 25; Palmer, *Journal of Travels,* 127; Flint, *Letters from America,* 272; Daubney, *Journal of a Tour,* 143–44; Flint, *Recollections of the Last Ten Years,* 67, 229; Hodgson, *Remarks During a Journey,* 142, 286–87; Hall, *The New Purchase* 1: 199; Olmsted, *A Journey Through Texas,* 48, 430. Fortescue Cuming disagreed, asserting that the backwoodsmen "are very similar in their habits and manners to the aborigines, only perhaps more prodigal and more careless of life. They depend more on hunting than on agriculture." Cuming, *Sketches of a Tour to the Western Country,* 137.

47. Bernard Mayo, "Lexington: Frontier Metropolis," in Eric Goldman, ed., *Historiography and Urbanization: Essays in American History in Honor of W. Stull Holt* (Baltimore, MD, 1941), 31–40; Richard C. Wade, "Urban Life in Western America, 1790–1830," *American Historical Review* 64 (1858): 25; Charles H. Shinn, *The Story of the Mine: As Illustrated by the Great Comstock Lode of Nevada* (New York, 1898), 67–68; W. Turrentine Jackson, *Treasure Hill,* 26–27; *Texas in 1840: Or, the Emigrant's Guide to the New Republic, . . . By an Emigrant* (New York, 1840), 40–41, 66–67; LeRoy R. Hafen, ed., *Colorado and Its People: A Narrative and Topical History of the Centennial State,* 4 vols. (New York, 1948), 1: 192–94, 231–35; Power, *Impressions of America* 2: 119–22; Robert R. Dykstra, *The Cattle Towns* (New York, 1968).

48. Quoted in Buley, *The Old Northwest* 2: 563; Billington, *America's Frontier Heritage,* 87–94; Richard Hofstadter, *Anti-intellectualism in American Life* (New York, 1963), 24–51; Merle Curti, "Intellectuals and Other People," *American Historical Review* 60 (1955): 259–82; F. Garvin Davenport, "Culture versus Frontier in Tennessee, 1825–1850," *Journal of Southern History* 5 (1939): 18–33.

49. Hall, *The New Purchase* 2: 83. See especially any page of Trollope, *Domestic Manners;* for a long excerpt, see Trollope, "Domestic Manners of the Americans" in Bellesiles, ed., *BiblioBase.* See also Ashe, *Travels in America* 1: 225–32; Hamilton, *Men and Manners* 1: 228–35.

50. Marryat, *A Diary in America,* 462; Woods, *Two Years' Residence,* 295; Ashe, *Travels in America* 1: 298; Flint, *Letters from America,* 144; Latrobe, *The Rambler* 1: 259–60.

51. By 1793 books were being published in the frontier town of Pittsburgh. Every state could boast in turn its successful publishers within twenty years of white

settlement. Peckham, "Books and Reading," 652–56; Rusk, *Literature of the Middle Western Frontier,* 25–57.

52. Frederick Jackson Turner, *Rise of the New West, 1819–1829* (New York, 1906), 103; *Western Monthly Review* 1 (May 1827): 25.

53. Latrobe, *The Rambler* 1: 287; Robert R. Dykstra, "Field Notes: Overdosing on Dodge City," *Western Historical Quarterly* 27 (1996): 505–14. See also de Grandfort, *The New World,* 77–81; Steele, *A Summer Journey,* 223–29; McDermott, ed., *Before Mark Twain,* 58–69, 166–86.

54. Lilly, *The History of the Western States,* 35–36; John Bakeless, *Daniel Boone* (New York, 1939), 55; Osburne Russell, *Journal of a Trapper, or Nine Years in the Rocky Mountains* (Boise, ID, 1921), 55, 109; Frances F. Victor, *The River of the West* (Hartford, CT, 1870), 83–84; William H. Goetzmann, "The Mountain Man as Jacksonian Man," *American Quarterly* 15 (1963): 402–15. Many of the same generalizations can be made for the cowboys. Don D. Walker, "Reading on the Range: The Literary Habits of the American Cowboy," *Arizona and the West* 2 (1960): 307–18.

55. "Diary of a Scot," 30 September 1822, *Collections of the New-York Historical Society* 1: 147–50, 339–41. Frederick Marryat was also convinced of the basically harmless character of Americans by watching two militia musters. Marryat, *A Diary in America,* 59–61, 120–26.

56. George Bancroft, *History of the United States of America, From the Discovery of the Continent,* 6 vols. (New York, 1886); Henry Howe, *Historical Collections of the Great West* (Cincinnati, OH, 1854); Robert Greenhow, *The History of Oregon and California, and the Other Territories of the North-West Coast of North America* (New York, 1845); Richard Hildreth, *The History of the United States of America,* 6 vols. (New York, 1880); John Bach McMaster, *A History of the People of the United States from the Revolution to the Civil War,* 8 vols. (New York, 1885); Charles A. Goodrich, *History of the United States of America* (Boston, 1867); Benson J. A. Lossing, *A Common-School History of the United States from the Earliest Period to the Present Time* (New York, 1865).

57. *The Western Monthly Magazine* 1 (1833): 2–3, 49–55, 238–39, 313, 318; ibid. 2 (1834): 268; *Western Miscellany* 1 (1849): 49–55. See also *Southern Quarterly Review* 14 (1848): 242; *Holden's Dollar Magazine* 1 (1848): 188; *Literary World* 2 (1847): 283. On knives, see Russell, *Firearms, Traps, & Tools,* 164–231. On relative levels of violence, see Dykstra, *Cattle Towns,* 112–48; Luc Sante, *Low Life: Lures and Snares of Old New York* (New York, 1991), 197–235; Elliot J. Gorn, "'Good-Bye Boys, I Die a True American': Homicide, Nativism, and Working-Class Culture in Antebellum New York City," *Journal of American History* 74 (1987): 388–410; Paul A. Gilje, *The Road to Mobocracy: Popular Disorder in New York City, 1763–1834* (Chapel Hill, NC, 1987), 235–64; Carl E. Prince, "The Great 'Riot Year': Jacksonian Democracy and Patterns of Violence in 1834," *Journal of the Early Republic* 5 (Spring 1985): 1–19; David Grimsted, "Rioting in its Jacksonian Setting," *American Historical Review* 77 (April 1972): 361–97.

58. Arlin Turner, "Seeds of Literary Revolt in the Humor of the Old Southwest," *Louisiana Historical Quarterly* 39 (1956): 143–51; Derek Colville, "History and Humor: The Tall Tale in New Orleans," ibid., 155–67; Eugene Current-Garcia, "Thomas Bangs Thorpe and the Literature of the Ante-Bellum Southwestern Frontier," ibid., 200–22; J. B. Hubbell, "The Frontier in American Literature," *Southwest Review* 10 (1925): 84–92; Percy Boynton, *The Rediscovery of the Frontier* (Chicago, 1931). The western market formed a significant component of every publisher's sales. But readers in the western part of the country seemed oddly uninterested in books

about the frontier, which sold rather well in the East. Not until the dime novel of the later nineteenth century would western settlers indicate much interest in books about their way of life. Logan Esarey, "The Literary Spirit Among the Early Ohio Valley Settlers," *Mississippi Valley Historical Review* 5 (1918): 143–57; Buley, *The Old Northwest* 2: 558–62; Rusk, *Literature of the Middle Western Frontier* 2: 272–351; William Charvat, *Literary Publishing in America, 1790–1850* (Philadelphia, 1959), 18–25

59. James Fenimore Cooper, *The Pioneers: or, the Sources of the Susquehanna* (Albany, NY, 1980, orig. 1823), 20–25.

60. To take just one example, see Bernard Bush, ed., *Laws of the Royal Colony of New Jersey,* 5 vols. (Trenton, NJ, 1980), 2: 294–95, 3: 181, 186–90, 253, 489–90, 580, 4: 52–53, 237, 326–27, 582–85, 5: 52–53, 69–72, 162–63. In general see Paul C. Phillips, *The Fur Trade,* 2 vols. (Norman, OK, 1961), 1: 377–430; Thomas E. Norton, *The Fur Trade in Colonial New York, 1686–1776* (Madison, WI, 1974), 60–82.

61. As Stephen Aron wrote, "In addition to encouraging degeneracy and triggering violence, hunting by backcountry settlers challenged established authority." Aron, *How the West Was Lost,* 14. See also J. Hector St. John de Crevecoeur, *Letters from an American Farmer,* ed. Warren B. Blake (New York, 1957), 214–15; Russell, *Firearms, Traps, & Tools,* 97–163.

62. *The Atheneum,* 3rd ser., 1 (1828): 207–08. See also 1st ser., 1 (1817): 260–61, 6 (1819): 13–17, and 2d ser., 7 (1827): 29–34, 53–59, 167–68, 276–77, 408, 426–27; *Godey's Lady's Book* 2 (1831): 150; *Hazard's Register of Pennsylvania* 7 (1831): 191; *Museum of Foreign Literature, Science and Art* 27 (1835): 525–26; *Army and Navy Chronicle* 5 (1837): 59–60; *The American Penny Magazine, and Family Newspaper* 1 (1845): 609–11, 2 (1846): 73–74, 102–03; *The Anglo-American* 5 (1845): 200–01, 390–91; *Brother Jonathan* 6 (1843): 43; *The Eclectic Magazine of Foreign Literature, Science, and Art* 4 (1845): 358–64, 33 (1854): 563; Norton, *The Fur Trade in Colonial New York,* 83–99; Patrick Malone, *The Skulking Way of War: Technology and Tactics Among the New England Indians* (Lanham, MD, 1991), 60–66; Sarah F. McMahon, "A Comfortable Subsistence: The Changing Composition of Diet in Rural New England, 1620–1840," *William and Mary Quarterly* 42 (1985): 26–65; Henry M. Miller, "An Archaeological Perspective on the Evolution of Diet in the Colonial Chesapeake, 1620–1745," in *Colonial Chesapeake Society,* ed. Lois Green Carr et al. (Chapel Hill, NC, 1988), 176–99.

63. "A Buffalo Hunt," *The Knickerbocker, or New York Monthly Magazine* 23 (1844): 114–18; "Sporting," *The Atheneum,* 2nd ser., 2 (1825): 444; *The Ariel* 3 (1829): 94, 100; *The Casket* 9 (1830): 390–95. Occasionally these themes became mixed, to make hunting appear both exotic and foolish. In 1800 Donald Campbell wrote an essay on "Hunting the Wild Boar in the East Indies," which contrasted the social utility of hunting for pleasure and necessity. Campbell talked of his first hunt with his friends when "I was but eighteen years of age, and had not the judgment to reflect, that if I had been killed, my fate would be attended only with pity or scorn for my folly: whereas, had I succeeded, the whole reward of my danger would have been the useless applause of some youngsters, idle and inconsiderate as myself. . . . Often when I have heard, in coffee-houses and play-houses, some of our sporting sparks boasting of their prowess over a timid hare or a feeble fox, I could not help recollecting with respect the hunters of India, who chase the destructive monsters of the forest—the boar, the tyger, the hyena, the bull, or the buffalo; and . . . render essential service to their fellow-creatures, and save the lives and property of thousands." *Baltimore Weekly Magazine* 1 (26 April 1800): 4–5 .

64. *New England Farmer* 2 (1824): 301, 317, 5 (23 February 1827): 243. The journal felt that "The game laws of England and other countries are subject to great scorn in this country" as not "agreeable to republican notions. . . . Nevertheless they are attended with immense advantage to the farmer." *New England Farmer* 2: 317.

65. In general see Dickson D. Bruce Jr., *Violence and Culture in the Antebellum South* (Austin, TX, 1979), 196–211; Nicolas Wolfe Proctor, "Bathed in Blood: Hunting in the Antebellum South" (Ph.D. diss., Emory University, 1998). To state the obvious, not all southern planters enjoyed hunting. Virginian John T. Barraud wrote his mother about a miserable hunting trip with his brother Byrd, who "is so poor a hand with the gun, that it affords him little pleasure," and after a whole group of them back with "not even a snow bird" to show for their efforts, Byrd Barraud rejected hunting as a waste of time. Proctor, "Bathed in Blood," 123.

66. *American Turf Register* 1 (1829): 1. In 1856 Henry William Herbert looked back and said that when he first began hunting, the word "sportsman" was understood to be a gambler. Frank Forester [Henry William Herbert], *Complete Manual for Young Sportsmen: With Directions for Handling the Gun, the Rifle, and the Rod* (New York, 1856), 26. The English press entered this arena earlier. See E. V. Bovill, *The England of Nimrod and Suretees, 1815–1854* (New York, 1959). For a general study of the American sporting press see Ernest Gee, *Early American Sporting Books, 1734 to 1844* (New York, 1928); Norris Yates, *William T. Porter and the Spirit of the Times: A Study of the Big Bear School of Humor* (Baton Rouge, LA, 1957); Norris Yates, "The *Spirit of the Times*: Its Early History and Some of Its Contributors," *Papers of the Bibliographical Society of America* 48 (1954): 117–48.

67. *Spirit of the Times* 7 (1837): 4; N. Bosworth, *A Treatise on the Rifle, Musket, Pistol, and Fowling Piece* (New York, 1846), 64, 97. See also *Spirit of the Times* 7 (1837): 5 (1835): 1; *Spirit of the Times* 9 (1839): 1; *American Turf Register and Sporting Magazine* 1 (1829–30): 240, 441; *American Turf Register* 5 (1834): 371–73, 474–75, 615; "fowling piece" in G. G. and J. Robinson, *The Sportsman's Dictionary; Or, The Gentleman's Companion* (London, 1800). Kenneth S. Greenberg, in a book with a ridiculously long title, argued that hunting stories largely were southern in venue. Yet the sporting magazines indicate a much wider geographical range, including New England. Greenberg focused on Thoreau's amazement over William Elliott, *Carolina Sports by Land and Water* (New York, 1859). But Thoreau can hardly be held as typical of anything. Greenberg, *Honor & Slavery: Lies, Duels, Noses, Masks, Dressing as a Woman, Gifts, Strangers, Humanitarianism, Death, Slave Rebellions, the Proslavery Argument, Baseball, Hunting, and Gambling in the Old South* (Princeton, NJ, 1996), 130–31; Bradford Torrey, ed., *The Writings of Henry David Thoreau: Journal, August 1, 1860–November 3, 1861* (Boston, 1906), 20: 315–19.

68. *American Turf Register and Sporting Magazine* 1 (1829–30): 240, 2 (1830): 131 (quote), 131–36, 183–85, 2 (1831): 395–96, 438–39, 491–93, 541–45, 5 (1834): 371–73, 474–755, 615 (quote). For justifications of fox hunting, see also *The Casket* 2 (1830): 49–51; William Elliott, *Carolina Sports,* 269. Porter modeled *Spirit of the Times* on the London journal *Bell's Life*. Yates, "The *Spirit of the Times,*" 117–21.

69. *American Turf Register* 4 (1832): 130–31, 4 (1833): 239, 355. There are a very few articles describing outrageous feats of shooting, such as a target shoot in which the target was at the end of a musket barrel at thirty paces and each of the thirty-five contestants put at least two of their five balls through that barrel. It is very difficult to credit such a story. *American Turf Register* 3 (1831): 66–67.

70. *American Turf Register* 2 (1830–1831): 87–88, 287, 4 (1832): 27–28; Elliott, *Carolina Sports,* 179–80. See also *American Turf Register* 4 (1832): 161, 4 (1833): 237–38,

352–54, 401–02, 587–90; *Western Monthly Magazine* 3 (1835), 65–66; *Brother Jonathan* 6 (1843): 43; *The American Penny Magazine* 1 (1845): 387–88; *Hazard's Register of Pennsylvania* 15 (7 February 1835): 86, 388; *Spirit of the Times* 10 (1840): 97; Elliott, *Carolina Sports,* 161, 173, 178, 182–88, 193–213, 219–27. On another occasion, Elliott was astounded when his party killed three deer "without the aid of a dog!" Ibid., 189.

71. *American Turf Register* 2 (1831): 450, 485–86; 4 (1833): 241, 244, 306. See also 4 (1833): 241–47, 301–04, 348–51, 411; Elliott, *Carolina Sports,* 240. The other favored source was the *Sportsman's Cyclopeadia* (London, 1831). The leading expert on rifle use in America, N. Bosworth, praised the New York City militia as fine marksmen because of their regular practice. Bosworth, *Treatise on the Rifle,* 101.

72. Elliott, *Carolina Sports,* 184, 187–88.

73. Ibid., 222–23.

74. *American Turf Register* 1 (1829): 29, 44–46, 84–85, 88, 236, 292–94, 342, 388–89, 440–41, 500–03, 546–48, 595, 2 (1830): 72, 122 (quote), 123–24, 180, 186, 2 (1831): 285, 332 (quote), 342 (quote), 391, 3 (1831): 25–26, 29, 88, 3 (1832): 300, 346, 352–54, 399, 515 (quote), 4 (1833): 305, 349–50, 416 (quote), 587 (quote), 5 (1834): 40–41, 477–80, 618–19; Elliott, *Carolina Sports,* 260–61, 283 (quote), 284–90; Henry Peck, "Deer," *De Bow's Commercial Review* 5 (1848): 220–29; Hawker, *Instructions to Young Sportsmen,* 286; *Western Miscellany* 1 (1849): 330; *The American Penny Magazine* 1 (1845): 388. Franklin was often quoted: "Be kind to the swallow, And profit will follow." But then most writers seemed to be plagiarizing from Johnson's *Shooter's Companion.*

75. *American Turf Register* 2 (1830): 68–69, 124–25. The magazine even printed a letter from the wife of a southern gentleman hunter, signing herself "Julianna Rosebud," in opposition to hunting. "The brute," Rosebud wrote of her husband, spent all their money on "powder and shot, and whiskey." She wanted the *Turf Register* to recommend that men exchange their guns for fishing rods and other useful devices. *American Turf Register* 2 (1831): 339–40. See also Hawker, *Instructions to Young Sportsmen,* 272, 282; *Western Monthly Magazine* 1 (1833): 90–92; "The Swiss Hunter," *Godey's Lady's Magazine* 2 (1831): 150.

76. *American Turf Register* 2 (1831): 282, 3 (1832): 475, 632; Thompson, "My First and Last Fire Hunt," *Spirit of the Times* 15 (1845): 13. See also *American Turf Register* 4 (1832): 143; *Hazard's Register* 15 (7 February 1835): 86; Elliott, *Carolina Sports,* 264–66.

77. *American Turf Register* 4 (1833): 355, 359–60.

78. Ibid., 4 (1833): 410–17, quotes 410.

79. *American Turf Register* 3 (1832): 463; McNutt, "The Chase in the South West," *Spirit of the Times* 15 (1845): 225–26. See also Herbert, *Complete Manual for Young Sportsmen,* 31; Henry William Herbert, *Frank Forester's Field Sports of the United States,* 2 vols. (New York, 1852), 1: 26–27; *The Ladies' Companion* 17 (May 1842): 7; *Holden's Dollar Magazine* 2 (1848): 669–70.

80. *American Turf Register* 1 (1829–30): 400; 2 (1830): 33–34.

81. Ibid., 2 (1831): 486, 3 (1831): 177. See also Henry Peck, "Deer," *De Bow's Commercial Review* 5 (1848): 225.

82. A Gentleman of Philadelphia County [Lee Kester], *The American Shooter's Manual* (Philadelphia, 1827), 19–25, 31–32 (quote 24). A favored book, judging from references in *Spirit of the Times,* was John Mills, *The Sportsman's Library* (Edinburgh, 1845). This Scottish guide was far more detailed than any American instruction manual published by that time.

83. *American Turf Register* 4 (1833): 244; Herbert, *Complete Manual for Young Sportsmen,* 97; Elliott, *Carolina Sports,* 221.

84. *American Turf Register* 1 (1829–30): 88, 2 (1830): 68; *Army and Navy Chronicle* 6 (1838): 209; Kester, *The American Shooter's Manual,* 227; Herbert, *Complete Manual for Young Sportsmen,* 100. See also Frank Forester [Herbert], *The Warwick Woodlands* (New York, 1930, orig. 1845), 119–22.

85. *American Turf Register* 2 (1831): 587–90, 4 (1833): 416; Kester, *The American Shooter's Manual,* 210, 228. See also *American Turf Register* 2 (1831): 334, 533–35, 587–88, 3 (1832): 228.

86. *Spirit of the Times* 20 (1850): 519; Herbert, *Frank Forester's Field Sports* 1: 28; in general see 11–29. See also, Forester, *The Warwick Woodlands,* 107–09.

87. Bosworth, *Treatise on the Rifle,* 82, 101; *American Turf Register* 2 (1830): 186–87 (quote), 3 (1831): 67, 78–79, 3 (1832): 239–40, 346, 464, 4 (1833): 637–38; *Spirit of the Times* 9 (1839): 271–72, 10 (1841): 607, 13 (1843): 319, 15 (1846): 609–10, 27 (1857): 27–29, 29 (1859): 350–51. In 1844 eighty gentlemen from New York organized the New York Sportsmen's Club. James B. Trefethen, *An American Crusade for Wildlife* (New York, 1975), 73–74. On a southern hunting club see Francis Marion Kirk, *A History of the St. John's Hunting Club* (n.p., 1950).

88. Sacramento *Union,* 6 July 1853 (quote), 6 July 1854; Lawrence P. Shelton, *California Gunsmiths, 1846–1900* (Fair Oaks, CA, 1977), 10–12. In 1859 the club changed its name to the Sacramento Rifle Club.

89. Herbert, *Complete Manual for Young Sportsmen,* 31; *American Turf Register* 2 (1830): 77, 88–90, 129, 181–83, 187, 2 (1831): 296, 395–96, 438–39, 3 (1832): 241, 472, 4 (1832): 133–42, 191. In his introduction to Hawker, *Instructions to Young Sportsmen,* William T. Porter declared this work by an English authority, first printed in the United States in 1792, to be the first book "of a purely sporting character, ever published in the United States" (viii).

90. Bosworth, *Treatise on the Rifle,* 57, 69, 102; *Turf Register* 2 (1830): 73 (quote), 3 (1831): 123–24, 4 (1833): 240 (quote); Hooper, *Dog and Gun,* 15–16; Kester, *The American Shooter's Manual,* 104, 203–05 (quotes), 206–11, 220–21, 233–38; Charley Chase, "Three Chapters for Young Sportsmen," *Holden's Dollar Magazine* 6 (1850): 554–57, 687–90 (quote 554). The Scottish guide by John Mills also recommended English guns, only with greater detail as to the reasons than any of the American sources. Mills, *The Sportsman's Library,* 175–202. Even their clothes should be English. Hawker, *Instructions to Young Sportsmen,* 194.

91. Herbert, *Complete Manual for Young Sportsmen,* 51–52, 57–59, 61, 63, 67. See also Herbert, *Frank Forester's Field Sports* 1: 316–17, 2: 143–44, 225–28; Frank Forester, *My Shooting Box* (New York, 1930, orig. 1845), 5, 161. On Herbert see Frank Forester, *The Deerstalkers,* ed. Harry Worcester Smith (New York, 1930, orig. 1849), 141–73. On fake English guns, see *Holden's Dollar Magazine* 6 (1850): 689.

92. *American Turf Register* 2 (1830): 73, 122–23, 181 (quote), 2 (1831): 229–30, 282–86, 3 (1832): 228, 399–400, 620–21 (quote), 4 (1832): 17 (quote), 18–22, 4 (1833): 410–17, 637; Kester, *The American Shooter's Manual,* 13, 214, 217; Herbert, *Complete Manual for Young Sportsmen,* 69. See also Herbert, *Complete Manual for Young Sportsmen,* 110–17; Forester, *The Warwick Woodlands,* 162–70; *Holden's Dollar Magazine* 6 (1850): 688; *The New-England Magazine* 2 (July 1832): 42–48.

93. The West appears mostly in the context of the military (usually officers) or the most adventurous hunting stories. As one notes: "Our officers, stationed at the western posts, have opportunities of finer and more various field sports than are to be

enjoyed elsewhere in the world. It is gratifying to think that they have such delightful means of dissipating the otherwise dull monotony of a soldier's life, ... without,
for years together, even a speck of war, to sustain and animate him." *American Turf
Register* 3 (1831): 42. See also *American Turf Register* 2 (1831): 286–87, 3 (1832):
352–54, 4 (1833): 236–39, 305–06.

94. *American Turf Register* 1 (1829–30): 237. As Nicolas Proctor wrote, "Although slaves accompanied almost every white hunt, their presence never created
anything approaching a sense of interracial camaraderie." Proctor, "Bathed in
Blood," 148, see also 211–29. There was the occasional boasting over the superiority
of hunting in the South. "Ye city sportsmen! ... who with abundant pains and
troubles, and with note of fearful preparation, marshal your forces for a week's campaign among the plains of Long Island, or the barrens of Jersey—and in reward of
your toil, bag one brace of grouse, or enjoy a glorious snap at some straggling deer,
that escapes, of course, to tempt another party of your hopes and disappointments!"
In the South it can all be done within "five miles ... of our winter homes." Elliott
invites them to visit, "and mark the throb of a new delight springing in your
bosoms." Elliott, *Carolina Sports,* 191–92.

95. *American Turf Register* 1 (1829–30): 444, 5 (1834): 397–99; *The Ariel* 3 (1829):
117.

96. *American Turf Register* 1 (1829–30): 238, 4 (1833): 305–06. For a less positive
experience, see *Spirit of the Times* 10 (1840): 97, 22 (1852): 146.

97. Elliott, *Carolina Sports,* 266, 268–69, 281–82. The application of marital
metaphors to hunting becomes most noticeable in the 1850s. See, for example, *Spirit
of the Times* 23 (1853): 422, 24 (1854): 544, 25 (1855): 122, 29 (1859): 121–22, 350–51.
Davy Crockett had reversed the metaphor, using hunting phrases to describe combat. David Crockett, *A Narrative of the Life of David Crockett of the State of Tennessee*
(orig. 1834, Lincoln, NE, 1987), 107–08, 128.

98. Elliott, *Carolina Sports,* 278, 281–82.

99. Ibid., 157; Hunter quoted, Proctor, "Bathed in Blood," 204; *American Turf
Register* 4 (1833): 247. See also, *Spirit of the Times* 11 (1841): 349, 355, 15 (1846): 609–10,
17 (1847): 4, 19 (1849): 319–20; 29 (1859): 433.

100. *Army and Navy Chronicle* 6 (1838), 209–11; *American Turf Register* 1
(1829–30): 79, 338–39, 4 (1833): 352; *Spirit of the Times* 7 (1837): 364–65. See also *American Turf Register* 2 (1830): 38–42, 70–73, 130–31, 2 (1831): 286–89, 331–33, 342–44,
599–600, 3 (1831): 66, 4 (1833): 410–17; Elliott, *Carolina Sports,* 158, 241. There is
often an overtone of sexuality in these descriptions: "Three sportsmen, while it was
yet early, met at their trysting-place, to perpetuate a raid against the deer!" Elliott,
Carolina Sports, 182.

101. Kester, *The American Shooter's Manual,* ix–x. In fact, the country was not
"destitute of game laws." See Thomas A. Lund, *American Wildlife Law* (Berkeley,
CA, 1980), 19–54; James A. Tober, *Who Owns the Wildlife?: The Political Economy of
Conservation in Nineteenth-Century America* (Westport, CT, 1981); Stuart A. Marks,
*Southern Hunting in Black and White: Nature, History, and Ritual in a Carolina Com-
munity* (Princeton, NJ, 1991), 27–35.

102. See for instance *Turf Register* 1 (1829–30): 88, 238, 400, 443–45, 2 (1831): 72, 2
(1832): 288 , 592–97, 3 (1831): 29, 3 (1832): 352–54, 4 (1833): 305, 5 (1834): 298–99; *The
American Penny Magazine* 1 (1845): 387; *The Ariel* 3 (1829): 117; *Army and Navy
Chronicle* 6 (1838), 209–11; Elliott, *Carolina Sports,* 157, 168; Hawker, *Instructions to
Young Sportsmen,* 208–09. Every issue of the *Turf Register* carried horse obituaries.

103. *American Turf Register* 1 (1829–30): 352. See also 447–50, 595–96; *The Ariel* 5

(1832), 308–09; *The American Penny Magazine* 1 (1845): 388. "The sportsman, who gives a true description of his sports, must be an egoist. It is his necessity. The things which he has seen or done are precisely those which make the liveliest impression; and with none other, but such as are thus brightly enshrined in his memory, should he attempt the difficult task of interesting the careless or preoccupied." Elliott, *Carolina Sports,* 181.

104. *American Turf Register* 3 (1832): 477, 563, 628.

105. *Spirit of the Times* 28 (1858): 128; Hooper, *Dog and Gun,* 16–19. See also *Spirit of the Times* 12 (1843): 596–97, 15 (1845): 13, 171, 225–26, 16 (1846): 331, 19 (1849): 56, 24 (1854): 524–25, 25 (1856): 618, 28 (1858): 375–76, 30 (1860): 371–72; *Turf Register* 4 (1833): 305–06, 7 (1836): 314–23; *Southern Literary Messanger* 17 (1851): 44–49; Elliott, *Carolina Sports,* 253–60; Hooper, *Dog and Gun,* 60–63; Forester, *The Warwick Woodlands,* 42, 70–80; Proctor, "Bathed in Blood," 24–55.

106. Elliott, *Carolina Sports,* 258, 284–86, 290, 292. Elliot often contrasted the calm gentleman hunter with the hysterical pothunter and slave. Out fishing in the tide waters, Elliot's slave Cain screamed in terror at the sight of a shark. Elliot calmly said, "My spear." He then speared the shark. Elliott, *Carolina Sports* 142. See also Hawker, *Instructions to Young Sportsmen,* 286–89.

107. *Niles Weekly Register* 53 (9 September 1837): 32, 54 (25 August 1838): 416, 58 (11 July 1840): 304. *The Southern Literary Journal* and the *Gentleman's Magazine* printed many hunting stories during the 1840s.

108. *American Turf Register* 4 (1833): 419. As one example of a mainstream press publishing hunting articles, see *Graham's American Monthly Magazine* 37 (1850): 61–64, 126–28, 256–58, 317–20, 382–85, 38 (1851): 65–67, 152–55, 335–37, 457–59; *Knickerbocker* 48 (1856): 290–94; *Harper's Magazine* 1 (1850): 352–53, 393–95; *The Literary World* 7 (31 August 1850): 172–73.

109. *Brother Jonathan* 6 (1843): 43; *The Eclectic Magazine* 33 (1854): 563.

110. *Texas in 1840,* 270–72; Peter H. Burnett, "Letters of Peter H. Burnett," *Oregon Historical Quarterly* 3 (1902): 419; Blegen, trans. and ed., *Ole Rynning's True Account,* 99. See also Lansford W. Hastings, *The Emigrants' Guide to Oregon and California, Containing Scenes and Incidents of a Party of California Emigrants* (Cincinnati, OH, 1845), 143–47; Robert Baird, *View of the Valley of the Mississippi*; John M. Peck, *A New Guide*; Caroline Kirkland, *A New Home*; J. M. Shively, *The Route and Distances to Oregon and California* (Washington, DC, 1846); James H. Perkins, *Annals of the West: Embracing a Concise Account of Principal Events . . .* (Cincinnati, OH, 1846); Sidney Smith, *The Settler's New Home*; Oliver, *Eight Months in Illinois,* 125–26. John Jacob Aston's inventory of tools for his Columbia River base in 1812–13 does not include any gunsmith's tools. Inventory in Russell, *Firearms, Traps, & Tools,* 402–07.

111. Darby, *Emigrant's Guide*; also *Texas in 1840,* 257–66; Oliver, *Eight Months in Illinois,* 80.

112. Peter H. Burnett, "Letters," 420; Lansford W. Hastings, *The Emigrants' Guide,* 144; Faragher, *Women and Men on the Overland Trail,* 85.

113. George R. Brooks, ed., *The Southwest Expedition of Jedediah S. Smith: His Personal Account of the Journey to California, 1826–1827* (Glendale, CA, 1977), 161, 182, 186–91, 195; Zenas Leonard, *Narrative of the Adventures of Zenas Leonard* (Clearfield, PA, 1839), 68–71; Quaife, ed., *Kit Carson's Autobiography,* 20–22, 37–39; Linnie M. Wolfe, *Son of the Wilderness: The Life of John Muir* (New York, 1945), 177; Francis P. Farquhar, *History of the Sierra Nevada* (Berkeley, CA, 1965), 25, 31, 34, 46–47, 51, 56; Frank Mullen, *The Donner Party Chronicles: A Day by Day Account of a Doomed Wagon Train, 1846–1847* (Reno, NV, 1997), 184–311. Even after the Civil

War, *The Hunter's Guide, and Trapper's Companion* (Hinsdale, NH, 1869) held that "shooting . . . is the principal method [of hunting] in Russia, but it is a wasteful method" (6). This book recommended a number of different traps for Western hunters.

114. James Longmire, "Narrative of James Longmire, A Pioneer of 1853," *Washington Historical Quarterly* 23 (1932): 51–53; Faragher, *Women and Men on the Overland Trail,* 99–100, 103; Stephen E. Ambrose, *Crazy Horse and Custer: The Parallel Lives of Two American Warriors* (New York, 1975), 3–13.

115. Lucy R. Cooke, *Crossing the Plains in 1852* (Modesto, CA, 1923), 58; Harriet S. Ward, *Prairie Schnooner Lady* (Los Angeles, 1959), 66–67; Agnes Stewart, "The Journey to Oregon—A Pioneer Girl's Diary [1853]," ed. Claire Warner Churchill, *Oregon Histocial Quarterly* 29 (1928): 86; Faragher, *Women and Men on the Overland Trail,* 98–102.

116. Ward, *Prairie Schnooner Lady,* 46; Faragher, *Women and Men on the Overland Trail,* 101; Stephen E. Ambrose, *Crazy Horse and Custer,* 37–81; Anthony McGinnis, *Counting Coup and Cutting Horses: Intertribal Warfare on the Northern Plains, 1738–1889* (Evergreen, CO, 1990), 49–84; Reid, *Policing the Elephant,* 42–50, 171–73, 198–99. Faragher quotes from one account in which three men catch up with an Indian horse thief and want to shoot him, but are dissuaded from doing so by some other men "to make the women in camp feel easy." Faragher, *Women and Men on the Overland Trail,* 102.

117. Washington Irving, *The Adventures of Captain Bonneville; or, Scenes Beyond the Rocky Mountains of the Far West* (New York, c. 1837), 12; Shively, *Route and Distances,* 6. Examining a similar source, Faragher writes, "Here on the trail was an opportunity to bring to life that male self-image" of the heroic frontiersman. Hunting took its meaning "in this context of male fantasy and the measurement of masculine identity against the standard of earlier, heroic generations of men." *Women and Men on the Overland Trail,* 135. On the often tame nature of the migration, see for example, Blegen, trans. and ed., *Ole Rynning's True Account,* 90–91.

118. J. Gerald Kennedy, *The Astonished Traveler: William Darby, Frontier Geographer and Man of Letters* (Baton Rouge, LA, 1981).

119. "The Hunter's Tale" in Kennedy, *The Astonished Traveler,* 159. First published in *The Casket* (December 1831). See also Forester, *The Deerstalkers,* 46–54, 68, 71–72, 77, 118–19.

120. "The Hunter's Tale," 163–66, 172.

121. Ibid., 168.

122. Ibid., 172–73, 178.

123. "The Moravian Indians," in Kennedy, *The Astonished Traveler,* 185. Originally published in *The Casket* (May 1833).

124. Darby, *The Emigrant's Guide to the Western and Southwestern States and Territories* in Kennedy, *The Astonished Traveler,* 214–15.

125. "Pike's Letters," *The American Magazine of Useful and Entertaining Knowledge* 2 (1836): 286.

126. *The Army and Navy Chronicle* 6 (1838): 7.

127. *Western Miscellany* 1 (1849): 213–14; *De Bow's Commercial Review* 4 (1847): 553–54. See also *Western Monthly Magazine* 1 (1833): 90–92.

128. William C. Davis, *A Way Through the Wilderness: The Natchez Trace and the Civilization of the Southern Frontier* (New York, 1995), 88–89. See especially Mark Twain's marvelous essay, "Fenimore Cooper's Literary Offenses."

129. *Western Monthly Magazine* 1 (1833): 391, 3 (1835): 63–66.

130. *Museum of Foreign Literature, Science, and Art* (New York and Philadelphia) 19 (1831): 351–56. Audubon dismissed hunting as "a very unprofitable trade" that led to "idleness, intemperance, and poverty." John James Audubon, *Ornithological Biography, or an Account of the Habits of the Birds of the United States of America*, 2 vols. (Edinburgh, 1831), 1: 232.

131. Tocqueville, *Democracy in America* 2: 267; Daniel Walker Howe, *The Political Culture of the American Whigs* (Chicago, 1979).

132. Davis, *A Way Through the Wilderness*, 278–79; James Lal Penick Jr., "John A. Murrell: A Legend of the Old Southwest," *Tennessee Historical Quarterly* 48 (1989): 174–83; James Lal Penick, *The Great Western Land Pirate: John A. Murrell in Legend and History* (Columbia, MO, 1981), 9–31; Christopher Waldrep, "Word and Deed: The Language of Lynching, 1820–1953," in Bellesiles, ed., *Lethal Imagination*, 234–35.

133. Daniel Walker Howe, *The Political Culture of the American Whigs*, 126–29, 240–49; Louis Pendleton, *Alexander H. Stephens* (Philadelphia, 1908), 85–88; Rudolph Von Abele, *Alexander H. Stephens: A Biography* (New York, 1946), 115–17. Stephens's friend, Herschel V. Johnson of Georgia, declined to duel Stephens, as did William L. Yancey of Alabama and Benjamin H. Hill. Hill stated, "I regard dueling as no evidence of courage, no vindication of truth, and no test of the character of a true gentleman." Pendleton, *Alexander H. Stephens*, 87.

134. Howe, *The Political Culture of the American Whigs*, 127; Henry Clay, "On Mr. Foote's Motion," 1850, Calvin Colton, ed., *The Works of Henry Clay*, 10 vols. (New York, 1904), 9: 418; Aron, *How the West was Lost*, 195–96.

135. Davis, *A Way Through the Wilderness*, 263–67; Robert V. Haynes, "Law Enforcement in Frontier Mississippi," *Journal of Mississippi History* 22 (1960), 30, 34.

136. John F. H. Claiborne, *Mississippi as a Province, Territory and State* (Jackson, MS, 1880), 225–28; Haynes, "Law Enforcement in Frontier Mississippi," 40–41; Raymond M. Bell, *Samuel Mason, 1739–1803* (Washington, PA, 1985); Thomas B. Thorpe, "Remembrances of the Mississippi," *Harper's New Monthly Magazine* 12 (December, 1855), 25–41. Claiborne wrote that with the death of Mason, "highway robbery ceased, and the Natchez Trace became perfectly secure. This was due mainly to the settlement on the road of numerous respectable Indians." *Mississippi as a Province*, 228.

137. Davis, *A Way Through the Wilderness*, 276.

138. Haynes, "Law Enforcement in Frontier Mississippi," 36, 39–42.

139. David Grimsted has written, "There is some irony that, in American history, the only area where it is respectable to pass such vicious verbal judgements on the poor is vigilantism." Grimsted, "Ne D'Ilici. American Vigilantism, Communal Rebirth and Political Traditions," in *People and Power: Rights, Citizenship and Violence*, ed. Loretta Valtz Mannucci (Milan, 1992), 78. On violence among the lower class, see Richard Maxwell Brown, *Strain of Violence: Historical Studies of American Violence and Vigilantism* (New York, 1975), 104–12; Grady McWhiney, *Cracker Culture: Celtic Ways in the Old South* (Tuscaloosa, AL, 1988), 146–70.

140. Salley E. Hadden, "Colonial and Revolutionary Era Slave Patrols of Virginia," in Bellesiles, ed., *Lethal Imagination*, 69–85; Nicole Etcheson, "Good Men and Notorious Rogues: Vigilantism in Massac County, Illinois, 1846–1850," in Bellesiles, ed., *Lethal Imagination*, 149–69; Robert M. Sankewicz, *Vigilantes in Gold Rush San Francisco* (Stanford, CA, 1985).

141. James W. Bragg, "Captain Slick, Arbiter of Early Alabama Morals," *Alabama Review* 11 (1958): 125–34; Nicole Etcheson, "Good Men and Notorious

Rogues," 129–69. English crowds used guns well before American mobs. During the Spa Field riot of December 2, 1816, gun shops were ransacked, and one customer was shot in W. A. Beckwith's shop. Howard L. Blackmore, *A Dictionary of London Gunmakers, 1350–1850* (Oxford, 1986), 50.

142. Featherstonhaugh, *Excursion through the Slave States,* 250–54; *Niles' Weekly Register,* 1 August 1835; Waldrep, "Word and Deed," 232–39; McDermott, ed., *Before Mark Twain,* 200–21.

143. Grimsted, "Ne D'Hier," 96, 112; Alexandre Barde, *L'Histoire des comites de la vigilance des Attakapas* (1861), trans. Henrietta G. Rogers (M.A. thesis, Louisiana State University, 1936), 31–37.

144. Michael S. Hindus, *Prison and Plantation: Crime, Justice, and Authority in Massachusetts and South Carolina, 1767–1876* (Chapel Hill, NC, 1980), 59–84.

145. Vermont Superior Court records (County Courthouse, Rutland, VT). A study of Ohio County, Virginia, 1801–10, found a total of 240 criminal indictments, three (1.2 percent) of which were for murder. Edward M. Steel, "Criminality in Jeffersonian America—A Sample," Eric H. Monkkonen, ed., *Crime and Justice in American History: The Colonies and Early Republic,* 2 vols. (Westport, CT, 1991), 2: 720–26. The recent, unpublished research of Randolph Roth of Ohio State University indicates a similar low murder rate and few instances of the gun as a murder weapon. For instance, "Why Northern New Englanders Seldom Commit Murder," paper delivered at the Annual Conference of the Society of Historians of the Early American Republic, 1987. See also Lawrence M. Friedman, *Crime and Punishment in American History* (New York, 1993), 172–92; Roger Lane, *Murder in America: A History* (Columbus, OH, 1997), 117–35.

146. As David Grimsted noted, this fact was omitted from the county history. Grimsted, "Ne D'Hier," 110; Davis, *A Way Through the Wilderness,* 263, 266, 270, 276; Gerald W. McFarland, *The "Counterfeit" Man: The True Story of the Boorn-Colvin Murder Case* (New York, 1990).

147. See appendix. Prominent cases are defined as those that made the major newspapers. Five hundred one cases are drawn from Thomas M. McDade, *The Annals of Murder: A Bibliography of Books and Pamphlets on American Murders from Colonial Times to 1900* (Norman, OK, 1961); an additional 184 cases were drawn from the following newspapers: *Baltimore Weekly Magazine; Niles' Weekly Register* (Baltimore); *Boston Gazette; Southern Patriot* (Charleston, SC); *Western Monthly Magazine* (Cincinnati); *Western Miscellany* (Dayton, OH); *Connecticut Courant* (Hartford); *Southern Recorder* (Milledgeville, GA); *New York World; New York Tribune; Graham's American Monthly Magazine* (Philadelphia); *Pennsylvania Packet* (Philadelphia); *Southern Literary Messanger* (Richmond, VA); *Vermont Journal* (Windsor). The execution of rebellious slaves has not been included in these statistics, though they certainly were unjustifiable homicide. A few prominent beating deaths of slaves have been included, though the law did not always consider these murders. Also excluded from this data are all Civil War–related murders including the New York City Draft Riot of July 1863. On murder rates see Eric H. Monkkonen, "New York City Homicides," *Social Science History* 19 (1995): 201–12.

148. *An Authentic Life of John C. Colt, Now Imprisoned for Killing Samuel Adams* (Boston, 1842); William B. Edwards, *The Story of Colt's Revolver* (Harrisburg, PA, 1953), 139–75, 191–275. Every issue of *The Non-Resistant* had a section titled "Refuge of Violence," recording all the violence in the country they could locate. Many issues contain no deaths, and the weapon used in the few murder cases they record generally involved a knife or ax.

149. Gregory Sanford, "Begging your Pardon: Early 19th Century Petitions for Pardon in Vermont," manuscript article, 1999, courtesy of author.

150. Robert V. Remini, *Andrew Jackson: The Course of American Democracy, 1833–1845,* vol. 3 of *Andrew Jackson,* 3 vols. (Baltimore, MD, 1988), 228–29; David Grimsted, *American Mobbing, 1828–1861: Toward Civil War* (New York, 1998), 132. When Daniel Sickles killed his wife's lover Philip Barton Key in 1859, his five-shot revolver misfired twice. Nat Brandt, *The Congressman Who Got Away with Murder* (Syracuse, NY, 1991), 121–22.

151. Thomas Hart Benton, *Thirty Years' View; Or, A History of the Working of the American Government for Thirty Years, From 1820 to 1850,* 2 vols. (New York, 1854), 1: 71–77. Supposedly Randolph accused Clay of forging a document from a Mexican general. Benton denied that he ever said any such thing (pp. 72–73).

152. *The Non-Resistant,* 3 August 1839.

153. John Hope Franklin, *The Militant South, 1800–1861* (Cambridge, MA, 1956), 49; John L. Wilson, *The Code of Honor; or, Rules for the Government of Principals and Seconds in Dueling* (Charleston, SC, 1858, orig. 1838); Hamilton Cochran, *Noted American Duels and Hostile Encounters* (New York, 1963), 19, 45–48, 131, 231–32; Bruce, *Violence and Culture,* 21–43.

154. Bruce Baird, "The Social Origins of Dueling in Virginia," in Bellesiles, ed., *Lethal Imagination,* 93–94; J. A. Leo Lemay, "Southern Colonial Grotesque: Robert Bolling's Neanthe," *Mississippi Quarterly* 35 (1982): 97–126; Richard J. Hooker, ed., *The Carolina Backcountry on the Eve of the Revolution: The Journal and Other Writings of Charles Woodmason, Anglican Itinerant* (Chapel Hill, NC, 1953), 154–59; Crockett, *A Narrative of the Life of David Crockett;* McDermott, ed., *Before Mark Twain,* 248–56.

155. Michael Kaplan, "New York City Tavern Violence and the Creation of a Working-Class Male Identity," *Journal of the Early Republic* 15 (1995): 591–617; Gorn, " 'Good-Bye Boys"; Gorn, *The Manly Art: Bare-Knuckle Prize Fighting in America* (Ithaca, NY, 1986).

156. Peter Way, review of Paul Gilje, *Rioting in America,* in *William and Mary Quarterly* 54 (1997): 677. "The United States had known only few and scattered riots in the nineteenth century prior to Andrew Jackson's presidency." Grimsted, *American Mobbing,* 3.

157. A review of C. McFarlane, *Lives of Banditti and Robbers* in *Western Monthly Magazine* (Cincinnati) 1 (1833): 238–39.

158. Emmons Clark, *History of the Seventh Regiment of New York 1806–1889,* 2 vols. (New York, 1890), 1: 254–55.

159. Grimsted, *American Mobbing,* 207–09.

160. Marvin E. Gettleman, *The Dorr Rebellion: A Study in American Radicalism: 1833–1849* (New York, 1973), 125–38; Grimsted, *American Mobbing,* 213–17, 230–31; Ray Allen Billington, *The Protestant Crusade, 1800–1860* (Chicago, 1964), 225–30.

161. Clark, *History of the Seventh Regiment* 1: 214–15; Paul A. Gilje, *The Road to Mobocracy,* 138–41; Grimsted, *American Mobbing,* 203–4. In the attack on Lewis Tappan's house, the crowd fled before the regiment's bayonets. No one was seriously injured; no shots were fired. Clark, *History of the Seventh Regiment* 1: 220–24; Gilje, *The Road to Mobocracy,* 162–70.

162. An Act supplemental to the several acts to organise . . . the Militia, 14 January 1833, *Laws of a Public and General Nature . . . of the State of Missouri, 1824–1836 2* (Jefferson City, 1842): 320–22; *The Revised Statutes of the State of Missouri* (St. Louis, 1845).

163. *Congressional Globe* 38th Cong., 1st sess., 2037; Frederick T. Wilson, *Federal Aid in Domestic Disturbances, 1787–1903* (Washington, DC, 1903), 32–100.

164. *American State Papers: Documents, Legislative and Executive, of the Congress of the United States,* class 5: *Military Affairs,* 7 vols. (Washington, DC, 1832–61), 5: 633, 763–65, 824, 827.

165. *American State Papers, Military Affairs* 5: 725, 873–74, 895.

166. Paul Tincher Smith, "Militia of the United States from 1846 to 1860," *Indiana Magazine of History* 15 (1919): 20–47; C. Edward Skeen, *Citizen Soldiers in the War of 1812* (Lexington, KY, 1999), 184.

167. David Reynolds, *Report of the Adjutant General of the Indiana Militia . . . [for 1845]* (Indianapolis, 1846), 37; Reynolds, *Report of the Adjutant General of the Indiana Militia . . . [for 1846]* (Indianapolis, 1846), 7.

168. Executive Document #60, 30th Congress, 1st sess., 91. Of course using the militia in an aggressive war was strictly unconstitutional under Art. 1 sect. 8, which states that Congress has the authority "for calling forth the Militia to execute the Laws of the Union, suppress Insurrections and repel Invasions."

169. Marvin A. Kreidberg and Marton G. Henry, *History of Military Mobilization in the U.S. Army, 1775–1945* (Washington, DC, 1955), 74–75; John S. D. Eisenhower, *So Far From God: The U.S. War with Mexico, 1846–1848* (New York, 1990), 87, 101–02.

170. Emory Upton, *The Military Policy of the United States* (Washington, DC, 1912), 202–03; Anthony Marro, "Vermont's Local Militia Units, 1815–1860," *Vermont History* 40 (1972): 29–39; George C. Bittle, "In the Defense of Florida: The Organized Florida Militia from 1821 to 1920" (Ph.D. diss., Florida State University, 1965), 180–81; Charles W. Hall, *Regiments and Armories of Massachusetts,* 2 vols. (Boston, 1899), 1: 141–48; Leuck to Oliver, 24 November 1846, "Militia Reports and Recommendations, 1846," Military Records, Reel 64, Massachusetts Adjutant General's Office; Clark, *History of the Seventh Regiment* 1: 326–35.

171. Edward G. Ryan to the Racine *Advocate,* 29 October 1846, X to the Platteville *Independent American,* 29 October 1846, Milo M. Quaife, ed., *The Struggle over Ratification, 1846–47,* vol. 28 of the *Collections of the Historical Society of Wisconsin* (Madison, WI, 1920), 29, 111; Milo M. Quaife, ed., *The Convention of 1846,* vol. 27 of *Collections of the Historical Society of Wisconsin* (Madison, WI, 1919), 305–6; Milo M. Quaife, ed., *The Attainment of Statehood,* vol. 29 of *Collections of the Historical Society of Wisconsin* (Madison, WI, 1928), 400–6; Ulysses S. Grant, *Personal Memoirs of U.S. Grant,* 2 vols. (New York, 1885–86), 1: 53.

172. A. T. Andreas, *History of Cook County, Illinois* (Chicago, 1884), 213; Ezra M. Price, "The 4th Illinois Infantry in the War with Mexico," *Transactions of the Illinois State Historical Society* 11 (1906): 173–75; Wilbur G. Kurtz Jr., "The First Regiment of Georgia Volunteers in the Mexican War," *The Georgia Historical Quarterly* 27 (1943); Kenneth O. McCreedy, "Palladium of Liberty: The American Militia System, 1815–1861" (Ph.D. diss., University of California, Berkeley, 1991), 354–59; Eisenhower, *So Far From God,* 25. A total of 13,768 Americans died in the war. Upton, *The Military Policy of the United States,* 216–18.

173. Carey McWilliams, *North from Mexico: The Spanish-Speaking People of the United States* (New York, 1990), 101; Luther Giddings, *Sketches of the Campaign in Northern Mexico* (New York, 1853) 223, 225–27. For other negative assessments of the shooting abilities of these volunteers, see William S. Myers, ed., *The Mexican War Diary of George B. McClellan* (Princeton, NJ, 1917), 16; George W. Smith and Charles

Judah, eds., *Chronicles of the Gringos: The United States Army in the Mexican War, 1846–1848* (Albuquerque, NM, 1968), 274–75.

174. Paul A. C. Koistinen, *Beating Plowshares into Swords: The Political Economy of American Warfare, 1606–1865* (Lawrence, KS, 1996), 89–98. For a detailed description of the variety of weaponry employed by U.S. forces during the Mexican War, see Richard B. Winders, *Mr. Polk's Army: The American Military Experience in the Mexican War* (College Station, TX, 1997), 88–103.

175. George Talcott to W. L. Marcy, 18 March 1848, Stephen Vincent Benet, comp., *A Collection of Annual Reports and Other Important Papers Relating to the Ordnance Department, 1812–1889,* 4 vols. (Washington, DC, 1890), 2: 218; Justin H. Smith, *The War with Mexico,* 2 vols. (New York, 1919), 1: 139–40, 450–51; H. W. Halleck, *Elements of Military Art and Science: or, Course of Instruction in Strategy, Fortification, Tactics of Battles, &c.* (Westport, CT, 1971, orig. 1846); Winfield Scott, *Infantry Tactics; or Rules for the Exercise and Manoeuvres of the Infantry of the U.S. Army,* 2 vols. (Washington, DC, 1825); Taylor quoted, Eisenhower, *So Far From God,* 76. For similar orders emphasizing the use of the bayonet, see ibid., 135; Smith, *The War with Mexico* 1: 250–51; Zachary Taylor, *Letters of Zachary Taylor, From the Battle-fields of the Mexican War* (Rochester, NY, 1908), 1–2, 178.

176. Eisenhower, *So Far From God,* 326. See also ibid., 246–47, 279–83, 325–42; Grady McWhiney and Perry D. Jamieson, *Attack and Die: Civil War Military Tactics and the Southern Heritage* (University, AL, 1982), 41–47.

177. Smith, *The War with Mexico* 1: 298–302; Eisenhower, *So Far From God,* 247.

178. Grant, *Personal Memoirs* 1: 95.

179. A point developed at length in Lester R. Dillon Jr., *American Artillery in the Mexican War, 1846–1847* (Austin, TX, 1975); Eisenhower, *So Far From God,* see esp. 379–80. A few officers spoke to this issue at the time; see Taylor to R. C. Wood, 9 May 1846, Taylor, *Letters of Zachary Taylor,* 1; Giddings, *Sketches of the Campaign,* 40–41.

180. Additional evidence that most frontier settlers still lacked firearms can be found in the Indian attack on the white Americans of Taos and Mora on January 19, 1847. Nine Americans, including Governor Charles Bent, were killed in these attacks; there is no evidence that any guns were used on either side. Eisenhower, *So Far From God,* 236–37.

181. Letter from Yerba Buena, 24 October 1846, printed in *The Friend,* 16 November 1846, in Oscar Lewis, ed., *California in 1846* (San Francisco, 1934), 31–36 (quote 32); Eisenhower, *So Far From God,* 212–19; Smith, *The War with Mexico* 1: 331–40.

182. Eisenhower, *So Far From God,* 219–32; Smith, *The War with Mexico* 1: 340–46.

183. Charles Edward Chapel, *Guns of the Old West* (New York, 1961), 271–74; Don Russell, *The Life and Legends of Buffalo Bill* (Norman, OK, 1960), 164–65; Kent L. Steckmesser, *The Western Hero in History and Legend* (Norman, OK, 1965), 175–77; John Francis McDermott, ed., *Audubon in the West* (Normon, OK, 1965), 47; William Hosley, *Colt: The Making of an American Legend* (Amherst, MA, 1996), 66–97.

184. Taylor, *Eldorado* 1: 101; Charles Howard Shinn, *Mining Camps: A Study of American Frontier Government* (New York, 1965, orig. 1885), 230; Oscar O. Winther, *Via Western Express and Stagecoach* (Lincoln, NE, 1968), 81, 98; John L. McConnel, *Western Characters: or, Types of Border Life in the Western States* (New York, 1853), 171–76, 244–45; Lynn I. Perrigo, "Law and Order in Early Colorado Mining

Camps," *Mississippi Valley Historical Review* 28 (1941): 41–62; Thomas M. Marshall, "The Miners' Laws of Colorado," *American Historical Review* 25 (1919–20): 426–40; Lynn I. Perrigo, "Law and Order in Early Colorado Mining Camps"; Roger D. McGrath, *Gunfighters, Highwaymen, and Vigilantes: Violence on the Frontier* (Berkeley, CA, 1984), 267–68; Robert R. Dykstra, "To Live and Die in Dodge City: Body Counts, Law and Order, and the Case of *Kansas v. Gill,*" in Michael Bellesiles, ed., *Lethal Imagination,* 211–26.

185. George R. Stewart, *Committee of Vigilance: Revolution in San Francisco, 1851* (Boston, 1964), 327. Stewart added that "There has been a tendency among historians to exaggerate the amount of crime" in California, but that a close study of the newspapers led him to conclude that homicide was extremely rare. In contrast, Hubert H. Bancroft claimed 583 murders occurred in frontier California in 1855. If accurate, this figure makes California in 1855 the most homicidal place in the antebellum period. Bancroft listed Hubert Howe Bancroft, *Popular Tribunals,* 2 vols. (San Francisco, 1887), 1: 131–32. Stewart dismissed Bancroft since he offered no sources for this murder record and used "constructed conversations . . . and remarkable details for which no source is given and for which I can find no contemporary authority." Stewart, *Committee of Vigilance,* 325.

186. Leonard Pitt, *The Decline of the Californios: A Social History of the Spanish-Speaking Californians, 1846–1890* (Berkeley, CA, 1966), 60. Even nativist violence seems to have had some relation with slavery. David Grimsted calculated that seventy-seven people were killed in riots involving the Know-Nothings, seventy-two of them in slave states. Grimsted, *American Mobbing,* 226.

187. Gunther Barth, *Bitter Strength: A History of the Chinese in the United States, 1850–1870* (Cambridge, MA, 1964), 94–95; Robert Seager II, "Some Denominational Reaction to Chinese Immigration to California, 1856–1892," *Pacific Coast Historical Review* 28 (1959): 61; W. Eugene Hollon, *Frontier Violence: Another Look* (New York, 1974), 87.

188. Clark, *History of the Seventh Regiment* 1: 365.

189. Faragher, *Sugar Creek,* 212; *Daily State Register* (Springfield, IL), 31 July 1860.

190. Grimsted, *American Mobbing,* 230.

191. Kingsford, *Impressions of the West and South,* 53; Murray, *Lands of the Slave and the Free,* 135–37. Grady McWhiney made use of travel accounts to describe antebellum southern violence, though he treated southern culture as undifferentiated and unchanging despite the implication of his own evidence that violence increased in the South in the late 1840s and 1850s. McWhiney took this ahistorical approach in order to argue that southern violence is the product of a "Celtic heritage," which is also not subject to alteration over the centuries. "The South was and still is a violent society because violence is one of the cultural traditions that Southerners brought with them to America." Proof of the Celtic heritage of violence is found in the observations of the English, who label the Irish and Scots "a barbourous and . . . a warlike people." This is rather like using the opinions of slaveowners to describe the character of their slaves. Anyone familiar with the English conquest and occupation of Ireland and Scotland will have difficulty accepting that violence was unusual to these latter peoples. Slavery and its defense seem sufficient explanation for this increased southern violence of the 1850s. It is certainly an error to confuse stereotype and reality. McWhiney, *Cracker Culture,* 149, 152. Thomas Jefferson perceived this connection in 1791 in his *Notes on the State of Virginia.* Andrew A. Lipscomb and Albert E.

Bergh, eds., *The Writings of Thomas Jefferson* (Washington, DC, 1904), 2: 191–201, 225–28.

192. Grimsted, *American Mobbing*.

193. Stephens to Thomas H. Thomas, 25 May 1856, Stephens Papers, Emory University.

194. Waldrep, "Word and Deed," 230–35; Leonard L. Richards, *Gentlemen of Property and Standing: Anti-abolition Mobs in Jacksonian America* (New York, 1970), 6–52; Grimsted, *American Mobbing*, 3–32, 101–3; Bruce, *Violence and Culture*, 114–60.

195. Junius P. Rodriguez, "Complicity and Deceit: Lewis Cheney's Plot and Its Bloody Consequences," in Bellesiles, ed., *Lethal Imagination*, 139–47; Grimsted, "Ne D'Hier," 79n; Grimsted, *American Mobbing*, 138–47.

196. Grimsted, *American Mobbing*, 97. See also Eugene D. Genovese, *A Consuming Fire: The Fall of the Confederacy in the Mind of the White Christian South* (Athens, GA, 1998), 3–33.

197. John Schneider, "Mob Violence and Public Order in the American City, 1830–1865" (Ph.D. diss., University of Minnesota, 1971), 45, 66, 82, 132, 153; Richards, *Gentlemen of Property and Standing*, 8–9, 124–27; Nicholas B. Wainwright, ed., *A Philadelphia Perspective, the Diary of Sidney George Fisher Concerning the Years 1841–1871* (Philadelphia, 1967), 168; William J. Bopp and Donald O. Schultz, *A Short History of American Law Enforcement* (Springfield, IL, 1972), 33; Grimsted, *American Mobbing*, 62–64.

198. The earliest such advertisement emphasizing self-defense that I can locate is one for the New York hardware store A. W. Spies & Co., which appeared in the *National Police Gazette*, 28 February 1846.

199. W. Darrell Overdyke, *The Know-Nothing Party in the South* (Baton Rouge, LA, 1950), 240–60. David Grimsted has counted 115 antiabolitionist crowd actions claiming twelve lives in the two years prior to the Civil War—just seven abolitionists had been killed in the previous thirty years. Grimsted, *American Mobbing*, 101, 233–40. In general see Tyler Gregory Anbinder, *Nativism and Slavery: The Northern Know-Nothings and the Politics of the 1850s* (New York, 1992).

200. Gladstone, *The Englishman in Kansas*, 80; Grimsted, *American Mobbing*, 247–48, 259; Charles Robinson, ed., *The Kansas Conflict* (New York, 1892), 265–67, 392–406.

201. James Montgomery to George L. Stearns, 11 March 1861, George L. Stearns Papers, Kansas State Historical Society, Topeka, KS. Thanks to Michael Johnson for this citation.

202. "Connecticut Kansas Colony," 1856 signed by C. B. Lines, William H. Russell, S. W. S. Dutton, Edward Strong, Broadsides Collection, American Antiquarian Society; Beecher quoted in Hosley, *Colt*, 70. In general see Allan Nevins, *Ordeal of the Union*, 2 vols. (New York, 1947), 2: 380–411.

203. Grimsted, *American Mobbing*, 241–42.

Chapter Ten

The Arming of the American People

1. Samuel Colt to Charles Manby, 18 May 1852, Colt Collection, Connecticut Historical Society, Hartford, CT.

2. Frank Raymond Secoy, *Changing Military Patterns of the Great Plains Indians* (Lincoln, NE, 1992), 96–97; John E. Parsons, "Gunmakers for the American Fur Company," *The New-York Historical Society Quarterly* 36 (1952): 183–86.

3. Secoy, *Changing Military Patterns,* 98–100; Arcadi Gluckman, *United States Muskets, Rifles, and Carbines* (Buffalo, 1948), 56–57, 348–49; E. C. Lenz, *Muzzle Flashes* (Huntington, WV, 1944), 136–37.

4. Secoy, *Changing Military Patterns,* 99; R. I. Dodge, *Our Wild Indians* (Hartford, CT, 1882), 450.

5. *American State Papers: Documents, Legislative and Executive, of the Congress of the United States,* class 5: *Military Affairs,* 7 vols. (Washington, DC, 1832–61), 6: 104–11, 987; Philip B. Sharpe, *The Rifle in America* (New York, 1938), 12–13; James E. Hicks, *Notes on United States Ordnance,* 2 vols. (Mount Vernon, NY, 1940), 1: 59; Simeon N. D. North and Ralph H. North, *Simeon North, First Official Pistol Maker of the United States* (Concord, NH, 1913), 142–57; Merritt Roe Smith, *Harpers Ferry Armory and the New Technology: The Challenge of Change* (Ithaca, NY, 1977), 198–216; David A. Hounshell, *From the American System to Mass Production, 1800–1932: The Development of Manufacturing Technology in the United States* (Baltimore, MD, 1984), 42.

6. *American State Papers, Military Affairs* 7: 466–82, 525–32, 763, 789 (quote p. 468); Smith, *Harpers Ferry Armory,* 216–18.

7. *American State Papers: Military Affairs* 7: 471–72.

8. Newton Bosworth, *A Treatise on the Rifle, Musket, Pistol, and Fowling Piece* (New York, 1846), 22. For a summary of this research, see George Raudzens, "Firepower Limitations in Modern Military History," *Journal of the Society for Army Historical Research* 67 (1989): 130–53. For specific studies see Hans Busk, *The Rifle and How to Use It* (London, 1859), 17–19; Sir Thomas Longmore, *Gunshot Injuries, Their History, Characteristic Features, Complications, And General Treatment* (London, 1895), 688–89; B. P. Hughes, *Firepower: Weapons Effectiveness on the Battlefield, 1630–1850* (New York, 1974), 165–68; Paddy Griffith, *Forward into Battle: Fighting Tactics from Waterloo to Vietnam* (Chichester, UK, 1981); Martin L. Van Creveld, *Supplying War: Logistics from Wallenstein to Patton* (Cambridge, 1977). See also John Keegan's brilliant *The Face of Battle* (London, 1976).

9. *Eclaireur* 1 [1853]: 14–15. The numbering system of the *Eclaireur* changed often and erratically. Poinsett quoted, William Hosley, *Colt: The Making of an American Legend* (Amherst, MA, 1996), 44; Felicia J. Deyrup, *Arms Makers of the Connecticut Valley* (Northampton, MA, 1948), 22–24; Justin H. Smith, *The War With Mexico,* 2 vols. (New York, 1919), 1: 450.

10. Deyrup, *Arms Makers of the Connecticut Valley,* 26; Hounshell, *From the American System to Mass Production,* 25–32; Smith, *Harpers Ferry Armory,* 92, 113–17, 241–46; Claude Blair, ed., *Pollard's History of Firearms* (New York, 1983), 161–87.

11. Lee to the Ordnance Department, 20 November 1817 Springfield Armory Records, National Archives, Washington, DC; Deyrup, *Arms Makers of the Connecticut Valley,* 55–57; Michael S. Raber, "Conservative Innovators, Military Small Arms, and Industrial History at Springfield Armory, 1794–1918," *Industrial Archeology* 14 (1988): 1–21.

12. "Improvement in Fire Arms, by John W. Cochran," *The American Magazine of Useful and Entertaining Knowledge* 3 (1837): 160–62.

13. *Hartford Daily Times,* 5 January 1852. See also Henry Howe, *Adventures and Achievements of Americans: A Series of Narratives Illustrating Their Heroism, Self-Reliance, Genius and Enterprise* (New York, 1859), 148–49.

14. Deyrup, *Arms Makers of the Connecticut Valley,* 26; Charles T. Haven and Frank A. Belden, *A History of the Colt Revolver, and the Other Arms Made by Colt's Patent Firearms Manufacturing Company from 1836 to 1940* (New York, 1940), 46–49; Hosley, *Colt,* 82–84.

15. The leading British expert on early firearms, H. L. Blackmore, had written "The flintlock pistol was always of questionable value. As a personal weapon carried in the pocket it had more psychological value than any other. . . . In fact, according to some contemporary writers, it was better to rely on a sword or bludgeon for personal protection rather than a pistol. The introduction of the percussion cap altered all this." Blair, ed., *Pollard's History of Firearms,* 178.

16. Samuel Colt, "On the Application of Machinery to the Manufacture of Rotating Chambered-Breech Fire-Arms" (London, 1851), in Haven and Belden, *History of the Colt Revolver,* 312–26 (quote p. 316); Walter Prescott Webb, *The Great Plains* (New York, 1931), 167–79; Hosley, *Colt,* 13–14. In general, on Colt's advertisements and testimonials, see the Colt Manuscripts, Wadsworth Atheneum, Hartford, CT.

17. Carl P. Russell, *Guns on the Early Frontiers* (Berkeley, CA, 1957), 96; Deyrup, *Arms Makers of the Connecticut Valley,* 24. Russell bases this influence on the Colt Model 1836, of which only a few hundred were ever made, and those sold almost entirely to the army.

18. Colt quoted in Hosley, *Colt,* 81; Talcott, Annual Report of the Chief of Ordnance, 3 December 1850, Talcott to Conrad, 30 December 1850, Stephen Vincent Benet, comp., *A Collection of Annual Reports and Other Important Papers Relating to the Ordnance Department, 1812–1889,* 4 vols. (Washington, DC, 1890), 2: 353, 361; Haven and Belden, *History of the Colt Revolver,* 254–67, 300–11.

19. James E. Serven, *Colt Firearms, 1836–1958* (Santa Ana, CA, 1954), xx–xxx; Hosley, *Colt,* 80–92; Hounshell, *From the American System to Mass Production,* 47; Haven and Belden, *History of the Colt Revolver,* 339–43, 368–70, 374–81.

20. John W. Oliver, *History of American Technology* (New York, 1956), 255–56; Haven and Belden, *A History of the Colt Revolver,* 82–89, 312–26, 334–45; William B. Edwards, *The Story of Colt's Revolver* (Harrisburg, PA, 1953); Hosley, *Colt,* 27.

21. Hosley, *Colt,* 84–86, 98–115; Haven and Belden, *A History of the Colt Revolver,* 345–67; Nathan Rosenberg, comp., *The American System of Manufactures: The Report of the Committee on the Machinery of the United States 1855* (Edinburgh, 1969). Nathan Rosenberg credits the arms industry with introducing machine tool industry to other areas of American production, from sewing machines to bicycles. Rosenberg "Technological Change in the Machine Tool Industry, 1840–1910," *Journal of Economic History* 23 (1963): 414–43. A point well demonstrated in Hounshell, *From the American System to Mass Production,* 15–123.

22. Hounshell, *From the American System to Mass Production,* 42–45, 49; Carolyn C. Cooper, " 'A Whole Battalion of Stockers': Thomas Blanchard's Production Line and Hand Labor at Springfield Armory," *Industrial Archeology* 14 (1988): 37–57.

23. W. W. Greener, *The Gun and Its Development* (New York, 1967), 130–33; John E. Parsons, *Smith & Wesson Revolvers: The Pioneer Single Action Models* (New York, 1957), 6–14; Blair, ed., *Pollard's History of Firearms,* 239–41.

24. Deyrup, *Arms Makers of the Connecticut Valley,* 19–21.

25. Bosworth, *Treatise on the Rifle,* 19–28 (quotes pp. 13–14, 28).

26. Blair, ed., *Pollard's History of Firearms,* 183–87.

27. Claud E. Fuller, *Springfield Muzzle-Loading Shoulder Arms: A Description of the Flint Lock Muskets, Musketoons and Carbines* (New York, 1930), 113–15; Brian J.

Given, *A Most Pernicious Thing: Gun Trading and Native Warfare in the Early Contact Period,* (Ottawa, 1994), 102; Claud E. Fuller, *The Rifled Musket* (Harrisburg, PA, 1958), 3–11.

28. Given, *A Most Pernicious Thing,* 104–05; Hughes, *Firepower* (New York, 1974), 3, 64; Carl L. Davis, *Arming the Union: Small Arms in the Civil War* (Port Washington, NY, 1973), 38–40.

29. Bosworth, *Treatise on the Rifle,* 56–57; Deyrup, *Arms Makers of the Connecticut Valley,* 60–75; Smith, *Harpers Ferry Armory,* 76–82.

30. Work Returns, Notice of Superintendent 13 September 1827, Springfield Armory Records, National Archives, Washington, DC; Memorandum Book of Contracts and Nathan Starr's Day Book, 1823–52, Starr Papers, Middlesex County Historical Society; Deyrup, *Arms Makers of the Connecticut Valley,* 102–04; Benet, comp., *A Collection of Annual Reports* 1: 395–96; Hosley, *Colt,* 114–25. Not that workers were always pleased with the transition to clock-based labor. Smith, *Harpers Ferry Armory,* 271–74.

31. Bosworth, *A Treatise on the Rifle,* 106; G. Gregory, *A New and Complete Dictionary of Arts and Sciences, Including the Latest Improvement and Discovery,* 3 vols. (New York, 1819), II: see "musket"; A Gentleman of Philadelphia County [Lee Kester], *The American Shooter's Manual* (Philadelphia, 1827), 214–17.

32. North and North, *Simeon North,* 10–36; Merrill Lindsay, *The New England Gun: The First Two Hundred Years* (New Haven, CT, 1975); Smith, *Harpers Ferry Armory,* 52–103.

33. Ripley quoted Hosley, *Colt,* 42; Hounshell, *From the American System to Mass Production,* 45–47. The power of image overwhelms reality in discussing early firearms. Paul B. Jenkins, a prominent gun expert early in this century, wrote that the Sharps rifle "accompanied every wagon train from the Mississippi to the Rio Grande, . . . and taught alike Pawnee, Ute, . . . and Blackfoot that . . . their Canute-like attempts to check the incoming tide of white men were predestined to be a losing game." Harold F. Williamson, *Winchester, the Gun that Won the West* (Washington, DC, 1952), 25.

34. United States Census Office, *Statistical View of the United States: Embracing Its Territory, Population—White, Free Colored, and Slave—Moral and Social Condition, Industry, Property, and Revenue* (Washington, DC, 1854); United States Census Office, *Manufactures in 1860* (Washington, DC, 1865); J. Leander Bishop, *A History of American Manufactures, from 1608 to 1860: Comprising Annals of the Industry of the United States in Machinery, Manufactures and Useful Arts,* 2 vols. (Philadelphia, PA, 1864).

35. Based on U.S. Census Office, *Manufactures in 1860;* Deyrup, *Arms Makers of the Connecticut Valley,* 218.

36. Lawrence P. Shelton, *California Gunsmiths, 1846–1900* (Fair Oaks, CA, 1977), 3–5. This book contains a large number of advertisements.

37. Robert W. Bingham, *Early Buffalo Gunsmiths* (Buffalo, NY, 1934), 15–16; Ebenezer Stone, *Annual Report of the Adjutant General of the Commonwealth of Mass for the Year Ending Dec. 31, 1852* (Boston, 1853), 31.

38. United States Congress, *Tariff Acts Passed By the Congress of the United States from 1789 to 1909* (Washington, DC, 1909).

39. Secretary of the Treasury McLane, *Documents Relative to the Manufactures in the United States* (Washington, DC, 1833), vols. 3–7 of Thomas C. Cochran, ed. *The New American State Papers: Manufactures,* 9 vols. (Wilmington, DE, 1972), 3: 318–19, 4: 19–20, 181–82, 201–02, 205–06, 251–52, 5: 35–36, 119–20, 359–61; Joseph C. G.

Kennedy, *Abstract of the Statistics of Manufactures, According to the Returns of the Seventh Census* (Washington, DC, 1858), vol. 9 of Cochran, ed., *New American State Papers: Manufactures* 9: 548. For a precise breakdown of these statistics, see the appendix. There is also a much briefer listing in 1845: Secretary of Treasury George M. Bibb, *Statistics of the Agriculture and Manufactures . . . of the United States* (Washington, DC, 1845) in Cochran, ed., *The New American State Papers: Manufactures* 8: 375, 391, 416, 442, 516.

40. On this new productivity see Deyrup, *Arms Makers of the Connecticut Valley,* 115–215; Michael S. Raber, "Conservative Innovators, Military Small Arms, and Industrial History at Springfield Armory, 1794–1918," *The Journal of the Society for Industrial Archeology* 14 (1988): 1–21; David A. Hounshell, *From the American System to Mass Production,* 46–50; Robert A. Howard, "Interchangeable Parts Reexamined: The Private Sector of the American Arms Industry on the Eve of the Civil War," *Technology and Culture* 19 (October 1978), 633–49.

41. See appendix on pages 445–54.

42. Jacob Abbott, "The Springfield Armory," *Harper's Magazine* 5 (1852): 143–61, quote p. 161.

43. Haven and Belden, *A History of the Colt Revolver,* 389; Davis, *Arming the Union,* 100–04.

44. William C. Davis, *A Way Through the Wilderness: The Natchez Trace and the Civilization of the Southern Frontier* (New York, 1995), 24, 319–20.

45. The last militia return for Delaware was in 1827, Indiana in 1832, Maryland and Mississippi in 1838, Tennessee in 1840, Vermont in 1843, D.C. and North Carolina in 1845, Texas in 1847; Oregon and Iowa issued no returns before the Civil War. Paul Tincher Smith, "Militia of the United States from 1846 to 1860," *Indiana Magazine of History* 15 (1919): 23, 34–36.

46. William H. Zierdt, *Narrative History of the 109th Artillery Pennsylvania National Guard, 1775–1930* (Wilkes-Barre, PA, 1932), 66; Mark Pitcavage, "An Equitable Burden: The Decline of the States Militias" (Ph.D. diss., Ohio State University, 1995), 716–20; Tom Dillard, "'An Arduous Task to Perform': Organizing the Territorial Arkansas Militia," *Arkansas Historical Quarterly* 41 (1992): 174–90; Cyril B. Upham, "Historical Survey of the Militia in Iowa, 1838–1865," *Iowa Journal of History and Politics* 17 (1919): 299–405; Dan Elbert Clark, "Frontier Defense in Iowa, 1850–1865," *The Iowa Journal of History and Politics* 16 (1918): 315–86.

47. *Laws of New York, 1857,* 1: 416; *Quincy Patriot* quoted in *The Non-Resistant* 1 June 1839; Stone, *Annual Report of the Adjutant General . . . 1852,* 15; *Annual Report of the Adjutant General of the Commonwealth of Massachusetts for the Year Ending Dec. 31, 1855* (Boston, 1856), 23; Charles W. Hall, *Regiments and Armories of Massachusetts,* 2 vols. (Boston, 1899), 1: 160–64.

48. Adjutant General of Virginia, *Report of the Adjutant-General for . . . 1853* (Richmond, VA, 1854), 1–4; Smith, "Militia of the United States from 1846 to 1860," 31, 33, 45; Adjutant General W. H. Richardson to Kemper, 5 January 1857, Kemper Papers, 4098, Box 2, University of Virginia (Charlottesville, VA).

49. Stewart L. Gates, "Disorder and Social Organization: The Militia in Connecticut Public Life, 1660–1860" (Ph.D. diss., University of Connecticut, 1975), 2; Marcus Cunliffe, *Soldiers and Civilians: The Martial Spirit in America, 1775–1865* (Boston, 1968), 203; Kenneth O. McCreedy, "Palladium of Liberty: The American Militia System, 1815–1861" (Ph.D. diss., University of California, Berkeley, 1991), 267–324. Members of volunteer companies did not even have to be from the immediate vicinity. In 1846 the legislature passed an act that would have terminated all the

voluntary militia by requiring men to serve in companies within their districts. The volunteer companies fought back, convincing the governor to delay enforcement of the act until it was repealed. Emmons Clark, *History of the Seventh Regiment of New York, 1806–1889* 2 vols. (New York, 1890), 1: 323–24.

50. Clark, *History of the Seventh Regiment* 1: 327–29. The 7th Regiment began 1847 as the 27th, but in the reorganization became the 7th Regiment of the 3d Brigade of the 1st Division of the New York State Militia.

51. The regiment had not grown much in the 1840s, rarely varying by much from its 1840 strength of 349. In 1845 the regiment held an encampment and only two hundred men showed up, which was considered disastrous, almost to the point of dissolving the regiment. Clark, *History of the Seventh Regiment* 1: 277, 319, 335, 340, 353, 363, 374, 384, 390.

52. This proposal replicated the suggestions of Henry Knox and George Washington back in the 1790s. There had been a few such "select militia" units in the Colonial period, but they had died out in the years after the War of 1812. *American State Papers, Military Affairs* 1: 7–8; McCreedy, "Palladium of Liberty," 16–46; Lyle D. Brundage, "The Organization, Administrations, and Training of the United States Ordinary and Volunteer Militia, 1792–1861" (Ph.D. diss., University of Michigan, 1958), 52–55, 142–47.

53. See, for example, "Report of Committee on Volunteer Companies," 18 September 1856, "Petition of Volunteer Companies of St. Philip's and St. Michael's" [1849], Military Affairs Committee Files, Legislative Group, South Carolina Department of Archives and History, Columbia, SC; Annual Report of the Massachusetts Adjutant General, 1840–1844, Commonwealth of Massachusetts Military Division, Military Records, National Guard Armory, Natick, MA.

54. Shooting at a target had never been particularly popular, usually involving just the 8th Company. Clark, *History of the Seventh Regiment* 1: 306, 322, 338–39, 465, 2: 452. In 1835 the regiment started a contest among the companies, the "Trial of Skill." The "Order of Merit" went to the company that drilled best, with shooting no part of that evaluation. The 7th Company did so poorly in 1836 that it disbanded; many of its members quit the militia entirely. The regiment dropped the Order of Merit. Ibid. 1: 235–37, 245–47, 249.

55. "Minority Report of the Commission Appointed . . . to Examine the Militia System of the State," 28 November 1859, Military Affairs Committee Files, Legislative Group, South Carolina Dept. of Archives and History; Henry W. B. Howard, ed., *The Eagle and Brooklyn,* 2 vols. (Brooklyn, NY, 1893), 2: 820; Hartford *Daily Times,* 8 November 1860; Hosley, *Colt,* 71; McCreedy, "Palladium of Liberty," 291–302; Pitcavage, "An Equitable Burden," 315–404. A major controversy arose in 1846 when sergeants were ordered to appear at musters with muskets rather than swords. The sergeants spent weeks lobbying against this change, and succeeded in getting it overturned. Clark, *History of the Seventh Regiment* 1: 323.

56. Clark, *History of the Seventh Regiment* 1: 330.

57. McCreedy, "Palladium of Liberty," 267–324; Michael Feldberg, *The Philadelphia Riots of 1844: A Study of Ethnic Conflict* (Westport, CT, 1975); Richard Moody, *The Astor Place Riot* (Bloomington, IN, 1958); Clark, *History of the Seventh Regiment* 1: 341–51. The Astor Place riot created a long-standing "feeling of bitter hostility . . . toward the Seventh Regiment among the reckless and disorderly classes" of New York, while the regiment became a "favorite" among "respectable citizens." The hostility of "the dangerous classes" was so great that the city canceled

the Fourth of July parade and when the 7th next paraded, in September, they were met with a constant stream of verbal abuse, but no violence. One captain, James Waugh, had refused to order out his company during the riots and resigned rather than face a court-martial. Clark, *History of the Seventh Regiment* 1: 349–51.

58. David Grimsted, *American Mobbing, 1828–1861: Toward Civil War* (New York, 1998) 227–28.

59. Mark Pitcavage offers a careful study of the militia "casting aside its traditional role as a defense against foreign invaders . . . in favor of the role of civil police." Pitcavage, "An Equitable Burden," 740–72 (quote p. 758). Most revealing in this context are the sermons delivered to the Boston Artillery Company, a tradition that goes back to the mid-seventeenth century. A number of these ministers started to appeal to this elite volunteer unit to defend social order against internal dangers. See, particularly, Artemas B. Muzzey, *A Sermon Preached Before the Ancient and Honorable Artillery Company on Their 199th Anniversary, June 5, 1837* (Boston, 1837); Otis A. Skinner, *A Discourse Preached Before the Ancient and Honorable Artillery Company, June 3, 1839* (Boston, 1839); John S. C. Abbot, *A Discourse Preached Before the Ancient and Honorable Artillery Company, June 6, 1842* (Boston, 1842); Thomas M. Clark, *A Discourse Delivered Before the Ancient and Honorable Artillery Company* (Boston, 1849).

60. Clark, *History of the Seventh Regiment* 1: 227, 244, 299–300.

61. *Citizen Soldier,* 15 January 1841, 198, quoted in Gates, "Disorder and Social Organization," 235, 239. See also *Citizen Soldier,* 22 January 1840, 204; 29 July 1840, 1212; 28 March 1841, 253.

62. Pauline Maier, "Popular Uprisings and Civil Authority in Eighteenth-Century America," *William and Mary Quarterly* 27 (1970): 33–35; Clark, *History of the Seventh Regiment* 1: 244, 276. The centrality of the militia to the preservation of order in New York City is evident in the city's turning over the top floor of the new Central Market for their use as a headquarters and armory in 1839. Ibid. 1: 258–59, 262, 266.

63. This editorial came in the aftermath of the mob attack on the Ursuline Convent. *Boston Evening Transcript,* 14 August 1834.

64. Clark, *History of the Seventh Regiment* 1: 216.

65. Gideon Tomlinson, *Message of the Governor, to the General Assembly of Connecticut, May Session, 1829* (Hartford, CT, 1829), 12; *Report of the Joint Standing Committee on the Militia* (Hartford, CT, 1835), 3; Isaac Toucey, *Message from His Excellency, Isaac Toucey, to the Legislature of Connecticut* (Hartford, CT, 1846), 15–16. See also William W. Ellsworth, *Speech of His Excellency, William W. Ellsworth, Governor of Connecticut* (Hartford, CT, 1839), 11–14; Roger S. Baldwin, *Speech of His Excellency, Roger S. Baldwin, Governor of Connecticut* (Hartford, CT, 1845), 8–9; Clark Bissell, *Speech of His Excellency, Clark Bissell, Governor of Connecticut* (New Haven, CT, 1848), 10–12; William A. Buckingham, *Message of His Excellency William A. Buckingham, Governor of Connecticut* (Hartford, CT, 1859), 13; Joseph D. Williams, *Annual Report of the Adjutant General of the State of Connecticut for the Year 1858* (New Haven, CT, 1859), 26–27.

66. *United States Magazine and Democratic Review* 25 (1849): 484; Dennis Charles Rousey, *Policing the Southern City: New Orleans, 1805–1889* (Baton Rouge, LA, 1997), 66–101; DeFrancias Folsom, ed., *Our Police: A Study of the Baltimore Force from the First Watchmen to the Latest Appointee* (Baltimore, MD, 1888), 28; Clement Eaton, *The Growth of Southern Civilization, 1790–1860* (New York, 1961), 273–74. See also Roger Lane, *Policing the City, Boston, 1822–1885* (Cambridge, MA, 1967), 103–04,

118, 142–45, 187–88, 203; Blake McKelvey, *The Urbanization of America, 1860–1915* (New Brunswick, NJ, 1963), 92; Howard O. Sprogle, *The Philadelphia Police, Past and Present* (Philadelphia, 1887), 169.

67. *New York Herald,* 14 July 1857, 1; 15 July 1857, 1 (quote); 6 November 1857; *New York Times,* 18 May 1856, 4; 12 November 1856, 8; 15 November 1858, 4; James F. Richardson, "The History of Police Protection in New York City, 1800–1870" (Ph.D. diss., New York University, 1961), 290–311; Wilbur R. Miller, *Cops and Bobbies: Police Authority in New York and London, 1830–1870* (Chicago, 1977), 50–52, 185–86; Clark, *History of the Seventh Regiment* 1: 410–14. For a contemporary satire of the police, see Q. K. Philander Doesticks, *Doesticks' Letters: And What He Says* (Philadelphia, 1855), 283–91.

68. *Eclaireur* 1 (1853): 2, 8, 1 (1854): 54.

69. H. W. S. Cleveland, "Rifle Clubs," *Atlantic Monthly* 10 (September 1862): 303–08; Hosley, *Colt,* 73–74; Russell S. Gilmore, "'Another Branch of Manly Sport': American Rifle Games, 1840–1890," in *Hard at Play: Leisure in America, 1840–1940,* ed. Kathryn Grover (Amherst, MA, 1992), 93–95. Jack London wrote about the *schutzenfest* and was struck by the fact that the best shooters are always city men. In King Hendrick and Irving Shepard, eds., *Jack London Reports: War Correspondence, Sports Articles, and Miscellaneous Writings* (New York, 1970), 226.

70. Guyer to Starr, 25 March 1852, Militia, Box 101, Records of the Military Dept., Connecticut State Library, Hartford, CT; *Hartford Courant,* 27 September 1855, quoted in Carroll J. Noonan, *Nativism in Connecticut, 1829–1860* (Washington, DC, 1985), 220–21; McCreedy, "Palladium of Liberty," 286–89. Capt. Abram Duryee of the 27th Regiment wrote an angry denunciation of the Germans in the *Military Argus,* which led to his court-martial. He appealed his conviction to the governor, who dismissed the charges on the grounds that the militia law did not authorize night drills, and was thus not subject to military law. Clark, *History of the Seventh Regiment* 1: 304–05.

71. *Public Acts, Passed by the State of Connecticut, May Session, 1846* (New Haven, CT, 1846), 29, 54–68; *Public Acts, . . . 1847* (Hartford, 1847), 39–57; *Public Acts, . . . 1850* (New Haven, CT, 1850), 47–54; *Public Acts, . . . 1851* (Hartford, CT, 1851), 38–40; *Public Acts, . . . 1852* (New Haven, CT, 1852), 70; *Public Acts, . . . 1854* (New Haven, CT, 1854), 99–100; *Public Acts, . . . 1857* (Hartford, CT, 1857), 49; Gates, "Disorder and Social Organization," 220–28, 236–63.

72. Gates, "Disorder and Social Organization," 168–69, 249; Marcus Cunliffe, *Soldiers and Civilians,* 223–30; Henry Dutton, *Message from His Excellency Henry Dutton, Governor of Connecticut, to the Legislature of the State* (New Haven, 1854), 7; Joseph D. Williams, *Annual Report of the Adjutant General of the State of Connecticut for the Year 1857* (Hartford, CT, 1858), 26–27; Noonan, *Nativism in Connecticut,* 273.

73. William T. Minor, *Message of His Excellency William T. Minor, Governor of Connecticut* (New Haven, CT, 1856), 19; Williams, *Annual Report of the Adjutant General of the State of Connecticut for the Year 1857* 26–27; Gates, "Disorder and Social Organization," 251–55.

74. *Eclaireur* 18 and 24 (January and February 1855); Clark, *History of the Seventh Regiment* 1: 261; Ebenezer Stone, *Annual Report of the Adjutant General of the Commonwealth of Massachusetts for the Year Ending Dec. 31, 1855* (Boston, 1856), 30–32; Cunliffe, *Soldiers and Civilians,* 227; Buckingham, *Message of His Excellency William A. Buckingham,* 13; Jerome B. Lucke, *History of the New Haven Grays* (New Haven, CT, 1876), 135.

75. Gates, "Disorder and Social Organization," 251–60.

76. *Eclaireur* 2 (1854): 64, 68, 71–72, 75, 80, see also 76–79, 85–87; Clark, *History of the Seventh Regiment* 1: 288.

77. Sumner to Daniels, 28 February 1832, Letterbooks of the Adjutant General, Massachusetts Military Records Office; Marengo Blues, quoted in Pitcavage, "An Equitable Burden," 452; Randolph Campbell, *An Empire for Slavery: The Peculiar Institution in Texas* (Baton Rouge, LA, 1989), 109–10; Sally E. Hadden, "Law Enforcement in a New Nation: Slave Patrols and Public Authority in the Old South, 1700–1865" (Ph.D. diss., Harvard University, 1993), 133–36; George C. Bittle, "In the Defense of Florida: The Organized Florida Militia from 1821 to 1920" (Ph.D. diss., Florida State University, 1965), 187–89; Allan Robert Purcell, "The History of the Texas Militia, 1835–1903" (Ph.D. diss., University of Texas at Austin, 1981), 94–97.

78. *Eclaireur* 2 (1855): 205–09, quote 208.

79. Hall's column "City Intelligence" quoted in Clark, *History of the Seventh Regiment* 1: 321.

80. *Eclaireur* 2 (1854): 63; Clark, *History of the Seventh Regiment* 1: 352, 397.

81. Increase N. Tarbox, *Winnie and Walter's Evening Talks with Their Father About Old Times* (Boston, 1861), 69–71. See also Doesticks, *Doesticks' Letters,* 76–83; H. H. Riley, *The Puddleford Papers, Or, Humors of the West* (New York, 1860), 226–46; Ikabod Izax, *My Satchel and I, or Literature on Foot* (Springfield, MA, 1873), 297–303.

82. *Boston Evening Transcript,* 15 June and 1 November 1837; Boston *Morning Post,* 31 August 1837. See also the *Eclaireur* 18 and 24 (January and February 1855); John Charles Schneider, "Mob Violence and Public Order in the American City, 1830–1865" (Ph.D. diss., University of Minnesota, 1971), 37–41.

83. T. Cadwallader, *Adjutant General's Report for 1855* (Trenton, NJ, 1856), 35; *Laws Relating to the Organization and Regulation of the Militia of the State of New Jersey from 1846–1860* (Trenton, NJ, 1863), 3–43; William, *Annual Report of the Adjutant General of the State of Connecticut for the Year 1857,* 27; Joseph J. Holmes, "The Decline of the Pennsylvania Militia, 1815–1870," *The Western Pennsylvania Historical Magazine* 57 (1974): 209; Joseph C. Abbott, *Report of the Adjutant General* (Concord, NH, 1860), 11; Everett Stackpole, *History of New Hampshire* (New York, 1916), 159.

84. "Report of Committee on Volunteer Companies," 18 September 1856, "Petition of Volunteer Companies of St. Philip's and St. Michael's" [1849], Military Affairs Committee Files, Legislative Group, South Carolina Dept. of Archives and History, Columbia, SC.

85. Lucke, *History of the New Haven Grays,* 212; McCreedy, "Palladium of Liberty," 188–89; Augustus T. Francis, ed., *History of the 71st Regiment, National Guard of New York* (New York, 1919), 79; George G. Benedict, *Vermont in the Civil War,* 2 vols. (Burlington, VT, 1886), 1. 9–11.

86. Adjutant General W. H. Richardson to Kemper, 5 January 1857, Kemper Papers, 4098, Box 2, University of Virginia, Charlottesville, VA; McCreedy, "Palladium of Liberty," 322; Record of the Worcester County Regiment of Cavalry, Worcester, MA, Collection, American Antiquarian Society; *Niles' Weekly Register,* 29 August 1840, 407; ibid. 5 September 1840, 4–5.

87. Clark, *History of the Seventh Regiment* 1: 400–06.

88. *Annual Report of the Adjutant General of the Commonwealth of Massachusetts for the Year Ending Dec. 31, 1856* (Boston, 1857), 18; Wisconsin Militia Law, 1858, 31; *Adjutant-General's Report for 1857,* Wisconsin, 3–4; Laws of New York, 1854, 1031; Smith, "Militia of the United States from 1846 to 1860," 32, 43–45; Frederick Townshend, *Annual Report of the Adjutant General of the State of New York* (Albany, NY, 1861), 50–57.

89. Pitcavage, "An Equitable Burden," 1–3; Bittle, "In the Defense of Florida," 213; McCreedy, "Palladium of Liberty," 367. In this context, the argument of many scholars that the South was peculiarly militaristic does not make a great deal of sense. John Franklin, *The Militant South, 1800–1861* (Cambridge, MA, 1956), 245–48; Grady McWhiney and Perry D. Jamieson, *Attack and Die: Civil War Military Tactics and the Southern Heritage* (University, AL, 1982), 170–79.

90. Dickson D. Bruce, *Violence and Culture in the Antebellum South* (Austin, TX, 1979), 162.

91. Clark, *History of the Seventh Regiment* 1: 431, 441–42, 455–56, 462; William Schouler, *Annual Report of the Adjutant General of the Commonwealth of Massachusetts for the Year Ending Dec. 31, 1861* (Boston, 1862), 6–19.

92. Anthony Marro, "Vermont's Local Militia Units, 1815–1860," *Vermont History* 40 (1972): 28–42.

93. Clyde N. Wilson, *Carolina Cavalier: The Life and Mind of James Johnston Pettigrew* (Athens, GA, 1990), 123–29 (quote p. 123); McCreedy, "Palladium of Liberty," 366; Bittle, "In the Defense of Florida," 218–19; Jack Gunn, "Mississippi in 1860 as Reflected in the Activities of the Governor's Office," *Journal of Mississippi History* 23 (1960): 185–86; Giles Cromwell, *The Virginia Manufactory of Arms* (Charlottesville, VA, 1975), 61–62; Smith, *Harpers Ferry Armory*, 305–10; Stephen B. Oates, *To Purge This Land with Blood: A Biography of John Brown* (New York, 1970), 274–306; Donald E. Reynolds, *Editors Make War: Southern Newspapers in the Secession Crisis* (Nashville, TN, 1970), 97–101; Clarence L. Mohr, *On the Threshold of Freedom: Masters and Slaves in Civil War Georgia* (Athens, GA, 1986), 20–21, 49–51.

94. McCreedy, "Palladium of Liberty," 371–72, 375; T. R. Fehrenbach, *Lone Star* (New York, 1968), 352; Frank E. Vandiver, *Ploughshares into Swords: Josiah Gorgas and Confederate Ordnance* (Austin, TX, 1952), 56–57; Smith, *Harpers Ferry Armory*, 316–22.

95. Fitzhugh, "Frederick the Great, by Thomas Carlyle," *De Bow's Review* 29 (1860): 155–56.

96. Quoted, Bruce, *Violence and Culture*, 163. Bruce adds, "To the extent that there was a Southern martial spirit, it was late in developing, and even then, fraught with inconsistencies." See in general, ibid., 161–77.

97. *Daily Richmond Whig*, 26 August 1862; William Howard Russell, *My Diary North and South*, 2 vols. (London, 1863), 1: 250.

98. Pitcavage, "An Equitable Burden," 423–25; Bittle, "In the Defense of Florida," 221–35, 251–52, 261–66; Vandiver, *Ploughshares into Swords*, 58–60. The Virginia legislature had first ordered the conversion of these guns in 1854, but did not have the resources or a gunsmith to make the changes. Cromwell, *The Virginia Manufactory of Arms*, 61–65.

99. William Seth to J. L. Kemper, 11 January 1861, Kemper Papers, University of Virginia. See also W. S. Parran to Kemper, 8 January 1861, ibid.

100. Paul Tincher Smith, "Militia of the United States from 1846 to 1860," 37–38; George D. Moller, *Massachusetts Military Shoulder Arms, 1784–1877* (Lincoln, RI, 1988), 19, 59, 72–74.

101. Clark, *History of the Seventh Regiment* 1: 393, 432, 470–77, 492, 498.

102. United States War Department, *The War of the Rebellion: A Compilation of the Official Records of the Union and Confederate Armies*, 128 vols. (Washington, DC, 1880–01), ser. 1, 3: 1–2, 18–33, 42–44, 51–60, 4: 290–92; Benet, comp., *A Collection of Annual Reports* 2: 687–89, 3: 448; Davis, *Arming the Union*, 39–41, 97; Vandiver, *Ploughshares into Swords*, 60–61; A. Howard Meneely, *The War Department, 1861: A*

Study in Mobilization and Administration (New York, 1928), 27–29, 37–50; Fred R. Shannon, *The Organization and Administration of the Union Army,* 2 vols. (New York, 1928), 1: 107–48.

103. John Mack Faragher, *Sugar Creek: Life on the Illinois Prairie* (New Haven, CT, 1986), 139.

104. Shannon, *Organization and Administration* 1: 23–31; John Niven, *Connecticut for the Union* (New Haven, CT, 1965), 40–70; Terrell, *Annual Report* (1869), 433–34; William Hasseltine, *Lincoln and the War Governors* (New York, 1948), 153–60; Meneely, *The War Department, 1861,* 114–15, 141–51.

105. Townshend, *Annual Report of the Adjutant General of the State of New York,* 8–11; Meneely, *The War Department, 1861,* 118–26.

106. Jones to Butler, 5 February 1861, Benjamin F. Butler Papers, Mss. Division, Library of Congress; Benedict, *Vermont in the Civil War* 1: 19–26; Abbott, *Report of the Adjutant General,* 11; H. C. Ampbell, *Wisconsin in Three Centuries, 1634–1905,* 3 vols. (New York, 1906), 3: 144–69; McCreedy, "Palladium of Liberty," 396, 403.

107. Townshend, *Annual Report* (1861), 70–94.

108. Stephen W. Sears, *George B. McClellan: The Young Napoleon* (New York, 1988), 70; McCreedy, "Palladium of Liberty," 370, 394; Joseph A. Parsons Jr., "Indiana and the Call for Volunteers, April, 1861," *Indiana Magazine of History* 54 (1958): 2; W. H. H. Terrell, *Annual Report of the Adjutant General of the State of Indiana* (Indianapolis, IN, 1869), 427–29; E. L. Kimball, "Richard Yates: His Record as Civil War Governor of Illinois," *Journal of the Illinois State Historical Society* 23 (1930): 31–32; Cyril B. Upham, "Arms and Equipment for the Iowa Troops in the Civil War," *The Iowa Journal of History* 16 (1918): 5; N. Brewer, *Report of the Adjutant General of Maryland to the General Assembly* (Annapolis, MD, 1860), 7–8; Jack Gunn, "Mississippi in 1860," 185–86; Terry L. Jones, *Lee's Tigers: The Louisiana Infantry in the Army of Northern Virginia* (Baton Rouge, LA, 1987), 3–4; Bittle, "In the Defense of Florida," 213–24, 266; Robert V. Bruce, *Lincoln and the Tools of War* (Indianapolis, IN, 1956), 37–58. Cyril B. Upham's opening sentence is succinct: "At the outbreak of the Civil War the State of Iowa was in a condition of almost total disarmament." Upham, "Arms and Equipment," 3.

109. *New York Tribune,* 17 April 1861, quoted in Phillip Shaw Paludan, *"A People's Contest": The Union and Civil War, 1861–1865* (New York, 1988), 23. See also Cecil Perkins, ed., *Northern Editorials on Secession* (New York, 1942), 732–36, 757–59, 811.

110. James McPherson, *The Struggle for Equality: Abolitionists and the Negro in the Civil War and Reconstruction* (Princeton, NJ, 1964), 29–51; W. Eugene Hollon, *Frontier Violence: Another Look* (New York, 1974), 47; Richard Hofstadter and Michael Wallace, eds., *American Violence: A Documentary History* (New York, 1970), 202–03.

111. Jackson quoted, William Earl Parrish, *Turbulent Partnership: Missouri and the Union, 1861–1865* (Columbia, MO, 1963), 17; Hicks and Magoffin quoted in Anthony Montachello, "Missouri in the Balance: Struggle for St. Louis," *America's Civil War* (March 1998): 44–47.

112. Hans Christian Adamson, *Rebellion in Missouri: 1861* (Philadelphia, 1961), 24–33 (quote p. 32); Parrish, *Turbulent Partnership,* 18–22.

113. Michael Fellman, *Inside War: The Guerrilla Conflict in Missouri During the American Civil War* (New York, 1989), 9–11.

114. Montachello, "Missouri in the Balance," 44–74; Fellman, *Inside War,* 23–80, 132–230; Parrish, *Turbulent Partnership,* 22–32.

115. Daniel Stevenson, "General Nelson, Kentucky, and Lincoln Guns," *Magazine of American History* 7 (1883): 118–21; Fremont quoted Davis, *Arming the Union*, 46; Benet, comp., *A Collection of Annual Reports* 1: 445–48; Meneely, *The War Department, 1861*, 100–14, 148–50.

116. War Department, *The War of the Rebellion*, ser. 1, 3: 277–78, 484–86, 593–95; Report on the Commission on Ordnance, U.S. Congress, *Senate Executive Document Number 72*, 37th Congress, 2d Session (Washington, DC, 1862), 68–93; Contracts made by the Ordnance Department, U.S. Congress, *House Executive Document Number 99*, 40th Congress, 2nd Session (Washington, DC, 1868), 166–67, 284–85, 661, 756–58, 764–65, 845–48, 953–58, 979; Benet, comp., *A Collection of Annual Reports* 4: 1572; Davis, *Arming the Union*, 50–67; Daniel M. Roche, "The Acquisition and Use of Foreign Shoulder Arms by the Union Army, 1861–1865" (Ph.D. diss., University of Colorado, 1949); Meneely, *The War Department, 1861*, 280–308.

117. Davis, *Arming the Union*, 61; Report on the Commission on Ordnance, *Senate Executive Document Number 72*, 434–55, see also 247–74, 485–95, 508–20; Contracts made by the Ordnance Department, *House Executive Document Number 99*, 962–63; R. Gordon Wasson, *The Hall Carbine Affair: A Study in Contemporary Folklore* (New York, 1948), 6–73; Benet, comp., *A Collection of Annual Reports* 4: 855–56, 1063–65, 1572.

118. Ripley quoted, Davis, *Arming the Union*, 99; Fuller, *Springfield Muzzle-Loading Shoulder Arms*, 116–21; Contracts made by the Ordnance Department, *House Executive Document Number 99*, 730–36, 818–23, 861–64, 922–30, 945–46; Haven and Belden, *A History of the Colt Revolver*, 93, 119; Hosley, *Colt*, 43; Williamson, *Winchester*, 15–26. These contracts and actual gun deliveries are collected in contracts made by the Ordnance Department, *House Executive Document Number 99* and Report on the Commission on Ordnance, *Senate Executive Document Number 72*. Smith & Wesson and Whitney bought most of the equipment from the Robbins and Lawrence plant. *Hartford Daily Times*, 16 May 1860.

119. McCreedy, "Palladium of Liberty," 404; Bittle, "In the Defense of Florida," 252–54.

120. Vandiver, *Ploughshares into Swords*, 60–61; Cromwell, *Virginia Manufactory of Arms*, 62–63, 67–68, 81. Claud E. Fuller and Richard D. Steuart, *Firearms of the Confederacy* (Huntington, WV, 1944), 110–13.

121. Vandiver, *Ploughshares into Swords*, 61–63, 79–89, 93–98, 104; Caleb Huse, *The Supplies for the Confederate Army: How They Were Obtained in Europe and How Paid For* (Boston, 1904), 9–21; Gary W. Gallagher, *The Confederate War* (Cambridge, MA, 1997), 28–29. Huse traveled to Europe by way of New York. On the train he met Caleb Cushing, who had been chair of the Charleston Democratic Convention that had nominated John C. Breckenridge for president, splitting the Democratic Party. Huse remembered Cushing telling him that the South had no chance, as "the money is all in the North; the manufactories are all in the North; the ships are all in the North; the arms and arsenals are all in the North." Gallagher, *Confederate War*, 14.

122. Frank E. Vandiver, ed., *Confederate Blockade Running through Bermuda, 1861–1865: Letters and Cargo Manifests* (New York, 1970), xii–xxi; William Diamond, "Imports of the Confederate Government from Europe and Mexico," *Journal of Southern History* 6 (1940): 470–503; Cynthia Myers, "The Cotton Road between Houston and Matamoros," *America's Civil War* (March 1998): 10–16.

123. Vandiver, *Ploughshares into Swords,* 72–73, 81–82, 93, 103, 196–97, 235.

124. Matthew W. Norman, *Colonel Burton's Spiller & Burr Revolver: An Untimely Venture in Confederate Small-Arms Manufacturing* (Macon, GA, 1996), 17–90, 130 (quote p. 31).

125. Bittle, "In the Defense of Florida," 293; Davis quoted, Gallagher, *The Confederate War,* 144; Stephen V. Ash, *When the Yankees Came: Conflict and Chaos in the Occupied South, 1861–1865* (Chapel Hill, NC, 1995), 20–23.

126. Davis, *Arming the Union,* 36; Shannon, *The Organization and Administration of the Union Army* 1: 151–92; Paddy Griffith, *Battle Tactics of the Civil War* (New Haven, CT, 1989), 29–52.

127. Bittle, "In the Defense of Florida," 289.

128. Moller, *Massachusetts Military Shoulder Arms,* 95–97.

129. Charles B. Norton, *American Inventions and Improvements in Breech-Loading Small Arms . . .* (Springfield, MA, 1880), 19; Davis, *Arming the Union,* 76–78; Benet, comp., *A Collection of Annual Reports* 4: 1572; Bruce, *Lincoln and the Tools of War,* 75–88, 118–23.

130. Dyer to Secretary of War Stanton, 5 December 1864, Benet, comp., *A Collection of Annual Reports* 4: 894; Davis, *Arming the Union,* 77–81, 122–32; Bruce, *Lincoln and the Tools of War,* 99–117.

131. Haven and Belden, *A History of the Colt Revolver,* 118–21; Williamson, *Winchester,* 28–41; Benet, comp., *A Collection of Annual Reports* 4: 851–52, 880–84, 890–94, 1572; Contracts made by the Ordnance Department, *House Executive Document Number 99,* 573–74, 963; Davis, *Arming the Union,* 132–45; J. O. Buckeridge, *Lincoln's Choice* (Harrisburg, PA, 1956), 9–45.

132. Deyrup, *Arms Makers of the Connecticut Valley,* 233; Benet, comp., *A Collection of Annual Reports* 3: 465–66, 572, 4: 844–45, 857–89; Henry I. Kurtz, "Arms for the South," *Civil War Times* 4 no. 1 (1960): 12–19; Fuller, *Springfield Muzzle-Loading Shoulder Arms,* 116–21, 142; Contracts made by the Ordnance Department, *House Executive Document Number 99,* 730–36, 818–23, 861–64, 922–30.

133. Robert C. Cheeks, "John Hunt Morgan's Ill-Fated Ohio Raid," *America's Civil War* (March 1998): 44–49; James A. Ramage, *Rebel Raider: The Life of General John Hunt Morgan* (Lexington, KY, 1986), 168–82.

134. C. A. Stevens, *Berdan's United States Sharpshooters in the Army of the Potomac, 1861–1865* (St. Paul, MN, 1892), 12–31; John W. Whitman, "Lorenzo Barber was the Eagle-Eyed 'Fighting Parson,' of Hiram Berdan's famous U.S. Sharpshooters," *America's Civil War* (September 1998): 12–18. Ironically, Barber died when he accidentally shot himself while hunting near Troy in 1874.

135. McWhiney and Jamieson, *Attack and Die.* The authors did a brilliant job demonstrating that commanders North and South adhered to this basic approach to warfare, though with more exceptions on the northern side. But they then added a last chapter that insists that the South *really* liked charging because of their Celtic heritage, an argument that borders on the perverse. McWhiney and Jamieson, *Attack and Die,* 170–91.

136. McWhiney and Jamieson, *Attack and Die,* 12; Griffith, *Battle Tactics of the Civil War,* 137–63.

137. Winfield Scott, *Memoirs of Lieut.-General Scott, LL.D. Written by Himself,* 2 vols. (New York, 1864), 1: 259; Winfield Scott, *Infantry Tactics; or, Rules for the Exercise and Manoeuvres of the Infantry of the U.S. Army,* 3 vols. (New York, 1846), 1: 5–10, 79–81. Scott's later editions, including the one published in 1861, did not change in

the essentials. William J. Hardee, soon to be a Confederate general, wrote his manual supposedly in response to Jefferson Davis's request for a work that would consider the new technology. But Hardee seemed no better attuned to the advantages of the rifle than Scott—or to the meaning of plagiarism, since his work was mostly a translation of a French manual. Hardee, *Rifle and Light Infantry Tactics; For the Exercise and Manoeuvres of Troops When Acting as Light Infantry or Riflemen*, 2 vols. (Philadelphia, 1855).

138. H. W. Halleck, *Elements of Military Art and Science: or, Course of Instruction in Strategy, Fortification, Tactics of Battles, &c.* (Westport, CT, 1971, orig. 1846), 127, 260. See also George B. McClellan, *Regulations and Instructions for the Field Service of the U.S. Cavalry in Time of War* (Philadelphia, 1861), 11–14; McWhiney and Jamieson, *Attack and Die*, 126–39; Stephen E. Ambrose, *Crazy Horse and Custer: The Parallel Lives of Two American Warriors* (New York, 1975), 195–215; Griffith, *Battle Tactics of the* Civil War, 179–88.

139. John Gibbon, *The Artillerist's Manual* (New York, 1860), 219–22, quote p. 220. Another promoter of the new rifles was Cadmus M. Wilcox, but he did not consider its military impact closely. Wilcox, *Rifles and Rifle Practice* (New York, 1959). And even once the war started, proponents of rifle use continued to consider it limited to special service with sniper units. Cleveland, "Rifle Clubs," 306–07.

140. Rosecrans, General Orders, 31 December 1862, War Department, *The War of the Rebellion*, ser. 1, 20: 183; *Missouri Army Argus*, 12 May 1862, quoted in McWhiney and Jamieson, *Attack and Die*, 144; Thomas L. Livermore, *Numbers and Losses in the Civil War in America, 1861–1865*, 2nd ed. (Boston, 1901), 132; Vandiver, *Ploughshares into Swords*, 105–06; McWhiney and Jamieson, *Attack and Die*, 76–80. On the continued preference for the bayonet, see also *The War of the Rebellion*, ser. 1, 10: 395, 11: 344, 20: 786, 827, 21: 431, 34: 567, 38: 871, 876, 882. On the debate over battle tactics, see also Thomas L. Connelly and Archer Jones, *The Politics of Command: Factions and Ideas in Confederate Strategy* (Baton Rouge, LA, 1973); McWhiney and Jamieson, *Attack and Die;* John K. Mahon, "Civil War Infantry Assault Tactics," *Military Affairs* 25 (1961): 57–68; Alan T. Nolan, *Lee Considered: General Robert E. Lee and Civil War History* (Chapel Hill, NC, 1991); Gallagher, *The Confederate War*, 15–59, 115–53.

141. Raudzens, "Firepower Limitations," 148–53; Van Creveld, *Supplying War*, 102–03; Andrew Wheatcroft, "Technology and the Military Mind: Austria, 1866–1914," in Geoffrey Bast and Andrew Wheatcroft, eds., *War, Economy and the Military Mind* (Totowa, NJ, 1976), 45. For a good example of continued resistance to modern rifles, see [Major] G. L. Willard, *Comparative Value of Rifled and Smooth-Bored Arms* (Washington, DC, 1863).

142. *The War of the Rebellion*, ser. 1, 38: 184, 199; John S. Mosby, *Memoirs*, ed. Charles Wells Russell (Bloomington, IN, 1959, orig. 1887), 30; McWhiney and Jamieson, *Attack and Die*, 71–77, 99–111; Gallagher, *The Confederate War*, 28–29; Jay Luvaas, *The Military Legacy of the Civil War: The European Inheritance* (Chicago, 1959), 73–74, 166–80, 226–33. For some examples of rifles halting massive Confederate attacks, see Stevens, *Berdan's United States Sharpshooters*, 95–97, 117–20, 166–67, 300–12.

143. Joseph G. Rosa, *The Gunfighter: Man or Myth?* (Norman, OK, 1969), 39; Joe B. Frantz and Julian E. Choate Jr., *The American Cowboy, the Myth and the Reality* (Norman, OK, 1955), 76–78.

144. *Richmond Whig*, 20 June 1865, quoted in David F. Allmendinger, *Ruffin:*

Family and Reform in the Old South (New York, 1990), 154. The governor of Florida, John Milton, also blew his brains out in April 1865. Dan T. Carter, *When the War Was Over: The Failure of Self-Reconstruction in the South, 1865–1867* (Baton Rouge, LA, 1985), 33–34.

145. Officially, Union soldiers had to purchase their firearms before taking them home. But the army did not make a concerted effort to collect this money. Even most Confederate soldiers took guns home with them when the war ended. Noah Andre Trudeau, *Out of the Storm: The End of the Civil War, April–June, 1865* (New York, 1994), 379; Edith Abbott, "The Civil War and the Crime Wave of 1865–70," *Social Service Review* 1 (1929): 212–34.

Epilogue

1. Colt to T. C. Brownell, 1861, Colt Collection, Connecticut Historical Society, Hartford, CT.

2. Nyle H. Miller and Joseph W. Snell, *Great Gunfighters of the Kansas Cowtowns, 1867–1886* (Lincoln, NE, 1963), 4; Jay Monaghan, ed., *Book of the American West* (New York, 1960), 408; Charles T. Haven and Frank A. Belden, *A History of the Colt Revolver, and the Other Arms Made by Colt's Patent Firearms Manufacturing Company from 1836 to 1940* (New York, 1940), 145–50; Harold F. Williamson, *Winchester, the Gun that Won the West* (Washington, DC, 1952), 102.

3. Gordon S. Wood, *The Radicalism of the American Revolution* (New York, 1992), 336.

4. H. W. S. Cleveland, "Rifle Clubs," *Atlantic Monthly* 10 (September 1862): 303–04.

5. R. L. Wilson, *Colt: An American Legend* (Artabras, NY, 1985), 153–97; Williamson, *Winchester,* 47–80.

6. J. O. Buckeridge, *Lincoln's Choice* (Harrisburg, PA, 1956), 238–39.

7. William B. Edwards, *Civil War Guns* (Harrisburg, PA, 1962), 400–12; Alden Hatch, *Remington Arms in American History* (New York, 1956), 82; Williamson, *Winchester,* 74–80. Adding to the gunmakers' problems, the Springfield Armory also maintained its wartime production levels. Michael S. Raber, "Conservative Innovators, Military Small Arms, and Industrial History at Springfield Armory, 1794–1918," *Industrial Archeology* 14 (1988): 16.

8. Nathan Rosenberg, comp., *The American System of Manufactures: The Report of the Committee on the Machinery of the United States, 1855* (Edinburgh, 1969), 193.

9. Williamson, *Winchester,* 62–66, Roger Burlingame, *March of the Iron Men. A Social History of Union Through Invention* (New York, 1938), 429–31; L. Sprague de Camp, *The Heroic Age of American Invention* (New York, 1961), 90.

10. Donald B. Webster Jr., *Suicide Specials* (Harrisburg, PA, 1958), 1–35; *New York Times,* 26 March 1879, 4.

11. J. T. Headley, *The Great Riots of New York, 1712–1863* (New York, 1873); David M. Barnes, *The Draft Riots in New York, July, 1863* (New York, 1863).

12. Wilbur R. Miller, *Cops and Bobbies: Police Authority in New York and London, 1830–1870* (Chicago, 1977), 53; Dan T. Carter, *When the War Was Over: The Failure of Self-Reconstruction in the South, 1865–1867* (Baton Rouge, LA, 1985), 35; Robert W. Shook, "The Battle of the Nueces, August 10, 1862," *Southwestern Historical Quarterly* 66 (1962): 31–42; James Smallwood, "Disaffection in Confederate Texas: The

Great Hanging at Gainesville," *Civil War History* 22 (1976): 349–60; Phillip Shaw Paludan, *Victims: A True Story of the Civil War* (Knoxville, 1981).

13. H. V. Redfield, *Homicide, North and South* (Philadelphia, 1880), 193–207; Jane Dailey, "Deference and Violence in the Postbellum Urban South: Manners and Massacres in Danville, Virginia," *Journal of Southern History* 68 (1997): 568, 578–80; Michael Kaplan, "New York City Tavern Violence and the Creation of a Working-Class Male Identity," *Journal of the Early Republic* 15 (1995): 591–617; Elliot J. Gorn, *The Manly Art: Bare-Knuckle Prize Fighting in America* (Ithaca, NY, 1986), 129–47; Elizabeth Pleck, *Domestic Tyranny: The Making of American Social Policy against Family Violence from Colonial Times to the Present* (New York, 1987), 49–66; Jerome Nadelhaft, "Wife Torture: A Known Phenomenon in Nineteenth-Century America," *Journal of American Culture* 10 (1987): 39–59; Ralph L. Peek, "Lawlessness in Florida, 1868–1871," *Florida Historical Quarterly* 40 (1961): 164–85; Eric H. Monkkonen, "New York City Homicides," *Social Science History* 19 (1995): 201–12; Edith Abbott, "The Civil War and the Crime Wave of 1865–70," *The Social Service Review* 1 (1929): 212–34; Luc Sante, *Low Life: Lures and Snares of Old New York* (New York, 1991); Waldo L. Cook, "Murders in Massachusetts," *Journal of the American Statistical Association* 3 (1893): 357–78; Harry G. Nutt, "Homicide in New Hampshire," *Journal of the American Statistical Association* 9 (1905): 220–30.

14. W. Eugene Hollon, *Frontier Violence: Another Look* (New York, 1974), 115; Carl W. Brieheim, *Quantrill and His Civil War Guerrillas* (Denver, CO, 1959), 168–74; Paul I. Wellman, *A Dynasty of Western Outlaws* (Garden City, NY, 1961).

15. Joseph G. Rosa, *The Gunfighter: Man or Myth?* (Norman, OK, 1969), 64, 125; Robert R. Dykstra, *The Cattle Towns* (New York, 1968), 144.

16. Hollon, *Frontier Violence,* 52.

17. Ibid., 197–203, 220–21; Rosa, *The Gunfighter,* 122; John Pleasant Gray, *When All Roads Led to Tombstone: A Memoir,* ed. W. Lane Rogers (Boise, ID, 1998), 18–26; Kent Ladd Stechmesser, *The Western Hero in History and Legend* (Norman, OK, 1965), 139; Joe B. Frantz and Julian E. Choate Jr., *The American Cowboy: The Myth and the Reality* (Norman, OK, 1955), 95n. Hollon compares this number to the twenty-two men, women, and children Lieutenant William Calley admits to having killed at close quarters within the space of a few minutes. Hollon, *Frontier Violence,* 228n.

18. W. Eugene Hollon, "Rushing for Land: Oklahoma 1889," *The American West* 3 no. 4 (1966): 4–15; Hollon, *Frontier Violence,* 202–05; A. S. Mercer, *The Banditti of the Plains; or, The Cattlemen's Invasion of Wyoming in 1892: The Crowning Infamy of the Ages* (Norman, OK, 1954, orig., 1894), 6–7; Harry Sinclair Drago, *The Great Range Wars: Violence on the Grasslands* (New York, 1970); Dykstra, *Cattle Towns.*

19. Hollon, *Frontier Violence,* 118.

20. Robert R. Dykstra, "Field Notes: Overdosing on Dodge City," *Western Historical Quarterly* 27 (1996): 505–14.

21. Hollon, *Frontier Violence,* 62; Alvin M. Josephy Jr. et al., *The American Heritage Book of Indians* (New York, 1961), 305.

22. House of Representatives Report #16, 39th Congress, 1866–67 (V. 1: 220), 76–78; *Chicago Tribune,* 26 July 1877, 1, 4 August 1877, 8; Allan Pinkerton, *Strikers, Communists, Tramps and Detectives* (New York, 1878), 13–24, 216–60, 282–84; Frederick T. Wilson, *Federal Aid in Domestic Disturbances, 1787–1903* (Washington, DC, 1903), 189–205.

23. Wall display, Gene Autry Museum of Western Heritage, Los Angeles; Hugh

Grey and Ross McCloskey, eds., *Field and Stream Treasury* (New York, 1961), 240–41; Haven and Belden, *A History of the Colt Revolver,* 427; *Frank Leslie's Illustrated Newspaper,* 7 April 1877.

24. Mark Twain, *Innocents Abroad,* chapter 51.

25. Whitelaw Reid, *After the War: A Southern Tour* (Cincinnati, OH, 1866), 422; Sidney Andrews, *The South Since the War* (Boston, 1866), 288–300; John William De Forest, *A Union Officer in the Reconstruction,* ed. James H. Croushore and David M. Potter (New Haven, CT, 1948), 153–54, 181–82.

26. E. Merton Coulter, *The South During Reconstruction, 1865–1877* (Baton Rouge, LA, 1947), 49–50; John Hope Franklin, *Reconstruction: After the Civil War* (Chicago, 1961), 49; William A. Paul, "The Shadow of Equality: The Negro in Baltimore" (Ph.D. diss., University of Wisconsin, 1972), 195. Allen Trelease wrote that "Some Negro men began carrying guns. White men did this too, more and more frequently. It became so common that young men of both races felt undressed without a pistol stuck into their belts or hip pocket." Allen Trelease, *Reconstruction: The Great Experiment* (New York, 1971), 23, 66.

27. See in general, Carter, *When the War Was Over,* 6–23.

28. Quoted, Eric Foner, *Reconstruction: America's Unfinished Revolution, 1863–1877* (New York, 1988), 119; Lou Falkner Williams, *The Great South Carolina Ku Klux Klan Trials, 1871–1872* (Athens, GA, 1996), 22–29. On irrational white fears of the freedmen, see Carter, *When the War Was Over,* 127–29, 189–203, 215–21.

29. The *Charleston Mercury,* 26 January 1865, quoted Lawrence J. Friedman, *The White Savage: Racial Fantasies in the Postbellum South* (Englewood Cliffs, NJ, 1970), 15; Otis A. Singletary, *Negro Militia and Reconstruction* (New York, 1963), 3–24.

30. Williams, *Great South Carolina Ku Klux Klan Trials,* 26 (quote), 29–40; Allen W. Trelease, *White Terror: The Ku Klux Klan Conspiracy and Southern Reconstruction* (New York, 1971), 362–80. The Klan always insisted that they organized to defend themselves from these armed blacks, which was a reversal of causality, since the militia had been created in 1870, the Klan in 1868. Williams, *Great South Carolina Ku Klux Klan Trials,* 27, 78–79.

31. James Richardson, comp., *A Compilation of the Messages and Papers of the Presidents,* 20 vols. (New York, 1897–1917), 9: 4089–92; Williams, *Great South Carolina Ku Klux Klan Trials,* 125–135 (quote, 129); Wilson, *Federal Aid in Domestic Disturbances,* 183–88.

32. House of Representatives Report #265, 43rd Congress, 2nd Session, 1875 (V.1: 225), 7–9. See in general, Foner, *Reconstruction,* 119–23, 425–59.

33. Anon., *The Pistol as a Weapon of Defense in Its Home and on the Road* (New York, 1875), 7, 10.

34. Ted Tunnell, *Crucible of Reconstruction: War, Radicalism, and Race in Lousiana, 1862–1877* (Baton Rouge, LA, 1984), 185–202.

35. United States *v.* Cruikshank, 92 U.S. 542 (1876). For more examples of white violence against blacks and their white supporters in these years, see Wilson, *Federal Aid in Domestic Disturbances,* 107–88.

36. Pat T. Tucker, "Buffalo in the Judith Basin," in H. G. Merriam, ed., *Way Out West: Recollections and Tales* (Norman, OK, 1969), 69; Monaghan, ed., *Book of the American West,* 436; *Hartford Daily Times,* 4 July 1866; William Hosley, *Colt: The Making of an American Legend* (Amherst, MA, 1996), 71–73.

37. Williamson, *Winchester,* 183–85; Pete Kuhloff, *Kuhloff on Guns* (New York,

1970), 64–66; Walter Havighurst, *Annie Oakley of the Wild West* (New York, 1954), 81–94; Harold L. Peterson, *The Remington Historical Treasury of Historical Guns* (New York, 1966), 121.

38. "The Minuteman" statue is at Minuteman National Historical Park, Concord, MA.

39. *New York Times,* 12 March 1911, 8; James E. Serven and James B. Trefethen, eds., *Americans and Their Guns* (Harrisburg, PA, 1967), 174; Arthur A. Ekirch Jr., *The Civilian and the Military* (New York, 1956), 154.

40. There is surprisingly little historical study of the National Rifle Association (NRA): two dissertations, an official history, and a biography. Russell S. Gilmore's "Crackshots and Patriots: The National Rifle Association and America's Military-Sporting Tradition" (Ph.D. diss., University of Wisconsin, 1974); Donald G. LeFave, "The Will to Arm: The National Rifle Association in American Society, 1871–1970" (Ph.D. diss., University of Colorado, 1970); Serven and Trefethen, eds., *Americans and Their Guns,* 20–56, 82; Donald N. Bigelow, *William Conant Church and the Army and Navy Journal* (New York, 1952). On the modern NRA, see Osha Gray Davidson, *Under Fire: The NRA and the Battle for Gun Control* (New York, 1993).

41. *New York Herald,* 23 July 1876; Dee Brown, *The Year of the Century* (New York, 1966), 182–85, 197; William E. Connelley, *Wild Bill and His Era: The Life & Adventures of James Butler Hickok* (New York, 1933), 190–93; U.S. Congress, 44th, 1st Session, Senate Executive Doc. 85 (Washington, DC, 1876), 26–37; Wilson, *Federal Aid in Domestic Disturbances,* 182–83; D. W. Stevens, *The James Boys in Minnesota* (New York, 1882).

42. Ironically, this information is from D. C. McChristian, *An Army of Marksmen: The Development of United States Army Marksmanship in the 19th Century* (Fort Collins, CO, 1981), 32.

43. Stephen E. Ambrose, *Crazy Horse and Custer: The Parallel Lives of Two American Warriors* (New York, 1975), 234–43, 411–47, 462.

Acknowledgments

For there is nothing covered, that shall not be revealed; neither hid, that shall not be known.

—Luke 12:2

Page Smith, my undergraduate advisor, once told me of a nightmare he had immediately after he sent in the manuscript for his biography of John Adams. In the dream, a friend called to criticize Page's new book for not even looking at a collection of letters that had been published years before, and for missing the recent book by a prominent scholar. Page said he awoke in a cold sweat and jotted a note to himself to get these books first thing in the morning. And here his wife, Eloise Pickard Smith, broke in, "And he looked, too. They didn't exist. It was just a dream."

Perhaps this is a nightmare common among scholars who know full well that every action has an equal and opposite criticism. After ten years working on this book, visiting numerous archives, searching through dozens of document collections, reading scores of books and articles, I realize that there is much left to be done, much yet to read. But that will always be the case. Every volume I open reveals yet more information of use to this study of the creation of America's gun culture. At least another ten years could be happily spent continuing this research. But Jane Garrett of Knopf persuaded me that it was time to publish the findings of this research. For that encouragement I am forever grateful. It is the nature of the historian to always want to look further, to uncover more buried truths, to allow those who once lived to speak again in their own voices. I hope that I have done justice to these people.

Though historians tend to work alone, we do rely on one another for counsel, information, and support. In this regard I have been very lucky, and not just for the advice I have received from those scholars I know personally. This project began in the margins of books (or on Post-its, if a library book); it has built on the work of many scholars. My respect for my predecessors and colleagues has grown enormously with my research, and I acknowledge myself the beneficiary of their labors and wisdom. Hopefully my esteem for the work of many scholars, especially the often underappreciated military historians, will be evident. I cannot, of course, thank everyone, and I apologize for not being able to properly express my gratitude to all who have assisted me. With only one exception, every scholar I've asked for help has been generous in sharing his or her time and knowledge. Just to have read the books of so many fine scholars has been a delight, to have also exchanged views with so many over the years enhances the pleasure of being an historian.

It should be obvious that this work has made liberal use of the insights of a range of superb historians like Fred Anderson, Don Higginbotham, Alice Hanson Jones, Jack Rakove, Harold Selesky, Robert Dykstra, Lois Schwoerer, John Phillip Reid, Richard White, and Alan Taylor. Less obvious may be the influence of a number of brilliant dissertations, which I hope will soon be books. To mention just four among many, the research of Mark Pitcavage, Nick Proctor, Steve Hahn, and Bill Carrigan has proved invaluable in the development of this book. Along the way I published an article in the *Journal of American History* on America's gun culture, and benefited from their careful reading and editing, and David Thelen's enthusiasm. My thanks also to the memory of Ray Allen Billington for suggesting to me that I examine travel accounts, which were the most fascinating part of this research.

Any long-term project like this tests the bounds of friendship. I have been remarkably fortunate in my friends, though I regret deeply that the teacher who first inspired me with a love of learning, Paul Liley, died before I finished this work. More happily, my great and good friends Peter Onuf, Laura Edwards, Greg Nobles, Gregory Sanford, Mary Odem, Margot Finn, Jim Roark, Mark Ravina, Tom Chaffin, Andrew Kull, and Greg Thompson have always treated my inquiry with enthusiasm and skepticism, and kept me from getting carried away with the subject. And on the latter point, special thanks to John Juricek, who provided a close, critical reading of the first four chapters. My officemates from graduate school days, Janet Ruprecht and Paul Roach, persist in upholding the highest standards of friendship, and have been there for me for more years than I care to recall. Chris Davis and Sheila Cavanagh have been noble neighbors, reliable friends, and witty critics. My other neighbors and good friends, the historians John and Andrea Tone, have been marvelous dinner companions and insightful listeners; my special thanks to Andrea for convincing me to trust my evidence. Bill Deverell read the entire first draft and reminded me that "gun" often appeared as "fun," the least of his many valuable corrections. Jack Rakove kindly went through the second draft with a keen eye and improved every page he read. And, as always, my warmest thanks to Christine Heyrman, my graduate advisor, who taught me to check the sources myself. Good point.

While working to create and direct Emory University's interdisciplinary Violence Studies Program, I met an astounding array of scholars all concerned with the nature of violence. I have benefited enormously from their diverse understandings of the essential human problem, and am delighted that I have gotten to know Arthur Kellermann, Patricia Brennan, Irwin Waldmann, Scott Lilienfeld, Bobbi Patterson, Bob Agnew, and Matt Bernstein, among others. I would also like to thank one excellent source of information who prefers to remain anonymous because of his position within the National Rifle Association—such is the nature of this subject.

The generosity of the American Antiquarian Society, the Huntington Library, the American Philosophical Society, and the Stanford Humanities Center were essential for the completion of this manuscript. As their many admirers know, the Huntington and the Antiquarian Society are every scholar's fantasy (which just shows what kind of people we are)— marvelous centers of research with supportive staffs and invigorating intellectual companionship. My special thanks to Roy Ritchie and John Hench; they are treasures to scholarship. My gratitude also to William Hosley of the Wadsworth Atheneum, who shares my fascination with Samuel Colt. I wrote this book during a year at the Stanford Humanities Center, and I can never give thanks enough to Bliss Carnochan, Susan Dunn, Susan Sebbard, Gwen Lorraine, and the rest. The center's fellows were great colleagues and sources of the most amazing variety of intellectual opinions, many of which I understood. Their good cheer proved essential as I battled to bring my hundreds of pages of notes into some order; I am still flattered that they labeled me "the empiricist in fuzzyland." It was all great fun, and had the added advantage of bringing me into the same area as much of my family. Matt, Kathleen, Lisa, and Antonio know how important it was for me to have spent time with them. And at last I can tell my father that, yes, I am done with that book.

And of course with family I must end this self-indulgence. Without the love of Kate Dornhuber and our daughter Lilith Claire, I would never have bothered with such a huge subject. I respect Kate's dignity and unique clarity of vision as much today as I did when I met her thirty-four years ago. Her sagacity and unshakable integrity make Kate my beacon in a chaotic world. I dedicate this book to our daughter Lilith Claire. My most sharp-tongued critic, she keeps me humble and never lets me forget the power of contingency in human affairs. She has spent almost her whole life hearing about guns and has traveled with me on research trips and through the dusty aisles of libraries and bookstores, and has never lost her good humor or, what I respect most, her absolute honesty. I wrote this book for her in fulfillment of a promise made years ago at Mt. Ranier. And I end it here with another promise, that soon we will stand again on Ireland's western shore, watch some sunsets, ask for more.

Index

A Note About the Author

Michael Bellesiles received his B.A. from the University of California, Santa Cruz, in 1975, and his Ph.D. at the University of California, Irvine, in 1986. He has taught at University of California, Irvine; University of California, Los Angeles; Universität Augsburg; and University College, Oxford. He is currently Professor of History at Emory University and founding Director of their Center for the Study of Violence. He is the author of *Revolutionary Outlaws: Ethan Allen and the Struggle for Independence on the Early American Frontier* and numerous articles and reviews; developer of BiblioBase, an on-line documents reader; and editor of *Ethan Allen and His Kin* and *Lethal Imagination: Violence and Brutality in American History.*

A Note on the Type

This book was set in Granjon, a type named in compliment to Robert Granjon, a type cutter and printer active in Antwerp, Lyons, Rome, and Paris from 1523 to 1590. Granjon, the boldest and most original designer of his time, was one of the first to practice the trade of type-founder apart from that of printer. Linotype Granjon was designed by George W. Jones, who based his drawings on a face used by Claude Garamond (ca. 1480–1561) in his beautiful French books. Granjon more closely resembles Garamond's own type than do any of the various modern faces that bear his name.

Composed by
Stratford Publishing Services, Incorporated,
Brattleboro, Vermont

Printed and bound by
R. R. Donnelley & Sons,
Harrisonburg, Virginia

Designed by Ralph L. Fowler